The Wiley-Blackwell Handbook of Infant Development

Wiley-Blackwell Handbooks of Developmental Psychology

This outstanding series of handbooks provides a cutting-edge overview of classic research, current research, and future trends in developmental psychology.

- Each handbook draws together 25–30 newly commissioned chapters to provide a comprehensive overview of a sub-discipline of developmental psychology.
- The international team of contributors to each handbook has been specially chosen for its expertise and knowledge of each field.
- Each handbook is introduced and contextualized by leading figures in the field, lending coherence and authority to each volume.

The *Wiley-Blackwell Handbooks of Developmental Psychology* will provide an invaluable overview for advanced students of developmental psychology and for researchers as an authoritative definition of their chosen field.

Published

Blackwell Handbook of Childhood Social Development
Edited by Peter K. Smith and Craig H. Hart

Blackwell Handbook of Adolescence
Edited by Gerald R. Adams and Michael D. Berzonsky

The Science of Reading: A Handbook
Edited by Margaret J. Snowling and Charles Hulme

Blackwell Handbook of Early Childhood Development
Edited by Kathleen McCartney and Deborah A. Phillips

Blackwell Handbook of Language Development
Edited by Erika Hoff and Marilyn Shatz

Wiley-Blackwell Handbook of Childhood Cognitive Development, 2nd edition
Edited by Usha Goswami

Wiley-Blackwell Handbook of Infant Development, 2nd edition
Edited by J. Gavin Bremner and Theodore D. Wachs

Forthcoming

Blackwell Handbook of Developmental Psychology in Action
Edited by Rudolph Schaffer and Kevin Durkin

Wiley-Blackwell Handbook of Adulthood and Aging
Edited by Susan Krauss Whitbourne and Martin Sliwinski

Wiley-Blackwell Handbook of Childhood Social Development, 2nd edition
Edited by Peter K. Smith and Craig H. Hart

The Wiley-Blackwell Handbook of Infant Development

Second Edition

Volume 2

Applied and Policy Issues

Edited by J. Gavin Bremner and Theodore D. Wachs

A John Wiley & Sons, Ltd., Publication

This second edition first published 2010
© 2010 Blackwell Publishing Ltd

Edition history: Blackwell Handbook of Handbook of Infant Development, edited by J. Gavin Bremner and Alan Fogel, Blackwell Publishers Ltd (1e, 2001)

Blackwell Publishing was acquired by John Wiley & Sons in February 2007. Blackwell's publishing program has been merged with Wiley's global Scientific, Technical, and Medical business to form Wiley-Blackwell.

Registered Office
John Wiley & Sons Ltd, The Atrium, Southern Gate, Chichester, West Sussex, PO19 8SQ, United Kingdom

Editorial Offices
350 Main Street, Malden, MA 02148-5020, USA
9600 Garsington Road, Oxford, OX4 2DQ, UK
The Atrium, Southern Gate, Chichester, West Sussex, PO19 8SQ, UK

For details of our global editorial offices, for customer services, and for information about how to apply for permission to reuse the copyright material in this book please see our website at www.wiley.com/wiley-blackwell.

The right of J. Gavin Bremner and Theodore D. Wachs to be identified as the authors of the editorial material in this work has been asserted in accordance with the UK Copyright, Designs and Patents Act 1988.

Library of Congress Cataloging-in-Publication Data

The Wiley-Blackwell handbook of infant development / edited by J. Gavin Bremner and Theodore D. Wachs. – 2nd ed.
    p. ; cm. – (Blackwell handbooks of developmental psychology)
  Other title: Handbook of infant development
  Rev. ed. of: Blackwell handbook of infant development / edited by Gavin Bremner and Alan Fogel. 2001.
  Includes bibliographical references and index.
  ISBN 978-1-4051-7874-7 (set : hardcover : alk. paper) – ISBN 978-1-4443-3273-5 (v. 1 : hardcover : alk. paper) – ISBN 978-1-4443-3274-2 (v. 2 : hardcover : alk. paper)   1. Infants–Development–Handbooks, manuals, etc.   2. Infants–Health and hygiene–Handbooks, manuals, etc.   I. Bremner, J. Gavin, 1949-   II. Wachs, Theodore D., 1941-   III. Blackwell handbook of infant development.   IV. Title: Handbook of infant development.   V. Series: Blackwell handbooks of developmental psychology.
  [DNLM: 1. Child Development.   2. Infant Care.   3. Infant.   WS 105 W676 2010]
  RJ131.B475 2010
  305.231–dc22
                                                2010016203

A catalogue record for this book is available from the British Library.

Set in 10.5 on 12.5 pt Adobe Garamond by Toppan Best-set Premedia Limited
Printed in Singapore by Markono Print Media Pte Ltd

1   2010

Contents

List of Contributors   vii

Introduction to Volume 2: Applied and Policy Issues   1
J. Gavin Bremner and Theodore D. Wachs

Part I   Bioecological Risks   **5**

Introduction   7

1   Fetal Development   9
    Raye-Ann deRegnier and Shivani Desai

2   Infant Nutrition   33
    Maureen M. Black and Kristen M. Hurley

3   Health   62
    R. J. Karp

4   Development of Communication in Children with Sensory
    Functional Disabilities   87
    Gunilla Preisler

Part II   Psychosocial Risks   **111**

Introduction   113

5   Growing Up in Poverty in Developed Countries   115
    Jondou J. Chen, Nina Philipsen Hetzner, and Jeanne Brooks-Gunn

6   Infant Development in the Developing World   140
    Patrice Engle

7   Child Abuse and Neglect   165
    Kelli Connell-Carrick

8   Effects of Postnatal Depression on Mother–Infant Interactions
    and Child Development   192
    Lynne Murray, Sarah Halligan, and Peter Cooper

Part III   Developmental Disorders   **221**

    Introduction   223

9   Infant Assessment   226
    Susan P. Berger, Joyce Hopkins, Hyo Bae, Bryce Hella, and Jennifer Strickland

10 The Early Development of Autism Spectrum Disorders   257
    Gregory S. Young and Sally Ozonoff

11 Infant Psychosocial Disorders   280
    Melissa R. Johnson and Karen Appleyard

12 Genetic Disorders Associated with Intellectual Disability:
    An Early Development Perspective   308
    Deborah J. Fidler, Lisa Daunhauer, David E. Most, and Harvey Switzky

Part IV   Intervention and Policy Issues   **335**

    Introduction   337

13 Early Intervention   339
    Douglas R. Powell

14 Childcare Research at the Dawn of a New Millennium: An Update   359
    Sarah L. Friedman, Edward Melhuish, and Candace Hill

15 Infancy Research, Policy, and Practice   380
    Marguerite Barratt and Erica Fener

Author Index   401
Subject Index   430

Contents of Volume 1: Basic Research   443

List of Contributors

Volume 2

Karen Appleyard, Duke University.

Hyo Bae, Illinois Institute of Technology.

Marguerite Barratt, The George Washington University.

Susan P. Berger, Children's Memorial Hospital & Northwestern University, Feinberg School of Medicine.

Maureen M. Black, University of Maryland School of Medicine.

J. Gavin Bremner, Lancaster University.

Jeanne Brooks-Gunn, Columbia University.

Jondou J. Chen, Columbia University.

Kelli Connell-Carrick, University of Houston.

Peter Cooper, University of Reading.

Lisa Daunhauer, Colorado State University.

Raye-Ann deRegnier, Northwestern University Feinberg School of Medicine.

Shivani Desai, Northwestern University Feinberg School of Medicine.

Patrice Engle, California Polytechnic State University.

Erica Fener, The George Washington University.

Deborah J. Fidler, Colorado State University.

Sarah L. Friedman, Institute for Public Research.

Sarah Halligan, University of Reading.

Bryce Hella, Illinois Institute of Technology.

Nina Philipsen Hetzner, Columbia University.

Candace Hill, CAN.

Joyce Hopkins, Illinois Institute of Technology.

Kristen M. Hurley, University of Maryland School of Medicine.

Melissa R. Johnson, WakeMed Health and Hospitals & University of North Carolina – Chapel Hill.

Robert J. Karp, SUNY-Downstate Medical Center.

Edward Melhuish, Birkbeck, University of London.

David E. Most, Colorado State University.

Lynne Murray, University of Reading.

Sally Ozonoff, University of California, Davis.

Douglas R. Powell, Purdue University.

Gunilla Preisler, University of Stockholm.

Jennifer Strickland, Illinois Institute of Technology.

Harvey Switzky, Northern Illinois University.

Theodore D. Wachs, Purdue University.

Gregory S. Young, University of California, Davis.

Introduction to Volume 2: Applied and Policy Issues

In the time between the publication of the original *Handbook of Infant Development* in 2001 and the current publication of the two-volume revised *Handbook* there have been continued major gains in our knowledge of basic infant development. The contents of volume 1 document these gains. There also has been significant progress in applied areas, such as an increased understanding of what constitutes developmental risk in infancy, the nature and etiology of problems in infant cognitive and social-emotional development, and approaches to prevent or remediate developmental problems in infancy. The contents of the present volume reflect such progress.

While our knowledge base in the areas of developmental risk, developmental problems, and developmental interventions in infancy continues to increase, progress in these applied areas is often slower than progress in basic research in infant development. There are certain reasons for this discrepancy that are inherent to the area of research in applied infant development. One such issue involves the nature of research strategies used to investigate applied questions in infant development. Focusing on specific basic developmental processes such as infant perception or infant imitation, while a daunting task, nonetheless can be carried out using a relatively narrow "bandwidth" strategy. In contrast, by its very nature, research in applied infant development must be both multifaceted and involve multiple determinants. For example, as documented in several chapters in this volume, poverty is a major developmental risk factor. To understand how growing up in poverty translates into early and continuing developmental deficits requires assessing both early cognitive and social-emotional development, as well as integrating both biological and psychosocial risk factors nested under poverty (e.g., increased exposure to environmental toxins, reduced cognitive stimulation in the home). By its very nature such research is more difficult to carry out, thus slowing the pace of progress. A number of chapters in this volume illustrate both the multifaceted (chapters 5, 7–9, 12, and 14) and multi-determined nature of infant development (chapters 1, 5, 6, 8, and 11).

Further, as amply documented in volume 1, many of the major advances in our knowledge of basic processes of infant development are partly due to major advances in the procedures by which we are able to study infant development (e.g., see volume 1 chapters on auditory development, perceptual categorization and brain development). Unfortunately, many of these procedures are not appropriate for studying many critical applied developmental questions (e.g., direct measures of early brain development are appropriate for studying the neural consequences of child abuse in infancy, but tell us little about the multiple conditions that lead to child abuse), or are inappropriate for contexts that are linked to applied developmental problems (e.g., use of sophisticated computer-driven equipment is problematical in populations of infants growing up in low-income countries, where electricity is either not available or current flow is often disrupted). Thus, many of the procedures used to study applied developmental issues involve some form of observational methodology, which can be very time-consuming if done correctly (e.g., chapters 2, 4–6, 9, and 11–13).

The above two issues reflect the nature of the scientific process in the domain of applied early human development. Applied early developmental scientists continue to wrestle with them, but these issues are inherent in the field and are thus not likely to change dramatically in the near future. However, there is a third dynamic that must be considered, namely the relatively low level of communication between developmental scientists studying basic processes in infant development, and those studying more applied issues. Basic and applied developmental scientists publish in and read different journals, attend different specialty conferences, and, even if attending the same conference, usually attend very different sessions. One consequence of reduced communication is a lower likelihood of translation of basic research findings into solutions for applied problems in infancy. The reverse also holds. Reduced communication reduces the likelihood of generating new basic research questions, as a result of findings from applied developmental studies not fitting what might be expected from basic research findings.

There are a variety of reasons for reduced communication between basic and applied scientists interested in early human development. One such reason involves the use of very different theoretical models. For example, developmental scientists interested in basic processes such as the emergence of patterns of object manipulation in infancy (volume 1, chapter 5) and developmental scientists interested in child abuse and neglect in infancy (volume 2, chapter 7) both refer to ecological theories. However, in the former case the ecological theory referred to is that of Eleanor Gibson, while in the latter case the ecological theory referred to is that of Urie Bronfenbrenner. In this case the same term refers to radically different theories, which does not facilitate the process of communication.

Regardless of the causes of reduced communication (and there are many) we believe that both basic and applied developmental scientists interested in early human development will benefit to the extent that each group knows what the other group is doing, both conceptually and empirically. This benefit is certainly documented by known examples where basic research findings clearly inform our understanding of applied issues. One such example is in the area of autism spectrum disorders, where understanding of the nature and etiology of autism has been significantly advanced by basic knowledge in the areas of preverbal communication, language development, emotional development, and sensory processing processes. Similarly, our understanding of the etiology of early deficits in school readiness has been advanced by knowledge from basic infancy research in the cognitive (e.g., executive function) and temperament domains (e.g., self-regulation).

To maximize exposure of readers in both the basic and applied infancy areas to findings both within and outside of their primary interests we have chosen to publish this revision of the *Handbook of Infant Development* in two volumes rather than the traditional single volume. By maximizing exposure to basic and applied findings we hope to reduce the basic–applied communication gap referred to in the previous paragraphs. On the face of it, separating the *Handbook* into two volumes would seem to be a strategy that would reduce rather than enhance communication. However, we do not believe this will be the case. Given the variety of topic areas in early human development that are studied by basic and applied researchers, publishing everything in a single volume meant either leaving out some critical areas, or publishing a volume of inordinate length (and weight). Publishing in two volumes allows us to cover the breadth of both basic and applied infancy research and, as such, is a more accurate representation of the field. For example, in the original single-volume version of the *Handbook* there were eight chapters on applied issues. In volume 2 of the current *Handbook* there are 15 chapters covering a variety of important topics on applied developmental issues. By increasing the breadth of coverage we increase the likelihood that researchers, professionals, and students with specific basic or applied interests will encounter information from other areas of study in infancy that will be relevant to their own work.

Volume 2 of the current revision is organized into four major parts. The first two deal with risk factors occurring in the prenatal and infancy periods that can compromise both early and later development: part I is concerned with different biomedical risks, and part II with a variety of psychosocial risks. Part III deals with the nature of disorders of early cognitive and social-emotional development, as well as issues in the assessment of these disorders. Part IV contains chapters on early intervention, both at an individual and at a population (public policy) level. To maximize exposure to different topics, in each chapter we refer readers to relevant topics in other chapters in both volumes. As with volume 1 our target audiences are advanced undergraduates, graduate students, practitioners and scientific researchers interested in infant development.

For cataloguing purposes, the editorial order is alphabetic for both volumes. However, Gavin Bremner had editorial responsibility for most chapters in volume 1 and Ted Wachs had editorial responsibility for all chapters in volume 2.

Theodore D. Wachs and J. Gavin Bremner

PART I

Bioecological Risks

Introduction

The four chapters in this part of the book detail the nature and consequences of infant exposure to pre- or postnatal bioecological risk factors, which have the potential to compromise both early and later developmental outcomes. Chapter 1 by deRegnier and Desai on fetal development begins with a description of normal brain development during the prenatal period. The chapter then describes the various influences that can impair normal brain development during this period, including genetic defects, maternal nutritional deficiencies during pregnancy, the impact of fetal exposure to both legal (e.g., antidepressants) and illegal drugs (e.g., cocaine) or environmental toxins, and maternal stress during pregnancy. The chapter concludes with a presentation of recent evidence on the developing functional capacities of the fetus, including auditory processing, learning and memory.

Chapter 2 is by Black and Hurley, and covers the many aspects of infant nutrition, as viewed within the framework of developmental-ecological theory (e.g., Bronfenbrenner). This framework is evident in a number of topics discussed in the chapter such as the problem of infant failure to thrive and the development of child eating patterns. The chapter begins with a discussion of the role of macro- (e.g., protein, calories) and micro-nutritional deficiencies (e.g., trace minerals, vitamins) and breastfeeding in infant physical growth and cognitive and social-emotional development. Cutting across the nutritional spectrum, Black and Hurley then deal with the relation of parental feeding styles to the development of obesity in infancy, and conclude the chapter with a discussion of public policy contributions to programs designed to promote infant nutrition.

Chapter 3 by Karp focuses on relations between health and illness in infancy and various dimensions of infant development. Topics covered include the postnatal consequences of maternal diabetes during pregnancy, bacterial and viral infections during infancy (including issues centered around vaccination of infants), infant exposure to environmental toxins (e.g., lead), physical injuries, metabolic disease and infant colic. The chapter concludes with a discussion of how issues in infant health must be viewed within a larger social and cultural framework, including the availability of health care.

Chapter 4 by Preisler deals with the developmental consequences for infants who have significant auditory or visual impairments, with specific emphasis on infant–caregiver communication and infant language development. Preisler points out a shift in focus away from a deficit model (what children with sensory impairments cannot do) to a competence model (how children with auditory or visual impairments are able to communicate with their caregivers). Based on this distinction, a large portion of the chapter is dedicated to presenting evidence on the functional communicative capacities of children with sensory impairments. In addition, consideration is given to the impact on parents of having a child with auditory or visual impairment, the fundamental role parents play in helping their sensory impaired child establish communication, and means through which parental caregiving can be facilitated.

1

Fetal Development

Raye-Ann deRegnier and Shivani Desai

Introduction

In years past, the study of human development began at birth, as the weeks of gestation were a "black box" and the development of a live fetus *in utero* was largely invisible to psychologists interested in early development. Fetal anatomic brain development was described by pathologists many years ago and some aspects of hearing and motor development could be inferred by the reports of pregnant women. However, many aspects of the sensory, cognitive, and emotional development of the fetus were unknown. This situation changed dramatically with the advent of fetal ultrasound and heart rate monitoring. First used by obstetricians to evaluate fetal anatomic development (Figure 1.1) and well-being, these techniques have been significantly refined and are now used by psychologists to evaluate fetal responses to external events and to show evidence of fetal learning.

   This chapter will review what is currently known about the normal development of the fetal brain, including both the anatomy and function. It will also be important to understand how brain development is affected by genetic problems, nutritional deficiencies, maternal medical problems, and toxins such as alcohol. This chapter also will deliberate the thorny question of whether fetal experiences are important in setting up the basic framework of the brain or whether genetics rules the fetal period, bringing the nature vs. nurture question into a new realm for the twenty-first century.

Anatomic Development

The timetable of a normal, healthy pregnancy begins two weeks after the mother's last menstrual period. At this time, ovulation occurs as the egg is released from the ovary.

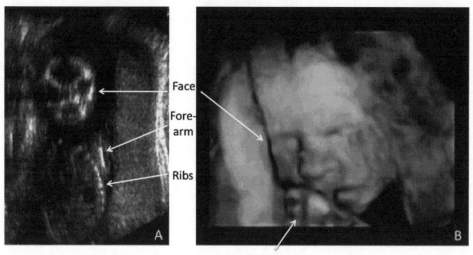

Figure 1.1   Two-dimensional (A) and three-dimensional (B) ultrasound pictures of the fetus, showing the fetal face (A and B) as well as fetal chest and abdomen (A).

The egg can be fertilized within several days of release from the ovary and the process of fetal development begins, culminating with the birth of the baby approximately 38–41 weeks after the mother's last menstrual period. This time *in utero* is known as gestation and the age of specific occurrences is known as gestational age.

The sperm and the egg contain half the genetic material (chromosomes) of each parent that combines to create a full complement of chromosomes for the new baby. Each set of chromosomes is composed of the sex chromosomes (XX for a girl, XY for a boy) plus 22 pairs of autosomes (nonsex chromosomes). Chromosomal arrangement in the newly fertilized egg is a process that frequently goes astray; approximately 20% of pregnancies end in first trimester miscarriages, and 50% of these are due to abnormal chromosomes (Goddijn & Leschot, 2000). Later miscarriages may also result from fetal chromosomal abnormalities, but some fetuses with less severe chromosomal abnormalities may survive till birth. This is particularly true for infants with trisomy of chromosomes 21, 13, and 18 or monosomy of the X chromosome in a female. In a baby with a trisomy, rather than the pair of chromosomes, there are three chromosomes, whereas in a monosomy, there is only one copy. Chromosomal abnormalities are important as they may result in alterations in the normal trajectory of brain development, resulting in significant differences in central nervous system function (Volpe, 2001).

The anatomy of brain development

Brain development has been traditionally divided into four processes: formation and differentiation of the neural tube; formation and migration of neurons; formation and elaboration of synapses; and myelination. In general, these processes occur sequentially, but there is temporal overlap, particularly between synaptogenesis and myelination (Nelson, 2002).

Formation and differentiation of the neural tube.   Formation of the neural tube begins very early in development, at 13–17 days after fertilization, with the development of a neural plate that folds in upon itself, and "zips" closed beginning near the base of the brain at about 22 days, and then proceeding simultaneously up toward the head (cranially) and down toward the base of spine (caudally). Failure of normal neural tube formation in the fetus leads to severe abnormalities; some of these result in stillbirth or early neonatal death (e.g., anencephaly), whereas others lead to the birth of an infant with an abnormal nervous system, such as spina bifida (meningomyelocele).

Differentiation of the brain continues through the second to third month as the neural tube folds on itself and cleaves to form the optic vesicles which will form the eye, olfactory bulbs (for smell) and major parts of the brain, including the cerebral hemispheres, basal ganglia, ventricles, and hypothalamus. In general, abnormal differentiation of the neural tube results in severe neurologic disorders in the fetus, often leading to stillbirth or death during infancy. Surviving infants may suffer from seizure disorders, severe developmental delay, hormonal abnormalities, blindness and difficulties with temperature regulation.

Neuronal migration.   Neurons begin to form in an area of the brain called the ventricular zone, peaking during the second to fourth months of gestation and finishing by 24–25 weeks' gestation, which is close to the age of viability for preterm infants. After formation, the neurons migrate out to initiate formation of a cortical plate that differentiates and organizes to form the layers of the cerebral cortex. Programmed cell death or apoptosis of some of the newly formed neurons occurs in human fetuses; generally this occurs to the greatest extent in the earliest developing areas of the cortex (Rakic & Zecevic, 2000). Surviving cells will form six overlapping and interconnected layers of cells that characterize the cerebral cortex. Each layer has distinct patterns of afferent (incoming) and efferent (outgoing) connections to other parts of the brain. Occasionally, the process of neuronal formation and migration does not proceed normally and this results in brains (and skulls) that are smaller or larger than usual. Affected infants often have severe seizure disorders and mental retardation. The formation and migration of neurons are processes that are sensitive to environmental conditions, which will be discussed in later sections.

Synaptic elaboration.   Initially, the differentiation of neurons and production of synapses are under genetic control and proceed similarly in all fetuses and infants in order to set up the basic neural networks that are important for neurobehavioral function. During development, each neuron elaborates dendrites and an axon. The axon is used as a superhighway by the transmitting neuron to rapidly send a signal that causes the release of neurotransmitters across a synapse to the dendrites of receiving neurons. These relays across specific neurons in different parts of the brain make up neuronal networks for specific brain functions such as auditory perception, memory, and voluntary motor function. The building of these neuronal networks begins in the fetus as neurons differentiate axons and dendrites and subsequently begin to form synapses with other neurons.

In nonhuman primates such as rhesus monkeys, all regions of the cerebral cortex appear to undergo synaptogenesis in a burst that occurs during a relatively short time interval. Two investigators in the 1990s suspected that this would not be true in human beings because specific brain functions come "on line" at different points of development. For example, even very young infants can hear and respond to sounds (auditory cortex) whereas some types of memory, such as working memory (prefrontal cortex), develop much later. Huttenlocher and Dabholkar (1997) proposed that synaptogenesis would proceed at different rates in different parts of the brain. Their research showed that synaptogenesis proceeded more rapidly in the auditory cortex than in the prefrontal cortex during the fetal period, with prefrontal synaptogenesis continuing on until about 3.5 years when the density of synapses was similar in these two areas. As these young synapses are used, they are strengthened. Those that are not used will die back (Haydon & Drapeau, 1995). The pruning of synapses occurs postnatally after the early infantile burst of synaptogenesis and is thought to be highly influenced by environmental inputs. How the fetal environment may affect the formation of synapses will be discussed later in this chapter.

Myelination.   The last process of brain development involves the production and laying down of myelin. Myelin is a fatty substance that is produced from glial cells. In the cerebral cortex, glial cells develop in the germinal matrix during the latter half of gestation and migrate out, align themselves along axons, and begin to form myelin. Myelination of axons results in an increased speed of transmission that allows for faster transmission of neural impulses. Relatively little myelination occurs in the fetus, and this occurs predominantly in the peripheral nervous system, spinal cord and brainstem (Paus et al., 2001). In the spinal cord and brainstem, myelination of the sensory areas precedes that of the motor systems. Myelination continues on for decades after birth.

Influences on Brain Development

Chromosomal abnormalities

The chromosomes can be thought of as the blueprint for brain development, and therefore chromosomal abnormalities can interfere with brain development at all stages. The most commonly recognized chromosomal abnormality, trisomy of chromosome 21, results in Down syndrome. Fetal studies of Down syndrome have shown normal brain development through 22 weeks' gestation, but by the time of birth, 20–50% fewer neurons are noted, and those have abnormal distributions, particularly in cortical layers V and VI (Wisniewski, 1990). Additionally, the prenatal development of synapses within the cortical layers proceeds abnormally, with decreases in protein markers of synaptogenesis noted during fetal life (Weitzdoerfer, Dierssen, Fountoulakis, & Lubec, 2001). However, most of the neuropathologic abnormalities seen in the brains of people with Down syndrome arise after birth as synaptogenesis and myelination proceed. There have been few studies of neurobehavioral function of newborn infants with Down syndrome, but low muscle tone is consistently noted after birth. Other neurobehavioral impairments in infants with Down syndrome may be relatively subtle in the first year of life, progressing over time and correlating with the more subtle abnormalities of fetal brain development in these infants. For detailed discussion of the postnatal development of infants with Down syndrome see chapter 12 in this volume.

Nutrition and brain development

The fetal brain grows more rapidly than other body organs; in a newborn infant, 12% of the body mass is due to the weight of the brain, compared to 2.8% of an adult's body mass (Bogin, 1999). Furthermore, the newborn brain accounts for 87% of the total resting metabolic rate (Leonard, Snodgrass, & Robertson, 2007) which is higher than requirements seen in older children and adults and higher than seen in other species. This means that the process of normal fetal brain development and the synthesis and release of fetal neurotransmitters requires the ongoing provision of relatively high amounts of all nutrients. However, protein, energy, specific types of fats, iron, zinc, copper, iodine, selenium, vitamin A, choline, and folate are particularly important for fetal brain development and subsequent neurobehavioral function. The importance of nutrition during gestation was illustrated by experience with a severe famine in Holland in 1944–5. Women who did not receive sufficient rations of food during midgestation and the third trimester had infants with smaller head circumferences (reflecting poor brain growth) than infants born to Dutch women before or after the famine (Roseboom et al., 2001). It should be noted that although malnutrition of pregnant women is not particularly common in developed countries, deficiencies of specific nutrients do occur as a result of maternal medical conditions such as diabetes, or medications such as oral contraceptives.

Early in fetal life, nutrient deficiencies may result in severe impairments. For example, folate is a vitamin that may become depleted with the use of birth control pills. Folate deficiency during the first few months of pregnancy can result in neural tube defects such as spina bifida (Rayburn, Stanley, & Garrett, 1996). Later in gestation, deficiencies of nutrients that are utilized globally, such as protein and energy, will result in a general lack of neuronal proliferation, differentiation and synapse formation (Georgieff, 2007). Poor transplacental transfer of both oxygen and nutrients occurs in infants with intrauterine growth restriction. Severely affected infants are at risk for low intelligence, behavioral problems, and poor memory abilities (Geva, Eshel, Leitner, Fattal-Valevski, & Harel, 2006; Walker & Marlow, 2008). These problems may lead to school difficulties and lowered economic potential in adulthood (Low et al., 1992; Strauss, 2000).

In contrast, some nutrients are utilized predominantly in specific neural pathways to synthesize neurotransmitters or in pathways that are particularly metabolically active at certain times in development. These deficiencies may have more specific effects. For example, iron is important in the function in parts of the neural pathways for recognition memory. Fetal iron deficiency may occur in the fetus, particularly in infants of diabetic mothers who are in poor control of their diabetes (Petry et al., 1992). These infants have been shown to have memory deficits starting at birth and persisting over the first year of life (DeBoer, Wewerka, Bauer, Georgieff, & Nelson, 2005; Sidappa et al., 2004). Although there are few specific studies of iron deficient fetuses, in animal models, iron deficiency disturbs a number of developmental processes, including the synthesis of monamine neurotransmitters and myelination. Information on the consequences of post-natal nutritional deficiencies is found in chapter 2 in this volume.

Effect of drugs, medications, and toxins on brain development

A wide variety of drugs, medications, and toxins have been shown to affect the fetus (Trask & Kosofsky, 2000). Fetal effects can occur via several mechanisms. First, drugs, medications, and toxins that can cross the placenta may result in acute intoxication of the fetus at the time of the ingestion. If the ingestion is near the time of birth, the newborn may show transient signs of drug intoxication. Second, regular use of physically addictive drugs during pregnancy can result in drug withdrawal in the newborn infant. Finally, specific exposures early in pregnancy or chronically throughout gestation may result in disturbances in brain developmental processes and subsequent cognitive and behavioral sequelae. The effects of such exposures may be variable, depending on the timing, dose, duration, and genetic vulnerability. In addition to the biologic effects of drug and alcohol exposure on the fetus, women who drink or use drugs during pregnancy may suffer from poverty, chronic stress, poor nutrition, and mental health problems. Women who use drugs and alcohol also have high rates of attention deficit hyperactivity disorder that may be inherited by their infants or affect their parenting skills (Schubiner et al., 2000). Thus, the use of drugs and alcohol by pregnant women may be accompanied by complex mental health problems and social factors that may independently affect brain development during or after pregnancy and have important effects upon parenting skills after birth. Interventions to improve outcomes for infants with fetal drug and alcohol exposure need to address both infant development and the home environment.

Alcohol.   Alcohol is one of the most commonly abused substances in the world, and unfortunately it is a known neurotoxin with severe effects during gestation. It has been difficult to quantify the amount of alcohol constituting a risk to the fetus, though clearly chronic alcoholism and heavy drinking carry higher risks than light social drinking. Infants born to alcoholics and heavy drinkers (less than 1% of pregnant women in the US) are at risk for the most severe symptoms classified as fetal alcohol syndrome (Substance Abuse and Mental Health Services Administration, 2008). Binge drinking was reported by 6.6% of American women during the first trimester of pregnancy in 2006–7 and is of concern due to the fetal exposure to a large amount of alcohol over a short period of time. Alcohol exposure between 4 and 10 weeks' gestation may disrupt neuronal migration, resulting in a loss of neurons and a small brain and head (Volpe, 2001). Brain imaging in children and adults with fetal alcohol exposure has revealed abnormal development in many parts of the brain important for learning, memory, and behavioral regulation, including the cerebellum, basal ganglia, and corpus callosum (Roebuck, Mattson, & Riley, 1998). Although there is a wide range of intelligence, fetal alcohol syndrome is the most common recognizable cause of mental retardation (Niccols, 2007). Further information on the long-term consequences of fetal alcohol syndrome is found in chapter 3 in this volume.

Illicit drugs. Though some decreases in illicit drug use have been noted in recent years, illicit drug use is still a major public health issue with implications for the fetus. Marijuana is the most commonly used drug, used by about half of drug-users, followed by prescription-type psychotherapeutics used nonmedically (including narcotic pain relievers), cocaine, hallucinogens, inhalants, and heroin. In 2006 and 2007, 5.2% of women reported using illicit drugs during pregnancy, with significantly higher rates (16.6%) reported by pregnant teenagers (Substance Abuse and Mental Health Services Administration, 2008).

Though it is the most commonly used drug of abuse, studies of fetal effects of maternal marijuana use have either shown no effects or conflicting mild effects on growth (Schempf, 2007). Nevertheless, marijuana use is still of concern as it may be associated with the use of tobacco or other drugs, the specific effects of which are described below.

Cocaine use during pregnancy received a great deal of media attention during the "crack" epidemic of the 1980s. There have been hundreds of studies on the effects of cocaine on pregnancy. It has been difficult to isolate the effects of cocaine on the development of the brain in the fetus due to the myriad of factors associated with cocaine use during pregnancy, including polydrug use, poor nutrition, and maternal mental health problems. However, cocaine does have physiologic effects on placental function, the fetus and the newborn infant (Woods, Plessinger, & Clark, 1987). Many of these effects result from the drug's effects on blood vessels. Cocaine causes constriction or narrowing of the maternal blood vessels in the placenta. This in turn reduces the blood flow to the fetus, reducing the oxygen and nutrients supplied to the fetus. Cocaine use also may lead to severe increases in blood pressure in the mother that may lead to premature birth due to separation of the placenta from the uterine wall (placental abruption). Prompt delivery of the fetus in this situation is often necessary due to life-threatening bleeding in the mother and loss of the fetal blood supply. Regular use of cocaine by pregnant women can cause poor fetal growth, which is the most consistently reported effect. Cocaine also causes premature labor as well as early rupture of the membranes surrounding the baby, which leads to a loss of amniotic fluid, infection, and subsequent premature birth (Schempf, 2007).

Cocaine also has direct effects on the class of neurotransmitters known as monoamines – norepinephrine, dopamine and seratonin (Mayes, 1999). These are important in brain development, and therefore alterations of neurotransmitter levels and release during gestation may alter the trajectory of brain development. In nonhuman primates, cocaine administration has been associated with abnormalities of neuronal migration (Lidow, 1998). It is difficult to determine whether this occurs in human infants as well, though there have been a few scattered and uncontrolled reports of brain developmental abnormalities . In contrast, destructive events such as strokes and brain hemorrhages have been well described as a result of the effects of cocaine in raising blood pressure and narrowing blood vessels (Volpe, 2001).

Studies of newborn infants exposed to cocaine *in utero* often show abnormal findings that sometimes dissipate when corrected for common confounding factors such as gestational age, use of tobacco or other drugs and social factors. Newborn infants exposed to cocaine shortly before birth may show signs of cocaine intoxication (Mastrogiannis, Decavalas, Verma, & Tejani, 1990), including abnormal muscle tone, tremor, hyperalertness, excessive sucking, high pitched crying, irritability, and autonomic (blood pressure and heart rate) instability (Bauer et al., 2005; Chiriboga, Brust, Bateman, & Hauser, 1999). These effects appear to be dose-dependent, with higher doses associated with more severe symptoms. It is not clear whether these symptoms are predominantly an effect of cocaine intoxication or drug withdrawal as most of the symptoms resolve after a few days, but in some studies neurologic abnormalities persisted for a number of months.

Isolating the long-term effects of cocaine on cognitive function and behavior becomes even more difficult as children grow older because the effects of the environment on development become stronger. Recent studies of preschool and early school-aged children exposed to cocaine prenatally have evaluated a wide range of developing abilities. Some of these studies have statistically adjusted for polydrug and alcohol use as well as the social environment. These adjusted analyses generally have not shown significant differences in intelligence or school achievement as a result of prenatal cocaine exposure, but poorer language development and subtle decrements in more discrete cognitive abilities have been demonstrated (Bauer et al., 2005; Behnke et al., 2006; Morrow et al., 2003; Singer et al., 2004, 2008). In several studies, cocaine-exposed children with smaller head sizes at birth had poorer long-term outcomes (Bauer et al., 2005; Singer et al., 2008). Positive effects of a good home environment have been noted in many studies, but unfortunately improvements in the home environment typically are associated with adoption or non-family foster care (Singer et al., 2008), as drug use and social problems may continue in the biological family after birth.

Narcotic use during pregnancy may occur in mothers addicted to heroin or methadone as well as in pregnant women with chronic pain syndromes who take prescription narcotics during pregnancy. Narcotics are physically addictive and higher maternal doses generally result in withdrawal symptoms in the newborn infant, including both neurologic symptoms such as excessive crying and high muscle tone, as well as physical symptoms such as diarrhea, rapid breathing, and sneezing. Uncontrolled narcotic withdrawal can result in seizures and death, and so newborn infants exhibiting physical symptoms of withdrawal must be placed in a dark, quiet environment and treated with sedatives or narcotics such as methadone (Sarkar & Donn, 2006). The medication dose is gradually decreased over a period of weeks to months and then discontinued. Neurologic symptoms may persist without physical symptoms even after the period of physical withdrawal is past (Desmond & Wilson, 1975).

Longer term studies of infants exposed to narcotics *in utero* have shown minimal effects upon long-term development compared with control groups raised in similar social environments (Kaltenbach & Finnegan, 1984, 1987; Ornoy, Michailevskaya, Lukashov, Bar-Hamburger, & Harel, 1996), suggesting that for narcotic drugs, the social environment associated with maternal drug use is of more concern than the effects of the drug on fetal brain development.

Antidepressant drugs.   Depression is common in women of childbearing age. Because untreated depression is a serious illness, many women are treated during pregnancy using a class of drugs known as selective serotonin reuptake inhibitors (SSRIs). These drugs block the reuptake of the neurotransmitter serotonin in the central nervous system. The use of these medications during pregnancy has increased in the past 10–15 years (Bakker, Kolling, van den Berg, de Walle, & de Jong van den Berg, 2008). Although the absolute risk of birth defects associated with the use of SSRIs appears to be small (Green, 2007), SSRIs used later in pregnancy have been shown to affect neurobehavioral function in the newborn infant. Infants may experience tremors, abnormal muscle tone, irritability, poor feeding, and breathing problems. These problems are usually mild, although seizures have been reported. Symptoms may occur as direct effects of the medication or due to withdrawal, as similar symptoms have been reported in adults under these conditions. They usually resolve spontaneously within two weeks (Moses-Kolko et al., 2005).

Because neurotransmitters are important in brain development, there is concern that any drug that alters neurotransmitter levels in the fetus may have effects on brain development and subsequent neurobehavioral function. However, in the existing studies of human infants, there have been no clear long-term neurobehavioral effects of SSRI use during pregnancy (Gentile, 2005). This is an important area of investigation for the future as there are few other therapeutic options for depressed pregnant women. Hormonal effects of maternal depression will also be discussed later in the section on fetal programming. Detailed discussion of the postnatal consequences of maternal depression can be found in chapter 8 in this volume.

Environmental toxins. In addition to drugs and medications, other environmental chemicals and pollutants may affect the development of the fetal brain and subsequent neurobehavioral function. Pollutants such as polychlorinated biphenyls (PCBs) and methylmercury may remain in the environment for many years, contaminating food and water supplies. Pregnant women may ingest these chemicals by eating contaminated foods. The pollutant methylmercury tends to accumulate in the fetal blood in higher concentrations than in maternal blood, and the brain accumulates concentrations higher than the blood, predisposing the fetus to neurotoxicity. The massive Japanese food poisoning that occurred in the 1950s and 1960s resulted in very high levels of methylmercury in pregnant women. Although the pregnant women had no symptoms, their newborns were at high risk for severe consequences, including small heads and brains at birth, cerebral palsy, blindness, deafness, and motor, speech, and cognitive dysfunction. Some of the effects had delayed onset (Castoldi et al., 2008). These effects appear to be dose-dependent as high levels of methylmercury in umbilical cord blood are associated with deficits in language, attention, and memory at 7 years of age, whereas lower levels have shown milder or less consistent effects (Castoldi et al., 2008; Grandjean et al., 1999). Interestingly, although fish may be contaminated with mercury, it also contains specific types of fat that are beneficial for brain development in the fetus (Daniels et al., 2004). The neurotoxicity of lower levels of mercury from fish may therefore be buffered by the benefits of the long chain fats that are also present in high concentrations in fish.

Summary: drugs, medications and toxins. The aforementioned studies make it clear that drug and chemical exposures in a pregnant woman can affect the developmental trajectory of the fetal brain, resulting in transient or longer-term effects on neurobehavioral development. Specific neurotoxins such as alcohol and methylmercury have particularly severe effects on development in high doses. Various psychotropic drugs and medications that alter neurotransmitter function in the mother and fetus are of concern due to the fact that neurotransmitters stimulate the development of the brain, but the effects of these drugs and medications in human beings appear to be subtle and difficult to isolate. It is theoretically possible that some of the psychotropic medications discussed in this chapter may have effects on adult mental health and behavior, but longer time lags between exposures and outcomes tend to increase the strength of intervening factors and make it difficult to conduct valid studies on these topics. For individual women and their infants, multiple risk factors or beneficial modulating factors before and after birth tend to create difficulties in attributing outcomes to specific factors. However, the good news within this complex problem is that adverse fetal exposures are not destiny, as a positive, nurturing environment after birth can help normalize outcomes in many newborns exposed to mild to moderate risk factors.

Fetal programming

Barker and Osmond (1986) reported that geographic patterns of death from heart disease in England in 1968–78 were correlated with previous neonatal mortality rates in those same geographic areas in 1921–5. They hypothesized that their findings indicated that poor nutrition very early in life increases a person's susceptibility to the later effects of the unhealthy eating habits associated with a Westernized lifestyle. This finding spawned thousands of epidemiologic studies that have confirmed and extended the findings of fetal or developmental origins of adult diseases. The basic concept of fetal programming is that fetal adaptation to adverse conditions during pregnancy may lead to lasting changes in physiologic functions that leave the brain or body vulnerable to later conditions. In addition to evaluation of adult medical diseases such as obesity and heart disease, later investigators have evaluated how maternal mental health problems or life stressors during pregnancy might lead to long-term emotional and behavioral effects in the child.

The fetal effects of maternal mental status are an important area of investigation because up to 20% of pregnant women have mental health problems such as depression and anxiety (Hollins, 2007). However definitively showing cause and effect in these types of studies is an extremely difficult proposition for several reasons. First, to establish plausible etiologic factors, it is important to use valid measures to quantify both life stressors during pregnancy and later outcomes. Maternal mental illness or life stresses during pregnancy are not likely to resolve simply with the birth of the child. Therefore, the postnatal environment may be just as important as the pregnancy. Complex or subtle effects require large numbers of subjects in order to disentangle fetal conditions from other risk factors. Large longitudinal studies, while difficult to conduct, are particularly important because the early developmental effects on the fetus and newborn may be tempered by the process of ongoing brain development in the context of postnatal environmental experiences. Finally, once a set of risk factors has been identified, it is necessary to prove some type of biologic mechanism in order to move toward prevention or therapy. Given these difficulties, many investigators have turned to the use of animal models of fetal stress during pregnancy. Although the applicability of fetal neurobehavioral studies in animals is necessarily limited due to species-specific physiology, these studies can provide useful complementary information about physiologic mechanisms and structural changes in the brain. Furthermore, animal studies can be completed in a shorter period of time than human studies and the information gleaned from animal studies can then be used to develop more focused, hypothesis-driven human studies.

Prenatal hormonal influences. The hypothalamic pituitary axis of the brain appears to hold the key to understanding how maternal stressors can lead to changes in fetal brain development that may affect later function. The hypothalamus is an area of the brain that links neural activity to hormonal activity through the pituitary gland. In situations of stress or perceived danger, the hypothalamus secretes a hormone called corticotrophin-releasing hormone (CRH). This hormone in turn stimulates the pituitary gland to secrete a second hormone, adrenocorticotropic hormone (ACTH), which stimulates the adrenal glands to secrete cortisol, a stress hormone that prepares the body for stress. As cortisol levels rise, they serve as negative feedback for the hypothalamus and pituitary glands to then decrease secretion of CRH and ACTH. Neuronal receptors in the hippocampus and frontal cortex appear to be important in this feedback loop and in animal studies (Talge et al., 2007).

One current working theoretical model begins with increasing cortisol levels in response to maternal stress (Diego et al., 2006). Maternal cortisol then passes through the placenta to enter the fetal bloodstream and activates the same receptors in the fetal and maternal brains. In the fetus, high levels of cortisol permanently alter the development of the glucocorticoid receptors in the hippocampus and frontal cortex by chemically altering the expression of the fetal genes and permanently decreasing or downregulating the number of receptors. Fewer receptors means there is less negative feedback to the hypothalamus and pituitary gland and therefore cortisol secretion continues without tight regulation in the fetus. This may leave the fetus hypersensitive to stress due to lack of timely termination of the cortisol response.

Prenatal maternal stress. Although confirmatory research is difficult to conduct in humans, preliminary reports indicate that maternal stress during pregnancy may have long-lasting implications for cognitive and emotional development. Studies taking advantage of natural disasters are particularly beneficial in this respect as the timing and severity of the stressor can be located precisely during gestation, and confounding with postnatal stress or mental health problems is less likely. LaPlante, Brunet, Schmitz, Ciampi, and King (2008) reported on the effects of a severe ice storm in Quebec in 1998 in which 3 million people lost power for up to 40 days. Women who were pregnant during this time were queried about specific events that occurred and their feelings of distress in response to these events. LaPlante et al. recently reported that full-scale and verbal intelligence scores were lower for 5½-year-old children whose mothers reported higher levels of objective stress (e.g., more days without electricity, moving to a shelter) during the ice storm, whereas subjective feelings of distress were not predictive.

This study design has also been used to evaluate long-term effects of prenatal stress on emotional development and mental health in adult offspring of women who went through a severe earthquake in Tangshan, China. Male (but not female) offspring had a later increased risk of depression if the earthquake occurred in the second trimester of pregnancy (Watson, Mednick, Huttunen, & Wang, 1999). Male (but not female) offspring were also found to have a greater risk of schizophrenia if they were in the second trimester of gestation during the 5-day German invasion of the Netherlands in 1940 (Van Os & Selten, 1998).

Other studies that have been helpful in understanding the effects of fetal stress have been those that have measured cortisol levels in pregnant women. Follow-up evaluations of their offspring were correlated with maternal cortisol levels. Although newborn assessments are not necessarily predictive of later function, newborn assessments do allow for quantification of fetal effects without the confounding of postnatal maternal mental illness or life stressors. Field and colleagues evaluated cortisol levels in pregnant women and found that women with higher cortisol levels were more likely to be depressed. Their infants were more likely to be premature, have lower birthweights, lower Brazelton habituation scales, and higher reflex scores than infants born to women with lower cortisol levels (Field et al., 2006). It is important to recognize that the possible effects of hormones other than cortisol have not been as well characterized, although some evidence suggests that norepinephrine levels are increased and dopamine levels are decreased in depressed women and their infants, compared with nondepressed women (Field et al., 2008). In addition, anxiety, anger and depression commonly occur together, and women with these conditions bear infants who show greater right frontal EEG activation, lower vagal tone, and altered sleep states with more time spent in deep sleep (Field et al., 2003).

Figure 1.2 summarizes the major stages of brain development during gestation and the effects of genetic abnormalities, maternal conditions, and drugs and environmental toxins.

Fetal Neurobehavioral Development

In the past it was thought that development of sensory function began at birth and that cognitive development did not develop until later in infancy. With the advent of more sophisticated methods of behavioral and neurophysiologic testing, it has become clear that neurons begin to fire during development, resulting in rudimentary sensory and cognitive functions during fetal life. Indeed, this incoming sensory neural activity may in turn promote further development of some areas of the brain (Mennerick & Zorumski, 2000). This section will review what is known about fetal neurobehavioral development. Information on postnatal brain development is found in chapter 9 in volume 1.

Techniques for evaluation of the fetus include fetal ultrasound and fetal heart rate monitoring. Fetal ultrasound reveals both static views of fetal anatomy and dynamic views of fetal movement, blood flow, and breathing. Postnatal evaluation of preterm infants allows for additional techniques, including evaluation of heart rate, motor activity, and behavior. Motor and behavioral responses to stimuli require not only that infants process incoming sensory and cognitive events but also that they have the ability to act upon this information by changing behavior. Where behavioral skills are limited, it is also possible

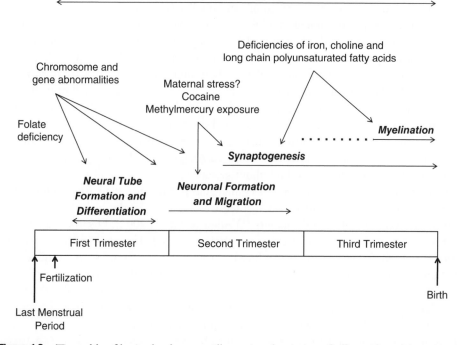

Figure 1.2 Timetable of brain development illustrating the timing of effects of nutrition, genetic abnormalities, maternal conditions, and drugs and environmental toxins. Note that myelination of the fetus is generally limited to the peripheral nervous system and brainstem until near full-term gestation.

to evaluate responses to the environment by recording brain activity in response to stimuli and environmental conditions. The two most common techniques for evaluating brain responses in preterm infants are the electroencephalogram (EEG), which monitors brain activity in a continuous fashion over multiple areas of the brain by recording from overlying skull and scalp, and evoked and event-related potentials (EPs and ERPs), which monitor brain activity occurring in response to discrete stimuli or events. Other techniques that have been used to evaluate the developing abilities of the fetus include functional magnetic resonance imaging (evaluation of blood flow patterns through the brain) and magnetoencephalography (detection of biomagnetic fields from the brain). These techniques are technically challenging but have been used to provide some information about development of the fetus and preterm infant.

Development of sleep states and the EEG

The development of sleep is an essential part of human development. One of the first manifestations of maturation of the fetal nervous system is the development of sleeping and waking states. The development of normal sleep–wake cycling occurs with normal maturation, and it is important to note that infants who suffer from brain damage will have sleep–wake cycles of different timing and quality (Osredkar et al., 2005).

The typical sleep states noted in adults such as rapid eye movement (REM) sleep do not develop until later in the first year of life. Early on, the fetal state is indeterminate. As the fetus matures and brain activity becomes more organized, differentiated sleep states are discernible by evaluating fetal cardiac activity and movements seen on ultrasound recordings. In the state of active sleep, fetal heart rate and fetal breathing movements are variable and twitchy or jerky movements are noted. In quiet sleep, the heart rate and breathing movements are regular and there is little movement, though startles may be noted. As the fetus matures, indeterminate sleep gradually becomes less common due to an increase in quiet sleep (Mirmiran, Maas, & Ariagno, 2003), though active sleep is more common than quiet sleep throughout gestation.

In preterm infants, it is possible to evaluate sleep states using an EEG. This is frequently used in nurseries and neonatal intensive care units at the bedside since it is a noninvasive way to look at brain activity (D'Allest & Andre, 2002). Electrodes are placed on the surface of the scalp and electrical activity is recorded. This electrical activity originates in the cerebral cortex and is conducted through the overlying tissues to the surface of the scalp. The EEG measures spontaneous brain activity that is composed of post-synaptic electrical potentials that are conducted through the scalp to the brain structures. The development of the EEG reflects the development of the brain. In the youngest preterm infants, the brain activity is discontinuous, meaning that activity alternates between high and low but sleep cycling is not observed. As the brain matures, between 28 and 31 weeks, the signal becomes more continuous and some differentiation is noted between active and quiet sleep. Initially, activity in the right and left hemispheres of the brain is not synchronous. Synchrony develops near the end of gestation, coincident with the development of the corpus callosum, a brain structure that links the two hemispheres (D'Allest & Andre, 2002).

In children and adults, EEG patterns of sleep state are well correlated with behavioral manifestations such as motor activity, eye movements, heart rate, and respiration. In preterm and full-term newborn infants, behavioral manifestations of sleep and the EEG recordings do not correlate well until later in infancy. Behavioral evaluations of sleep are considered to be the "gold standard" (Thoman, 1990) and five behavioral stages of sleep have been described (Table 1.1). Similar to the developmental pattern seen on the EEG, using behavioral evaluations, preterm infants show increasing amounts of quiet sleep as gestation progresses, with less time spent in transitional sleep.

Auditory Development of the Fetus

The fetal sound environment includes noises associated with the mother (speech, heart sounds, placental blood flow, and digestive sounds) as well as external noises that are transmitted through the uterus. The uterus filters airborne extrauterine sounds, moderately attenuating low-pitched (400–1000 Hz) sounds and further attenuating high-pitched

Table 1.1   Infant behavioral sleep states.

Drowse or daze. Infant's eyes are open but are opening and closing. Motor activity is low.

Active sleep. Infant's eyes are closed. Respiration can be uneven and REMs occur intermittently. Muscle tone is low. This stage will transition to REM sleep.

Active–quiet transition sleep. The type of sleep in between active and quiet sleep. The baby shows behavioral signs of both states. Muscle tone may vary, there is little motor activity, and respiration is not as regular as quiet sleep and more regular than active sleep.

Quiet sleep. The baby's eyes are closed and respirations are slow and regular. Normal motor tone is present and motor activity includes startles, sighs, or rhythmic mouthing. The baby may also move body parts and limbs. Premature infants have more limb movement than term infants. This quiet sleep is immature non-REM sleep in the baby.

Sleep–wake transition. The baby shows behavior of both wakefulness and sleep. There is motor activity, the eyes may closed or open and close rapidly. This state happens when the baby is waking up from sleep, usually active sleep.

(10 kHz) sounds (Lecanuet & Schaal, 1996). Environmental voices near the uterus are audible to the fetus, but because the higher frequencies are attenuated, vowel sounds are preserved more than consonant sounds, voices are muffled, and male voices are more intelligible than female voices. The rhythm and intonation patterns of speech and music are preserved (Gerhardt & Abrams, 2000). Querleu, Renard, Versyp, Paris-Delrue and Crepin (1988) estimated that up to 30% of extrauterine speech is intelligible *in utero*. For the maternal voice, a special situation exists because her voice is transmitted through the airborne route as well as through body tissue and bone, which results in less filtering of higher frequencies (Lecanuet & Schaal, 1996). The net result of this is that the maternal voice is louder *in utero* than *ex utero* and less subject to distortion of the acoustic properties than are the airborne voices of others.

Sound travels through the ear canal to the middle ear, inner ear, and brainstem before reaching the auditory cortex, where perception is thought to occur. All parts of the ear begin to develop in the embryo with the middle ear appearing to be functional by 18–20 weeks' gestation and the inner ear mature by 36 weeks' gestation (Lecanuet & Schaal, 1996). The brainstem also forms relatively early and has a short time course of myelination starting near 23–24 weeks' gestation and completing at about 37 weeks' gestation (Eggermont, 1988). The auditory cortex has a more prolonged period of development. Early synapse formation is seen in all six layers of the auditory cortex beginning at about 28 weeks' gestation (Huttenlocher & Dabholkar, 1997). Synaptic density is maximal in this area at 3 months of postnatal age. Thus, synaptic connections are present from the auditory nerve through primary auditory cortex by mid- to late gestation in the fetus, suggesting that fetal awareness of sounds may develop during the latter half of pregnancy.

Fetal hearing has been tested using a variety of methods (reviewed in Lecanuet & Schaal, 1996), with the most common responses being fetal cardiac responses and motor responses. By 23–24 weeks' gestation, some fetuses show an increase in heart rate or motor activity in response to sound. Fetal responses to sound become more uniformly present by about 27–28 weeks' gestation (Hepper & Shahidullah, 1994; Lecanuet &

Schaal, 1996). Fetal responses to sound include changes in heart rate (both increases and decreases), movement, and eye blinks. Fetal responses to sound appear to vary according to position of the head and ears (breech infants have different responses than infants who are head down) and sleep state.

Further information about the development of hearing later in gestation can be gained through neurophysiologic assessment of premature infants, who are able to survive outside of the womb by about 23–24 weeks' gestation (deRegnier, 2002). The auditory brainstem response (ABR) methodology has been used in a number of studies to evaluate the maturation of the auditory nerve through the brainstem. In an ABR, an electrode is placed on the scalp and thousands of clicks are presented to the infant through a tiny earphone. Brain activity is recorded and time-locked to the presentation of each click. Any artifacts due to movement are removed from consideration and the remaining brain activity is averaged together. When this is finished, the ABR shows a series of well-described, numbered peaks which track the transmission of neural impulses from the auditory nerve (wave I) through the medial geniculate body of the thalamus (wave VI) (Taylor, Saliba, & Laugier, 1996). Some infants as young as 24 weeks' gestation have shown reproducible waveforms indicating transmission of neural impulses through the brainstem (Amin, Orlando, Dalzell, Marle, & Guillet, 1999; Starr, Amlie, Martin, & Sanders, 1977), but the responses become more robust by 27–28 weeks' gestation. A great deal of maturation occurs in the auditory brainstem pathway, continuing through gestation and the first year of life (Salamy & McKean, 1976). Hearing thresholds improve (i.e., quieter sounds can be heard) and the speed of conduction within the brainstem improves dramatically between 24 weeks' gestation and term.

Sound transmits through the newborn brainstem in the first 10–15 milliseconds after the sound onset, but transmission through to the cerebral cortex takes much longer. This can be studied using long latency ERP studies. These studies are technically similar to ABR studies, as electrodes are placed on the surface of the scalp and sounds are played repeatedly while brain activity is recorded. However, in an ERP study, multiple areas of the scalp are sampled, complex sounds are used as stimuli and the interval between sounds is longer to allow for more time to reach the cerebral cortex. Using this process, cortical ERP responses to sounds have been generated as early as 23 weeks' gestation (Weitzman, Graziani, & Duhamel, 1967). In these extremely premature infants the waveforms are very simple, consisting of a large negative wave that peaks at about 180–270 ms over the midline and lateral parts of the scalp. The waveforms of the ERP show maturation as gestational age advances. In full-term infants, the waveforms show a positive peak over the midline, with either a negative or positive peak over the lateral scalp (deRegnier, Wewerka, Georgieff, Mattia, & Nelson, 2002; Kurtzberg, Hilpert, Kreuzer, & Vaughan, 1984; Novak, Kurtzberg, Kreuzer, & Vaughan, 1989). These changes in the waveforms indicate ongoing and rapid development of the cerebral cortex that will allow the fetus to begin to process environmental sounds.

Fetal sound processing has been also studied using fetal magnetic resonance imaging (MRI). MRI is a medical imaging technique used to develop detailed anatomic pictures of the brain using magnetic fields. Because there is no radiation, this technique can be safely used in the fetus. There is also a functional version of MRI (fMRI) that evaluates patterns of blood flow through the brain during neural processing (Davidson, Thomas, & Casey, 2003). The use of this technique is limited by the restriction that the fetus or infant needs to remain immobile during the study. However, making use of the natural immobilization that occurs with engagement of the fetal head in the maternal pelvic bones, fMRI was used by Hykin et al. (1999) to evaluate hearing in the fetus in response to the maternal voice at 38–39 weeks' gestation. Of the three subjects with technically satisfactory scans, two showed significant activation of the temporal lobe (presumably auditory cortex) that was also seen in adult control subjects. This study demonstrated fetal voice processing prior to birth in a manner similar to that seen in adults, showing that laying down adult neural networks begins before birth.

Experience and Fetal Brain Development

Given that the late-gestation fetus has the neuroanatomic connections to process incoming sounds, a natural question arises as to whether the fetal sound environment is associated with lasting effects on later development. Basic cognitive and emotional neural networks begin to form during the fetal period, but it is important to remember that these networks develop predominantly after birth and fetal cognitive functions are very rudimentary precursors of later abilities. When considering the influence of experience on development, it is useful to consider the concepts of experience-independent, experience-expectant and experience-dependent brain development and learning (Greenough, Black, & Wallace, 1987). Experience-independent development refers to brain developmental processes that are independent of experience (i.e., the genetic blueprints). Experience-expectant development occurs when neural networks are hardwired by experience, typically occurring in response to experiences that invariably occur during early postnatal development. Experience-dependent brain development is the result of learning that occurs as a result of experiences that are unique to each person.

In the fetus, experience-independent genetic factors predominate in development. The sequences of cortical development and early synapse formation described above show the same patterns in all humans. This is necessary to ensure that all humans have the same basic brain structures and abilities such as vision, hearing, and memory. Although *postnatal* visual and auditory experiences appear to be important in hardwiring some aspects of the sensory abilities, there is no evidence to suggest that fetal sensory experiences are important for long-term brain development.

A related question is whether the fetal environment is important in laying down early neural networks. If the environment is considered broadly to include hormonal and nutritional influences on brain development (discussed earlier in this chapter), there is emerging evidence that the environment in which the brain develops is very important in determining later function. Furthermore, based on studies of fetal learning and memory, there is evidence from a variety of sources that experience-dependent brain development occurs during the later fetal period.

Prenatal Learning and Memory

Neuroanatomically, development of the explicit memory network begins *in utero*. Recognition memory, a form of explicit memory, is the earliest type of memory to develop. It is a function of the hippocampus and medial temporal lobe structures, with inputs from sensory cortices. The human hippocampus begins to develop during fetal life, with development continuing to adulthood. Fetal development of the hippocampus has been elegantly described by Seress, Abrahám, Tornóczky, and Kosztolányi (2001). Most of the neurons in the hippocampal formation are formed in the first half of gestation, the exception being the dentate gyrus, where the neurons develop later. Projections from the hippocampus to other brain regions (e.g., entorhinal cortex) are noted during midgestation (Hevner & Kinney, 1996). These connections appear to be among the first cortico-cortical connections in the human brain. Although the human hippocampus is quite immature at birth, it appears that sufficient synaptic connections are present to support at least rudimentary recognition memory at term gestation.

Auditory learning is the most likely type of learning in the fetus, due to constraints in the visual, tactile, and olfactory environments. The most frequent types of auditory experiences will be those associated with maternal physiology and the maternal voice. Since the fetus hears the maternal voice whenever she speaks, the fetus has many weeks of experience by the time of birth. Although the duration of experience required for encoding in the newborn is not known, the fetal experience with the maternal voice should result in encoding if the neural mechanisms are sufficiently developed. For any comparisons of the fetal responses to the maternal voice and a stranger's voice, it is important to utilize recordings of both the maternal voice and the stranger's voice. This is important because if the mother is speaking naturally, the maternal voice will be louder than the stranger's voice and will have different acoustic properties due to tissue and bone conduction. Kisilevsky et al. (2003) tested term fetuses with 2-minute tape recordings of the maternal voice, a stranger's voice, and silence. The voice of the previous mother used in the study served as the stranger. They reported an increase in the fetal heart rate for the maternal voice for the 90 seconds post stimulus onset, whereas the stranger's voice led to a fetal heart rate deceleration. No differences in body movements were noted for the two voices. These data show that at term, the fetus is able to respond differently to the maternal voice than to a stranger's voice, suggestive of recognition memory.

After birth, recognition of the maternal voice and other fetal experiences has been tested by several authors. Querleu et al. (1984) videotaped 25 newborn infants (less than 2 hours of age) with no prior postnatal exposure to the maternal voice. Each infant listened to recordings of five voices, including that of the mother. The videotapes were scored by blinded observers who documented orienting movements to the maternal voice more often than to the strangers' voices. DeCasper and Fifer (1980) tested 2-day old infants with an operant sucking procedure and noted that the infants could learn to suck at a specific rate that would produce a recording of the maternal voice rather than a stranger's voice. DeRegnier, Nelson, Thomas, Wewerka, and Georgieff (2000) studied maternal voice recognition in 2-day-old newborns using ERP and described specific patterns of activity associated with the maternal voice. These patterns strengthened with increasing postnatal experience (deRegnier et al., 2002). In these studies, it was unclear whether the results reflected fetal or neonatal learning. However, DeCasper and Spence (1986) later showed that prenatal stimulation with specific speech sounds was associated with changes in newborns' perceptions of those sounds. Fifer and Moon (1995) also tested newborn infants with a filtered version of the maternal voice created to mimic conditions *in utero* compared with an unfiltered version. The newborns sucked preferentially to elicit the filtered version, providing additional evidence that intrauterine experience is encoded. Therefore, current psychobiologic and behavioral evidence supports the concept that late-gestation fetuses and newborns are capable of encoding auditory stimuli and show behavioral evidence of recognition memory.

Although it is more difficult to manipulate the fetal visual, olfactory, tactile, and gustatory environments, it seems likely that if regularly exposed to specific sensory experiences, the fetus would be capable of learning about these as well. Some researchers have devised clever studies to evaluate fetal gustatory learning by manipulation of the taste of amniotic fluid. The fetus is surrounded by amniotic fluid throughout pregnancy. The kidneys begin to function at about 12 weeks and by 20 weeks the amniotic fluid is composed nearly entirely of fetal urine, with a minimal amount derived from fetal lung fluid and some fluid filtered through the placenta (Cunningham et al., 2005). Fetal breathing and swallowing of amniotic fluid assist in the development of the lungs and the gastrointestinal tract and allow the fetus to smell and taste different flavors before birth. Food flavors (garlic, spices) that pass into the maternal blood can pass into the fetal blood and subsequently the fetal urine and amniotic fluid. This allows the fetus different taste experiences before birth as the fetus swallows and then tastes the amniotic fluid. If the fetus learns from this experience, it may result in the prenatal development of early food preferences. There is evidence that fetal taste experiences can result in alterations of later feeding behavior. For example, infants whose mothers drank carrot juice during pregnancy were evaluated months after birth for their first feeding of cereal mixed with carrot juice. These infants showed fewer negative facial expressions and more enjoyment of carrot-flavored cereal than infants whose mothers drank no carrot juice during pregnancy or after birth (Mennella, Jagnow, & Beauchamp, 2001). These data suggested that these infants recognized the carrot flavor as a result of their prenatal experience. In general, young infants show preferences for familiar stimuli and this may represent a mechanism for the early development of food preferences.

Conclusions

Exciting advances in our ability to evaluate the fetus in the last 20 years indicate that fetal brain development is marked both by uniformity and variability. Uniformity of the basic processes of brain development is genetically driven and allows for all humans to have the same basic brain structures. Individual variability is introduced due to the sensitivity of brain developmental processes to maternal nutrients, drugs, medications, and hormones that cross the placenta and alter brain development. It has also become apparent that the fetal brain develops functional abilities gradually as development progresses and that rudimentary learning can occur *in utero*. In the next 20 years, it will be vital to gain a further understanding of these complex interacting processes in brain development in order to develop better preventative measures for pregnant women (such as improved nutritional and mental health screening and treatment) as well as early interventions for preterm and full-term newborn infants from high-risk pregnancies.

References

Amin, S. B., Orlando, M. S., Dalzell, L. E., Merle, K. S., & Guillet, R. (1999). Morphological changes in serial auditory brain stem responses in 24 to 32 weeks' gestational age infants during the first week of life. *Ear and Hearing, 20,* 410–418.

Bakker, M. K., Kolling, P., van den Berg, P. B., de Walle, H. E., & de Jong van den Berg, L. T. (2008). Increase in use of selective serotonin reuptake inhibitors in pregnancy during the last decade, a population-based cohort study from the Netherlands. *British Journal of Clinical Pharmacology, 65,* 600–606.

Barker, D. J., & Osmond, C. (1986). Infant mortality, childhood nutrition, and ischaemic heart disease in England and Wales. *Lancet, 8489,* 1077–1081.

Bauer, C. R., Langer, J. C., Shankaran, S., Bada, H. S., Lester, B., Wright, L. L., Krause-Steinrauf, H., Smeriglio, V. L., Finnegan, L. P., Maza, P. L., & Verter, J. (2005). Acute neonatal effects of cocaine exposure during pregnancy. *Archives of Pediatric and Adolescent Medicine, 159,* 824–834.

Behnke, M., Eyler, F. D., Warner, T. D., Garvan, C. W., Hou, W., & Wobie, K. (2006). Outcome from a prospective, longitudinal study of prenatal cocaine use: Preschool development at 3 years of age. *Journal Pediatric Psychology, 31,* 41–49.

Bogin, B. (1999). *Patterns of human growth* (2nd ed.). New York: Cambridge University Press.

Castoldi, A. F., Johansson, C., Onishchenko, N., Coccini, T., Roda, E., Vahter, M., Ceccatelli, S., & Manzo, L. (2008). Human developmental neurotoxicity of methylmercury: Impact of variables and risk modifiers. *Regulatory Toxicology and Pharmacology, 51,* 201–214.

Chiriboga, C. A., Brust, J. C., Bateman, D., & Hauser, W. A. (1999). Dose-response effect of fetal cocaine exposure on newborn neurologic function. *Pediatrics, 103*(1), 79–85.

Cunningham, F. G., Leveno, K. L., Bloom, S. L., Hauth, J. C., Gilstrap, L. C. III, & Wenstrom, K. D. (2005). Fetal growth and development. In F. G. Cunningham, K. J. Leveno, S. L. Bloom, J. C. Hauth, L. C. Gilstrap III, and K. D. Wenstrom (Eds.), *Williams Obstetrics* (22nd ed.). New York: McGraw-Hill Professional.

D'Allest, A. M., & Andre, M. (2002). Electroencephalography. In H. Langercrant, M. Hanson, P. Evrard, & C. Rodeck (Eds.), *The newborn brain: Neuroscience and clinical applications* (pp. 339–367). Cambridge: Cambridge University Press.

Daniels, J. L., Longnecker, M. P., Rowland, A. S., Golding, J. & ALSPAC Study Team, University of Bristol Institute of Child Health (2004). Fish intake during pregnancy and early cognitive development of offspring. *Epidemiology, 15,* 394–402.

Davidson, M. C., Thomas, K. M., & Casey, B. J. (2003). Imaging the developing brain with fMRI. *Mental Retardation and Developmental Disabilities Research Reviews, 9,* 161–167.

DeBoer, T., Wewerka, S., Bauer, P. J., Georgieff, M. K., & Nelson, C. A. (2005). Explicit memory performance in infants of diabetic mothers at 1 year of age. *Developmental Medicine and Child Neurology, 47,* 525–531.

DeCasper, A. J., & Fifer, W. P. (1980). Of human bonding: Newborns prefer their mothers' voices. *Science, 208,* 1174–1176.

DeCasper, A. J., & Spence, M. J. (1986). Prenatal maternal speech influences newborns' perception of speech sounds. *Infant Behavioral and Development, 6,* 19–25.

DeRegnier, R. A. (2002). Morbidity and mortality of the extremely preterm infant. In L. K. I. Blickstein (Ed.), *Triplet pregnancy* (pp. 307–318). New York: Parthenon.

DeRegnier, R. A., Nelson, C. A., Thomas, K., Wewerka, S., & Georgieff, M. K. (2000). Neurophysiologic assessment of auditory discrimination and memory in healthy newborn infants and infants of diabetic mothers. *Journal of Pediatrics, 137,* 777–784.

DeRegnier, R., Wewerka, S., Georgieff, M. K., Mattia, F., & Nelson, C. A. (2002). Influences of postconceptional age and postnatal experience on the development of auditory recognition memory in the newborn infant. *Developmental Psychobiology, 41,* 216–225.

Desmond, M. M., & Wilson, G. S. (1975). Neonatal abstinence syndrome: Recognition and diagnosis. *Addictive Diseases, 2,* 113–121.

Diego, M. A., Jones, N. A., Field, T., Hernandez-Reif, M., Schanberg, S., Kuhn, C., & Gonzalez-Garcia, A. (2006). Maternal psychological distress, prenatal cortisol, and fetal weight. *Psychosomatic Medicine, 68,* 747–753.

Eggermont, J. J. (1988). On the rate of maturation of sensory evoked potentials. *Electroencephalography and Clinical Neurophysiology, 70,* 293–305.

Field, T., Diego, M., Hernandez-Reif, M., Figueiredo, B., Deeds, O., Ascencio, A., Schanberg, S., & Kuhn, C. (2008). Prenatal dopamine and neonatal behavior and biochemistry. *Infant Behavior and Development, 31,* 590–593.

Field, T., Diego, M., Hernandez-Reif, M., Schanberg, S., Kuhn, C., Yando, R., & Bendell, D. (2003). Pregnancy anxiety and comorbid depression and anger: Effects on the fetus and neonate. *Depression and Anxiety, 17*(3), 140–151.

Field, T., Hernandez-Reif, M., Diego, M., Figueiredo, B., Schanberg, S., & Kuhn, C. (2006). Prenatal cortisol, prematurity and low birthweight. *Infant Behavior and Development, 29,* 268–275.

Fifer, W. P., & Moon, C. M. (1995). The effects of fetal experience with sound. In J. P. Lecanuet, W. P. Fifer, N. A. Krasnegor, & W. P. Smotherman (Eds.), *Fetal development: A psychobiologic perspective* (pp. 351–356). Hillsdale, NJ: Lawrence Erlbaum Associates.

Gentile, S. (2005). SSRIs in pregnancy and lactation: Emphasis on neurodevelopmental outcome. *CNS Drugs, 19,* 623–633.

Georgieff, M. K. (2007). Nutrition and the developing brain: Nutrient priorities and measurement. *American Journal of Clinical Nutrition, 85,* 604S–620S.

Gerhardt, K. J., & Abrams, R. M. (2000). Fetal exposures to sound and vibroacoustic stimulation. *Journal of Perinatology, 20,* S20–S29.

Geva, R., Eshel, R., Leitner, Y., Fattal-Valevski, A., & Harel, S. (2006). Memory functions of children born with asymmetric intrauterine growth restriction. *Brain Research, 1117,* 186–194.

Goddijn, M., & Leschot, N. J. (2000). Genetic aspects of miscarriage. *Baillieres Best Practice & Research. Clinical Obstetrics & Gynaecology, 4,* 855–865.

Grandjean, P., Budtz-Jørgensen, E., White, R. F., Jørgensen, P. J., Weihe, P., Debes, F., & Keiding, N. (1999). Methylmercury exposure biomarkers as indicators of neurotoxicity in children aged 7 years. *American Journal of Epidemiology, 150,* 301–305.

Green, M. F. (2007). Teratogenicity of SSRIs – serious concern or much ado about little? *New England Journal of Medicine, 356,* 2732–2733.

Greenough, W. T., Black, J. E., & Wallace, C. S. (1987). Experience and brain development. *Child Development, 58,* 539–559.

Haydon, P. G., & Drapeau, P. (1995). From contact to connection: Early events during synaptogenesis. *Trends in Neurosciences, 18,* 196–201.

Hepper, P. G., & Shahidullah, B. S. (1994). Development of fetal hearing. *Archives of Disease in Childhood, 71*, F81–87.

Hevner, R. F., & Kinney, H. C. (1996). Reciprocal entorhinal-hippocampal connections established by human fetal midgestation. *Journal of Comparative Neurology, 372*, 384–394.

Hollins, K. (2007). Consequences of antenatal mental health problems for child health and development. *Current Opinions in Obstetetrics and Gynecology, 19*, 568–572.

Huttenlocher, P. R., & Dabholkar, A. S. (1997). Regional differences in synaptogenesis in human cerebral cortex. *Journal Comparative Neurology, 387*, 167–178.

Hykin, J., Moore, R., Duncan, K., Clare, S., Baker, P., Johnson, I., Bowtell, R., Mansfield, P., & Gowland, P. (1999). Fetal brain activity demonstrated by functional magnetic resonance imaging. *Lancet, 354*, 645–646.

Kaltenbach, K., & Finnegan, L. P. (1984). Developmental outcome of children born to methadone maintained women: A review of longitudinal studies. *Neurobehavioral Toxicology and Teratology, 6*, 271–275.

Kaltenbach, K., & Finnegan, L. P. (1987). Perinatal and developmental outcome of infants exposed to methadone in-utero. *Neurotoxicology and Teratology, 9*, 311–313.

Kisilevsky, B. S., Hains, S. M., Lee, K., Xie, X., Huang, H., Ye, H. H., Zhang, K., & Wang, Z. (2003). Effects of experience on fetal voice recognition. *Psychological Science: A Journal of the American Psychological Society/APS, 14*, 220–224.

Kurtzberg, D., Hilpert, P. L., Kreuzer, J. A., & Vaughan, H. G. Jr. (1984). Differential maturation of cortical auditory evoked potentials to speech sounds in normal fullterm and very low-birth-weight infants. *Developmental Medicine and Child Neurology, 26*, 466–475.

Laplante, D. P., Brunet, A., Schmitz, N., Ciampi, A., & King, S. (2008). Project Ice Storm: Prenatal maternal stress affects cognitive and linguistic functioning in $5\frac{1}{2}$-year-old children. *Journal of the American Academy of Child and Adolescent Psychiatry, 47*, 1063–1072.

Lecanuet, J. P., & Schaal, B. (1996). Fetal sensory competencies. *European Journal of Obstetrics, Gynecology and Reproductive Biology, 68*, 1–23.

Leonard, W. R., Snodgrass, J. J., & Robertson, M. L. (2007). Effects of brain evolution on human nutrition and metabolism. *Annual Review of Nutrition, 27*, 311–327.

Lidow, M. S. (1998). Nonhuman primate model of the effect of prenatal cocaine exposure on cerebral cortical development. *Annals of the New York Academy of Sciences, 846*, 182–193.

Low, J. A., Handley-Derry, M. H., Burke, S. O., Peters, R. D., Pater, E. A., Killen, H. L., & Derrick, E.J. (1992). Association of intrauterine fetal growth retardation and learning deficits at age 9 to 11 years. *American Journal of Obstetrics and Gynecology, 167*, 1499–1505.

Mastrogiannis, D. S., Decavalas, G. O., Verma, U., & Tejani, N. (1990). Perinatal outcome after recent cocaine usage. *Obstetrics and Gynecology, 76*, 8–11.

Mayes, L. C. (1999). Developing brain and in utero cocaine exposure: Effects on neural ontogeny. *Development and Psychopathology, 11*, 685–714.

Mennella, J. A., Jagnow, C. P., & Beauchamp, G. K. (2001). Prenatal and postnatal flavor learning by human infants. *Pediatrics, 107*, E88.

Mennerick, S., & Zorumski, C.F. (2000). Neural activity and survival in the developing nervous system. *Molecular Neurobiology, 22*, 41–54.

Mirmiran, M., Maas, Y. G., & Ariagno, R. L. (2003). Development of fetal and neonatal sleep and circadian rhythms. *Sleep Medicine Reviews, 7*, 321–334.

Morrow, C. E., Bandstra, E. S., Anthony, J. C., Ofir, A. Y., Xue, L., & Reyes, M. B. (2003). Influence of prenatal cocaine exposure on early language development: Longitudinal findings from four months to three years of age. *Journal of Developmental and Behavioral Pediatrics, 24*, 39–50.

Moses-Kolko, E. L., Bogen, D., Perel, J., Bregar, A., Uhl, K., Levin, B., & Wisner, K. L. (2005). Neonatal signs after late in utero exposure to serotonin reuptake inhibitors: Literature review and implications for clinical applications. *Journal of the American Medical Association, 18,* 2372–2383.

Nelson, C. A. (2002). Neural development and life-long plasticity. In R. M. Lerner, F. Jacobs, & D. Wertlieb (Eds.), *Promoting positive child, adolescent, and family development: Handbook of program and policy interventions* (pp. 31–60). Thousand Oaks, CA: Sage.

Niccols, A. (2007). Fetal alcohol syndrome and the developing socio-emotional brain. *Brain and Cognition, 65,* 135–142.

Novak, G. P., Kurtzberg, D., Kreuzer, J. A., & Vaughan, H. G. Jr. (1989). Cortical responses to speech sounds and their formants in normal infants: Maturational sequence and spatiotemporal analysis. *Electroencephalography and Clinical Neurophysiology, 73,* 295–305.

Ornoy, A., Michailevskaya, V., Lukashov, I., Bar-Hamburger, R., & Harel, S. (1996). The developmental outcome of children born to heroin-dependent mothers, raised at home or adopted. *Child Abuse & Neglect, 20,* 385–396.

Osredkar, D., Toet, M. C., van Rooij, L. G., van Huffelen, A. C., Groenendaal, F., & de Vries, L. S. (2005). Sleep–wake cycling on amplitude-integrated electroencephalography in term newborns with hypoxic-ischemic encephalopathy. *Pediatrics, 115,* 327–332.

Paus, T., Collins, D. L., Evans, A. C., Leonard, G., Pike, B., & Zijdenbos, A. (2001). Maturation of white matter in the human brain: A review of magnetic resonance studies. *Brain Research Bulletin, 54,* 255–266.

Petry, C. D., Eaton, M. A., Wobken, J. D., Mills, M. M., Johnson, D. E., & Georgieff, M. K. (1992). Iron deficiency of liver, heart, and brain in newborn infants of diabetic mothers. *Journal of Pediatrics, 121,* 109–114.

Querleu, D., Lefebvre, C., Titran, M., Renard, X., Morillion, M., & Crepin, G. (1984). Reaction of the newborn infant less than 2 hours after birth to the maternal voice. *Journal de Gynécologie, Obstétrique et Biologie de la Reproduction, 13,* 125–134.

Querleu, D., Renard, X., Versyp, F., Paris-Delrue, L., & Crepin, G. (1988). Fetal hearing. *European Journal of Obstetrics, Gynecology and Reproductive Biology, 28,* 191–212.

Rakic, S., & Zecevic, N. (2000). Programmed cell death in the developing human telencephalon. *European Journal of Neuroscience, 12,* 2721–2734.

Rayburn, W. F., Stanley, J. R., & Garrett, M. E. (1996). Periconceptional folate intake and neural tube defects. *Journal of the American College of Nutrition, 15,* 121–125.

Roebuck, T. M., Mattson, S. N., & Riley, E. P. (1998). A review of the neuroanatomical findings in children with fetal alcohol syndrome or prenatal exposure to alcohol. *Alcoholism, Clinical and Experimental Research, 22,* 339–344.

Roseboom, T. J., van der Meulen, J. H., Ravelli, A. C., Osmond, C., Barker, D. J., & Bleker, O. P. (2001). Effects of prenatal exposure to the Dutch famine on adult disease in later life: An overview. *Molecular and Cellular Endocrinology, 185,* 93–98.

Salamy, A., & McKean, C. M. (1976). Postnatal development of human brainstem potentials during the first year of life. *Electroencephalography and Clinical Neurophysiology, 40,* 418–426.

Sarkar, S., & Donn, S. M. (2006). Management of neonatal abstinence syndrome in neonatal intensive care units: A national survey. *Journal of Perinatology, 26,* 15–17.

Schempf, A. H. (2007). Illicit drug use and neonatal outcomes: A critical review. *Obstetric and Gynecological Survey, 62,* 749–757.

Schubiner, H., Tzelepis, A., Milberger, S., Lockhart, N., Kruger, M., Kelley, B. J., & Schoener, E. P. (2000). Prevalence of attention-deficit/hyperactivity disorder and conduct disorder among substance abusers. *Journal of Clinical Psychiatry, 61,* 244–251.

Seress, L., Abrahám, H., Tornóczky, T., & Kosztolányi, G. (2001). Cell formation in the human hippocampal formation from mid-gestation to the late postnatal period. *Neuroscience, 105,* 831–843.

Sidappa, A., Georgieff, M. K., Wewerka, S., Worwa, C., Nelson, C. A., & deRegnier, R. (2004). Iron deficiency alters auditory recognition memory in newborn infants of diabetic mothers. *Pediatric Research, 55*, 1034–1041.

Singer, L. T., Minnes, S., Short, E., Arendt, R., Farkas, K., Lewis, B., Klein, N., Russ, S., Min, M. O., & Kirchner, H. L. (2004). Cognitive outcomes of preschool children with prenatal cocaine exposure. *Journal of the American Medical Association, 26*, 2448–2456.

Singer, L. T., Nelson, S., Short, E., Min, M. O., Lewis, B., Russ, S., & Minnes, S. (2008). Prenatal cocaine exposure: Drug and environmental effects at 9 years. *Journal of Pediatrics, 153*, 105–111.

Starr, A., Amlie, R. N., Martin, W. H., & Sanders, S. (1977). Development of auditory function in newborn infants revealed by auditory brainstem potentials. *Pediatrics, 60*, 831–839.

Strauss, R. S. (2000). Adult functional outcome of those born small for gestational age: Twenty-six-year follow-up of the 1970 British Birth Cohort. *Journal of the American Medical Association, 283*, 625–632.

Substance Abuse and Mental Health Services Administration, Office of Applied Studies. (2008). *Results from the 2007 National Survey on Drug Use and Health: National Findings*. Retrieved from http://oas.samhsa.gov.

Talge, N. M., Neal, C., Glover, V. & the Early Stress Translational Research and Prevention Science Network: Fetal and Neonatal Experience on Child and Adolescent Mental Health (2007). Antenatal maternal stress and long-term effects on child neurodevelopment: How and why? *Journal of Child Psychology and Psychiatry, 48*(3–4), 245–261.

Taylor, M. J., Saliba, E., & Laugier, J. (1996). Use of evoked potentials in preterm neonates. *Archives of Disease in Childhood. Fetal and Neonatal Edition, 74*, F70–76.

Thoman, E. B. (1990). Sleeping and waking states in infants: A functional perspective. *Neuroscience & Biobehavioral Reviews, 14*, 93–107.

Trask, C. L., & Kosofsky, B. E. (2000). Developmental considerations of neurotoxic exposures. *Neurologic Clinics, 18*, 541–562.

Van Os, J., & Selten, J. P. (1998). Prenatal exposure to maternal stress and subsequent schizophrenia. The May 1940 invasion of The Netherlands. *British Journal of Psychiatry, 172*, 324–326.

Volpe, J. J. (2001). *Neurology of the newborn* (4th ed.). Philadelphia: W. B. Saunders.

Walker, D. M., & Marlow, N. (2008). Neurocognitive outcome following fetal growth restriction. *Archives of Disease in Childhood. Fetal and Neonatal Edition, 93*, F322–325.

Watson, J. B., Mednick, S. A., Huttunen, M., & Wang, X. (1999). Prenatal teratogens and the development of adult mental illness. *Development and Psychopathology*, 457–466.

Weitzdoerfer, R., Dierssen, M., Fountoulakis, M., & Lubec, G. (2001). Fetal life in Down syndrome starts with normal neuronal density but impaired dendritic spines and synaptosomal structure. *Journal of Neural Transmission Supplementum, 61*, 59–70.

Weitzman, L., Graziani, L., & Duhamel, L. (1967). Maturation and topography of the auditory evoked response of the prematurely born infant. *Electroencephalography and Clinical Neurophysiology, 23*, 82–83.

Wisniewski, K. E. (1990). Down syndrome children often have brain with maturation delay, retardation of growth, and cortical dysgenesis. *American Journal of Medical Genetics, Supplement, 7*, 274–281.

Woods, J. R. J., Plessinger, M. A., & Clark, K. E. (1987). Effect of cocaine on uterine blood flow and fetal oxygenation. *Journal of the American Medical Association, 257*, 957–961.

2

Infant Nutrition

Maureen M. Black and Kristen M. Hurley

Infancy is a period of rapid growth and development. In the first year of life, birth weight triples and infants progress from few voluntary movements and information processing skills to walking independently and communicating with caregivers. During this period, not only are infants' nutritional demands high to meet their increasing physical and developmental skills, but also infants are acquiring sophisticated feeding skills. They gain the postural skills to sit, the fine motor skills to self-feed, the oral motor skills to advance from a milk or formula-based liquid diet to a diet characterized by complex textures and flavors, and the social skills to respond to routines and interact with others during family meals.

This chapter addresses the nutritional and developmental transitions that infants experience during the first years of life that guide their early growth, feeding behavior, and development. We discuss: (1) human growth, including measurement; (2) the link between developmental theory and infant nutrition; (3) infant nutritional needs; (4) failure to thrive; (5) infant feeding behavior; (6) infant–caregiver feeding interactions; (7) policies and programs to promote infant nutrition; and (8) recommendations for future research related to infant growth and nutrition.

Human Growth

Human growth is influenced by multiple factors, ranging from genetic endowment and internal metabolism to environmental and cultural factors. Children require adequate nutrients to achieve expected indices of early growth and development.

Growth charts

Growth charts enable healthcare providers to determine whether children are achieving their physiological needs for growth. Growth charts are gender-specific and are used to compare children's growth with a reference population that includes children of all ages and racial or ethnic groups. Using standardized measurement procedures, growth charts are used to determine children's rate of increase in weight, length or height, and other measurements, such as head circumference and body mass index (BMI, defined, for children aged 2 or over, as weight in kilograms divided by the square of height in meters). Children's growth is commonly expressed in terms of percentiles or z-scores (the 50th percentile is at the median, the 5th percentile is at the lower level, and the 95th percentile is at the upper level of the reference population). Weight-for-age is an indicator of children's weight in comparison to other children of the same age. Although it is commonly used in pediatric practice and is a good indicator of change in weight over time, it is a confounded measure because it does not account for differences in length or height. Thus, conclusions about children's growth patterns cannot be made without information about their stature.

Height-for-age is an indicator of children's linear growth in comparison to other children of the same age (recumbent length for children under age 2 years, standing height for children aged 2 years or older). Children who experience chronic or severe undernutrition often experience a slowdown in the rate of weight gain as their body conserves energy, followed by a slow down in the rate of linear growth. Children whose height-for-age drops below a z-score of −2 below the median are considered to be stunted. Children who experience stunting prior to 2 years of age are at risk for academic and behavioral problems during school age. Cross-sectional and longitudinal studies have found associations between stunting and children's health and development, caused by underlying factors, such as undernutrition, and infections, such as diarrhea (Berkman, Lescano, Gilman, Lopez, & Black, 2002; Mendez & Adair, 1999; Walker, Chang, Powell, Simonoff, & Grantham-McGregor, 2007). For example, a pooled analysis of nine longitudinal studies from five countries showed that five or more episodes of diarrhea prior to 24 months led to a 25% increase in the risk of stunting at 24 months (Checkley et al., 2008). The consequences associated with early stunting include metabolic changes, depressed immune function, morbidity, mortality, delayed motor skills, delayed and irregular school attendance, low cognitive scores, and poor academic achievement. Adults with a history of stunting are at risk for obesity, reduced glucose tolerance, coronary heart disease, hypertension, and osteoporosis, as well as decreased work performance and productivity, thereby limiting economic capacity (Uauy, Kain, Mericq, Rojas, & Corvalan, 2008; Victora et al., 2008). In settings in which stunting is prevalent, the economic capacity of the entire society may be diminished.

Weight-for-length or weight-for-height is the third indicator that is commonly used to measure children's growth. It provides an estimate of fat stores. Failure to thrive is sometimes defined as weight-for-height below the 5th percentile, and wasting, a marker of acute weight loss, is defined as weight-for-height below a z-score of −2 below the median. At the other end of the spectrum, among children under 2 years of age, obesity is defined by weight-for-length at or above the 95th percentile (Krebs et al., 2007).

Among children 2 years and over, obesity is defined as BMI at or above the 95th percentile and overweight is defined BMI at or above the 85th and below the 95th percentile (Kuczmarski et al., 2000).

The United States relies on growth charts developed by the National Center for Health Statistics and made available through the Centers for Disease Control and Prevention (http://www.cdc.gov/GROWTHCHARTS/). The charts were developed in 1977 and have been updated periodically. The most recent update, conducted in 2000, includes breastfed babies and provides BMI charts for children over age 2 years.

Multicenter Growth Reference Study

Other countries have been reluctant to use growth charts based exclusively on children from the United States. Between 1997 and 2003 the World Health Organization (WHO) undertook a Multicenter Growth Reference Study (MGRS) to examine whether they could define an international growth standard for children (de Onis et al., 2007). A standard differs from a reference in that a standard defines how children *should* grow, rather than how they *do* grow. The MGRS was based on healthy children from middle-class families recruited from six diverse countries (Brazil, Ghana, India, Norway, Oman, and the United States). Mothers agreed to participate in health-promoting practices, including breastfeeding and not smoking. Children were weighed and measured longitudinally. Analyses showed that there was little variability in children's linear growth across the six sites. Most of the variability in growth could be attributed to individual characteristics. These findings highlight that in the context of healthy caregiving practices, there is little variability in young children's growth.

Birth weight

Birth weight serves as an initial indicator of infant nutritional status. In a recent review of five longitudinal cohort studies from Brazil, Guatemala, India, the Philippines, and South Africa, indices of child undernutrition (birth weight, intrauterine growth restriction, weight, length, and BMI at 2 years) were related to adult stature and to outcomes that extended to health, educational, and economic indices (Victora et al., 2008). Outcomes also extended to the next generation. Women with few indices of undernutrition from their own childhood were more likely to give birth to infants with a normal birth weight than women with multiple indices of child undernutrition (Victora et al., 2008).

Theory and Methods: Link between Infant Development and Infant Nutrition

Developmental-ecological theory (DET) is a useful theoretical basis for the study of early growth, feeding behavior, and development because it conceptualizes infant

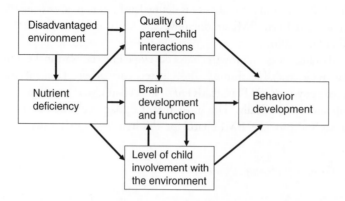

Figure 2.1 Association between nutritional deficiency and children's behavior and development. *Source*: Adapted from Wachs (2002).

behavior and development through an interactive process in which infants and their caregivers influence one another and, in turn, are influenced by multiple physical, social, and cultural factors (Bronfenbrenner & Ceci, 1994; Budetti, Berry, Butler, Collins, & Abrams, 2000). Based on DET, characteristics of the infant (e.g., birth weight, age, size, and temperament), the caregiver (e.g., beliefs regarding food and early child behavior and development), the household, and the community combine to influence parenting and feeding practices (Belsky, 1984; Black & Hurley, 2008; Hurley, Black, Papas, & Caulfield, 2008).

DET emphasizes the consideration of both direct and indirect models. In direct models, environmental factors, such as nutrition, impact children's development. There is striking evidence from animal research demonstrating the direct effects of nutritional deprivation on structural and functional changes in the developing brain (Bianco, Wiesinger, Earley, Jones, & Beard, 2008; Dobbing, 1972). The negative effects of nutritional deprivation on children's growth are another example of direct effects.

Evidence from both human and animal studies also supports indirect models (Levitsky & Barnes, 1972; Wachs, 2002). For example, nutritional deprivation may interfere with children's interactions with caregivers and opportunities for environmental stimulation. Thus, in addition to the direct effects of nutritional deprivation on development, undernourished infants who are unable to elicit or respond to environmental stimulation may also be denied the environmental enrichment that promotes development (Figure 2.1).

Nutrients for Infant Growth and Development

Nutrient requirements, influenced by rapid cell division and growth, are higher on a per-kilogram basis during infancy than at any other developmental stage, making infants particularly vulnerable to micro- and macronutrient deficiencies (Kleinman, 2004). Recommendations for infant feeding (including those set forth by the American Academy

Table 2.1 Infant feeding recommendations.

Breastfeed exclusively for the first 6 months, continue for at least 12 months.

Substitute iron-fortified infant formula for breast milk, if necessary.

Delay introduction of water until 6 months of age (requirements are met when adequate amounts of breast milk or infant formula are consumed).

Introduce iron-rich complementary foods (via spoon) at 6 months (i.e. infant cereal).

Gradually introduce a variety of pureed fruits and vegetables.

Introduce whole-fat cow's milk at 1 year of age.

Introduce reduced-fat cow's milk at 2 years of age.

of Pediatrics) support optimal infant nutrition, growth, and development through breast-feeding, the use of iron-fortified infant formula when breast milk is not available, and the appropriate introduction of complementary foods (Table 2.1).

Human milk alone provides sufficient amounts of the carbohydrates, fats, proteins, vitamins, and minerals needed for normal growth and development during early infancy. In the first six months, water, juice, and other foods are generally unnecessary. While infants are usually born with enough stored iron for four to six months, iron and vitamin D may need to be given before 6 months of age in selected groups of infants (iron for infants with low iron stores or anemia; vitamin D for infants whose mothers are vitamin D deficient or infants not exposed to adequate sunlight).

Most babies are ready to start supplemental foods at 6 months of age. Single-grain cereal is often the first food offered, followed by other single-ingredient foods. New foods should be added one at a time, at intervals of a few days. This progression allows infants to get used to the flavors of new foods and can help caregivers determine if specific foods disagree with their infant. Special efforts should be made to provide infants with iron and zinc during the first two years. The best sources of iron are meats, poultry, and iron-fortified infant cereal. Dietary sources of zinc include oat cereals, meats and poultry, wheat germ, egg yolk, and cheddar cheese. Calcium is abundant in milk and other dairy products. During the first year of life infants should not receive cow's milk, but should receive human milk or iron-fortified infant formula.

Macronutrients

Nutrients are chemicals needed for growth or metabolism which are obtained from the environment, typically through food. Macronutrients are required in large quantities; the primary macronutrients are carbohydrates, proteins, and fats. While carbohydrates, primarily lactose, are the principal source of dietary energy between 7 and 12 months of age, dietary fat provides up to 50% (from human milk and/or infant formula) of the calories supplied between 0 and 6 months (Kleinman, 2004). Dietary fat requirements decrease across infancy and the lifespan as energy needs for growth and brain development decrease. Protein requirements (providing approximately 6% of total calories) increase with age and in infants undergoing catch-up growth (i.e., premature infants).

Micronutrients

Micronutrients are nutrients required in small quantities. They include essential vitamins and minerals that are not produced by the body and must be acquired through diet, fortification, or supplementation. Iodine, iron, and zinc have been linked to growth, cognition, and social development in infants and young children. In addition, at least four vitamins (A, B6, B9, and B12) have been associated with infant development.

Iodine deficiency.   Iodine deficiency is a major problem that affects children in areas where iodine is depleted from the soil. Iodine deficiency occurs primarily in mountainous regions, such as the Himalayas and the Andes, and in flood plains. A report from the WHO (2007) estimates that nearly 2 billion people are iodine-deficient worldwide.

When iodine deficiency occurs *in utero*, it leads to fetal hypothyroidism and irreversible neurological and cognitive deficits, manifested as cretinism. Neurological cretinism includes mental retardation, primitive reflexes, visual problems, facial deformities, stunted growth, and diplegia (WHO, 1993). When iodine deficiency occurs postnatally, the child may experience thyroid failure that can lead to hypothyroidism and an enlarged thyroid gland, a goiter. Most of the studies examining the relation between iodine deficiency and cognitive performance have been conducted among school-age children. However, a study from Belgium demonstrated that infants (aged 6–36 months) experience iodine deficiency at the same rate as older children and adults and are therefore at risk for the negative consequences of iodine deficiency (Delange, Wolff, Gnat, Dramaix, Pilchen, & Vertongen, 2001). In two meta-analyses of observational studies that compared school-age children based on the iodine status of their community, children who lived in iodine-deficient areas had IQ scores that averaged 12.5–13.5 points lower than children who lived in iodine-sufficient areas (Bleichrodt & Resing, 1994; Halpern, 1994). In a well-controlled observational study in Bangladesh, investigators found that school-age children with mild levels of hypothyroidism had deficits in spelling and reading, compared to healthy controls (Huda, Grantham-McGregor, Rahman, & Tomkins, 1999). Although evidence from these studies is compelling, families who live in iodine-deficient areas are often more impoverished than families in areas where iodine is adequate, highlighting the importance of considering nutritional–environmental interactions, as portrayed in Figure 2.1.

Several randomized trials have been conducted to examine the impact of iodine supplementation on the cognitive performance of school-age children in iodine-deficient areas. However, results have not been consistent. In a recent longitudinal follow-up of school-age children, all of whom received iodine, those who received iodine *in utero* prior to the third trimester had better scores on a measure of psychomotor performance than children who received iodine later in pregnancy or at age 2 years (O'Donnell et al., 2002). There was a similar trend when measures of cognitive performance were considered; however, the differences did not reach significance. Thus, the effects of postnatal iodine deficiency on children's cognitive performance are less clear than the effects of prenatal iodine deficiency, suggesting an important role of iodine during early brain development and function. Further studies examining the effects of iodine supplementation during the first two years of life on children's cognitive performance are warranted. In addition, many of the previous studies have had methodological problems that interfere with interpretation, including inconsistent definition of iodine deficiency.

Iron deficiency.   Iron deficiency is the most common nutritional deficiency in the world, and often results in anemia (Yip, 1994). A joint report by the WHO and UNICEF (2004) estimated that 2 billion people are experiencing anemia, 50% caused by iron deficiency and the remaining caused by chronic diseases, such as malignancies, HIV infection, and other infections. High risk of iron deficiency occurs during times of rapid growth and nutritional demand, particularly during infancy (ages 6–24 months).

Iron is necessary for hemoglobin synthesis. Iron deficiency leads to reduced oxygen carrying capacity and can impact immunity, growth, and development. Iron has multiple roles in neurotransmitter systems and may affect behavior through its effects on dopamine metabolism (Beard, 2001). The association between iron deficiency and dopamine metabolism is highly relevant to children's early cognitive development as dopamine clearance has strong effects on attention, perception, memory, motivation, and motor control (Beard, 2001).

Multiple observational studies have found that infants who experience anemia early in life have low scores on tests of mental performance and are fearful, inattentive, and solemn with low levels of initiation and exploration (Honig & Oski, 1984; Iannotti, Tielsch, Black, & Black, 2006; Lozoff et al., 1998, 2007; Lozoff, Klein, & Prabucki, 1986). Many children continue to demonstrate lower academic performance during their school-age years, even when the anemia has been treated. The Special Nutritional Supplemental Program for Women, Infants, and Children (WIC) routinely evaluates hemoglobin for anemia after infants are 9 months of age. In an evaluation of low-income infants enrolled in the Florida WIC Program, those who were anemic early in life were more likely to experience academic problems at 10 years of age, compared to children who were not anemic (Hurtado, Claussen, & Scott, 1999). Concurrent iron status among school-age children is also related to academic performance, as demonstrated in an investigation from over 5000 children aged 6–16 from NHANES III (Halterman, Kaczorowski, Aligne, Auinger, & Szilagyi, 2001). When standardized math test scores were examined controlling for background variables, children with iron deficiency with and without anemia had lower scores than children with normal iron status. Thus, iron deficiency, even without anemia, may place children at risk for cognitive delays.

Iron-deficiency anemia (IDA) has been associated with poor and slow cognitive performance among college women in the United States (Murray-Kolb & Beard, 2007) and with depression and parenting behavior characterized by low responsivity and controlling behavior among South African women (Beard et al., 2005; Perez et al., 2005). Iron treatment improved the women's iron status, cognitive processing, depressive symptoms, and parenting behavior. Thus, while IDA among infants may impact their development directly, IDA among caregivers may alter caregiving behavior, with indirect effects on the infant, consistent with predictions from DET (Figure 2.1).

Zinc deficiency.   Zinc is a trace mineral that is involved with DNA and RNA synthesis and the metabolism of proteins, carbohydrates, and fat. Findings on the cognitive effects from the zinc supplementation studies lack clarity (Black, 1998). Four published trials reported beneficial effects of zinc supplementation on infants' activity, motor quality, or motor development (Bentley et al., 1997; Castillo-Duran et al., 2001; Friel et al., 1993; Sazawal et al., 1996), one reported that zinc-supplemented infants were more cooperative (Ashworth, Morris, Lira, & Grantham-McGregor, 1998), three found no differences in mental development (Ashworth et al., 1998; Castillo-Duran et al., 2001; Friel et al., 1993), and one reported that supplemented infants had slightly lower scores on mental development than comparison children (Hamadani et al., 2001). One study found beneficial effects of zinc supplementation on general infant development, but only in the context of psychosocial stimulation (Meeks Gardner et al., 2005), suggesting that the beneficial effects of the supplement may only be apparent in the context of a stimulating environment. These findings are consistent with DET, highlighting the importance of considering the environmental context and indirect effects when evaluating the relation between nutritional status and infant development (Figure 2.1).

At least two studies have examined zinc supplementation in combination with iron supplementation. One found beneficial effects of the two micronutrients on infants' motor development and behavior (Black et al., 2004) and the other did not (Lind et al., 2004). More work is necessary to clarify the role of zinc supplementation on infants' performance, particularly in the context of other micronutrients and a stimulating environment.

Vitamin A.   Vitamin A deficiency has long been associated with vision problems, but it is also an important agent in protecting the human body from infections and illnesses (i.e. diarrhea and measles) by enhancing the epithelial tissues. Evidence from multiple sites has shown that dosing infants with vitamin A during the pre- and postnatal period reduces mortality (West, 2003).

Vitamin B6.   Vitamin B6 (pyridoxine) converts foods into stored carbohydrates or fat. Mothers with low vitamin B6 concentrations in their breast milk have been observed to be less responsive caregivers and their infants showed more temperamental difficulties than mothers with adequate concentrations of vitamin B6 (McCullough et al., 1990; Ooylan, Hart, Porter, & Driskell, 2002). Recent studies have examined the impact of vitamin B6 on the behavior of children with autism. However, a recent Cochrane Review (Nye & Brice, 2005) concluded that there was no evidence to suggest that B6 supplementation improved the behavior of children with autism.

Vitamin B9.   Vitamin B9 (folic acid) plays a critical role in neural tube formation. Vitamin B9 is recommended for all women, not only pregnant women, because neural tube formation occurs during the first month of pregnancy before many women know that they are pregnant. Folate levels are lowest among minority and socioeconomically disadvantaged women. Thus, public health messages, targeting populations at risk, are needed to prevent folate deficiencies during the child-bearing years (Kaiser, Allen, & American Dietetic Association, 2008).

Vitamin B12. Vitamin B12 (cobalamin) is involved in red cell production and in myelination. Under normal circumstances, infants are born with adequate stores of vitamin B12 for the first several months post partum. However, infants of vitamin B12 deficient breastfeeding mothers or infants receiving low animal source foods may be vulnerable to vitamin B12 deficiency between 6 and 12 months of age. Among infants, vitamin B12 deficiency has been associated with neurological symptoms, including delayed motor skills and lethargy. Recovery following treatment is variable, with some infants experiencing permanent disabilities. Most of the information regarding vitamin B12 deficiency in infancy is from case studies of infants exclusively breastfed by mothers on vegan, vegetarian, or lactovegetarian diets. Although the mechanisms linking vitamin B12 deficiency to disruptions in infant development are not clear, vitamin B12 deficiency appears to interfere with early brain development, possibly through demyelination. Additional research is needed to better understand the associations between vitamin B12 deficiency and early development, along with strategies to prevent deficiencies (Black, 2008).

Long-chain polyunsaturated fatty acids. Long-chain polyunsaturated fatty acids (LCPUFAs), including docosahexaenoic acid (DHA) and arachidonic acid, are preferentially incorporated into neural cells and are important for retinal and cortical development (Gibson, Chen, & Makrides, 2001). Evidence from animal studies has demonstrated the importance of fatty acids in brain structure and function. For example, rodent studies have shown that reduced brain DHA concentrations are related to functional changes, including poor cognitive and behavioral ability (McNamara & Carlson, 2006). In addition, rodent studies have shown that restriction of LCPUFAs during early infancy may result in impaired neural function and performance that cannot be reversed by improvements in diet, suggesting that LCPUFAs may play an important role during critical periods of development (McNamara & Carlson, 2006). Related to infant development, LCPUFAs have been linked to infant visual acuity and neurodevelopment and to maternal depression.

LCPUFAs are most actively accreted into the fetal brain during the last trimester of pregnancy, making preterm infants especially vulnerable for LCPUFA deficiency (Clandinin et al., 1980). However, there is concern that preterm infants may be unable to synthesize enough LCPUFA. In a recent Cochrane review, Simmer, Schulzke, and Patole (2008) reviewed 15 randomized controlled trials of LCPUFA supplementation to preterm infants (most infants were relatively mature and healthy); 11 of the 15 trials met stringent inclusion criteria. Although findings differed, the authors concluded that there were no clear effects of LCPUFA supplementation on preterm infants' visual acuity, neurodevelopment, or growth.

DHA content is higher in breast milk than in infant formula, leading to the production of LCPUFA-supplemented formulas. However, data on the effects of LCPUFAs during pregnancy, lactation, and infancy for term infants are controversial. One recent review concluded that LCPUFA supplementation during pregnancy and lactation has beneficial effects on infants' cognitive development, but not on their visual acuity (Eilander, Hundscheid, Osendarp, Transler, & Zock, 2007). However, the Eilander review and another review (Uauy, Hoffman, Mena, Llanos, and Birch, 2003) concluded that supplementation during infancy benefits visual acuity as early as 4 months of age. Thus, further studies are needed to understand the moderating effect of birth weight and gestational age on the relationship between LCPUFAs and neurodevelopment.

Maternal depression can interfere with responsive parenting and lead to poor development and physical health in children (Albright & Tamis-LeMonda, 2002; Bosquet & Egeland, 2001; Gorden, 2003; Lyons-Ruth, Wolfe, & Lyubchik, 2000; McCarty & McMahon, 2003; McClure, Brennen, Hammen, & Le Brocque, 2001; see also chapter 8, this volume). LCPUFAs may influence maternal depression through their effects on serotonin and pro-inflammatory cytokines which play key roles in the pathophysiology of depression. Several observational studies suggest a relationship between dietary consumption of LCPUFAs in sea food and low risk of maternal depression. However, a recent systematic review and meta-analysis of at least 12 randomized control trials found small or no effects of LCPUFA supplementation on depression (Appleton et al., 2006). However, a significant effect was observed in the subset of eight studies that were conducted among subjects diagnosed with clinical depression (Appleton et al., 2006). While evidence from animal and observation studies suggests an important role for LCPUFAs in maternal and child health, the data from well-control studies are limited.

Failure to Thrive

Failure to thrive (FTT) refers to infants whose weight gain is significantly lower than age- and gender-specific norms (Kleinman, 2004). FTT begins with a deceleration in weight gain, measured by changes in weight-for-age or weight-for-height. Under chronic conditions, FTT also includes a deceleration in linear growth, resulting in declines in height-for-age. FTT typically begins during the second six months of life, as children are transitioning from a liquid to a semi-solid or solid diet and learning to feed themselves (Shrimpton et al., 2001).

In the past, FTT was dichotomized into organic or nonorganic, based on the perceived etiology. Organic FTT referred to medical problems and nonorganic FTT referred to psychosocial problems, often conceptualized as maternal neglect or deprivation. The organic/nonorganic dichotomy is no longer used because, in most cases, malnutrition is the proximal cause of FTT. Treatment should be planned with information gathered from a comprehensive evaluation that addresses multiple contributing factors, including medical, nutritional, developmental, and social issues (Kessler, 1999).

Until recently, many investigators relied on hospitalized or referred samples of children with FTT (Drotar, 1990). However, most children with FTT are not hospitalized, but are treated as outpatients, consistent with recommendations from the American Academy of Pediatrics Committee on Nutrition, published in the *Pediatric Nutrition Handbook* (Kleinman, 2004). FTT is often managed successfully in specialized, interdisciplinary clinics (Bithoney et al., 1991). Thus, much of the existing literature, which was based on hospitalized children, represents the most extreme and complex cases of FTT, rather than the majority of children with FTT.

Several recent follow-up evaluations have found that by school age, most children with a history of FTT have experienced growth recovery (Black & Krishnakumar, 1999). Although many children with a history of FTT continue to be shorter than age-matched peers, they rarely experience growth deficits severe enough to be classified as wasted or stunted, indicators of severe malnutrition. When cognitive and academic performance have been considered, by school age, children with FTT recruited from primary care or community sites achieved IQ scores that were approximately 4.2 points lower than children with a history of adequate growth (Black, Dubowitz, Krishnakumar, & Starr, 2007; Corbett & Drewett, 2004; Drewett, Corbett, & Wright, 1999, Rudolf & Logan, 2005). These findings suggest that early FTT may result in a small, though potentially important, impact on cognitive performance, but not the severe deficits implied by earlier studies that evaluated primarily hospitalized children.

Although FTT is more common among infants from low-income families with limited resources, it can be found in all segments of the population. In keeping with DET theory, poverty can affect children directly through lack of basic resources, such as food, healthcare, and educational opportunities, and indirectly through family stress, which may interfere with parents' ability to provide nutritious meals on a regular basis or in a responsive style. Food insecurity, defined as the lack of access to enough food for an active and healthy lifestyle for all household members (Nord, Andrews, & Carlson, 2005), has been associated with increased hospitalizations during infancy and parental perceptions that their infants are in poor health (Cook et al., 2004), at developmental risk (Rose-Jacobs et al., 2008), and have behavior problems (Whitaker, Phillips, & Orzol, 2006). Mothers of infants and toddlers in food-insecure households are at risk for symptoms of depression and anxiety (Casey et al., 2004; Whitaker et al., 2006) and may limit the quality and quantity of food available to family members, filling up on low-cost foods with low nutritional value.

Infant Feeding Behavior

Breastfeeding

The AAP and WHO recommend exclusive breast milk for infants during the first six months and continued breastfeeding for at least the first year of life (American Academy of Pediatrics Work Group on Breast-feeding, 2005; WHO, 2001). Although rates of breastfeeding initiation in the United States are approaching the Healthy People 2010 national goals of 75%, the rates of breastfeeding duration at 6 and 12 months post partum are still below the national goals of 50% and 25%, respectively (Hurley, Black, Papas, & Quigg, 2008; Li, Darling, Maurice, Barker, & Grummer-Strawn, 2005; see also chapter 15, this volume). The health and immunological benefits of breast milk for infants are well established (American Academy of Pediatrics Work Group on Breast-feeding, 2005; American Dietetic Association, 2005), thereby making breastfeeding the normative model against which to measure children's growth and development.

Methodological problems.   Multiple methodological problems interfere with interpretation of studies that examine associations between breastfeeding and subsequent infant outcomes. First, many of the maternal factors associated with breastfeeding (e.g., intelligence, motivation, responsivity, education) are also associated with infant development. Most studies have not recruited women prior to delivery and have not controlled adequately for potentially confounding factors. Second, the definition of breastfeeding varies across studies, often ranging from ever breastfed for any period of time to exclusively breastfed for a specified period of time. Third, it would be unethical to randomly assign women to breastfeed or bottlefeed. Since most breastfeeding studies have been observational, it is impossible to separate maternal motivation and behavioral factors from the nutritional aspects of breast milk on infant growth and development. In addition to inadequate control for confounding variables, which may explain reported differences between breastfed and formula-fed infants, there is evidence suggesting a publication bias favoring studies that find beneficial effects of breastfeeding (Kramer et al., 2007).

Breastfeeding and growth.   Differences in the growth pattern of breastfed and formula-fed infants are well established (De Onis & Onyang, 2002; Dewey, 1998; Kramer et al., 2003), with breastfed infants experiencing lower weight gains than formula-fed infants (Butte, Wong, Hopkinson, Smith, & Ellis, 2000). In comparison to formula-fed infants, breastfed infants are leaner at 12 months of age (Dewey, 1998). There are several potential explanations for growth differences by method of feeding. Breastfed babies may take in less energy, protein, and micronutrients than bottlefed infants (Butte et al., 2000; Heinig, Nommsen, Peerson, Lonnerdal, & Dewey, 1993; Michaelsen, Larsen, Thomsen, & Samuelson, 1994). One possibility is that the relatively high nutrient density of formulas may promote higher intakes and rates of weight gain (Butte et al., 2000). Another possibility is that breastfed infants self-regulate their energy intake at lower levels than formula-fed infants. Although infants regulate their energy intake through cues of hunger and satiety, caregiver feeding behaviors may override their cues. The tendency to encourage infants to finish a bottle may inhibit infant regulatory processes, specifically hunger and satiety cues, and may be a predisposing factor for rapid weight gain and the development of obesity. A third possibility is that mothers who breastfeed may be more sensitive to their infants' appetite signals related to volume of feedings than mothers who bottlefeed (Taveras et al., 2006). Some studies have documented protective effects of breastfeeding on obesity and chronic diseases later in life (Arenz, Ruckerl, Koletzko, & von Kries, 2004; Dewey, 2003; Gillman et al., 2001; Grummer-Strawn & Mei, 2004; Harder, Bergmann, Kallischnigg, & Plagemann, 2005; Kramer, 1981; Owen, Martin, Whincup, Smith, & Cook, 2005; von Kries et al., 1999). However, others have not found long-term effects of breastfeeding (Butte, 2001; Kramer et al., 2007; Owen et al., 2005). More research is needed to understand the effects of breastfeeding on growth beyond infancy.

Breastfeeding and intellectual functioning.   There has been a great deal of attention on the association between breastfeeding and intelligence. Epidemiological evidence, based on observational studies, has suggested a positive association. Although there is evidence linking breastfeeding with cognitive performance from studies that controlled for confounding by adjusting for socioeconomic status and home stimulation (Angelsen, Vik, Jacobsen, & Bakketeig, 2001; Jain, Concato, & Leventhal, 2002; Quinn et al., 2001), some authors have criticized the quality of the methodological controls and have urged caution (Jain et al., 2002) and others have suggested that the home environment is responsible for the cognitive advantage (Zhou, Baghurst, Gilson, & Makrides, 2007). A recent large-scale trial was conducted in Belarus involving over 13,000 infants; breastfeeding promotion was randomized at the hospital level (Kramer et al., 2008). Infants in the experimental condition were exclusively breastfed longer and at age 6.5 years had higher cognitive scores based on standardized tests and higher academic performance based on teacher reports than children in the control condition. Evidence from three studies on school performance in late adolescents or young adulthood also suggests that breastfeeding is positively associated with small but significant effects on educational attainment (Horwood & Fergusson, 1998; Richards, Hardy, & Wadworth, 2002; Victora, Barros, Horta, & Lima, 2005).

Studies that have examined the association between breastfeeding and infant–mother attachment have found that attachment security is dependent on the quality of the interaction, rather than the type of feeding (Britton, Britton, & Gronwaldt, 2006; Klaus, 1998; Renfrew, Lang, & Woolridge, 2000). For example, one study found that longer breastfeeding duration was associated with higher maternal sensitivity (Britton et al., 2006), which could contribute to psychological benefits, perhaps through the promotion of a secure attachment. These studies illustrate the importance of considering the quality of the mother–infant relationship in linking early feeding patterns to cognitive and psychological functioning.

Developmental Progression of Eating Skills

Learning to eat is a challenging developmental task that requires the integration of multiple systems, from neurological to musculoskeletal, to gastrointestinal and endocrine, as well as to social-emotional. In addition, eating requires the integration of all the senses: smell, sight, touch, hearing, and taste. Children's hunger and satiety, regulatory processes that are established early in life, guide eating behavior. For newborns, feeding is usually the primary parent–child activity and can be the source of mutual joy or frustration.

An infant's transition to the family diet and meal patterns occurs simultaneously with the rapid developmental changes that take place during the first year of life. As oral and fine motor skills increase, infants progress from being fed in a supine or semi-reclined position to a seated position. This change requires skills in balance and the proprioceptive system. Infants also progress from being fed exclusively by others to at least partial self-feeding, moving from exclusive breast milk or formula, through specially prepared weaning (i.e., pureed) foods, to more complex textures and foods (Bosma, 1997; Morris, 1989). By 12 months of life, children can sit independently, can chew and swallow a range of textures, are learning to feed themselves, and are transitioning to the family diet and meal patterns (Black & Hurley, 2008).

By late infancy children are striving for autonomy and independence as they attempt to do things themselves. Applied to eating, infants might be neophobic (hesitant to try new foods) and insist on a limited repertoire of foods (Birch, 1995), thus leading to the description of children as picky eaters. Feeding problems occur in 25–35% of children, particularly when children are acquiring new skills and are challenged with new foods (Linscheid, Budd, & Rasnake, 1995). Although most problems are self-limiting, those that persist can undermine growth and development and lead to behavioral problems or even psychopathology (Keren, Feldman, & Tyano, 2001).

Family environments can influence children's eating behavior, dietary variety, and nutritional status (Arimond & Ruel, 2004; Skinner et al., 1997). Parents help their children by establishing routines around mealtimes, such as eating in the same place and at the same time; by ensuring that children are seated in a supportive and comfortable position; and by modeling appropriate mealtime behavior, such as making healthy choices for themselves. Young children raised by caregivers who model healthy eating behaviors, such as a diet rich in fruits and vegetables, establish patterns of eating behaviors and food preferences that include fruits and vegetables (Skinner, Carruth, Bounds, Ziegler, & Reidy, 2002). In contrast, children of mothers who model unhealthy dietary behaviors (i.e., diets high in refined carbohydrates and saturated fats) are likely to develop unhealthy diets themselves (Papas, Hurley, Quigg, Oberlander, & Black, 2009).

Feeding behavior through infant–caregiver interactions

Family environments influence children's mealtime behavior and weight gain through three mechanisms: (1) the foods that are offered (composition of diet, textures and tastes); (2) parenting behaviors such as modeling eating behavior; and (3) feeding styles or the socioemotional environment that the family establishes around meals (Black & Hurley, 2008). Interactive feeding styles begin in infancy, as infants and their caregivers establish a partnership in which they recognize and interpret both verbal and nonverbal communication signals from one another. This reciprocal process forms a basis for the emotional bonding or attachment between infants and caregivers that is essential to healthy social functioning (see chapter 16 in volume 1). If there is a disruption in the communication between children and caregivers, characterized by inconsistent, nonresponsive interactions, attachment may not be secure, and feeding may become an occasion for unproductive and upsetting battles over food.

Feeding styles.   Feeding styles are a function of overall parenting styles (Baumrind, 1971; Costanzo & Woody, 1985; Maccoby & Martin, 1983) and refer to the interactive pattern of behavior between caregivers and children that occurs during meals. As with parenting styles, feeding styles are embedded in the dimensions of parental nurturance/responsiveness and parental demandingness/control (Baumrind, 1971; Hughes, Power, Fisher, Mueller, & Nicklas, 2005). Parental nurturance/responsiveness refers to the support and affection that a parent displays, including warmth, acceptance, sensitive attunement, and reciprocity. Parental demandingness/control refers to the amount of regulation or control parents display, including clear expectations, structure, intrusive-directiveness, and a

Table 2.2   Patterns of parenting and feeding styles.

		NURTURANCE / RESPONSIVENESS	
		HIGH	*LOW*
DEMANDING / CONTROLLING	**HIGH**	AUTHORITATIVE • Involved • Nurturing • Structured **Responsive Feeding Style**	AUTHORITARIAN • Controlling • Restricting • Structured **Controlling Feeding Style**
	LOW	INDULGENT • Accepting • Nurturing • Unstructured **Indulgent Feeding Style**	UNINVOLVED • Unengaged • Insensitive • Unstructured **Uninvolved Feeding Style**

pattern of firm, consistent discipline with high maturity demands (Hughes et al., 2005; Hurley, Black, Papas, & Caulfield, 2008; Maccoby & Martin, 1983).

Four parenting styles have been described: (1) authoritative (high demandingness/high responsiveness), characterized by parental involvement, nurturance, reasoning, and structure; (2) authoritarian (high demandingness/low responsiveness), characterized by restrictive, punitive, and controlling behaviors; (3) indulgent (low demandingness/high responsiveness), characterized by warmth and acceptance in conjunction with a lack of monitoring of the child's behavior; and (4) uninvolved (low demandingness/low responsiveness), characterized by little control and involvement with the child (Darling & Steinberg, 1993; Hughes et al., 2005). Feeding behaviors form four patterns that are consistent with the overall or domain specific "style" of parenting: sensitive/responsive, controlling, indulgent, and uninvolved (Table 2.2).

A *sensitive/responsive* feeding style, high in nurturance/responsiveness and demandingness, represents a relationship that involves clear caregiver demands and mutual interpretation of signals and bids for mealtime interaction. Responsivity on its own may or may not be sensitive (e.g., yelling at a toddler in response to food refusal); whereas sensitive responsitvity refers to contingent, developmentally appropriate, and consistent responses to toddler's cues (Leyendecker, Lamb, Scholmerich, & Fricke, 1997). The sensitive/responsive style is a derivative of the authoritative parenting style (Baumrind, 1989; Maccoby & Martin, 1983). Although toddlers of sensitive/responsive parents may be expected to have optimal growth and behavior, in comparison with toddlers of parents with other styles (Landry, Smith, Swank, Assel, & Vellet, 2001), relations between feeding styles and toddler weight gain and behavior have not been well studied and the data that do exist are controversial (Faith, Scanlon, Birch, Francis, & Sherry, 2004).

A *controlling* feeding style, high in demandingness and low in nurturance/responsiveness, represents forceful or restrictive strategies to control mealtimes. Controlling feeding styles are embedded in an overall authoritarian pattern of parenting. Control may also include overstimulating behavior, such as trying to get the toddler's attention by speaking loudly, forcing foods, or otherwise overpowering the child (Beebe & Lachmann, 2002). Infants and toddlers of overstimulating mothers show distress and/or avoidance (Beebe & Lachmann, 2002).

Among preschool children, forceful and restrictive techniques are often counterproductive – children pressured to eat more fruits and vegetables do not (Fisher, Mitchell, Smiciklas-Wright, & Birch, 2002), and children of parents who use restrictive feeding practices tend to overeat (Birch, Fisher, & Davison, 2003). When families are controlling, particularly around food, they may override their children's internal regulatory cues regarding hunger and satiety (Birch & Fisher, 2000). Infants have an innate capacity to self-regulate their energy intake, which diminishes during early childhood in response to family and cultural patterns (Birch, Johnson, Andresen, Peters, & Schulte, 1991). Although the mechanisms that guide regulatory changes are not entirely clear, when parents override their children's regulatory processes, eating occurs in the absence of hunger, which in turn is associated with rapid weight gain and pediatric overweight (Birch et al., 2003).

An *indulgent* feeding style, high in nurturance/responsiveness and low in demandingness, is embedded in an overall indulgent style of parenting and occurs when children are permitted to make decisions around meals, such as when and what they will eat. Without parental guidelines, children are not socialized to cultural nutritional patterns, but are likely to be attracted to their genetic predisposition for foods high in salt and sugar, rather than to a more balanced variety including vegetables (Hughes et al., 2005). We are not aware of studies of an indulgent feeding style among infants, but one study among preschoolers has shown that children of indulgent mothers have higher BMI *z*-scores than children of nonindulgent mothers (Anderson, Hughes, Fisher, & Nicklas, 2005).

An *uninvolved* feeding style, low in both nurturance/responsiveness and demandingness, is embedded in an overall uninvolved style of parenting. It often represents caregivers who have limited knowledge and involvement in their child's mealtime behavior, lack of reciprocity between the mother and toddler, a negative feeding environment, and a lack of feeding structure or routine (Hughes et al., 2005). Caregivers using an uninvolved feeding style often ignore both feeding recommendations and toddlers' cues of hunger and satiety and may be unaware of what or when their toddler is eating. Infants of psychologically unavailable mothers are more likely to be anxiously attached when compared with infants of available mothers (Egeland & Sroufe, 1981). The absence of a secure attachment relationship threatens the tasks of autonomy and self-development (Sroufe & Waters, 1977). At least one study has reported that African American mothers are at increased risk for use of uninvolved feeding styles (Hughes et al., 2005).

Feeding styles and child obesity.   The relation between feeding styles and weight among infants and young children is controversial. Some authors have found no association (Baughcum et al., 2001; Wardle, Sanderson, Guthrie, Rapoport, & Plomin, 2002), and others have found associations, primarily with restrictive feeding and childhood overweight (Birch & Fisher, 2000; Johnson & Birch, 1994). Faith et al. (2004) reviewed 22 studies that examined feeding styles. Most were cross-sectional (19 out of 22) and measured feeding styles using parent report (15 out of 22), primarily the Child Feeding Questionnaire. The few studies that used observational measures focused on child feeding behaviors (e.g., bites, refuses food, etc.) and parent behaviors (e.g., offers food, encourages eating) in relatively small samples of children (Klesges, Woolfrey, & Vollmer, 1985), and did not focus on the quality of the overall relationship. The most common finding was an association between restrictive feeding and child weight, such that mothers who were restrictive had heavy children. However, because most studies were cross-sectional, it is not clear whether parents reacted to their child's overweight by attempting to restrict their intake or children reacted to parental restrictions by overeating. In either case, restrictive feeding may interfere with children's ability to self-regulate (Johnson & Birch, 1994).

Feeding styles are a fundamental component of parenting and may reflect underlying maternal psychiatric disorders (Albright & Tamis-LeMonda, 2002; Bosquet & Egeland, 2001; Lyons-Ruth et al., 2000; McClure et al., 2001). A recent study found that mothers with mental health symptomatology (e.g., stress, depression, and anxiety) report using nonresponsive feeding styles (e.g., controlling, restrictive, and indulgent) with their infants, and among mothers who perceive their infant as temperamentally fussy, those with mental health symptoms report restrictive feeding styles (Hurley, Black, Papas, & Caulfield, 2008). Although parenting and feeding styles have been described as stable parental characteristics (Baumrind, 1989; Maccoby & Martin, 1983), Costanzo and Woody (1985) have suggested variation in parenting styles based on personal or domain-specific issues. For instance, a parent may generally use an authoritative parenting style, but may be highly authoritarian or controlling based on specific demands of the situation, such as fear that a child is in danger or may be engaging in a behavior with negative health consequences. Applied to obesity proneness, parents may be controlling when they (1) have weight and eating issues of their own, (2) perceive their child to be under- or overweight, and (3) are concerned their child may develop a problem with weight (Costanzo & Woody, 1985; Francis, Hofer, & Birch, 2001).

Policies and Programs to Promote Infant Nutrition

International organizations, such as the World Bank, have focused their attention on the first two years of life, when nutrition has a strong impact on infants' growth, health, and development (World Bank, 2006). For example, a recent follow-up of a village-based nutritional supplementation program implemented in the 1970s in Guatemala found that males who had been exposed to the higher nutritional supplement prior to 3 years of age were more likely to have higher hourly wages than males who were exposed to the lower nutritional supplement (Hoddicott, Maluccio, Behrman, Flores, & Martorell, 2008). Exposure at older ages had no long-term economic effects and there were no effects for females, perhaps because many of the women were engaged in low-productivity positions.

Attention to adequate infant nutrition begins during the prenatal period as women prepare for childbirth. The Institute of Medicine and the American College of Obstetricians and Gynecologists has published guidelines on nutrition during pregnancy. Making this information readily available to women before and during pregnancy may promote healthier pregnancies and prenatal growth and development. Low-income pregnant women are often eligible to receive services through the Special Supplemental Nutrition Program for Women, Infants, and Children. WIC was initiated by the United States Department of Agriculture (USDA) in 1974 and currently provides food, nutrition education, and health referrals to over 8 million pregnant and postpartum women, infants, and children who meet income, residency, and nutritional criteria. On average, 1.95 million infants per month, or approximately 50% of all infants in the US, receive WIC services (USDA, 2006). Evidence has documented that WIC is effective in preventing low birth weight and iron deficiency and promoting healthy growth among infants (Black et al., 2004; Buescher, Larson, Nelson, & Lenihan, 1993; Devaney, Bilheimer, & Schore, 1992; El-Bastawissi, Peters, Sasseen, Bell, & Manolopoulos, 2007; Owen & Owen, 1997).

Although rates of breastfeeding initiation have been improving in recent years, strategies are needed to promote breastfeeding, exclusivity and duration, including baby-friendly hospitals and workplaces. Information on the introduction of complementary foods should ensure that children receive foods that contain recommended quantities of macro- and micronutrients.

Programs to improve infant nutrition should focus on feeding styles and practices, emphasizing the importance of building healthy eating habits and eating to satisfy nutritional, not emotional, needs. Mealtimes that are enjoyable, interactive, and part of regular family routines will contribute to children's nutrition and development. Zero To Three (Lerner & Parlakian, 2006) has published guidelines on infant and parent feeding behaviors that emphasize how infants contribute to and learn from mealtime interactions (Table 2.3). In addition, evidence suggests that reducing the underlying determinants of food insecurity, such as poverty, poor education, disease burden, and lack of women's empowerment will benefit children's nutrition and development (Bhutta et al., 2008), particularly if opportunities for emotional and cognitive development are included (Black et al., 2008).

Recommendations for Future Research Related to Infant Nutrition

Nutrition is an essential component of infant development, yet the two topics are rarely integrated. Recommendations for future research are to integrate the two topics by incorporating infant development into nutritional studies, incorporating nutrition into infant developmental studies, and developing and evaluating programs that integrate nutrition and development. The tenets of DET provide guidance for integrating nutrition and child development by illustrating the interactive relationships between infants and caregivers, and considering both direct and indirect models.

Both undernutrition and overweight/obesity have been associated with negative developmental consequences for children. Further research is needed, extending beyond recommendations related to food and nutrients, to examine how feeding styles and parenting practices are related to children's growth and development.

Table 2.3 Mealtime opportunities for young children and parents.

	What Child Can Do	What Parent Can Do	What Child Is Learning
0–6 months	• Signal hunger/satiety through voice, facial expression, and actions	Respond to signals: • Feed child when hungry • Calm child so she can focus on eating • Hold child and make eye contact • Stop feeding when she signals fullness • Avoid feeding in response to every cry – may not be hungry	• To trust that parent will meet her needs • That she can communicate • That parents listen • That she is important to parents • To eat on a predictable schedule • To calm herself • That milk is for nutrition, not calming
6–12 months	• Sit up • Self-feed with fingers	• Ensure child is well supported and comfortably positioned to use her hands • Establish family mealtimes and routines • Start with semi-solid food from the spoon. Move to thicker and lumpier, then to soft pieces • Offer safe finger foods to promote self-feeding • Use two spoons so child learns to self-feed • Turn off TV. Use mealtimes to interact and share about daily activities	• To self-feed • To decide how much to eat • To experience tastes and textures and decide favorites • To focus on eating during mealtimes • That eating and mealtimes are fun and feel good
12–24 months	• Self-feed many different foods • Begin to use baby-safe fork, spoon, etc.	• Offer 3–4 healthy choices/meal • Offer 2–3 healthy snacks/day • Offer foods that can be picked up, chewed, or gummed and swallowed easily • Offer child-size utensils and provide help when needed	• To try new foods • To do things for herself • To ask for help • To trust that parent will help her when she needs help

Table 2.3 *Continued*

	What Child Can Do	What Parent Can Do	What Child Is Learning
	• Use actions and words to communicate thoughts and feelings, including hunger and satiety	• Make meals a time to connect with your child • Point to and name foods or objects on the table • Talk about things beyond food, such as daily activities	• New words • That she can effectively communicate • That parent will listen and respect her • That her feelings matter
24–36 months	• Choose which foods to eat from among parent choices	• Prepare one family meal with 3–4 healthy choices, including some the child likes. Avoid preparing separate meals • Offer 2–3 healthy snacks/day • Model eating healthy snacks in front of child	• To make healthy food choices • That she knows her own body • To eat when she is hungry and stop when she is full
	• Use words to express her thoughts and feelings	• Talk with child • Ask questions and listen to child's explanations • Use words to help child describe ideas, feelings, experiences • Encourage polite behavior	• New words • That mealtime is fun • That her ideas matter • Good behavior at the table
	• Help during mealtime	• Offer simple tasks such as putting napkins on table, placing pre-cut vegetables into the salad, or helping to mix the batter	• That she is an important member of the family • That she is very capable • That helping others feels good

References

Albright, M., & Tamis-LeMonda, C. (2002). Maternal depressive symptoms in relation to dimensions of parenting in low-income mothers. *Applied Developmental Science, 6*, 24–34.

American Academy of Pediatrics Work Group on Breast-feeding (2005). Breastfeeding and the use of human milk. *Pediatrics, 115*, 496–506.

American Dietetic Association. (2005). Position of the American Dietetic Association: Promoting and supporting breastfeeding. *Journal of the American Dietetic Association, 105*, 810–818.

Anderson, C. B., Hughes, S. O., Fisher, J. O., & Nicklas, T. A. (2005). Cross-cultural equivalence of feeding beliefs and practices: The psychometric properties of the child feeding questionnaire among Blacks and Hispanics. *Preventive Medicine, 41*, 521–531.

Angelsen, N. K., Vik, T., Jacobsen, G., & Bakketeig, L. S. (2001). Breastfeeding and cognitive development at age 1 and 5 years. *Archives of Disease in Childhood, 85*, 183–188.

Appleton, K. M., Hayward, R. C., Gunnell, D., Peters, T. J., Rogers, P. J., Kessler, D., et al. (2006). Effects of n-3 long-chain polyunsaturated fatty acids on depressed mood: Systematic review of published trials. *American Journal of Clinical Nutrition, 84*(6), 1308–1316.

Arenz, S., Ruckerl, R., Koletzko, B., & von Kries, R. (2004). Breast-feeding and childhood obesity: A systematic review. *International Journal of Obesity and Related Metabolic Disorders, 28*, 1247–1256.

Arimond, M., & Ruel, M. T. (2004). Dietary diversity is associated with child nutritional status: Evidence from 11 demographic and health surveys. *Journal of Nutrition, 134*, 2579–2585.

Ashworth, A., Morris, S. S., Lira, P. I., & Grantham-McGregor, S. M. (1998). Zinc supplementation, mental development and behaviour in low birth weight term infants in northeast Brazil. *European Journal of Clinical Nutrition, 52*(3), 223–227.

Baughcum, A. E., Power, S. W., Bennett Johnson, S., Chamberlin, L. A., Deeks, C. M., Jain, A., et al. (2001). Maternal feeding practices and beliefs and their relationships to overweight in early childhood. *Developmental and Behavioral Pediatrics, 22*, 391–408.

Baumrind, D. (1971). Current patterns of parental authority. *Developmental Psychology Monograph, 4*, 1–103.

Baumrind, D. (1989). Rearing competent children. In W. Damon (Ed.), *Child development today and tomorrow*. San Francisco: Jossey-Bass.

Beard, J. L. (2001). Iron biology in immune function, muscle metabolism and neuronal functioning. *Journal of Nutrition, 131*(2S-2), 568S–579S; discussion 580S.

Beard, J. L., Hendricks, M. K., Perez, E. M., Murray-Kolb, L. E., Berg, A., Vernon-Feagans, L., et al. (2005). Maternal iron deficiency anemia affects postpartum emotions and cognition. *Journal of Nutrition, 135*(2), 267–272.

Beebe, B., & Lachmann, F. (2002). *Infant research and adult treatment: Co-constructing interactions.* Hillsdale, NJ: Analytic Press.

Belsky, J. (1984). The determinants of parenting: A process model. *Child Development, 55*(1), 83–96.

Bentley, M. E., Caulfield, L. E., Ram, M., Santizo, M. C., Hurtado, E., Rivera, J. A., et al. (1997). Zinc supplementation affects the activity patterns of rural Guatemalan infants. *Journal of Nutrition, 127*(7), 1333–1338.

Berkman, D. S., Lescano, A. G., Gilman, R. H., Lopez, S. L., & Black, M. M. (2002). Effects of stunting, diarrhoeal disease, and parasitic infection during infancy on cognition in late childhood: A follow-up study. *Lancet, 359*(9306), 564–571.

Bhutta, Z. A., Ahmed, T., Black, R. E., Cousens, S., Dewey, K., Giugliani, E., et al. (2008). What works? Interventions for maternal and child undernutrition and survival. *Lancet, 371*(9610), 417–440.

Bianco, L. E., Wiesinger, J., Earley, C. J., Jones, B. C., & Beard, J. L. (2008). Iron deficiency alters dopamine uptake and response to L-DOPA injection in Sprague-Dawley rats. *Journal of Neurochemistry, 106*(1), 205–215.

Birch, L. L. (1995). Appetite and eating behavior in children. *Pediatric Clinics of North America, 42,* 931–953.

Birch, L. L., & Fisher, J. O. (2000). Mothers' child-feeding practices influence daughters' eating and weight. *American Journal of Clinical Nutrition, 71,* 1054–1061.

Birch, L. L., Fisher, J. O., & Davison, K. K. (2003). Learning to overeat: Maternal use of restrictive feeding practices promotes girls' eating in the absence of hunger. *American Journal of Clinical Nutrition, 78,* 215–220.

Birch, L. L., Johnson, S. L., Andresen, G., Peters, J. C., & Schulte, M. C. (1991). The variability of young children's energy intake. *New England Journal of Medicine, 324,* 232–235.

Bithoney, W. G., McJunkin, J., Michalek, J., Snyder, J., Egan, H., & Epstein, D. (1991). The effect of a multidisciplinary team approach on weight gain in nonorganic failure-to-thrive children. *Journal of Development Behavioral Pediatrics, 12,* 254–258.

Black, M. M. (1998). Zinc deficiency and child development. *American Journal of Clinical Nutrition, 68*(2 Suppl.), 464S–469S.

Black, M. M. (2008). Effects of vitamin B12 and folate deficiency on brain development in children. *Food and Nutrition Bulletin, 29*(2 Suppl.), S126–131.

Black, M. M., Baqui, A. H., Zaman, K., Ake Persson, L., El Arifeen, S., Le, K., et al. (2004). Iron and zinc supplementation promote motor development and exploratory behavior among Bangladeshi infants. *American Journal of Clinical Nutrition, 80*(4), 903–910.

Black, M. M., Dubowitz, H., Krishnakumar, A., & Starr, R. H. (2007). Early intervention and recovery among children with failure to thrive: Follow-up at age 8. *Pediatrics, 120,* 59–69.

Black, M. M., & Hurley, K. M. (2008). Helping children develop healthy eating habits. In R. E. Tremblay, R. G. Barr, & R. DeV. Peters (Eds.), *Encyclopedia on early childhood development* [online]. Montreal: Centre of Excellence for Early Childhood Development. Available at: www.excellence-earlychildhood.ca/documents.

Black, M. M., & Krishnakumar, A.(1999). Predicting longitudinal growth curves of height and weight using ecological factors for children with and without early growth deficiency. *Journal of Nutrition, 129*(Suppl. 2), 539S–543S.

Black, M. M., Walker, S. P., Wachs, T. D., Ulkuer, N., Gardner, J. M., Grantham-McGregor, S., et al. (2008). Policies to reduce undernutrition include child development. *Lancet, 371*(9611), 454–455.

Bleichrodt, N., & Resing, W. (1994). Measuring intelligence and learning potential in iodine-deficient and noniodine deficient populations. In J. B. Stanbury (Ed.), *The damaged brain of iodine deficiency* (pp. 27–36). Elmsford, NY: Cognizant Communication.

Bosma, J. F. (1997). Development and impairments of feeding in infancy and childhood. In M. E. Groher (Ed.), *Dysphagia: Diagnosis and management* (3rd ed., pp. 131–138). Boston: Butterworth-Heinemann.

Bosquet, M., & Egeland, B. (2001). Associations among maternal depressive symptomatology, state of mind and parent and child behaviors: Implications for attachment-based interventions. *Attachment and Human Development, 3,* 173–199.

Britton, J. R., Britton, H. L., & Gronwaldt, V. (2006). Breastfeeding, sensitivity, and attachment. *Pediatrics, 118,* e1436–e1443.

Bronfenbrenner, U., & Ceci, S. J. (1994). Nature-nurture reconceptualized in developmental perspective: A bioecological model. *Psychological Review, 101*(4), 568–586.

Budetti, P., Berry, C., Butler, P., Collins, K. S., & Abrams, M. (2000). *Assuring the healthy development of young children: Opportunities for states.* Issue Brief, Commonwealth Fund, New York.

Buescher, P. A., Larson, L. C., Nelson, M. D., Jr., & Lenihan, A. J. (1993). Prenatal WIC participation can reduce low birth weight and newborn medical costs: A cost-benefit analysis of WIC participation in North Carolina. *Journal of the American Dietetic Association, 93*(2), 163–166.

Butte, N. F. (2001). The role of breastfeeding and obesity. *Pediatric Clinics of North America, 48*, 189–198.

Butte, N. F., Wong, W. W., Hopkinson, J. M., Smith, E. O., & Ellis, K. J. (2000). Infant feeding mode affects early growth and body composition. *Pediatrics, 106*, 1355–1366.

Casey, P., Goolsby, S., Berkowitz, C., Frank, D., Cook, J., Cutts, D., et al. (2004). Maternal depression, changing public assistance, food security, and child health status. *Pediatrics, 113*(2), 298–304.

Castillo-Duran, C., Perales, C. G., Hertrampf, E. D., Marin, V. B., Rivera, F. A., & Icaza, G. (2001). Effect of zinc supplementation on development and growth of Chilean infants. *Journal of Pediatrics, 138*(2), 229–235.

Checkley, W., Buckley, G., Gilman, R. H., Assis, A. M., Guerrant, R. L., Morriss, S. S., et al. (2008). Multi-country analysis of the effects of diarrhoea on childhood stunting. *International Journal of Epidemiology, 37*, 816–830.

Clandinin, M. T., Chappell, J. E., Leong, S., Heim, T., Swyer, P. R., & Chance, G. W. (1980). Intrauterine fatty acid accretion rates in human brain: Implications for fatty acid requirements. *Early Human Development, 4*(2), 121–129.

Cook, J., Frank, D., Berkowitz, C., Black, M., Casey, P., Cutts, D., et al. (2004). Food insecurity is associated with adverse health outcomes among human infants and toddlers. *Journal of Nutrition, 134*(6), 1432–1438.

Corbett, S. S., & Drewett, F. R. (2004). To what extent is failure to thrive in infancy associated with poorer cognitive development? A review and meta-analysis. *Journal of Child Psychology and Psychiatry, 45*, 641–654.

Costanzo, P., & Woody, E. (1985). Domain specific parenting styles and their impact on the child's development of particular deviance: The example of obesity proneness. *Journal of Social and Clinical Psychology, 3*, 425–445.

Darling, N., & Steinberg, L. (1993). Parenting style as context: An integrative model. *Psychological Bulletin, 113*(3), 487–496.

Delange, F., Wolff, P., Gnat, D., Dramaix, M., Pilchen, M., & Vertongen, F. (2001). Iodine deficiency during infancy and early childhood in Belgium: Does it pose a risk to brain development? *European Journal of Pediatrics, 160*, 251–254.

De Onis, M., Garza, C., Onyango, A. W., & Borghi, E. (2007). Comparison of the WHO child growth standards and the CDC 2000 growth charts. *Journal of Nutrition, 137*, 144–148.

De Onis, M., & Onyango, A. W. (2002). The Centers for Disease Control and Prevention 2000 growth charts and the growth of breastfed infants. *Acta Paediatrica, 92*, 413–419.

Devaney, B., Bilheimer, L., & Schore, J. (1992). Medicaid costs and birth outcomes: The effects of prenatal WIC participation and the use of prenatal care. *Journal of Policy Analysis and Management, 11*(4), 573–592.

Dewey, K. (1998). Growth characteristics of breast-fed compared to formula-fed infants. *Biological Neonate, 74*, 94–105.

Dewey, K. G. (2003). Is breastfeeding protective against child obesity? *Journal of Human Lactation, 19*, 9–18.

Dobbing, J. (1972). Undernutrition and the developing brain. The relevance of animal models to the human problem. *Bibliotheca Nutritio et Dieta, 17*, 35–46.

Drewett, R. F., Corbett, S. S., & Wright, C. M. (1999). Cognitive and educational attainments at school age of children who failed to thrive in infancy: A population-based study. *Journal of Child Psychology and Psychiatry, 40*, 551–561.

Drotar, D. (1990). Sampling issues in research with nonorganic failure-to-thrive children. *Journal of Pediatric Psychology, 15,* 255–272.

Egeland, B., & Sroufe, L. A. (1981). Attachment and early maltreatment. *Child Development, 52,* 44–52.

Eilander, A., Hundscheid, D. C., Osendarp, S. J., Transler, C., & Zock, P. L. (2007). Effects of n-3 long chain polyunsaturated fatty acid supplementation on visual and cognitive development throughout childhood: A review of human studies. *Prostaglandins, Leukotrienes, and Essential Fatty Acids, 76,* 189–203.

El-Bastawissi, A. Y., Peters, R., Sasseen, K., Bell, T., & Manolopoulos, R. (2007). Effect of the Washington Special Supplemental Nutrition Program for Women, Infants and Children (WIC) on pregnancy outcomes. *Maternal and Child Health J, 11*(6), 611–621.

Faith, M., Scanlon, K. S., Birch, L. L., Francis, L. A., & Sherry, B. (2004). Parent–child feeding strategies and their relationships to child eating and weight status. *Obesity Research, 12,* 1711–1722.

Fisher, J. O., Mitchell, D. C., Smiciklas-Wright, H., & Birch, L. L. (2002). Parental influences on young girls' fruit and vegetable, micronutrient, and fat intakes. *Journal of the American Dietetic Association, 102,* 58–64.

Francis, L. A., Hofer, S. M., & Birch, L. L. (2001). Predictors of maternal child-feeding style: Maternal and child characteristics. *Appetite, 37*(3), 231–243.

Friel, J. K., Andrews, W. L., Matthew, J. D., Long, D. R., Cornel, A. M., Cox, M., et al. (1993). Zinc supplementation in very-low-birth-weight infants. *Journal of Pediatric Gastroenterology and Nutrition, 17*(1), 97–104.

Gibson, R. A., Chen, W., & Makrides, M. (2001). Randomized trials with polyunsaturated fatty acid interventions in preterm and term infants: Functional and clinical outcomes. *Lipids, 36*(9), 873–883.

Gillman, M. W., Rifas-Shiman, S. L., Camargo, C. A., Jr, Berkey, C. S., Frazier, A. L., Rockett, H. R., et al. (2001). Risk of overweight among adolescents who had been breastfed as infants. *Journal of the American Medical Association, 285,* 2461–2467.

Gorden, M. (2003). Roots of empathy: Responsive parenting, caring societies. *Keio Journal of Medicine, 52,* 236–243.

Grummer-Strawn, L. M., & Mei, Z. (2004). Does breastfeeding protect against pediatric overweight? Analysis of longitudinal data from the Centers for Disease Control and Prevention Pediatric Nutrition Surveillance System. *Pediatrics, 113,* 81–86.

Halpern, J. (1994). The neuromotor deficit in endemic cretinism and its implications for the pathogenesis of the disorder. In J. B. Stanbury (Ed.), *The damaged brain of iodine deficiency* (pp. 15–24). Elmsford, NY: Cognizant Communication.

Halterman, J. S., Kaczorowski, J. M., Aligne, C. A., Auinger, P., & Szilagyi, P. G. (2001). Iron deficiency and cognitive achievement among school-aged children and adolescents in the United States. *Pediatrics, 107*(6), 1381–1386.

Hamadani, J. D., Fuchs, G. J., Osendarp, S. J., Khatun, F., Huda, S. N., & Grantham-McGregor, S. M. (2001). Randomized controlled trial of the effect of zinc supplementation on the mental development of Bangladeshi infants. *American Journal of Clinical Nutrition, 74*(3), 381–386.

Harder, T., Bergmann, R., Kallischnigg, G., & Plagemann, A. (2005). Duration of breastfeeding and risk of overweight: A meta-analysis. *American Journal of Epidemiology, 162,* 397–403.

Heinig, M. J., Nommsen, L. A., Peerson, J. M., Lonnerdal, B., & Dewey, K. G. (1993). Energy and protein intakes of breastfed and formula-fed infants during the first year of life and their association with growth velocity: The DARLING Study. *American Journal of Clinical Nutrition, 58,* 152–161.

Hoddicott, J., Maluccio, J. A., Behrman, J. R., Flores, R., & Martorell, R. (2008). Effect of a nutrition intervention during early childhood on economic productivity in Guatemalan adults. *Lancet*, *371*, 411–416.

Honig, A. S., & Oski, F. A. (1984). Solemnity: A clinical risk index for iron deficient infants. *Early Child Development and Care*, *16*(1–2), 69–83.

Horwood, L. J., & Fergusson, D. M. (1998). Breastfeeding and later cognitive and academic outcomes. *Pediatrics*, *101*, E9.

Huda, S. N., Grantham-McGregor, S. M., Rahman, K. M., & Tomkins, A. (1999). Biochemical hypothyroidism secondary to iodine deficiency is associated with poor school achievement and cognition in Bangladeshi children. *Journal of Nutrition*, *129*(5), 980–987.

Hughes, S., Power, T. G., Fisher, J. O., Mueller, S., & Nicklas, T. (2005). Revisiting a neglected construct: Parenting styles in a child-feeding context. *Appetite*, *44*, 83–92.

Hurley, K. M., Black, M. M., Papas, M. A., & Caulfield, L. E. (2008). Maternal symptoms of stress, depression, and anxiety are related to nonresponsive feeding styles in a statewide sample of WIC participants. *Journal of Nutrition*, *138*, 799–805.

Hurley, K., Black, M., Papas, M., & Quigg, A. (2008). Variation in breastfeeding behaviours, perceptions, and experiences by race/ethnicity among a low-income statewide sample of Special Supplemental Nutrition Program for Women, Infants, and Children (WIC) participants in the United States. *Maternal and Child Nutrition*, *4*, 95–105.

Hurtado, E. K., Claussen, A. H., & Scott, K. G. (1999). Early childhood anemia and mild or moderate mental retardation. *American Journal of Clinical Nutrition*, *69*(1), 115–119.

Iannotti, L. L., Tielsch, J. M., Black, M. M., & Black, R. E. (2006). Iron supplementation in early childhood: Health benefits and risks. *American Journal of Clinical Nutrition*, *84*(6), 1261–1276.

Jain, A., Concato, J., & Leventhal, J. (2002). How good is the evidence linking breastfeeding and intelligence? *Pediatrics*, *109*, 1044–1053.

Johnson, S. L., & Birch, L. L. (1994). Parents' and children's adiposity and eating style. *Pediatrics*, *94*, 653–661.

Kaiser, L., Allen, L. H., & American Dietetic Association (2008). Position of the American Dietetic Association: Nutrition and lifestyle for a healthy pregnancy outcome. *Journal of the American Dietetic Association*, *108*, 553–561.

Keren, M., Feldman, R., & Tyano, S. (2001). Diagnoses and interactive patterns of infants referred to a community-based infant mental health clinic. *Journal of the American Academy of Child and Adolescent Psychiatry*, *40*(1), 27–35.

Kessler, D. B. (1999). Failure to thrive and pediatric undernutrition: Historical and theoretical context. In D. Kessler & P. Dawson (Eds.), *Failure to thrive and pediatric undernutrition* (pp. 3–18). Baltimore, MD: Paul H. Brookes.

Klaus, M. (1998). Mother and infant: Early emotional ties. *Pediatrics*, *102*, 1244–1246.

Kleinman, R. E. (Ed.) (2004). *Pediatric nutrition handbook* (5th ed.). Elk Grove Village, IL: American Academy of Pediatrics.

Klesges, R. C., Woolfrey, J., & Vollmer, J. (1985). An evaluation of the reliability of time sampling versus continuous observation data collection. *Pediatrics*, *1994*, 303–307.

Kramer, M., Guo, T., Platt, R., Sevkovskaya, Z., Dzikovich, I., Collet, J., et al. (2003). Infant growth and health outcomes associated with 3 compared with 6 months of exclusive breastfeeding. *American Journal of Clinical Nutrition*, *78*, 291–295.

Kramer, M. S. (1981). Do breast-feeding and delayed introduction of solid foods protect against obesity? *Journal of Pediatrics*, *98*, 883–887.

Kramer, M. S., Aboud, F., Mironova, E., Vanilovich, I., Platt, R. W., Matush, L., et al. (2008). Breastfeeding and child cognitive development: New evidence from a large randomized trial. *Archives of General Psychiatry*, *65*(5), 578–584.

Kramer, M. S., Matush, L., Vanilovich, I., Platt, R. W., Bogdanovich, N., Sevkovskaya, Z., et al. (2007). Effects of prolonged and exclusive breastfeeding on child height, weight, adiposity, and blood pressure at age 6.5 y: Evidence from a large randomized trial. *American Journal of Clinical Nutrition, 86*(6), 1717–1721.

Krebs, N. F., Himes, J. H., Jacobson, D., Nicklas, T. A., Guilday, P., & Styne, D. (2007). Assessment of child and adolescent overweight and obesity. *Pediatrics, 120*(Suppl. 4), S193–228.

Kuczmarski, R. J., Ogden, C. L., Grummer-Strawn, L. M., Flegal, K. M., Guo, S. S., Wei, R., et al. (2000). *CDC Growth Charts: United States.* Advance Data from Vital and Health Statistics, no. 314. Hyattsville, MD: National Center for Health Statistics. www.cdc.gov/nchs/data/ad/ad314.pdf.

Landry, S. H., Smith, K. E., Swank, P. R., Assel, M. A., & Vellet, S. (2001). Does early responsive parenting have a special importance for children's development or is consistency across early childhood necessary? *Developmental Psychology, 37,* 387–403.

Lerner, C., & Parlakian, R. (2006). *Healthy from the start: How feeding nurtures your young child's body, heart and mind.* Washington, DC: Zero To Three.

Levitsky, D. A., & Barnes, R. H. (1972). Nutritional and environmental interactions in the behavioral development of the rat: Long-term effects. *Science, 176*(30), 68–71.

Leyendecker, B., Lamb, M., Scholmerich, A., & Fricke, D. (1997). Context as moderators of observed interactions: A study of Costa Rican mothers and infants from differing socioeconomic backgrounds. *International Journal of Behavioral Development, 21,* 15–24.

Li, R., Darling, N., Maurice, E., Barker, L., & Grummer-Strawn, L. (2005). Breastfeeding rates in the United States by characteristics of the child, mother, or family: The 2002 National Immunization Survey. *Pediatrics, 115,* e31–e37.

Lind, T., Lonnerdal, B., Stenlund, H., Gamayanti, I. L., Ismail, D., Seswandhana, R., et al. (2004). A community-based randomized controlled trial of iron and zinc supplementation in Indonesian infants: Effects on growth and development. *American Journal of Clinical Nutrition, 80*(3), 729–736.

Linscheid, T. R., Budd, K. S., & Rasnake, L. K. (1995). Pediatric feeding disorders. In M. C. Roberts (Ed.), *Handbook of pediatric psychology* (2nd ed.). New York: Guilford Press.

Lozoff, B., Corapci, F., Burden, M. J., Kaciroti, N., Angulo-Barroso, R., Sazawal, S., et al. (2007). Preschool-aged children with iron deficiency anemia show altered affect and behavior. *Journal of Nutrition, 137*(3), 683–689.

Lozoff, B., Klein, N. K., Nelson, E. C., McClish, D. K., Manuel, M., & Chacon, M. E. (1998). Behavior of infants with iron-deficiency anemia. *Child Development, 69*(1), 24–36.

Lozoff, B., Klein, N. K., & Prabucki, K. M. (1986). Iron-deficient anemic infants at play. *Journal of Developmental and Behavioral Pediatrics, 7*(3), 152–158.

Lyons-Ruth, K., Wolfe, R., & Lyubchik, A. (2000). Depression and parenting of young children: Making the case for early preventive mental health services. *Harvard Review of Psychiatry, 8,* 148–153.

Maccoby, E., & Martin, J. (1983). Socialization in the context of the family: Parent–child interaction. In P. H. Mussen (Series Ed.) & E. M. Hetherington (Vol. Ed.), *Handbook of child psychology* (4th ed., pp. 1–101). New York: Wiley.

McCarty, C. A., & McMahon, R. J. (2003). Mediators of the relation between maternal depressive symptoms and child internalizing and disruptive behavior disorders. *Journal of Family Psychology, 17*(4), 545–556.

McClure, B., Brennen, P., Hammen, C., & Le Brocque, R. (2001). Parental anxiety disorder, child anxiety disorder, and the perceived parent–child relationship in an Australian high risk sample. *Journal of Abnormal Child Psychology, 29,* 1–10.

McCullough, A. L., Kirksey, A., Wachs, T. D., McCabe, G. B., Basly, N. S., Bishry, Z., Galal, O., M., Harrison, G. G., & Jerome, N. W. (1990). Vitamin B-6 status of Egyptian mothers: Relation to infant behavior and maternal–infant interactions. *American Journal of Clinical Nutrition, 51,* 1067–1074.

McNamara, R. K., & Carlson, S. E. (2006). Role of omega-3 fatty acids in brain development and function: Potential implications for the pathogenesis and prevention of psychopathology. *Prostaglandins, Leukotrienes, and Essential Fatty Acids, 75*(4–5), 329–349.

Meeks Gardner, J., Powell, C. A., Baker-Henningham, H., Walker, S. P., Cole, T. J., & Grantham-McGregor, S. M. (2005). Zinc supplementation and psychosocial stimulation: Effects on the development of undernourished Jamaican children. *American Journal of Clinical Nutrition, 82*(2), 399–405.

Mendez, M. A., & Adair, L. S. (1999). Severity and timing of stunting in the first two years of life affect performance on cognitive tests in late childhood. *Journal of Nutrition, 129*(8), 1555–1562.

Michaelsen, K. F., Larsen, P. S., Thomsen, B. L., & Samuelson, G. (1994). The Copenhagen Cohort Study on Infant Nutrition and Growth: Breast-milk intake, human milk macronutrient content, and influencing factors. *American Journal of Clinical Nutrition, 59,* 600–611.

Morris, S. E. (1989). Development of oral motor skills in the neurologically impaired child receiving non-oral feedings. *Dysphagia, 3,* 135–154.

Murray-Kolb, L. E., & Beard, J. L. (2007). Iron treatment normalizes cognitive functioning in young women. *American Journal of Clinical Nutrition, 85*(3), 778–787.

Nord, M., Andrews, M., & Carlson, S. J. (2005). *Household food security in the United States, 2004.* Washington, DC: United States Department of Agriculture.

Nye, C., & Brice, A., (2005). Combined vitamin B6-magnesium treatment in autism spectrum disorder. *Cochrane Database of Systematic Reviews,* CD 003497.

O'Donnell, K. J., Rakeman, M. A., Zhi-Hong, D., Xue-Yi, C., Mei, Z. Y., DeLong, N., et al. (2002). Effects of iodine supplementation during pregnancy on child growth and development at school age. *Developmental Medicine and Child Neurology, 44*(2), 76–81.

Ooylan, L. M., Hart, S., Porter, K. B., & Driskell, J. A. (2002). Vitamin B-6 content of breast milk and neonatal behavioral functioning. *Journal of the American Dietetic Association, 102,* 1433–1438.

Owen, A. L., & Owen, G. M. (1997). Twenty years of WIC: A review of some effects of the program. *Journal of the American Dietetic Association, 97*(7), 777–782.

Owen, C. G., Martin, R. M., Whincup, P. H., Smith, G. D., & Cook, D. G. (2005). Effect of infant feeding on the risk of obesity across the life course: A quantitative review of published evidence. *Pediatrics, 115,* 1367–1377.

Papas, M., Hurley, K., Quigg, A., Oberlander, S., & Black, M. (2009). Low-income African American adolescent mothers and their toddlers exhibit similar dietary variety patterns. *Journal of Nutrition Education and Behavior, 41*(2), 87–94.

Perez, E. M., Hendricks, M. K., Beard, J. L., Murray-Kolb, L. E., Berg, A., Tomlinson, M., et al. (2005). Mother–infant interactions and infant development are altered by maternal iron deficiency anemia. *Journal of Nutrition, 135*(4), 850–855.

Quinn, P., O'Callaghan, M., Williams, C., Najman, J., Andersen, M., & Bor, W. (2001). The effect of breastfeeding on child development at 5 years: A cohort study. *Journal of Paediatrics and Child Health, 37,* 465–469.

Renfrew, M. J., Lang, S., & Woolridge, M. W. (2000). Early versus delayed initiation of breast-feeding. *Cochran Database of Systematic Reviews, 2*: CD000043.

Richards, M., Hardy, R., & Wadworth, M. E. (2002). Long-term effects of breastfeeding in a national birth cohort: Educational attainment and midlife cognitive function. *Public Health Nutrition, 5,* 631–635.

Rose-Jacobs, R., Black, M. M., Casey, P. H., Cook, J. T., Cutts, D. B., Childton, M., et al. (2008). Household food insecurity: Associations with at-risk infant and toddler development. *Pediatrics, 121*, 65–72.

Rudolf, M. C., & Logan, S. (2005). What is the long term outcome for children who fail to thrive? A systematic review. *Archives of Disease in Childhood, 90*, 925–931.

Sazawal, S., Bentley, M., Black, R. E., Dhingra, P., George, S., & Bhan, M. K. (1996). Effect of zinc supplementation on observed activity in low socioeconomic Indian preschool children. *Pediatrics, 98*(6 Pt 1), 1132–1137.

Shrimpton, R., Victora, C. G., de Onis, M., Lima, R. C., Blossner, M., & Clugston, G. (2001). Worldwide timing of growth faltering: Implications for nutritional interventions. *Pediatrics, 107*, E75.

Simmer, K., Schulzke, S. M., & Patole, S. (2008). Longchain polyunsaturated fatty acid supplementation in preterm infants. *Cochrane Database Systematic Review*, CD000375.

Skinner, J., Carruth, B., Bounds, W., Ziegler, P., & Reidy, K. (2002). Do food-related experiences in the first two years of life predict dietary variety in school-aged children? *Journal of Nutrition Education and Behavior, 34*, 310–315.

Skinner, J. D., Carruth, B. R., Houck, K. S., Coletta, F., Cotter, R., Ott, D., et al. (1997). Longitudinal study of nutrient and food intakes of infants aged 2 to 24 months. *Journal of the American Dietetic Association, 97*(5), 496–504.

Sroufe, L. A., & Waters, O. (1977). Attachment as an organizational construct. *Child Development, 48*, 1184.

Taveras, E. M., Rifas-Shiman, S. L., Scanlon, K. S., Grummer-Strawn, L. M., Sherry, B., & Gillman, M. W. (2006). To what extent is the protective effect of breastfeeding on future overweight explained by decreased maternal feeding restriction? *Pediatrics, 118*, 2341–2348.

Uauy, R., Hoffman, D. R., Mena, P., Llanos, A., & Birch, E. E. (2003). Term infant studies of DHA and ARA supplementation on neurodevelopment: Results of randomized controlled trials. *Journal of Pediatrics, 143*(4 Suppl. 1), S17–25.

Uauy, R., Kain, J., Mericq, V., Rojas, J., & Corvalan, C. (2008). Nutrition, child growth, and chronic disease prevention. *Annals of Medicine, 40*(1), 11–20.

United States Department of Agriculture (2006). WIC: The Special Supplemental Nutrition Program for Women, Infants, and Children [Electronic Version]. Available from www.fns.usda.gov/fns.

Victora, C. G., Adair, L., Fall, C., Hallal, P. C., Martorell, R., Richter, L., et al. (2008). Maternal and child undernutrition: Consequences for adult health and human capital. *Lancet, 371*(9609), 340–357.

Victora, C. G., Barros, F. C., Horta, B. L., & Lima, R. C. (2005). Breastfeeding and school achievement in Brazilian adolescents. *Acta Paediatrica, 94*, 1656–1660.

von Kries, R., Koletzko, B., Sauerwald, T., von Mutius, E., Barnert, D., Grunert, V. & von Voss, H. (1999). Breast feeding and obesity: Cross-sectional study. *British Medical Journal, 98*, 883–887.

Wachs, T. D. (2002). Nutritional deficiencies as a biological context for development. In W. Hartup & R. Silbereisen (Eds.), *Growing points in developmental science* (pp. 64–84). Hove: Psychology Press.

Walker, S. P., Chang, S. M., Powell, C. A., Simonoff, E., & Grantham-McGregor, S. M. (2007). Early childhood stunting is associated with poor psychological functioning in late adolescence and effects are reduced by psychosocial stimulation. *Journal of Nutrition, 137*(11), 2464–2469.

Wardle, J., Sanderson, S., Guthrie, C. A., Rapoport, L., & Plomin, R. (2002). Parental feeding style and the inter-generational transmission of obesity risk. *Obesity Research, 10*, 453–462.

West, K. P. (2003). Vitamin A deficiency disorders in children and women. *Food and Nutrition Bulletin, 24*(4 Suppl.), S78–90.

Whitaker, R. C., Phillips, S. M., & Orzol, S. M. (2006). Food insecurity and the risks of depression and anxiety in mothers and behavior problems in their preschool-aged children. *Pediatrics, 118*(3), e859–868.

World Bank (2006). *Repositioning nutrition as central to development: A strategy for large-scale action.* Washington, DC: The International Bank for Reconstruction and Development/The World Bank.

World Health Organization (1993). *Global prevalence of iodine deficiency disorders.* Geneva: WHO.

World Health Organization (2001). *The optimal duration of exclusive breastfeeding: Report of an expert consultation,* WHO/NHD/01.09. Geneva: WHO.

World Health Organization (2007). *Global prevalence of iodine deficiency disorders.* Geneva: WHO.

World Health Organization/UNICEF (2004). *Focusing on anaemia: Towards an integrated approach for effective anaemia control.* Available from www.who.int/topics/anaemia/en/who_unicef-anaemiastatement.pdf.

Yip, R. (1994). Iron deficiency: Contemporary scientific issues and international programmatic approaches. *Journal of Nutrition, 124*(8 Suppl.), 1479S–1490S.

Zhou, S. J., Baghurst, P., Gilson, R. A., & Makrides, M. (2007). Home environment, not duration of breast-feeding, predicts intelligence quotient of children at four years. *Nutrition, 23*(3), 236–241.

3

Health

R. J. Karp

Overview

The focus of this chapter is on the relationship of postnatal health and illness to infant development. Specific topics to be covered in this chapter include: (1) periconceptual diabetes mellitus; (2) infectious illnesses; (3) gastrointestinal (diarrheal) disorders; (4) toxins such as alcohol and lead; (5) intentional and unintentional injuries; (6) inborn errors of metabolism; and (7) infantile colic. The chapter concludes with a pediatrician's model, from Calvin Sia, on the "Medical Home" as a resource available to provide a full panoply of resources to families in need (Sia, 1992).

While malignancies and their treatments do affect neurodevelopment, these disorders are relatively rare in infancy and thus will not be covered here. The papers by Meadows (2006) and Grunfeld (2006) are suggested for a comprehensive overview of this topic. Other medically related issues linked to topics shown in Table 3.1 that will not be presented in this chapter are prenatal development, nutrition, sensory or motor impairments, psychosocial disorders, and genetic disorders resulting in intellectual disabilities; see chapters 1, 2, 4, 11 and 12 in this volume, respectively. In addition, the focus of this chapter will be on infants in developed countries. Detailed discussion of biological risk factors commonly encountered by infants in developing countries (e.g., nutritional deficiencies, infectious diseases, and environmental toxins) can be found chapter 6 in in this volume (see also Walker et al., 2007).

The essential dilemma in dealing with such questions on the relationship of postnatal health and illness to infant development is best described by an aphorism attributed to the Greek poet Archilochus (seventh century BC): "The fox knows many things, but the hedgehog knows one big thing" (Berlin, 1953). To appreciate the full scope of this chapter requires the broad view of a fox. To appreciate the pathophysiology of specific diseases, however, requires the focused understanding of a hedgehog. To carry out this dual focus, this chapter incorporates the approach of Gonnella (1993) and colleagues, which provides

Table 3.1   Child illness domains with developmental consequences.

Infection	Bacterial, viral, tuberculosis, protozoan diseases
Immunologic	Rheumatoid and allergic diseases
Traumatic	Unintentional or intentional ("child abuse")
Congenital – inherited	Inborn errors of metabolism and enzyme defects (cystic fibrosis)
Congenital –*in utero*	Fetal alcohol syndrome, gestational diabetes
Toxicological	Ingestion of toxic or teratogenic agent
Iatrogenic	Provider decisions leading to untoward consequences
Psychobiologic	Interaction between psychology and biology
Psychosocial	Interaction between experience in the environment and biology
Nutritional	Nutrient deficiencies or excesses
Oncologic	Malignancies and their treatment
Idiopathic	Not sure of origins

Note. This list can be expanded to include almost any condition. To be included the disease must fulfill either of the following two criteria to be presented in the body of this chapter: *either* it is likely *or* it is dangerous.

an overarching paradigm for categories of illness including immunologic, infectious, traumatic, and metabolic. This approach is shown in Table 3.1, in which potential causes are listed followed by comments on prevalence ("how likely") and an assessment of "how dangerous." For example, under infection viral illness would be "common" while meningitis would be "dangerous."

In addition to the framework shown in Table 3.1, there are two additional considerations in understanding the interaction of early disease and subsequent development. The first is that "social gradients" affect developmental outcomes. Social gradient theory is based on "causes of the causes" (Marmot, 2003; Waterston, Alperstein, & Stewart Brown, 2004). As Marmot (2003, p. 9) writes:

> The social gradient in health is influenced by such factors as social position, relative versus absolute deprivation, and control and social participation. To understand causality and generate policies to improve health, we must consider the relationship between social environment and health and especially the importance of early life experiences.

The second consideration is that while all chronic illnesses carry the risk of affecting development, there are both direct and indirect effects of disease on development. Social gradients are less likely to affect direct causes of developmental delay, such as meningitis, than indirect ones, such as chronic illness unrelated to central nervous system function. Birch and Gussow (1970, pp. 261–262) list three indirect effects: "loss of learning time … , interference with learning during critical [or sensitive] periods of development, [and maternal] motivation and [infant] personality change." For example, studies of low birth weight infants suggest that outcomes are enhanced by availability of resources and the social structure of the family (Shonkoff & Phillips, 2000; Wachs, 2000; Holditch-Davis, Schwartz, Black, & Scher, 2007). Examples of both direct and indirect effects are seen in the following sections.

Gestatational Diabetes Mellitus

Incidence

In 2005, almost 18 million adults in the United States were known diabetics, with 80% having "adult onset" (type 2) diabetes mellitus (National Diabetes Quality Improvement Alliance, 2005). However, national data for the prevalence of gestatational diabetes mellitus (GDM) are not helpful as the range is too great, from 0.5% to 12.6% (Anderson, 2005). At SUNY Downstate Medical Center in central Brooklyn, 131 (7.6%) of the 1,728 women who delivered infants in 2007 were recorded as having "gestational diabetes." Another 11 women (0.6% of total) were listed as having "chronic diabetes."

In a seminal article, Pedersen (1954) described the metabolic changes occurring with gestational diabetes. He hypothesized that maternal *hyper*glycemia triggers insulin production in the fetus with concomitant macrosomia (organ enlargement) and postnatal *hypo*glycemia (low blood sugar). Freinkel (1988) later expanded Pedersen's observation to include any transplacental passage of metabolically active substances as "fuel-mediated teratogenesis," specifically noting:

> [M]ultifactorial possibilities may account for the multiple birth defects that can occur in individual offspring, and the seemingly non-specific pattern of diabetic embryopathy. Insulin therapy diminishes the dysmorphogenic effects of 'the diabetic state' in rodents with experimental or spontaneous diabetes (Freinkel, 1988, p. 463).

Simply stated, the passing of excess glucose from a poorly controlled hyperglycemic gravid woman through the placenta has both immediate effects on the growing fetus as well as postnatal complications, including "subtle nervous system delay" (Weintrob, Karp, & Hod, 1996).

Prenatal consequences

The fetus does not have the capacity to respond to hyperglycemia before 20 weeks' gestation (Nold & Georgieff, 2004). Thus, early hyperglycemia, as would be found with poorly controlled type 1 or type 2 diabetes mellitus, is in itself the trigger for dysfunction. The most common consequences would be early growth delay and congenital anomalies (Weintrob et al., 1996; Nold & Georgieff, 2004).

Post 20 weeks' gestation, however, there are substantial *in utero* effects of the increased anabolic stimulation from available substrate (amino acids, glucose, and fatty acids) and insulin associated with GDM. Post 20 weeks hyperglycemia results in increased fat deposition in heart and liver and alteration in the composition and function of neural tissues in the central nervous system (CNS).

Thus, it is necessary to appreciate that untoward events are likely to affect the fetus even with optimal medical control. Hod, Merlob, Friedman, Rusecki, Schoenfeld and Ovadia (1991), in their study of 878 women with GDM, 132 with pre-gestational

Table 3.2 Consequences to the fetus resulting from maternal diabetes mellitus by trimester of pregnancy (derived from Weintrob et al., 1996).

Period of exposure	Complication
1st trimester – generally associated with preexisting diabetes mellitus	Early growth delay Congenital anomalies
2nd trimester – either preexisting or gestational diabetes mellitus	Macrosomia, Organomegaly, "Subtle nervous system delay"
3rd trimester – generally associated with gestational diabetes mellitus	Macrosomia, Chronic hypoxemia, Stillbirth, "Subtle nervous system delay"

diabetes, and 380 healthy pregnant women, showed significant differences in postnatal consequences of diabetes in pregnancy. These included organ enlargement ("macrosomia" – 25.0% for diabetic women compared to 5.6 % for the unaffected), low blood sugar ("hypoglycemia" – 7.8% compared to 0.9%), elevated bilirubin levels ("hyperbilirubinemia" – 16.7% compared to 8.2%), low calcium levels ("hypocalcemia" – 5.5% compared to 2.7%), and increased red blood cell mass ("polycythemia" – 13.3% compared to 3.8%). Similar, though not so drastic, differences were described by Nold and Georgieff (2004) in their review of the literature.

Table 3.2 shows consequences to the fetus resulting from maternal diabetes mellitus by trimester of pregnancy and in the newborn period. In addition to what is presented in Table 3.2, it is important to recognize that congenital malformations are increased two- to fourfold in infants born to diabetic mothers. The actual rate depends on the level of control at the time of body organ formation (Landon & Gabbe, 1992).

Postnatal and early childhood consequences

The primary direct effect of gestational diabetes is macrosomia in the newborn infant (Nold & Georgieff, 2004). Increased availability of amino acids, glucose and fatty acids (substrate) permits the insulin produced in response to fetal hyperglycemia to fulfill its anabolic function. As described by Creasy and Resnik (1995), the resulting macrosomia places the infant of a diabetic mother at greater risk for birth trauma because of the head and shoulder being held up by "cephalopelvic disproportion" (e.g., shoulder dystocia), as well as trauma to nerves running through the axilla (the "brachial plexus" is likely to be compressed with resultant injuries such as "Erb palsy"). There are also injuries at the juncture of the cervical and lumbar spine (a "Klumpke palsy"), diaphragmatic nerve paralysis, and recurrent laryngeal nerve paralysis.

A second direct effect in the newborn is hypoglycemia. An expected response to islet cell hyperplasia is increased insulin, which, without a source of glucose post partum, results in a steep fall in serum glucose. This drop is accentuated in macrosomic infants because of a lack of sympathetic system responses to hypoglycemia (Artal et al., 1982). This phenomenon can be prevented by control of blood glucose during pregnancy among gravidas with GDM. Small infants of prepregnancy gravidas also have decreased blood sugars because of depleted stores of glycogen and fat (Artal et al., 1982).

As noted above, most infants of mothers with poorly treated GDM are macrocosmic. In addition, some experience premature delivery or intrauterine growth retardation (IUGR) of the symmetric variety (a concomitant reduction in weight, length, and head circumference), which can also have adverse consequences (Nold & Georgieff, 2004). For example, in a recent study by Schlotz, Jones, Phillips, Godfrey, and Phillips (2007), motor activity under stress at 7–9 years of age was evaluated for 127 IUGR babies. Effects were found on motor activity of both asymmetric (weight diminished more than length or head circumference) and symmetric (all anthropometric measure are reduced) body proportions in infancy, as well as effects of IUGR (reduced head circumference at birth). However, there were greater effects on motor activity in the school-age children with the symmetric form of IUGR in infancy:

> Motor activity during the nonstress situation was unrelated to birth weight in boys and girls. In contrast, lower birth weight was associated with higher motor activity scores in boys ($P = .048$), whereas no association was observed in girls when the subjects were placed under stress conditions. … [T]here were greater effects in the children whose IUGR was symmetric (head circumference as well as weight) than there were for the infants whose IUGR was asymmetric. (Schlotz et al., 2007, p. e1240)

The fact that their results were significant for *boys* but not for *girls* suggests specific gender sensitivities during the intrauterine experience (Schlotz et al., 2007). Thus diabetes in pregnancy, resulting in either macrosomia or IUGR, has the potential to affect long-term development (Petry, Eaton, Wobken, Mills, Johnson, & Georgieff, 1992; Nold & Georgieff, 2004; Shonkoff & Phillips, 2000).

A third direct effect is polycythemia. Elevated glucose and insulin levels *in utero* increase formation of red cells ("hematopoiesis") and red cell mass ("polycythemia"). As a result the child becomes polycythemic and has an increased blood viscosity – the "hyperviscosity syndrome." The consequences of this syndrome are described by Nold and Georgieff (2004, p. 627): "Chronically accelerated erythropoeisis results in poly-cythemia, which in turn contributes to the increased incidence of stroke, seizures, necro-tizing enterocolitis, and renal vein thrombosis" as potential hazards for infants of diabetic mothers.

Moreover, the fetus draws iron stores primarily from the liver, and redistributes them to support the increased hematopoiesis (Petry et al., 1992). Depletion in iron stores results in an iron deficiency at the cellular level in heart and brain. Iron deficiency in infancy has both immediate and ongoing consequences for later development (Lozoff et al., 2007; see also chapter 2 in this volume). A recent study by Dionne, Boivin, Séguin, Pérusse, and Tremblay (2008) in a French-speaking population in Quebec provides data showing that infants whose mother had gestational diabetes were twice as likely to show limitations in language development when assessed at 18 and 84 months of age. These infants of diabetic mothers "performed 0.27 to 0.41 SD > below controls" (Dionne et al., 2008,

p. e1079). Their data, however, show protective effects of both genetic patterns affecting vulnerability as well as higher levels of maternal education achieved. Their explanations for these findings include the iron depletion noted above (Lozoff et al., 2007; see also chapter 2 in this volume) as well as the impact of fluctuating glucose levels in pregnancy.

There are several additional concerns that follow from GDM, including deposition of heme pigments in brainstem nuclei from elevations in unconjugated bilirubin in the neonatal period. The consequence, kernicterus, is a devastating condition (Oski & Naiman, 1982). Cardiac defects are also associated with both prepregnancy and GDM (Holm, Fredriksen, Fosdahl, Olstad, & Vøllestad, 2007).

Infectious Illnesses

Overview

Preventing infectious illness by providing clean water, preventive screening and immunizations to mothers and infants has a profound impact on child development (American Academy of Pediatrics (AAP), 2006; Shonkoff & Phillips, 2000, p. 34; Ali et al., 2005, 2008). Direct advantages of these measures include the prevention of *in utero* rubella and post-meningitis deafness (Letson, Gellin, Bulkow, Parks, & Ward, 1992; Goetghebuer et al., 2000; AAP, 2006). Other effects are indirect, such as improved growth and survival itself. Children who are ill are not attentive and do not explore their environment. (Shonkoff & Phillips, 2000; Wachs, 2000). Particularly critical for infant morbidity and mortality in developing countries are the interactions between specific risk factors such as diarrheal disease, nutritional deficiencies, and infection (Galler & Barrett, 2002; Grantham-McGregor & International Child Development Committee, 2007; Johnston and Markowitz, 1993; McLaren, 1981). There also is an increased susceptibility to diseases associated with vitamin A deficiency, particularly measles and tuberculosis (McLaren, 1981), which together have a historically well-known association (Holt, 1911).

The effectiveness of vaccines in preventing complications of infectious illnesses that affect children can best be understood by recalling when only antibiotics were available (Letson et al., 1992). Bradford, in the 1968 edition of the *Nelson Textbook of Pediatrics*, reports that antibiotics decreased mortality for both *Hemophilius influenzae* and *Streptococcus pneumoniae*, "but the incidence of serious and permanent consequences has increased" (Bradford, 1968, p. 575). Bacterial infections likely to affect neurodevelopment include *S. pneumoniae* and *H. influenzae* type b (AAP, 2006; Letson et al., 1992). Inactive cell wall vaccines are now used as preventives for these two diseases. As a result of immunization, smallpox has disappeared and the spread of many others diseases including polio, measles, rubella and varicella has been limited (AAP, 2006). Active immunization with attenuated viruses has similarly prevented viral illnesses such as rubella, measles, and varicella (AAP, 2006). In developing countries, combining a clean water supply with the use of vaccines and oral rehydrating solutions has prevented the complications of diarrheal disease (Kossmann, Nestel, Herrera, El Amin, & Fawzi, 2000).

Of special concern is a widespread, though undocumented, belief that either preservatives in vaccines or vaccines themselves, specifically the measles, mumps and rubella vaccine (MMR), are a direct antecedent to pervasive developmental disorder (PDD) spectrum disorders (for further discussion, see Elliman & Bedford, 2007; Institute of Medicine Safety Review Committee, 2004). This belief is based on parental report that infants who develop PDD slide under an accepted two standard deviations below the mean in language and social development and increase repetitive behaviors at about 12 months of age following MMR vaccination. However, retrospective analyses of these children's development suggest that the signs were there prior to immunization. As Elliman and Bedford (2007, p. 1055) write: "There is no scientific evidence of a link between bowel disease and/or autism and MMR vaccine. Attainment of a high uptake of the vaccine should be encouraged."

One consequence of the lack of universal immunization is loss of the herd immunity phenomenon, when individuals in a community are sufficiently immunized such that a vulnerable person will not be exposed (Stephens, 2008). The loss of herd immunity will put unimmunized children at increased risk for measles and other illnesses (May & Silverman, 2003; Ali et al., 2005). For example, in the most recent measles epidemic in New York City, there was an overall death rate of 7.2 per 1,000 cases in 1990 and 3.2 per 1,000 cases in 1991 (Davis et al., 1994). In contrast, as reported by the *New York Times*, the 1991 measles death rate among 500 infected children attending a Philadelphia church that promoted nonimmunization was 10 per 1,000 cases.

Prenatal and congenital infections

The incidence of infectious and prevalence of parasitic diseases are affected by the existence and availability of vaccines, preventive and therapeutic services, clean water, and removal of sewage. Clinical smallpox has actually disappeared globally, and the spread of many others diseases including polio, measles, and rubella has been limited (AAP, 2006).

Important sets of diseases occurring prenatally are toxoplasmosis, rubella, cytomegalic inclusion disease, herpes simplex, and syphilis. The neurodevelopmental outcomes from these infectious diseases have been found to be "highly variable, ranging from no effect to severe and profound intellectual disability" (Scola, 1991). Table 3.3 lists infectious prenatal illnesses of common concern with preventive steps for each; for a comprehensive review of each entity, see AAP (2006).

Postnatal and early childhood infectious illnesses

Vaccinations. Until the advent of effective vaccines, *H. Influenzae* b (HIB, advent of vaccine in 1988) and *S. pneumoniae* (advent of polysaccharide conjugate vaccine in 2000) were the most common causes of meningoencephalitis that occurred between 3 months and 3 years of age, and deafness was the most common consequence (Bradford, 1968, p. 576; Letson et al., 1992; AAP, 2006). Both morbidity and mortality were considerable, particularly among disadvantaged populations (Letson et al., 1992). However, even with

Table 3.3 Infectious agents likely to affect infant development.

Infectious agent affecting fetus	Action
Syphilis	Have VDRL or RPR screening before pregnancy, prenatal visits and at birth. If positive, treat mother and infant.
Mycobacterium tuberculosis	Have PPD screening before pregnancy with chest radiograph confirmation. Recognize risk to infant.
Group B *Streptococcus*	Screen mother at term and treat 4 hours prior to delivery. Treat or observe infant according to protocol.
Rubella and varicella	Immunize before pregnancy. Obtain maternal titers. Immunize all children likely to expose others.
Herpes, cytomegalic inclusion disease, toxoplasmosis, and others	Provide an awareness of risk. Limit exposure.

effective vaccines available, some populations of infants may not be adequately protected against these and other forms of infectious illnesses.

Jafari, Adams, Robinson, Plikaytis, and Wenger (1999) list the phenomena associated with limited vaccination and invasive HIB disease. These include living in a single-parent, overcrowded household, exposure to tobacco smoke, and other indicators of social disadvantage. These authors show that while two or three doses of the HIB vaccine provide a remarkably effective immunity rate of 86%, the occurrence of low immunization rates in disadvantaged families creates continual risk for transmittal of HIB.

With respect to *S. pneumoniae*, O'Brien et al. (2004) report that Native Americans in the southwestern United States have among the highest globally reported rates. These authors divided 8,292 Native American infants below 7 months of age into those receiving heptavalent polysaccharide conjugate vaccine (PnCRM7) and placebo controls (O'Brien et al., 2003). All but two of the vaccinated infants were disease-free at 2 years of age; eight of the control children developed invasive *S. pneumoniae* disease. However, O'Brien et al. (2003, p. 355) also report that the "per protocol primary efficacy of PnCRM7 was 76.8% (95% CI −9.4% to 95.1%)," leading to concerns about the somewhat diminished primary prevention efficacy for this vaccine. Supporting this concern, serotypes for *S. pneumoniae* not included in the heptavalent vaccine have emerged in high-risk Alaskan Native children, emphasizing the need to maintain surveillance and keep vaccine development active in the pursuit of expanded valency (Singleton et al., 2007).

As noted above, a critical concern for vaccine-based interventions is that the phenomenon of herd immunity is lost when a critical mass of infants and children are not sufficiently immunized (May & Silverman, 2003; Ali et al., 2005). The effect of intentional or inadvertent failure to immunize upon herd immunity increases risk to all children. For example, in a Colorado community, 11% of children who contracted measles were fully vaccinated. Moreover, a community norm of noncompliance with immunization will inevitably increase the proportion of children who are vulnerable to infection, including the fully immunized (May & Silverman, 2003). Community accessibility to healthcare is thus an essential element in preventing infectious illnesses and their developmental consequences (Rodewald et al., 1999).

Gastrointestinal (diarrheal) disorders.   Diarrheal disorders are not a major developmental risk factor in high-income countries such as the United States. However, the scope of the problem clearly deserves discussion, given that estimates indicate that approximately 5 million children from developing countries die as the result of diarrheal disease (World Health Organization, 2008a). As reported by the World Health Organization, many of these deaths are preventable: "In the long term, improvements in water supply, sanitation, food safety and community awareness of preventive measures are the best means of preventing cholera and other diarrheal diseases" (World Health Organization, 2008a).

Particularly in developing countries, two kinds of infectious agents in the water supply, parasites and bacteria, precipitate gastrointestinal/diarrheal disease. Some have a direct impact on CNS structure or function. Both chronic and episodic diarrheal diseases reduce nutritional status, and impaired nutritional status clearly has adverse developmental consequences associated with the developmental consequences of protein energy malnutrition (Scholl, Johnston, Cravioto, & DeLicardie, 1983; see also chapter 2 in this volume). As Scholl et al. (1983, p. 721) point out: "Decrements in the growth rate of young children, often so serious as to constitute growth failure, are frequently seen in association with episodes of disease."

Parasitic infection.   Parasites that invade neural tissues include *Naegleria fowleri* and several *Acanthamoeba* species. One route of parasitic invasion of the CNS by species such as *Tainas* (tape worms), *Toxoplasma gondii*, and *Trichinella* (causing trichinosis) is ingestion of raw or undercooked food. Another route is via insects carrying the parasite. The classic example here is malaria. Malaria is a devastating disease in developing countries with a cerebral form that is often lethal, and even less severe but repeated attacks can also have adverse developmental consequences (Walker et al., 2007; see also chapter 6 in this volume). In addition to direct effects on the CNS there may also be indirect effects, as seen when malnutrition results from parasitic infection by species such as *Entamoeba histolitica*, *Ascaris lumbricoides*, and *Giardia lamblia*. For example, *Necator* and *Ancylostoma* (hookworm) species and *Strongeloides stercoralis* are parasites that live in contaminated soil and reach children through their bare feet. These disorders cause a profound iron deficiency anemia, compounding the effect of diets that may already be iron deficient.

It is important to note that treatment for these disorders is with drugs categorized as "C," "D," or "X," meaning that these drugs have known toxicity ("C"), likely toxicity ("D"), or toxicity of such severity as to preclude use during pregnancy or while breast feeding. Thus primary prevention of parasitic disease is essential (see www.perinatology.com/exposures/Drugs/FDACategories.htm).

Bacterial infection.   Gastrointestinal illness caused by bacterial infection has a profound effect on the mortality and associated disease morbidity in developing countries (Ali et al., 2005, 2008). The major infectious agent in developing countries is *Cholera vibrio*.

This organism contaminates the water supply in major population centers. Nevertheless, as Borroto and Martinez-Piedra (2000) point out, the incidence of cholera was inversely associated with urbanization and directly with poverty level. Specifically, the least urban stratum showed a fourfold rate ratio over the most urban one and the incidence rate of the poorest stratum was about six times as high as that of the least poor stratum. While there are clear biomedical consequences associated with cholera, at present little is known about the developmental consequences of this disorder.

In addition to the usually recommended control measures such as provision of safe water and adequate sanitation, oral cholera vaccine has been shown to be an effective public health tool (Ali et al., 2005, 2008). However, the same issues that lead to the spread of the disease also make immunization difficult, including poverty, lack of education and unavailability of healthcare (World Health Organization, 2008b; for further discussion of issues related to poverty in developing countries, see chapter 6 in this volume).

Viral agents are the most common cause for infant diarrhea in industrial societies (Morishima et al., 1978; Butz, Fosarelli, Dick, Cusack, & Yolken, 1993; Fischer & Mølbak, 2001). Poor hand washing technique by adults and fecal–oral contact from child to child spreads these agents among children in day-care (AAP, 2006; Butz et al., 1993). In addition, even in developed countries young children are also at risk for some forms of parasitic exposure that cause diarrheal disease (Novotny, Hopkins, Shillam, & Janoff, 1990).

Lead Poisoning and Fetal Alcohol Syndrome

Overview

Two particularly important precursors to child development are exposure to alcohol and lead before and during pregnancy. Maternal nutritional status affects absorption and the teratogenic impact of alcohol (Lieber, 1993; Abel and Hannigan, 1995), while the nutritional status of the child, specifically iron deficiency, will enhance lead absorption and compound the consequences, which will be reviewed in this section (Clark, Royal, & Seeler, 1988; Wright, Tsaih, Schwartz, Wright, & Hu, 2003).

Lead

The prevalence of lead poisoning has varied as the maximal accepted blood lead levels diminished from approximately 60µg/dL before 1970, when the first official limit for lead of 40µg/dL was set by the Centers for Disease Control and Prevention (CDC; Rogan & Ware, 2003). The subsequent progression of decrements went to 30µg/dL in 1970, and 25µg/dL in 1984. At present the limit for blood lead level is 10µg/dL (CDC, 1991). However, recent research by Mendelsohn et al. (1998) with children in New York City and Lanphear et al. (2005) using pooled national data has shown neurodevelopmental delay with lead levels as low as 5 µg/dL. These findings call into question a model using stepwise decrements for establishing minimum acceptable levels (Brent & Weitzman, 2004). Substantial evidence exists that toxicity occurs at 5 µg/dL, with some authors concluding that the only safe level for lead is zero (Mendelsohn et al., 1998; Brent & Weitzman, 2004; Lanphear et al., 2005).

Prenatal and in utero *exposure.*   Because of its charge as a "divalent cation," lead (Pb^{++}) substitutes for similarly charged nutrients such as calcium, iron, magnesium, and zinc (Rosen, 1985). Lead is stored in cartilage, bones, and teeth, and lead poisoning is associated with anemia and growth failure as well as neurodevelopmental abnormalities (Rosen, 1985; Lanphear et al., 2005; Hu et al., 2006). Delayed effects can occur because of the slow release of stored body lead through childhood (Gardella, 2001; Hu et al., 2006).

Elevated lead levels in childhood for girls carry elevated risk for the fetus when the female becomes pregnant, and as well during pregnancy with continued impact on subsequent generations (Gardella, 2001; Schnaas et al., 2006; Hu et al., 2006). As Schnaas et al. (2006, p. 791) write: "Lead exposure around 28 weeks' gestation is a critical period for later child intellectual development, with lasting and possibly permanent effects. There was no evidence of a threshold; the strongest lead effects on IQ occurred within the first few micrograms of [blood lead]."

Postnatal lead exposure.   Postnatally, lead impairs global intellectual development. There are sustained decrements in infants exposed to blood levels of 5 µg/dL or above (Mendelsohn et al., 1998; Liu, Dietrich, Radcliffe, Ragan, Rhoads, & Rogan, 2002; Lanphear et al., 2005). The global developmental consequences of low lead exposure are shown in Figure 3.1. However, the impact of lead on child development is not limited to decrements in global measures of intelligence. Rather, the replacement of iron with lead in the CNS stems is associated with malfunctions in auditory information processing and executive function (Bellinger, 1996; David, Clark, & Voeller, 1972). This may reflect the fact that the principal enzyme systems used for transport of information in the CNS are iron catalyzed cytochrome and monoamine oxidase (Lozoff, 1990).

Lead in relatively low doses can also affect temperament and behavior (Needleman, 1988; Bellinger, 1996). As Needleman (1988, p. 781) notes, studies of lead exposed primates

> correspond to the findings in humans of impaired reaction time under longer intervals of delay and teachers' reports of impaired classroom behaviors ... stand in close parallel to the reports of [lead exposed] children with impaired reaction time under varying intervals of delay, and teachers' reports of increased destructibility, impulsiveness, aggressiveness and hyperactivity in classroom.

These experimental findings lend clear support to the results from multiple epidemiologic studies linking lead to a variety of adverse developmental consequences (Bellinger, 1996).

Even though the focus of the present chapter is on infancy, it is important to recognize that the impact of lead exposure can occur after infancy as well. Lead levels in older children show close correlation with developmental testing regardless of whether chelation

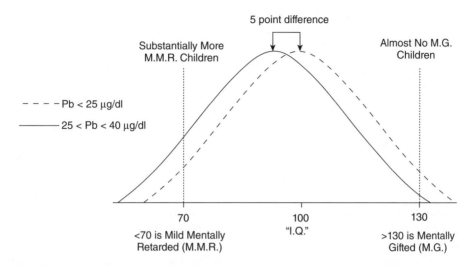

Figure 3.1 Seemingly small differences at the mean belie the consequences of lead poisoning at the extremes. Note that the small difference leaves no child in the category of "mentally gifted," with many children in the category of "mild mentally retarded." *Source*: Adapted from Harris, Clark, & Karp (1993), p. 95.

therapy has been provided (Liu et al., 2002). For example, as described by Chen, Dietrich, Ware, Radcliffe, & Rogan (2005, p. 600), "despite the immediate drops in the chelated group, there was no association between change in blood lead level and change in cognitive test score."

Fetal alcohol syndrome

International data suggest that one in every 600–700 babies in the general population (1.3 per 1,000 live births) are born with the stigmata of fetal alcohol syndrome (FAS), with an equal number of children showing effects of *in utero* exposure – fetal alcohol effects or alcohol-related birth defects (Streissguth, 1997). The Centers for Disease Control (CDC, 2007) have reported that FAS rates range from 0.2 to 1.5 per 1,000 live births in different communities in the United States. For Native Americans, overall rates may be higher. As described by May, Hymbaugh, Aase and Samet (1988), the risk of FAS infants ranges from a low of 1.3 per 1,000 live births among the Navajo to 10.3 per 1,000 live births among Plains Indians. Rates of *in utero* exposure may be even higher. For example, data provided by Marino, Scholl, Karp, Yanoff, and Hetherington (1987) suggest that 10% of the children in the schools of an industrial town in New Jersey have some expression of alcohol exposure *in utero*.

Historically, at the turn of the twentieth century, at the height of the eugenics movement, studies of families with multiply affected members – the "Jukes" and the "Kallikaks" – led to an assumption that mental retardation (called "hereditary feeble-mindedness" by

Henry H. Goddard) caused alcoholism (Goddard, 1914, 1916; Kevles, 1985; Karp, Qazi, Hittelman, & Charier, 1993; Karp, Qazi, Moller, Angelo, & Davis, 1995). According to Goddard (1914, p. 11), writing in a book that provides an overview of eugenic thinking in its own time, "the same inability to control one's actions leads these defectives inevitably to alcoholism whenever the environment is suitable." However, data taken from his studies of the "Kallikak" family suggest the converse, namely that alcohol can be a cause of intellectual deficit (Karp et al., 1993, 1995).

FAS is a constellation of effects seen in children with a history of prenatal ethanol (alcohol) exposure. It is a permanent condition characterized by facial deformities, growth retardation, and neurodevelopmental delay (Jones, Smith, Ulleland, & Streissguth, 1973; Astley & Clarren, 2001; Karp et al., 1993; Streissguth, 1997). Besides general cognitive delay, there may also be specific cognitive impairments associated with FAS, such as decreased working memory (Streissguth, 1997). Children who have only some of the characteristics of FAS have either fetal alcohol effects where there are developmental problems or alcohol-related birth defects where there are congenital anomalies (Streissguth, 1997). The high prevalence and preventability of FAS makes it imperative that healthcare professionals focus on identifying *both* communities at risk for the range of alcohol effects *and* women who drink during pregnancy (Streissguth, 1997).

Prenatal exposure.   Recognition of FAS in newborns is a major concern. Figure 3.2 shows characteristic dysmorphic features in a newborn with FAS. Besides alcohol exposure

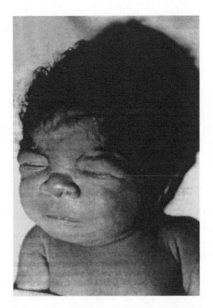

Figure 3.2   In diagnosing FAS a helpful measure is to use a full frontal photograph to measure the "palpebral fissure" (lateral to medial canthal fold) and compare to the inter-canthal distance. The ratio should be >1:1:>1 (width of eyes are each larger than distance between). Also note the long flat philtrum, which is the space between upper lip and nose (Astley & Clarren, 2001). *Source:* Karp et al. (1993), p. 102.

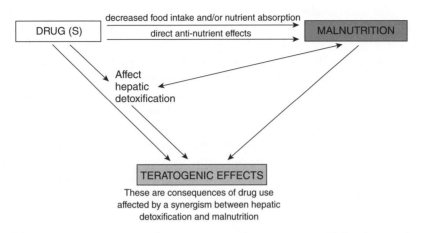

Figure 3.3 Alcohol consumption affects nutrient intake, nutrient availability, hepatic function and concomitant fetal development. *Source*: Karp (1999).

per se, evidence indicates that the severity of the alcohol effects on the fetus can be moderated by the nutritional status of the mother. Other potential moderators include the mother's age, hepatic function, other toxic ingestions, and parity (Abel & Hannigan, 1995; Lieber, 1993; Karp, 1999; Hashimi & Karp, 2007). For example, older women are more likely to have an affected infant because of deterioration in their nutritional status (Hashimi & Karp, 2007; Abel & Hannigan, 1995), while hepatic dysfunction associated with chronic alcoholism alters the detoxification process for other drugs of abuse as well as for environmental pollutants, allowing toxic metabolites to reach the fetus.

A contemporary view, from Lieber (1993), is that "at cellular, biochemical and molecular levels, the nutritional and toxic effects of alcohol converge." Thus, polydrug abuse concomitant to aging of mothers creates a nutrient-deprived *in utero* environment that increases the risk for teratogenic consequences of drug exposure on the growing fetus. A model of teratogen [×] malnutrition effects for FAS, derived by Karp (1999) from the work of Lieber (1993), is shown in Figure 3.3.

Long-term consequences of FAS. Besides intellectual disability, there are also a variety of consequences not inherently present at birth that may occur as a result of FAS. These include an increased risk for psychiatric problems, criminal behavior, inability to conform to accepted social norms of behavior and conduct, unemployment, and incomplete education (Grisham & Estes, 1986; Streissguth, 1997). Once a child has been diagnosed with FAS, the goal of management and early intervention should be to help the child achieve independence and to avoid the long-term consequences listed (Streissguth, 1997; Streissguth & O'Malley, 2000).

Cumulative influences

While treated independently in the present chapter, the impact of biomedical risk factors such as IUGR, FAS, and lead poisoning may be synergistic in nature. For example, lead exposure after birth might differentially affect an infant with exposure to alcohol prior to birth, a premature infant, or a child small for her gestational age. Similarly, the increased risk of neurodevelopmental delay found for premature infants or infants with *in utero* growth failure may be compounded by subsequent growth failure in early infancy (Emond, Blair, Emmett, & Drewett, 2007). In addition, the biomedical risk factors discussed in this chapter provide the biological milieu in which the cluster effects of poverty can play out (Sameroff & Chandler, 1975; Rutter & Madge, 1976; Johnston & Markowitz, 1993). Taken together, they add to the probability of a child's developing cognitive or social-emotional deficits as part of a cluster of multiple risk factors (Shonkoff & Phillips, 2000; Wachs, 2000). The cumulative consequences of multiple biological and psychosocial risk factors also can result in the maintainance of disadvantage from one generation to another (Birch & Gussow, 1970; Rutter & Madge, 1976; Karp, 1993).

Injury

Overview

Injury protection is a critical factor affecting children's future development. In 2001, the trauma fatality rate for infants and toddlers (from birth to 4 years of age) was 18.4 per 100,000 population, with a nonfatal injury rate of 10,200 per 100,000 (Vyrostek, Annest, & Ryan, 2004). Although information was not provided on the statistical significance of gender differences, the rate of unintentional injury for boys (16.0) is somewhat higher than for girls (11.7). Similarly, for intentional injuries (e.g., assault or abuse), boys (11.1) are substantially more affected than girls (3.3). Using this data set, the rates and number of affected infants and toddlers are shown in Table 3.4. The infancy and toddler period may be particularly risky for injuries, given evidence that fatal injury rates were lowest among children aged 5–9 years (6.3 for unintentional and 0.7 for intentional); see Vyrostek et al. (2004).

The approach to dealing with unintentional injury is quite distinct from that proposed for intentional injuries. For unintentional injuries the Injury Prevention Program of the American Academy of Pediatrics (2008) focuses on social engendering as well as on education of the parent and family. For example, much injury occurs because of design failures (e.g., easily opened medicine bottles, open access of cars to residential streets, failure to enforce laws requiring seat belt use or nonuse of-cell phones while driving, etc.).

In 1957, John Caffey reported radiologic evidence we now recognize as pathognomonic for abuse. "In the absence of trauma in the history, however," he wrote, "these same findings are now construed to be signs of scurvy" and other causes including "atypical chondrodystrophy" (Caffey, 1957). Child abuse was brought from "suspicion and doubt" to recognition by Kempe, Silverman, Steele, Droegemueller, and Silver (1962). Prior to that date, unexplained injuries were considered as unintentional. The developmental consequences of child abuse are detailed in chapter 7 in this volume. With regard to biomedical consequences, at most risk would be infants who sustain CNS damage from what is called "shaken baby" syndrome. In shaken baby syndrome the back-and-

Table 3.4   Trauma to infants and children: Unintentional and intentional injury.

Rate per 100,000 (actual number)

Source of Injury	Fatal Injury	Nonfatal Injury
Unintentional	13.9 (2,690)	9,650 (2,390,299)
Intentional (Assault)	3.9 (742)	215 (41,661)

Data taken from Vyrostek et al. (2004).

forth motion of an infant's relatively large head and weak neck muscles leads to vessels tearing or oozing blood into the subdural spaces. The triad of encephalopathy, thin subdural hemorrhages, and retinal hemorrhages is pathognomonic of shaken baby syndrome (Richards et al., 2006). Diagnosis is from clinical and radiologic evidence or presence of cerebral swelling with swelling of the optic disc ("papilledema"). Survivors experience a range of disabilities, from focal losses to spastic quadriplegia.

Inborn Errors of Metabolism

It would be presumptuous to limit the infirmities of infancy and early childhood with developmental consequences to those listed herein. As noted earlier in this chapter, there are whole categories of illness that have untoward effects. One such category involves inborn errors of metabolism (Saudubray, Nassogne, de Lonlay, & Touati, 2002; Rezvani, 2004; Panambulam, Wershil & Gurwitz, 2007).

Overview

Unrecognized metabolic disorder can cause lasting neurological damage in a neonate. At the present time newborn screening reports are available to the clinician for many of the common inborn errors of metabolism before the disorder presents. While these disorders are *caused* by a deficient enzyme, the *consequence* of that deficiency is a result of a combination of accumulation of substrate, toxic metabolites of the substrate, *and* a deficiency of the end product. The consequences of inborn errors of metabolism may present after the first year of life (Saudubray et al., 2002).

The variability of inborn errors is influenced greatly by (1) the acceptance of known consanguinity, as seen in first cousin and uncle–niece marriages, and (2) colony effects when there is a relatively limited gene pool. As an example of the first situation, Ashkenazic Jews are likely to marry the equivalent of a fifth cousin (about 3% of common genetic background), while French Canadians are approximately third cousins (about 10%). With regard to colony effects, the Amish are descended from about 80 Swiss Germans who migrated to Central Pennsylvania; all are closely related without consanguineous marriages (see Table 1 in Panambulam et al., 2007, for further details).

Phenylketonuria

The prototypical disease is phenylketonuria (PKU). This disorder is caused by a defect in the enzyme phenylalanine hydroxylase or its coenzyme. Failure of hydroxylation means an accumulation of phenylalanine (PHA) and its principal metabolite, phenylketone, which is not toxic. One reason for the emphasis on newborn screening for metabolic diseases like PKU is that, unrecognized, this genetic defect produces a severely handicapped adult (Panambulam et al., 2007). Therapy early on in life will prevent most, but not all, of the sequelae. As Maillot, Lilburn, Baudin, Morley, & Lee (2008) point out, to be truly effective, therapy must be maintained from prepregnancy and be closely monitored through to delivery. The metabolic pathway for transformation of PHA to tyrosine (TYR) shown in Figure 3.4 requires the enzyme PHA hydroxylase to remove a hydroxyl group from PHA. Of note, both PHA and TYR are essential amino acids that cannot be constructed *de novo* and must be supplied in the diet.

The accumulation of PHA, which is neurotoxic, adversely impacts on the development and function of the CNS, which in turn leads to a gradual onset of mental retardation (Rezvani, 2004). Children with this disorder begin life normally, and, while the disease progresses slowly, the consequences of untreated disease are signs of developmental delay by 4–6 months of age. Affected children are characteristically blond, fair, and somewhat listless because the next steps in the metabolic pathway result in formation of melanin (pigment producing) and dopamine (DOPA, activity stimulating). Pregnancy is a particularly difficult time for women with PKU due to PHA being in multiple foods. For example, aspartamine, a created amino acid that contains PHA, is a commonly used sugar substitute. Usage must be labeled in bold letters: "**Phenylketonurics: contains phenylalanine**."

Over-restriction of PHA leads to developmental consequences similar to those seen in protein energy malnutrition. Successful early diagnosis and treatment requires removal of most, *but not all*, phenylalanine from the diet, while also providing appropriate levels of tyrosine (Rezvani, 2004; Waisbren et al., 2007). Thus, both inadequate and overly aggressive control of PHA intake will adversely affect neurodevelopment (Rezvani, 2004; Maillot et al., 2008). Contemporary therapies are successful in keeping levels of both PHA and TYR at nontoxic and adequate levels, respectively.

From a public health perspective, PKU illustrates the importance of newborn screening for early diagnosis *and* an availability of sophisticated medical care for affected infants and their families. The costs of failing to either identify or properly treat PKU are enormous in both monetary terms and in terms of pain and suffering. No financial value can

$$\text{PHA} \quad \to // \to \text{TYR} \to \text{DOPA} \to \text{Melanine}$$
$$\downarrow$$
$$\downarrow$$
$$\text{PK's}$$

Figure 3.4   A schema for the metabolism of phenylalanine. The enzymatic defect between phenylalanine and tyrosine leads to an accumulation of phenylalanine, which is toxic. Of equal importance is the depletion of tyrosine, an essential product of the enzymatic reaction.

be placed on the loss of a child's future to a preventable consequence of an inherited disorder.

The PKU model applies to many inborn metabolic errors. To avoid long-term adverse consequences it is essential to maintain a system of such errors for diagnosis before, at, or just after birth, with a therapy that combines appropriate restriction of substrate and provision of product whenever possible (Panambulam et al., 2007). This requires a robust system for public health and patient care (R. J. Karp, 2002).

Colic

There have been concerns raised that infantile colic may be associated with developmental delay or behavioral changes (Sloman, Bellinger, & Krentzel, 1990; Rao, Brenner, Schisterman, Vik, & Mills, 2004). Colic has a formal definition from the "rule of threes" – crying for "at least 3 hours a day, 3 days in a week, 3 weeks in a row" (H. Karp, 2002).

Crying and discomfort are *not* critical with respect to possible subsequent developmental effects. For example, Rao et al. (2004) documented no adverse developmental consequence for colic occurring at less than 3 months of age when it is expected to occur. However, Sloman et al. (1990) recognized *potential* indirect relationships between colic and subsequent development and behavior. They suggested that a mismatch between parental temperament and parental expectations for infant temperament increased risk (see chapter 20 in volume 1 for further discussion of the issue of parent–infant fit). In addition, Rao et al. (2004) reported that long-term pain and discomfort as a function of colic were shown to be a predicator of developmental consequences.

Rao et al. (2004) hypothesize two possible mechanisms to explain the developmental consequences associated with colic. The first is a continuation of the parent–infant temperament mismatch described by Sloman et al. (1990). The second was that the colic was associated with underlying gastrointestinal illness. With regard to colic occurring during the first 3 months of life, parents should be reassured and given instructions on effective care during this time period (H. Karp, 2002). However, long-standing colic symptoms require careful evaluation of parent–child interaction and evaluation for potential illness.

Providing a "Medical Home"

The developmental consequences of prenatal, congenital, and early childhood illnesses are heavily influenced by the quality of healthcare available to the community, family, and child. Calvin Sia, a pediatrician in Hawaii, has developed a concept that he called the "Medical Home" (Sia, 1992). Sia's work is similar to that of Sally Grantham-McGregor (1998) in Jamaica, and Deborah Frank (2004; Wilbur & Frank, 2007) in Boston. Illustrating this approach Grantham-McGregor (1998, pp. 257) wrote: "It is naive to expect mono-focal interventions, in the presence of extremely deprived environments, to produce substantial and long-term benefits to the children's development."

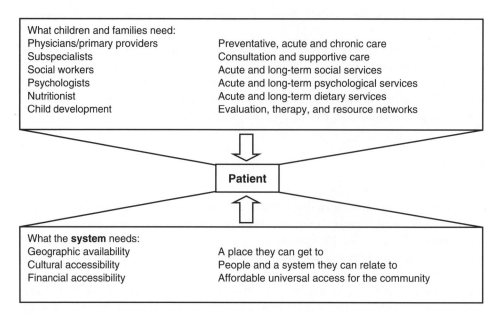

Figure 3.5   Interacting resources. Healthcare is more than a physician in his or her office. It is the provision of a broad panoply of related services promoting prevention and care with careful attention to location, cost, and cultural factors. *Sources*: Frank (2004); Grantham-McGregor (1998); Karp (2002); Sia (1992).

How this model plays out in practice is shown in Figure 3.5. In Sia's model, the physician does not dominate care. Rather, the family is the center of attention with a resource-rich network that includes, but is no means limited to, physician services. As shown in Figure 3.5, the elements of financial, geographic, and cultural accessibility are necessary parts of service (Nelson et al., 2005; Smith, Santoli, Chu, Ochoa, & Rodewald, 2005).

Illness is not an isolated occurrence in the lives of affected children. It often signals that other social or medical problems exist in the family, community or society at large. Built into the healthcare given to a child is a recognition that abnormal tests require more than additional diagnostic tests and medication. These are "necessary but not sufficient" (Wachs, 2000). What is clear from the model shown in Figure 3.5 is that no single person or institution has all of the skills or resources necessary to care for the larger social and psychological problems of the physically ill disadvantaged child. Such children are best treated by an interdisciplinary team including physician, nurse, nutritionist, social worker, home health worker, and others from outside the medical community such as planners of agriculture, economists, sociologists, and educators (R. Karp, 1993).

Acknowledgments

The careful review and suggestions of Laura Bruno, Harris Huberman, and Linda Oppenheim are gratefully acknowledged, as are the contributions of Ted Ferenczy, Cesar Mejia, and the figure-making skills of Sebastian Stanescu and Ted Ferenczy.

References

Abel, E., & Hannigan, B. (1995). Maternal risk factors in fetal alcohol syndrome: Provocative and permissive influences. *Neurotoxicology and Teratology, 17,* 445–462.

Ali, M., Emch, M., von Seidlein, L., Yunus, M., Sack, D. A., Rao, M., et al. (2005). Herd immunity conferred by killed oral cholera vaccines in Bangladesh: A reanalysis. *Lancet, 366*(9479), 44–49.

Ali, M., Emch, M., Yunus, M., Sack, D., Lopez, A. L., Holmgren, J., & Clemens, J. (2008). Vaccine protection of Bangladeshi infants and young children against cholera: Implications for vaccine deployment and person-to-person transmission. *Pediatric Infectious Disease Journal, 27,* 33–37.

American Academy of Pediatrics (2006). *Red book: 2006 Report of the Committee on Infectious Diseases* (27th ed.). L. K. Pickering, C. J. Baker, S. S. Long et al. (Eds). Elk Grove Village, IL: American Academy of Pediatrics.

American Academy of Pediatrics (2008). *The Injury Prevention Program (TIPP).* http://pediatrics. about.com/od/aaptippsheets/AAP_Injury_Prevention_Program.htm.

Anderson, J. W. (2005) Diabetes mellitus: Medical nutrition therapy. In M. E. Shils, M. Shike, A. C. Ross, B. Caballero, & R. J. Cousins (Eds.), *Modern nutrition in health and disease* (10th ed., pp. 1043–1066). Baltimore, MD: Lippincott Williams Wilkins.

Artal, R., Platt, L. D., Kammula, R. K., Strassner, H. T., Gratacos, J., & Golde, S. H. (1982). Sympathoadrenal activity in infants of diabetic mothers. *American Journal of Obstetrics & Gynecology, 142,* 436.

Astley, S., & Clarren, S. (2001). Measuring the facial phenotype of individuals with prenatal alcohol exposure: Correlations with brain dysfunction. *Alcohol, 36,* 147–159.

Bellinger, D. (1996) Learning and behavioral sequelae. In S. M. Pueschal, J. G. Linakis, & A. C. Anderson (Eds.), *Lead poisoning in childhood* (pp. 97–116). Baltimore, MD: Paul Brookes.

Berlin, I. (1953). *The hedgehog and the fox: An essay on Tolstoy's view of history.* Chicago: Ivan R. Dee.

Birch, H. G., & Gussow, J. D. (1970). *Disadvantaged children: Health, nutrition and school failure.* New York: Harcourt Brace & World.

Borroto, R. J., & Martinez-Piedra, R. (2000). Geographical patterns of cholera in Mexico, 1991–1996. *International Journal of Epidemiology, 29,* 764–772.

Bradford, W. H. (1968). Influenza meningitis. In W. Nelson, V. C. Vaughn, & R. McKay (Eds.), *Nelson textbook of pediatrics* (9th ed.). Philadelphia: WB Saunders.

Brent, R. L., & Weitzman, M. (2004). The current state of knowledge about the effects, risks, and science of children's environmental exposures. *Pediatrics, 113*(Suppl.), 1158–1166.

Butz, A. M., Fosarelli, P., Dick, J., Cusack, T., & Yolken, R. (1993). Prevalence of rotavirus on high-risk fomites in day-care facilities. *Pediatrics, 92,* 202–205.

Caffey, J. (1957). Some traumatic lesions in growing bones other than fractures and dislocations: Clinical and radiological. *British Journal of Radiology, 30,* 225–238.

Centers for Disease Control and Prevention (1991, October). *Preventing lead poisoning in young children.* http://wonder.cdc.gov/wonder/Prevguid/p0000029/p0000029.asp (accessed March 2010).

Centers for Disease Control and Prevention (2007). *Fetal alcohol spectrum disorders (FASDs).* www. cdc.gov/ncbddd/fasd/index.html (accessed March 2010).

Chaudhuri, J. (2000). Alcohol and the developing fetus – a review. *Medical Science Monitor, 6,* 1031–1041.

Chen, A., Dietrich, K. N., Ware, J. H., Radcliffe, J., & Rogan, W. J. (2005). IQ and blood lead from 2 to 7 years of age: Are the effects in older children the residual of high blood lead concentrations in 2-year-olds? *Environmental Health Perspectives, 113,* 597–601.

Clark, M., Royal, J., & Seeler, R. (1988). Interaction of iron deficiency and lead and the hematologic findings in children with severe lead poisoning. *Pediatrics, 81*, 247–254.

Creasy, R. K., & Resnik, R. (1995). Intrauterine growth restriction. In R. K. Creasy & R. Resnik (Eds.), *Maternal-fetal medicine* (4th ed., pp. 793–803). Philadelphia: WB Saunders.

David, O., Clark, J., & Voeller, K. (1972). Lead and hyperactivity. *Lancet, 7783*, 900–903.

Davis, S. F., Strebel, P. M., Atkinson, W. L., Markowitz, L. E., Sutter, R. W., Scanlon, K. S. et al. (1994). Reporting efficiency during a measles outbreak in New York City. *American Journal of Public Health, 84*, 868–869.

Dionne, G., Boivin, M., Séguin, J. R., Pérusse, D., & Tremblay, R. E. (2008). Gestational diabetes hinders language development in offspring. *Pediatrics, 122*, e1073–e1079.

Elliman, D., & Bedford, H. (2007). MMR: Where are we now? *Archives of Disease in Childhood, 92*, 1055–1057.

Emond, A. M., Blair, P. S., Emmett, P. M., & Drewett, R. F. (2007). Weight faltering in infancy and IQ levels at 8 years in the Avon Longitudinal Study of Parents and Children. *Pediatrics, 120*, e1051–1058.

Fischer, T. K., & Mølbak, K. (2001). The costs of an outbreak – an example from a Danish day care setting. *Vaccine, 20*, 637–638.

Frank, D. A. (2004). Failure to thrive. In S. Parker, B. Zuckerman, & M. Augustyn (Eds.), *Developmental and behavioral pediatrics* (pp. 183–187), Philadelphia: Lippincott Williams Wilkins.

Freinkel, N. (1988). Diabetic embryopathy and fuel-mediated organ teratogenesis: Lessons from animal models. *Diabetes/Metabolism Research and Reviews, 20*, 463–475.

Galler, J. R., & Barrett, L. R. (2002). Children and famine: long-term effects on behavioral development. *Ambulatory Child Health, 7*, 85–95.

Gardella, C. (2001). Lead exposure in pregnancy: A review of the literature and argument for routine prenatal screening. *Obstetrical & Gynecological Survey, 56*, 231–238.

Goddard, H. H. (1914). *Feeble-mindedness: Its causes and consequences*. New York: Macmillan.

Goddard, H. H. (1916). Alcoholism and feeble-mindedness. *Interstate Medical Journal, 26*, 1–4.

Goetghebuer, T., West, T. E., Wermenbol, V., Cadbury, A. L., Milligan, P., Lloyd-Evans, N., et al. (2000). Outcome of meningitis caused by Streptococcus pneumoniae and Haemophilus influenzae type b in children in The Gambia. *Tropical Medicine & International Health, 5*, 207–213.

Gonnella, J. S. (1993). Clinical disease staging. In J. S. Gonnella, M. Hojat, J. B. Erdmann, J. J. Veloski, & G. Miller II (Eds.), *Assessment measures in medical school, residency, and practice: The connections*. New York: Springer Publishing.

Grantham-McGregor, S. (1998). Summary. In *Nutrition, health, and child development. Scientific Publication, No. 566* (pp. 256–257). Washington, DC: Pan American Health Organization.

Grantham-McGregor, S., & International Child Development Committee (2007). Early child development in developing countries. *Lancet, 10*, 369.

Grisham, K., & Estes, N. (1986). Dynamics of alcoholic families. In N. Estes & M. E. Heinemann (Eds.) *Alcoholism: Development, consequences and interventions* (3rd ed., pp. 303–316). St. Louis, MO: Mosby.

Grunfeld, E. (2006). Looking beyond survival: How are we looking at survivorship? *Journal of Clinical Oncology, 24*, 5166–5169.

Harris, P., Clark, M., & Karp, R. J. (1993). Prevention and treatment of lead poisoning. In R. J. Karp (Ed.). *Malnourished children in the United States: Caught in the cycle of poverty* (pp. 91–100). New York: Springer Publishing.

Hashimi, S., & Karp, R. J. (2007). Fetal Alcohol Syndrome. In R. J. Karp, E. Shepard, & S. Hassink (Eds.), *A teacher's guide to pediatric nutrition*. Washington, DC: Academic Pediatric Association.

Hod, M., Merlob, P., Friedman, S., Rusecki, Y., Schoenfeld, A., & Ovadia, J. (1991). Prevalence of congenital anomalies and neonatal implications in the offspring of diabetic mothers in Israel. *Israel Journal of Medical Sciences, 27,* 498–502.

Holditch-Davis, D., Schwartz, T., Black, B., & Scher, J. (2007). Correlates of mother–premature infant interactions. *Research in Nursing & Health, 30,* 333–346.

Holm, I., Fredriksen, P. M., Fosdahl, M. A., Olstad, M., & Vøllestad, N. (2007). Impaired motor competence in school-aged children with complex congenital heart disease. *Archives of Pediatrics & Adolescent Medicine, 161,* 945–950.

Holt, L. E. (1911). Tuberculosis. In *Diseases of infancy and childhood* (6th ed.). New York: D. Appelton and Co.

Hu, H., Téllez-Rojo, M. M., Bellinger, D., Smith, D., Ettinger, A. S., Lamadrid-Figueroa, H., et al. (2006). Fetal lead exposure at each stage of pregnancy as a predictor of infant mental development. *Environmental Health Perspectives, 114,* 1730–1735.

Institute of Medicine Safety Review Committee (2004). *Immunization safety review: Vaccines and autism, 2004.* Washington, DC: National Academy of Sciences.

Jafari, H. S., Adams, W. G., Robinson, K. A., Plikaytis, B. D., & Wenger, J. D. (1999). Efficacy of Haemophilus influenzae type b conjugate vaccines and persistence of disease in disadvantaged populations. The Haemophilus Influenzae Study Group. *American Journal of Public Health, 89,* 364–368.

Johnston, F., & Markowitz, D. (1993). Do poverty and malnutrition affect children's growth and development: Are the data there? In R. J. Karp (Ed.), *Malnourished children in the United States: Caught in the cycle of poverty* (pp. 3–12). New York: Springer Publishing.

Jones, K. L., Smith, D. W., Ulleland, C., & Streissguth, A. P. (1973). Patterns of malformation in offspring of chronic alcoholic mothers. *Lancet, 1,* 1267.

Karp, H. (2002). *The happiest baby on the block.* New York: Bantam Books.

Karp, R. J. (1993). Introduction and overview. In R. J. Karp (Ed.). *Malnourished children in the United States: Caught in the cycle of poverty* (pp. xix–2). New York: Springer Publishing.

Karp, R. J. (1999). Malnutrition among children in the United States. The impact of poverty. In M. E. Shils, J. A. Olson, M. Shike, & A. C. Ross (Eds.). *Modern nutrition in health and disease* (9th ed., pp. 989–1001). Baltimore, MD: Williams and Wilkins.

Karp, R. J. (2002). *Epilogue: The dimensions of poverty among children in the United States: An exposition of causes and consequences.* Curriculum for Poor and Underserved Children. McLean, VA: Academic Pediatric Association. www.servingtheunderserved.org.html. (accessed September 2008).

Karp, R. J., Qazi, Q., Hittelman, J., & Charier, L. (1993). Fetal alcohol syndrome. In R. J. Karp (Ed.), *Malnourished children in the United States: Caught in the cycle of poverty* (pp. 101–108). New York: Springer Publishing.

Karp, R. J., Qazi, Q. H., Moller, K. A., Angelo, W. A., & Davis, J. M. (1995). Fetal alcohol syndrome at the turn of the 20th century: An unexpected explanation of the Kallikak family. *Archives of Pediatric & Adolescent Medicine, 149,* 45–48.

Kempe, C. H., Silverman, F. N., Steele, B. F., Droegemueller, W., & Silver, H. K. (1962). The battered-child syndrome. *Journal of American Medical Association, 181,* 17–24.

Kevles, D. (1985). *In the name of eugenics: Genetics and the uses of human heredity.* New York: Knopf.

Kossmann, J., Nestel, P., Herrera, M. G., El Amin, A., & Fawzi, W. W. (2000). Undernutrition in relation to childhood infections: A prospective study in the Sudan. *European Journal of Clinical Nutrition, 54,* 463–472.

Landon, M. B., & Gabbe, S. G. (1992). Diabetes mellitus and pregnancy. *Obstetrics & Gynecology Clinics of North America, 19,* 633–654.

Lanphear, B. P., Hornung, R., Khoury, J., Yolton, K., Baghurst, P., Bellinger, D. C., et al. (2005). Low-level environmental lead exposure and children's intellectual function: An international pooled analysis. *Environmental Health Perspectives, 113,* 894–899.

Letson, G. W., Gellin, B. G., Bulkow, L. R., Parks, D. J., & Ward, J. I. (1992). Severity and frequency of sequelae of bacterial meningitis in Alaska Native infants. Correlation with a scoring system for severity of sequelae. *American Journal of Disease in Childhood, 146,* 560–566.

Lieber, C. S. (1993). Herman Award Lecture, 1993: A personal perspective on alcohol, nutrition, and the liver. *American Journal of Clinical Nutrition, 58,* 430–442.

Liu, X., Dietrich, K. N., Radcliffe, J., Ragan, N. B., Rhoads, G. G., & Rogan, W. J. (2002). Do children with falling blood lead levels have improved cognition? *Pediatrics, 110,* 787–791.

Lozoff, B. (1990). Has iron deficiency been shown to cause altered behavior in infants? In J. Dobbing (Eds.), *Brain, behavior, and iron in the infant diet* (pp. 107–131). London: Springer Verlag.

Lozoff, B., Corapci, F., Burden, M. J., Kaciroti, N., Angulo-Barroso, R., Sazawal, S., & Black, M. (2007). Pre-school age children with iron deficiency anemia show altered affect and behavior. *Journal of Nutrition, 137,* 683–689.

Maillot, F., Lilburn, M., Baudin, J., Morley, D. W., & Lee, P. J. (2008). Factors influencing outcomes in the offspring of mothers with phenylketonuria during pregnancy: The importance of variation in maternal blood phenylalanine. *American Journal of Clinical Nutrition, 88,* 700–705.

Marino, R. V., Scholl, T. O., Karp, R. J., Yanoff, J. M., & Hetherington, J. (1987). Minor physical anomalies and learning disability: What is the prenatal component? *Journal of the National Medical Association, 79,* 37–39.

Marmot, M. G. (2003). Understanding social inequalities in health. *Perspectives in Biology & Medicine, 46*(3 Suppl.), S9–23.

May, P. A., Hymbaugh, K. J., Aase, J. M., & Samet, J. M. (1988). Epidemiology of fetal alcohol syndrome among American Indians of the Southwest. *Social Biology, 30,* 374–385.

May, T., & Silverman, R. D. (2003). Clustering of exemptions as a collective action threat to herd immunity. *Vaccine, 21,* 1048–1051.

McLaren, D. S. (1981). *A colour atlas of nutritional disorders.* London: Wolfe Medical.

Meadows, A. T. (2006). Pediatric cancer survivorship: Research and clinical care. *Journal of Clinical Oncology, 24,* 5160–5165.

Mendelsohn, A. L., Dreyer, B. P., Fierman, A. H., Rosen, C. M., Legano, L. A., Kruger, H. A., et al. (1998). Low-level lead exposure and behavior in early childhood. *Pediatrics, 101,* E10.

Morishima, T., Ichikawa, T., Hideaki, M., Miyazu, M., Nagayoshi, S., Ozaki, T., et al. (1978). Acute infantile gastroenteritis caused by rotavirus in Japan. *European Journal of Pediatrics, 129,* 1432–1476.

National Diabetes Quality Improvement Alliance (2005) *National Diabetes Quality Improvement Alliance performance measurement set for adult diabetes.* Chicago: National Diabetes Quality Improvement Alliance. www-nehc.med.navy.mil/bumed/diabetes/document%20folders/diabetes/cpg/dqia.msrs.pdf (accessed March 2010).

Needleman, H. L. (1988). The persistent threat of lead: Medical and sociological issues. *Current Problems in Pediatrics, 18,* 703–744.

Nelson, C. S., Higman, S. M., Sia, C., McFarlane, E., Fuddy, L., & Duggan, A. K. (2005). Medical homes for at-risk children: parental reports of clinician-parent relationships, anticipatory guidance, and behavior changes. *Pediatrics, 115,* 48–56.

Nold, J. L., & Georgieff, M. K. (2004). Infants of diabetic mothers. *Pediatric Clinics of North America, 51,* 619–630.

Novotny, T., Hopkins, R., Shillam, P., & Janoff, E. (1990). Prevalence of giardia lamblia and risk factors for infection among children attending day-care facilities in Denver. *Public Health Reports, 105,* 72–75.

O'Brien, K. L., Moulton, L. H., Reid, R., Weatherholtz, R., Oski, J., Brown, L., et al. (2003). Efficacy and safety of seven-valent conjugate pneumococcal vaccine in American Indian children: Group randomised trial. *Lancet, 362,* 355–361.

O'Brien, K. L., Shaw, J., Weatherholtz, R., Reid, R., Watt, J., Croll, J., et al. (2004). Epidemiology of invasive *Streptococcus pneumoniae* among Navajo children in the era before use of conjugate pneumococcal vaccines, 1989–1996. *American Journal of Epidemiology, 160,* 270–278.

Oski, F., & Naiman, J. L. (1982). *Hematologic problems in the newborn* (3rd ed.). Philadelphia: Saunders.

Panambulam, A., Wershil, B., & Gurwitz, A. (2007). Inborn errors of metabolism. In R. J. Karp, E. Shepard, & S. Hassink (Eds.), *A teacher's guide to pediatric nutrition.* McLean, VA: Academic Pediatric Association.

Pedersen, J. (1954). Weight and length at birth of infants of diabetic mothers. *Acta Endocrinologica, 16,* 330–342.

Petry, C. D., Eaton, M. A., Wobken, J. D., Mills, M. M., Johnson, D. E., & Georgieff, M. K. (1992). Iron deficiency of liver, heart and brain iron in newborn infants of diabetic mothers. *Journal of Pediatrics, 121,* 109–114.

Rao, M. R., Brenner, R. A., Schisterman, R. F., Vik, T., & Mills, J. L. (2004). Long term cognitive development in children with prolonged crying. *Archives of Disease in Childhood, 89,* 989–992.

Rezvani, I. (2004). Defects in metabolism of amino acids: Phenylketonuria. In R. E. Bierman, R. M. Kliegman & H. B. Jenson (Eds.), *Nelson textbook of pediatrics* (17th ed., pp. 398–402). Philadelphia: Saunders.

Richards, P. G., Bertocci, G. E., Bonshek, R. E., Giangrande, P. L., Gregson, R. M., Jaspan, T., et al. (2006). Shaken baby syndrome. *Archives of Disease in Childhood, 91,* 205–206.

Rodewald, L. E., Szilagyi, P. G., Humiston, S. G., Barth, R., Kraus, R., & Raubertas, R. F. (1999). A randomized study of tracking with outreach and provider prompting to improve immunization coverage and primary care. *Pediatrics, 103,* 31–38.

Rogan, W. J., & Ware, J. H. (2003). Exposure to lead in children – how low is low enough? *New England Journal of Medicine, 348,* 1515–1516.

Rosen, J. F. (1985). Metabolic and cellular effects of lead: A guide to low level lead toxicity in children. In K. R. Mahaffey (Ed.), *Dietary and environmental lead. Human health effects* (pp. 157–185). New York: Elsevier.

Rutter, M., & Madge, N. (1976). *Cycles of disadvantage.* London: Heinemann.

Sameroff, A., & Chandler, N. (1975). Reproductive risk and the continuum of care taking causality. In F. Horowitz (Ed.), *Review of child development research.* Chicago: University of Chicago Press.

Saudubray, J. M., Nassogne, M. C., de Lonlay, P., & Touati, G. (2002). Clinical approach to inherited metabolic disorders in neonates: An overview. *Seminars in Neonatology, 7,* 3–15.

Schlotz, W., Jones, A., Phillips, N. M., Godfrey, K. M., & Phillips, I. W. (2007). Size at birth and motor activity during stress in children aged 7 to 9 years. *Pediatrics, 120,* e1237–1244.

Schnaas, L., Rothenberg, S. J., Flores, M. F., Martinez, S., Hernandez, C., Osorio, E., et al. (2006). Reduced intellectual development in children with prenatal lead exposure. *Environmental Health Perspectives, 114,* 791–797.

Scholl, T. O., Johnston, F. E., Cravioto, J., & DeLicardie, E. R. (1983). The utility of cross-sectional measurements of weight and length for age in screening for growth failure (chronic malnutrition) and clinically severe protein-energy malnutrition. *Acta Paediatrica Scandinavica, 72,* 867–872.

Scola, P. (1991). Infections. In J. Maton & J. Mulick (Eds.). *Handbook of mental retardation* (2nd ed.). Elmsford, NY: Pergamon Press.

Shonkoff, J. P., & Phillips, D. A. (Eds.) (2000). *From neurons to neighborhoods: The science of early child development.* Committee on Integrating the Science of Early Childhood Development. Washington, DC: National Academy Press.

Sia, C. C. (1992). Abraham Jacobi Award address. The medical home: Pediatric practice and child advocacy in the 1990s. *Pediatrics, 90,* 419–423.

Singleton, R. J., Hennessy, T. W., Bulkow, L. R., Hammitt, L. L., Zulz, T., Hurlburt, D. A., et al. (2007). Invasive pneumococcal disease caused by nonvaccine serotypes among Alaska native children with high levels of 7-valent pneumococcal conjugate vaccine coverage. *Journal of the American Medical Association, 297,* 1825–1826.

Sloman, J., Bellinger, D. C., & Krentzel, C. P. (1990). Infantile colic and transient developmental lag in the first year of life. *Child Psychiatry and Human Development, 21,* 25–36.

Smith, P. J., Santoli, J. M., Chu, S. Y., Ochoa, D. Q., & Rodewald, L. E. (2005). The association between having a medical home and vaccination coverage among children eligible for the vaccines for children program. *Pediatrics, 116,* 130–139.

Stephens, D. S. (2008). Vaccines for the unvaccinated: Protecting the herd. *Journal of Infectious Diseases, 197,* 643–645.

Streissguth, A. P. (1997). *Fetal Alcohol Syndrome: A guide for families and communities.* Baltimore, MD: Paul H. Brookes.

Streissguth, A. P., & O'Malley, K. (2000). Neuropsychiatric implications and long-term consequences of fetal alcohol spectrum disorders. *Seminars in Clinical Neuropsychiatry, 5,* 177–190.

Vyrostek, S. B., Annest, J. L., & Ryan, G. W. (2004). Surveillance for fatal and nonfatal injuries – United States, 2001. *MMWR Surveillance Summaries, 3,* 1–57.

Wachs, T. D. (2000). *Necessary but not sufficient: The respective roles of single and multiple influences on individual development.* Washington, DC: American Psychological Association.

Waisbren, S. E., Noel, K., Fahrbach, K., Cella, C., Frame, D., Dorenbaum, A., & Levy, H. (2007). Phenylalanine blood levels and clinical outcomes in phenylketonuria: A systematic literature review and meta-analysis. *Molecular Genetics and Metabolism, 92,* 63–70.

Walker, S. P., Wachs, T. D., Meeks Gardner, J., Lozoff, B., Wasserman, G., Pollitt, E., Carter, J., & the International Child Development Steering Group (M. Black, P. Engle, S. Grantham-McGregor, B. Lozoff, T. D. Wachs, & S. P. Walker) (2007). Child development in developing countries 2: Risk factors for adverse outcomes in developing countries. *Lancet, 369,* 145–157.

Waterston, T., Alperstein, G., & Stewart Brown, S. (2004). Social capital: A key factor in child health inequalities. *Archives of Disease in Childhood, 89,* 456–459.

Weintrob, N., Karp, M., & Hod, M. (1996). Short and long-range complications in offspring of diabetic mothers. *Journal of Diabetes Complications, 10,* 294–301.

Wilbur, M. A., & Frank, D. A. (2007). Failure to thrive. In R. J. Karp, S. Hassink, & E. Shepard (Eds.), *A teacher's guide to pediatric nutrition.* McLean, VA: Academic Pediatric Association.

World Health Organization (2008a). *Cholera vaccines.* www.who.int/topics/cholera/vaccines/en/index.html (accessed September 2008).

World Health Organization (2008b). *Joint WHO/UNICEF statement for cholera vaccine use in tsunami-affected areas.* www.who.int/cholera/tsunami_choleravaccine/en/index.html (accessed September 2008).

Wright, R. O., Tsaih, S. W., Schwartz, J., Wright, R. J., & Hu, H. (2003). Association between iron deficiency and blood lead level in a longitudinal analysis of children followed in an urban primary care clinic. *Journal of Pediatrics, 142,* 9–14.

4

Development of Communication in Children with Sensory Functional Disabilities

Gunilla Preisler

Introduction

Questions concerning the consequences of deafness and blindness and even deaf-blindness on a person's mind have fascinated philosophers and scientists for centuries. In the English language the term "deaf and dumb" was, and sometimes still is, used for people who are deaf or profoundly hearing impaired. Blindness has often been thought of as associated with wisdom. The prophet Tiresias from Thebes was blind, as were many other sages in ancient and medieval times.

What are the implications for development if the child lacks one of these important senses, or even both of them? Can a deaf child develop language without access to auditory input? Can a blind child participate in the world outside without being able to perceive it visually? Can a deaf-blind child develop any competencies without access to either hearing or vision? Questions of how auditory, visual, and combinations of sensory disorders and additional functional disabilities affect the development of communication and language in infancy, as well as socioemotional development, will be discussed in this chapter. First, however, it is necessary to set this work in the context of current infant research.

The competent infant

It was not many decades ago that pediatricians maintained that newborns and young infants experienced a totally confusing perceptual world in which they perceived nothing or almost nothing at all. During the last 35–40 years experimental as well as observational studies of early mother–infant interaction, with improved methods of studying the interplay between the two, have given us new insights not only into the perceptual capacities of the infant, but also about their emotional, communicative, social, and cognitive abilities (e.g., see chapters 8, 9, 13, 14, 16, and 19 in volume 1). This in turn has meant that we have a new view of the potentialities of the growing child. We now talk about the competent child, and even the competent infant. Writing in 1960, Winnicot (1987, p. 39) maintained that "There is no such thing as a baby," meaning that the baby requires the presence of another for its secure existence. We now know more than ever about both the inborn and autonomous capabilities of infants and about the inseparability of everyone from each other. Today researchers also say that "there is no such thing as a mother" (Brown, 2005).

Development is regarded as a process involving caregiver and child, where both play an active role in the interaction (Fogel, 1993; Tronick, 1998; Stern, 2000; Trevarthen, 2004). According to Trevarthen (2004), these results indicate that infants are ready to pick up the motives of other people. Today there is also physiological evidence of an innate ability to understand another's motives. Humans have been found to be equipped with cells in the cortex with neural mirroring elements. These appear to anticipate the evolution of imitations that make the learning of human speech and language possible (Rizzolatti & Arbib, 1998).

Infant–caregiver communication

From birth, infants enter into an exchange of feelings and communicative acts with the mother or the father. Eye contact is sought and movements of eyes and mouth, hand gestures, and vocalizations can be imitated by the infant (Meltzoff, 1986; Kugiumutzakis, 1998; Nadel, Guérini, Pezé, & Rivet, 1999). During the first months of life caregivers and infants mutually create sequences of reciprocal behaviors, so-called social dialogues. In these dialogues parents are responding to their infants in the same modality as the infant is using – a smile from the infant is met by a smile from the parent. At approximately 9 months caregivers start to add a new dimension to their imitation-like behaviors and expand their way of communicating into a new category of behavior that Stern (2000) calls affect attunement: the smile is not only met by a smile but also with an exaggerated facial expression, and always with vocalizations. After a period of presymbolic communication, the infant can start to enter into a world of symbols and to use a language code in communication. Intersubjectivity, a synchronized attention to and understanding of events and others' emotions, is viewed as essential to other developing competencies such as language and social cognition (Studdert-Kennedy, 1991). Intersubjective experiences begin in the first year of life and continue to be refined as children and their relationships mature and become more complex. One important determinant of the later quality of the infant–caregiver relationship is how sensitive the caregiver is to the infant's communicative attempts (Ainsworth, Blehar, Waters, & Wall, 1978). In the first months of life infants have expectations of particular patterns of behavior from their caregivers (Stern, 1995, 2000; Trevarthen, 2004).

However, if the caregiver behaves in a way that is unusual to the infant, the infant reacts very quickly. The first response that infants try to modify is usually their way of communicating, testing different means to attract caregivers' attention and affection (Trevarthen, 2001). If infants do not succeed in attracting the attention and care of their caregivers, they may become withdrawn (Tronick & Weinberg, 1997; Tronick, 2005).

It is obvious that both vision and hearing are the primary senses for input of information about the surrounding world. Motor actions, like being able to grasp, to hold, to explore with hands and body, to be able to move around in the environment are other important prerequisites for a child's cognitive, communicative and social development as well as language development (see chapter 5 in volume 1).

The traditional way of conducting studies of children with functional disabilities has been to compare them with children without disabilities, resulting in a view that they have appeared less able and competent. Today many researchers have changed focus from this deficit model to a competence model, studying what children in fact can do, resulting in a quite different view of these children's abilities. A competence model will be emphasized in this chapter.

Being Deaf or Hard of Hearing in Infancy

Being deaf means having severe difficulties or no abilities at all to perceive speech, even using a hearing aid. In Western countries approximately one child out of every 1,000 newborns has a severe sensory-neural hearing loss. Two to three children per 1,000 are born with a congenital hearing impairment over 40 dB, which for most individuals means having difficulties in perceiving normal speech (Cunningham & Cox, 2003). Children can also suffer from auditory processing disorders (APDs). In a broad sense, APD refers to how the central nervous system uses auditory information. Children with APD may exhibit a variety of listening and related complaints. They may have difficulties understanding speech in noisy environments, following directions and discriminating similar speech sounds. Thus, in many ways they face similar problems to children with hearing impairment. Then there are children who have a progressive or an acquired hearing impairment identified at a later age.

The older the population of children, the more incidents of hearing impairment will emerge. In approximately one-third of the population of deaf infants the etiology is "unknown," but probably due to genetic factors. About 25% of the cases have known hereditary causes. Other causal factors in hearing loss can be congenital defects or early damage to the auditory system resulting from meningitis, prematurity, or viral infections. The etiology of APD is often unknown. Difficulties in auditory processing may be associated with other conditions such as dyslexia, attention deficit disorder (ADD), autism or autism spectrum disorder, specific language impairment, pervasive developmental disorder or developmental delay (for detailed discussion of autism spectrum disorders and intellectual delay, see chapters 10 and 12 in this volume).

Identification

Until recently suspicion of deafness or a profound hearing impairment was seldom made before the age of 6–12 months, often much later (Davis, Bamford, Wilson, Ramkalawan, Forshaw, & Wright, 1997). When parents have tried to recall the time prior to suspicion and diagnosis, many of them report that they noticed that their child did not seem to react to noises or very loud sounds, but when they started to cuddle and play and talk to their infants they cooed and smiled and answered, in much the same way a hearing infant would do. There are now a growing number of early neonatal screening programs which aim to identify, as early as two days after birth, whether the child has a hearing loss or not. For example, diagnosis of hearing impairments is now made in England on average at 2 months of age by using universal newborn hearing screening (Young & Tattersall, 2007).

An important research focus has involved studying the developmental gains deriving from early identification. Despite difficulties associated with the diverse nature of family and linguistic interventions (Young & Tattersall, 2007), there seem to be substantial advantages with early identification with respect to linguistic and socioemotional develop-ment (Yoshinaga-Itano, 2003). While there are still few studies on parents' reactions to early identification, existing studies indicate that there are positive effects. Parents have stated that they can take action quickly, can start learning new skills and can start being part of a new context (Young & Tattersall, 2007). But many parents have also reported that nothing has happened for a long period of time after identification; they receive the identification, but are then left alone. For these parents it has been a negative experience and they have had difficulties enjoying their baby (Young & Tattersall, 2007). One important question to be discussed in this context is whether an early diagnosis will affect caregivers' sensitivity to their infants' way of communicating during a period of natural bonding, when even mothers of normally developing babies are at risk for depression, such that the attachment-bonding process might be in danger (Young & Tattersall, 2007; see also chapter 8 in this volume for discussion on the issue of maternal depression and infant attachment). Caregivers of infants are also at risk for depression or other psychiatric disorders when two independent life events occur closely in time: a new baby in the family as well as the infant being identified as having a disability (Copper & Stein, 1989; Murray, Kempton, Woolgar, & Hooper, 1993). In addition, there is a risk that if the infant has a functional disability the parents' intuitive parenting skills might be less appropriate. In combination with the infant's special needs, the parents may feel inadequate as caregivers. This in turn might result in a self-fulfilling prophecy of unsatisfactory interaction (Meadow-Orlans & Spencer, 1996).

The advantages of early identification have been emphasized primarily by medical and technical experts. From a psychological point of view the advantages seem less obvious.

Approaches to intervention

The most common question that parents of deaf infants ask their doctors at the time of diagnosis is whether their infant's hearing loss can be medically or surgically treated. Until recently, the answer was no. In the 1970s, however, a new technique called cochlear implant was developed, first on adults and then, at the end of the 1980s, tested on young children. This intervention can briefly be described as a hearing aid surgically placed in the cochlea. As a result parents are now faced with the question whether to choose surgery or not for their newborn baby (see Spencer & Marschark, 2003; Spencer, 2004). Parents have said that this has been the most difficult and stressful event that they have ever experienced (Incesulu, Vural, & Erkam, 2003; Li, Baind, & Steinberg, 2004; Spencer, 2004; Preisler, 2007).

After this decision other stressful events follow, such as the worry about the consequence of the surgery and anesthetics (Chute & Nevins, 2002). Parents also get information that they have to take an active part in a demanding habilitation process, at least if they choose an oral method of communication (Incesulu et al., 2003). Research on the needs of the parents in this situation has shown that they expressed a strong need for emotional support and psychosocial interventions (Zaidman-Zait & Most, 2005; Zaidman-Zait, 2007). All of this happens during the very first months of their newborn baby's life. That all these issues will affect the relationship between infant and caregiver seems evident, but how is still unknown.

Today, most deaf children in Sweden and in many other countries receive a cochlear implant at an early age, unilaterally or bilaterally. In most countries the lower age limit for receiving an implant was initially 2 years of age, but now children aged 1 year and even younger are being implanted. The rationale for an early implant is to give the child auditory experiences as early as possible in order to stimulate his or her speech perception and later speech production.

For many years there has been a detailed plan in Sweden for how to meet the psychological needs of parents coming to the hospital with a suspicion that their child might not be able to hear. This plan has been worked out by a group of professionals with long experience of psychological, psychotherapeutic, as well as educational, work with parents of deaf children and is based on scientific research on early relationships, attachment, and sign language. Many parents have said that this support system has been important for them in adapting to their new life. Today, many parents hope that by opting for an implant, they do not have to face the fact that their infant is deaf.

Communication with a deaf child

In addition to the trauma of adjusting to the diagnosis and the challenges of planning for both present and future, parents of deaf infants must also make decisions about mode of communication (Meadow-Orlans & Sass-Lehrer, 1995). This is a difficult decision for parents, because opinions differ on whether to use a manual–gestural–visual language code (i.e., a sign language), or to make the deaf child lip-read and to learn a language based on oral/aural skills. The argument behind using sign language is that this is the natural language of deaf people, being based on a code of communication, appropriate for a person who cannot perceive speech sounds. On the other hand, the majority of deaf children's parents (90%) are hearing (Schein, 1996), and in most cases have no earlier experience of sign language. Therefore they have to learn an entirely new language in order to be able to share a common language code with their child. Another reason why there has been, and still is, a negative attitude to sign language is the belief that a proper language can only be a spoken language and that language (i.e., speech) is a prerequisite for thinking. However, intensive linguistic studies of signed languages have shown that sign language has all the characteristics of a proper language, although the rules differ (Stokoe, 1972). On the other hand, sign language is used by a minority group in almost all societies, and therefore in many countries it is recommended that parents use speech and hearing in communication with their deaf child. As cochlear implants have now become the rule rather than the exception for deaf children, parents do not seem to be as motivated to learn sign language as they were prior to the introduction of this new hearing device.

Most studies of early interaction between deaf infants and their parents emanate from pre-implant times. Research from the 1970s, 1980s, and 1990s showed that if habilitation of the deaf child became focused on the use of communicative signals that are suited to auditory perception and difficult to interpret, visually mutual understanding was often impeded, and breakdowns in communication were the rule rather than the exception. Studies of toddlers or preschoolers have shown that hearing parents using an oral/aural approach in communication use more directives and different control techniques in interaction with their deaf child (Meadow-Orlans, 1987). Deaf children were considered to be more passive, and less attentive than hearing children, and tended to withdraw from social interaction. When sign language was recommended as the mode used for communication, the situation altered.

During the first year of life, studies of mother–deaf infant interaction have shown that these infants are able to share in communication with their hearing others to much the same extent as hearing infants (Jamieson & Pedersen, 1993; Robinshaw & Evans, 1995). Deaf infants take part in body games, play give-and-take, and peek-a-boo games with their parents, explore toys, imitate their mother's actions, start to take part in early pretend play, show their intentions and wants, and take an active part in proto-conversations (Preisler, 1995). Hearing impairment is seldom a serious obstacle to communication until the age when hearing children normally begin to talk.

Early language development in deaf children

In deaf children exposed to sign language, the first stages of conventional and referential communication are more easily established than in deaf children exposed to oral/aural communication. Objects are directly in view and each partner can signal his or her intentions visually to the other. But deaf children learning sign language must divide their attention between the mother's signs and the objects or activities to which these relate if they are to note the analogous correspondences between signs and familiar routines. Several studies of early interaction between deaf parents and their deaf infants have shown how deaf parents use touch in various ways to reinforce interaction and to help their infants to attend visually (Erting, Prezioso, & O'Grady Hynes,1990; Maestas y Moores, 1980; Preisler, 1995; Harris, 2001). For example, mothers have been observed to sign on the infant's body or to form the infant's hand into the shape of signs. The mothers' signing also is more simplified and mothers emphasize the key signs in utterances (Harris, Clibbens, Tibbitts, & Chasin, 1987; Harris, 2001). Mothers have also been observed paying careful attention to their infants' faces and eye direction, ensuring that their children could see most of their signed utterances. Deaf mothers have been shown to use more tactile contact with their infants compared to hearing mothers in order to attract their infant's attention (Koester, Brooks & Traci, 2000). They also signed in such a way that the child could observe the sign while still attending to the context to which the sign related. For example, mothers most frequently signed within the child's preexisting focus of attention (Harris et al., 1987, Harris, 2001; Preisler, 1995).

Deaf parents who are native signers of American Sign Language or Swedish Sign Language report that their children start to produce signs as early as 6 months of age (Folven & Bonvillian, 1991; Preisler, 1995). One suggestion is that the 6-month-old's signs are comparable with manual babbling. These manual forms can be conventional if the parents respond to them in a systematic way. One common measure of language development is to note when children produce up to 10 words. The signing children in Folven and Bonvillian's study attained a vocabulary of 10 different signs at an average age of 13.5 months (range 11.0–16.5 months), a mean age significantly earlier than the 15.1 months for hearing children's first 10 words reported by Nelson (1973). The content of the initial 10-item vocabularies was highly similar; each child's first sign production occurred within a nonreferential context as an imitation or as a request for action. The children did not use signs as representations (e.g., signs for Mummy, lamp, dog) on average until they were 12.6 months of age. This age of onset therefore does not appear to differ from the typical age of 13 months reported for first spoken representational words in hearing children (Bates, O'Connel, & Shore, 1987).

Studies of communication and language development in deaf children with cochlear implants

Studies of communication and language development in deaf children with cochlear implants have primarily compared speech perception and speech production between children using an implant and children using different conventional hearing aids (see, for example, Geers and Moog, 1994; Miyamoto et al., 1995; Meyer, Svirsky, Kirk, & Miyamoto, 1998; Allen, Nikolopoulos, & O'Donoghue, 1998; Svirsky, Robbins, Kirk, Pisoni, & Miyamoto, 2000; Blamey et al., 2001). However, it has been difficult to draw valid conclusions from these studies, as information about the degree of comparability between the groups before receiving an implant (e.g., measures of hearing status, language ability, or the families' level of education or socioeconomic status) is seldom or never made available (Spencer & Marschark, 2003).

The above studies report that deaf children make progress with the implant and that a cochlear implant is more effective than ordinary hearing aids for the development of children's perception and production of speech. Specifically, results show that the children can perceive sounds in their surroundings, that they can perceive spoken words and sentences, and that they can also produce words and sentences in laboratory conditions or in well-known contexts with one partner (Osberger, Maso, & Sam, 1993; Walzman, Cohen,

Gomolin, Shapiro, Shelly, & Hoffman, 1994). Further, the children studied have mainly been engaged in different oral programs and the ultimate aim is to be able to integrate them into preschools and schools for the hearing. Discriminating certain target words or being able to utter single words and simple sentences is not sufficient when you want to take part in social activities with others. In a longitudinal study of 22 deaf children starting when the children were between 2 and 5, it was found that after three years' experience of wearing a cochlear implant, most of the children could produce three- to five-word sentences and could take part in oral dialogues if the content was about the here-and-now and if the context was well defined. However, detailed transcriptions from video-recorded observations in natural interactional situations in the home, preschool, and school setting showed that the children had severe difficulties in taking part in spoken conversations with parents, siblings, peers, and teachers (Preisler, Tvingstedt, & Ahlström, 1997, 2002).

Conclusions

For deaf children brought up in a sign-language environment, the development of communication and language shows a very similar pattern compared to that for hearing children. For children with cochlear implants, the situation seems somewhat more complicated if they are obliged to primarily use speech in communication. Studies have shown that vision can compensate for the hearing loss in early dialogue-like exchanges and in various forms of social play. Therefore, a logical question is how blind children, who have to rely mainly on the auditory sense, communicate with their parents and how parents manage to stimulate their blind infant.

Being Born Blind

Blindness – defined as the total absence of sight – is fairly infrequent in Western countries, whereas it is still more common in the developing countries due to specific micronutrient deficiencies such as vitamin A as well as lack of medical facilities (for detailed discussion of nutritional deficiencies and the impact of poverty in developing countries, see chapters 2 and 6 in this volume). The incidence rate among Western countries has been estimated at fewer than 15 per 100,000 children born (Rosenberg et al., 1996). There are many different causes of visual defects, but in most cases of severe visual impairment something is wrong with the eyes. In the most severe case, anophthalmia, the eyes are actually missing. In retinoblastoma, a malignant tumor develops early in the retina. If treatment, which involves removal of one eye (or, in very rare cases, both eyes) and/or radiation therapy of the tumor, is not begun immediately, the tumor can spread along the optic nerve to the brain and cause visual impairment (Ek, 2000). Brain damage can cause blindness, although in such cases the eyes are usually normally developed. Retinopathy of prematurity (ROP) is a disease affecting the immature visual system that may cause severe visual impairment, sometimes total blindness. Prematurely born babies have been and still are at risk of having ROP. A strong association between ROP and autistic disorder has been found. This association is most probably mediated by brain damage and is largely independent of the blindness *per se* (Ek, Fernell, Jacobson, & Gillberg, 1998). A common cause of blindness is congenital cataract, in which the lens of the eye is cloudy. Congenital glaucoma is a further condition that is usually inherited.

Development of communication in blind infants

Diagnosis of blindness is seldom made before the age of 4–5 months. Therefore, studies of very early patterns of interaction between parents and blind infants are rare. Exceptions are if the child has a defect, such as anophthalmia, or if there is a congenitally hereditary illness in the family. But there are some studies which can give an idea of early mother–infant communication. Als, Tronick, and Brazelton (1980) regularly observed a child born without eyes from soon after birth up to the age of 15.5 months in interaction with her mother and father in the home setting. They carefully describe how the mother interacted with her baby and how the mother addressed her baby in an intimate manner, in a way that also occurs in the interaction of sighted infants and their parents. Through continuous tactile and vocal input, the mother stimulated the infant to take part in communication. At 3 weeks of age the infant was able to modulate her state when in face-to-face situations with her parents. She could become very attentive, "her face softening and brightening with raised cheeks and open mouth, her arms relaxing, either opening to the side of her body or resting on her chest" (Als et al., 1980, p. 27). This infant's development in general was characterized by step-like spurts of new organization and periods of consolidation. At times there were also periods of disorganization and seeming regression before the next level of organization was reached. Als et al. (1980) commented on specific adults' expectations about the signals and displays coming from an infant, even if the infant is blind, and also noted that it takes a great deal of skill and patience on the part of the parent to read and understand the infant's expressions.

In one of the most extensive longitudinal studies of blind children's development, Fraiberg (1977) focused on infants' different communicative expressions. She studied the development of 10 congenitally blind children for a period of three years, starting from the age of 1 month. She observed the children in interaction with their mothers by means of filming as well as by direct observation. Analyses of these filmed interactions showed that blind infants exhibited a restricted repertoire of facial expressions. Only two different expressions could be registered – a happy and an unhappy face. The social smile was found to occur irregularly in blind infants as a reaction to their mother's voice. Fraiberg also found that the mothers of blind infants had difficulties in reading their infant's nonvisual expressions. Only two out of ten mothers could interpret their infant's actions and reactions without special support. These mothers were considered "extraordinary" mothers, with great experience of children. The remaining eight mothers had severe difficulties in reading and interpreting their infant's intentions and wants. Other researchers have also found that blind infants exhibit a more limited repertoire of facial expressions, show less responsiveness, and initiate contact with their mothers less frequently compared to sighted infants (Tröster & Brambring, 1992). However, a lack of behaviors that require visual information processing cannot be interpreted as an indicator of a delay in social-emotional development. In many cases the blind infant's level of social-emotional development is expressed in reactions that differ from those in sighted infants (Tröster & Brambring, 1992). But blindness can also cause difficulties for infants in reading and understanding their caregivers' emotional expressions, as well as in knowing whether their actions and reactions have an effect on others (Bigelow, 1995). Again, the sensitivity of the caregiver is of utmost importance for the formation of a relationship between caregiver and child.

Communicative expressions used by blind infants and their parents

In order to study which communicative behaviors blind children use in interaction with their parents, as well as which means of communication parents use, seven blind infants were observed from 5 months of age up to early school age (Preisler, 1991, 1995, 1997). Analyses of the interactions showed that, when first observed at the age of 5–6 months, the blind children reacted to and elicited contact initiatives from their parents. They took active part in proto-conversations by means of smiles and cooing, with articulation-like lip movements as though they were imitating their mothers' speech sounds. They used body movements and even eyebrows to signal turns in conversations. Expectancy aware-ness in rhythmic body-touching songs was also observed in these infants. When the mothers initiated contact with their babies they primarily used their voice, but also used tactile communicative means. Observations showed that at 5–6 months of age infants preferred being with another person rather than manipulating objects or toys. With few exceptions, mothers were responsive to their infants' facial expressions, body movements, and vocalizations, interpreting them as meaningful parts or as turns in dialogue-like exchanges. Mothers made comments on their infants' emotional states or they referred to their relationship with their infant. The way these mothers behaved when the children were 5–6 months old did not differ in any significant way from the way mothers of sighted babies communicate with their children.

From approximately 6–7 months of age, blind children's interest in exploring the environment increased. They manipulated toys with fingers and mouth and they started to explore the characteristics of objects. At this age, mothers and infants started to share affects and the mothers, just like mothers of sighted infants, gradually started to use affect-attunement behaviors. This phenomenon has also been described in a study of two blind infants observed from the age of 7 months of age (Urwin, 1983). Urwin observed how the mothers mock-imitated their babies' fusses, coughs, splutters, and sneezes and in this way "dramatized" their babies' actions.

However, differences have also been noted. Children who are blind gesture less fre-quently than do sighted children during infancy and they express fewer distal gestures than sighted children. They do not use gestures like pointing, either with their eyes or their hands, and they do not spontaneously use hand gestures like showing or giving (Iverson, Tencer, Landy, & Goldin-Meadow, 2000). In some instances, pointing with the head or upper part of the body can be observed when the infant becomes attentive to sounds (Preisler, 1995). But these means of communication are not always registered or even understood by their parents and are therefore not very effective means of communication.

The absence of coordination of eye pointing with finger and hand pointing reduces the natural opportunities to refer to external events. It also makes it more difficult for caregivers to read the preferences and interests of the child (Landau & Gleitman, 1985; Preisler, 1991, 1995, 1997; Rowland, 1983; Urwin, 1983). The blind child cannot see the caregiver's world of referents and cannot easily determine when the caregiver is trying to establish joint reference (Iverson et al., 2000). This apparent lack of attention toward the outside world by the blind child might in turn discourage caregivers from initiating activities involving external referents. Perhaps for this reason early communication between blind children and their parents seems to consist primarily of physical games and routines in which the referent is the interaction itself (e.g., repetitive games of bouncy-bouncy in which the child learns to anticipate the parent's physical position at different points in time).

In her study of two blind infants, Urwin (1983) found that prior to the emergence of speech both babies' blindness posed constraints on establishing communication about objects and events located outside their own immediate sphere of action. Urwin found that the two mothers' way of communicating with their child differed somewhat from each other, particularly in their use of techniques in order to establish a smooth interaction. The mothers initially responded to their infants' facial expressions and body movements and made comments on their babies' actions, intentions, and experiences. However, even if the mothers acted somewhat differently, the rules of interpersonal communication between the mothers and their infants were similar up to the age of 1 year. After this age there was a change. In one case the mother was very eager to use toys in interaction. This child had some residual vision in one eye, which could explain a greater interest in the surrounding world than if the child had been totally blind. The toys were used in give-and-take games as well as in pretend play. The mother made the toys the content of the interaction and in this way mother and child could establish joint attention and joint reference. In the other case, the interaction was mainly without toys, as the mother did not find that the child showed any interest in them. This child's world of experience was very restricted. When he started to talk, his speech was repetitive and imitative. It referred mostly to his own body and to phrases. Many investigators have identified this as characteristic of blind children's speech. Urwin's interpretation was that the form of social interaction will have consequences for the language acquisition of blind children.

Observations of blind infants' play show that they seldom engage in pretend play until toward the second half of the second year (Fraiberg, 1977; Preisler, 1995; Urwin, 1983). This is also the time when blind children start to use language in communication.

Caregivers' communicative style

The emotional development of blind children may be at risk because of the constraints on the children's capacity to share and to respond to the feelings of others (Campbell, 2007; Loots, Devisé, & Sermijn, 2003). This lack of early social experiences may lead to difficulties in the future in social understanding. Thus, the way the parents interact with their blind infants and the way they adapt to the capacities of the child can be crucial for later developmental outcomes.

Thorén (2002) analyzed the verbal input of the parents of seven blind children participating in the longitudinal study mentioned earlier (Preisler, 1991, 1995, 1997), categorizing a vast number of mothers' verbal utterances when their children were between 18 and 36 months old. One finding was that the parents of those children who later were found to have developed normally in a socioemotional-communicative sense used more confirmations than directives in their verbal communication to the child during the observation period. These parents' communicative patterns also showed a high degree of regularity and stability, independent of time or situation. In those cases where the child's later socioemotional and communicative development was found to be less optimal, the parent's early communication showed an opposite pattern. Their utterances consisted of more directives than affirmatives, or were in some cases equally distributed between the two. These parents' communication also showed a more varied and unstable pattern, with frequent changes depending on the context. Thus, it was probably more difficult for these children to anticipate their parents' reactions and responses, resulting in confusion and uncertainty in the children.

Campbell (2007) explored the quality of interaction in two mother–child dyads in a play context. The aim was to study the emotional availability of mothers and their children to each other. Two cases were selected and their video-recorded interactions were analyzed in detail as they showed contrasting interaction styles. Both mothers made themselves emotionally available in the interaction but by different means: one showed availability through active involvement and one through acceptance of the child's initiatives. These findings demonstrate that the parents of blind children use different strategies to meet their children's needs (Pérez-Pereira & Conti-Ramsden, 2001; Preisler, 1997).

There are also studies focusing on the communicative styles or language input of blind children's parents in relation to their children's language development. Blind children have to rely even more on the linguistic input of their parents than sighted children to get information and to gain understanding of the surrounding world. Kekelis and Andersen (1984) compared the language directed to visually impaired children as well as to sighted children. Their results indicated that the parents of visually impaired children used more imperatives and fewer declaratives than the parents of sighted children. They thereby provided their children with less information about the functions and the attributes of objects. There was also a tendency for these parents to ask their blind child to repeat labels or to request labeling of objects from the child.

There is a common view among researchers that there is a relationship between caregiver's speech to their infants and the nonverbal context in which it occurs. This relationship is difficult to establish if the child is blind. The relationship is most naturally established by caregivers making comments on activities and objects on which their children are focusing their visual attention. It has been suggested that the rate of children's early language development can be influenced by the extent to which adult speech provides opportunities to relate linguistic input to a familiar nonverbal context (see chapter 14 in volume 1). This provides the infant with an opportunity to note correspondences between familiar routines and accompanying linguistic descriptions. For sighted caregivers of blind children, it is a difficult task to attain this correspondence between linguistic input and nonverbal context, as they can have difficulties in reading what their children are paying attention to.

Early language development in blind children

Some studies of blind children's early language development suggest that the onset of speech is relatively late (Warren, 1984). In an extensive study of 86 neurologically intact blind children's early language development, Norris, Spaulding, and Brodei (1957) showed that more than 25% of these children produced two words when they were 15 months old, more than 50% achieved this vocabulary in the period from 18 to 21 months, and more than 75% by 24 months. This is roughly 8 months later than sighted full-term normal infants usually reach the same language level (Lenneberg, 1967). But 85% of the subjects in Norris et al.'s (1957) study were premature births (with ROP), which might explain some of the delay. In other studies, differences between blind and sighted children's early speech development have not been found. Bigelow (1990) asked mothers to record their blind children's words from before they had recognizable words to the acquisition of a 50-word vocabulary, which is approximately the time when children start combining words into two-word sentences. Bigelow found no differences between blind and sighted children's early language development. The blind children acquired their 50-word vocabularies between 16 and 21 months of age. Sighted children generally acquire their 50-word vocabularies between 15 and 20 months of age, which suggests a delay of 1 month (Nelson, 1973).

McConnachie and Moore (1994) found a delay of several months in the acquisition of the first 10 words used by a sample of 16 severely visually impaired children. In contrast, Mulford (1988) collected data from 16 individual case studies and found no major delay in these children's language development. Moore and McConnachie (1994) suggest that the children in the case studies were an unusually successful group, which could explain this difference. Researchers also have found a qualitative difference in the type of nouns used by blind and by sighted children (Brambring, 2003; Pérez-Pereira & Conti-Ramsden, 1999). Blind children seem to have difficulty in recognizing the similarity of different objects within the same semantic category.

In a longitudinal early intervention study, Brambring (2007) studied 10 children from the age of 1–3 years up to the age of 4–6 years. The researcher used participant observations in the home environment, using specially developed scales for assessing and promoting development in blind infants and preschoolers (Bielefeld Observations Scales). The results on these scales were compared to age norms for sighted children. Brambring found that language development in these 10 blind children was only slightly delayed compared to that of sighted children, although they seem to have had some initial difficulty in starting with language. There were developmental divergences in some individual skills or categories between blind children and the norms for sighted children (Brambring, 2007), with some in favour of the blind children. For example, Brambring found that blind children learned to name objects spontaneously at an earlier age than do sighted children. As discussed above, one explanation could be different parental communicative style of parents of blind children compared to that of parents of sighted children. For example, parents of blind children often pose questions to their children and ask them to name objects they are handling (Brambring, 2003, 2007).

Blind children's first words usually refer to food and to items they act upon, such as puppy, doll, key, and so on. This is also what many sighted children refer to in their first words. But blind children often choose to label objects that can be characterized as having the properties of perceptual change. They name items that produce auditory change or give tactual sensation. Compared to sighted children, blind children have more labels that refer to specific referents rather than classes of objects. Self-action and perceptual change are salient variables for young blind children, as they are for young sighted children. The major difference is that perceptual change for blind children comes from other modalities than vision (see also Dunlea, 1989; Mulford, 1988).

Conclusions

Studies of early patterns of communication between blind infants and their parents show that the absence of visual information about the world, and therefore the dependence on auditory and haptic stimulation, diminishes the blind infant's opportunities to learn and to understand interpersonal rules in communication, the relation between objects and symbols, as well as knowledge about the environment. The auditory sense does not seem to compensate for the lack of vision in the same way as vision can compensate for the lack of auditory input in early child development.

Being Born Deaf-Blind

How can children who lack both vision and hearing communicate with their parents about their feelings and experiences as well as about the physical world around them? Deafness *per se* does not have to be a serious obstacle to early caregiver–infant communication if children are allowed to use their intact senses, while blindness poses more constraints on the interaction. A combination of a severe hearing impairment or deafness and a visual impairment or blindness makes the life situation even more complicated. Early patterns of communication are affected and that is an impairment that remains throughout life.

Helen Keller, who was both deaf and blind, describes in her book, *The Story of My Life* (1903), her awakening awareness of the world when her young teacher started to spell words in her hand. Gradually she understood that everything had a name. This happened over a century ago. What is the situation for deaf-blind children today?

There are few cases reported where the child is both totally blind and deaf (Andrew, 1989), the group as a whole being most heterogeneous. Within the population of young children diagnosed as deaf-blind, there are children with varying degrees of hearing and visual impairment, with or without additional disabilities, but also children with cortical visual and or central auditory disabilities (Michael & Paul, 1991). Approximately 94% of these children have some residual vision and hearing (Fredericks & Baldwin, 1987).

As the group of children who are deaf-blind is both small in number, as well as heterogeneous in character, most research is based on single or small-scale case studies. The children have often been older than 1.5–2 years and have thus passed the infancy period. Most studies of these children as well as other children with multiple functional disabilities have focused on different intervention and educational programs to promote communication as well as socioemotional development (Aitkens, 2000; Chen & Haney, 1995; Daelman, Nafstad, Rodbroe, Souriau, & Visser, 1996; Janssen, Riksen-Walraven, & van Dijk, 2002, 2003, 2006; Michael & Paul, 1991; Nafstad & Rodbroe, 1996), but there are a few studies focusing on the natural development of communication in deaf-blind children from a longitudinal perspective.

Development of communication in deaf-blind children

Infants who are deaf-blind are generally reported to be less responsive and less active in communication than nondisabled infants of comparable age. Their parents must work to elicit responses from them, even though studies have shown that a caregiver can develop social interaction through movements and by haptic means. But as the infant cannot hear the voice of the caregiver or see her or his face, not only the physical but also the social world is severely restricted for the child. A further complication for parents is the difficulty of reading and interpreting the infant's signals. This in turn can result in a feeling of failure or helplessness by the parent. In addition, these children often have severe medical problems, making the situation even more difficult to cope with for their parents. One of the main problems for parents in the early interaction process is responding to the infant's actions and reactions. This is a serious matter, because it is through the responsiveness of the caregiver that the infant can gradually begin to anticipate that his or her actions will cause a change. Experiences of contingency in social interaction are difficult to achieve in interplay with deaf-blind children as they cannot hear the voice or see the facial expressions of their caregiver.

Six children and their parents participated in a longitudinal study of the development of communication between deaf-blind children and their parents (Preisler, 2005). The children were between 6 months and 3.9 years old when first video-observed in natural interactional settings with their parents. They were studied for a period of two years. Common to the children was the fact that they were blind or severely visually impaired as well as severely hearing impaired. Four had additional functional disabilities, such as mental retardation and/or cerebral palsy.

Detailed transcriptions of the video-recorded interactions showed that the children could communicate with their parents and the parents with their child. Even if the expressions varied and sometimes were difficult to interpret, the analyses showed that the development of communication followed the same path as that for "normal" children, from interest in social interaction and social plays with the caregiver, to interest in the physical environment and an intent to share their experiences with somebody else. Some of the children already used symbols in communication at the commencement of the study, while others did so toward the end of the observed period. The social plays most frequently observed were different turn-taking and body-movement games. Movements, sounds, and touch were important communicative expressions in these playful activities. Thereafter the children started to show an interest in and attention to the environment. They started to touch, taste, smell, or in other ways investigate and test characteristics and functions of objects and toys. After an intensive period of exploration, their interest in social interaction returned, but now on a somewhat more advanced level as they wanted to share their interest in something with somebody else. The children's expressions as well as the content of the communication varied, but the aim seemed to be the same: to establish and maintain a meaningful and joyful interaction. But every single achievement took a long time to acquire for these children. It was also difficult for the parents to observe and discover that their child had made progress, and also to understand how these achievements could fit into a normal chain of child development.

The parents of the deaf-blind children faced further difficulties in translating a spoken language into a tactile sign language. But even if the number of signs or the variation of the signs used were limited, it could be registered how important the hands were as a channel of communication – the children's own hands, as well as the caregivers'. Initially parents grasped the children's hands and formed them into a sign. But in these instances there was a risk of hindering children's free use of their hands. When the parents instead started to offer their own hands to their children, the dialogue became more extended. When their communicative style became more child-centered and affirmative and less directive, communication became more functional and smooth. Despite severe functional disabilities in several cases, the children could take part in communication and share meaning. The results of this study confirm those of other caregiver–infant interaction studies – that infants' perceptions seem to be tuned into human and social stimuli and that all children have a congenitally hereditary ability to communicate with the social environment (Trevarthen, 2001). But results also point to the difficulties the deaf-blind child has in interpersonal encounters.

Approaches to interaction

Chen and Haney (1995) have developed a model for promoting learning through active interaction (PLAI) in order to support deaf-blind infant–caregiver interaction. They maintain that much of the stimulation given to deaf-blind children is of a far too passive character, with the focus often on stimulating the infant's residual vision and/or hearing. Chen and Haney question the meaningfulness of this approach from the infant's perspective. Their model instead is aimed at creating an environment for learning and for mutually satisfying exchanges through intervention strategies focusing on developing contingent responsiveness in caregivers. By first observing parent–infant interaction by means of video recordings and then identifying what is typical for each pair, parents are given feedback on their own as well as on their babies' communicative behaviors. The most important part of the model is to concentrate on the caregivers' ability to give immediate responses to their infants' expressions. In the feedback sessions with parents those instances where there is a reciprocal and joyful interaction between infant and caregiver are focused on, in order to promote and strengthen parents' capacity for responding to and interpreting their child's expressions.

The Early Development of Communication in Children with Multiple Functional Disabilities

Hearing and vision are our main senses for communication and learning. Suffering from motor disorders or other functional disabilities, often in combination, means even more constraints on the parent–child interaction. Intentionality, which is so easily read in a young infant's movements, vocalizations, and early gestures and attributed communicative meaning by parents, is often more subtle and can be difficult to read in children with different types of motor disorders such as cerebral palsy. In a study of the interplay between children with severe visual impairments in combination with functional disabilities such as mental retardation and cerebral palsy and their parents, these difficulties were displayed (Preisler, Karlsson & Norström, 1994). Four of the children were between 7 and 15 months at the time of the first observation, one was 2.5 years old. The dyads were regularly video-recorded in natural settings in their homes for a period of two years. Detailed registrations of the children's and the parents' communicative expressions showed that the children used vocalizations, body movements, and facial expressions to communicate with their parents. As four of the children had some residual vision, visual behaviors were also important communicative behaviors in these children. The children's means of communication were highly individual. Play and routine activities were important for all of the children, as well as for the parents. However, the children seldom imitated the parents' expressions, which in turn made the adults unsure of their own competence as able or good-enough parents of a child with severe functional disabilities. In some cases this resulted in a tendency of the parents to overstimulate their child. Video feedback turned out to be one way of making the parents aware of their own way of communicating as well as their child's way of both eliciting and responding to their communicative initiatives.

Conclusions and Future Research Directions

Communication between blind, deaf, and deaf-blind children and their parents as well as between children with other functional disabilities shows a pattern of early interaction similar to that of nondisabled children. Even if development proceeds slowly for children with severe and multiple sensory disabilities, it follows the same path as those for a normal child: from person–person communication to person–object to person–person–object communication. The results of detailed analyses further show that the potential for a child with sensory disabilities to engage in meaningful interaction is to a great extent dependent on the sensitivity of the caregiver and the ability to adapt to the infant's capabilities and to give space for the child to take an active part in the interaction – to follow rather than direct the child. Joyful interaction seems to be of special importance for the child's psychological well-being, not to mention that of the parents.

Research on normal caregiver–infant interaction has led to a gradual change in our perspective on the child's development. A sensitive caregiver who responds to the infant's initiatives and who develops them further can have a positive effect on development. In those families where a baby is born with sensory functional disabilities, the situation is somewhat or even radically different. Most of these parents have never met an adult who is deaf or blind, let alone a child, and almost certainly not one who is both deaf and blind. Traditionally, support services for families with children with sensory disabilities have focused on the children's lack of performance and skills. This is also the type of support that is requested by many parents, as they notice that their child's development is delayed compared to nondisabled children of comparable age. The problem with such an approach is that there is a risk that the focus will be on the disability, not on the child. An alternative approach is to strengthen the relationship between parents and child. Video recordings of the caregiver and the infant interacting have become a frequently used means for giving feedback to parents as well as making them – and often also researchers – aware of what the child in fact can do, achieve, and communicate. Such data indicate also that most parents are sensitive and responsive to their deaf, blind, or deaf-blind child's communicative expressions. This in turn can have positive effects on the parent's feeling of being a good-enough parent. And this is perhaps the best starting point for positive development in the child.

Early diagnosis of different functional disabilities has now become possible with new neonatal screening techniques. The aim is to provide families with early habilitation, minimizing the effects of the disability/ties. But too little notice has been given to the effect of early diagnosis on the attachment-bonding process, when the parents themselves have not yet suspected their child's deficit. There is a growing research interest in the effects of early attachment – or lack of attachment – for later psychological development (e.g., Lyons-Ruth, 2003; see also chapter 16 in volume 1 on attachment). It would be valuable if families with children with different functional disabilities were also included in these studies. This could give new perspectives on attachment processes and a better understanding of how to meet the needs of these families.

Research on different aspects of psychosocial development in children with sensory disabilities has primarily focused on the first years of life. This is probably due to the fact that these years are considered the most important for later development. But as children grow up, other children become important actors in the psychosocial arena. In order to learn social rules and practices, children need to interact with peers. But many children with sensory impairments like deafness and blindness have difficulty in finding peers to interact with. Deaf children exposed to sign language attending a sign language school program have no problems communicating with other deaf signing children. Today, many deaf children receive a cochlear implant and are mainstreamed in the ordinary school system with hearing children. What are the consequences on their socioemotional development if these children as well as other hard-of-hearing children cannot communicate in a smooth and fluent way with peers?

Growing up as a blind child means having very different experiences of the world compared to a sighted child. Blind children experience the physical and social world primarily by auditory and haptic means, which is reflected in their play and use of language. How is it possible to share in a meaningful way this auditory and haptic world with a sighted child? These are some of the issues that need to be explored further in order to promote positive socioemotional development in such children.

References

Ainsworth, M. D. S., Blehar, M. C., Waters, E., & Wall, S. (1978). *Patterns of attachment: A psychological study of the Strange Situation*. Hillsdale, NJ: Erlbaum.

Aitkens, S. (2000). Understanding deafblindness. In S. Aitkens, M. Buultjens, C. Clark, J. T. Eyre & L. Pease (Eds.), *Teaching children who are deafblind* (pp. 1–34). London: David Fulton.

Allen, M., Nikolopoulos, T., & O'Donoghue, G. (1998). Speech intelligibility in children after cochlear implantation. *American Journal of Otology, 19*(6), 742–746.

Als, H., Tronick, E., & Brazelton, B. (1980). Affective reciprocity and the development of autonomy. *American Academy of Child Psychiatry, 19,* 22–40.

Andrew, A. K. (1989). Meeting the needs of young deaf-blind children and their parents: Part II. *Child: Care, Health and Development, 15*(4), 251–267.

Bates, E., O'Connel, B., & Shore, C. (1987). Language and communication in infancy. In J. D. Osofsky (Ed.), *Handbook of infant development* (pp. 149–203). New York: Wiley.

Bigelow, A. (1990). Relationship between the development of language and thought in young blind children. *Journal of Visual Impairment and Blindness, 84*(8), 414–419.

Bigelow, A. E. (1995). The effect of blindness on the early development of the self. In P. Rochat (Ed.), *The self in infancy: Theory and research* (pp. 327–347). Amsterdam: Elsevier.

Blamey, P. J., Sarant, J. Z., Paatsch, L. E., Barry, J. G., Bow, C. P., Wales, R. J., et al. (2001). Relationships among speech perception, production, language, hearing loss, and age in children with impaired hearing. *Journal of Speech, Language and Hearing Research, 44*(2), 264–285.

Brambring, M. (2003). *Early interventions with infants and preschoolers who are blind.*, 2 volumes. Würzburg: Edition Bentheim.

Brambring, M. (2007). Divergent development of verbal skills in children who are blind or sighted. *Journal of Visual Impairment and Blindness, 101*(12), 212–225.

Brown, S. F. (2005). *There is no such thing as a mother: A review of "what do mothers want? Developmental perspectives, clinical challenges."* Hillsdale, NJ: Analytic Press.

Campbell, J. (2007). Understanding the emotional needs of children who are blind. *Journal of Visual Impairment & Blindness, 101,* 351–355.

Chen, D., & Haney, M. (1995). An early intervention model for infants who are deaf-blind. *Journal of Visual Impairment and Blindness, 89*(3), 213–221.

Chute, P. M., & Nevins, M. E. (2002). *The parent's guide to cochlear implant.* Washington, DC: Gallaudet University Press.

Copper, P. J., & Stein, A. (1989). Life events and postnatal depression: The Oxford Study. In J. Cox & E. S. Paykel (Eds.), *Life events and postpartum psychiatric disorder.* Southampton: Southampton University Press.

Cunningham, M., & Cox, E. O. (2003). Hearing assessment in infants and children: Recommendations beyond neonatal screening. *Pediatrics, 111*(2), 436–440.

Daelman, M., Nafstad, A., Rodbroe, I., Souriau, J., & Visser, A. (1996). *Social interaction and the emergence of communication.* London: DbI-European Working Group on Communication.

Davis, A., Bamford, J., Wilson, I., Ramkalawan, T., Forshaw, M., & Wright, S. (1997). A critical review of the role of neonatal hearing screening in the detection of congenital hearing impairment. *Health Technology Assessment, 1*(10), 1–77.

Dunlea, A. (1989). *Vision and the emergence of meaning: Blind and sighted children's early language.* Cambridge: Cambridge University Press.

Ek, U. (2000). *Children with visual disorders. Cognitive development, developmental disorders and consequences for treatment and counselling.* Stockholm University: Department of Psychology (doctoral dissertation).

Ek, U., Fernell, E., Jacobson, L., & Gillberg, C. (1998). Relation between blindness due to retin-opathy of prematurity and autistic spectrum disorders: A population-based study. *Developmental Medicine and Child Neurology, 40*, 297–301.

Erting, C., Prezioso, C., & O'Grady Hynes, M. (1990). The interactional context of deaf mother–infant communication. In V. Volterra & C. Erting (Eds.), *From gesture to language in hearing and deaf children* (pp. 97–106). New York: Springer Verlag.

Fogel, A. (1993). *Developing through relationships. Origins of communication, self, and culture.* New York: Harvester Wheatsheaf.

Folven, R. J., & Bonvillian, J. D. (1991). The transition from nonreferential to referential language in children acquiring American sign language. *Developmental Psychology, 27*(5), 806–816.

Fraiberg, S. (1977). *Insights from the blind.* New York: Basic Books.

Fredericks, H., & Baldwin, V. (1987). Individuals with sensory impairments: Who are they? In L. Goetz, D. Guess, & K. Stremel-Campbell (Eds.), *Innovative program design for individuals with dual sensory impairments* (pp. 3–15). Baltimore, MD: Paul H. Brookes.

Geers, A., & Moog, J. (1994). Effectiveness of cochlear implant and tactile aids for deaf children: The sensory aids study at Central Institute for the Deaf. *Volta Review, 96*(5).

Harris, M. (2001). It's all a matter of timing: Sign visibility and sign reference in deaf and hearing mothers of 18-month-old children. *Journal of Deaf Studies and Deaf Education, 6*(3), 177–185.

Harris, M., Clibbens, J., Tibbitts, R., & Chasin, J. (1987). *Communication between deaf mothers and their deaf infants.* Paper presented at the Child Language Seminar, University of York, UK.

Incesulu, A., Vural, M., & Erkam, U. (2003). Children with cochlear implants: Parental perspective. *Otology & Neurotology, 24*, 605–611.

Iverson, J., Tencer, H., Lany, J., & Goldin-Meadow, S. (2000). The relation between gesture and speech in congenitally blind and sighted language learners. *Journal of Nonverbal Behavior, 24*, 105–130.

Jamieson, J. R., & Pedersen, E. D. (1993). Deafness and mother–child interaction. Scaffolded instruction and the learning of problem-solving skills. *Early Child Development and Parenting, 2*, 229–242.

Janssen, M. J., Riksen-Walraven, J. M., & van Dijk, J. P. M. (2002). Enhancing the quality of interaction between deafblind children and their educators. *Journal of Development and Physical Disabilities, 14*(1), 87–109.

Janssen, M. J., Riksen-Walraven, J. M., & van Dijk, J. P. M. (2003). Contact: Effects of an intervention program to foster harmonious interaction between deaf-blind children and their educators. *Journal of Visual Impairment and Blindness, 97*, 215–229.

Janssen, M. J., Riksen-Walraven, J. M., & van Dijk, J. P. M. (2006). Applying the diagnostic intervention model for fostering harmonious interactions between deaf-blind children and their educators: A case study. *Journal of Visual Impairment and Blindness, 100*(2).

Kekelis, L., & Andersen, E. (1984). Family communication styles and language development. *Journal of Visual Impairment and Blindness, 78*, 54–64.

Keller, H. (1903). *The story of my life.* New York: Doubleday, Page & Co.

Koester, L. S., Brooks, L., & Traci, M. A. (2000). Tactile contact by deaf and hearing mothers during face-to-face interactions with their infants. *Journal of Deaf Studies and Deaf Education, 5*(2), 127–139.

Kugiumutzakis, G. (1998). Neonatal imitation in the intersubjective companion in space. In S. Bråten (Ed.), *Intersubjective communication and emotion in early ontogeny* (pp. 63–88). Cambridge: Cambridge University Press.

Landau, B., & Gleitman, L. (1985). *Language and experience.* Cambridge, MA: Harvard University Press.

Lenneberg, E. H. (1967). *Biological foundations of language.* New York: Wiley.

Li, Y., Baind, L., & Steinberg, A. G. (2004). Parental decision-making in considering cochlear implant technology for a deaf child. *International Journal of Pediatric Otorhinolaryngology, 68,* 1027–1038.

Loots, G., Devisé, I., & Sermijn, J. (2003). The interaction between mothers and their visually impaired infants: An intersubjective developmental perspective. *Journal of Visual Impairment and Blindness, 97,* 403–417.

Lyons-Ruth, K. (2003). Dissociation and the parent–infant dialogue: A longitudinal perspective from attachment research. *Journal of the American Psychoanalytic Association, 51*(3), 883–911.

Maestas y Moores, J. (1980). Early linguistic environment: Interactions of deaf parents with their infants. *Sign Language Studies, 26,* 1–13.

McConnachie, H. R., & Moore, V. (1994). Early expressive language of severely visually impaired children. *Developmental Medicine and Child Neurology, 36,* 230–240.

Meadow-Orlans, K. (1987). *Deaf and hearing mothers of deaf and hearing infants: Interaction during the first year.* Paper presented at the World Conference for the Deaf, Helsinki.

Meadow-Orlans, K. P., & Sass-Lehrer, M. (1995). Support services for families with children who are deaf: Challenges for professionals. *Topics in Early Childhood Special Education, 15*(3), 314–334.

Meadow-Orlans, K. P., & Spencer, P. (1996). Maternal sensitivity and the visual attentiveness of children who are deaf. *Maternal Development and Parenting, 5*(4), 213–223.

Meltzoff, A. N. (1986). Imitation, intermodal representation and the origins of the mind. In I. B. Lindblom & R. Zetterström (Eds.), *Precursors of early speech* (pp. 245–265). New York: Stockton Press.

Meyer, T., Svirsky, M., Kirk, K., & Miyamoto, R. (1998). Improvements in speech perception by children with profound prelingual hearing loss: Effects of device, communication mode and chronological age. *Journal of Speech, Language, & Hearing Research, 41*(4), 846–858.

Michael, M. G., & Paul, P. V. (1991). Early intervention for infants with deaf-blindness. *Exceptional Children, 57*(3), 200–210.

Moore, V., & McConnachie, H. R. (1994). Communication between blind and severely visually impaired children and their parents. *British Journal of Developmental Psychology, 12,* 491–502.

Mulford, R. (1988). First words of the blind child. In M. Smith & J. Locke (Eds.), *The emergent lexicon* (pp. 293–338). London: Academic Press.

Murray, L., Kempton, C., Woolgar, M., & Hooper, R. (1993). Depressed mothers' speech to their infants and its relation to infant gender and cognitive development. *Journal of Child Psychology and Psychiatry, 34,* 1083–1101.

Miyamoto, R., Robbins, A., Osberger, M. J., Todd, S., Allyson, I., Riley, M., & Kirk, K. (1995). Comparison of multichannel tactile aids and multichannel cochlear implants in children with profound hearing impairments. *American Journal of Otology, 16*(1), 8–13.

Nadel, J., Guérini, C., Pezé, A., & Rivet, C. (1999). The evolving nature of imitation as a format for communication. In J. Nadel & G. Butterworth (Eds.), *Imitation in infancy* (pp. 209–234). Cambridge: Cambridge University Press.

Nafstad, A., & Rodbroe, I. (1996). Congenital deafblindness, interaction and development towards a model of intervention. In M. Laurent (Ed.), *Communication and congenital deafblindness* (pp. 179–195). Paris: Centre National de Suresnes.

Nelson, K. (1973). *Structure and strategy in learning to talk.* Monographs of the Society for Research in Child Development, 38. Chicago: University of Chicago Press for the Society for Research in Child Development.

Norris, M., Spaulding, P. J., & Brodei, F. H. (1957). *Blindness in children.* Chicago: University of Chicago Press.

Osberger, M. J., Maso, M., & Sam, L. K. (1993). Speech intelligibility of children with cochlear implants, tactile aids or hearing aids. *Journal of Speech and Hearing Research*, *36*, 186–203.

Pérez-Pereira, M., & Conti-Ramsden, G. (1999). *Language development and social interaction in blind children*. Hove: Psychology Press.

Pérez-Pereira, M., & Conti-Ramsden, G. (2001). The use of directives in verbal interactions between blind children and their mothers. *Journal of Visual Impairment and Blindness*, *95*, 133–149.

Preisler, G. (1991). Early patterns of interaction between blind infants and their mothers. *Child: Care, Health and Development*, *17*, 65–90.

Preisler, G. (1995). The development of communication in blind and in deaf infants: Similarities and differences. *Child: Care, Health and Development*, *21*(2), 79–110.

Preisler, G. (1997). Social and emotional development. Blindness and psychosocial development 0–10 years. In V. Lewis & G. Collis (Eds.), *Blindness and psychological development in young children* (pp. 69–85). Leicester: BPS Books.

Preisler, G. (2005). The development of communication in deaf-blind children. *Scandinavian Journal of Disability Research*, *7*(1), 41–62.

Preisler, G. (2007). The psychosocial development in deaf children with cochlear implants, In L. Komesaroff (Ed.), *Surgical consent: Bioethics and cochlear implantation* (pp. 120–136). Washington, DC: Gallaudet University Press.

Preisler, G., Karlsson, J.-O., & Norström, H. (1994). Alla barn kommunicerar [All children communicate]. *Rapporter*, No. 80. Stockholm University: Department of Psychology.

Preisler, G., Tvingstedt, A.-L., & Ahlström, M. (1997). The development of communication and language in deaf preschool children with cochlear implants. *International Journal of Pediatric Otorhinolaryngology*, *41*, 263–272.

Preisler, G., Tvingstedt, A-L., & Ahlström, M. (2002). A psycho-social follow-up study of deaf preschool children using cochlear implants. *Child: Care, Health and Development*, *28*(5), 403–418.

Rizzolatti, G., & Arbib, M. A. (1998). Language within our grasp. *Trends in the Neurosciences*, *21*, 188–194.

Robinshaw, H. M., & Evans, R. (1995). Caregivers' sensitivity to the communicative and linguistic needs of their deaf infants. *Early Child Development and Care*, *109*, 23–41.

Rosenberg, T., Flage, T., Hansen, E., Riise, R., Rudanko, S.-R., Viggosson, G. & Thornqvist, K. (1996). Incidence of registered visual impairment in the Nordic child population. *British Journal of Opthalmology*, *80*, 49–53.

Rowland, C. (1983). Patterns of interaction between three blind infants and their mothers. In A. Wills (Ed.), *Language acquisition in the blind child* (pp. 114–132). Beckenham: Croom Helm.

Schein, J. (1996). The demography of deafness. In P. C. Higgins & J. E. Nash, *Understanding deafness socially* (2nd ed., pp. 21–43). Springfield, IL: Thomas.

Spencer, P. E. (2004). Individual differences in language performance after cochlear implantation at one to three years of age: Child, family and linguistic factors. *Journal of Deaf Studies and Deaf Education*, *9*, 395–412.

Spencer, P. E., & Marschark, M. (2003). Cochlear implants: Issues and implications. In M. Marschark & P. E. Spencer (Eds.), *Oxford handbook of deaf studies, language and education* (pp 434–448). New York: Oxford University Press.

Stern, D. (1995). *The motherhood constellation*. New York: Basic Books.

Stern, D. (2000). *The interpersonal world of the infant: A view from psychoanalysis and developmental psychology*. New York: Basic Books. (Originally published in 1985.)

Stokoe, W. (1972). *Semiotics and human sign languages*. The Hague: Mouton.

Studdert-Kennedy, M. (1991). Language development from an evolutionary perspective. In N. Krasnegor, D. Rumbaugh, R. Schiefelbusch, & M. Studdert-Kennedy (Eds.), *Language acquisition: Biological and behavioral determinants* (pp. 5–28). Hillsdale, NJ: Lawrence Erlbaum Associates.

Svirsky, M., Robbins, A. K., Kirk, K. I., Pisoni, D. B., & Miyamoto, R. T. (2000). Language development in profoundly deaf children with cochlear implants. *Psychological Science, 11*(2), 153–158.

Thorén, A. (2002). *Blinda barn och seende föräldrar i utveckling och kommunikation [Blind children and sighted parents in interaction and communication].* Doctoral dissertation, Department of Psychology, Stockholm University.

Trevarthen, C. (2001). Intrinsic motives for companionship in understanding: Their origin, development and significance for infant mental health. *International Journal of Infant Mental Health, 22*(1–2), 95–131.

Trevarthen, C. (2004). How infants learn how to mean. In M. Tokoro and L. Steels (Ed.), *A learning zone of one's own* (pp. 37–70). Amsterdam: IOS Press.

Tronick, E. Z. (1998). Dyadically expanded states of consciousness and the process of therapeutic change. *Infant Mental Health Journal, 19*(3), 290–299.

Tronick, E. Z. (2005). Why is connection with others so critical? The formation of dyadic states of consciousness and the expansion of individual's states of consciousness: Coherence governed selection and the co-creation of meaning out of messy meaning making. In J. Nadel and D. Muir (Eds.), *Emotional development,* (pp. 293–315). Oxford: Oxford University Press.

Tronick, E. Z., & Weinberg, K. (1997). Depressed mothers and infants: Failure to form dyadic states of consciousness. In L. Murray and P. Cooper (Eds.), *Postpartum depression and child development* (pp. 54–82). New York: Guilford.

Tröster, H., & Brambring, M. (1992). Early social-emotional development in blind infants. *Child: Care, Health and Development, 18,* 207–227.

Urwin, C. (1983). Dialogue and cognitive functioning in the early language development in blind children. In A. Wills (Ed.), *Language acquisition in the blind child* (pp. 142–161). Beckenham: Croom Helm.

Walzman, S., Cohen, N., Gomolin, R. H., Shapiro, W. H., Shelly, R. O., & Hoffman, R. A. (1994). Long-term results of early cochlear implantation in congenitally and prelingually deafened children. *Journal of Otology, 15*(Suppl. 2), 9–13.

Warren, D. (1984). *Blindness and early childhood development.* New York: American Foundation for the Blind.

Winnicot, D. (1987). The theory of the parent–infant relationship. In D. Winnicott, *The maturational processes and the facilitating environment.* London: Hogarth Press. (Original work published 1960.)

Yoshinaga-Itano, C. (2003). From screening to early identification and intervention: Discovering predictors to successful outcomes for children with significant hearing loss. *Journal of Deaf Studies and Deaf Education, 8*(1), 11–30.

Young, A., & Tattersall, H. (2007). Universal newborn hearing screening and early identification of deafness: Parents' response to knowing early and their expectations of child communication development. *Journal of Deaf Studies and Deaf Education, 12*(2), 209–220.

Zaidman-Zait, A. (2007). Parenting a child with cochlear implant: A critical incident study. *Journal of Deaf Studies and Deaf Education, 12*(2), 221–241.

Zaidman-Zait, A., & Most, T. (2005). Cochlear implants in children with hearing loss: Maternal expectations and impact on the family. *Volta Review, 105,* 129–150.

PART II

Psychosocial Risks

Introduction

Part II has four chapters detailing the nature and consequences of infant exposure to a variety of psychosocial risk factors, which can increase the likelihood of compromised cognitive and/or social-emotional development. Chapter 5 by Chen, Hetzner, and Brooks-Gunn deals with the impact of growing up in poverty for young children living in developed countries. As initially noted by the authors, defining poverty is not a simple issue of establishing a specific income cut-off level. Rather, issues such as relative versus absolute cut-off levels, the chronicity of poverty and the timing of the child's exposure to poverty must also be considered. This discussion of definitional issues is followed by a systematic review documenting the multifaceted association between growing up in poverty and physical development, social-emotional development, cognitive development and academic achievement. Chen and colleagues propose a variety of mechanisms underlying the multiple associations between poverty and development, including family stress, maternal depression, family structure, parenting style, quality of the home environment and community characteristics. The chapter concludes with a discussion of interventions that may reduce the consequences of growing up in poverty.

Chapter 6 by Engle deals with a relatively understudied population, namely infants from low-income developing countries. The importance of this topic is highlighted by the fact that nearly 90% of the world's infants are growing up in such countries. The chapter beings with a discussion of the economic and noneconomic distinctions between developed and developing countries. This is followed by presentation of the multiple and major biological risks encountered by young children from developing countries who are growing up in poverty. Engle notes that exposure to biological risks not only directly compromises young children's development, but also increases the exposure of young children to powerful psychosocial risk factors such as being orphaned. Based on a cumulative risk framework, Engle then goes on to present other psychosocial risk factors that have also been shown to adversely impact upon young children from developing countries, such as maternal depression and reduced child stimulation and learning opportunities. Drawing from international human rights resolutions, the chapter concludes with policy recommendations for interventions for young children from developing countries and identifies characteristics of effective early child development interventions that have been carried out in such countries.

Chapter 7 by Connell-Carrick deals with child abuse and child neglect. The chapter is framed by the use of ecological models that identify and link multiple influences that lead to maltreatment of infants and young children, including parental characteristics, the nature of the family environment, the nature of the parent's work environment, and community and cultural characteristics. Within this framework the operation of risk factors that can increase the risk of child maltreatment and protective factors that can reduce the likelihood of child maltreatment are discussed. Connell-Carrick then focuses on the multiple biological and social-emotional consequences of different types of child maltreatment, with specific reference to neglect, physical abuse and sexual abuse. The chapter concludes with presentation of intervention strategies that support families and have the potential to reduce the incidence of maltreatment of infants and young children.

Chapter 8 by Murray, Halligan, and Cooper is on the topic of postnatal maternal depression. The chapter begins with a brief presentation on the incidence and characteristics of postnatal maternal depression, noting the high incidence rate of this disorder. This is followed by a detailed review of the impact of postnatal maternal depression on mother–infant interactions, infant and child brain function, infant and child cognitive development, infant and child social-emotional development, and the emergence of child behavioral or psychiatric problems. Murray and colleagues next propose mechanisms through which maternal depression can impact upon infant and child development, including infant modeling of maternal affective state, an inability of depressed mothers to help their infants regulate their own emotions, increased hostility or coercive behavior by depressed mothers, and disruptions in the infant's stress reactivity. Murray and colleagues then review evidence on psychological and biological interventions with depressed mothers, with specific reference to the impact of such interventions on mother–infant interactions. The chapter concludes with identification of several areas where more research is needed, such as maternal depression in developing countries and paternal depression.

5

Growing Up in Poverty in Developed Countries

Jondou J. Chen, Nina Philipsen Hetzner, and Jeanne Brooks-Gunn

Introduction: Why Study Children in Poverty?

Child poverty has been identified as an immediate concern in a number of developed countries (Biterman & Börjeson, 2002; Kahn & Kamerman, 2002; Phipps, 1999; Waldfogel, 2002). Children living in poverty are more likely to experience food, health-care, family nurturance, and educational deprivation relative to their nonpoor counter-parts. These disadvantages are linked with compromised development on many fronts including health, cognitive functioning, and socioemotional development (Kamerman, Neuman, Waldfogel, & Brooks-Gunn, 2003; Leventhal & Brooks-Gunn, 2002). As children who experience poverty become adults, they are more likely to have children early, be unemployed, receive low pay, and experience poor physical and mental health. These outcomes, in turn, serve as developmental risk factors for the next generation of children, perpetuating the cycle of poverty (Duncan & Brooks-Gunn, 1997; Hobcraft & Kiernan, 2001; Vleminckx & Smeeding, 2001).

In many developed countries, children are more likely than adults to live in poverty. For example, in the United States, children are twice as likely as adults and 70% more likely than the elderly to live in poverty (Brooks-Gunn, Duncan, & Maritato, 1997; Song & Yu, 2002). In the European Union, children are over 30% more likely to live in poverty than adults (Mejer & Siermann, 2000). Additionally, poverty experienced by children across developed countries tends to be deeper and more persistent than poverty experienced by adults (Bradbury, Jenkins, & Micklewright, 2001; Leventhal & Brooks-Gunn, 2002; Mejer & Linden, 2000).

Child poverty is associated with decreased human capital and economic productivity, giving industrialized countries the economic incentive to alleviate these social costs (Bradbury et al., 2001; Heckman, 2007). Indeed, developed countries with lower rates of child poverty tend to measure higher on indicators of child well-being including school retention and graduation, maintenance of child health, and higher cognitive skills as well as lower child abuse and neglect (Organization for Economic Co-operation and Development (OECD), 1999a, 1999b). Given this, several countries have the stated goal of reducing and even eliminating child poverty: the UK aims to eliminate it by 2020, and Belgium and Japan aim to halve it by 2010 and 2015, respectively (Kamerman et al., 2003). There remains, however, great variability in developed countries' attempts to redress child poverty (Bradbury et al., 2001; Phipps, 1999).

Studies of children living in poverty in the developed world have demonstrated a robust association between economic hardship and suboptimal development in infancy, through adolescence, and into adulthood. Moreover, children living in poverty typically experience increased stress and additional risk factors, which have a cumulative effect, making recovery and resilience virtually impossible (Luthar, 2003). Nevertheless, many children who grow up poor manage to adapt and become successful adults (Werner & Smith, 1982). Ongoing research continues to illuminate the pathways underlying the associations between poverty and child development (Duncan, Ludwig, & Magnuson, 2007).

This chapter is organized with five goals in mind: (1) to consider different measures of poverty in developed countries; (2) to discuss methodological challenges in studying poverty; (3) to review findings from longitudinal studies regarding associations between poverty and developmental outcomes in developed countries; (4) to explore hypothesized pathways by which poverty influences children; (5) to review potential strategies for remediating the effects of poverty on children. A discussion of poverty and child development in developing countries can be found in the next chapter in this volume.

The Nature of Poverty

Relative poverty

Poverty is not uniformly defined across countries (Kamerman et al., 2003). In countries where the government uses a relative definition to identify people living in poverty, family incomes are measured relative to the median income of all households in the measurement area. Income in developed countries tends to be positively skewed, meaning that a small percentage of wealthy individuals drive the mean income to be significantly higher than the earnings of the majority of individuals. Wealth becomes even more skewed as debt and wealth other than income (e.g., stock ownership) are considered (Banks, Blundell, & Smith, 2003). Consequently, median rather than mean income has been the preferred description of the typical individual in developed countries. Governments then establish a threshold below which families are considered to live in poverty. The European Union countries, Japan, and the OECD have established their poverty thresholds at 50% of that country's median income.[1]

Questions remain regarding the percentage of the median income at which the poverty threshold should be established and whether the income level and the median level of income are the best standards by which to measure poverty (Iceland, 2005; Rainwater, Smeeding, & Coder, 2001; Tachibanaki, 2006). Also, as the distribution of wealth becomes more skewed or perhaps bimodal, the utility of the median to establish the poverty threshold must be reassessed. In these cases, researchers must adjust analyses that rely on parametric distributions (Walberg, Strykowski, Rovai, & Hung, 1984).

Absolute poverty

Traditionally, English-speaking countries and South Korea have relied on absolute measures of poverty, which rely on formulas to calculate the anticipated cost of living in a given area (Hong & Song, 2006).[2] For example, in the United States, this threshold was originally calculated in 1960 as three times the cost of an adequate diet as determined by the US Department of Agriculture (Committee on Ways and Means, 2000). The original estimation has been updated periodically to account for increases in costs of living. In 2007, the poverty threshold established for a family consisting of one adult and two related children was set at $16,705 (US Census Bureau, 2008).

Critics have questioned the meaningfulness of this measure because the calculation of an adequate diet rests on several assumptions about nutrition, time spent on food preparation, and the cost of food (Rose, 2007). In addition, the adjustments for cost of living have been critiqued as inadequate, with variance in food prices by region unaccounted for. For example, the original calculation was based on the premise that food should constitute 30% of a family's purchases. This figure is outdated, as food costs have decreased over time while other costs (e.g., housing and medical) have increased (Currie, 2006).

Relative versus absolute poverty

Policy-makers and researchers have debated whether poverty should be defined absolutely or relatively (Kamerman et al., 2003; Mayer, 1997a). Does typical, healthy human development depend on the absolute presence of certain resources? Or does relative poverty, above and beyond absolute poverty, affect the psychological well-being of individuals living in poverty by adding a perception of unfair distribution of wealth? Research has shown relative poverty to be a stronger predictor of teenage childbearing rates in the US and UK than absolute poverty (Pickett & Wilkinson, 2007). Researchers have also found that wealth does not always have continuous effects, as unique findings have been uncovered while studying extreme groups of people living in affluence (Browning & Cagney, 2003; Morenoff, Sampson & Raudenbush, 2001) versus people living in poverty and deep poverty (Duncan, Yeung, Brooks-Gunn & Smith, 1998; Smith, Brooks-Gunn, & Klebanov, 1997). Mayer (1997a) states that poverty experienced in developed countries is not actually poverty when compared to conditions in developing countries (e.g., the availability of education, running water, and electricity). Iceland (2005) has argued that both models, as well as quasi-relative models, have their advantages and should be seen as complementary rather than interchangeable or comparable.

This debate among researchers also involves policy-makers, as welfare program eligibility is almost universally determined relative to the poverty line. As policy-makers continue to debate whether these programs serve as parts of a morally mandated safety net, cost-saving preventative interventions, or poverty-enabling crutches, so too will the discussion over how best to define poverty (Currie, 2006; Mabughi & Selim, 2006.) A number of policy-makers have begun following the lead of social scientists in using ranges around poverty thresholds to measure social trends and program eligibility. These scholars and policy-makers have recognized that a significant number of individuals can be described as the "working poor" who live above the poverty threshold but still experience economic hardship (Heclo, 1994). For example, a number of US states currently provide free early childhood education and subsidized healthcare for children from families living below 200% of the US poverty level (Byck, 2000).

Variation in poverty rates across developed countries

Regardless of the poverty measure used, child poverty levels vary across developed countries. Whether using a relative or absolute measure of poverty, the Nordic countries tend to have lower child poverty rates (Finland at 3.4% and Norway at 4.5%, using a relative measure of poverty set at 50% of national income). Using the same relative measure, the US leads developed countries with a child poverty rate at 26.3% (Bradbury et al., 2001). Reflecting the applicable differences in the two measurements of poverty, the Czech Republic, Poland, and Hungary have comparatively low relative child poverty but high absolutely poverty. That is, the wealth in these countries is more narrowly distributed and lower relative to other developed countries. While few people are significantly poorer than the rest of the population, there are still many people who live with less than the absolute measure of wealth that has been calculated to be necessary for adequate living. Countries with higher levels of median income tend to have lower child poverty rates. There are notable deviations from this trend, however, including the US having higher than expected child poverty and Taiwan having lower than expected (Bradbury & Jäntti, 2001).

The added cost of poverty for children

Poverty is not a permanent state for most families. Usually families experience poverty in one or more bouts. Children who experience persistent, as opposed to occasional or transitory, poverty see worse effects (Brooks-Gunn et al., 1997; Duncan & Brooks-Gunn, 1997). Rates of persistent poverty vary between countries independent of rates of overall poverty – for example, post-reunification Germany saw similar rates of poverty to the UK but lower rates of persistent poverty (Schulter, 2001); in Italy, child poverty has remained high relative to the general population even as fertility rates have declined (Brandolini, Cannari, D'Alessio, & Faiella, 2004). Differential effects for the depth of poverty experienced (deep poverty is defined as families living below 50% of the poverty line) have also been reported (Yeung, Linver, & Brooks-Gunn, 2002; Song & Yu, 2002).

Finally, the timing of poverty has also been found to be critical, with poverty experienced early in life, and especially during the first two years of life, being more strongly correlated with development than poverty experienced later in life (Bradbury et al., 2001;

Duncan & Brooks-Gunn, 1997). This is especially disconcerting given the increased likelihood that younger children (under age 6) will live in poverty in the US: 18% compared to 16% for all children (Proctor & Dalaker, 2002). As many developmental processes are sequential, poverty experienced earlier in life can result in delayed, stunted, or maladaptive development. While some of these processes are reversible – for example, current low weight for height (Korenman & Miller, 1997) and antisocial behavior (Laub & Sampson, 2001) – others are not – for example, infant and earlier low weight for height (Korenman & Miller, 1997 and iron deficiency anemia (Hurtado, Claussen & Scott, 1999). Persistence, depth, and timing are important moderating factors of poverty that must be methodologically addressed when studying the development of children in poverty. The links established using these three moderators will be discussed in more detail in the following sections of this chapter.

Limitations in Studying Poverty and Children

Addressing additional aspects of wealth and cost of living

Problematic for both definitions of poverty is that the established poverty lines do not take into consideration government-subsidized income transfers such as food stamps, housing, healthcare, or other tax benefits (Hernandez, 1997). Regional differences in cost of living and availability of resources also go unconsidered as well as the added material needs and costs of having children and dependents with special needs (Rainwater et al., 2001). Additionally, over the past half-century, there has been a shift toward employment of women including, in some countries, poor mothers (Hernandez, 1997). This development requires that poverty calculations include the cost of childcare or high-quality early childhood education in those countries which do not provide such services (for a detailed discussion of the role of early childcare, see chapter 14 in this volume).

Social scientists have thus sought to create stronger measures of poverty by creating composite measures of socioeconomic status (SES), which include a family's economic well-being, occupational status, social class and social capital as factors influencing a family's future economic and well-being potential (Ensminger & Fothergill, 2003). Although these additional variables provide a more comprehensive picture, they are also distinct from income, and some have argued for their inclusion in predictive models as separate variables rather than as a composite SES measure.

Problems of selection

A number of factors covary with poverty status in developed countries: parental unemployment (and especially long-term unemployment), reliance on a single income source, large family size, low parental education, parental absence and receipt of government welfare support (Aber & Ellwood, 2001; Brooks-Gunn et al., 1997; McLanahan, 1997). These factors are associated not only with being in poverty, but also with negative child outcomes. As a result, it is difficult to make causal claims about the association between poverty and negative child outcomes (Mayer, 1997a), since it is possible that negative child outcomes are a result of the family characteristics predictive of child poverty. A number of developmental studies have posited that these family characteristics might be explained as mediators between poverty and child development (Brooks-Gunn, Berlin, Leventhal, & Fuligni, 2000; Duncan et al., 1998).[3] However, detecting causal relationships has proven challenging due to the observational nature of the data available. While experimental data on poverty do not exist (as it would require randomly assigning people to live in poverty), innovative researchers have taken advantage of natural experiments and the random assignment of cash transfers and other benefits to strengthen conclusions (e.g., Costello, Compton, Keeler, & Angold, 2003; Duncan et al., 1998). That research will be reviewed in the following sections.

Prevalence of US research

While much descriptive data exist regarding poverty rates across developed countries, research on the associations between poverty and the pathways through which poverty influences child development was found to be largely based in the United States. Most of the poor in European Union countries receive enough income supplements to drastically reduce if not eliminate poverty (OECD, 2002). In Japan and South Korean, poor people are initially the legal responsibility of their immediate families before the government, which still provides similar supplements to EU countries for those who are still poor after extended family support (Hong & Song, 2006; Tachibanaki, 2006).

The US stands in stark contrast to these other developed countries. While the US has the highest level of wealth and the lowest levels of unemployment relative to other developed countries, it also has one of the highest levels of income inequality and spends the lowest percentage of its gross domestic product on poverty-reduction payments and programs (Smeeding, 2005). This contrast leaves the US as the ideal setting for studying poverty (which has largely been eliminated in other developed countries through family assistance and government income supplements). Furthermore, the ongoing policy debate has required the means-testing of welfare interventions, which has encouraged greater amounts of research (Currie, 2006; Duncan, Ludwig, & Magnuson, 2007).

Child Development Outcomes

Individual countries and studies vary in their categorization of child outcomes (Phipps, 1999). For example, the Longitudinal Study of Australian Children categorizes outcomes as behavioral and emotional, language and cognitive, readiness to learn, overall health, motor/physical and social competence (Sanson et al., 2002). In contrast, the Canadian National Children's Agenda measures normal child development with physical and emotional health, safety and security, successful learning, and social engagement and responsibility (Human Resources Development Canada, 2000). As physical outcomes are discussed in chapter 3 of this volume, we shall focus primarily on socioemotional and cognitive outcomes.

Longitudinal studies are predominantly referenced because they provide the best evidence of the pathways linking child poverty to later outcomes (Brooks-Gunn et al., 2000). After establishing the developmental domains influenced by poverty, we go on to consider several pathways that may explain how poverty influences child development.

Physical outcomes

In the US, being born into poverty has been associated with food insecurity and low birth weight (Borders, Grobman, Amsden, & Holl, 2007), but these correlations were found to fade if families move out of poverty (Korenman & Miller, 1997). While food surpluses exist in most OECD countries, food scarcity is still experienced by 11% of US families even as provision of an adequate diet is guaranteed through federal programs such as Women, Infants and Children (WIC) and the Food Stamp Program (FSP) (Committee on Ways and Means, 2000; OECD, 1998). In addition to food scarcity and low birth weight, poor families in developed countries must also address the low availability of healthy food options, nutrition education, and exercise opportunities (Fox & Cole, 2004). Combined these lead to higher obesity rates among children living in poverty as found in Australia and the US (Gibson, 2006; Wake, Hardy, Canterford, Sawyer, & Carlin, 2006).[4] Poor nutrition and food insecurity have also been associated with higher rates of infant hospitalization in the US (Cook et al., 2004).[5]

An additional nutritional consequence of poverty is iron deficiency. A study of 12-month-old infants in nine EU countries found that 5% of poor infants suffered from iron deficiency in contrast with 0% of infants from high-income families (Male, Persson, Freeman, Guerra, van't Hof, & Haschke, 2001). Iron deficiency at such an early stage has in turn been associated with mental retardation and cognitive function deficits across child and adolescent development (Grantham-McGregor & Ani, 2001; Hurtado et al., 1999). One US study has calculated that nutritional deficits account for 13–20% of the difference in IQ between poor and nonpoor children (Brooks-Gunn et al., 1997), while another found that poor children were 50% more likely to experience iron deficiencies than nonpoor children (Looker, Cogswell, & Gunter, 2002). One explanation for higher levels of iron deficiency among infants from poor families is the lower level of breastfeeding in low-income families in the US (Zubieta, Melgar-Quinonez, & Taylor, 2006). However, immigrant status may function as a protective factor for these families, given that immigrant mothers were more likely to breastfeed their infants (Neault et al., 2007).

Socioemotional outcomes

Socioemotional development is most often measured in children by using parent and teacher reports of child friendliness, cooperation, task engagement, temper tantrums, defiance, and aggression. Overall, research has produced mixed evidence for an association between socioemotional outcomes and poverty. This is largely because many correlations between income and socioemotional outcomes tend to disappear when controlling for variables associated with income such as home environment, maternal depression, maternal education, single parenthood, and family stress (Mayer, 1997a). However, as will be addressed later, this may be because income influences socioemotional outcomes through these factors (McLanahan, 2004; Yeung et al., 2002).

Socioemotional skills such as recognizing hostility and self-regulation are developed during infancy and early childhood (Dodge, 2006; National Scientific Council of the Developing Child, 2005; Nelson, 2000). Children from Canada living in poverty are less likely to develop these skills and are more likely to exhibit physical hostility as early as at 17 months of age (Tremblay et al., 2004). These findings remained even after maternal factors such as education, antisocial behavior, smoking, depression, and marital status were controlled for. Physical hostility, in turn, is associated with adult onset of alcohol and drug abuse, violent crimes, depression, suicide attempts, and abuse of partners and children (Tremblay et al., 2004). In the US, a National Institute of Health and Child Development (NIHCD) study of children aged 1–3 years measured similar externalizing negative behavior (e.g., violence and defiance), as well as internalizing negative behaviors (e.g., depression and withdrawal) and school readiness, to test for associations with change in income level over a three-year period (Dearing, McCartney, & Taylor, 2001). Positive changes in income were associated with improved prosocial behavior, expressive and receptive language, and school readiness for poor but not nonpoor families. However, effect sizes on behavior were small (0.0143 standard deviations; Taylor, Dearing, & McCartney, 2004). Similar results were found using the US National Longitudinal Survey of Youth (NLSY) data, where short-term poverty was linked to externalizing behavior problems, but poverty since birth or infancy was a stronger predictor of internalizing problems for children aged 4–8 (Smith et al., 1997).

As addressed earlier, one of the primary limitations of most poverty research is the observational nature of the data available. However, Costello et al. (2003) also found income to have significant effects on youth behavior based on a natural experiment. During an existing eight-year longitudinal study of youth aged 9–13, from poor rural families in the US, a casino was established on a Native American reservation. The casino provided supplemental incomes for Native American families who comprised approximately one-quarter of the families in the study. Relative to youth whose families experienced continuous poverty over the eight years of the study, youth whose family had moved out of poverty showed drops in externalizing behaviors such as conduct and oppositional defiance disorder, though drops in internalizing behaviors such as anxiety or depression symptoms were not found. While this study did not involve infants, the use of natural manipulations might prove similarly useful for future research on infants living in poverty.

Cognitive outcomes

Associations between poverty and child development are the strongest with regard to cognitive outcomes and school achievement (Duncan et al., 1998). Standardized assessments such as the Bayley Scales of Infant Development, IQ tests, the Woodcock–Johnson math and reading assessments, the Peabody Picture Vocabulary Test, and the Peabody Individual Assessment Tests in math and reading are common measures of cognitive performance. In the US, IQ scores have been found to be associated with poverty as early as age 2 (for a review of the literature, see Bradley & Corwyn, 2002). For example, the NLSY Child Supplements and the Infant Health and Development Program (IHDP) are both longitudinal data sets with information available from birth through adolescence. Using these data, Klebanov, Brooks-Gunn, McCarton, and McCormick (1998) found negative associations between poverty and child IQ and receptive vocabulary scores at ages 2 and 3 in the US.

Cognitive deficits seen during infancy are persistent through childhood as children enter schools. Coll, Buckner, Brooks, Weinreb, and Bassuk (1998) found that cognitive deficits existing in a population of poor homeless and housed infants in the US remained stable from 4 through 30 months. Using data from a British cohort born in 1958, McCulloch and Joshi (2001, 2002) also found lower cognitive test scores both for children aged 5–17 living in poverty and children who experienced poverty during infancy. Duration of poverty also has been found to affect child cognitive outcomes. Children in the US living in poverty for one to three years test four IQ points lower on average relative to children who never experienced poverty, while children living in poverty for four to five years test nine points lower (Brooks-Gunn et al., 1997). Cognitive performance has been tied to school achievement in the US and UK (Blanden & Gregg, 2004), with the association between income and school achievement strengthening over the past half century in the UK.

Also relying on the IHDP data set, Smith et al. (1997) used measures of school readiness to determine the links between poverty and cognitive development for children between the ages of 3 and 5.[6] Cognitive, verbal and achievement outcomes were all associated with living in poverty for young children, with children living in persistent poverty experiencing effects sizes three times greater than other children living in poverty (Smith et al., 1997). As early as age 2, and even after controlling for family structure, these differences were consistent with cognitive gaps seen at ages 3 and 5 in other studies (Smith et al., 1997).

Poverty and educational outcomes

School-related measures have also been shown to be associated with poverty. Using US data from the Panel Study of Income Dynamics, Duncan et al. (1998) compared siblings, controlling for environment even as income changed (family income typically increases 40% over an individual's childhood). Family income was associated with school attainment, and graduation for children from birth to age 20. Poverty during early childhood was a stronger predictor of high school graduation than poverty later in childhood. Duncan et al. (1998) argued that differences between poor and nonpoor youth in cognitive outcomes found later in childhood and adolescence may reflect the association between poverty experienced during infancy and socioemotional development.

Illustrating this point, poverty has also been associated with differences across life transitions. Fergusson and Woodward (2000) found that New Zealand youth from poor families were only one fifth as likely as their peers with parents in professional occupations to attend post-secondary education. An analysis of youth from EU countries found more modest links, with a 10% decrease in family income being associated with a 1.4% decrease in the likelihood of attending a four-year college (Acemoglu & Pischke, 2001). Maurin (2002) found in a French sample of three generations of primary school students that living in poverty was a stronger predictor of being forced to repeat a grade than age, sex, and even parental education. Nonincome-related aspects of poverty were controlled for using parental education and grandparent SES status. Poverty was also found to be negatively associated with school attendance in a study of children age 6–14 living in the former West Germany (Buchel, Frick, Krause, & Wagner, 2001). Ultimately, school dropout rates have also been tied to future economic success across developed countries (Micklewright & Stewart, 2000).

The overall pattern of evidence documents the association between poverty and negative child development outcomes, beginning with infancy and continuing across childhood.

Pathways of Poverty on Development

We now turn to the pathways by which poverty may influence child development. Baron and Kenny's (1986) mediational model requires possible explanatory variables to be first correlated with poverty and then with at least one developmental outcome. Researchers have examined the role of a number of potential mediators of the relationship between poverty and infant development. These include infant–parent attachment, parenting quality, availability and quality of childcare and early childhood education, accessibility and use of healthcare, parental mental health, exposure to violence, presence of fathers and child support, parental residence patterns, income sources, employment patterns, and neighborhood/community characteristics (Rouse, Brooks-Gunn, & McLanahan, 2005). Data for these indicators continue to be useful across childhood, along with additional variables such as cognitive reports and socioemotional observations from schools, and educational and social services received (Brooks-Gunn et al., 2000).

Two major theories exist describing how family poverty might affect children. The family stress model is often associated with Bronfenbrenner's (1979) ecological systems theory, and hypothesizes that economic hardship experienced by adults influences the parent–child relationship (Elder, 1999; Conger and Elder, 1994). The parental investment model measures discrete variables (time, materials, physical environment) as potential mediators, and has been more frequently associated with economic and intervention studies measuring long-term earnings (Heckman, 2006, 2007; Mayer, 1997a; Yeung et al., 2002).

The family stress model and family structure

Adult poverty in the developed world is typically accompanied by unstable work, low income, and unemployment, all of which cause stress. Parenthood can enhance stress as parents must look for ways to feed, house, and educate their children, often having limited options available to them. Child outcomes are known to covary with child psychosocial stressors such as family turmoil, early childhood separation, and exposure to violence both at home and in the community (Evans & English, 2002; Evans, Gonnella, Marcynyszyn, Gentile, & Salpekar, 2005). Research in the US shows that children in diverse racial and ethnic groups develop optimally in home environments characterized as stable, safe, and with parenting characterized as warm and responsive (Berlin, Brady-Smith, & Brooks-Gunn, 2002; Berlin and Cassidy, 2000). The potential stress of living in poverty can manifest itself through lack of maternal sensitivity, maternal depression, marital conflict, and maladaptive parenting styles, affecting developing infants.

Maternal sensitivity. One US study found maternal sensitivity to be negatively correlated with poverty during the first three years of life, with longer lengths of poverty being associated with lower maternal sensitivity (NIHCD, 2005). Lower maternal sensitivity was then associated with lower cognitive and language performance at age 5.

Maternal depression and marital conflict. Maternal depression[7] has been linked to increased marital conflict, and the negative effects for parental stress have been shown to be greater for infants living in poverty than for nonpoor infants (Petterson & Albers, 2001). Persistent poverty in the Petterson and Albers (2001) study of US mothers was associated with especially negative socioemotional effects for adolescent females. Similarly, other studies have also found economic stress to affect maternal depression, which is strongly related to adolescent socioemotional functioning in both rural and urban US settings (Conger, Wallace, Sun, Simons, McLoyd, & Brody, 2002; McLeod & Nonnemaker, 2000).

Studies of family economic loss in the US (Conger & Elder, 1994; Elder, 1999) have found that income loss leads to parental emotional distress, which results in marital conflict between parents as well as punitive parenting styles, particularly by fathers. Especially for boys, this change in family stress often resulted in the poor adjustment to adolescence and interpersonal relationships throughout adult life. Following mothers with children leaving welfare, Smith, Brooks-Gunn, Kohen, and McCarton (2001) found income loss to be linked to maternal depression. Similar to the previously discussed Costello et al. (2003) study, these natural experiments focused on older children but are included here as an effective research method, which might be implemented in future research on infants. Also useful to consider are the lifespan studies of Werner and Smith (1982) following high-risk families over half a century in the US state of Hawaii.

Family structure. Historically, unwed motherhood has also been seen as an added stress factor (Furstenberg, Brooks-Gunn, & Morgan, 1987). Across English-speaking developed countries, poor, unwed, adolescent mothers are more likely to live in poverty than older and married mothers, more likely to be mothers than nonpoor adolescents, and more likely to be unwed that adult mothers (Biterman & Börjeson, 2002; Carothers, Borkowski, & Whitman, 2006; Christopher, England, McLanahan, Ross, & Smeeding, 2001; Furstenberg et al., 1987; Plotnik, 2007). A thorough investigation of maternal parenting style found that these younger mothers were less likely to be supportive and more likely to be detached, intrusive and hostile toward their 14-month-old children than older mothers in the US (Berlin et al., 2002). Findings from Canada support this conclusion, with children from poor single-parent families being more likely to experience social impairment and lower math scores (Lipman, Boyle, Dooley & Offord, 1998).

However, a shift is underway across developed countries regarding the association with poverty and social acceptability of being born to unwed parents. Being born to unwed parents is still associated with poverty and negative child development in some countries (e.g., the US and New Zealand report births out of marriage to represent one third of all births, while this number has been established at 40% for the UK and France; Kamerman et al., 2003). In other EU countries, however, it is associated with neither and has become not only socially acceptable but the social norm (as is the case in Sweden, where 55% of births occur out of wedlock) and is not as strongly associated with child poverty (Kamerman et al., 2003).

Barber (2003) found rates of single parenthood to be positively correlated with a developed countries' gross national product. In these countries, increased female literacy is associated with increased likelihood of single motherhood, suggesting that educated women are more likely to be employed at an income level where single parenthood is feasible. For these more educated and better-paid women, there is a disincentive to be married and dependent on a partner. However, poor mothers who were required to return to work in the US do not reflect the same trend (Kaushal, Gao, & Waldfogel, 2007). While these women have an incentive to marry for their own and their children's financial security, they are more likely to live in areas with high male unemployment (reducing the incentive to be married).

Parenting style.   Research on infants from poor and nonpoor families has shown that infants in US samples from poor families did not experience continuity of attachment in contrast to nonpoor infants, and this, in turn, was associated with violent behavior at ages 5 and 7 and with lower attachment at age 19 (Gauthier, 2003; Weinfield, Whaley, & Egeland, 2004). Paternal absence and attachment withdrawal have also been associated with family stress and found to negatively impact family environment during prenatal and infant development (Cox & Paley, 2003; Paley, Cox, Kanoy, Harter, Burchinal, & Margand, 2005). These associations hold across time: parent mental health, marital distress, and parenting style have been more consistently associated with socioemotional outcomes than cognitive outcomes (Linver, Brooks-Gunn, & Kohen, 2002; Yeung et al., 2002). However, Linver et al. (2002) found that family stress factors (as manifested in parenting style) only account for 2% of the IQ difference in 3- and 5-year-old US children living in poverty. This effect size, though small, has been consistently found, leaving researchers and policy-makers to debate its social and political significance. School readiness, related to both socioemotional and cognitive development, has also been negatively connected with low parent support due to financial stress (Guo & Harris, 2000; Jackson, Brooks-Gunn, Huang, & Glassman, 2000). From an economic perspective, Heckman, Krueger, and Friedman (2003) and Heckman and Masterov (2004) have revealed that this is especially disconcerting as poor family environment has been associated with adult crime, illiteracy, and unemployment, with poor results for adult remediation interventions. More effective intervention designs would seek to address these negative developments during early childhood, during which time parenting style can be addressed.[8]

While much research supports the connections among poverty, family stress, and child development, it must be emphasized that family relationships can also serve as a buffer for the effects of poverty on child development. In those families that manage to provide support, guidance and nurturance in the face of poverty, children are found to experience fewer effects of poverty and are more likely to transition to adolescence and adulthood (Conger & Conger, 2002; Elder, 1999; Shonkoff & Phillips, 2000).

The investment model and the home environment

There is a direct connection between poverty and the level of financial investment parents can make in a child's life. These investments include materials, experiences, and services associated with providing children with a rich and stimulating environment in which to learn both cognitive and socioemotional skills. A meta-analysis of 63 studies of nonresident fathers in the US (Amato & Gilbreth, 1999) found stronger evidence for the positive effect of child support payments than father–child contact on both socioemotional and cognitive outcomes.

Investment in time.   For many families living in poverty, parents must spend time working that they might otherwise spend with their children. In the US, welfare reform has required mothers to be employed to receive continued welfare benefits, with maternal employment already on the rise before reform (Hernandez, 1997). Researchers have sought to understand the influence of maternal employment on child development with mixed results. A study of working European American mothers found that 3-year-olds whose mother worked 30 or more hours per week had lower school-readiness scores than other children, controlling for quality of childcare, quality of the home environment, and maternal sensitivity (Brooks-Gunn, Han, & Waldfogel, 2002). Results from other US studies, however, showed no effects on young children for mothers returning to work and leaving welfare and found improved mental health for mothers who found satisfaction in their work (Chase-Lansdale et al., 2003; Coley, Lohman, Votruba-Drzal, Pittman, & Chase-Lansdale, 2007).

Investment in the home environment.   Independent of parenting style, a stimulating and safe home environment is associated with both poverty and child outcomes (Dunifon, Duncan, & Brooks-Gunn, 2001). The most commonly used measure of the quality of the home environment in the US is the Home Observation for Measurement of the Environment (HOME). The HOME assessment tests availability of learning materials (e.g., books and puzzles), learning opportunities (e.g., trips to museums), the physical condition of the home (e.g., how cluttered, cramped, dirty, or unsafe it is), parental warmth, and family routine. In US samples, scores on this measure are consistently lower among families in poverty than those not in poverty (Mott, 2004; NIHCD, 2005). Another US study found home environment to be negatively correlated with poverty during the first three years of life, with longer lengths of poverty being associated with worse home environment (NIHCD, 2005). Further evidence of the relationship between income and home environment comes from studies showing that changes in family income level over time correspond to similar changes in home environment scores (Dearing et al., 2001; Korenman, Miller, & Sjaastad, 1995; Yeung et al., 2002).

During the first year of life, a combined measure of family risk (home environment and parent-reported family member health) has been found to be significantly associated with IQ and cognitive development (Burchinal, Vernon-Feagans, & Cox, 2008; Klebanov et al., 1998). Once again, the deficits that emerge during infancy appear to hold, if not increase, across childhood. At ages 3 and 5 findings from a US sample of low-birth-weight children found home environment to mediate the relationship between low income and child cognitive outcomes (Linver et al., 2002). Home environment during middle childhood has been associated with negative associations with both cognitive and socioemotional outcomes in the US (Votruba-Drzal, 2006). Similar results for socioemotional outcomes were found in a British cohort at age 7 (McCulloch, 2006). Home environment, like maternal sensitivity, served as a mediator for the association between poverty and cognitive and language outcomes at age 5.

Also using the HOME, Bradley, Corwyn, McAdoo, and Garcia Coll (2001) found that US children living in poverty are less likely to be taken by parents to enjoy enriching activities such as trips to a museum. Infants living in poverty are half as likely to be read to more than three times a week, and less likely to be taught about colors, shapes, sizes and letters. Exposure to stimulating toys and experiences positively influences child cognitive development well before children reach primary school. As these infants live in less safe, less clean, more cluttered, and darker homes than their nonpoor counterparts, their cognitive development is further stunted. The home environment has been calculated to account for 50% of the effect of poverty on young children's IQ scores and other cognitive outcomes when comparing children living in poverty and nonpoor children (Korenman et al., 1995; Linver et al., 2002; Yeung et al., 2002). While IQ measures are not typically used for infants, Coll et al. (1998) found consistent cognitive results for infants using the Bayley Scales of Infant Development.

Operating from a deficit model, a number of negative characteristics such as lack of central heating and septic system and the presence of cracks, holes, and leaks in family housing have been positively associated with families living in poverty (Evans, 2004; Mayer, 1997b). Taken together, these findings suggest that as wealth increases, families are better able to invest in a safe and enriching environment in which infants can develop.

Neighborhood- or community-level effects.   Expanding the scope of the family investment model, neighborhood characteristics, over and above individual- and family-level variables, also have a unique influence on child development. Neighborhood disadvantage has also been found to have an especially negative effect for single mothers in the US, who are more likely to manifest depression, which in turn negatively influences child socioemotional development (Ross, 2000). Further research using nested models of families in neighborhoods is needed to understand how mean neighborhood-level SES, above and beyond individual-level SES, is associated with infant development.

Current research using such techniques has focused on adolescents and children with regard to academic achievement in the US (Caldas & Bankston, 1997; Kohen, Brooks-

Gunn, Leventhal, & Hertzman, 2002) and England (McCulloch & Joshi, 2001, 2002); community physical resources (Leventhal & Brooks-Gunn, 2000; Sampson, Morenoff, & Gannon-Rowley, 2002); and physical activity and obesity in Australia (Timperio, Salmon, Telford, & Crawford, 2005).[9] These associations of neighborhood characteristics with income are particularly troubling considering the increase in neighborhood income inequality over the past three or four decades in the US, Canada, and Australia (Hunter, 2003). Such increasing disparities should further compel researchers to investigate neighborhood effects on infant development.

Conclusion: Policy Implications

In summary, poverty can be measured and studied in a number of ways. Regardless of method, poverty has been associated with negative child outcomes including physical, socioemotional, and cognitive development in developed countries. This is especially true if the poverty experienced is deep, persistent, and occurs early in a child's life. In addition, family and neighborhood characteristics are also useful in understanding how poverty affects child development. Family stress and parental investment are two such powerful pathways.

As previously discussed, European Union countries have addressed poverty with income supplements and welfare programs addressing specific needs such as healthcare and education (Kamerman et al., 2003; Oxley, Dang, Forster, & Pellizzari, 2001; Smeeding, 2005; Solera, 2001).[10] The high poverty rates and low government wealth redistribution rates in the US have resulted in much available data for research and designing interventions. Studies of interventions to alleviate the negative impact of poverty on children have shown that many have beneficial short- and long-term impacts on children, and are advantageous to society from a cost–benefit perspective, satisfying both economic and developmental interests (Heckman, 2007). Utilizing the European model of transferring income as well as services to families, one randomized, controlled US experiment offered job training and income transfer to a treatment group of poor families with children aged 2–9. The intervention resulted in improved school engagement and prosocial behavior for the children, as reported by mothers (Morris & Gennetian, 2003).

Positive effects of early childhood education also have been found in two US randomized controlled trials, reducing the effects of poverty at an early age and throughout childhood and into adulthood (Campbell, Pungello, Miller-Johnson, Burchinal, & Ramey, 2001; Schweinhart, Montie, Xiang, Barnett, Belfield, & Nores, 2005). These early childhood education programs, the Perry Preschool Project in Yipsilanti, Michigan, and the Abecedarian Study in North Carolina, provided high-quality settings with low child-to-adult ratios and stimulating toys and planned activities for a combined sample size of approximately 200 children aged 3 who have been followed thus far for 37 years and 18 years, respectively. In particular, the Abcedarian intervention began in the first year of life with high-quality care provided 8 hours per day, 5 days per week, and 50 weeks per year, with a 1 : 3 ratio of adults to infants (Campbell et al., 2001). Differences in cognition between treatment and nontreatment children were noted at age 3, and cognitive and academic outcomes differences remained even at age 21. Similar results were also found in the Perry Preschool Project (Campbell et al., 2001; Schweinhart et al., 2005). In addition, positive effects were found with mothers being able to return to work and with children's future criminal activity being greatly reduced. This last factor alone accounted for 8 : 1 investment returns, and the overall investment returns approached 13 : 1 (Committee on Ways and Means, 2000; Currie, 2006). Home visits have also shown to be effective when combined with center-based care for infants (Love et al., 2005).

Repeated meta-analyses of early childhood interventions have shown annual rates of overall return as high as 16% and rates of public return as high as 12% (Rolnick & Grunewald, 2003). From an economic perspective, investments in early childhood development are linked to improvements in educational outcomes, which have been associated with increased labor productivity (Schweke, 2004). Thus it can be argued that public investment in poor children benefits society at large and saves taxpayer outlays (Heckman, 2007). At the same time, even if educational programs and income transfers are made available to families and children living poverty, there is no guarantee that these services will be utilized (Leventhal, Brooks-Gunn, McCormick, & McCarton, 2000). Ever-changing program eligibility requirements, difficult application processes, and social stigma have all been offered as possibly explanations for this (Currie, 2006).

Without appropriate support and intervention strategies, it is likely that poor children will continue to lag behind their nonpoor peers. It is imperative that policy-makers attend to the extensive body of research literature emphasizing linkages between poverty and child development, as well as options for intervening in and enhancing the lives of poor children.

Notes

1. While it is not a country, the OECD has provided much descriptive research on poverty across its 30 member countries, with membership often being synonymous with being a developed country (OECD, 2005). The OECD includes: Australia, Austria, Belgium, Canada, Czech Republic, Denmark, Finland, France, Germany, Greece, Hungary, Iceland, Ireland, Italy, Japan, South Korea, Luxembourg, Mexico, the Netherlands, New Zealand, Norway, Poland, Portugal, Slovakia, Spain, Sweden, Switzerland, Turkey, the United Kingdom, and the United States.

2. However, the United Kingdom has increasingly used relative poverty measures in conjunction with other EU countries.

3. A newer deficit-based construct called "social exclusion" has recently become more commonly used in European research (Burchardt, Le Grand, & Pichaud, 2002; Roosa, Deng, Nair, & Lockhart-Burrell, 2005). This latent construct considers the level of participation individuals are unable to achieve in society, which is highly associated with financial poverty, food insecurity, material need, as well as social alienation.

4. Infants are not typically labeled as obese or overweight until after the age of 2 years, although this practice is beginning to shift (e.g., Kimbro, Brooks-Gunn, & McLanahan, 2007).

5. Across development countries, additional atypical childhood physical outcomes associated with poverty include reports of child abuse and neglect, infant mortality, obesity, teen preg-

nancy and parenting rates (Micklewright & Stewart, 2000). For a detailed discussion of child abuse and neglect, see also chapter 7 in this volume.

6. It is important to note that some scholars and policy-makers view school readiness as more than simply readiness to learn. It is believed that social and behavioral skills are also important in a child's ability to adapt to and thrive in the school environment so that learning can be maximized (Kagan & Rigby, 2003). For example, if a child is able to focus in class, develop proper rapport with fellow students and teachers, and cope with new stimuli and adverse situations, the child will be more likely to show gains in cognitive functioning compared with students with similar initial cognitive abilities but having fewer socioemotional and behavioral skills. Evidence for this perspective has been found with regard to socioemotional characteristics such as self-esteem, anxiety, antisocial behavior, and hyperactivity (Blanden, Gregg, & Macmillan, 2007). Data from two British cohorts (1958 and 1970) revealed that, combined with family income and cognitive abilities, these socioemotional characteristics predicted not only school achievement but also future earnings. In contrast to these findings, Duncan, Dowsett, et al. (2007) found that school-entry reading and math levels, along with attention skills, were the strongest predictors of future academic success, while socioemotional indicators were typically insignificant. These analyses included data from six cohorts across the US, Canada and one of the two British cohorts used by Blanden et al. (2007).

7. For a review of postnatal depression, a major type of maternal depression, see chapter 8 in this volume.

8. The influence of family stress on children has also been framed from the perspective of parent–child attachment, with negative measures including arbitrary and harsh discipline and emotional detachment. These indicators have been associated with poverty and with negative effects on child well-being and development (Shonkoff & Phillips, 2000). For a review of parent–child attachment, a major aspect of socioemotional development, see chapter 16 in volume 1.

9. Neighborhood effects on child abuse against infants are discussed in chapter 7 in this volume.

10. These income transfers do not entirely eliminate the effects of child poverty, however, and additional programs and interventions have been called for to address these deficits (Bradbury & Jäntti, 2001).

References

Aber, J. L., & Ellwood, D. (2001). Thinking about children in time. In B. Bradbury, S. P. Jenkins, & J. Micklewright (Eds.), *The dynamics of child poverty in industrialized countries* (pp. 281–300). Cambridge: Cambridge University Press.

Acemoglu, D., & Pischke, J. S. (2001). Changes in the wage structure, family income and children's education. *European Economic Review, 45*, 890–904.

Amato, P. R., & Gilbreth, J. G. (1999). Non-resident fathers and children's well-being: A meta-analysis. *Journal of Marriage and the Family, 61*(3), 557–573.

Banks, J., Blundell, R., & Smith, J. P. (2003). Understanding differences in household financial wealth between the United States and Great Britain. *Journal of Human Resources, 38*(2), 241–279.

Barber, N. (2003). Paternal investment prospects and cross-national differences in single parenthood. *Cross-Cultural Research, 37*(2), 163–177.

Baron, R. M., & Kenny, D. A. (1986). The moderator-mediator variable distinction in social psychological research: Conceptual, strategic, and statistical considerations. *Journal of Personality and Social Psychology, 51*(6), 1173–1882.

Berlin, L. J., Brady-Smith, C., & Brooks-Gunn, J. (2002). Links between child-bearing age and observed maternal behaviors with 14-month-olds in the Early Head Start Research and Evaluation Project. *Infant's Mental Health Journal, 23*(1–2), 104–129.

Berlin, L. J., & Cassidy, J. (2000). Understanding parenting: Contributions of attachment theory and research. In J. Osofsky & H. E. Fitzgerald (Eds.), *The World Alliance for Infant Mental Health handbook of infant mental health, Vol. 3: Parenting and child care* (pp. 133–170). New York: John Wiley & Sons, Inc.

Biterman, D., & Börjeson, M. (Eds.). (2002). Social report 2001: The national report on social conditions in Sweden. *International Journal of Social Welfare, 11*(Special Supplement).

Blanden, J., & Gregg, P. (2004). Family income and educational attainment: A review of approaches and evidence for Britain. *Oxford Review of Economic Policy, 20*(2), 245–263.

Blanden, J., Gregg, P., & Macmillan, L. (2007). Accounting for intergenerational income persistence: Noncognitive skills, ability and education. *Economic Journal, 117*, C3–C60.

Borders, A. E. B., Grobman, W. A., Amsden, L. B., & Holl, J. L. (2007). Chronic stress and low birth weight neonates in a low income population of women. *Obstetrics & Gynecology, 109*, 331–338.

Bradbury, B., & Jäntti, M. (2001). Child poverty across the industrialized world: Evidence from the Luxembourg Income Study. In K. Vleminckx & T. Smeeding (Eds.), *Child well-being, child poverty, and child policy in modern nations: What do we know?* (pp. 11–32). Bristol: Policy Press.

Bradbury, B., Jenkins, S. P., & Micklewright, J. (Eds.). (2001). *The dynamics of child poverty in industrialized countries.* Cambridge: Cambridge University Press.

Bradley, R. H., & Corwyn, R. F. (2002). Socioeconomic status and child development. *Annual Review of Psychology, 53*, 371–399.

Bradley, R. H., Corwyn, R. F., McAdoo, H. P., & Garcia Coll, C. T. (2001). The home environments of children in the United States part I: Variations by age, ethnicity, and poverty status. *Child Development, 72*(6), 1844–1867.

Brandolini, A., Cannari, L., D'Alessio, G., & Faiella, I. (2004). *Household wealth distribution in Italy in the 1990s.* Economic Working Papers. Rome: Bank of Italy.

Bronfenbrenner, U. (1979). *The ecology of human development.* Cambridge, MA: Harvard University Press.

Brooks-Gunn, J., Berlin, L. J., Leventhal, T., & Fuligni, A. S. (2000). Depending on the kindness of strangers: Current national data initiatives and developmental research. *Child Development, 71*(1), 257–268.

Brooks-Gunn, J., Duncan, G., & Maritato, N. (1997). Poor families, poor outcomes: The well-being of children and youth. In G. J. Duncan & J. Brooks-Gunn (Eds.), *Consequences of growing up poor* (pp. 1–17). New York: Russell Sage Foundation.

Brooks-Gunn, J., Han, W. J., & Waldfogel, J. (2002). Maternal employment and child cognitive outcomes in the first three years of life: The NICHD Study of Early Child Care. *Child Development, 73*(4), 1052–1072.

Browning, C., & Cagney, K. A. (2003). Neighborhood structural disadvantage, collective efficacy, and self-rated physical health in an urban setting. *Journal of Health and Social Behavior, 43*, 383–399.

Buchel, F., Frick, J. R., Krause, P., & Wagner, G. G. (2001). The impact of poverty on children's school attendance: Evidence from West Germany. In K. Vleminckx & T. Smeeding (Eds.), *Child well-being, child poverty, and child policy in modern nations: What do we know?* (pp. 151–173). Bristol: Policy Press.

Burchardt, T., Le Grand, J., & Pichaud, D. (2002). Degrees of exclusion: Developing a multidimensional, dynamic measure. In J. Hills, J. Le Grand, & D. Pichaud (Eds.), *Understanding social exclusion* (pp. 30–43). New York: Oxford University Press.

Burchinal, M., Vernon-Feagans, L., & Cox, M. (2008). Cumulative social risk, parenting, and infant development in rural low-income communities. *Parenting: Science & Practice, 8*(1), 41–69.

Byck, G. R. (2000). A comparison of the socioeconomic and health status characteristics of uninsured States Children's Health Insurance Program-eligible children in the United States with those of other groups of insured children: Implications for policy. *Pediatrics, 106*(1), 14–21.

Caldas, S. J., & Bankston III, C. (1997). Effects of school population socioeconomic status on individual academic achievement. *Journal of Educational Research, 90*(5), 269–277.

Campbell, F. A., Pungello, E. P., Miller-Johnson, S., Burchinal, M., & Ramey, C. T. (2001).The development of cognitive and academic abilities: Growth curves from an early childhood educational experiment. *Developmental Psychology, 37*(2), 231–242.

Carothers, S. S., Borkowski, J. G., & Whitman, T. L. (2006). Children of adolescent mothers: Exposure to negative life events and the role of social supports on their socioemotional adjustment. *Journal of Youth and Adolescence, 35*(5), 827–837.

Chase-Lansdale, P. L., Moffitt, R. A., Lohman, B. J., Cherlin, A. J., Coley, R. L., Pittman, L. D., et al. (2003). Mothers' transition from welfare to work and the well-being of preschoolers and adolescents. *Science, 299*(5612), 1548–1552.

Christopher, K., England, P., McLanahan, S., Ross, K., & Smeeding, T. M. (2001). In K. Vleminckx & T. Smeeding (Eds.), *Child well-being, child poverty, and child policy in modern nations: What do we know?* (pp. 199–220). Bristol: Policy Press.

Coley, R. L., Lohman, B. J., Votruba-Drzal, E., Pittman, L. D., & Chase-Lansdale, P. L. (2007). Maternal functioning, time and money: The world of work and welfare. *Child and Youth Services Review, 29*(6), 721–741.

Coll, C. G., Buckner, J. C., Brooks, M. G., Weinreb, L. F., & Bassuk, E. L. (1998). The developmental status and adaptive behavior of homeless and low-income housed infants and toddlers. *American Journal of Public Health, 88*(9), 1371–1373.

Committee on Ways and Means, United States House of Representatives. (2000). *The 2000 Green Book*. Washington, DC: US Government Accounting Office.

Conger, R. D., & Conger, K. J. (2002). Resilience in Midwestern families: Selected finings from the first decade of a prospective longitudinal study. *Journal of Marriage and Family, 64*(2), 361–373.

Conger, R. D., & Elder, G. H. (1994). *Families in troubled times: Adapting to change in rural America*. New York: Aldine de Gruyter.

Conger, R. D., Wallace, K. E., Sun, Y., Simons, R. L., McLoyd, V. C. C., & Brody, G. H. (2002). Economic pressure in African American families: A replication and extension of the family stress model. *Developmental Psychology, 38*(2), 179–193.

Cook, J. T., Frank, D. A., Berkowitz, C., Black, M. M., Casey, P. H., Cutts, D. B., et al. (2004). Food insecurity is associated with adverse health outcomes among human infants and toddlers. *Journal of Nutrition, 134*, 1432–1438.

Costello, E. J., Compton, S. N., Keeler, G., & Angold, A. (2003). Relationships between poverty and psychopathology: A natural experiment. *Journal of the American Medical Association, 290*(15), 2023–2029.

Cox, M. J., & Paley, B. (2003). Understanding families as systems. *Current Directions in Psychological Science, 12*(5), 193–196.

Currie, J. M. (2006). *The invisible safety net*. Princeton, NJ: Princeton University Press.

Dearing, E., McCartney, K., & Taylor, B. A. (2001). Change in family income-to-needs matters more for children with less. *Child Development, 72*(6), 1779–1793.

Dodge, K. A. (2006). Translational science in action: Hostile attributional style and the development of aggressive behavior problems. *Development and Psychopathology, 18*, 791–814.

Duncan, G. J., & Brooks-Gunn, J. (Eds.). (1997). *Consequences of growing up poor*. New York: Russell Sage Foundation Press.

Duncan, G. J., Dowsett, C. J., Claessens, A., Magnuson, K., Huston, A. C., Klebanov, P., et al. (2007). School readiness and later achievement. *Developmental Psychology, 43*(6), 1428–1446.

Duncan, G. J., Ludwig, J., & Magnuson, K. A. (2007). Reducing poverty through preschool interventions. *Future of Children, 17*(2), 143–160.

Duncan, G. J., Yeung, W. J., Brooks-Gunn, J., & Smith, J. R. (1998). How much does childhood poverty affect the life chances of children? *American Sociological Review, 63*(3), 406–423.

Dunifon, R., Duncan, G. J., & Brooks-Gunn, J. (2001). As ye sweep, so shall ye reap. *American Economic Review, 91*(2), 150–154.

Elder, G. H. (1999). *Children of the Great Depression: Social change of life experience* (25th anniversary ed.). Chicago: University of Chicago Press.

Ensminger, M. E., & Fothergill, K. E. (2003). A decade of measuring SES: What it tells us and where to go from here. In M. H. Bornstein & R. H. Bradley (Eds.), *Socioeconomic status, parenting, and child development* (pp. 13–27). Mahwah, NJ: Lawrence Erlbaum Associates.

Evans, G. W. (2004). The environment of childhood poverty. *American Psychology, 59*(2), 77–92.

Evans, G. W., & English, K. (2002). The environment of poverty: Multiple stressor exposure, psychophysiological stress, and socioemotional adjustment. *Child Development, 73*(4), 1238–1248.

Evans, G. W., Gonnella, C., Marcynyszyn, L. A., Gentile, L., & Salpekar, N. (2005). The role of chaos in poverty and children's socioemotional adjustment. *Psychological Science, 16*(7), 560–565.

Fergusson, D. M., & Woodward, L. J. (2000). Family socioeconomic status at birth and rates of university participation. *New Zealand Journal of Educational Studies, 35*(1), 25–36.

Fox, M. K., & Cole, N. (2004, December). *Nutrition and health characteristics of low-income populations: Volume I, Food Stamp Program participants and nonparticipants* (USDA ERS Publication No. E-FAN-04–014–1). Washington, DC: US Government Printing Office.

Furstenberg, F. J., Brooks-Gunn, J., & Morgan, S. P. (1987). *Adolescent mothers in later life*. New York: Cambridge University Press.

Gauthier, Y. (2003). Infant mental health as we enter the third millennium: Can we prevent aggression? *Infant Mental Health Journal, 24*(3), 296–308.

Gibson, D. (2006). Long-term Food Stamp Program participation is positively related to simultaneous overweight in young daughters and obesity in mothers. *Journal of Nutrition, 136*(4), 1081–1085.

Grantham-McGregor, S., & Ani, C. (2001). A review of studies on the effect of iron deficiency on cognitive development in children. *Journal of Nutrition, 131*(2S-2), 649S–666S.

Guo, G., & Harris, K. M. (2000). The mechanisms mediating the effects of poverty on children's intellectual development. *Demography, 37*(4), 431–447.

Heckman, J. J. (2006). Skill formation and the economics of investing in disadvantaged children. *Science, 312*(578), 1900–1902.

Heckman, J. J. (2007). The economics, technology, and neuroscience of human capability formation. *Proceedings of the National Academy of Science, 104*(33), 13250–13255.

Heckman, J. J., Krueger, A. B., & Friedman, B. (2003). *Inequality in America: What role for human capital policies?* Cambridge, MA: MIT Press.

Heckman, J. J., & Masterov, D. V. (2004). *The productivity argument for investing in young children* (Working Paper #5). Washington, DC: Committee on Economic Development.

Heclo, H. (1994). Poverty politics. In S. H. Danziger, G. D. Sandefur, and D. H. Weinberg (Eds.), *Confronting poverty: Prescriptions for change* (pp. 396–437). Cambridge, MA: Harvard University Press.

Hernandez, D. (1997). Poverty trends. In G. J. Duncan & J. Brooks-Gunn (Eds.), *Consequences of growing up poor* (pp. 18–34). New York: Russell Sage Foundation.

Hobcraft, J., & Kiernan, K. (2001). Childhood poverty, early motherhood and adult social exclusion. *British Journal of Sociology, 52*(3), 495–517.

Hong, K. Z., & Song, H. K. (2006). Continuity and change in the Korean welfare system. *Journal of Social Policy, 35*, 247–265.

Human Resources Development Canada (2000). *What Canadians are telling us about the National Children's Agenda.* Ottawa: HRDC.

Hunter, B. (2003). Trends in neighbourhood inequality of Australian, Canadian and United States of America cities since the 1970s. *Australian Economic History Review, 43*(1), 22–44.

Hurtado, E. K., Claussen, A. H., & Scott, K. G. (1999). Early childhood anemia and mild or moderate mental retardation. *American Journal of Clinical Nutrition, 69*(1), 115–119.

Iceland, J. (2005). Measuring poverty: Theoretical and empirical consideration. *Measurement: Interdisciplinary Research and Perspectives, 3*(4), 199–235.

Jackson, A. P., Brooks-Gunn, J., Huang, C. C., & Glassman, M. (2000). Single mothers in low-wage jobs: Financial strain, parenting, and preschoolers' outcomes. *Child Development, 71*(5), 1409–1423.

Kagan, S. L., & Rigby, E. (2003). *Policy matters: Setting and measuring benchmarks for state policies.* Washington, DC: Center for the Study of Social Policy.

Kahn, A. J., & Kamerman, S. B. (Eds.) (2002). *Beyond child poverty: The social exclusion of children.* New York: Institute for Child and Family Policy, Columbia University.

Kamerman, S. B., Neuman, M., Waldfogel, J., & Brooks-Gunn, J. (2003). *Social policies, family types, and child outcomes in selected OECD countries.* OECD Social, Employment and Migration Working Papers, No. 6. Paris: OECD.

Kaushal, N., Gao, Q., & Waldfogel, J. (2007). Welfare reform and family expenditures: How are single mothers adapting to the new welfare and work regime? *Social Service Review, 81*(3), 369–396.

Kimbro, R. T., Brooks-Gunn, J., & McLanahan, S. (2007). Racial and ethnic differentials in overweight and obesity among 3-year-old-children. *American Journal of Public Health, 97*, 298–305.

Klebanov, P. K., Brooks-Gunn, J., McCarton, C., & McCormick, M. C. (1998). The contribution of neighborhood and family income to developmental test scores over the first three years of life. *Child Development, 69*(5), 1420–1436.

Kohen, D., Brooks-Gunn, J., Leventhal, T., & Hertzman, C. (2002). Neighborhood income and physical and social disorder in Canada: Associations with young children's competencies. *Child Development, 73*(6), 1844–1860.

Korenman, S., & Miller, J. E. (1997). Effects of long-term poverty on physical health of children in the National Longitudinal Survey of Youth. In G. J. Duncan & J. Brooks-Gunn (Eds.), *Consequences of growing up poor* (pp. 70–99). New York: Russell Sage Foundation.

Korenman, S., Miller, J. E., & Sjasstad, J. E. (1995). Long-term poverty and child development in the United States: Results from the NLSY. *Children and Youth Services Review, 17*(1), 127–155.

Laub, J. H., & Sampson, R. J. (2001). Understanding desistance from crime. *Crime and Justice, 28*, 1–69.

Leventhal, T., & Brooks-Gunn, J. (2000). The neighborhoods they live in: The effects of neighborhood residence on child and adolescent outcomes. *Psychological Bulletin, 126*(2), 309–37.

Leventhal, T., & Brooks-Gunn, J. (2002). Poverty and child development. In N. J. Smelser & P. B. Baltes (Eds.), *The International Encyclopedia of the Social and Behavioral Sciences*, Vol. *17* (pp. 11889–11894). Amsterdam: Elsevier.

Leventhal, T., Brooks-Gunn, J., McCormick, M. C., & McCarton, C. M. (2000). Patterns of service use in preschool children: Correlates, consequences, and the role of early intervention. *Child Development, 71*(3), 802–819.

Linver, M. R., Brooks-Gunn, J., & Kohen, D. E. (2002). Family processes as pathways from income to young children's development. *Developmental Psychology, 38*(5), 719–734.

Lipman, E. L., Boyle, M., Dooley, M., & Offord, D. (1998). *What about children in lone mother families?* Paper presented at the conference on Investing in Children, Ottawa.

Looker, A. C., Cogswell, M. E., & Gunter, E. W. (2002). Iron deficiency – United States, 1999–2000. *Morbidity and Mortality Weekly Report, 51*(40), 897–899.

Love, J. M., Kisker, E. E., Ross, C., Raikes, H., Constantine, J., Boller, K., et al. (2005). The effectiveness of Early Head Start for 3-year-old children and their parents: Lessons for policy and programs. *Developmental Psychology, 41*(6), 885–901.

Luthar, S. (Ed.). (2003). *Resilience and vulnerability: Adaptation in the context of childhood adversities*. New York: Cambridge University Press.

Mabughi, N., & Selim, T. (2006). Poverty as social deprivation: A survey. *Review of Social Economy, 64*(2), 181–204.

Male, C., Persson, L. A., Freeman, V., Guerra, A. van't Hof, M. A., & Haschke, F. (2001). Prevalence of iron deficiency in 12-mo-old infants from 11 European areas and influence of dietary factors on iron status (Euro-Growth study). *Acta Paediatrica, 90*(5), 492–498.

Maurin, E. (2002). The impact of parental income on early schooling transitions: A re-examination using data over three generations. *Journal of Public Economics, 85*, 301–332.

Mayer, S. E. (1997a). *What money can't buy: Family income and children's life chances*. Cambridge, MA: Harvard University Press.

Mayer, S. E. (1997b). Trends in the economic well being and life chances of America's children. In G. J. Duncan & J. Brooks-Gunn (Eds.), *Consequences of growing up poor* (pp. 62–63). New York: Russell Sage Foundation.

McCulloch, A. (2006). Variation in children's cognitive and behavioural adjustment between different types of place in the British National Child Development Study. *Social Science and Medicine, 62*(8), 1865–1879.

McCulloch, A., & Joshi, H. E. (2001). Neighbourhood and family influences on the cognitive ability of children in the British National Child Development Study. *Social Science & Medicine, 53*(5), 579–591.

McCulloch, A., & Joshi, H. E. (2002). Child development and family resources: Evidence from the second generation of the 1958 British birth cohort. *Journal of Population Economics, 15*, 283–304.

McLanahan, S. (1997). Parent absence or poverty: Which matters more? In G. J. Duncan & J. Brooks-Gunn (Eds.), *Consequences of growing up poor* (pp. 35–48). New York: Russell Sage Foundation.

McLanahan, S. (2004). Diverging destinies: How children are faring under the second demographic transition. *Demography, 41*(4), 607–627.

McLeod, J. D., & Nonnemaker, J. M. (2000). Poverty and child emotional and behavioral problems: Racial/ethnic differences in processes and effects. *Journal of Health and Social Behavior, 41*(2), 137–161.

Mejer, L., & Linden, G. (2000). Persistent income poverty and social exclusion in the European Union. *Statistics in Focus*. Luxembourg: Eurostat.

Mejer, L., & Siermann, C. (2000). Income poverty in the European Union: Children, gender and poverty gaps. *Statistics in Focus, Population and Social Conditions*, Theme 3. Luxembourg : Eurostat.

Micklewright, J., & Stewart, K. (2000). *The welfare of Europe's children: Are EU member states converging?* Bristol: Policy Press.

Morenoff, J. D., Sampson, R. J., & Raudenbush, S. W. (2001). Neighborhood inequality, collective efficacy, and the spatial dynamics of urban violence. *Criminology, 39*(3), 517–559.

Morris, P. A., & Gennetian, L. A. (2003). Identifying the effects of income on children's development using experimental data. *Journal of Marriage and the Family, 65*(3), 716–729.

Mott, F. L. (2004). The utility of the HOME-SF scale for child development research in a large national longitudinal survey: The National Longitudinal Survey of Youth 1979 cohort. *Parenting: Science and Practice, 4*(2–3), 259–270.

National Institute of Child Health and Human Development Early Child Care Research Network (NIHCD) (2005). Duration and developmental timing of poverty and children's cognitive and social development from birth through third grade. *Child Development, 76*(4), 795–810.

National Scientific Council of the Developing Child (2005). *Excessive stress disrupts the architecture of the developing brain* (Working Paper #3). http://www.developingchild.net/pubs/wp/Stress_Disrupts_Architecture_Developing_Brain.pdf (accessed March 2008).

Neault, N. B., Frank, D. A., Merewood, A., Philipp, B., Levenson, S., Cook, J. T., et al. (2007). Breastfeeding and health outcomes among citizen infants of immigrant mothers. *Journal of the American Dietetic Association, 107*(12), 2077–2086.

Nelson, C. A. (2000). Neural plasticity and human development. *Developmental Science, 3*(2), 115–136.

Organization for Economic Co-operation and Development (1998). *The future of food: Long term prospects for the agro-food sector*. Paris: OECD Publications.

Organization for Economic Co-operation and Development (1999a). *Early childhood education and care: Norway background report and country note*. Paris: OECD Publications.

Organization for Economic Co-operation and Development (1999b). *Early childhood education and care: Sweden background report and country note*. Paris: OECD Publications.

Organization for Economic Co-operation and Development (2002). *1980–1998: Twenty years of social expenditures*. Paris: OECD Publications.

Organization for Economic Co-operation and Development (2005). *Making poverty reduction work*. Paris: OECD Publications.

Oxley, H., Dang, T. T., Forster, M. F., & Pellizzari, M. (2001). Income inequalities and poverty among children and households with children in select OECD countries. In K. Vleminckx & T. Smeeding (Eds.), *Child well-being, child poverty, and child policy in modern nations: What do we know?* (pp. 371–406). Bristol: Policy Press.

Paley, B., Cox, M. J., Kanoy, K. W., Harter, K. S. M., Burchinal, M., & Margand, N. A. (2005). Adult attachment and marital interaction as predictors of whole family interactions during the transition to parenthood. *Journal of Family Psychology, 19*(3), 420–429.

Petterson, S. M., & Albers, A. B. (2001). Effects of poverty and maternal depression on early child development. *Child Development, 72*(6), 1794–1813.

Phipps, S. (1999). *An international comparison of policies and outcomes for young children*, Canadian Policy Research Network study no. F 05. Ottawa: Renouf Publishers.

Pickett, K. E., & Wilkinson, R. G. (2007). Child wellbeing and income inequality in rich societies: Ecological cross sectional study. *British Medical Journal, 335*(7629), 1080–1086.

Plotnik, R. D. (2007). Adolescent expectations and desires about marriage and parenthood. *Journal of Adolescence, 30*(6), 943–963.

Proctor, B. D., & Dalaker, J. (2002). *Poverty in the United States: 2001.* U.S. Census Bureau, Current Population Reports, P60219. Washington, DC: US Government Printing Office.

Rainwater, L., Smeeding, T. M., & Coder, J. (2001). Poverty across states, nations, and continents. In K. Vleminckx & T. Smeeding (Eds.), *Child well-being, child poverty, and child policy in modern nations: What do we know?* (pp. 33–74). Bristol: Policy Press.

Rolnick, A., & Grunewald, R. (2003). Early childhood development: Economic development with a high public return. *FedGazette*, March.

Roosa, M. W., Deng, S., Nair, R. L., & Lockhart-Burrell, G. (2005). Measures for studying poverty in family and child research. *Journal of Marriage and Family, 67*(4), 971–988.

Rose, D. (2007). Food stamps, the Thrifty Food Plan, and meal preparation: The importance of the time dimension for US nutrition policy. *Journal of Nutrition Education and Behavior, 39*(4), 226–232.

Ross, C. E. (2000). Neighborhood disadvantage and adult depression. *Journal of Health and Social Behavior, 41*(2), 177–187.

Rouse, C. E., Brooks-Gunn, J., & McLanahan, S. (2005). Introducing the issue. In C. E. Rouse, J. Brooks-Gunn, & S. McLanahan (Eds.), School readiness: Closing racial and ethnic gaps. *Future of Children, 15*(1), 5–14.

Sampson, R. J., Morenoff, J. D., & Gannon-Rowley, T. (2002). Assessing neighbourhood effects: Social processes and new directions in research. *Annual Review of Sociology, 28*, 443–478.

Sanson, A., Nicholson, J., Ungerer, J., Zubrick, S., Wilson, K., Ainley, J., et al. (2002). *Introducing the Longitudinal Study of Australian Children*, LSAC Discussion Paper No. 1. Melbourne: Australian Institute of Family Studies.

Schulter, C. (2001). Child poverty in Germany: Trends and persistence. In B. Bradbury, S. P. Jenkins, & J. Mickewright (Eds.), *The dynamics of child poverty in industrialized countries.* Cambridge: Cambridge University Press.

Schweinhart, L. J., Montie, J., Xiang, Z., Barnett, W. S., Belfield, C. R., & Nores, M. (2005). *Lifetime effects: The High/Scope Perry Preschool study through age 40* (Monographs of the High/Scope Educational Research Foundation, 14). Ypsilanti, MI: High/Scope Press.

Schweke, W. (2004). *Smart money: Education and economic development.* Washington, DC: Economic Policy Institute.

Shonkoff, J. P., & Phillips, D. A. (Eds.). (2000). *From neurons to neighborhoods: The science of early child development.* Washington, DC: National Academy of Sciences.

Smeeding, T. M. (2005). Public policy, economic inequality, and poverty: The United States in comparative perspective. *Social Science Quarterly, 86*(5), 955–983.

Smith, J. R., Brooks-Gunn, J., & Klebanov, P. (1997). Consequences of living in poverty for young children's cognitive and verbal ability and early school achievement. In G. J. Duncan & J. Brooks-Gunn (Eds.), *Consequences of growing up poor* (pp. 132–189). New York: Russell Sage Foundation.

Smith, J. R., Brooks-Gunn, J., Kohen, D., & McCarton, C. (2001). Transitions on and off AFDC: Implications for parenting and children's cognitive development. *Child Development, 72*(5), 1512–1533.

Solera, C. (2001). Income transfers and support for mothers' employment: The link to family poverty risks. In K. Vleminckx & T. Smeeding (Eds.), *Child well-being, child poverty, and child policy in modern nations: What do we know?* (pp. 459–484). Bristol: Policy Press.

Song, Y., & Yu, S. (2002). *Early childhood poverty: A statistical profile.* New York: National Center for Children in Poverty.

Tachibanaki, T. (2006). Inequality and poverty in Japan. *Japanese Economic Review, 57*(1), 1–27.

Taylor, B. A., Dearing, E., & McCartney, K. (2004). Income and outcomes in early childhood. *Journal of Human Resources, 39*(4), 980–1007.

Timperio, A., Salmon, J., Telford, A., & Crawford, D. (2005). Perceptions of local neighbourhood environments and their relationship to childhood overweight and obesity. *International Journal of Obesity and Related Metabolic Disorders, 29*(2),170–175.

Tremblay, R. E., Nagin, D. S., Séguin, J. R., Zoccolillo, M., Zelazo, P. D., Boivin, M., et al. (2004). Physical aggression during early childhood: Trajectories and predictors. *Pediatrics, 114*(1), e43–e50.

United States Census Bureau, Housing and Household Economic Statistics Division. (2008). *Poverty Thresholds 2007*. http://www.census.gov/hhes/www/poverty/threshld/thresh07.html (accessed March 2008).

Vleminckx, K., & Smeeding, T. (Eds.). (2001). *Child well-being, child poverty and child policy in modern nations: What do we know?* Bristol: Policy Press.

Votruba-Drzal, E. (2006). Economic disparities in middle childhood development: Does income matter? *Developmental Psychology, 42*(6), 1154–1167.

Wake, M., Hardy, P., Canterford, L., Sawyer, M., & Carlin, J. B. (2006). Overweight, obesity and girth of Australian preschoolers: Prevalence and socioeconomic correlates. *International Journal of Obesity, 31*, 1044–1051.

Walberg, H. J., Strykowski, B. F., Rovai, E., & Hung, S. S. (1984). Exceptional performers. *Review of Educational Research, 54*(1), 87–112.

Waldfogel, J. (2002). Research on poverty and anti-poverty policies. In S. Danziger & R. Haveman (Eds.), *Understanding poverty*. Cambridge, MA: Harvard University Press.

Weinfield, N. S., Whaley, G. J. L., & Egeland, B. (2004). Continuity, discontinuity, and coherence in attachment from infancy to late adolescence: Sequelae of organization and disorganization. *Attachment & Human Development, 6*(1), 73–97.

Werner, E. E., & Smith, R. S. (1982). *Vulnerable but invincible: A longitudinal study of resilient children and youth*. New York: Adams, Bannister & Cox.

Wilson, J. Q., & Kelling, G. L. (1989). Making neighborhoods safe: Sometimes "fixing broken windows" does more to reduce crime than conventional "incident-oriented" policing. *Atlantic Monthly, 256*(2), 46–52.

Xue, Y., Leventhal, T., Brooks-Gunn, J., & Earls, F. J. (2005). Neighborhood residence and mental health problems of 5 to 11-year olds. *Archives of General Psychiatry, 62*, 554–563.

Yeung, W. J., Linver, M. R., & Brooks-Gunn, J. (2002). How money matters for young children's development: Parental investment and family processes. *Child Development, 73*(6), 1861–1879.

Zubieta, A. C., Melgar-Quinonez, H., & Taylor, C. (2006). Breastfeeding practices in U.S. households by food security status. *Journal of the Federation of American Societies for Experimental Biology, 20*(5), A1004–A1005.

6

Infant Development in the Developing World

Patrice Engle

The evidence for the importance of the first two to three years of life for a child's cognitive, motor, social, and emotional development is widely recognized (Shonkoff & Phillips, 2000). So too are the major risk factors facing a child during these critical years, ranging from the most proximal (e.g., nonresponsive parenting, unsafe environment, abuse or neglect) to the more distal (low level of education of parents, housing conditions, poverty, lack of services, etc.). However, these are risks facing children in the US, where less than 3% of the world's children live. An additional 8% of children live in the rest of the industrialized countries (UNICEF, 2006b). This chapter describes the conditions of the remaining 89% of the world's infants, the risks they face, the effects on their development, and possible interventions.

The chapter first discusses the economic categorization of developing countries. After a discussion of the developmental needs of infants and young children, the chapter then examines the risks that infants and young children face in developing countries, including both biological and social risks. Finally, the chapter integrates human rights considerations and the existing knowledge base and makes recommendations for program and policy options for the improved development of young children.

Economic and Noneconomic Characteristics of Developing Countries

In order to examine risks in the development of infants and young children, four different kinds of comparison are made. Many studies compare countries differing broadly by income and poverty level. Others compare economically similar countries that differ on child-rearing values and attitudes. A third group uses comparisons within a country, such as rural versus urban, which captures many environmental factors as well as the attitudes and beliefs of caregivers (Bornstein et al., 2008) related to the caregiving context. Finally, studies compare ethnic groups or economic groups within countries or types of country. The overall question is to determine risks and interventions in globally representative populations.

Economic comparisons between industrialized and developing countries

UNICEF divides the 192 UN countries into industrialized and developing countries. The 39 industrialized countries include Europe, the US, Canada, Australia, New Zealand, and Japan. The developing countries cover a wide range, including many of fairly high income, such as South Korea, Barbados, and the United Arab Emirates, as well as very low-income countries, such as Afghanistan and Guinea. The UN further defines a subset of 52 least developed countries, mainly from sub-Saharan Africa and South Asia (UNICEF, 2006b).

The World Bank's main criterion for classifying economies is gross national income (GNI) per capita (previously gross national product). Based on its GNI per capita, every economy is classified as low income, middle income (subdivided into lower middle and upper middle), or high income. Specifically, countries are classified as: low income, $935 or less; lower middle income, $936–$3,705; upper middle income, $3,706–$11,455; and high income, $11,456 or more. There is a close overlap between the UN-defined "least developed countries" and the 43 World Bank low-income countries. Many, but by no means all, of these countries are in sub-Saharan Africa. Countries in each category can be found on the World Bank website (www.worldbank.org).

The term "developing" country has problems. The World Bank notes that:

> Low-income and middle-income economies are sometimes referred to as developing economies. The use of the term is convenient; it is not intended to imply that all economies in the group are experiencing similar development or that other economies have reached a preferred or final stage of development. Classification by income does not necessarily reflect development status. (www.worldbank.org)

This chapter will use the terms "industrialized" and "developing" countries following the World Bank and UNICEF.

Noneconomic comparisons

In the 1960s, there was a clear demarcation between industrialized and developing countries on almost all measures of children's well-being, but this has changed. Some countries have developed quickly, whereas others have progressed more slowly or gone backward. This can be illustrated by the most widely used and most salient indicator of child well-being: the under-5 mortality rate, or the number of children who die before the age of 5 per thousand births. In 1970, the average rate for industrialized countries was 27 deaths per 1,000 births, compared to 167 for developing countries, a ratio of 6 to 1 (UNICEF, 2006b). By 2004, the ratio was 14 to 1, with a rate of 87 for all developing countries and 6 for industrialized countries. Progress was made in both areas, but the developing countries improved more slowly. But these differences mask wide individual differences by region and country. The largest reductions have been in the Middle East and North Africa, East Asia, and Latin America, all above a 70% change, whereas in sub-Saharan Africa the changes have been modest at best, perhaps a 30% reduction in under-5 mortality.

The small reduction has been due in large part to the AIDS pandemic which has reversed gains made in previous years (UNICEF, 2006a), and there is considerable variation among countries depending on the percentage of mothers who are HIV+. For example, in Zimbabwe, there was a 61% increase in child mortality from 1990 to 2004, and in Botswana, one of the hardest-hit countries, a 100% increase. On the other hand, African countries such as Guinea and the Gambia are showing reductions in infant mortality of above 30% (UNICEF, 2006b). Thus, we no longer have two kinds of countries, the rich and the poor; rather, there are a number of countries that have shown tremendous gains, whereas others are lagging behind, and there are also increasing disparities within countries (World Bank, 2005). The rate of children attending some form of preschool is another measure of child well-being and access to services. This rate has tripled over the past three decades, but still stands at only 35%, with wide regional disparities.

The former Soviet countries and Soviet sphere countries are exceptions to the dichotomy described above. Currently they are classified as "developing countries" or "countries in transition," possibly because their GNI per capita is relatively low ($2,667 in 2004 dollars) compared to industrialized countries ($32,232 in 2004 dollars) and even to Latin America ($3,649) (UNICEF, 2006b). However, in many ways the well-being of their children has followed a different path from other countries. Under the Soviet influence, overall well-being was relatively high. Primary school education levels still tend to be as high as in industrialized countries, with 99% of males and 96% of females literate and 96% completing fifth grade. Differences begin to emerge in secondary school, with 91% of males and 83% of females attending, compared to over 100% in industrialized countries. Health and nutrition are also good, with only 5% underweight, and 93% receiving three DPT immunizations, compared to 96% in industrialized countries (UNICEF, 2006b). The Soviet tradition of home visits to families by health workers during the first two years of a child's life continues to be a goal, although many countries can no longer sustain the practice (Engle, 2007). Preprimary education has fared less well. A high proportion of children were attending preschool prior to the end of the Soviet era. The proportion dropped dramatically after the fall of the Soviet system, but has rebounded in all but the Central Asian countries (Global Monitoring Report Team, 2006).

In sum, disparities among countries are increasing rapidly, and there are no longer just "rich" and "poor" countries. However, at the same time, disparities within countries are also growing across the world (World Bank, 2005). From an economic perspective, it will continue to be important to examine the ecological context within as well as between countries.

Infant Development: What Do Children Need?

It is generally recognized in the US literature that emotional availability is one of the most basic needs of the infant (Bornstein and Lamb, 2008; Bornstein et al., 2008). Parental emotional displays engage and communicate to children, and children provide multiple cues that express their emotional states and needs to their parents (Bornstein et al., 2008). Dimensions of emotional availability of particular relevance to infant development include maternal variables of sensitivity, responsiveness, structuring or scaffolding of experiences, nonintrusiveness (not overprotective or overdirective), and nonhostility (not rejecting or antagonistic). These dimensions are consistent with three aspects of parenting that Shonkoff and Phillips (2000) found to be consistently related to young children's cognitive and social emotional competence: (1) cognitive stimulation; (2) caregiver sensitivity and responsiveness to the child; and (3) caregiver affect (emotional warmth or rejection of the child). From the infant's perspective critical outcome dimensions are age-appropriate exploring and enjoyment as well as involvement, interest, ability, and success in engaging the mother.

Somewhat similar conclusions were reached by researchers in South Africa evaluating the effects of the HIV/AIDS pandemic on young children (Richter & Foster, 2006). They concluded that every child needs a continuing relationship with at least one person for whom that child is special. However, these researchers also emphasized two other basic requirements: that the mother–infant dyad have adequate sources of support (economic as well as social), and that they belong to a larger social group (Richter, Foster, & Sherr, 2006). In many developing countries, access to resources and to the wider context of social support is absolutely essential to survival and development. In a well-resourced society, policy supports may be strong enough that the latter two requirements are more likely to be fulfilled, and so do not become a basic requirement.

Other characteristics of the environment and the characteristics of the infant can also influence the emerging trajectory of the child's development (Bradley, 1994). These environments are generally described in terms of proximal characteristics such as house quality, educational level of family, or crowding, and distal characteristics, including neighborhood, services, and economic conditions (Wachs, 2000). Child characteristics may include temperament, disability or delay, gender, and perhaps physical appearance. Further, given that the ecological perspective (Bronfenbrenner & Morris, 1998) is now "central to developmental study" (Bornstein et al., 2008), culture also must be taken into account. Given that the largest percentage of research on infants is done on the 11% of the world's children under 5 living in industrialized countries, there is much that needs to be learned about the effects of varying ecocultural contexts on infant development for the other 89%. Ecocultural contexts are defined by culture, by the means of production (e.g., agricultural, nomadic, urban), and ecological conditions (desert or forest, drought-prone or secure, etc.). If we are to have a developmental theory for all infants, we must look beyond the cultural context of the US and other industrialized societies, or even the various ethnic, income, and geographic groupings, to be able to make generalizations about infant development in many different contexts.

Many questions emerge when attempting to integrate culture into studies of infant development. How many cultures must we examine? What are the categories that should be used and are they best defined by researchers within a country? How different is the process of child development itself, compared to the differences that occur because economic and geographic differences, as well as family size and structure, are different?

In the US, major environmental risk factors include poverty, family disruption, exposure to violence, abuse and neglect (see chapters 5 and 7 in this volume). Characteristics of the child which increase risk include genetic differences, developmental delay, inability to self-regulate, and other temperamental issues (see chapter 20 in volume 1 on temperament; and chapter 12 in this volume on the genetics of developmental delay). As will be discussed below, in developing countries one finds a much wider variety of risk factors. Environmental risk factors include not only those presented above, but also food insecurity, greater health risks, conflict, more likelihood of migration, exposure to toxins, infections and the HIV pandemic. In the poorest countries, children are at much greater risk as a result of the death of their mothers than is an American child. They also face greater risks of poor health and nutritional status, and absence of contingent stimulation, than children from the US. The tragedy is that infants who are most vulnerable – because of poor nutrition or health, low birth weight (LBW), or inadequate growth *in utero* – are likely to be raised in the most challenging environments. When macroenvironmental changes, such as global warming, result in increases in drought or inundations, those who have done the least to create these conditions, and are least prepared to adapt to them, are the most exposed. As will be discussed in the final section of this chapter, it is impossible to examine the development of infants in the developing world without a focus on social justice.

Risks to Children in the Developing World

Grantham-McGregor et al. (2007) estimate that over 200 million children under 5 in the developing world are not developing to their full potential. Walker et al. (2007) identified four key risk factors that are causally and consistently linked to child development, affect large numbers of infants and young children from developing countries, and can be modified. The four risk factors that fit these criteria are: malnutrition that is chronic and severe enough to cause stunting; inadequate cognitive stimulation or learning opportunities; iodine deficiency; and iron deficiency anemia. These risks, their prevalence in developing countries, and our current level of knowledge about each one are shown in Table 6.1 (Engle, Grantham-McGregor, Black, Walker, & Wachs, 2007; Walker et al., 2007). The table summarizes the risk, a rough estimate of the prevalence, effects on children, and the strength of the evidence. The strongest risk factors, as well as some of the other factors, will be discussed.

Biological risk factors

Nutritional deficiencies.   Malnutrition includes inadequate growth (stunting, or short stature), underweight, or a series of micronutrient deficiencies such as iron deficiency,

Table 6.1 Risk factors for poor development in the first two or three years of life (from Engle, Grantham-McGregor, et al., 2007; references in Walker et al., 2007).

Risk	Prevalence	Effects on children	Strength of evidence
Stunting	25–30%	6–13 DQ points (0.4–0.8 SD), social and emotional effects	Strong
Iodine deficiency	35%	9–13 IQ points (1 SD)	Strong
Iron deficiency anemia	20–30%	1.73 IQ/10 g/L Hb Some supplementation trials show benefits to motor, socioemotional and cognitive development of 0.3–0.4 SD	Strong
Lack of child stimulation and learning opportunities	60–90% of parents do not stimulate	Provision of stimulation/learning opportunities has benefits of 0.5–1.0 SD in IQ	Strong
Maternal depression	17%, rates may be higher	0.5–1.0 SD in cognitive development scores	Correlations clear; need for treatment approaches
Exposure to violence	Major armed conflict in 27–38% countries from 1990–2003, affects 20 million children	Behavior problems, post-traumatic stress disorder	Urgent need for research particularly on interventions
Intrauterine growth retardation	11%	0.25–0.5 SD compared to non-LBW	Associated with developmental deficits to age 3; need for longitudinal studies
Malaria	40% of population in 90 countries – 300–600 million	Significant cognitive impairments associated with severe malaria or cerebral malaria, or number of episodes of malaria	Negative associations clear; needs further study
Lead levels	40%	2–5 IQ points	Correlational studies in developed and developing countries
Lack of breastfeeding	40–50%	Small effects on cognition (2–5 IQ pts), may affect bonding	Consistent but small to moderate effects; hard to design good studies

Table 6.1 *Continued*

Risk	Prevalence	Effects on children	Strength of evidence
Parental loss or parental illness; community affected by HIV	Over 43 million orphans in sub-Saharan Africa, 16% below age 6 (7 million) in 2003	Descriptive studies show higher rates of mortality, some behavior problems, sense of vulnerability, depression; improves over time	Need for interventions and intervention research
Lack of maternal responsiveness	Unknown	Associated with less secure attachment, lower cognitive ability and more behavior problems	Need for more intervention studies
Zinc deficiency	33%	Cognitive development and activity	Mixed results
Intestinal helminths	33%	Cognitive development	Inconsistent results
HIV infection	2%	Can be severe; developmental delays, language delays, mortality in first 5 years if untreated	Evidence for risk is strong; little data on interventions
Diarrhea	Common	Some associations with cognitive development found	Suggestive; needs further study
Arsenic	High in areas such as Bangladesh	Lowered IQ	Correlational data; only investigated in older children
Manganese, pesticides	Depends on area	Lowered IQ	Some data but need for more
Abuse and neglect	Data for young children not readily available	Multiple; increase in aggression, long-term deficit in productivity	Strong in industrialized countries; not much data in developing countries

zinc deficiency, iodine deficiency, or vitamin A deficiency. Of all of these, the only one which has not been found to be associated with cognitive development is vitamin A deficiency. Chapter 2 in this volume describes the effects of nutritional impacts more fully. A brief summary is included here.

Stunting or low height for age, often beginning with LBW, has been associated with cognitive as well as social and emotional effects, including apathy, less positive affect, less play, and more insecure attachment compared to well-nourished children (Walker et al.,

2007). Stunting affects approximately 25–30% of young children in the developing world (UNICEF, 2006b).

Worldwide 35% of people have insufficient iodine intake (World Health Organization (WHO), 2004). Iodine deficiency can cause irreversible mental retardation, making it the most common preventable cause of mental retardation (WHO, 2004). Iodine-deficient children show deficits of up to 13 IQ points (almost 1 standard deviation), and even modest levels of iodine deficiency have been shown to have an effect on cognitive functioning (Choudhury & Gorman, 2003).

Anaemia affects 45–65% of children under 4, of which half is iron deficiency anaemia (Stoltzfus, Mullany, & Black, 2005). There is conclusive evidence that infants with iron deficiency anaemia are developmentally at risk in the short term, and consistent evidence that they continue to be at risk in the long term despite iron therapy (Walker et al., 2007).

Lack of breastfeeding has been associated with poorer cognitive outcomes, although the causal argument is difficult to make, given design difficulties (Grantham-McGregor, Fernald, & Sethuraman, 1999). However, a study in Belarus used a cluster randomized control design comparing the Wechsler IQ scores of 6.5-year-old children whose mothers had been in a breastfeeding promotion program and a control group to test the hypothesis that breastfed children would perform better on cognitive tests. The intervention had resulted in significant changes in the rates of exclusive breastfeeding. Significantly higher IQ scores were reported for breastfed children in the sample of almost 14,000 children, and the hypothesis was supported (Kramer et al., 2008).

Low birth weight.   Data on infant weight at birth are often difficult to obtain in cultures in which mothers give birth at home and are not assisted by birth attendants equipped to obtain weights. The available data suggest that 7% of infants are born below 2500 g in industrialized countries, compared to 31% in South Asia, and around 15% in most other regions (UNICEF, 2006b). However, it is critical to distinguish different kinds of LBW. By far the most common reason for LBW in industrialized countries is prematurity. On the other hand, LBW infants in developing countries tend to be small for gestational age, born at term but lower weight. Thus LBW is not a homogeneous pregnancy outcome (Goldenberg & Culhane, 2007), but instead is composed of infants who are either born too early (i.e., preterm birth) or too small (i.e., fetal growth restriction). LBW causes and consequences for infants in the US are dealt with in chapters 1 and 3 in this volume. The present chapter focuses on infant LBW risks in developing countries.

Approximately 16–17% of births worldwide are LBW, that is, below 2.5 kg (Morris, Grantham-McGregor, Lira, Assunção, & Ashworth, 1999; UNICEF, 2006b). De Onis, Blössner, and Villar (1998) estimate that LBW infants born at term (interuterine growth retarded) represent 11% of births in developing countries (see also Villar & Belizán, 1982). In contrast, in developed countries, most LBW infants are preterm and appropriately grown for their gestational age (Morris et al., 1999).

In northeast Brazil, intrauterine growth retardation was associated with lower cognitive development (Grantham-McGregor, Lira, Ashworth, Morris, & Assunção, 1998), and diarrhea in the first six months of life among LBW term infants, although not high birth weight infants, had an effect on cognitive development at 6 and 12 months. Two other groups of studies in Guatemala (Gorman & Pollitt, 1992; Villar, Smeriglio, Martorell, Brown, & Klein, 1984) and Jamaica (Meeks Gardner, Walker, Powell, & Grantham-McGregor, 2003; Wachs, Chang-Lopez, Walker, & Meeks Gardner, 2007; Walker, Chang, Powell, & Grantham-McGregor, 2004) showed that LBW term infants were lower in cognitive ability than a matched group of adequate birth weight infants in the first two years of life. These children are also more vulnerable to other risks, and more likely to profit from interventions. LBW term infants were detrimentally affected by unstimulating home environments, whereas higher birth weight infants were not (Grantham-McGregor et al., 1998). Wachs et al. (2007) found that the postnatal rearing environment, including maternal verbal interactions, was associated with subsequent cognitive development of the infants at 24 months. Moreover, the risks associated with LBW were more evident when the mother did not facilitate the child's development with interactions, and parents with lower levels of cognitive development were less effective in stimulating their infants' development (Wachs et al., 2007). In addition, Black, Sazawal, Black, Khosla, Kumar, and Menon (2004) reported more significant effects of zinc and iron supplementation on the development of LBW infants than adequate birth weight infants in northern India. These results suggest that there are synergistic or multiplicative consequences of LBW.

Micronutrient interventions have been able to reduce the incidence of LBW in developing countries (Fawzi et al., 2007, in Tanzania; Shankar et al., 2008, in Indonesia). Additional cognitive stimulation through a psychosocial intervention program resulted in higher levels of functioning at 7 months in LBW term infants in Jamaica (Meeks Gardner et al., 2003). However, there is a need for long-term follow-up of these interventions, similar to the US Infant Health and Development Program which tested the ameliorating effects of early intervention on LBW infants through age 18 (McCormick et al., 2006).

Exposure to toxins.   Infants are more likely to be exposed to toxins in the developing world than in the industrialized world – but much exposure is unknown. Stein, Schettler, Wallinga, and Valenti (2002) point out that although there are 80,000 chemicals in regular use, with about 3,000 new ones each year, we have studied the effects on child development of only 12. Although some think of pollution as being greater in industrialized countries, a recent summary of the top 10 most polluted cities in the world found that *all* were in developing countries – two in China, two in India, one in Peru, four in Russia and the former Soviet republics, and one in Zambia (Blacksmith Institute, 2007). Such cities often have unregulated manufacturing and mining plants (e.g., Linfen, China, with 3 million residents) with coal and particulates pollution or with mines and industries spewing out lead, heavy metals, chromium, or cadmium. Too often the safeguards for toxins are not present or even recognized as important, as in the former Soviet Union, or people live in desperate circumstances including toxic exposures far beyond what is acceptable.

Mercury was one of the first substances to have its toxicity identified (Stein et al., 2002). More recently, Walker et al. (2007) documented negative effects of manganese, arsenic, lead, and pesticides on cognitive development in developing countries. In a study in Tongling, China, Tang et al. (2008) found that 2-year-olds who had higher levels of polycyclic aromatic hydrocarbons (PAH) from coal-burning plants and lead in their umbilical cord blood scored significantly lower on a Gesell DQ than those who had had no signs of either lead or PAH.

One of the most tragic cases of toxin exposure resulted from thousands of wells dug in Bangladesh and eastern India to help the region deal with water shortages. Later it was learned that these wells were contaminated with arsenic. Studies on the long-term effects of arsenic suggest that there will probably be impacts of various kinds on exposed children (Calderón et al., 2001; Tsai, Chou, The, Chen, & Chen, 2003; Wasserman et al., 2004). These children are particularly at risk of suffering from adverse effects of high exposures (at concentrations of 100 µg/L and more) to arsenic that are widespread in well water, since no alternative drinking water sources are accessible to them.

The effects of *alcohol* and *nicotine* on the developing fetus are now well recognized; not only do they cause LBW, but there is evidence of short- and long-term effects on mental functioning (Stein et al., 2002; WHO, 2003). In the US the rate of women's smoking dropped from 34% in 1965 to 22% in 1999, but the rate continues to be high in many developing countries, and is likely to increase (WHO, 2003). Further, rates of smoking by men are extremely high in many developing countries, with more than 60% of men smoking in western Asia, Russia, Mongolia, Yemen, and Kenya (WHO, 2003). Thus, even though women on the whole are smoking relatively little, they are exposed to a tremendous amount of passive smoke. The losses due to cigarette smoking include not only health risks to parents, risks to children's health and development, but also a loss of income for the family, deforestation for growing tobacco, and misuse of agricultural land.

Similarly, while there is increasing awareness of the negative effects of alcohol on fetal development in the industrialized countries, alcohol use is on the rise in some developing regions. The WHO Department of Mental Health and Substance Abuse (2004) reported that the highest rates of alcohol dependence among women were in South Africa (9.9%) and Brazil (5.9%), only slightly higher than the US (4.8%). Heavy drinking among women was highest in Uganda (20%), Columbia (21%), Nigeria (36%), and the UK (42%). These rates refer to all women, and do not distinguish pregnant from nonpregnant women. Current figures suggest that, overall, rates are decreasing in the European and American regions, but increasing slightly in the East Asia and West Asia regions, although from a low level.

Maternal alcohol consumption during pregnancy can result in fetal alcohol syndrome in children, and parental drinking is correlated with child abuse and impacts a child's environment in many social, psychological and economic ways (for discussion of fetal alcohol syndrome, see chapter 3 in this volume). Drinking can impair performance as a parent, as a spouse or partner, and as a contributor to household functioning. There are also other aspects of drinking that may impair functioning as a family member. In many societies, drinking may be carried out primarily outside the family and the home. In this circumstance, time spent while drinking often competes with the time needed to carry on family life. Drinking also costs money and thus can significantly reduce family economic resources, leading to less money being available for essentials such as food and clothing (WHO, 2004). In addition, child neglect is an increasing problem when parents are intoxicated so early in the day that they are not able to prepare food for their children or will give alcohol to their children as a food substitute and to stave off hunger. Further, the neglect of young children due to alcohol abuse means that these children often are undersocialized, leading to reduced school attendance, begging or stealing for food (Molamu & MacDonald, 1996, cited in WHO, 2004).

Infection.   Infants suffer from a number of different infections that may affect cognitive development, including diarrhea, helminths, malaria, and HIV/AIDS. As Walker et al. (2007) conclude, there is some indication of impacts of the first two on cognitive development, but more research is needed. The evidence for cognitive effects of severe malaria, which is a risk for over 40% of the world's population, in 90 countries, has been found in many studies. Neurological and cognitive impairments are associated with severe or cerebral malaria (Boivin, 2002; Carter et al., 2005, 2006), with more disease severity associated with greater degree and duration of impairment (Kihara, Carter, & Newton, 2006). Impairment may also be associated with repeated uncomplicated attacks in school-aged children, potentially affecting millions (Fernando et al., 2003).

An emerging risk for all children is HIV infection either of the child or his/her mother. Between 2.1 and 2.9 million children are currently infected with HIV (UNICEF, 2006a). Given fertility and HIV prevalence rates at the time, it can be estimated that more than 2.5 million South African children had a mother who was alive but infected with HIV (Richter & Foster, 2006). Untreated, most children born with HIV will die before their fourth birthday, most likely in the first two years of life (Richter & Foster, 2006). They are much more likely to suffer from neurodevelopmental delays than non-infected children. In a matched comparison of infants from Kinshasa, Democratic Republic of the Congo, 60% children with HIV infection had a severe delay in cognitive function, and 85% had a delay in language expression. Younger HIV-infected children (18–29 months) were more likely to be delayed (91%) than older children (82%), possibly because the most severely infected children had not survived (Van Rie, Mupuala, & Dow, 2008).

To reduce the number of HIV-infected infants, the prevention of transmission of HIV from mother to child is a high priority. It is estimated that 90% of HIV-infected children worldwide became infected via mother-to-child transmission; this rate increases to 95% in sub-Saharan Africa (African Network for the Care of Children Affected by HIV/AIDS, 2006; UNAIDS, 2006). However, by 2005, fewer than 10% of HIV-positive pregnant women had access to prevention of mother-to-child transmission (PMTCT) services worldwide (UNAIDS, 2006). This low coverage rate is abysmal, considering that approximately 35–40% of infants born to HIV-positive mothers will acquire HIV infection without treatment before, during, and after birth (UNAIDS and World Health Organization, 2006). While 15–30% of infants born to HIV-positive mothers who do not breastfeed will acquire infection without provision of PMTCT regimens, the risk increases to 20–45% for breastfed infants in the absence of a treatment regimen (De Cock et al., 2000). Offering comprehensive PMTCT services can result in HIV transmission of less than 2% (Cooper, Landman, Tomlinson, Molteno, Swartz, & Murray, 2002).

The social and psychological environment

Covariance of biological and psychosocial risks.   Biomedical factors also can increase a child's exposure to psychosocial risks. This is clearly illustrated by reference to the large numbers of children orphaned and affected by HIV/AIDS. In 2005, an estimated 48 million children aged 0–18 years – 12% of all children in sub-Saharan Africa – were orphans, and that number is expected to rise to 53 million by 2010 (UNICEF, 2006a). One quarter of all orphans are orphaned because of AIDS. Over half of these orphans are under age 12, and 7 million (16%) of the orphans in Africa are under age 6 (UNICEF, 2006a). Moreover, it is estimated that 25% of the orphans in sub-Saharan Africa experienced a parent's death before the age of 5 (UNICEF, 2006a). UNICEF (2006a, p. 6) concludes that, although they represent a smaller percentage of all orphans, the youngest orphans are the least resilient and have the greatest need for physical care and emotional nurturing.

In addition, Richter and Foster (2006) point out:

> the impact of HIV/AIDS goes beyond orphaning or having the disease. Even if not orphaned or infected themselves children whose parents were infected may be at increased developmental risk due to household economic and emotional resources being directed towards the infected parent(s), with a consequent reduction in children's nutrition, health, and education.

Supporting this prediction, in the Congo study HIV-affected (not infected) children also showed more cognitive delay than control children (van Rie et al., 2008).

The kinds of effects that might be seen for young children who are affected, but not necessarily infected, with HIV are reviewed in Engle and Dunkelberg (2007). In the "Speak for the Child" project in western Kenya, young children prior to an intervention were more likely to be withdrawn and passive – acting out, disobedient, or unable to pay attention to learning activities (Lusk, 2005). On the other hand, there is no clear evidence that these children are more likely to be malnourished (Stewart, 2007). Because poverty was found to be a greater risk factor for malnutrition in five countries in Eastern and Southern Africa, the author concluded that identification of vulnerable children should be based on indicators of household poverty, rather than on orphan status. Yet there may be exceptions. A recent evaluation in Zimbabwe (Watts, Gregson, Saito, Lopman, Beasley, & Monasch, 2007) found that stunting and being underweight were most common in double and maternal orphans compared to other children. Differences in poverty did not explain the greater exposure to chronic malnutrition, and, after further adjustment for exposure to extreme poverty, orphans and vulnerable children (OVCs) were still more likely to have diarrheal disease and acute respiratory infections. Maternal and double orphans were also less likely to have health cards than other children, and OVCs with acute respiratory infections were significantly more likely not to have received treatment, compared to non-OVCs.

Although there are support programs for young children affected by HIV/AIDS in areas with high percentages of children affected by AIDS, they are far below the level needed, and few have been evaluated (Engle & Dunkelberg, 2007; Engle, 2008). One intervention with young infected children in South Africa showed that a year-long program of parent support improved outcomes (Potterton, 2007). The "Speak for the Child" project also was able to improve the support environment for young children affected by AIDS (Lusk, 2005). This is an area of work that will need to be developed in the next few years with great urgency.

Further complicating the search for effective interventions is the fact that societies with a high social burden of HIV/AIDS also are at high risk for the "toxic stressors" that can impair a young child's brain architecture in the first few years of life (Joint Learning Initiative for Children, 2008). These toxic stressors have been demonstrated to directly affect a child's potential for language development as well as lifelong social and physical health. Chronic poverty as well as crises within the family such as maternal depression, caregiver illness or death, divorce, and family violence may cause persistent elevation of stress hormones in children that, without the buffered protection of adult support, disrupt brain chemistry and can lead to impaired learning, memory, social development and increased susceptibility to physical illness in adulthood (National Scientific Council on the Developing Child, 2007). These risks can be minimized and prevented by strengthening the family environment through means such as the provision of consistent, safe, high-quality programs for early childhood development and child and family educational opportunities (National Scientific Council on the Developing Child, 2007; Siddiqi, Irwin, and Hertzman, 2007).

Poverty.   Children growing up in poverty are frequently exposed to multiple and cumulative risks. These include the biological risks described above such as nutritional deficiencies, LBW and exposure to environmental toxins. Since the greater the number of risks a child is exposed to the more a child's development is compromised (Wachs, 2000; Walker et al., 2007), the impact of exposure to these biological risk factors can be exacerbated by poverty. Similarly, whereas known psychological risk factors such as of lack of stimulation, low maternal responsiveness, parental loss, abuse and neglect, and maternal depression may occur across a wide variety of economic levels, the combined effect of these problems with poverty exacerbates the problems.

How should poverty be defined – in solely economic terms, or as part of a broader social disadvantage? (For discussion of this issue in industrialized countries, see chapter 5 in this volume.) The economic definition of poverty is typically based on income measures, with the absolute poverty line calculated as the food expenditure necessary to meet dietary recommendations, supplemented by a small allowance for nonfood goods (Ravallion, 1992). However, many poverty researchers use a broader definition for "poor" including not only lack of material assets and health but also capabilities such as social belonging, cultural identity, respect and dignity, and information and education (Sen, 1995). Tilly (2007) adds social exclusion which prevents groups or categories of peoples from moving out of poverty The complex and multifaceted conditions that prevent people from moving out of poverty in developing countries are illustrated in 60,000 interviews from 60 countries in *Voices of the Poor* (Narayan & Petesch, 2002).

Poverty is a dynamic process with some families cycling in and out of poverty in a relatively short time, resulting in intermittent rather than persistent poverty. In a study of 30,000 households in India, Peru, and Uganda, Krishna (2007) reported that nearly one third of individuals currently living in poverty were not born poor. Mobility out of poverty has been described as the interaction of (1) changes in the *opportunity structure,* consisting of the dominant institutional climate and social structures within which disadvantaged actors must work to advance their interests, and (2) changes in the capabilities of poor individuals or groups to take purposeful actions, that is, to exercise *agency* (Narayan & Petesch, 2007). Agency depends on individual assets, such as education and self-confidence, and collective and family assets, such as organization, identity and having a voice. The risks described in this chapter relate for the most part to lack of agency, but the limited opportunity structure may have equal weight.

In developing countries, children in poverty are at much greater risk of never attending school than wealthier children, and these differences are wide; for example, in a sample of 80 countries, 12% of children in the top quintile of households never attended school, whereas 38% of children in the poorest quintile never attended school (Bruneforth, 2006; Global Monitoring Report Team, 2006). These differences are more highly related to wealth and mothers' education than to urban/rural residence and gender (Global Monitoring Report Team, 2006). Children raised in poverty also achieve less in school. Analyses show strong positive relationships between socioeconomic status and student achievement across countries, across age levels, and across academic areas of study (Global Monitoring Report Team, 2006). Further, socioeconomic differences in achievement scores, often called socioeconomic gradients, exist within most countries, reflecting socioeconomic status-related inequality in educational outcomes (Ross, Zuze, & Ratsatsi, 2005).

Social change and urbanization. The world is rapidly becoming urban. Over 70% of the population in industrialized countries and Latin America are urban, closely followed by Central and Eastern Europe and the Commonwealth of Independent States (63%) and the Middle East and North Africa (58%). East Asia is rapidly urbanizing (42%), as is sub-Saharan Africa (36%). The least urbanized area to date is South Asia (28%) (UNICEF, 2006). In simple comparisons of urban and rural children, urban children almost always have better outcomes, possibly due to greater wealth in urban families. However, there are other differences between rural and urban families besides wealth. Urban families tend to be smaller, more educated and have more access to services; in addition there are rural–urban differences in caregiver beliefs and rearing practices (Bornstein et al., 2008). For example, rural families tend to have more traditional child-rearing values, a greater belief in parental authority, and to emphasize children's incorporation or communion into a family unit (Keller, Abels, Lamm, Yovsi, Volker, & Lakhani, 2005). Further, Sachs (2005) has proposed that remoteness in itself is a risk factor, with greater poverty associated with more remote location even in rural areas.

Lack of child stimulation, learning opportunities, and maternal responsiveness. Substantial differences in cultural values, ecological conditions, and economic resources affect the environment that the infant faces in the developing world. However, responsiveness and opportunities for learning may be basic requirements for healthy infant development, with an underlying significance in both developed and developing countries.

Bradley and Corwyn (2005) provided a useful illustration of this point in their review of results from studies applying the Home Observation for Measurement of the Environment (HOME) scale in many cultures around the world. They define three key dimensions along which most cultures vary: warmth and responsiveness, discipline/harsh punishment, and stimulation/teaching. After a review of the variations both in how these concepts are expressed, and in the variability in scores, they find that both warmth/responsiveness and stimulation/teaching show strong associations with outcomes in almost every cultural context, the former more consistently with social and emotional development, and the latter with child competence, although less with social adjustment. Large differences were seen in the acceptance of harsh punishment, and these attitudes and behaviors covaried with a belief that children need to learn to respect authority. Harsh punishment was not always associated with demeaning a child or lack of acceptance; rather, it was a cultural norm. However, in spite of this caveat, Bradley and Corwyn (2005) conclude that the use of harsh punishment is still consistently associated with negative child outcomes.

In an attempt to measure quality of the home environment on a comparative scale, UNICEF developed a series of questions adapted from the HOME that could be used in a survey format to have a broad perspective of the variation in home environments globally (Kariger, Frongillo, Engle, Rebello, Sywulka, & Menon, 2008). These questions focused on the dimension of learning/stimulation as the most predictive dimension and the easiest to assess in a survey format. The questions included: (a) parental activities with children; (b) learning and play materials that children had; and (c) type of nonparental care. The measures were validated and shown to be associated with the HOME and with Bayley Scores in a study in Bangladesh (Hamadani, Tofail, Yesmin, Hud, Engle, & Grantham-McGregor, 2010).

Emergencies and conflict.   Emergencies, both natural disasters and conflict, have a huge cost for infants and young children. These costs are normally considered to be health and nutrition risks, but increasingly there is an awareness of psychosocial impacts on caregivers and on young children. Not only do risk factors include depression, but also exposure to violence may be more common in these situations. Lustig (2009) outlines the effects of the separations and chaotic experiences of refugee children and interventions that have been shown to make a difference.

Both internal migration (internally displaced persons) and international migration are associated with emergencies and conflict. Countries that have received the largest proportion of migrants are often those least able to handle them. This migration is often due to conflict and natural or man-made disasters. Efforts to develop programs for young children, such as the early child development (ECD) program in northern Uganda, will soon be evaluated to see if they have any impact beyond a health and nutrition effect (Jones, personal communication).

Maternal depression.   In a 10-country survey Lepine (2001) finds that 11% of women are depressed, with rates closer to 30–50% in some areas, such as in South Asia and in conditions of poverty. In addition to genetic predisposition and neurochemical imbalances, risk factors for maternal depression in developing countries include poverty and economic stress, conflict, disasters, exposure to violence including domestic violence, migration, and HIV infection. Other factors associated with maternal depression are the birth of a girl in a male-preference society and lack of autonomy, while education for women is a strong protective factor (Wachs, Black, & Engle, 2009).

The consequences of maternal depression for children's well-being in developing countries, and the evidence for significant negative impacts on child morbidity, birth weight, poor growth, and reduced cognitive and social-emotional development have also been documented (Wachs et al., 2009). It appears that these effects are mediated by poor caregiving of depressed mothers, reduced responsive and stimulating care, and early cessation of breastfeeding.

Again, multiple risks were shown to have a greater impact. When maternal depressive symptoms occurred in conjunction with perceptions of infant irritability, infants acquired fewer cognitive, motor, and behavioral skills than when mothers had neither or only one condition (Black et al., 2007). The relation between maternal depressive symptoms, perceived infant irritability, and infant cognitive skills was partially mediated by parental responsiveness and opportunities for play in the home, suggesting that caregiving behavior is influenced by both depressive symptoms and perceptions of infant temperament.

It is likely that treatment of maternal depression with medications will be judged prohibitively expensive in many developing countries. In these countries alternative treatments such as increasing social support, enhancing mother–infant interactions, and group therapy have been shown to be successful (Wachs et al., 2009). Other potential interventions that have been advocated include increasing women's status and power, and reducing alcohol consumption among males (Rahman & Creed, 2007). However, far more needs to be known about the most effective treatments in low-resource contexts and there is a critical need in developing countries for trained mental health personnel to identify women who are depressed and to carry out appropriate interventions.

Policy Recommendations for Resource-Poor Countries

A human rights perspective

There is a tension between a universalistic perspective that sees all children having essentially the same needs and potential developmental course, and an ecological framework that presumes that an optimal developmental path will occur through the interaction between child and context. In a recent publication, a group of researchers and practitioners who are trying to find the best strategies for children affected by AIDS illustrates how these perspectives might be combined through mothers with resources and tools to promote their infant's social and cognitive development (Joint Learning Initiative for Children, 2008). These researchers also concluded that providing mothers with support and the tools to promote the early development of their offspring can improve human dignity in general and maternal self-confidence in particular. However, a major barrier to providing such support and tools is a lack of awareness of the importance of such interventions (JLICA lg3, 2008).

The Convention for the Rights of the Child (CRC), which was adopted by the UN General Assembly in 1989, is perhaps the strongest tool for pressuring countries and the international community to improve the well-being of all children, and also manages to combine both perspectives (United Nations Committee on the Rights of the Child (UNCRC), UNICEF, & Bernard van Leer Foundation, 2006). Four main principles to ensure children's rights are specified in the CRC: the right to survival and development); the universality of rights (protection from discrimination); the indivisibility of rights; and the best interests of the child. Conventions also define who is responsible for fulfilling rights. Thus, while governments are responsible ("duty bearers") for ensuring that families have the livelihood and support needed to fulfill their responsibilities, families are also responsible.

In the past, most of the advocates for child rights focused on school-age children and adolescents, with a few exceptions such as birth registration. However, recently a clarification of the application of the CRC to young children was developed to increase understanding of early childhood and environmental risks and to help countries in their reporting. The General Comment for young children was prepared to underline the unique vulnerability of young children to contextual and biological risks (UNCRC et al., 2006). Articles with special significance for infant and young children include: the right to survival and development; education to develop the child's personality, talents and mental and physical abilities to their fullest potential; the right to leisure and play; the right to parenting by both mother and father; and childcare for working parents. It is important to stress that, rather than being a rigid set of rules, there are "variations in cultural expectations and treatment of children, including local customs and practices that should be respected, *except where they contravene the rights of the child*" (UNCRC et al., 2006, p. 36). There is a global universal standard of child rights that cannot be abridged by cultural practices, but also there is flexibility when these rights are not abridged.

In addition to the CRC, all governments agreed in 2000 to two sets of goals for children, some of which apply to infants. The Education for All Framework for Action developed in 2000 in Dakar expresses the international community's commitment to a broad-based strategy for ensuring that the basic learning needs of every child, youth, and adult are met within a generation and sustained thereafter. The goal most related to infant development is to "expand and improve comprehensive early childhood care and education, especially for the most vulnerable and disadvantaged children" (Global Monitoring Report Team, 2006, p. 13). The term "early childhood care and education" includes both early childhood education programs and support for parenting and child-rearing.

A second international agreement was the Millennium Development Declaration and Goals, approved by world leaders in 2000, to reduce poverty and improve lives. It defined eight major goals to be achieved by 2015. Most of the goals are related to children, although child development is not one of them, nor one of the 48 indicators to measure the achievement of the goals. However, child development is implicitly linked to the goals, since improved child development will result from achieving universal primary education to fifth grade, reduction of malnutrition, and promoting gender equity and empowering women.

Moving from human rights to policy

Policy recommendations include the need to make child development promotion a goal in developing countries, and use indicators to track progress in child cognitive and socio-emotional development. To achieve the Millennium Development Goals of reducing poverty and ensuring primary school completion for girls and boys, governments and civil society should consider expanding high-quality, cost-effective ECD programs.

Other factors may also improve ECD. Two related initiatives that could have enormous potential are strengthening the role of the father (e.g., Engle, Beardshaw, & Loftin, 2005) and empowering women to provide better care. The latter actually includes interventions such as raising the age at marriage, encouraging secondary schooling for girls, and employment for women with adequate childcare.

A major challenge in instituting programs for young children, particularly disadvantaged children, is the absence of resources to support basic healthcare, clean water, and nutrition. Confronted with these needs, policy-makers may be less eager to invest in ECD, even though there are clearly long-term benefits. A second challenge is that the concept of ECD is only gradually emerging in many countries as more programs are developed and professional training is done. Yet it is important for this development to occur. There is an emergence of new approaches to child-rearing as changing circumstances such as urbanization, migration, or new work roles demand changes in the traditional patterns of behavior. These patterns, which were effective in one kind of society, no longer provide support for children in more urbanized or education-focused societies. As fertility rates decline worldwide, women will spend fewer years in childbearing and child-rearing and changes will occur in investments for children.

Moving from policy to interventions

Because many young children from developing countries experience multiple risks, integrated interventions that address multiple identified risk factors are most likely to be effective. Two major initiatives in 2007 began to address the issues of what can be done in developing countries to support children's development in developing countries. First, Siddiq et al. (2007) were commissioned by the WHO Social Commission on Health to identify strategies for improving ECD globally. Second, the third paper in the Lancet Series on Child Development evaluated the effectiveness of ongoing programs for ECD (Engle, Grantham-McGregor, et al., 2007). This final section summarizes many of these points.

Although no single approach is a "magic bullet," the basic principles of developmental neuroscience and child development are assumed to be equally valid across societies and economies, whatever the program category and administrative structure (National Scientific Council on the Developing Child, 2007). For example, children's development depends on relationships that extend from the family to influence factors at the regional, national, and global levels (Siddiqi et al., 2007), and key principles of ECD such as the importance of brain development, critical periods, and the centrality of affective relationships and emotional availability in the process of healthy development are found across all societies (Siddiqi et al., 2007). However, a contrasting viewpoint expressed in a number of papers is the need to avoid the imposition of a Western-style response to improving ECD and thus undermine existing patterns of child-rearing, as well as the need to recognize the resilience of traditional social arrangements and cultural patterns of child-rearing (Siddiqi et al., 2007; Keller et al., 2005).

Hertzman and colleagues use charts of "gradients," or the degree of association of a child outcome with socioeconomic status, to assess progress toward equity for all children in a particular culture (Siddiqi et al., 2007). The steeper the gradient, the more the social and economic environment determines the outcome, and the less equality. If the goal is to increase equity or equality among families, we should strive for a flat gradient in which all have access to a program or service, regardless of income.

Interventions can make a difference. In the Walker et al. (2007) review, the authors conclude that all but one of 16 efficacy studies in developing countries showed that improving children's cognitive stimulation and learning opportunities resulted in improvements in children's cognitive development of between one half and one standard deviation. The evidence *strongly supports* the importance of early cognitive stimulation for young children's cognitive abilities. Follow-up studies in Turkey (Kagitcibasi, Sunar, & Bekman, 2001), South Africa (Magwaza & Edwards, 1991), and Jamaica (Walker, Chang, Powell, & Grantham-McGregor, 2005) show lasting intervention benefits for cognition, with some maintained for up to age 17. Four of five studies also report benefits for socioemotional development in areas such as social behavior, self-confidence, and positive affect. One mechanism may be increases in maternal sensitivity and responsiveness. Results from two small studies indicate that when caregivers are aware of their children's abilities, they are more responsive and their children do better in the short term (Cooper et al., 2002; Wendland-Carro, Piccinini & Millar, 1999).

In a recent review of programs and effectiveness studies in developing countries, Engle, Black, et al. (2007) identified 20 ECD programs that have been implemented in developing countries that had an adequate comparison group, measured children's outcomes, and occurred prior to age 6. The programs fall into three groups: center-based early learning; parenting or parent–child interventions; and community-based interventions. All include health and nutrition interventions. All of the eight evaluations of center-based programs found a significant effect on children's cognitive development, either through preschools or treatment centers for malnourished children. These programs also demonstrated noncognitive gains such as social skills, self-confidence, willingness to talk to adults, and motivation. Four of six parenting interventions using home visiting found positive effects on child development (Morenza, Arrazola, Seleme, & Martinez, 2005; Powell, 2004; Powell, Baker-Henningham, Walker, Gernay, & Grantham-McGregor, 2004; Waber et al., 1981), particularly those allowing mothers to practice their skills with their child under supervision. Four out of five community-based programs illustrated the beneficial effects of integrating ECD programs into existing community-based systems: Rao (2005) and Vazir and Kashinath (1999) in India; Cueto and Diaz (1999) in Peru; Ghuman, Behrman, Gultiano, and King (2006) in the Philippines; and Hamadani, Huda, Khatun, and Grantham-McGregor (2006) in Bangladesh. The effect sizes ranged from one third to almost two standard deviations. Given these effect sizes, if there were coverage of 90% of disadvantaged children with an ECD program, the result would be a net increase of a year of school per child. Preschool enrollment would contribute to increases of about 5–10% in lifetime labor income.

From these studies, Engle, Black, et al. (2007) concluded that effective ECD programs have the following characteristics: (1) they are targeted toward disadvantaged children; (2) they provide services for younger children (less than age 3); (3) they continue throughout early childhood; (4) they are of high quality, defined by structure (e.g., child staff ratio, staff training) and processes (e.g., responsive interactions, variety of activities); (5) they provide direct services to children and parents; (6) they are integrated into existing health, nutrition, or educational systems.

Despite convincing evidence, program coverage is low. Barriers include lack of awareness of children's loss of developmental potential, and its cost, lack of globally accepted indicators for child development to monitor progress or ensure accountability, difficulty of making long-term investments, the multiple stakeholders for young children, and the lack of a single strategy or "package" of interventions for ECD. Efforts are underway to address some of these concerns, such as the lack of a global indicator, and systems for calculating costs are improving. But more work is urgently needed to determine what kinds of interventions are most effective in which contexts.

Summary and Conclusion

The theme throughout this chapter is that those who have the least material resources to provide well for their children are often raising infants in the most difficult circumstances. The effects of multiple risks are clearly evident in many cases. We must be aware of the increasing risks to child-rearing that will emerge for families and communities as they begin to suffer from the consequences of climate change – extreme weather, floods, and, possibly most damaging, long periods of drought. Those likely to suffer most are those who did least to create the problem. We cannot ignore the well-being of 89% of the world's children. Enlightened self-interest will lead us to recognize that a higher proportion of children need to thrive as well as survive. A commitment to social justice and child rights should move us to action.

References

African Network for the Care of Children Affected by HIV/AIDS (2006). *Handbook on paediatric AIDS in Africa*. Kampala: ANECCA.

Black, M. M., Baqui, A. H., Zaman, K., McNary, S. W., Le, K., Arifeeen, S. E., et al. (2007). Depressive symptoms among rural Bangladeshi mothers: Implications for infant development. *Journal of Child Psychology and Psychiatry, 48*, 764–772.

Black, M. M., Sazawal, S., Black, R., Khosla, S., Kumar, J., & Menon, V. (2004). Cognitive and motor development among small-for-gestational-age infants: Impact of zinc supplementation, birth weight, and caregiving practices. *Pediatrics, 113*(5), 1297–1305.

Blacksmith Institute (2007). The world's worst polluted places: The top 10 of the dirty 30. http://www.blacksmithinstitute.org/ten.php.

Boivin, M. J. (2002). Effects of early cerebral malaria on cognitive ability in Senegalese children. *Journal of Developmental and Behavioral Pediatrics, 23*, 353–364.

Bornstein, M., & Lamb, M. E. (2008). *Development in infancy: An introduction* (5th ed.). Mahwah, NJ: Erlbaum.

Bornstein, M. H., Putnick, D. I., Heslington, M., Gini, M., Suwalsky, J. T. D., Venuti, P., et al. (2008). Mother–child emotional availability in ecological perspective: Three countries, two regions, two genders. *Developmental Psychology, 44*(3), 666–680.

Bradley, R. H. (1994). The HOME inventory: Review and reflections. In H. Reese (Ed.), *Advances in child development and behavior* (pp. 241–288). San Diego, CA: Academic Press.

Bradley, R. H., & Corwyn, R. F. (2005). Caring for children around the world: A view from HOME. *International Journal of Behavioral Development, 29*(6), 468–478.

Bronfenbrenner, U., & Morris, P. A. (1998). The ecology of developmental processes. In R. M. Lerner (Ed.) & W. Damon (Series Ed.), Handbook of child psychology, Vol. *1. Theoretical models of human development* (5th ed., pp. 993–1028). New York: Wiley.

Bruneforth, M. (2006). *Characteristics of children who drop out of school and comments on the drop-out population compared to the population of out-of-school population.* EFA Global Monitoring Report.

Calderón, J., Navarro, M. E., Jimenez-Capdeville, M. E., Santos-Diaz, M. A., Golden, A., Rodriguez-Leyva, I., et al. (2001). Exposure to arsenic and lead and neuropsychological development in Mexican children. *Environmental Research, 85*, 69–76.

Carter, J. A., Lees, J. A., Gona, J. K., Murira, G., Rimba, K., Neville, B. G., et al. (2006). Severe falciparum malaria and acquired childhood language disorder. *Developmental Medicine and Child Neurology, 48*, 51–57.

Carter, J. A., Mung'ala-Odera, V., Neville, B. G., Murira, G., Mturi, N., Musumba, C., et al. (2005). Persistent neurocognitive impairments associated with severe falciparum malaria in Kenyan children. *Journal of Neurology, Neurosurgery, and Psychiatry, 76*, 476–481.

Choudhury, N., & Gorman, K. S. (2003). Subclinical prenatal iodine deficiency negatively affects infant development in Northern China. *Journal of Nutrition, 133*, 3162–3165.

Cooper, P. J., Landman, M., Tomlinson, M., Molteno, C., Swartz, L., & Murray, L. (2002). Impact of a mother–infant intervention in an indigent peri-urban South African context: Pilot study. *British Joirnal of Psychiatry, 180*, 76–81.

Cueto, S., & Diaz, J. (1999). Impacto de la educación inicial en el rendimiento en primer grado de primaria en escuelas públicas urbanas de Lima. *Revista de Psicologia, 17*(1), 74–91.

De Cock, K. M., Fowler, M. G., Mercier, E., de Vincenzi, I., Saba, J., Hoff, E., et al. (2000). Prevention of mother-to-child HIV transmission in resource-poor countries: Translating research into policy and practice. *Journal of the American Medical Association, 283*(9), 1175–1182.

De Onis, M., Blössner, M., & Villar, J. (1998). Levels and patterns of intrauterine growth retardation in developing countries. *European Journal of Clinical Nutrition, 52*(Suppl. 1), S5–15.

Engle, P. L. (2007). *Final Report to Tajikistan.* UNICEF Dushanbe.

Engle, P. L. (2008). *National plans of action for orphans and vulnerable children in sub-Saharan Africa: Where are the youngest children?* Working Papers in Early Childhood Development 50. The Hague: The Bernard van Leer Foundation.

Engle, P. L., Beardshaw, T., & Loftin, C. (2005). The child's right to shared parenting. In L. Richter and R. Morell (Eds.), *BABA: Men and fatherhood in South Africa.* Cape Town: HSRC Press.

Engle, P. L., Black, M. M., Behrman, J. R., Cabral de Mello, M., Gertler, P. J., Kapiri, L., et al. (2007). Strategies to avoid the loss of developmental potential in more than 200 million children in the developing world. *Lancet, 369*, 229–242.

Engle, P. L., & Dunkelberg, E., with Issa, S. (2007). ECD and HIV/AIDS: The newest programming and policy challenge. In J. Evans, A. Pence, & M. Garcia (Eds.), *Early child development in Africa*. Washington, DC: World Bank.

Engle, P. L., Grantham-McGregor, S., Black, M., Walker, S. P., & Wachs, T. (2007). How to avoid the loss of potential in over 200 million young children in the developing world. *Child Health and Education, 1*(2), 68–87.

Fawzi, W. W., Msamanga, G. I., Urassa, W., Hertzmark, E., Petraro, P., Willett, W. C., & Spiegelman, D. (2007). Vitamins and perinatal outcomes among HIV-negative women in Tanzania. *New England Journal of Medicine, 356*(14), 1423–1431.

Fernando, S. D., Gunawardena, D. M., Bandara, M. R., De Silva, D., Carter, R., Mendis, K. N., et al. (2003). The impact of repeated malaria attacks on the school performance of children. *American Journal of Tropical Medicine and Hygiene, 69*, 582–588.

Ghuman, S., Behrman, J., Gultiano, S., & King, E. (2006). *Children's nutrition, school quality, and primary school enrollment in the Philippines*. New York: Population Council.

Global Monitoring Report Team (2006). *EFA Global Monitoring Report: Strong foundations: Early Childhood Care and Education*. Paris: UNESCO.

Goldenberg, R. L., & Culhane, J. F. (2007). Low birth weight in the United States. *American Journal of Clinical Nutrition, 85*(2), 584S–590S.

Gorman, K. S., & Pollitt, E. (1992). Relationship between weight and body proportionality at birth, growth during the first year of life, and cognitive development at 36, 48, and 60 months. *Infant Behavior and Development, 15*, 279–296.

Grantham-McGregor, S. M., Fernald, L., & Sethuraman, K. (1999). Effects of health and nutrition on cognitive and behavioral development in the first 3 years of life. Part 2. Infections and micronutrient deficiencies: Iodine, iron and zinc. *Food and Nutrition Bulletin, 20*, 76–99.

Grantham-McGregor, S. M., Lira, P. I. C., Ashworth, A., Morris, S. S., & Assunção, M. A. S. (1998). The development of low birth weight term infants and the effects of the environment in north-east Brazil. *Journal of Pediatrics, 132*, 661–666.

Grantham-McGregor, S. M., Cheung, Y. B., Cueto, S., Glewwe, P. L., Richter, L., Strupp, B., & the International Child Development Steering Group (2007). Developmental potential in the first 5 years for children in developing countries. *Lancet, 369*, 60–70.

Hamadani, J. D., Huda, S. N., Khatun, F., & Grantham-McGregor, S. M. (2006). Psychosocial stimulation improves the development of undernourished children in rural Bangladesh. *Journal of Nutrition, 136*, 2645–2652.

Hamadani, J. D., Tofail, F., Yesmin, S., Hud, S. N., Engle, P. & Grantham-McGregor, S. M. (2010). Validating family care indicators in Bangladesh. *Journal of Health, Population and Nutrition, 28*(1), 22–33.

Joint Learning Initiative for Children and HIV/AIDS Learning Group on Expanding Access to Services and Protecting Human Rights (JLICA-LG3) (2008, March). *Report I: Integration and expansion of PMTCT-plus and early childhood intervention services*. Francois Xavier Bagnoud Center for Health and Human Rights, Harvard School of Public Health.

Kagitcibasi, C., Sunar, D., & Bekman, S. (2001). Long-term effects of early intervention: Turkish low-income mothers and children. *Journal of Applied Developmental Psychology, 222*, 333–361.

Kariger, P., Frongillo, E. A., Engle, P. L., Rebello, P. B., Sywulka, S. M., & Menon, P. (2008). *Indicators of psychosocial caregiving practices and resources for use with multi-country surveys*. Paper submitted for publication.

Keller, H., Abels, M., Lamm, B., Yovsi, R. D., Volker, S., & Lakhani, A. (2005). Ecocultural effects on early infant care: A study in Cameroon, India, and Germany. *Ethos, 33*, 512–541.

Kihara, M., Carter, J. A., & Newton, C. R. (2006). The effect of Plasmodium falciparum on cognition: A systematic review. *Tropical Medicine & International Health, 11,* 386–397.

Kramer, M. S., Aboud, F., Mironova, E., Vanilovich, I., Platt, R. W., Matush, L., et al. (2008). Breastfeeding and child cognitive development: New evidence from a large randomized trial. *Archives of General Psychiatry, 65*(5), 578–584.

Krishna, A. (2007). Escaping poverty and becoming poor in three states of India, with additional evidence from Kenya, Uganda, and Peru. In D. Narayan & P. Petesch (Eds.), *Moving out of poverty: Cross-disciplinary perspectives on mobility* (pp. 165–198). Washington, DC: Palgrave Macmillan and the World Bank.

Lepine, J. (2001). Epidemiology, burden, and disability in depression and anxiety. *Journal of Clinical Psychiatry, 62,* 4–10.

Lusk, D. (2005). *Bungoma and Vihiga annual assessments: Key results.* Washington, DC: Academy for Educational Development.

Lustig, S. (2009). An ecological framework for the refugee experience: What is the impact on child development? In G. W. Evans and T. D. Wachs (Eds.), *Chaos and children's development: Levels of analysis and mechanisms.* Washington, DC: American Psychological Association.

Magwaza, A., & Edwards, S. (1991). An evaluation of an integrated parent-effectiveness training and children's enrichment programme for disadvantaged families. *South African Journal of Psychology, 21,* 21–25.

McCormick, M. C., Brooks-Gunn, J., Buka, S. L., Goldman, J., Yu, J., Salganik, M., et al. (2006). Early intervention in low birth weight premature infants: Results at 18 years of age for the Infant Health and Development Program. *Pediatrics, 117*(3), 771–780.

Meeks Gardner, J., Walker, S. P., Powell, C., & Grantham-McGregor, S. (2003). A randomized controlled trial of a home visiting intervention on cognition and behaviour in term low birth weight infants. *Journal of Pediatrics, 143,* 634–639.

Molamu, L., & MacDonald, D. (1996). Alcohol abuse among the Basarwa of the Kgalagadi and Ghanzi districts in Botswana. *Drugs: Education, Prevention and Policy, 3*(2), 145–152.

Morenza, L., Arrazola, O., Seleme, I., & Martinez, F. (2005). Evaluación proyecto Kallpa Wawa. Report to UNICEF.

Morris, S. S., Grantham-McGregor, S. M., Lira, P. I., Assunção, A. M., & Ashworth A. (1999). Effect of breastfeeding and morbidity on the development of low birthweight term babies in Brazil. *Acta Paediatrica, 88*(10), 1101–1106.

Narayan, D., & Petesch, P. (2002). *Voices of the poor: From many lands.* Washington, DC: World Bank.

Narayan, D., & Petesch, P. (2007). Agency, opportunity structure, and poverty escapes. In D. Narayan & P. Petesch (Eds.), *Moving out of poverty: Cross-disciplinary perspectives on mobility* (pp. 1–44). Washington, DC: Palgrave Macmillan and the World Bank.

National Scientific Council on the Developing Child. (2007). *The Science of Early Child Development.* Center for the Developing Child, Cambridge, MA: Harvard University.

Potterton, J. L. (2007). *A longitudinal study of neurodevelopmental delay in HIV-infected children.* Dissertation. Pretoria: Human Sciences Research Council.

Powell, C. (2004). An evaluation of the roving caregivers programme of the Rural Family Support Organization. Report to UNICEF.

Powell, C., Baker-Henningham, H., Walker, S. P., Gernay, J., & Grantham-McGregor, S. (2004). Feasibility of integrating early stimulation into primary care for undernourished Jamaican children: cluster randomised controlled trial. *British Medical Journal, 329*(7457), 89.

Rahman, A., & Creed, F. (2007). Outcome of prenatal depression and risk factors associated with persistence in the first postnatal year: Prospective study from Rawalpindi, Pakistan. *Journal of Affective Disorders, 100,* 115–121.

Rao, N. (2005). Children's rights to survival, development, and early education in India: The critical role of the integrated child development services programme. *International Journal of Early Childhood, 37*(3), 15–31.

Ravallion, M. (1992). *Poverty comparisons: A guide to concepts and methods*. Washington, DC: World Bank.

Richter, L., & Foster, G. (2006). *The role of the health sector in strengthening systems to support children's healthy development in communities affected by HIV/AIDS: A review*. Geneva: Department of Child and Adolescent Health and Development (CAH), WHO.

Richter, L., Foster, G., & Sherr, L. (2006). *Where the heart is: Meeting the psychosocial needs of young children in the context of HIV/AIDS*. The Hague: Bernard van Leer Foundation.

Ross, K., Zuze, L., & Ratsatsi, D. (2005, September–October). *The use of socioeconomic gradient lines to judge the performance of school systems*. Presented at SACMEQ Research Conference, Paris.

Sachs, J. (2005). *The end to poverty*. New York: Penguin Group.

Sen, A. (1995). The political economy of targeting. In D. van de Walle & K. Nead (Eds.), *Public spending and the poor: Theory and evidence*. Baltimore, MD: Johns Hopkins University Press for the World Bank.

Shankar, A. H., Jahari, A. B., Sebayang, S. K., Aditiawarman, Apriatni, M., Harefa, B., et al. (2008). Effect of maternal multiple micronutrient supplementation on fetal loss and infant death in Indonesia: A double-blind cluster-randomised trial. *Lancet, 371*(9608), 215–227.

Shonkoff, J. P., & Phillips, D. A. (2000). *From neurons to neighborhoods: The science of child development*. Washington, DC: National Academy Press.

Siddiqi, A., Irwin, L. B., & Hertzman, C. (2007). *Total environment assessment model for early child development: Evidence report*. For the World Health Organization's Commission on the Social Determinants of Health.

Stein, J., Schettler, T., Wallinga, D., & Valenti, M. (2002). In harm's way: Toxic threats to child development. *Developmental and Behavioral Pediatrics, 23*(18), s13–s20.

Stewart, S. (2007). *No worse than their peers? Orphans' nutritional status in five Eastern and Southern African countries*. Paper prepared for UNICEF Eastern and Southern Africa Regional Office, Nairobi.

Stoltzfus, R. J., Mullany, L., & Black, R. E. (2005). Iron deficiency anaemia. In *Comparative quantification of health risks: Global and regional burden of disease attributable to selected major risk factors. Volume 1* (pp. 163–209). Geneva: World Health Organization.

Tang, D., Li, T.-Y., Liu, J. J., Zhou, Z.-J., Yuan, T., Chen, Y.-H., et al. (2008). Effects of prenatal exposure to coal-burning pollutants on children's development in China. *Environmental Health Perspectives, 116*(5), 674–679.

Tilly, C. (2007). Poverty and the politics of exclusion. In D. Narayan & P. Petesch (Eds.), *Moving out of poverty: Cross-disciplinary perspectives on mobility* (pp. 45–76). Washington, DC: Palgrave Macmillan and the World Bank.

Tsai, S. Y., Chou, H. Y., The, H. W., Chen, C. M., Chen, C. J. (2003). The effects of chronic arsenic exposure from drinking water on the neurobehavioral development in adolescence. *Neurotoxicology, 24*, 747–753.

UNAIDS and World Health Organization (2006). *WHO and UNAIDS Secretariat Statement on HIV Testing and Counseling*. www.who.int/hiv/toronto2006/WHO-UNAIDSstatement_TC_081406_dh.pdf (accessed February 2007).

UNAIDS (2006). *Report on the Global HIV/AIDS Epidemic*. Geneva: UNAIDS.

UNICEF (2006a). *Africa's orphaned and vulnerable generations: Children affected by AIDS*. New York: UNICEF.

UNICEF (2006b). *The state of the world's children: Excluded and invisible*. New York: UNICEF.

United Nations Committee on the Rights of the Child, UNICEF, and Bernard van Leer Foundation (2006). *A Guide to General Comment 7: Implementing child rights in early childhood*. The Hague: Bernard van Leer Foundation.

Van Rie, A., Mupuala, A., & Dow, A. (2008). Impact of the HIV/AIDS epidemic on the neurodevelopment of preschool-aged children in Kinshasa, Democratic Republic of the Congo. *Pediatrics, 122*, 123–128.

Vazir, S., & Kashinath, K. (1999). Influence of the ICDS on psychosocial development of rural children in southern India. *Journal of the Indian Academy of Applied Psychology, 25*(1–2), 11–24.

Villar, J., & Belizán, J. (1982). The relative contributions of prematurity and fetal growth retardation to low birth weight in developing and developed countries. *American Journal of Obstetrics and Gynecology, 143*, 793–798.

Villar, J., Smeriglio, V., Martorell, R., Brown, C. H., & Klein, R. E. (1984). Heterogeneous growth and mental development of intrauterine growth-retarded infants during the first 3 years of life. *Pediatrics, 74*, 783–791.

Waber, D. P., Vuori-Christiansen, L., Ortiz, N., Clement, J. R., Christiansen, N. E., Mora, J. O., et al. (1981). Nutritional supplementation, maternal education, and cognitive development of infants at risk of malnutrition. *American Journal of Clinical Nutrition, 34*, 807–813.

Wachs, T. D. (2000). *Necessary but not sufficient: The role of individual and multiple influences on human development*. Washington, DC: American Psychological Association Press.

Wachs, T. D., Black, M. M., & Engle, P. L. (2009). Maternal depression: A global threat to children's health, development, and behavior and to human rights. *Child Development Perspectives, 3*(1), 51–59.

Wachs, T. D., Chang-Lopez, S. M., Walker, S. P., & Meeks Gardner, J. (2007). Relation of birth weight, maternal intelligence and mother–child interactions to cognitive and play competence of Jamaican two-year-old children. *Intelligence, 35*, 605–622.

Walker, S. P., Chang, S. M., Powell, C. A., & Grantham-McGregor, S. M. (2004). Psychosocial intervention improves the development of term low-birth-weight infants. *Journal of Nutrition, 134*, 1417–1423.

Walker, S. P., Chang, S. M., Powell, C. A., & Grantham-McGregor, S. M. (2005). Effects of early childhood psychosocial stimulation and nutritional supplementation on cognition and education in growth-stunted Jamaican children: Prospective cohort study. *Lancet, 366*, 1804–1807.

Walker, S. P., Wachs, T. D., Gardner, J. M., Lozoff, B., Wasserman, G. A., Pollitt, E., et al. (2007). Child development: Risk factors for adverse outcomes in developing countries. *Lancet, 369*, 145–157.

Wasserman, G. A., Liu, X., Parvez, F., Ahsan, H., Factor-Litvak, P., van Geen, A., et al. (2004). Water arsenic exposure and children's intellectual function in Araihazar, Bangladesh. *Environmental Health Perspectives, 112*, 1329–1333.

Watts, H., Gregson, S., Saito, S., Lopman, B., Beasley, M. & Monasch, R. (2007). Poorer health and nutritional outcomes in orphans and vulnerable young children not explained by greater exposure to extreme poverty in Zimbabwe. *Tropical Medicine and International Health, 12*(5), 584–593.

Wendland-Carro, J., Piccinini, C. A., & Millar, W. S. (1999). The role of an early intervention on enhancing the quality of mother–infant interaction. *Child Development, 70*, 713–721.

World Bank (2005). *World Development Report 2006: Equity and development*. Washington, DC: World Bank.

World Health Organization (2003). *Gender, tobacco and health*. Geneva: WHO.

World Health Organization (2004). *Global database on iodine deficiency. Iodine status worldwide*. Geneva: WHO.

World Health Organization Department of Mental Health and Substance Abuse (2004). *Global status report on alcohol*. Geneva: WHO.

7

Child Abuse and Neglect

Kelli Connell-Carrick

Since Henry Kempe and his colleagues coined the term "battered child syndrome," the phenomenon of child maltreatment has been embraced by the public and research community as a major social issue (Kempe, Silverman, Steele, Droegemueller, & Silver, 1962). The phrase "battered child syndrome" referred to a clinical condition of children with diagnosable medical and physical symptoms resulting from deliberate physical assault (Kempe et al., 1962). This was a landmark step in defining child abuse, and laid the groundwork for the later definition of other forms of maltreatment, such as sexual abuse, neglect, and emotional maltreatment.

There were almost 1 million confirmed victims of child maltreatment in 2005 in the United States, and the highest rate of victimization is for children aged 0–3 (US Department of Health and Human Services (USDHHS), 2007). The youngest children also experience the greatest rate of fatality due to child maltreatment. Children under the age of 4 account for 77% of maltreatment related fatalities, and 42% of child fatalities are the result of neglect (USDHHS, 2007). Many children are rendered disabled and developmental delayed because of child abuse and neglect in infancy and toddlerhood (Musheno, 2006), and recent law has even required children who are maltreated from 0 to 3 to be referred to early intervention services as part of Part C of the Individuals with Disabilities Education Act (PL 108-466) for services (see Connell-Carrick & Scannapieco, 2007, for a more thorough discussion).

During the first two years of life, a child experiences tremendous growth in all areas of development. They develop from newborns to walking, talking toddlers with complex play and social understanding. Child maltreatment during the early years compromises healthy child development. Child maltreatment includes physical abuse, neglect, and sexual abuse. Although conceptualized as a distinct form of maltreatment, emotional abuse transcends all of these areas during the first three years.

This chapter will provide an overview of the major theories that guide the study of child abuse and neglect, delineate the causes and consequences of neglect, child physical abuse, and sexual abuse, and identify the risk and protective factors in assessing and treating victims who are infants and toddlers.

Theoretical Perspective

Since the growing awareness of child maltreatment in the 1960s, the professional literature has attempted to give us a clearer understanding of the etiology of child physical abuse, sexual abuse, and neglect (Scannapieco & Connell-Carrick, 2005a). Recognizing child maltreatment as a multifaceted problem, a comprehensive theoretical approach is required, taking into account ecological risk factors at varying systemic levels, and the transactions within each developmental stage of the child. The two major theoretical frameworks that are the foundation for understanding and treating child maltreatment are the ecological and developmental perspectives. An ecological perspective allows for an interactional and conceptual understanding of human behavior and social functioning. The developmental perspective provides a framework for understanding the growth and functioning of children in the context of the family (Scannapieco & Connell-Carrick, 2005a). While no one theory has been identified as a conclusive unifying framework – largely due to the inability to empirically test the theories – the ecological/transactional model is currently a widely embraced theoretical perspective due in part to its integration of multiple perspectives (Cicchetti & Rizley, 1981; Cicchetti & Lynch, 1993; Pecora, Whittaker, Maluccio, Barth, & Plotnik, 2000).

Ecological model

Bronfenbrenner (1979) proposed an ecological perspective on human development which Belsky (1980) applied specifically to child maltreatment. What separates the ecological model from other theoretical models is its deviation from single focused processes to a transactional and multilevel explanation. The ecological model places an individual in an interdependent relationship with the culture and situation, where one influences the other.

The ecological perspective is organized in four levels: (1) ontogenic, (2) microsystem, (3) exosystem, and (4) macrosystem. The levels are ecologically nested within one another, and maltreatment is determined by the interaction of, and between, levels. Therefore, an understanding of maltreatment is only possible by examining all the levels and their interaction. The examination of any one level provides an insufficient etiology for maltreatment (Scannapieco & Connell-Carrick, 2005a). Each level will be described briefly.

Ontogenic development.   Belsky's primary contribution to the ecological perspective on child maltreatment is his addition of the ontogenic level. Ontogenic development explores the childhood histories of abusive parents (Belsky, 1980) to assess how a particular parent grows to behave in an abusive manner. The occurrence of abuse or neglect in childhood alone is insufficient to explain the phenomenon of child maltreatment, because the majority of those who were maltreated fail to maltreat their own children (Belsky, 1980). Yet the developmental history of the parents may predispose them to respond to certain situations in the microsystem or exosystem in ways that can lead to maltreatment.

One well-known issue in the ontogenic level about which much is known is attachment. Research shows that maltreated children are more likely to have insecure attachments, and many have disorganized-disoriented (Type D) attachment patterns (Crittenden, 1988; Carlson, Cicchetti, Barnett, & Braunwald, 1989; Eckenrode, Egeland, & Sroufe, 1981; Main & Solomon, 1986). Bowlby (1982) explained that children form mental representations of their relationship to others based on their attachment to their primary caregiver, which includes affect, cognition and expectations about future interactions. This primary relationship influences the internal working model (IWM), which serves as a template for other interpersonal relationships throughout one's life (Bowlby, 1982). One's expectations and views of relationships are impacted by the IWMs that began during childhood. This places parents who were maltreated with a possible predisposition to maltreat, depending upon circumstances in the other levels of the ecological model (Scannapieco & Connell-Carrick, 2005a). Attachment theory is discussed in detail in chapter 16 of volume 1, and a more thorough discussion on the relationship between child maltreatment and attachment is presented later in this chapter.

Microsystem.   Many of the additional factors that interact with the parents' developmental history occur within the family. The microsystem is the immediate context in which child maltreatment takes place, and includes the family system, the maltreatment itself, and both parent and child characteristics. Within the microsystem child maltreatment is considered an interactive process (Belsky, 1980), and while children may play a role in their own maltreatment, they cannot cause it themselves (Scannapieco & Connell-Carrick, 2005a). Certain child characteristics can serve as contributors to child maltreatment which can make parenting difficult and unrewarding (Green, 1968). For example, children can be at greater risk of maltreatment if they are born prematurely (DiScala, Sege, Li, & Reece, 2000; Vig & Kaminer, 2002); are perceived by their parents as being less attractive (Frodi & Lamb, 1980); or have physical and mental disabilities (Ousted, Oppenheimer, & Lindsay, 1974; Vig & Kaminer, 2002; Gil, 1970).

Characteristics of the parent can also impact the likelihood of maltreatment. Parents who maltreat are more likely than nonmaltreating parents to have a history of abuse or neglect themselves (Cadzow, Armstrong, & Fraser, 1999; Kaufman & Zigler, 1989), are less satisfied with their children, and perceive parenting as less enjoyable and more difficult (Trickett, Aber, Carlson, & Cicchetti, 1991). Interpersonal violence, such as domestic violence and spousal abuse, also increases the likelihood of maltreatment to occur (Eckenrode et al., 2000; Rumm, Cummings, Krauss, Bell, & Rivara, 2000).

Exosystem.   The exosystem encompasses the individual and family within larger social structures including work, neighborhood, school, formal and informal support networks, socioeconomic status, and social services. Several aspects of the exosystem have been correlated with child maltreatment including unemployment (Wolfner & Gelles, 1993), and low social support and low social contact within one's community (Brayden, Atlemeier, Tucker, Dietrich, & Vietze, 1992; Connell-Carrick, & Scannapieco, 2006; Coohey,

1996; Corse, Schmid, & Trickett, 1990). Social isolation is more characteristic of parents who neglect their children, while social conflict is indicative of abusive parents (Crittenden, 1985). In neighborhoods with equal socioeconomic disadvantage, neighborhoods with more social resources, such as high neighborhood social support, less drug and alcohol availability (i.e., fewer bars and fewer drug possession incidents (Freisthler, 2004)), and residential stability, experience less child maltreatment than neighborhoods with fewer social resources and less social contact (Belsky, 1978; Freisthler, Merritt & La Scala, 2006). In addition, families who lack a connection to their community have fewer opportunities for exposure to child-rearing practices that could improve their own parenting skills (Trickett & Susman, 1988). Without this social filter and opportunities for parental learning, at-risk parents lack a connection to emotional and material support during stressful times which may contribute to maltreatment.

Macrosystem.   The macrosystem examines the embeddedness of the individual, community and family within the larger cultural fabric (see chapter 21 in volume 1 for a discussion of cultural influences). Poverty and socioeconomic status have been shown to be related to the occurrence of maltreatment (Gelles & Straus, 1987; Scannapieco & Connell-Carrick, 2002; Wolfner & Gelles, 1993). Living in substandard conditions with few economic resources can create a stressful environment and exert negative influences on other levels of the ecosystem, thereby placing children more at risk of maltreatment.

The macrosystem also examines the larger cultural fabric of society including the acceptance of violence and attitudes toward children. The United States, compared to other countries, tolerates violence to a certain degree (Christoffel, 1990), and the line between violence and punishment is ambiguous (Scannapieco & Connell-Carrick, 2005a). For example, countries with the lowest rates of death from maltreatment also have low rates of adult homicide, and countries with high levels of child death have high adult homicide rates, reflecting a larger social fabric of violence (UNICEF, 2003).

Similarly, the value placed on physical punishment for child discipline varies by culture. Korean parents have been found to report negative attitudes toward physical abuse, but positive attitudes toward the use of physical punishment as a discipline (Park, 2001), and tend to feel that physical punishment is necessary for disciplining children (Chun, 1989). Differences may also arise in regard to socioeconomic disparity. For example, research has shown that working-class parents are less likely to promote curiosity and to use reasoning in discipline, while middle-class parents encourage child inquisition and provide greater detail in their explanations to their children (Wolkind & Rutter, 1985).

The ecological model of child maltreatment lends itself to a multidisciplinary approach to the phenomenon of child maltreatment by drawing from the fields of psychology, medicine, sociology and child development (Ammerman, 1990). The ecological perspective has utility for both practice and research because the ecological model avoids deterministic cause–effect explanations of behavior and allows for many different ways to view patterns of relationships and the context of maltreatment (Payne, 1997). The ecological model also allows for interactive thinking, which concentrates on the ecological place of each individual rather than focusing on the internal thoughts and feelings of a single perpetrator or victim. In addition to understanding how factors in each ecological level contribute to the occurrence of child maltreatment, it is also important to understand how the ecological context of child maltreatment manifests in consequences to the child.

Ecological/transactional model

Cicchetti and Lynch (1993) drew upon Belsky's (1980) ecological model and Cicchetti and Rizley's (1981) transactional framework to develop the ecological/transactional model of child maltreatment. The ecological/transactional model presents a broad and integrative framework for explaining the processes associated with both the occurrence of child maltreatment and developmental outcomes. While the ecological model focuses on the etiology of child maltreatment, the transactional model focuses more closely on the outcomes of child maltreatment, with special attention to developmental outcomes for children (Cicchetti & Lynch, 1993).

The underlying assumption of the framework is that children's multiple ecologies influence one another, which in turn affects development (Cicchetti & Lynch, 1993). Thus, the individual, community, family, and larger culture combine to influence the developmental outcomes for children and shape the probabilistic course of the development of maltreated children. It is important to understand that the presence of violence at one level does not sentence children to poor developmental outcomes, and this model acknowledges that risk factors and protective factors exist that either contribute to or protect the child from adverse developmental outcomes.

Risk and protective factors.   A combination of individual, community, societal, and family risk factors contribute to the occurrence of child maltreatment. Although risk factors correlate to child maltreatment, they do not cause it; they only increase the likelihood of a particular event occurring. Protective factors, on the other hand, moderate or buffer the risks and therefore should reduce the likelihood of child maltreatment. Protective factors also exist at the family, societal, and individual level. Numerous studies have examined the risk and protective factors that influence the occurrence of child maltreatment.

Several factors have been identified in the empirical literature to increase the risk of child maltreatment (Table 7.1) including poverty, young maternal age, low education, and domestic violence (Eckenrode et al., 2000; Famularo, Kinscherff, & Fenton, 1992; Hay & Jones, 1994; Stier, Leventhal, Berg, Johnson, & Mezger, 1993). Chronic childhood illness, premature birth, and congenital abnormalities have also been shown to be at increased risk of maltreatment (Vig & Kaminer, 2002). In fact, DiScala et al. (2000) found that children who were physically abused were seven times more likely to have been born prematurely than children without an intentional injury. Other risk factors include a history of parental maltreatment (Straus, 1994), problems during pregnancy (Barth, 1991), parental perception of parenting as not enjoyable (Scannapieco & Connell-Carrick, 2005b; Trickett et al., 1991), substance abuse (Chaffin, Kelleher, & Hollenberg, 1996; Gessner, Moore, Hamilton, & Muth, 2004; Scannapieco & Connell-Carrick, 2007), depression (Coohey, 1998), single parenthood (Cadzow et al., 1999;

Table 7.1 Risk factors for child maltreatment.

Parent
- Parental history of maltreatment
- Parent does not enjoy baby – negative perception of child
- Parent does not enjoy parenting
- Lack of understanding about role as caregiver
- Lack of understanding about complexity of human relationships and importance of attachment
- Lack of understanding about child development
- Deficits in empathy
- Substance abuse/dependence
- Low self-esteem
- Depression
- Anger management problems
- Lack of education
- Young maternal age
- History of parental abuse
- Parental mental illness
- Unemployment
- Inadequate prenatal care
- Previous adverse pregnancy experience

Child
- Young child age
- Child born prematurely
- Born with low birth weight
- Child with physical or mental disability
- Child tests positive for alcohol or other drugs
- Chronic illness in infancy/childhood
- Disability

Family
- Poverty
- Lack of social support and social isolation
- Single parenthood
- Domestic violence
- History of child abuse within family
- Substance abuse
- Poor parent–child relationship
- Receipt of Medicaid

Societal and environmental
- Culture that supports violence
- Culture that approves of corporal punishment
- Attitudes towards how mothers should behave as a parent
- Power differentials

Scannapieco & Connell-Carrick, 2005a), and parental mental illness (Cadzow et al., 1999).

In addition to parent and child factors, environmental factors also increase the risk of child maltreatment such as lack of social support and poor social environment (Brayden, et al., 1992; Connell-Carrick & Scannapieco, 2006; Coohey, 1996; Scannapieco & Connell-Carrick, 2005b). Wu et al. (2004) explored the risk factors specific for abuse during infancy and found Medicaid receipt, nonmarital status, low birth weight, low maternal education, inadequate prenatal care, and previous adverse pregnancy experience increase the risk of child maltreatment. After further statistical analyses, they found the two highest risk factors were smoking during pregnancy and more than two siblings.

On the other hand, several protective factors can help reduce the chance of child maltreatment occurring (Table 7.2). Parents whose pasts are free from violence are less likely to commit child abuse and neglect (Scannapieco & Connell-Carrick, 2005a). A child's easy temperament and personality/emotional attributes that match well with those

Table 7.2 Protective factors for child maltreatment.

Parent
- Secure attachment as a child
- Supportive partner in the home
- Stable relationships
- Parental employment
- Knowledge of parenting and child development

Child
- Goodness of fit with parent
- Easy temperament
- Lacks disabilities
- Intellectual ability
- Healthy social and emotional development
- Warm and secure family relationships

Family
- Connectedness in community
- Adequate formal and informal support
- Living in a nonviolent community
- Parental perception of neighborhood is positive
- Economic security
- Supportive family environment
- Adequate housing
- Access to healthcare and social services
- Extrafamilial support (peers, teachers)

Societal and environmental
- Cultural value of protecting children
- Culture that does not objectify children as sexual
- Communities that support parents and take responsibility for preventing abuse

of their caregiver promote attachment and can protect a child from abuse, as can a child's intellectual ability and responsiveness to a parent (Luthar & Zigler, 1991) and normal or above average development (Hodges, 1993). In addition, mothers in happy, violence-free relationships and the presence of fathers or father-figures decrease the likelihood of maltreatment (Gaudin & Dubowitz, 1997; Marshall, English & Stewart, 2001; Scannapieco & Connell-Carrick, 2005b). Families characterized by warm and secure family relationships and extrafamilial support, such as peers and teacher support, can serve as protective factors of child maltreatment (Heller, Larrieu, D'Imperio & Boris, 1999), as do access to healthcare and social services, adequate housing, employment, and supportive family environments (Heller et al., 1999). Overall, the community plays a large role in setting and enforcing cultural norms. Risk is reduced when communities support parents and take responsibility for preventing abuse (USDHHS, 2003).

Overall, the ecological/transactional model provides a sound theoretical framework that is important for understanding the causes and consequences of child maltreatment. This framework examines not only the ecology of child maltreatment, including risk and protective factors, but also the consequences to the child, which are discussed later in this chapter.

In addition to understanding child maltreatment within an ecological context, it is also important to closely examine how attachment affects both the occurrence and the consequences of child maltreatment. Because attachment is a primary developmental need in infancy, the implications of poor attachment can have lifelong consequences, which helps us conceptualize how attachment can be a factor in understanding why a parent maltreats her/his child, as well as gives us insight into the consequences to victims.

Child maltreatment and attachment

Attachment theory has informed child maltreatment practice and research for decades (Aber & Allen, 1987; Brazelton, 1988; Carlson et al., 1989; Cicchetti & Lynch, 1993; Egeland & Sroufe, 1981; Perry, 1994). It is well established in the empirical literature that the quality of the caregiver–child interaction during the first three years has important implications for child development (Beckwith, 1990; Belsky, Rovine, & Taylor, 1984; Brazelton, 1988; Carlson, 1998; Scannapieco & Connell-Carrick, 2005a; see also chapter 16 in volume 1). This chapter will focus on the relationship between attachment and child maltreatment.

Child maltreatment affects all areas of a child's development, not only at the time of the incident, but also across the lifespan. Attachment can be classified into two major categories, secure and insecure, the latter with three classifiable subtypes, resistant/ambivalent, avoidant, and disorganized/disoriented. Research shows that approximately two thirds of maltreated children have insecure attachments, and possibly as many as 80% of those children with insecure attachments (Cicchetti & Barnett, 1991) have disorganized-disoriented (Type D) attachment patterns (Baer & Martinez, 2007; Crittenden, 1988; Carlson et al., 1989; Egeland & Sroufe, 1981; Main & Solomon, 1986). Disorganized attachment patterns represent the absence of a single coping mechanism with which to deal with stress and separation/reunion with a caregiver. Caregivers who maltreat contribute to the development of this pattern in infants because the caregiver is often both the source of and the solution to the infant's anxiety. A disorganized attachment pattern has been shown to have long-term stability and predicts poor developmental outcomes (Carlson, 1998). Interestingly, maltreated children with insecure attachments have a more stable attachment pattern than maltreated children with secure attachments (Schneider-Rosen, Braunwald, Carlson, & Cicchetti, 1985).

Consequences of an impaired attachment

The cost of an impaired attachment to the individual ranges from the most severe loss of the capacity to form any meaningful relationships, to mild interpersonal, social, or emotional problems. The *Diagnostic and Statistical Manual of Mental Disorders* (DSM-IV-TR) indicates that lack of adequate care can lead to reactive attachment disorder (RAD) of infancy or early childhood (American Psychiatric Association, 1994). It is important to note that the diagnosis of RAD is controversial, primarily because some researchers feel that the diagnosis pathologizes children and the diagnosis of and treatment for RAD lack strong empirical support (Werner-Wilson & Davenport, 2003). However, at this time it is still a diagnosable condition in the DSM-IV-TR (for a detailed discussion of attachment disorders see chapter 11 in this volume).

An impaired attachment relationship in infancy can have long lasting consequences, primarily because of its influence on the child's overall development and internal working model. Children with secure attachments feel confident that the world will meet their needs; they trust that the world is a place for them to explore through physical and emotional means. On the other hand, children with insecure attachment do not have that same understanding of the world. Thus, a child with an insecure-avoidant attachment might interpret "neutral or even friendly behavior as hostile and show inappropriate aggressive behavior" (Widom, 2000, p. 351). Research has shown that the experience of physical abuse in childhood may lead to aggressive behavior because the individual's internal working model includes a tendency to process information through deficient and hostile-influenced mechanisms (Dodge, Bates, & Petit, 1990). Similarly, children with insecure attachments cope with their environments less well than children with secure attachments. They often behave more impulsively and lack problem-solving skills. Other maladaptive means of coping include running away, especially for abused and neglected adolescents, a negative view of self, an increased risk for internalizing and externalizing psychopathology (Muller, Lemieux, & Sciolo, 2001), and substance abuse (Harrison, Hoffmann, & Edwall, 1989). Although it is difficult to ascertain the actual causes of maladaptive coping and behavioral patterns, since an impaired attachment affects all aspects of development, research has shown a link between early childhood maltreatment and later personality disorders and psychopathology. Childhood emotional abuse and neglect have been shown to be related to borderline personality disorder in adulthood, and childhood sexual abuse and physical abuse have been found to be predictors of both paranoid and antisocial personality disorders (Bierer et al., 2003).

Some children endure horrendous abuse, but have a stable and loving attachment figure during their first three years. The presence of this person and the influence this relationship has on their relational template may help them overcome the negative effects that could have resulted from their abuse. Because not all victims of child maltreatment experience severe consequences, it is important to explore both the risk and protective factors in a family within an ecological context. In general, however, without the presence of multiple strong protective factors, healthy development is compromised by negative childhood experiences, especially child maltreatment.

Child Maltreatment in Infants and Toddlers

As noted earlier, infants and toddlers make tremendous developmental gains from 0 to 3 years of age. They evolve from primarily reflexive beings to walking and talking toddlers, and child maltreatment affects all areas of a child's development. More children die from maltreatment between the ages of 0 and 3 than during any other time (USDHHS, 2007). Besides death, children may suffer developmental delays, including cognitive, social, emotional and physical problems. Infants and toddlers who enter the state's custody due to child maltreatment have been shown to be at risk on developmental screenings (Dale, Kendall, & Humber, 1996), and significantly below average on Bayley Scales of Infant Development (Urquiza, Wirtz, Peterson, & Singer, 1994). While all three forms of maltreatment (physical abuse, neglect, and sexual abuse) overlap to a certain extent, especially when discussing such young victims, each type results in developmental consequences to its victims. This section presents the consequences of neglect, physical abuse, and sexual abuse during the first three years. Table 7.3 presents a representative, but not exhaustive, list of both common effects found across neglect, physical abuse and sexual abuse, and unique effects of each type of maltreatment.

Neglect

Consistently in the United States, neglect is the most prevalent form of maltreatment perpetrated on infants and toddlers. Approximately 75% of victims of child maltreatment between the ages of 0 and 3 experience neglect (UHDHHS, 2007), and research has shown children under the age of 1 suffer neglect twice that of other ages (Raiha & Soma, 1997). Neglect is difficult to define, and definitions often vary depending upon the perspective one takes, such as legal, medical, psychosocial, social service, or lay (Erickson & Egeland, 2002). In general, neglect is the failure of caregivers to provide for a child's basic needs and typically includes inadequate food, housing, clothing, medical care, and education. It is often defined as "omissions of care resulting in significant harm or the risk of significant harm to children" (Dubowitz, 2000, p. 10). Most definitions of neglect are derived from the Child Abuse Prevention and Treatment Act of 1974 (P.L. 93-247) which defines abuse and neglect as "the physical or mental injury, sexual abuse or exploitation, negligent treatment, or maltreatment of a child under the age of 18."

Neglect is significantly different from other forms of child maltreatment. It is the omission of behavior, rather than a commission as is the case of physical or sexual abuse.

Table 7.3 Effects of neglect, physical abuse, and sexual abuse.

Overlapping effects of neglect, physical abuse and sexual abuse	Effects of neglect	Effects of physical abuse	Effects of sexual abuse
Impaired brain development/ brain injury	Delayed language development/ language deficits	Physical injury, which may include burns, bite marks, abdominal injury	Genital area infected, irritated, red, or blistered
Impaired attachment/ insecure attachment	Small height and weight	Fractures – old and new	Genital tears
Depression	Little enthusiasm for play	Untreated injuries	Sexually transmitted disease
Behavioral and emotional problems	Passive/withdrawn	Delayed language development	Difficulty with bowel movements
Social withdrawal	Cognitive deficits	Cognitive deficits/low IQ	Anxiety
Peer problems/ trouble with peers	Easily frustrated in play	PTSD/PTSD symptomology	PTSD/PTSD symptomology
	Impulsive	Aggression and delinquency in childhood and adulthood	Sexualized behaviors and/or mimicking sexual acts
	Poor school performance	Likelihood of being either a victim or perpetrator in childhood and adulthood	
		Male arrest for violent crimes	
		Work problems	

It also tends to be more chronic, rather than episodic (Scannapieco & Connell-Carrick, 2005a); more of a lifestyle than an event. Because of the growing infant's need for tactile and environmental stimulation, the emotional and physical deprivation inherent in neglect is particularly damaging to both short- and long-term development. Although several different subtypes of neglect exist and can be found in the literature, this chapter will focus primarily on physical and emotional neglect, which accounts for the majority of cases of maltreatment in infancy and toddlerhood (see chapter 2 in this volume for discussion of nonorganic causes of failure to thrive).

Correlates of neglect.   Several family and environmental characteristics have been found in the empirical literature to be associated with child neglect (see Connell-Carrick, 2003, for a complete review) including young maternal age (Brown, Cohen, Johnson, & Salzinger, 1998; Chaffin et al., 1996; Lee & Goerge, 1999) and single parenthood (Chaffin et al., 1996; Scannapieco & Connell-Carrick, 2005b; Sedlak & Broadhurst, 1996). In homes where neglect occurs, caregivers has been shown to have poorer parental capacity, less parenting knowledge, and provide poorer-quality care to the children (Connell-Carrick & Scannapieco, 2006). They have been shown to express less warmth (Gaudin, Polansky, Kilpatrick, & Shilton, 1993), have less empathy, and show less positive affect (Gaudin, Polansky, Kilpatrick, & Shilton, 1996). Families in which neglect occurs also tend to have more persons living in the home than families that do not neglect (Brown et al., 1998; Sedlak, 1997); and one study found that the greater the number of children aged 0–36 months in the home the more likely neglect was to occur (Connell-Carrick & Scannapieco, 2006). Other correlates of neglect include substance abuse (Coohey, 1998; Sun, Shillington, Hohman, & Jones, 2001), low maternal education (Brown et al., 1998; Zuravin & DiBlasio, 1996), depression (Brown et al., 1998; Coohey, 1998; Zuravin & DiBlasio, 1996), and low social support (Connell-Carrick & Scannapieco, 2006; Coohey, 1996; Coohey, 1998; Gaudin et al., 1993), including isolation, negative relationships and violence. However, Dubowitz, Black, Kerr, Starr, and Harrington (2000) found that the presence of a father or father figure significantly decreased the likelihood of neglect, especially when the father was involved in the care of and responsibility for the child(ren) and household.

The literature has also found poverty to be a risk factor for neglect (Lee & Goerge, 1999; Scannapieco & Connell-Carrick, 2002; Sedlak & Broadhurst, 1996). In fact, of all types of maltreatment, neglect is the most closely associated with poverty (Crittenden, 1996). One study found that children born to mothers 17 years of age or younger who lived in high-poverty areas were 17 times more likely to have a substantiated case of neglect than children born to mothers who were 22 years of age or more in low-poverty areas (Lee & Goerge, 1999).

The home and social environments in which neglect occurs are poor (Connell-Carrick, 2003; Connell-Carrick & Scannapieco, 2006). Neglect is often characterized by a chaotic and disorganized home environment (Brown et al., 1998; Connell-Carrick & Scannapieco, 2006; Gaudin et al., 1996) with more environmental stressors such as overcrowding and more dangerous living conditions (Connell-Carrick & Scannapieco, 2006). There tends to be less family leadership and cohesion, lack of parental responsibility, and less closeness than in nonneglecting homes (Gaudin et al., 1996). Parents who neglect tend to lack understanding of the importance and complexity of human connectedness and relationships, especially their importance during infancy (Erickson & Egeland, 2002). They tend to have difficulty seeing things from the child's perspective and understanding the child's behavior within a developmental context. This lack of understanding often results in the failure to provide appropriate affective experiences for the infant and may result in material and emotional deprivation.

Short- and long-term consequences.   In the past, the consequences of child neglect were considered less severe than those of physical or sexual abuse. This is no longer the case and research has shown the profound effects of neglect on infants and toddlers. Neglect during the first years of life may lead to irreversible and severe damage to the developing child, and the more chronic and severe the neglect, the more severe the damage to the child.

An infant or toddler who has been neglected may have an array of effects that span all areas of the child's development (Scannapieco & Connell-Carrick, 2003, 2005a). Children who have been neglected may have delayed cognitive development (Scannapieco & Connell-Carrick, 2003), including expressive and receptive language delays and deficits (Gowen, 1994). Neglected children are often smaller in height and weight and have skin that is dull and hair that is thin. Both fine and gross motor skill development is often markedly delayed. In play, neglected toddlers tend to be angry, easily frustrated, impulsive and show little enthusiasm (Erickson & Egeland, 2002). Neglected children tend to be passive and withdrawn, have trouble with peer relationships, and have disciplinary problems in school settings.

Chronic neglect during infancy and toddlerhood can result in damage to the child's developing brain. Babies' brains grow and develop as they interact with their environments. A rich, stimulating environment is an essential element for brain development where neural pathways are formed. Consequently, neural pathways that are not stimulated decrease and pathways that are stimulated flourish (Nelson, Thomas & de Haan, 2006). The later functioning of a child may depend upon the development of critical pathways in infancy. Thus, chronic neglect and stimulation deprivation may result in less brain capacity, a smaller brain, fewer neural pathways, and intellectual damage that manifests later in life (Greenough, Black, & Wallace, 1987; Perry & Pollard, 1998).

Especially when neglect occurs before the age of 3, the child may have difficulty forming or maintaining close relationships due to the damage done to the attachment relationship and consequently the child's internal working model. Perry (1997) maintains that the lack of appropriate affective experiences through attachment in the early years of life misorganizes the child's attachment capabilities for later in life. Because some emotions such as empathy, remorse, and sympathy are experience-dependent (i.e., learning that is unique to a child's particular world; learning "depends" upon what a child encounters in her/his environment) (Pollak & Sinha, 2002), a child who lacks an appropriate emotional experience with a caregiver in the early years of life will fail to develop such emotions (Perry, 1997).

Neglect has a profound effect on a developing child. Infants are inherently dependent and a lack of provision or the inadequate provision of basic physical and emotional care results in serious developmental consequences. However, other forms of maltreatment, such as physical and sexual abuse, also seriously affect infant development in both similar and unique ways.

Physical abuse

The second most prevalent form of child maltreatment, child physical abuse remains a significant concern to the well-being of children. About 17% of victims of maltreatment in the United States are victims of physical abuse, and 24% of maltreatment-related fatalities in 2005 were the result of physical abuse (USDHHS, 2007). Physical abuse is often the result of harsh discipline and corporal punishment in order to control infant and toddler behavior, but extends beyond the point of discipline to physical injury or the risk of physical injury. A clear definition of physical abuse is still debated. General guidelines for identifying physical abuse include experiencing an injury (harm standard) or risk of an injury (endangerment standard) as a result of having been hit with a hand or other object or having been kicked, shaken, thrown, burned, stabbed, or choked by a parent or parent-surrogate (Kolko, 2002). A difficulty in summarizing the physical abuse literature is that research often fails to use consistent definitions, and does not always measure severity, duration of abuse, and frequency, which have a great impact on the outcomes seen among children. However, in spite of the challenges to maltreatment research in overcoming these methodological obstacles and the breadth of the topic, the following discussion covers the correlates and consequences of physical abuse. A unique form of physical abuse during infancy, shaken baby syndrome, is also discussed.

Physical abuse tends to occur during moments of great stress, and often the parental explanation of the adverse event is inconsistent with the injury. Families from all socioeconomic, racial, and educational backgrounds commit physical abuse, but it is most often confirmed for single parents and poor households (Belsky & Vondra, 1989; Whipple & Webster-Stratton, 1991). Parents who commit physical abuse also tend to have poor impulse control, a history of abuse or neglect in their childhood, low maternal education (Cadzow et al., 1999), and drug and alcohol abuse (Gessner et al., 2004; Scannapieco & Connell-Carrick, 2007). Although most incidences of physical abuse occur during times of great stress, one particular form of infant abuse – shaken baby syndrome – is typically caused during periods of inconsolable crying or irritability during infancy.

Effects of physical abuse.   Infants and toddlers who have been physically abused may have burns, bite marks, bruises, fractures, injuries in uncommon sites (Scannapieco & Connell-Carrick, 2005a), brain injury (Bruce, 1992), and abdominal injury (Ricci, 2000). They also appear lethargic, irritable, or may show signs of vomiting (Perry, Mann, Palker Corell, Ludy-Dobson, & Schick, 2002). A child may also have old and new fractures, and untreated injuries. Physical abuse may result in developmental delay (Scannapieco & Connell-Carrick, 2005a), delayed language development (McFayden & Kitson, 1996; Oates, Peacock, & Forrest, 1984), retardation and paralysis (Perry et al., 2002). Other studies have found that physically abused children develop post-traumatic stress disorder (PTSD) (Famularo, Kinscherff, & Fenton, 1990), and PTSD symptomatology (Landsford, Dodge, Pettit, Bates, Crozier, & Kaplow, 2002; Boney-McGoy & Finkelhor, 1995).

Children who have been maltreated also tend to develop insecure attachments to their primary caregivers, including avoidance and resistance (Crittenden, 1992), anxiety (Erickson & Egeland, 2002), and a Type D (disordanized/disoriented) attachment pattern (Barnett, Ganiban & Cicchetti, 1999). It is during the very early years that attachment and relationship patterns develop, and children exposed to violence and physical abuse learn relationship patterns within this context that contribute to their dysfunctional development (Patterson, 2002). As the child grows, physical abuse has been associated with peer problems, anxiety and depression (Landsford, Miller-Johnson, Berlin, Dodge,

Bates, & Petit, 2007), social withdrawal (Landsford et al., 2002), teen parenthood (Landsford et al., 2007), low IQ, and antisocial behavior (Grotevant et al., 2006).

One of the most widely acknowledged effects of physical abuse is increased aggression and delinquency during childhood and adulthood (Herrera & McCloskey, 2001; Landsford et al., 2007; Shaffer & Ruback, 2002; Widom & Maxfield, 2001). Early physical abuse has been associated with victimization and perpetration of violence in romantic relationships (Arias, 2004; White & Widom, 2003), work problems (Sasone, Dakroub, Pole & Butler, 2005), and male arrests for violent crimes (Widom & White, 1997).

During the first three years of life, physical abuse can also damage a child's brain. Physical abuse influences the child's brain to focus its resources on managing the fear and anxiety associated with the threat and potential harm of living in a hostile environment. As a result, other neural pathways and areas of the brain will be underdeveloped (Shore, 1997). Prolonged and unpredictable physical abuse over time will make a child's brain adapt to be ready for danger (National Clearinghouse on Child Abuse and Neglect (NCCAN), 2001). When the neural pathways involved in fear are constantly activated in a child, the child may cognitively perceive the world as a threatening place, and will act accordingly for survival (Perry, 2000c; Shore, 1997). Even in circumstances where a threat is minimal, the child's brain is organized as such to perceive the world as hostile and the child in need of protection. The brain becomes hyper-aroused to danger, which is especially common later in life among males and older children (Perry, 1996). Different from adults who utilize a "fight or flight" response to cope with a perceived threat, infants will instead use dissociation (Perry & Pollard, 1998), crying, and/or facial expressions, or body movements to indicate discomfort and manage unpredictable stress. In a typical situation, an infant's gestures provoke the assistance of a caregiver who helps the infant manage and overcome the perceived threat (Scannapieco & Connell-Carrick, 2005a). Maltreated infants, however, may not receive a comforting response and may actually receive no response or a threatening response. Over time, the brain responds to such violence so that some physically abused children adapt to the world by provoking aggression in an attempt to manage the predictability of their lives (Perry, 1997).

Although many of the effects of physical abuse can be directly observed including bruises, bite marks, burns and other physical indicators, some forms of physical abuse are less easily observable. Shaken baby syndrome is a particular type of physical abuse during infancy that often shows few physical indicators, but rather is diagnosed by medical forensics.

Shaken baby syndrome.   A unique form of physical abuse that occurs primarily in the first two years of life is shaken baby syndrome (SBS). SBS describes a number of signs and symptoms that result in some damage to the head. The degree of brain damage varies by the amount and duration of the shaking and the force of the shaking (National Center on Shaken Baby Syndrome (NCSBS), 2008). The duration of shaking that is necessary to result in head trauma is unknown, but the baby must be shaken violently back and forth. Shaking most often occurs during a period of stress, typically as a reaction to a child's inconsolable crying or irritability, with a peak time of SBS occurring during the 6-week to 4-month age period (Alexander, Levitt, & Smith, 2001). The perpetrator impulsively responds with anger and aggression toward the infant and shakes the child.

Because infants have weak head and neck muscles, shaking a baby causes the brain to bounce back and forth inside the skull which results in bruising, swelling, and bleeding. SBS must be diagnosed medically, using a computed tomography scan or magnetic resonance imaging. Injuries from SBS can lead to severe and permanent brain damage and even death (National Institute of Neurological Disorders and Stroke (NINDS), 2007).

Common symptoms of SBS include irritability, lethargy, poor feeding, vomiting, pale or bluish skin and convulsions (NINDS, 2007), with major effects including seizures, coma, stupor and death (NCSBS, 2008). Many children also present with retinal hemorrhages in one or both eyes (NCSBS, 2008). The classic presenting factors for SBS include subdural hemotoma, brain swelling and retinal hemorrhages, and some, but not all, children also have bruising on some part of the body that was used for holding the baby during shaking. Other symptoms commonly include spinal cord and neck damage and rib fractures.

The majority of children who survive SBS have long-term neurological problems and mental disability. Many effects are not fully apparent until the age of 6 (NINDS, 2008). Some effects are mild, such as learning disorders and behavioral problems, but others are more severe, including mental retardation, blindness, developmental paralysis, physical disabilities, hearing and speech impairments, seizures, and death (NCSBS, 2008).

Sexual abuse

While neglect and physical abuse are common forms of maltreatment during infancy and toddlerhood, a less common but equally as serious form of maltreatment, sexual abuse, also occurs. The impact of sexual abuse during infancy can also manifest in long-term consequences, and similar to physical abuse and neglect, disrupts primary and brain development during formative years.

Child sexual abuse (CSA) refers to children who are engaged in sexual activities beyond their maturational and developmental level and includes behaviors such as digital and object penetration of the vagina or anus, oral sex, folding, sexualized kissing, masturbation, and involvement of the child in prostitution. The Child Abuse Prevention and Treatment Act defines sexual abuse as:

> The employment, use, persuasion, inducement, enticement, or coercion of any child to engage in, or assist any other person to engage in, any sexually explicit conduct or simulation of such conduct for the purpose of producing a visual depiction of such conduct;

or

> The rape, and in cases of caretaker or interfamilial relationships, statutory rape, molestation, prostitution, or other forms of sexual exploitation of children, or incest with children.

It has been commonly, but incorrectly, thought that infant sexual abuse has no lasting impact on a victim because the child would not remember what happened. Infants, in fact, are more vulnerable to trauma than others (Perry, 2000a). Perry (2003) maintains infants are able to "recall" prior traumatic events even if they have no concrete awareness of them because over time their bodies respond physiologically to danger and fear that manifests from sexual touching. When infants have experiences with caregivers that involve fear, unpredictability, pain and abnormal genital sensations, their neural and brain organization is altered (Perry, 2000b). The difference between adults and infants is that an infant's brain is just organizing itself, while adult trauma changes how one's brain organizes events (Perry, 1994). Thus, children understand and organize victimization even though they may not be able to verbalize it, which has long-lasting consequences for development.

In general, sexual abuse during infancy presents a serious disruption to healthy caregiving behaviors and creates an extreme and prolonged stress response in the infant (Perry, 2000b). Common physical manifestations that should be considered suspicious for sexual abuse in infancy include (Scannapieco & Connell-Carrick, 2005a, p. 87): infection, irritation, or rupture of the genital area not attributed to diaper rash; excessive reddening of the genitals; excessive blistering of the genitals; tears or bruises on the surface of the genitals; anal areas that are swollen, torn, lacerated, or infected; bite marks on or around the genitals; and sexually transmitted disease (which can be transmitted at childbirth, such as genital warts and chlamydia).

Other injuries include anal trauma and difficulty with bowel movements, and problems walking and sitting in toddlerhood. Common behavioral and psychological manifestations include sexualized behaviors such as overt sexual acting-out behaviors or compulsive masturbation (Kendall-Tackett, Williams, & Finkelhor, 1993), mimicking sexual intercourse (Friedrich et al., 2001), PTSD (Dubner & Motta, 1999; Ruggiero, McLeer, & Dixon, 2000), depression (Berliner & Elliott, 2002), and anxiety (McLeer et al., 1998). Not all children, however, will experience immediate or long-term effects of sexual abuse, and some key factors in the development of sequelae include the duration of abuse, frequency, nature of the abusive acts, time during development, and presence of protective factors such as a stable, caring caregiver (Perry, 2000b).

When the abuse has occurred from an attachment figure or caregiver who is supposed to create an environment of safety and security, the child's understanding of relationships becomes one of exploitation and abuse (Perry, 2003). The child lives at a heightened sense of awareness and in an environment that is oftentimes unpredictable and unsafe (Scannapieco & Connell-Carrick, 2005a). The sexually abused infant or toddler, therefore, cannot develop trust in his/her caregiver or the safety and predictability of his/her environment.

Brain development is also affected by sexual abuse in early childhood. Because the brain is developing and organizing during a child's first three years, the brain is influenced by early sexual experiences. The brain creates memories of a traumatic event, and these memories are reactivated when a reminder of the traumatic event (e.g., specific perpetrator) is presented (Perry & Pollard, 1998). These memories may alter the child's perception of the world in which she/he lives. Therefore, the child may physically respond to a perceived threat and may maintain a status of hyper-arousal, similar to what is seen among physically abused children. The stress of sexual abuse may cause a child to focus their brain resources on survival and perceived environmental threats, which may make it less likely for her/him to focus energies on more adaptive and sophisticated learning (NCCAN, 2001).

Similar to all forms of maltreatment during this critical period, sexual abuse poses serious consequences to infants and toddlers. Further, it is a misconception that infant sexual abuse fails to occur and that sexual abuse has no lasting effects, as research has shown grave consequences to a child's overall development. Healthy development is compromised by negative early childhood experiences, especially the occurrence of child maltreatment. Therefore it is imperative that infants and toddlers are identified to be at risk or to have experienced maltreatment when it has occurred and that early intervention services be provided.

Interventions and Treatment

During infancy and toddlerhood the interventions and treatment for child abuse and neglect must be viewed from an ecological perspective and examine the child, parent, and social environment. Child maltreatment generally has a negative effect on the attachment relationship, especially when the perpetrator is a parent. In addition, poor attachment is almost always a component of child neglect, and research has shown the need for both parenting skill and concrete services in homes where neglect occurs (Connell-Carrick & Scannapieco, 2006). Therefore, teaching attachment and repairing the attachment relationship is a necessary part of any early intervention program for maltreated children. Caregivers need to be taught sensitivity to their child's needs and how to better communicate with their baby, including recognizing the infant's ability to signal needs, accurately reading infant cues, and consistently and predictably responding to the cues (Erickson & Kurz-Riemer, 1999). Other specific techniques include teaching the parent appropriate developmental expectations, the importance and method of communicating with an infant, appropriate play, and healthy discipline techniques (Connell-Carrick & Scannapieco, 2007). Interventions focusing on parental attachment behavior have been shown to be effective in increasing attachment (Bakermans-Kraneburg, Van IJzendoorn, & Juffer, 2003), as are programs that address targeted child and parent outcomes by focusing on future behaviors rather than reworking the past relationship (Fergusson, Grant, Horwood, & Ridder, 2006).

The stress of child-rearing coupled with social isolation and lack of support, can lead to child maltreatment (Brayden et al., 1992; Coohey, 1996, 2000; Gaudin et al., 1993). Interventions designed to strengthen the social support of families who maltreat have been shown to be successful, and especially successful with families who neglect their children (Gaudin, Wodarski, Atkinson, & Avery, 1990; Gershater-Molko, Lutzker, & Wesch, 2002; Lutzker, Bigelow, Doctor, & Kessler, 1998). The purpose of social support intervention is to connect families, strengthen support networks, and reduce social isolation (Connell-Carrick & Scannapieco, 2007). Scannapieco and Connell-Carrick (2005a; Connell-Carrick & Scannapieco, 2007) identified several levels of intervention for social support: personal social networks (family, friend); neighborhood and community groups connecting parents (self-help groups, church); professional programs (school, medical, child care); and specialized professional programs (early intervention, family preservation, substance abuse treatment).

Intervention in the areas listed above can focus on developing relationships, repairing and strengthening existing relationships, and teaching parents how to utilize community services. Educating parents in how to maintain and appropriately utilize relationships with individuals and community service agencies can be helpful in providing necessary support in stressful times. Many parents would benefit from concrete support, such as medical and dental care for their children, as well as appraisal support (Connell-Carrick & Scannapieco, 2007; Scannapieco & Connell-Carrick, 2005a). Referral alone, however, is not enough. Families who maltreat need a committed individual who helps them continue to practice newly acquired skills with increasing social support and in applying attachment behaviors at home to monitor their program and offer follow-up suggestions. A combination of interventions to increase both the attachment relationship between parent and child and to increase the social support of a family is necessary. This will facilitate the child's healthy overall growth and development and help the parent increase parental capacity and strengthen social support networks to reduce the recurrence of maltreatment.

Although early intervention is essential in remedying the effects of maltreatment, it is not without its challenges. Recent law has recognized the importance of early intervention by mandating children between 0 and 3 years of age who are maltreated to be referred for early intervention services (PL 108-466), and the developmental effects of maltreatment made this legislation desperately needed (Dicker & Gordon, 2006). However, intervention with such families poses challenges to practitioners, families, and the child welfare system itself. Often families who maltreat do not recognize the problems that exist in the parenting relationship (Faver, Crawford & Combs-Orme, 1999), which makes engaging the families in change difficult. Even when problems are recognized by parents, the stigma associated with child maltreatment makes parents reluctant to obtain help (Faver et al., 1999). Further, when service needs are identified and appropriate referrals are made, completion rates are often low (Risley-Curtiss, Combs-Orme, Chernoff, & Heisler, 1996), and professionals and client families often have different views about what services are needed (Faver et al., 1999). Perhaps most importantly, funds for child welfare are limited and the majority of funds are allocated to investigations and foster care, which leaves fewer and fewer funds for treatment and prevention (Faver et al., 1999).

Conclusion

Child maltreatment is a serious social problem affecting almost 1 million children annually, and children aged 0–3 are at greatest risk of not only experiencing maltreatment but also its severe developmental consequences (USDHHS, 2007). The consequences of child maltreatment span all areas of a child's development, but one of the most damaging effects is the harm done to the attachment relationship. The attachment relationship has consequences for both infant mental health and adult mental health, and early intervention is essential in repairing this bond. When identified early on, the negative effects of maltreatment during infancy and toddlerhood can be ameliorated with early intervention.

References

Aber, J. L., & Allen, J. P. (1987). Effects of maltreatment on young children's socioemotional development: An attachment theory perspective. *Developmental Psychology, 23*, 406–414.

Alexander, R., Levitt, C., & Smith, W. (2001). Abusive head trauma. In R. Reece & S. Ludwig (Eds.), *Child abuse: Medical diagnosis and management* (2nd ed.). Philadelphia: Lippincott Williams & Wilkins.

American Psychiatric Association (1994). *The diagnostic and statistical manual of mental disorders, Fourth Edition, DSM-IV*. Washington, DC: American Psychiatric Association.

Ammerman, R. (1990). Etiological models of child maltreatment. *Behavior Modification, 14*(3), 230–254.

Arias, I. (2004). The legacy of child maltreatment: Long-term health consequences for women. *Journal of Women's Health, 13*, 468–473.

Baer, J., & Martinez, C. (2007). Child maltreatment and insecure attachment: A meta-analysis. *Journal of Reproductive and Infant Psychology, 24*(3), 187–197.

Bakermans-Kraneburg, M., Van IJzendoorn, M., & Juffer, F. (2003). Less is more: Meta-analyses of sensitivity and attachment interventions in early childhood. *Psychological Bulletin, 129*, 195–215.

Barnett, D., Ganiban, J., & Cicchetti, D. (1999). Maltreatment, negative expressivity, and the development of Type D attachments from 12 to 24 months of age. *Monographs of the Society for Research in Child Development, 64*(3), 97–118.

Barth, R. (1991). An experimental evaluation of in-home child abuse prevention services. *Child Abuse and Neglect, 15*, 363–375.

Beckwith, L. (1990). Adaptive and maladaptive parenting: Implications for intervention. In S. Meisels & J. Shonkoff (Eds.), *Handbook of early childhood interventions* (pp. 53–77). New York: Cambridge University Press.

Belsky, J. (1978). Three theoretical models of child abuse. *Child Abuse and Neglect, 2*(1), 37–49.

Belsky, J. (1980). Child maltreatment: An ecological integration. *American Psychologist, 35*(4), 320–335.

Belsky, J., Rovine, M., & Taylor, D. G. (1984). The Pennsylvania infant and family development project, III: The origins of individual differences in infant–mother attachment: Maternal and infant contributions. *Child Development, 55*, 718–728.

Belsky, J., & Vondra, J. (1989). Lessons from child abuse: The determinants of parenting. In D. Cicchetti & V. Carlson (Eds.), *Child maltreatment: Theory and research on the causes and consequences of child abuse and neglect* (pp. 153–202). New York: Cambridge University Press.

Berliner, L., & Elliott, D. (2002). Sexual abuse of children. In J. Myers, L. Berliner, J. Briere, C. Hendriz, C. Jenny, & T. Reid (Eds.), *The APSAC handbook on child maltreatment* (2nd ed., pp. 55–78). Thousand Oaks, CA: Sage.

Bierer, L., Yehuda, R., Schmeidler, J., Mitropoulou, V., New, A., Silverman, J., & Siever, J. (2003). Abuse and neglect in childhood: Relationship to personality disorder diagnoses. *CNS Spectrum, 8*(10), 737–754.

Boney-McGoy, S., & Finkelhor, D. (1995). Psychosocial sequelae of violent victimization in a national youth sample. *Journal of Consulting and Clinical Psychology, 63*(5), 726–736.

Bowlby, J. (1982). Attachment and loss: Retrospect and prospect. *Annual Progress in Child Psychiatry and Child Development, 52*(4), 29–47.

Brayden, R., Atlemeier, W., Tucker, D., Dietrich, M., & Vietze, P. (1992). Antecedents of child neglect in the first 2 years of life. *Journal of Pediatrics, 120*, 426–429.

Brazelton, T. D. (1988). Importance of early intervention. In E. Hibbs (Ed.), *Children and families: Studies in prevention and interventions* (pp. 107–120). Madison, CT: International Universities Press.

Bronfenbrenner, U. (1979). *The ecology of human development: Experiments by nature and design.* Cambridge, MA: Harvard University Press.

Brown, J., Cohen, P., Johnson, J., & Salzinger, S. (1998). A longitudinal analysis of risk factors for child maltreatment: Findings of a 17 year prospective study of officially recorded and self-reported child abuse and neglect. *Child Abuse and Neglect, 22*(11), 1065–1078.

Bruce, D. (1992). Neurosurgical aspects of child abuse. In S. Ludwig & A. Kornberg (Eds.), *Child abuse: A medical reference* (2nd ed., pp. 117–130). New York: Churchill Livingston.

Cadzow, S., Armstrong, K., & Fraser, J. (1999). Stressed parents with infants: Reassessing physical abuse risk factors, *Child Abuse and Neglect, 15*(5), 647–659.

Carlson, V., Cicchetti, D., Barnett, D., & Braunwald, K. (1989). Finding order in disorganization: Lessons from research on maltreated infants attachments to their caregivers. In D. Cicchetti & V. Carlson (Eds.), *Child maltreatment: Theory and research on the causes and consequences of child abuse and neglect* (pp. 494–528). New York: Cambridge University Press.

Carlson, W. (1998). A prospective longitudinal study of disorganized/disoriented attachment. *Child Development, 69*, 249–261.

Chaffin, M., Kelleher, K., & Hollenberg, J. (1996). Onset of physical abuse and neglect: Psychiatric, substance abuse, and social risk factors from prospective community data. *Child Abuse and Neglect, 20*(3), 191–203.

Christoffel, K. (1990). Violent death and injury in US children and adolescents. *American Journal of Disease Control, 111*, 697–706.

Chun, B. (1989). Child abuse in Korea. *Child Welfare, 68*, 154–158.

Cicchetti, D., & Barnett, D. (1991). Attachment organization in maltreated preschoolers. *Development and Psychopathology, 3*, 397–411.

Cicchetti, D., & Lynch, M. (1993). Toward and ecological/transactional model of community violence and child maltreatment. *Psychiatry, 56*, 96–118.

Cicchetti, D., & Rizley, R. (1981). *Developmental perspective on child maltreatment: New directions for child development.* San Francisco: Jossey-Bass.

Connell-Carrick, K. (2003). A critical review of the empirical literature: Identifying risk factors for child neglect. *Child and Adolescent Social Work, 20*(5), 389–425.

Connell-Carrick, K., & Scannapieco, M. (2006). Ecological correlates of neglect in infants and toddlers. *Journal of Interpersonal Violence, 21*(3), 299–316.

Connell-Carrick, K., & Scannapieco, M. (2007). Practice strategies for early childhood practitioners: Developmental interventions for infants and toddlers who have been maltreated. *Early Childhood Services Journal, 1*(3), 189–204.

Coohey, C. (1996). Child maltreatment: Testing the social isolation hypothesis. *Child Abuse Neglect, 29*(3), 241–254.

Coohey, C. (1998). Home alone and other inadequately supervised children. *Child Welfare, 77*(3), 291–301.

Coohey, C. (2000). The role of friends, in-laws, and other kin in father-perpetrated child physical abuse. *Child Welfare, 79*, 373–402.

Corse, S., Schmid, K., & Trickett, K. (1990). Social network characteristics of mothers in abusing and nonabusing families and their relationships to parenting beliefs. *Journal of Community Psychology, 18*, 44–59.

Crittenden, P. (1985). Social networks, quality of parenting, and child development. *Child Development, 56*, 1299–1313.

Crittenden, P. (1988). Distorted patterns of relationships in maltreating families: The role of internal representation models. *Journal of Reproductive and Infant Psychology, 6*, 183–199.

Crittenden, P. (1992). Children's strategies for coping with adverse home environments: An interpretation using attachment theory. *Child Abuse and Neglect, 23*, 329–343.

Crittenden, P. (1996). Research on maltreating families. In J. Briere, L. Berliner, J. A. Bulkley, C. Jenny, & T. Reid (Eds.), *The APSAC Handbook on Child Maltreatment* (pp. 158–174). Thousand Oaks, CA: Sage.

Dale, G., Kendall, J., & Humber, K. (1996). Mental health screening in foster care: A model for community-based service delivery and research in Baltimore. In *Proceedings from The Eighth Annual Research and Training Center Conference, University of South Florida, Tampa* (pp. 199–204). http://www.fmhi.usf.edu/institute/pubs/pdf/cfs/rtc/8thproceedings/8thchap5.pdf (accessed March 2010).

Dicker, S., & Gordon, E. (2006). Critical connections for children who are abused and neglected: Harnessing the new federal referral provisions for early intervention. *Infants and Young Children, 19*, 170–178.

DiScala, C., Sege, R., Li, G., & Reece, R. (2000). Child abuse and unintentional injuries: A 10-year retrospective study. *Archives of Pediatric and Adolescent Medicine, 154*, 16–22.

Dodge, K., Bates, J., & Pettit, G. (1990). Mechanisms in the cycle of violence. *Science, 2*, 1678–1683.

Dubner, A., & Motta, R. (1999). Sexually and physically abused foster care children and post-traumatic stress disorder. *Journal of Consulting and Clinical Psychology, 67*, 367–373.

Dubowitz, H. (2000). What is child neglect? In H. Dubowitz and D. DePanfilis (Eds.), *Handbook for child protection practice* (p. 10). Thousand Oaks, CA: Sage.

Dubowitz, H., Black, M., Kerr, M., Starr, R., & Harrington, D. (2000). Fathers and child neglect. *Archives of Pediatric and Adolescent Medicine, 154*, 135–141.

Eckenrode, J., Egeland, B., & Sroufe, L. (1981). Developmental sequelae of maltreatment infancy. *New Directions for Child Development, 11*, 77–92.

Eckenrode, J., Ganzel, B., Henderson, C. R., Smith, F., Olds, D. L., Powers, J., et al. (2000). Preventing child abuse and neglect with a program of nurse home visitation: The limiting effects of domestic violence. *Journal of the American Medical Association, 284*, 1385–1391.

Egeland, B., & Sroufe, L. A. (1981). Attachment and early maltreatment. *Child Development, 52*, 44–52.

Erickson, M., & Egeland, B. (2002). Child neglect. In J. Myers, L. Berliner, J. Briere, C. Hendrix, C. Jenny, & T. Reid (Eds.), *The APSAC handbook on child maltreatment* (2nd ed., pp. 3–20). Thousand Oaks, CA: Sage.

Erickson, M., & Kurz-Riemer, K. (1999). *Infants, toddlers and families: A framework for support and intervention.* New York: Guilford.

Famularo, R., Kinscherff, R., & Fenton, T. (1990). Symptom differences in acute and chronic presentation of child post-traumatic stress disorder. *Child Abuse and Neglect, 14*, 439–444.

Famularo, R., Kinscherff, R., & Fenton, T. (1992). Psychiatric diagnoses of abusive mothers: A preliminary report. *Journal of Nervous and Mental Disease, 180*, 658–661.

Faver, C., Crawford, S., & Combs-Orme, T. (1999). Services for child maltreatment: Challenges for research and practice. *Children and Youth Services Review, 21*(2), 89–109.

Fergusson, D., Grant, H., Horwood, J., & Ridder , E. (2006). Randomized trial of the Early Start Program of Home Visitation: Parent and family outcomes. *Pediatrics, 117*(3), 781–786.

Freisthler, B. (2004). A spatial analysis of social disorganization, alcohol access, and rates of maltreatment in neighborhoods. *Children and Youth Services Review, 26*(9), 803–819.

Freisthler, B., Merritt, D. & La Scala, E. (2006). Understanding the ecology of child maltreatment: A review of the literature and directions for future research. *Child Maltreatment, 11*(3), 263–280.

Friedrich, W., Dittner, C., Action, R., Berliner, L., Butler, J., Damon, L., et al. (2001). Child Sexual Behavior Inventory: Normative, psychiatric and sexual abuse comparisons. *Child Maltreatment, 6*, 37–49.

Frodi, A., & Lamb, M. (1980). Infants at risk for child abuse. *Infant Mental Health Journal, 1*(4), 240–247.

Gaudin, J. M., & Dubowitz, H. (1997). Family functioning in neglectful families: Recent research. In J. D. Berrick, R. P. Barth, & N. Gilbert (Eds.), *Child welfare research review, Vol. 2* (pp. 28–62). New York: Columbia University Press.

Gaudin, J., Polansky, N., Kilpatrick, A., & Shilton, P. (1993). Loneliness, depression, stress and social supports in neglectful families. *American Journal of Orthopsychiatry, 63*(4), 597–605.

Gaudin, J., Polansky, N., Kilpatrick A., & Shilton, P. (1996). Family functioning in neglectful families. *Child Abuse and Neglect, 20*(4), 363–377.

Gaudin, J. M., Jr., Wodarski, J. S., Atkinson, M. K., & Avery, L. S. (1990). Remedying child neglect: Effectiveness of social network interventions. *Journal of Applied Social Sciences, 15*, 97–123.

Gelles, R., & Straus, M. (1987). Is violence toward children increasing? A comparison of 1975 and 1985 national survey rates. *Journal of Interpersonal Violence, 2*, 212–222.

Gershater-Molko, R., Lutzker, J., & Wesch, D. (2002). Using recidivism data to evaluate Project Safecare: Teaching bonding, safety and health skills to parents. *Child Maltreatment, 7*, 277–285.

Gessner, B., Moore, M., Hamilton, B., & Muth, P. (2004). The incidence of infant physical abuse in Alaska. *Child Abuse and Neglect, 28*(1), 9–23.

Gil, D. (1970). *Violence against children: Physical child abuse in the U.S.* Cambridge, MA: Harvard University Press.

Gowen, J. (1994). Study of the effects of neglect on the early development of the symbolic function. In *Chronic Neglect Symposium Proceedings, National Center on Child Abuse and Neglect. June 27–28, 1993.* Washington, DC: Government Printing Office.

Green, A. (1968). Self-destruction in physically abused schizophrenic children: Report of cases. *Archives of General Psychiatry, 19*, 171–197.

Greenough, W., Black, J., & Wallace, C. (1987). Experience and brain development. *Child Development, 58*, 539–559.

Grotevant, H., Van Dulmen, H., Dunbar, N., Nelson-Christinedaughter, J., Christensen, M., Fan, X., et al. (2006). Antisocial behavior of adoptees and nonadoptees: Prediction from early history and adolescent relationships. *Journal of Research on Adolescence, 16*, 105–131.

Harrison, P., Hoffmann, N., & Edwall, G. (1989). Differential drug use patterns among sexually abused adolescent girls in treatment for chemical dependency. *International Journal of Addictions, 24*, 499–514.

Hay, T., & Jones, L. (1994). Societal interventions to prevent child abuse and neglect. *Child Welfare, 73*, 379–403.

Heller, S., Larrieu, J., D'Imperio, R., & Boris, N. (1999). Research on resilience to child maltreatment: Empirical considerations. *Child Abuse & Neglect, 23*(4), 321–338.

Herrera, V., & McCloskey, L. (2001). Gender differences in the risk for delinquency among youth exposed to family violence. *Child Abuse and Neglect, 25*(8), 1037–1051.

Hodges, V. (1993). Assessing strengths and protective factors in child abuse and neglect: Risk assessment with families of color. In P. Pecora & D. English (Eds.), *Multi-cultural guidelines for assessing family strengths and risk factors in child protective services* (pp. I1–I11). Seattle: University of Washington.

Kaufman, J., & Zigler, E. (1989). The intergenerational transmission of child abuse. In D. Cicchetti & V. Carlson (Eds.), *Child maltreatment: Theory and research in the causes and consequences of child abuse and neglect* (pp. 129–150). New York: Cambridge University Press.

Kempe, C. H., Silverman, F. N., Steele, B. F., Droegemueller, W., & Silver, H. K. (1962). The battered child syndrome. *Journal of the American Medical Association, 181*, 17–24.

Kendall-Tackett, K., Williams, L., & Finkelhor, D. (1993). Impact of sexual abuse on children: A review and synthesis of recent empirical studies. *Psychological Bulletin, 113*, 164–180.

Kolko, D. J. (2002). Child physical abuse. In J. E. B. Myers, L. Berliner, J. Briere, C. T. Hendrix, C. Jenny, & T. Reid (Eds.), *APSAC handbook of child maltreatment* (2nd ed., pp. 21–54). Thousand Oaks, CA: Sage.

Landsford, J., Dodge, K., Petit, G., Bates, J., Crozier, J., & Kaplow, J. (2002). A 12-year prospective study of the long-term effects of early child physical maltreatment on psychological, behavioral, and academic problems in adolescence. *Archives of Pediatrics and Adolescent Medicine, 156*, 824–830.

Landsford, J., Miller-Johnson, S., Berlin, L., Dodge, K., Bates, J., & Pettit, G. (2007). Early physical abuse and later violent delinquency: A prospective longitudinal study. *Child Maltreatment, 12*(3), 233–245.

Lee, B., & Goerge, R. (1999). Poverty, early child bearing and child maltreatment: A multinomial analysis. *Child and Youth Services Review, 21*(9–10), 755–780.

Luthar, S., & Zigler, E. (1991). Vulnerability and competence: A review of research on resilience in childhood. *American Journal of Orthopsychiatry, 61*, 6–22.

Lutzker, J., Bigelow, K., Doctor, R., & Kessler, M. (1998). Safety, health care, and bonding within an ecobehavioral approach to treating and preventing child abuse and neglect. *Journal of Family Violence, 13*, 163–185.

Main, M., & Solomon, J. (1986). Discovery of a disorganized/disoriented attachment pattern. In T. B. Brazelton & M. W. Yogman (Eds.), *Affective development in infancy*. Westport, CT: Ablex.

Marshall, D. B., English, D. J., & Stewart, A. J. (2001). The effect of fathers or father figures on child behavioral problems in families referred to child protective services. *Child Maltreatment, 6*(4), 290–299.

McFayden, R., & Kitson, W. (1996). Language comprehension and expression among adolescents who have experienced childhood physical abuse. *Journal of Child Psychology and Psychiatry and Allied Disciplines, 37*, 551–562.

McLeer, S., Dixon, J., Henry, D., Ruggiero, K., Escovitz, K., Niedda, T., & Scholle, R. (1998). Psychopathology in non-clinically referred sexually abused children. *Journal of the American Academy of Child and Adolescent Psychiatry, 37*, 1326–1333.

Muller, R., Lemieux, K., & Sciolo, L. (2001). Attachment and psychopathology in formerly maltreated adults. *Journal of Family Violence, 16*(2), 151–169.

Musheno, K. (2006). Children with disabilities and the Child Abuse Prevention and Treatment Act. *Impact, 19*(1), 13. http://ici.umn.edu/products/impact/191/191.pdf (accessed August 2006).

National Center on Shaken Baby Syndrome (2008). *Medical facts about SBS.* www.dontshake.org/Audience.aspx?categoryID=8&PageName=MedicalFactsAnswers.htm (accessed January 2008).

National Clearinghouse on Child Abuse and Neglect (2001, October). *In focus: Understanding the effects of maltreatment on early brain development.* Washington, DC: Author.

National Institute of Neurological Disorders and Stroke (2007). *NINDS Shaken Baby Syndrome Information Page.* www.ninds.nih.gov/disorders/shakenbaby/shakenbaby.htm?css=print (accessed January 2008).

Nelson, C. A., Thomas, K. M., & de Haan, M. (2006). *Neuroscience and cognitive development: Experience and the developing brain.* Hoboken, NJ: Wiley.

Oates, R., Peacock, A., & Forrest, D. (1984). Development in children following abuse and non-organic failure to thrive. *American Journal of Diseases of Children, 138*(8), 764–767.

Ousted, C., Oppenheimer, R., & Lindsay, J. (1974). Aspects of bonding failure: The psychopathology and psychotherapeutic treatment of families of battered children. *Developmental Medicine in Child Neurology, 16*, 447–457.

Park, M. (2001). The factors of child physical abuse in Korean immigrant families. *Child Abuse and Neglect, 25*, 945–958.

Patterson, G. (2002). The early development of coercive family process. In J. B. Reid, G. R. Patterson, & J. Snyder (Eds.), *Antisocial behavior in children and adolescents: A developmental analysis and model for intervention* (pp. 25–44). Washington, DC: American Psychological Association.

Payne, M. (1997). *Modern social work theory* (2nd ed.). Chicago: Lyceum Books.

Pecora, P., Whittaker, J., Maluccio, A., Barth, R., & Plotnik, R. (2000). *The child welfare challenge: Practice, policy and research*. Hawthorne, NY: Aldine de Gruyter.

Perry, B. D. (1994). Neurobiological sequelae of childhood trauma: PTSD in children. In M. M. Murburg (Ed.), *Catecholamine function in posttraumatic stress disorder: Emerging concepts* (pp. 233–255). Washington, DC: American Psychiatric Press, Inc.

Perry, B. (1996). *Neurodevelopmental adaptations to violence: How children survive the intragenerational vortex of violence [online]*. www.childtrauma.org/ctamaterials/vortex_violence.asp. (accessed May 2004).

Perry, B. (1997). Incubated in terror: Neurodevelopmental factors in the "cycle of violence." In J. Osofsky (Ed.), *Children, youth and violence: A search for solutions* (pp. 124–148). New York: Guilford Press.

Perry, B. (2000a). *The early years last forever: The importance of brain development. Lectureship materials*. Corpus Christi, TX.

Perry, B., (2000b). Sexual abuse of infants. *Trauma, Violence and Abuse, 1*, 194–296.

Perry, B., (2000c). Traumatized children: How childhood trauma influences brain development. *Journal of the California Alliance for the Mentally Ill, 11*(1), 48–51.

Perry, B. (2003). *Sexual abuse of infants: A five part question focusing on sexual abuse during infancy*. www.childtrauma.org/CTAMATERIALS/infant_abuse.asp.

Perry, B., Mann, D., Palker Corell, A., Ludy-Dobson, C., & Schick, S. (2002). Child physical abuse. In D. Levinson (Ed.), *Encyclopedia of crime and punishment*, vol. *1* (pp. 197–202). Thousand Oaks, CA: Sage.

Perry, B., & Pollard, R. (1998). Homeostasis, trauma and adaptations – A neurodevelopmental view of childhood trauma. *Child and Adolescent Psychiatric Clinics of North America, 7*(1), 33–51.

Pollak, S., & Sinha, P. (2002). Effects of early experience on children's recognition of facial displays of emotion. *Developmental Psychology, 38*(5), 784–791.

Raiha, N., & Soma, D. (1997). Victims of child abuse and neglect in the US Army. *Child Abuse and Neglect, 21*(8), 759–768.

Ricci, L. (2000). Initial medical treatment of the physically abused child. In R. Reece (Ed.), *Treatment of child abuse: Common ground for mental health, medical and legal practitioners* (pp. 81–94). Baltimore, MD: Johns Hopkins University Press.

Risley-Curtiss, C., Combs-Orme, T., Chernoff, R., & Heisler, A. (1996). Health care utilization by children entering foster care. *Research on Social Work Practice, 6*, 442–461.

Ruggiero, K., McLeer, S., & Dixon, J. (2000). Sexual abuse characteristics associated with survivor psychopathology. *Child Abuse and Neglect, 24*, 951–964.

Rumm, P., Cummings, P., Krauss, M., Bell, M., & Rivara, F. (2000). Identified spouse abuse as a risk factor for child abuse. *Child Abuse and Neglect, 24*(1), 1375–1381.

Sasone, R., Dakroub, H., Pole, M., & Butler, M. (2005). Childhood trauma and employment disability. *International Journal of Psychiatry in Medicine, 35*, 395–404.

Scannapieco, M., & Connell-Carrick, K. (2002). Focus on the first years: An eco-developmental assessment of child neglect for children 0 to 3 years of age. *Child and Youth Social Services Review, 24*(8), 601–621.

Scannapieco, M., & Connell-Carrick, K. (2003). Families in poverty: Those who maltreat their children and those who do not. *Journal of Family Social Work, 7*(3), 49–70.

Scannapieco, M., & Connell-Carrick, K. (2005a). *Understanding child maltreatment.* New York: Oxford University Press.

Scannapieco, M., & Connell-Carrick, K. (2005b). Focus on the first years: Correlates of substantiation of child maltreatment for families with children 0 to 4. *Children and Youth Services Review, 27*(12), 1307–1323.

Scannapieco, M., & Connell-Carrick, K. (2007). Assessment of families who have substance abuse issues: Those who maltreat their infants and toddlers and those who do not. *Substance Use and Misuse, 42*, 1545–1553.

Schneider-Rosen, K., Braunwald, K., Carlson, V., & Cicchetti, D. (1985). Current perspectives in attachment theory: Illustration from the study of maltreated infants. In E. Bretherton & E. Waters (Eds.), *Growing points in attachment theory and research* (Monographs of the Society for Research in Child Development, 209, *50*(1/2), pp. 194–210). Chicago: University of Chicago Press.

Sedlak, A. (1997). Risk factors for the occurrence of abuse and neglect. *Journal of Aggression, Maltreatment & Trauma, 1*(1), 149–187.

Sedlak, A., & Broadhurst, D. (1996). *The Third National Incidence Study of Child Abuse and Neglect.* Washington, DC: National Center on Child Abuse and Neglect.

Shaffer, J. & Ruback, R. (2002, December). Violent victimization as a risk factor for violent offending among juveniles. *OJJDP Juvenile Justice Bulletin*, 1–10.

Shore, R. (1997). *Rethinking the brain.* New York: Families and Work Institute.

Stier, D. M., Leventhal, J., Berg, A. T., Johnson, L., & Mezger, J. (1993). Are children born to young mothers at risk of maltreatment? *Pediatrics, 91*(3), 642–648.

Straus, M. (1994). *Beating the devil out of them: Corporal punishment in American families.* San Francisco: Jossey-Bass.

Sun, A., Shillington, A., Hohman, M., & Jones, L. (2001). Caregiver AOD use, case substantiation and AOD treatment: Studies based on two southwestern counties. *Child Welfare, 80*(2), 121–128.

Trickett, P., Aber, J., Carlson, V., & Cicchetti, D. (1991). The relationship of socioeconomic status to the etiology and developmental sequelae of physical child abuse. *Developmental Psychopathology, 27*, 148–158.

Trickett, P., & Susman, E. (1988). Parental perceptions of child-rearing practices in physically abusive and nonabusive families. *Developmental Psychology, 24*(2), 270–276.

U.S. Department of Health and Human Services, Administration on Children, Youth, and Families (2003). *Emerging practices in the prevention of child abuse and neglect.* Washington, DC: Government Printing Office. www.childwelfare.gov/preventing/programs/whatworks/report/

United States Department of Health and Human Services (2005). *Child maltreatment 2003 [online].* Washington, DC: Government Printing Office. www.acf.hhs.gov/programs/cb/pubs/cm03.index.htm.

United States Department of Health and Human Services (2007). *Child maltreatment reports from the states 2005.* Washington, DC: Author.

UNICEF (2003, September). A league table of child maltreatment deaths in rich nations. *Innocenti Report Card, No. 5.* Florence: Innocenti Research Centre.

Urquiza, A., Wirtz, S., Peterson, M., & Singer, V. (1994). Screening and evaluating abused and neglected children entering protective custody. *Child Welfare, 73*(2), 155–171.

Vig, S., & Kaminer, R. (2002). Maltreatment and developmental disabilities in children. *Journal of Developmental and Physical Disabilities, 14*(4), 371–386.

Werner-Wilson, R. J., & Davenport, B. R. (2003). Distinguishing between conceptualizations of attachment: Clinical implications in marriage and family therapy. *Contemporary Family Therapy, 25*, 179–193.

Whipple, E., & Webster-Stratton, C. (1991). The role of parental stress in physically abusive family interactions. *Journal of Clinical Child Psychology, 19*, 302–312.

White, H. R., & Widom, C. S. (2003). Intimate partner violence among abused and neglected children in young adulthood: The mediating effects of early aggression, antisocial personality, hostility and alcohol problems. *Aggressive Behavior, 29*(4), 332–345.

Widom, C. (2000). Understanding the consequences of childhood victimization. In R. M. Reece (Ed.), *Treatment of child abuse: Common ground for mental health, medical, and legal practitioners* (pp. 339–361). Baltimore, MD: Johns Hopkins University Press.

Widom, C., & Maxfield, M. (2001). Child abuse, neglect and violent criminal behavior. *Criminology, 27*(2), 251–271.

Widom, C., & White, H. (1997). Problem behaviors in abused and neglected children grown up: Prevalence and co-occurrence of substance, abuse, crime and violence. *Criminal Behavior and Health, 7*, 287–310.

Wolfner, G., & Gelles, R. (1993). A profile of violence toward children: A national study. *Child Abuse and Neglect, 17*, 197–212.

Wolkind, S., & Rutter, M. (1985). *Sociocultural factors in child and adolescent psychiatry.* Boston: Blackwell Scientific.

Wu, S., Ma, C.-X., Carter, R., Ariet, M., Feaver, E., Rosnick, M., & Roth, J. (2004). Risk factors for infant maltreatment: A population-based study. *Child Abuse and Neglect, 28*(12), 1253–1264.

Zuravin, S., & DiBlasio, F. (1996). The correlates of child physical abuse and neglect by adolescent mothers. *Journal of Family Violence, 11*(2), 149–166.

8

Effects of Postnatal Depression on Mother–Infant Interactions and Child Development

Lynne Murray, Sarah Halligan, and Peter Cooper

Overview

Depression is the most common psychiatric condition among women of childbearing age, with over 8% being affected at any one time (Weissman, Wickramaratne, & Prusoff, 1988). Depression occurring specifically in the postnatal period has been found to be around 14% in the developed world (O'Hara & Swain, 1996), and is substantially more common in developing world populations (Wachs, Black, & Engle, 2009). The symptoms of depression occurring in the postnatal months are largely the same as at other times, and include a prolonged period of low mood, and a profound loss of interest and enjoyment. Other symptoms are mood-related disturbances in sleep, altered appetite, concentration impairment, retardation, agitation, feelings of guilt and hopelessness, and suicidal thoughts or impulses. The duration of episodes varies; some women experience only a short period of depression, while others continue to be affected throughout the first year post partum and beyond. Overall, depression-related impairments can be wide-ranging and persistent, and may have a profound effect on interpersonal functioning. Particular risk factors for postnatal depression include a past history of the disorder and a lack of confiding relationships. Other risk factors include social isolation and socioeconomic deprivation (Boyce, 2003). Infant characteristics, such as irritable behavior, can also increase risk (Murray, Stanley, Hooper, King, & Fiori-Cowley, 1996), although these require further investigation.

Concern about the possible adverse consequences for the developing child of exposure to postnatal depression has arisen principally as a result of evidence from normal populations demonstrating the sensitivity of young infants to the quality of their interpersonal environment, and the importance of social interactions in fostering optimal child psychological development. The fact that the infant's primary environment in the early weeks and months is, in many cases, largely constituted by their mother, together with the impact of depression on interpersonal functioning, has added to the concern about the possible effects of postnatal depression on the child. Accumulating evidence from both animal and human studies of the role of the caretaking environment in the development of neurobiological systems has provided further impetus to research in this area.

In this chapter we first review research on the effects of postnatal depression on maternal interactions with the infant and young child, and on biological outcomes. We then consider what is known about the development of children of postnatally depressed mothers in the domains of cognitive, emotional-behavioral and psychiatric functioning. In each section we note the role of other factors that commonly occur together with postnatal depression, and that are also associated with adverse infant and child outcome: socioeconomic adversity, marital conflict, and subsequent maternal depression. We also address the question of more proximal mechanisms mediating associations between postnatal depression and any adverse child outcome, and give particular attention to the role of parent–child interactions. Finally, we review intervention studies conducted in this field. We conclude by considering emerging findings on effects of paternal postnatal depression, and depression occurring in the developing world.

Effects of Postnatal Depression on Mother–Child Relationships

Early infancy

The seminal work in the 1980s by Field, Cohn, Tronick and their colleagues (Field, 1984; Field, Sandberg, Garcia, Vega-Lahr, Goldstein, & Guy, 1985; Field et al., 1988; Cohn, Matias, Tronick, Connell, & Lyons-Ruth, 1986) was largely conducted with populations living in conditions of high adversity, and it showed marked differences between groups of depressed and well women when observed during structured face-to-face play with their infants. The depressed mothers in these samples were found to deviate from the normal pattern of interaction where parents respond to infant cues by imitating and elaborating infant expressions and gestures, and adjusting the timing and form of response to help regulate the infant's attention and affect (Brazelton, Kozlowski, & Main, 1974; Jaffe, Beebe, Feldstein, Crown, & Jasnow, 2001; Papousek & Papousek, 1987; Stern, Beebe, Jaffe, & Bennett, 1977; Trevarthen, 1979). Instead, depressed mothers were generally insensitive, with the form of insensitivity varying from intrusive and hostile communication at one extreme, to flat, withdrawn and disengaged behavior at the other. In turn, the infants of depressed mothers in these samples showed high rates of distress and avoided social contact.

While subsequent research with lower-risk samples has shown less marked disturbance in the contacts between depressed mothers and their infants, more subtle deficits have been found (Campbell, Cohn, & Meyers, 1995; Murray, Fiori-Cowley, Hooper, & Cooper, 1996; Weinberg, Olson, Beeghly, & Tronick, 2006). These mainly involve reductions in depressed mothers' behavioral responsiveness and sensitivity to infant signals (Murray,

Stanley et al., 1996; Stanley, Murray, & Stein, 2004), particularly in cases where the depression persists (Campbell et al., 1995), or where the interaction takes place under challenging circumstances (Weinberg et al., 2006). Aside from maternal behavioral responsiveness, depressed mothers' speech to their infants has also been found to differ from that of nondepressed mothers. Slower and less responsive speech has been reported in a number of studies (Breznitz & Sherman, 1987; Murray, Kempton, Woolgar, & Hooper, 1993; Bettes, 1988; Zlochower & Cohn, 1996), as has a reduction in the use of both prosodically "exaggerated" intonation contours (Fernald, 1989) and modulations in fundamental frequency (Kaplan, Bachorowski, Smoski, & Hudenko, 2002; Kaplan, Bachorowski, Smoski, & Zinser, 2001). In these relatively low-risk samples infants of depressed mothers fail to show the gross disturbances apparent in high-risk groups, although disruptions in attention and behavioral regulation have been observed in response to maternal insensitivity (Murray, Fiori-Cowley, et al., 1996), particularly among boys (Weinberg et al., 2006).

Late infancy and beyond

One frequently assessed outcome in relation to maternal postnatal depression is the quality of infant attachment to the mother. While two meta-analyses (Martins & Gaffan, 2000; Atkinson, Paglia, Coolbear, Niccols, Parker, & Guger, 2000) showed an overall reduced likelihood of security in infants and young children of depressed mothers, the effects were modest. Subsequent studies by Campbell, Brownell, Hungerford, Speiker, Mohan, and Blessing (2004) and McMahon, Barnett, Kowalenko, and Tennant (2006) help to clarify these findings. First, they confirm that depressed mothers' functioning is highly variable, the degree of disturbance being largely linked to background risk. Second, they show that such variability is important in determining the development of child attachments. The Campbell et al. (2004) study conducted with the large National Institute of Child Health and Human Development (NICHD) sample showed that the chronicity, rather than the occurrence of early depression *per se*, was important in predicting child insecurity, and that when depressed mothers were able to be sensitive with their infant, the child generally escaped the risk for insecure attachment. Similarly, McMahon et al. (2006) found that children of depressed mothers who were themselves securely attached were buffered from the otherwise adverse effect of maternal depression on child attachment.

Other studies examining mother–child interactions in late infancy and early childhood have found residual impairments in child responsiveness to maternal communication. Thus, Stein, Gath, Butcher, Bond, Day, & Cooper (1991), conducting home-based observations at 19 months in a representative UK sample, found that infants of postnatally depressed women showed less sharing of emotion with their mothers and more anger than control group infants. While this pattern of infant behavior was particularly evident in cases where the mother was still depressed, the effect was also present in relationships where the mother's depression had remitted, particularly where there was a high degree of marital conflict. A very similar profile of less responsive engagement with the mother was found in children of postnatally depressed mothers in a follow-up at 5 years of the low-risk Cambridge (UK) longitudinal sample (Murray, Sinclair, Cooper, Ducournau, Turner, & Stein, 1999). In this study, the relationship impairments in the index group children occurred even when controlling for current and chronic maternal depression, marital conflict and the quality of the mother's current behavior toward the child, and were wholly mediated by the development of an insecure pattern of attachment in infancy. Similarly, Cox, Puckering, Pound, and Mills (1987) found that when mothers had experienced persistent depression up to two years post partum, but had recovered when followed up six months later, their children showed residual diminished responsiveness towards their mother, despite improvements in maternal communication.

Overall, research on the effects of maternal postnatal depression on the mother–infant relationship indicates that there may be long-term effects of early difficulties, particularly in contexts of marked adversity, where depression is more likely to be chronic, and where maternal responsiveness and sensitivity to the child is particularly impaired. Insecure infant attachment may be a particular risk, and may mediate longer-term effects of postnatal depression on difficulties in mother–child relationships.

Biological Outcomes

Neural development

Emerging research suggests that the marked difficulties in social interactions of postnatally depressed mothers with their infants may have direct effects on developing infant and child neurophysiological systems. EEG recordings taken from children of postnatally depressed mothers have shown reduced left frontal activation from the age of 1–3 months (Aaron Jones, Field, Fox, Lundy, & Davalos, 1997), through to 6 (Field, Fox, Pickens, Nawrocki, & Soutullo, 1995) and 15 months (Dawson, Frey, Panagiotides, Osterling, & Hessl, 1997a; Dawson, Frey, Panagiotides, Yamada, Hessl, & Osterling, 1999), with evidence of some stability through to the early childhood years (Jones, Field, Davalos, & Pickens, 1997). This pattern of activation has been observed in infants of depressed mothers from both low- and high-risk samples, shows systematic associations with the severity of the maternal disorder, and is not accounted for by prenatal depression (Dawson et al., 1997a). There is evidence that the association between reduced left frontal activation and maternal depression is mediated by the infant's experience of interaction with the mother, particularly by her noncontingent (Dawson, Frey, Panagiotides, Self, Hessl, & Yamada, 1997b; Dawson et al., 1999) and withdrawn behavior (Diego, Field, & Hernandez-Reif, 2001). However, by 13–15 months the differences between index and control infants in frontal activity are not confined to periods when the infant is interacting with the mother, but extend to both baseline conditions and to positive interactions with an unfamiliar stranger (Dawson et al., 1999).

HPA-axis functioning

A second area of investigation relates to infant and child stress responses, with the functioning of the HPA-axis stress response system being a particular focus. This has followed on from animal research indicating early programming of the HPA-axis by aspects of maternal behavior. In rodents, studies show that reduced levels of maternal tactile stimulation can result in a more reactive HPA-axis, at least in part due to reduced levels of central glucocorticoid receptors which provide negative feedback to the system (for a review see Kaffman & Meaney, 2007). While nonhuman primate research is at an earlier stage there are findings consistent with the rodent model (Coplan et al., 1996, 2001, 2006; Rosenblum, Coplan, Friedman, Bassoff, Gorman, & Andrews, 1994). Similarly, studies have examined human cortisol secretion in relation to maternal post-natal depression, again with broadly consistent findings. Field et al. (1988) observed elevated cortisol levels in both postnatally depressed mothers and their infants during face-to-face interactions, a finding attributed to the fact that interactions were nonsyn-chronous, and therefore stressful. Studies have also demonstrated longitudinal associa-tions between postpartum depression and offspring cortisol secretion, with elevations being observed in basal measures in children at 18 months (Bugental, Martorell, & Barraza, 2003), 3 years (Hessl et al., 1998) and 4.5 years of age (Essex, Klein, Cho, & Kalin, 2002). Finally, evidence for the long-term effects of depressed mothers' early interactions was found in a follow-up of the Cambridge sample: here, elevated morning cortisol secretion observed in the postnatally depressed mothers' children at 13 years (Halligan, Herbert, Goodyer, & Murray, 2004) was predicted by maternal withdrawal during early interactions, rather than by later interaction difficulties (Murray, Halligan, Goodyer, & Herbert, 2010).

While consistency in the findings regarding biological outcomes of children of post-natally depressed mothers is encouraging, given methodological variability across studies, some caution is required in their interpretation. Thus, in relation to cortisol, although there have been attempts to examine explicitly the relevance of early versus later exposure to maternal depression (Essex et al., 2002; Halligan et al., 2004), there is also evidence to suggest that *any* parental history of depression may be associated with similar effects (Mannie, Harmer, & Cowen, 2007; Young, Vazquez, Jiang, & Pfeffer, 2006). The same possibility, in principle, exists for EEG effects. Antenatal exposures may also be influ-ential (Field et al., 2004; O'Connor, Ben-Shlomo, Heron, Golding, Adams, & Glover, 2005), and genetic effects are likely (Bartels, Van den Berg, Sluyter, Boomsma, & de Geus, 2003); see later discussion on biological process mediators. Studies are therefore required that differentially link exposure to maternal depression during particular periods of development to biological changes in the offspring, as well as further research into the mechanisms by which effects are brought about.

Cognitive Development

Outcome studies

A number of prospective longitudinal studies of community samples have examined the effects of postnatal depression on preschool and school-age children, and several have identified associations with poor child cognitive functioning. Cogill, Caplan, Alexandra,

Robson, & Kumar (1986) assessed child IQ at 4 years in a London community sample. Both boys and girls whose mothers had been depressed in the first postnatal year had poorer scores than children of well mothers, and children of mothers who had been depressed later on. However, further analysis showed that the adverse effects of postnatal depression were confined to children whose mothers had a low level of education (Hay & Kumar, 1995). A second study of a London sample from a largely disadvantaged community also assessed child IQ at 4 years (Sharp, Hay, Pawlby, Schmucker, Allen, & Kumar, 1995). While girls were unaffected by postnatal depression, boys whose mothers had been depressed in the first year had significantly lower scores than those never exposed to depression, and those exposed to maternal depression subsequent to the postnatal period. A follow-up of this sample at 11 years looked specifically at the effects of exposure to depression in the first three postnatal months (Hay, Pawlby, Sharp, Asten, Mills, & Kumar, 2001). Although the number of children exposed only in the early months was small, findings did suggest persistent effects on boys' general and performance IQ, taking account of subsequent maternal depressive episodes. Similar findings were obtained in a follow-up by Milgrom, Westley, and Gemmill (2004) of an Australian inpatient sample who were depressed at 6 months, with index group boys having lower IQ at 42 months than index group girls and control children. Effects of later depression were not, however, assessed in this study. Murray and colleagues examined the cognitive functioning of postnatally depressed and well mothers' children in their Cambridge longitudinal sample. As in the studies of Sharp and Milgrom, boys of postnatally depressed mothers had lower scores than exposed girls and control group infants on the Bayley Mental Development Index at 18 months (Murray, 1992; Murray, Fiori-Cowley, et al. 1996). By five years, however, the cognitive performance of postnatally depressed mothers' children, including that of boys, was no longer significantly affected (Murray, Hipwell, Hooper, Stein, & Cooper, 1996).

Other studies have also failed to identify adverse long-term effects of maternal postnatal depression on child cognitive development, or have shown smaller effects. For example, Kurstjens and Wolke (2001) conducted cognitive assessments at 20 months, 4 years and 6 years in a large Bavarian community sample and found no adverse effects of postnatal depression *per se*. However, boys with additional risk factors (low socioeconomic status, neonatal risk) and whose mothers experienced subsequent depression in addition to the postnatal episode did have poorer scores at the final assessment (Kurstjens & Wolke, 2001). Cornish, McMahon, Ungerer, Barnett, Kowalenko, and Tennant (2005) assessed cognitive functioning in 15-month-old infants of mothers attending a mother–infant health clinic in Australia, and found no effect on infant outcome of maternal depression occurring only at 4 months post partum. However, infants of mothers who were depressed later on (at 12–15 months), as well as at 4 months, had reduced scores on the Bayley Scales.

The importance of the chronicity and severity of maternal depression for infant and child cognitive functioning is also shown by three large-scale studies. The US National Maternal and Child Health survey reported by Petterson and Burke-Albers (2001) found only modest associations between maternal depression after the birth and child cognitive functioning at 3 years. By contrast, severe and chronic maternal depression (i.e., present at birth and at the second assessment at 3 years) was associated with substantially poorer child cognitive outcome, regardless of family income. For moderately depressed mothers only those on low incomes had infants with poorer cognitive performance. In an Australian community sample of almost 5,000 mothers Brennan, Hammen, Andersen, Bor, Najman, and Williams (2000) made serial assessments of maternal mood in pregnancy, shortly after the birth, and at 6 months and 5 years. At the 5-year assessment, both the severity and chronicity of depression were associated with poorer child vocabulary development, although these effects were small. For the subsample of women depressed at only one assessment, effects of exposure to episodes in the postnatal months were comparable to those associated with later exposure, suggesting that early exposure has no special status (Brennan et al., 2000). Finally, while not specifically focusing on the question of postnatal exposure to depression, the US NICHD sample of more than 1,000 families showed that children whose mothers were chronically depressed over the first three years were adversely affected on a range of measures of cognitive functioning compared to nonexposed children, while those exposed intermittently were less adversely affected. Consistent with other studies, the impact of depression was more marked when occurring in the context of a low income/needs ratio (NICHD, 1999).

Taken together, the findings arising from diverse studies suggest that the occurrence of depression in the postnatal period poses a risk for long-term poor cognitive functioning in the child, principally in the context of wider socioeconomic difficulties, and particularly where the depression is chronic. In lower-risk community samples long-term effects of postnatal depression on child cognitive development are largely either absent or confined to subgroups experiencing additional risks.

Mechanisms mediating cognitive effects of postnatal depression

General responsiveness.   A large body of evidence with normal populations has shown the overall level of child-centered parental responsiveness, or contingency, during social interactions to be important for child cognitive development (Eshel, Daelmans, Cabral de Mello, & Martines, 2006). As such, impairments in maternal responsivity may contribute to poor cognitive functioning for children of postnatally depressed mothers. This possibility has been investigated in four studies.

Stanley, Murray, and Stein (2004) found short-term effects, with reduced maternal contingent responsiveness during face-to-face interactions in the first two to three postnatal months predicting infant performance in an operant learning task.

In their Cambridge longitudinal study Murray et al. (1993) and Murray, Fiori-Cowley, et al. (1996) showed that the reduction in depressed mothers' responsiveness to the infant mediated the adverse effects of the postnatal episode on boys' performance on the Bayley Scales at 18 months. Furthermore, at 5-year follow-up, those children whose mothers had shown a particularly marked reduction in responsiveness in the postnatal period were found to continue on a trajectory of poor cognitive functioning to 5 years. By contrast, the development of infants whose mothers had been more responsive early on, despite being depressed, appeared to become less canalized along a negative trajectory, and their cognitive development appeared to benefit more from later improvements in maternal functioning and mental state (Murray, Hipwell, et al., 1996).

In the 1999 NICHD study, variability in the interactions of depressed mothers was also highlighted, with those experiencing adversity having markedly lower levels of responsiveness. For cases where the interactions of depressed mothers were particularly poor, risk for poor child cognitive outcome was substantial. In contrast, children whose mothers maintained good interactions despite their depression were buffered from the potentially negative effects of the maternal disorder.

Finally, in their clinic-based Australian sample, Milgrom et al. (2004) found that low maternal responsiveness at 6 months mediated the adverse effect of maternal depression on boys' IQ at 42 months.

Attention regulation.   Difficulties in depressed mothers' interactions that concern infant attention regulation are also likely to contribute to poorer infant cognitive performance, since the infant's ability to sustain attention is one of the most robust predictors of IQ in later childhood (Slater, 1995). Parental vocal modulations appear particularly important for gaining and maintaining infant attention (Stern, Spieker, & MacKain, 1982). Kaplan, Bachorowski, & Zarlengo-Strouse (1999) found that segments of child-directed speech recorded from postnatally depressed mothers failed to promote associative learning in infants of nondepressed mothers in a conditioned attention paradigm. By contrast, speech samples from nondepressed mothers *did* promote infant learning. Kaplan et al. also found that the fundamental frequency of the final portion of the speech segments of mothers with more depressive symptoms was less modulated than that of other mothers, and suggest that this reduced modulation may have failed to increase infant arousal sufficiently to enable efficient processing of, and attention to, the information required.

Dysregulation of emotion.   Emotion regulation processes during parent–infant interactions may also be relevant to infant and child cognitive functioning. Dysregulated affect is likely to both impair attention and, as shown in studies by Fagen, Ohr, Fleckenstein, and Ribner (1985), to disrupt infant information retrieval. The increase in infant and child cortisol levels associated with depressed mothers' withdrawal and lack of support for infant emotion regulation (Field et al., 1988; Murray et al., 2010) may also be important in this connection. In a study of 3-month-old infants within-session increases in cortisol levels were associated with impaired learning and memory; however, infant cortisol levels were unrelated to maternal sensitivity (Thompson & Trevathan, 2008). This mechanism requires further investigation.

Conclusions.   Taken together, studies on the cognitive development of postnatally depressed mothers' children suggest that when the maternal disorder is accompanied by wider adversity particularly poor mother–child interactions are likely to occur. Where this is the case, child cognitive functioning may be affected in the longer term. While general deficits in maternal responsiveness have been widely linked to poor child outcome, research also indicates more specific features of parent–child interactions that may have differential effects on particular psychological processes underpinning optimal cognitive development. Further research is needed to investigate these specific processes in the context of maternal depression, and to explore the role of biological changes.

Behavioral, Socioemotional, and Psychiatric Problems

Outcome studies

Maternal reports in infancy, and the pre- and early school years.   Using maternal report measures of child difficulties to assess early development, Murray (1992) found that mothers who had been depressed in the first few postnatal months reported increased behavior problems in their infants at 18 months on an age-adjusted version of the Behaviour Screening Questionnaire (BSQ; Richman & Graham, 1971), despite the fact that most of the mothers had recovered by the time of assessment. Reported problems mainly concerned difficulties in infant behavioral regulation (e.g., sleep disturbance, separation difficulties, temper tantrums). Similarly, Cicchetti, Rogosch, and Toth (1998) found raised child behavior problem scores at 20 months on the Child Behavior Checklist (CBCL; Achenbach, 1991) to be associated with maternal depression occurring at some point following childbirth. Current severity of depressive symptoms was not, however, associated with child behavior problems. In this sample, the relationship between maternal depression and child behavior disturbance was mediated by general contextual risk.

With regard to preschool-aged children, Ghodsian, Zajicek, and Wolkind (1984) monitored the mental state of a London community sample of postpartum women at intervals over 42 months. Although depression at both 4 and 14 months was associated with maternal reports of child behavior problems (BSQ) at 42 months, only the effects of 14-month depression were significant when current maternal mental state was taken into account. Caplan, Cogill, Alexandra, Robson, Katz, and Kumar (1989) also investigated maternal reports of child behavior at 4 years in a low-risk community sample of North London women followed up from pregnancy. In addition to the impact of current depression, postnatal episodes showed some association with reports of child disturbance. However, as in the study of Cicchetti et al. (1998), this was principally accounted for by chronic difficulties co-occurring with postnatal depression (in this case, marital conflict and paternal psychiatric history).

The importance of chronic problems rather than early depression is suggested by three further studies of community samples. In the large Australian study conducted by Brennan et al. (2000), involving serial assessments of maternal mood through early childhood, maternal reports of child behavior disturbance on the CBCL at the final, 5-year assessment were associated with both chronicity and severity of maternal depression, and these effects were additive. When analysis was restricted to those experiencing only one episode of depression, there was little evidence for the impact of disorder in the immediate postpartum period, whereas later depressions were significantly associated with child behavior problems. Philipps and O'Hara (1991), following up a low-risk community sample in the US, similarly found no effect of postnatal depression on child behavior problems (assessed on the CBCL) at 4½ years, but did find that depression occurring subsequent to the postnatal episode was associated with child disturbance. Finally, similar findings emerged from maternal reports concerning somewhat older children from a disadvantaged London sample where, compared to children of never-depressed women, symptoms of "violent" behavior in 11-year-olds were associated with postnatal episodes only if the mother experienced subsequent depression (Hay, Pawlby, Angold, Harold, & Sharp, 2003).

In contrast to the research outlined above, where postnatal depression has not emerged as an independent risk factor for maternally-reported child behavior problems, four studies have found positive associations. In the high-risk US sample studied by Alpern and Lyons-Ruth (1993), both chronic (at 18 months and 5 years) and recent maternal depression were associated with an increase in reported problems at age 5. However, there was also evidence that maternal depression at the earlier period, in the absence of current symptoms, was associated with child fearfulness. Three further studies of low-risk samples of preschool children have similarly found effects of maternal depression occurring relatively early in the child's life. In a study of a Scottish community sample, Wrate, Rooney, Thomas, and Cox (1985) found that postpartum depressive episodes of relatively short duration (one month) were associated with maternal reports of child behavior problems at 3 years, even when controlling for current and recent depression. In this study, neither protracted postnatal episodes nor later occurrences of depression were associated with later child problems. The authors suggest that this counterintuitive finding may be explained by the fact that the mothers with brief episodes were particularly anxious about their role as mother, whereas those with more chronic disorder had general preoccupations not specifically focused on the child. Similarly, in the longitudinal study of Murray, Sinclair, et al. (1999), maternal reports of child behavior problems on the Rutter Scale at age 5 showed a significant association with postnatal depression, even when account was taken of recent and chronic episodes, the presence of marital conflict, and the current quality of the mother's interaction with the child. Finally, Dawson et al. (2003) found that exposure to maternal depression during the child's first two years was the strongest predictor of maternal reports of behavior problems at 3.5 years. Once early depression was taken into account, the degree of subsequent exposure was unrelated to child outcome.

Taken together, these maternal report studies indicate that chronic depressive disorder, particularly in the context of general adversity, generally emerges as a strong predictor of poor child outcome. Nevertheless, there is also some evidence suggestive of behavior difficulties in children of mothers who were depressed in the first one to two postnatal years, independent of subsequent depression.

Independent assessments in the pre- and early school years.   The findings from some maternal reports of persistent effects of early exposure to depression are in line with a number of studies that have used independent evidence concerning the child's behavior. These include teacher reports, direct observations of children's behavior, and child reports.

Using teacher reports, Alpern and Lyons-Ruth (1993) found that recent and chronic maternal depression was linked to raised rates of child behavior problems in school. Children who had been exposed to depression by 18 months, but not those exposed at 5 years, were reported to be more withdrawn and anxious than children whose mothers were well. Similar findings have been reported by Essex, Klein, Miech, and Smider (2001). In their prospective study of a low-risk US community sample, teacher reports at 6 years showed significant effects of the timing of the child's exposure to depression.

Children who had initially been exposed during their first year had high rates of comorbid internalizing and externalizing symptoms. In contrast, first exposure to maternal depression beyond infancy increased the risk only of externalizing problems (a finding confined to girls). These associations were not altered when the overall chronicity of maternal depression was taken into account. Subsequent analyses of this sample, when the effects of marital conflict were also considered, showed that boys who were exposed only to early maternal depression had raised rates of internalizing problems (assessed by combined teacher and mother reports), but developed externalizing difficulties if early maternal depression was succeeded by marital conflict (Essex, Klein, Cho, and Kraemer, 2003). Teacher reports of child adjustment in school were also obtained in the Cambridge longitudinal study (Sinclair & Murray, 1998). As in other findings, recent maternal depression was related to more immature and dysregulated behavior, but associations were also found between boys' behavior problems (antisocial and hyperactive symptoms) and postnatal depressive episodes, particularly in the context of low socioeconomic status. Finally, in a small-sample study that included clinic-referred women, Wright, George, Burke, Gelfand, and Teti (2000) found that 5–8-year-old children of mothers who had experienced depression between 3 and 30 months had more adverse outcomes than children of well mothers on teacher reports of adjustment, especially on measures of aggression and poor peer relationships, even when controlling for current symptoms.

Direct assessments of children of postnatally depressed mothers were made in a number of contexts in the longitudinal study of Murray and colleagues. In school-based observations, both boys and girls of postnatally depressed mothers showed low levels of creative play, and they were relatively unresponsive to the positive approaches of other children (Murray, Sinclair, et al., 1999), effects that obtained when recent depression and marital conflict were taken into account. More extreme social difficulties in the form of marked aggression were also shown by the children of postnatally depressed mothers in this sample during peer play, although in this case the presence of marital conflict accounted for the association (Hipwell, Murray, Ducournau, & Stein, 2005).

Research has also identified sociocognitive disturbances relevant to depression. Thus, when children in the Cambridge longitudinal study were exposed to a mild stressor (the threat of losing deals in a card game), those who had been exposed to early maternal depression were more likely than nonexposed children to show evidence of depressive thinking (hopelessness, pessimism, self-denigration), even when controlling for the effects of recent maternal depression (Murray, Woolgar, Cooper, & Hipwell, 2001). A similar finding emerged from the study of Maughan, Cicchetti, Toth, and Rogosch (2007), where early maternal depression (before 21 months) was significantly associated with the child's own reports of low self-competence at 5 years. There was also an indirect effect of initial depression on child perceptions of social acceptance, via its impact on earlier emotion regulation. Notably, later occurring maternal depression was related to neither of the child report measures (Maughan et al., 2007).

The findings derived from independent assessments, while often consistent with maternal reports in showing effects of current difficulties, are notable in that all show persistent effects of early maternal depression, even when controlling for later episodes, with the majority showing an impact on child internalizing problems in the preschool or early school years.

Psychiatric disturbance in adolescence.   Children whose parents experience depression are at substantially raised risk themselves for depression and anxiety (Weissman, Wickramaratne, Nomura, Warner, Pilowsky, & Verdeli, 2006). However, since first episodes of depression typically occur only from adolescence onwards, long-term follow-up is required to examine associations between maternal postnatal depression and offspring disorder. To date, three studies have been reported, although all have involved children below the age of greatest risk for occurrence of depression. Hammen and Brennan (2003) examined the psychiatric status of 15-year-old children of mothers in a large Australian community sample, overselected for maternal depression. Both severity and chronicity of maternal depression were important, with adolescent disorder (and particularly depression) being more likely in the context of severe maternal episodes, even when of short duration. Milder maternal depression posed risk only if it was prolonged. Timing of maternal depression was also considered, with the subsample of women experiencing only one depressive episode being categorized according to whether it occurred between 0–2, 3–5, or 6–10 years. Exposure to maternal depression during any of these periods increased risk for adolescent depressive disorder, whereas the occurrence of non-depressive disorder showed no effects of exposure in any single time period. These findings suggest that the occurrence of maternal depression at any time in the first 10 years is associated with adolescent risk for depressive disorder, but that there is no specific risk from exposure in infancy.

Offspring psychiatric disorder was also assessed in the Cambridge longitudinal sample. At 13 years, those who had been exposed to postnatal depression were at increased risk of both depression and anxiety disorder. However, when subsequent maternal depression was taken into account the postnatal maternal episode had no additional impact on adolescent depression. In contrast, the association between maternal postnatal depression and offspring anxiety was retained regardless of later maternal disorder (Halligan, Murray, Martins, & Cooper, 2007). Finally, assessments were made of psychiatric disorder in the disadvantaged London sample of Sharp and colleagues. At 11 years, postnatal depression was associated with a substantially raised risk of child disorder (seasonal affective disorder, social anxiety, depression and behavior disorders combined). However, since subsequent maternal depression was not considered, conclusions regarding specific links to the postpartum episode cannot be drawn (Pawlby, Sharp, Hay, & O'Keane, 2008). A subsequent report on this sample concerned offspring depression at 16 years. This focused on the effects of timing of *new onsets*, rather than on exposure to maternal depression *per se* during particular time periods (Pawlby, Hay, Sharp, Waters, & O'Keane, 2009); therefore the effects of postnatal episodes in general (rather than episodes occurring for the first time postnatally) cannot be determined. Nevertheless, as in the Cambridge sample, this study also found chronicity of child exposure to maternal depression to be important, with the majority of episodes having started antenatally.

Mechanisms mediating social-emotional outcomes

Some individual differences in infant emotional expressiveness and reactivity through the first year, such as the amount of crying, appear relatively independent of parenting (St.

James-Roberts & Plewis, 1996; see also chapter 20 in volume 1 on temperament). However, capacities concerned with the self-regulation of behavioral and emotional states, which are key to subsequent good adjustment (DeGangi, Breinbauer, Doussard-Roosevelt, Porges, & Greenspan, 2000; Kochanska, Murray, & Harlan, 2000; Kochanska, Tjebkes, & Forman, 1998), develop only gradually (Posner & Rothbart, 2000) and appear more responsive to parental intervention (Sameroff & Emde, 1989). Whereas good cognitive outcome is primarily promoted by high parental *responsiveness*, or contingency, good behavioral and emotional regulation appear to be particularly affected by parental *sensitivity*, where parenting is appropriately and affectively attuned to the child's behavior. This association holds in both depressed and normal samples. In the NICHD (1999) study, for example, behavior problems (poor cooperation) were predicted by maternal depression that was accompanied by insensitivity. Three specific ways in which parental interaction difficulties associated with postnatal depression may impede the development of emotional and behavioral regulation have been proposed.

Contagion of distress.   Field (1995) has suggested a contagion effect whereby infants show increased sad affect and distress, either through modeling their mothers' depressed behavior, or else being directly affected by the mother's sad presentation. This suggestion is consistent with the high levels of matching of negative emotional expressions in interactions between infants and depressed mothers (Field, Healy, Goldstein, & Guthertz, 1990). To date, direct evidence for the effects of distress contagion on longer-term regulatory problems is lacking, although studies with older children and adolescents of depressed parents are consistent with this mechanism (Joormann, Talbot, & Gotlib, 2007; Monk et al., 2008).

Failures of interactive repair.   In normal populations, mother and infant repeatedly shift from miscoordinated to coordinated states during social interactions, as the mother supports the infant's immature capacities to regulate their behavior and affect (Tronick & Gianino, 1986; Tronick, 1989; Jaffe et al., 2001). However, postnatally depressed mothers may fail to provide such experience (Tronick and Weinberg, 1997; Weinberg et al., 2006), as seen with depressed mothers of older children (Jameson, Gelfand, Kulcsar, & Teti, 1997). While there is evidence from normal populations for the longer-term beneficial effects of parental strategies to promote infant self-regulation, as assessed by secure attachment (Isabella & Belsky, 1991; Jaffe et al., 2001) and good sleep outcomes (Murray & Ramchandani, 2007), further research is required to investigate self-regulation outcomes in the context of postnatal depression.

Maternal hostility and coercion.   The hostile and intrusive, or coercive, behavior that is characteristic of some depressed mothers (especially those living in conditions of marked adversity) may act directly to bring about infant distress and behavioral dysregulation. A microanalysis of face-to-face interactions between depressed and well mothers and their infants in the Cambridge study showed that episodes of infant behavioral dysregulation were immediately preceded by the mother's negating the infant's experience, often through intrusive or hostile interventions (Murray, Fiori-Cowley, et al., 1996). Long-term associations were also found in this sample, with early maternal hostility predicting negative child self-cognitions at 5 years (Murray et al., 2001). Such an association was similarly identified in the study of Maughan et al. (2007). A path analysis of mother–infant/child interactions, and child behavior assessed over eight years in the Cambridge study, showed that infant emotional and behavioral dysregulation at 2 months, assessed independently of the mother, was unrelated to depressed mothers' hostile and coercive interactions at this time, but that by 4 months an association was present. This difficult infant behavior began to show continuity over time, and in turn precipitated further maternal negativity and intrusiveness, with the ensuing vicious cycle culminating in raised rates of conduct problems and attention deficit hyperactivity disorder symptoms by age 5–8 years (Morrell & Murray, 2003). Such findings are consistent with more general research with older children, showing the occurrence of disruptive behavior disorders to be associated with parental hostility and coercive control (see review by Hill, 2002).

Conclusions. Research on the effects of maternal postnatal depression on child behavioral and socioemotional development indicates the importance of the general parenting characteristic of sensitivity. In addition, a number of specific dimensions of interactions between depressed mothers and their infants in the postnatal months are implicated in adverse child functioning in this domain. Further longitudinal work is needed that directly examines the role of early mother–infant interactions in longer-term child outcomes.

Mediators of poor psychiatric outcomes

While preliminary research indicates that postnatal depression is associated with increased rates of psychiatric disorder in offspring, longer-term follow-up studies are required for more definitive estimation of risks. Furthermore, the limited nature of the evidence available to date necessarily constrains consideration of the mechanisms accounting for any increased risk. What does seem apparent, however, at least for child depressive disorder, is that the chronicity and severity of maternal depression are important, as they have been found to be for several earlier child outcomes. This may, in part, reflect genetic liability, since both these dimensions of disorder are associated with genetic risk (Kendler, 1996), but it is also likely to reflect greater environmental adversity (Brown & Harris, 1978). In addition to these broad influences, a number of specific processes initiated in the postnatal period itself are also suggested.

Biological processes. As noted earlier, the unresponsive or withdrawn interactions with the infant seen in subgroups of postnatally depressed mothers have been found to predict particular infant EEG profiles, namely, relative reduction in left versus right prefrontal EEG activity (Dawson et al., 1997a, 1999; Diego et al., 2001). In turn, this EEG activity profile is associated with adult exposure to negative emotion stimuli such as fear and disgust (Davidson, Ekman, Saron, Senulis, & Friesen, 1990; Tomarken, Davidson, & Henriques, 1990) as well as with adult depressive disorder itself (Henriques & Davidson, 1990; Schaffer, Davidson, & Saron, 1983). While the parallels between EEG responses in infants of depressed mothers and those of adults experiencing depression are notable, it is important that follow-up studies of the infant populations be conducted to establish whether there are indeed direct links between early EEG functioning and subsequent disorder.

Research on HPA-axis functioning also has begun to show associations with disturbances in parenting in the context of postnatal depression (Murray et al., 2010). The previously noted pattern of increase in basal cortisol secretion found to occur with exposure to postnatal depression has also been associated with both risk for depression (Goodyer, Tamplin, Herbert, & Altham, 2000; Halligan et al., 2004; Harris et al., 2000; Mannie et al., 2007) and the occurrence of adolescent and adult depressive disorder (Southwick, Vythilingam, & Charney, 2005). For example, the cortisol elevations at age 13 in offspring of postnatally depressed mothers in the Cambridge longitudinal study were found to prospectively predict depressive symptoms at 16 years (Halligan, Herbert, Goodyer, & Murray, 2007).

Social cognitions.   Aside from physiological processes, certain patterns of social cognition regarding close relationships and emotions, typically identified around adolescence, have been found to raise the risk for depression (Gjerde, 1995; Gore, Aseltine, & Colten, 1993). The question arises whether early relationships between postnatally depressed mothers and their infants may set in train such developing child social cognitions. In the Cambridge study, adolescent sociocognitive functioning was assessed to address this question (Murray, Halligan, Adams, Patterson, & Goodyer, 2006). In interviews about friendship difficulties, girls of postnatally depressed mothers showed substantially heightened emotional sensitivity, which in turn was associated with their experience of depressive symptoms. These social cognitions also showed continuity with both insecure attachment to the mother in infancy and with representations of family relationships at age 5 (Murray, Woolgar, Briers, & Hipwell, 1999).

Conclusion.   Findings from both biophysiological and social-cognitive research suggest that the particularly difficult patterns of interaction in the early postpartum months that can occur in the context of postnatal depression may set in train developmental processes that confer increased risk for depressive disorder in adolescent offspring. Whether these are translated into actual disorder, however, is likely to depend upon subsequent adverse experience, most notably on further exposure to maternal depression.

Treatment and Prevention

Treatment studies

Given the evidence concerning the adverse impact of postnatal depression on mother–infant relationships and child development, the provision of effective interventions for the depression itself, and for the disturbances in mother–child relationships, is a priority. A number of approaches are being explored.

Psychotherapeutic interventions. A review of randomized control trials (Dennis & Hodnett, 2007) concluded that both psychological interventions (cognitive behavior therapy (CBT) and interpersonal therapy) and psychosocial interventions (primarily nondirective counseling) were moderately effective and similarly beneficial. A recent meta-analysis of psychotherapeutic interventions (including CBT, social support, inter-personal therapy, nondirective counseling, psychoanalytic therapy) also concluded that psychotherapy is moderately effective for the treatment of postnatal depression (Cuijpers, Brannmark, & van Straten, 2008). However, both reviews highlighted the short-term nature of most trials and their follow-ups, with a consequent lack of information about longer-term outcomes.

Pharmacological interventions. Only limited data are available. One study (Appleby, Warner, Whitton, & Faragher, 1997) compared treatment for postnatal depression with fluoxetine (a selective serotonin reuptake inhibitor: SSRI), counseling, or fluoxetine plus counseling, and found the two individual treatments were similarly efficacious relative to placebo or single-session counseling conditions. No advantage of the combined treatment was shown, although there was limited power to test this possibility. Notably, more than half the women approached for this study declined to participate, primarily because of reluctance to take medication. A second study compared paroxetine (an SSRI) to paroxetine plus CBT for postnatal depression with comorbid anxiety (Misri, Reebye, Corral, & Milis, 2004), and found them to be associated with similar levels of improvement over the 12-week treatment period. While participation rates were good, findings were limited by the lack of a nontreated control group and small sample size. Overall, therefore, the efficacy of antidepressant medication for postnatal depression requires further evaluation (Hoffbrand, Howard, & Crawley, 2001). Importantly, the possibility of drug transmission to the infant via breastfeeding requires evaluation. One study of 26 mothers treated with SSRIs showed elevations in serotonin reuptake inhibitors (SRIs) in breast milk (Berle, Steen, Aamo, Breilid, Zahlsen, & Spigset, 2004). Further research is required with larger samples, in which effects of antenatal medication are also considered.

Effects of interventions on mother–infant relationships. A critical question regarding the treatment of postnatal depression concerns the extent to which treatment effects are reflected in improvements in mother–infant relationships and infant developmental outcomes. Several studies have specifically addressed this issue, with mixed results. A large-scale randomized control trial comparing 10 sessions of CBT, counseling, or psychoanalytic therapy found that while all active treatments were moderately effective in treating depression and brought about short-term benefits in the quality of the mother–infant relationship, there was no consistent improvement in infant outcomes; and effects were generally not sustained at 18-month and 5-year follow-ups (Cooper, Murray, Wilson, & Romaniuk, 2003; Murray, Cooper, Wilson, & Romaniuk, 2003). Clark, Tluczek, and Wenzel (2003) conducted a pilot study comparing mother–infant therapy or interpersonal therapy to a waiting list control condition. Although treatments were beneficial in improving depression, consistent effects on subsequent mother–child interactions were not observed, and infants in the treatment groups did not differ from controls in terms of cognitive development or observed temperament. Finally, a recent study (Forman, O'Hara, Stuart, Gorman, Larsen, & Coy, 2007) found that mother–infant dyads who received effective treatment for postnatal depression were no better than nontreated dyads in terms of observed mother–infant interactions, infant negative emotionality, and attachment security. The same pattern of results held at 18-month follow-up, and positive benefits of treatment were not observed even when treatment responders were considered separately.

A related approach has been to directly focus on improving parenting. Cicchetti, Rogosch, and Toth (2000) examined the impact of prolonged psychotherapy (average 57 weeks) compared to nontreated depressed and nondepressed control groups. The intervention, which focused on promoting positive maternal attachment representations and mother–infant interactions, resulted in infant cognitive abilities that were comparable to control group levels at the end of treatment, whereas the untreated depressed group showed a relative decline in cognitive performance over the same period. Several studies focusing exclusively on dyadic interventions to improve mother–infant interactions have also indicated improvements, with interactive coaching (Horowitz et al., 2001), relationship facilitation based on maternal administrations of the Neonatal Behavioral Assessment Scale (Hart, Field, & Nearing, 1998), and infant massage (Glover, Onozawa, & Hodgkinson, 2002; Onozawa, Glover, Adams, Modi, & Kumar, 2001) all showing short-term beneficial effects. However, neither longer-term benefits, nor implications for infant development, have been examined in these studies.

Provision of alternative care.   Given the limited potential to alter difficulties in mother–infant relationships and prevent adverse child outcome in the context of maternal depression, it is also worth considering the potential for promoting the role of alternative caregivers. Studies have shown, for example, that infants of postnatally depressed mothers will respond positively during interactions with their nondepressed fathers (Hossain, Field, Gonzalez, Malphurs, & Del Valle, 1994), or other familiar caregivers, such as childminders or daycare nurses (Pelaez-Nogueras, Field, Cigales, Gonzalez, & Clasky, 1994). Mother–infant relationships themselves were found in one study to be affected, with better engagement occurring in cases where the mother was not based at home full-time (Cohn, Campbell, Matias, & Hopkins, 1990). While not specifically assessing postnatal depression, results from the early child care NICHD sample (Study of Early Child Care) showed that levels of internalizing behavior problems were reduced at 24 and 36 months where the child received alternative care (Lee, Halpern, Hertz-Picciotto, Martin, & Suchindran, 2006). Provision of alternative caregivers may be important to institute in the first 6–9 months, before infants start to generalize the difficult behavior shown with their mother to interactions with other people.

Conclusions.   A number of treatments have been shown to be effective in helping mothers recover from postnatal depression itself. However, more limited success has been achieved in altering mother–infant interactions and in preventing poor child outcome in the longer term. Those that are more promising in this regard are interventions that focus specifically on difficulties in mother–infant interactions. To the extent that many adverse child outcomes associated with postnatal depression are particularly likely to occur in the context of chronic, or recurrent, depression, it is not surprising that shortening the infant's initial exposure to depression is not sufficient to prevent longer-term problems in child development. In high-risk contexts where depression is more likely to be prolonged or recurrent it may be more productive to set up long-term monitoring of vulnerable families, so that support can be provided quickly if depression recurs. Finally, in addition to efforts to support mother–infant relationships, it may also be beneficial to give infants experience of positive interactions with additional caregivers.

Preventive interventions

An alternative approach has been to intervene to prevent the occurrence of postpartum depression in high-risk groups. A recent review of pharmacological preventive studies (Howard, Hoffbrand, Henshaw, Boath, &, Bradley, 2005) identified only two that addressed their prophylactic efficacy in the postpartum period (Wisner, Perel, Peindl, Hanusa, Findling, & Rapport, 2001; Wisner, Perel, Peindl, Hanusa, Piontek, & Findling, 2004), and concluded that there was insufficient evidence to draw clear conclusions about the preventive benefits. The review also highlighted several problems in this area, including a lack of data on the implementation of treatments antenatally, limited evaluation of the impact of antidepressants on fetal or infant development, and a limited ability to detect "at-risk" women to target. The efficacy of psychological or psychosocial preventive interventions has been more comprehensively investigated, but evidence for a beneficial effect is limited. A meta-analysis that included any psychological/psychosocial intervention concluded that there was no overall preventive effect for postpartum depression (Dennis & Creedy, 2004). When analyses were limited to trials that targeted women at high risk for depression, there was some support for a reduction in subsequent symptoms in association with intervention, but effects were short term. There was no evidence to support benefits for infant development.

Overall, preventive interventions for postpartum depression are currently not supported. However, a key problem in this area relates to the targeting of interventions. There is some evidence to suggest that high-risk populations may benefit, but the identification of such populations is problematic. While predictive indices have been developed which can identify women who will become postnatally depressed with a high degree of sensitivity, specificity is typically poor (Austin & Lumley, 2003; Cooper, Murray, Hooper, & West, 1996), meaning that the majority of women identified as being at risk do not develop postpartum depression.

Emerging Areas of Research

Impact of paternal depression

Although not as common as in women, depression also affects men during the postnatal period (Goodman, 2004). Effects of paternal disorder on children's development are underresearched, particularly those in infancy and early childhood. Nevertheless, there is emerging evidence that depression in men in the perinatal period may predict disorder in their offspring. Specifically, using the large ALSPAC UK cohort, Ramchandani, Stein, Evans, O'Connor, and the ALSPAC Study Team (2005) and Ramchandani, Stein, O'Connor, Heron, Murray, and Evans (2008) found depression in fathers in the postnatal period was associated with increased rates of behavioral problems in their children at 3.5 and 7 years, controlling for maternal depression and other potential confounding factors, with associations appearing stronger for boys. Children whose fathers were chronically depressed were at higher risk of emotional and behavioral problems, and there was evidence from comparisons of the effects of ante- versus postnatal depression for these to be mediated via environmental means, rather than via genetic risk (Ramchandani, O'Connor, Evans, Heron, Murray, & Stein, 2008).

Effects of postnatal depression in the developing world

The prevalence of postpartum depression has been found to be two to three times higher in developing countries than in the developed world (Halbreich & Karkun, 2006; Wachs et al., 2009). For example, 34% of mothers were found to be postnatally depressed in Khayelitsha, a socioeconomically deprived settlement in South Africa (Cooper, Tomlinson, Swartz, Woolgar, Murray, & Molteno, 1999), as were 23% and 28% of indigent samples in Goa, India (Patel, Rodrigues, & DeSouza, 2002) and rural Pakistan (Rahman, Iqbal, & Harrington, 2003), respectively. As in developed world countries, the occurrence of maternal depression is associated with a range of developmental difficulties in the children, including cognitive delay (Black et al., 2007), poor growth and health (Rahman, Iqbal, Bunn, Lovel, & Harrington, 2004; Rahman et al., 2007), and insecurity of attachment (Tomlinson, Cooper, & Murray, 2005). Consistent with findings from developed countries, in the Black et al., and Tomlinson et al. studies, difficulties in mother–infant interactions associated with depression were found to mediate its effects on infant outcome. Several studies have found that depression can be alleviated by a variety of interventions (see the review by Wachs et al., 2009). For example, taking account of limited healthcare resources, home visiting by trained community mothers in the early postpartum months was found to bring about marked improvements in both mother–infant interactions (Cooper, Landman, Tomlinson, Molteno, Swartz, & Murray, 2002), and infant attachment security (Cooper et al., 2009). Such promising findings potentially have important implications for future practice.

Summary

Postnatal depression is a common and disabling disorder associated with a range of adverse infant and child outcomes. These occur principally where the maternal depression is chronic or recurrent, and in the presence of other background risks. Adverse patterns of parenting associated with postnatal depression are likely to play a major role in bringing about poor child outcome. Biological processes are also likely to be important in mediating effects of depression on the child, but require further investigation. Attempts to change parental interactions and improve the longer-term outcome for children of postnatally depressed mothers have met with limited success, and longer-term monitoring and support for families may be necessary; an additional therapeutic strategy could include enhancing the role of other caregivers. There is a need for further research on the role of fathers, and on the effects of depression in the developing world.

References

Aaron Jones, N., Field, T., Fox, N. A., Lundy, B., & Davalos, M. (1997). EEG activation in 1-month-old infants of depressed mothers. *Development and Psychopathology, 9*, 491–505.

Achenbach, T. M., (1991). *Manual for the Child Behavior Checklist/4–18 and 1991 Profile.* Burlington: University of Vermont, Department of Psychiatry.

Alpern, L., & Lyons-Ruth, K. (1993). Preschool children at social risk: Chronicity and timing of maternal depressive symptoms and child behavior problems at school and at home. *Development and Psychopathology, 5*(3), 371–387.

Appleby, L., Warner, R., Whitton, A., & Faragher, B. (1997). A controlled study of fluoxetine and cognitive-behavioural counselling in the treatment of postnatal depression. *British Medical Journal, 314*, 932–936.

Atkinson, L., Paglia, A., Coolbear, J., Niccols, A., Parker K. C. H., & Guger, S. (2000). Attachment security: A meta-analysis of maternal mental health correlates. *Clinical Psychology Review, 20*, 1019–1040.

Austin, M. P., & Lumley, J. (2003). Antenatal screening for postnatal depression: A systematic review. *Acta Psychiatrica Scandinavica, 107*, 10–17.

Bartels, M., Van den Berg, M., Sluyter, F., Boomsma, D. I. C., & de Geus, E. J. (2003). Heritability of cortisol levels: Review and simultaneous analysis of twin studies. *Psychoneuroendocrinology, 28*, 121–137.

Berle, J. O., Steen, V. M., Aamo, T. O., Breilid, H., Zahlsen, K., & Spigset, O. (2004). Breastfeeding during maternal antidepressant treatment with serotonin reuptake inhibitors: Infant exposure, clinical symptoms, and cytochrome P450 genotypes. *Journal of Clinical Psychiatry, 65*, 1288–1234.

Bettes, B. A. (1988). Maternal depression and motherese: Temporal and intonational features. *Child Development, 59*, 1089–1096.

Black, M. M., Baqui, A. H., Zaman, K., McNary, S. W., Le, K., Arifeen, S. E., Hamadani, J. D., Parveen, M., Yunus, M., & Black, M. E. (2007). Depressive symptoms among rural Bangladeshi mothers: Implications for infant development. *Journal of Child Psychology and Psychiatry, 48*(8), 764–772.

Boyce, P. M. (2003). Risk factors for postnatal depression: A review and risk factors in Australian populations. *Archives of Women's Mental Health, 6*(Suppl. 2), s43–s50.

Brazelton, T. B., Kozlowski, B., & Main, M. (1974). The origins of reciprocity. In M. Lewis and L. Rosenblum (Eds.), *The effect of the infant on its caregiver.* New York: Elsevier.

Brennan, P. A., Hammen, C., Andersen, M. J., Bor, W., Najman, J. M., & Williams, G. M. (2000). Chronicity, severity, and timing of maternal depressive symptoms: Relationships with child outcomes at age 5. *Developmental Psychology, 36*, 759–766.

Breznitz, Z., & Sherman, T. (1987). Speech patterning of natural discourse of well and depressed mothers and their young children. *Child Development, 58*(2), 395–400.

Brown, G., & Harris, T. (Eds.) (1978). *The social origins of depression*. New York: Free Press.

Bugental, D. B., Martorell, G. A., & Barraza,V. (2003). The hormonal costs of subtle forms of infant maltreatment. *Hormones and Behavior, 43*, 237–244.

Campbell, S. B., Brownell, C. A., Hungerford, A., Speiker, S. J., Mohan, R., & Blessing J. S. (2004). The course of maternal depressive symptoms and maternal sensitivity as predictors of attachment security at 36 months. *Development and Psychopathology, 16*, 231–252.

Campbell, S. B., Cohn, J. E., & Meyers, T. (1995). Depression in first time mothers: Mother–infant interaction and depression chronicity. *Developmental Psychology, 60*, 349–357.

Caplan, H. L., Cogill, S. R., Alexandra, H., Robson, K. M., Katz, R., & Kumar, R. (1989). Maternal depression and the emotional development of the child. *British Journal of Psychiatry, 154*, 818–822.

Cicchetti, D., Rogosch, F. A., & Toth, S. (1998). Maternal depressive disorder and contextual risk: Contributions to the development of attachment insecurity and behavior problems in toddlerhood. *Development and Psychopathology, 10*, 283–300.

Cicchetti, D., Rogosch, F. A., & Toth, S. L. (2000). The efficacy of toddler–parent psychotherapy for fostering cognitive development in offspring of depressed mothers. *Journal of Abnormal Child Psychology, 28*, 135–148.

Clark, R., Tluczek, A., & Wenzel, A. (2003). Psychotherapy for postpartum depression: A preliminary report. *American Journal of Orthopsychiatry, 73*, 441–454.

Cogill, S. R., Caplan, H. L., Alexandra, H., Robson, K. M., & Kumar, R. (1986). Impact of maternal postnatal depression on cognitive development of young children. *British Medical Journal, 292*(6529), 1165–1167.

Cohn, J. F., Campbell, S. B., Matias, R., & Hopkins, J. (1990). Face-to-face interactions of postpartum depressed and nondepressed mother-infant pairs at 2 months. *Developmental Psychology, 26*(1), 15–23.

Cohn, J. F., Matias, R., Tronick, E. Z., Connell, D., & Lyons-Ruth, K. (1986). Face-to-face interactions of depressed mothers and their infants. In E. Z. Tronick & T. Field (Eds.), *Maternal depression and infant disturbance* (pp. 31–46). San Francisco: Jossey-Bass.

Cooper, P., Landman, M., Tomlinson, M., Molteno, C., Swartz, L., & Murray, L. (2002). The impact of a mother–infant intervention in an indigent peri-urban South African context: Pilot study. *British Journal of Psychiatry, 180*, 76–81.

Cooper, P. J., Murray, L., Hooper, R., & West, A. (1996). The development and validation of a predictive index for postpartum depression. *Psychological Medicine, 26*, 627–634.

Cooper, P. J., Murray, L., Wilson, A., & Romaniuk, H. (2003). Controlled trial of the short- and long-term effect of psychological treatment of post-partum depression. I. Impact on maternal mood. *British Journal of Psychiatry, 182*, 412–419.

Cooper, P. J., Tomlinson, M., Swartz, L., Landman, M., Molteno, C., Stein, A. L., et al. (2009) Improving quality of mother–infant relationship and infant attachment in socioeconomically deprived community in South Africa: Randomised controlled trial. *British Medical Journal, 338*, b974.

Cooper, P. J., Tomlinson, M., Swartz, L., Woolgar, M., Murray, L., & Molteno, C. (1999). Postpartum depression and the mother–infant relationship in a South African peri-urban settlement. *British Journal of Psychiatry, 175*, 554–558.

Coplan, J. D., Andrews, M. W., Rosenblum, L. A., Owens, M. J., Friedman, S., Gorman, J. M., et al. (1996). Persistent elevations of cerebrospinal fluid concentrations of corticotropin-releasing factor in adult nonhuman primates exposed to early-life stressors: Implications for the pathophysiology of mood and anxiety disorders. *Proceedings of the National Academy of Sciences of the United States of America, 93*, 1619–1623.

Coplan, J. D., Smith, E. L., Altemus, M., Mathew, S. J., Perera, T., Kral, J. G., et al. (2006). Maternal–infant response to variable foraging demand in nonhuman primates: Effects of timing of stressor on cerebrospinal fluid corticotropin-releasing factor and circulating glucocorticoid concentrations. *Annals of the New York Academy of Sciences, 1071*, 525–533.

Coplan, J. D., Smith, E. L. P., Altemus, M., Scharf, B. A., Owens, M., Nemeroff, C. B., et al. (2001). Variable foraging demand rearing: Sustained elevations in cisternal cerebrospinal fluid corticotropin-releasing factor concentrations in adult primates. *Biological Psychiatry, 50*, 200–204.

Cornish, A. M., McMahon, C. A., Ungerer, J. A., Barnett, B., Kowalenko, N., & Tennant, C. (2005). Postnatal depression and infant cognitive and motor development in the second postnatal year: The impact of depression chronicity and infant gender. *Infant Behavior and Development, 4*, 407–417.

Cox, A. D., Puckering, A., Pound, A., & Mills, M. (1987). The impact of maternal depression in young children. *Journal of Child Psychology and Psychiatry, 28*(6), 917–928.

Cuijpers, P., Brannmark, J. G., & van Straten, A. (2008). Psychological treatment of postpartum depression: A meta-analysis. *Journal of Clinical Psychology, 64*, 103–118.

Davidson, R. J., Ekman, P., Saron, C. D., Senulis, J. A., & Friesen, W. V. (1990). Approach-withdrawal and cerebral asymmetry: Emotional expression and brain physiology. I. *Journal of Personality and Social Psychology, 58*, 330–341.

Dawson, G., Ashman, S. B., Panagiotides, H., Hessl, D., Self, J., Yamada, E., & Embry, L. (2003). Preschool outcomes of children of depressed mothers: Role of maternal behavior, contextual risk, and children's brain activity. *Child Development, 74*(4), 1158–1175.

Dawson, G., Frey, K., Panagiotides, H., Osterling, J., & Hessl, D. (1997a). Infants of depressed mothers exhibit atypical frontal brain activity: A replication and extension of previous findings. *Journal of Child Psychology and Psychiatry, 38*, 179–186.

Dawson, G., Frey, K., Panagiotides, H., Self, J., Hessl, D., & Yamada, E. (1997b). *Atypical frontal brain activity in infants of depressed mothers: The role of maternal behavior.* Poster presented at the 1997 Meeting of the Society for Research in Child Development, Washington, DC.

Dawson, G., Frey, K., Panagiotides, H., Yamada, E., Hessl, D., & Osterling, J. (1999). Infants of depressed mothers exhibit reduced left frontal brain activity during interactions with mother and a familiar non-depressed adult. *Child Development, 70*(5), 1058–1066.

DeGangi, G. A., Breinbauer, C., Doussard-Roosevelt, J., Porges, S., & Greenspan, S. (2000). Prediction of childhood problems at three years in children experiencing disorders of regulation during infancy. *Infant Mental Health Journal, 21*(3), 156–175.

Dennis, C. L., & Creedy, D. (2004). Psychosocial and psychological interventions for preventing postpartum depression. *Cochrane Database of Systematic Reviews* CD001134.

Dennis, C. L., & Hodnett, E. (2007). Psychosocial and psychological interventions for treating postpartum depression. *Cochrane Database of Systematic Reviews* CD006116.

Diego, M. A., Field, T., & Hernandez-Reif, M. (2001). BIS/BAS scores are correlated with frontal EEG asymmetry in intrusive and withdrawn depressed mothers. *Infant Mental Health Journal, 22*(6), 665–675.

Eshel, N., Daelmans, B., Cabral de Mello, M., Martines, J. (2006). Responsive parenting: Interventions and outcomes. *Bulletin of the World Health Organization, 84*(12), 992–998.

Essex, M. J., Klein, M. H., Cho, E., & Kalin, N. H. (2002). Maternal stress beginning in infancy may sensitize children to later stress exposure: Effects on cortisol and behavior. *Biological Psychiatry, 52*, 776–784.

Essex, M. J., Klein, M. H., Cho, E., & Kraemer, H. (2003). Exposure to maternal depression and marital conflict: Gender differences in children's later mental health symptoms. *Journal of the American Academy of Child & Adolescent Psychiatry, 42*(6), 728–737.

Essex, M. J., Klein, M., Miech, R., & Smider, N. A. (2001). Timing of initial exposure to maternal major depression and children's mental health symptoms in kindergarten. *British Journal of Psychiatry, 179*, 151–156.

Fagen, J. W., Ohr, P. S., Fleckenstein, L. K., & Ribner, D. R. (1985). The effect of crying on long-term memory in infancy. *Child Development, 56*(6), 1584–1592.

Fernald, A. (1989). Intonation and communicative intent in mothers' speech to infants: Is the melody the message? *Child Development, 60*, 1497–1510.

Field, T. M. (1984). Early interactions between infants and their postpartum depressed mothers. *Infant Behaviour and Development, 7*, 517–522.

Field, T. M. (1995). Infants of depressed mothers. *Infant Behaviour and Development, 18*, 1–3.

Field, T., Diego, M., Hernandez-Reif, M., Vera, Y., Gil, K., Schanberg, S., et al. (2004). Prenatal predictors of maternal and newborn EEG. *Infant Behavior and Development, 27*(4), 533–536.

Field, T., Fox, N., Pickens, J., Nawrocki, T., & Soutullo, D. (1995). Right front EEG activation in 3- to 6-month-old infants of "depressed" mothers. *Developmental Psychology, 31*, 358–363.

Field, T., Healy, B., Goldstein, S., & Guthertz, M. (1990). Behavior state matching and synchrony in mother–infant interactions of nondepressed versus "depressed" dyads. *Developmental Psychology, 26*, 7–14.

Field, T., Healy, B., Goldstein, S., Perry, S., Bendell, D., Schanberg, S., et al. (1988). Infants of depressed mothers show "depressed" behavior even with nondepressed adults. *Child Development, 59*, 1569–1579.

Field, T. M., Sandberg, D., Garcia, R., Vega-Lahr, N., Goldstein, S., & Guy, L. (1985). Pregnancy problems, postpartum depression, and early mother–infant interactions. *Developmental Psychology, 21*(6), 1152–1156.

Forman, D. R., O'Hara, M. W., Stuart, S., Gorman, L. L., Larsen, K. E., & Coy, K. C. (2007). Effective treatment for postpartum depression is not sufficient to improve the developing mother–child relationship. *Development and Psychopathology, 19*, 585–602.

Ghodsian, M., Zajicek, E., & Wolkind, S. (1984). A longitudinal study of maternal depression and child behaviour problems. *Journal of Child Psychology and Psychiatry, 25*(1), 91–10.

Gjerde, P. F. (1995). Alternative pathways to chronic depressive symptoms in young adults: Gender differences in developmental trajectories. *Child Development, 66*(5), 1277–1300.

Glover, V., Onozawa, K., Hodgkinson, A. (2002). Benefits of infant massage for mothers with postnatal depression. *Seminars in Neonatology, 7*, 495–500.

Goodman, J. H. (2004). Paternal postpartum depression, its relationship to maternal postpartum depression, and implications for family health. *Journal of Advanced Nursing, 45*(1), 26–35.

Goodyer, I. M., Tamplin, A., Herbert, J., & Altham, P. M. (2000). Recent life events, cortisol, dehydroepiandrosterone and the onset of major depression in high-risk adolescents. *British Journal of Psychiatry, 177*, 499–504.

Gore, S., Aseltine, R. H., & Colten, M. E. (1993). Gender, social-relationship involvement, and depression. *Journal of Research on Adolescence, 3* (2), 101–125.

Halbreich, U., & Karkun, S. (2006). Cross-cultural and social diversity of prevalence of postpartum depression and depressive symptoms. *Journal of Affective Disorders, 91*, 97–111.

Halligan, S. L., Herbert, J., Goodyer, I. M., & Murray, L. (2004). Exposure to postnatal depression predicts elevated cortisol in adolescent offspring. *Biological Psychiatry, 55*, 376–381.

Halligan, S. L., Herbert, J., Goodyer, I., & Murray, L. (2007). Disturbances in morning cortisol secretion in association with maternal postnatal depression predict subsequent depressive symptomatology in adolescents. *Biological Psychiatry, 62*, 40–46.

Halligan, S. L., Murray, L., Martins, C., & Cooper, P. J. (2007). Maternal depression and psychiatric outcomes in adolescent offspring: A 13-year longitudinal study. *Journal of Affective Disorders, 97*, 145–154.

Hammen, C., & Brennan, P. A. (2003). Severity, chronicity, and timing of maternal depression and risk for adolescent offspring diagnoses in a community sample. *Archives of General Psychiatry*, *60*, 253–258.

Harris, T. O., Borsanyi, S., Messari, S., Stanford, K., Brown, G. W., Cleary, S. E., et al. (2000). Morning cortisol as a risk factor for subsequent major depressive disorder in adult women. *British Journal of Psychiatry*, *177*, 505–510.

Hart, S., Field, T., & Nearing, G. (1998). Depressed mothers' neonates improve following the MABI and a Brazelton demonstration. *Journal of Pediatric Psychology*, *23*, 351–356.

Hay, D. F., & Kumar, R. (1995). Interpreting the effects of mothers' postnatal depression on children's intelligence: A critique and re-analysis. *Child Psychiatry and Human Development*, *253*, 165–181.

Hay, D. F., Pawlby, S., Angold, A., Harold, G. T., & Sharp, D. (2003). Pathways to violence in the children of mothers who were depressed postpartum. *Developmental Psychology*, *39*(6), 1083–1094.

Hay, D. F., Pawlby, S., Sharp, D., Asten, P., Mills, A., & Kumar, R. (2001). Intellectual problems shown by 11-year-old children whose mothers had postnatal depression. *Journal of Child Psychology and Psychiatry and Allied Disciplines*, *42*, 871–889.

Henriques, J. B., & Davidson, R. J. (1990). Regional brain electrical asymmetries discriminate between previously depressed and healthy control subjects. *Journal of Abnormal Psychology*, *99*, 22–31.

Hessl, D., Dawson, G., Frey, K., Panagiotides, H., Self, H., Yamada, E., et al. (1998). A longitudinal study of children of depressed mothers: Psychobiological findings related to stress. In D. M. Hann, L. C. Huffman, K. K. Lederhendler, & M. Bethseda (Eds.), *Advancing research on developmental plasticity: Integrating the behavioral sciences and the neurosciences of mental health*. Bethseda, MD: National Institutes of Mental Health.

Hill, J. (2002). Biological, psychological and social processes in the conduct disorders. *Journal of Child Psychology and Psychiatry and Allied Disciplines*, *43*(1), 133–164.

Hipwell, A. E., Murray, L., Ducournau, P., & Stein, A. (2005). The effects of maternal depression and parental conflict on children's peer play. *Child: Care, Health and Development*, *31*(1), 11–23.

Hoffbrand, S., Howard, L., & Crawley, H. (2001). Antidepressant drug treatment for postnatal depression. *Cochrane Database of Systematic Reviews* CD002018.

Horowitz, J. A., Bell, M., Trybulski, J., Munro, B. H., Moser, D., Hartz, S. A. et al. (2001). Promoting responsiveness between mothers with depressive symptoms and their infants. *Journal of Nursing Scholarship*, *33*, 323–329.

Hossain, Z., Field, T., Gonzalez, J., Malphurs, J., & Del Valle, C. (1994). Infants of "depressed" mothers interact better with their nondepressed fathers. *Infant Mental Health*, *15*(4), 348–357.

Howard, L. M., Hoffbrand, S., Henshaw, C., Boath, L., & Bradley, E. (2005). Antidepressant prevention of postnatal depression. *Cochrane Database of Systematic Reviews* CD004363.

Isabella, R. A., & Belsky, J. (1991). Interactional synchrony and the origins of infant–mother attachment: A replication study. *Child Development*, *62*(2), 373–384.

Jaffe, J., Beebe, B., Feldstein, S., Crown, C. L., & Jasnow, M. D. (2001). Rhythms of dialogue in infancy. In W. F. Overton (Ed.), *Monographs of the Society for Research in Child Development*, *66*(2).

Jameson, P. B., Gelfand, D. M., Kulcsar, E., & Teti, D. M. (1997). Mother–toddler interaction patterns associated with maternal depression. *Development and Psychopathology*, *9*, 537–550.

Jones, N. A., Field, T., Davalos, M., & Pickens, J. (1997). EEG stability in infants/children of depressed mothers. *Child Psychiatry and Human Development*, *28*(2) 59–70.

Joormann, J., Talbot, L., & Gotlib, I. H. (2007). Biased processing of emotional information in girls at risk for depression. *Journal of Abnormal Psychology, 116,* 135–143.

Kaffman, A., & Meaney, M. J. (2007). Neurodevelopmental sequelae of postnatal maternal care in rodents: Clinical and research implications of molecular insights. *Journal of Child Psychology, and Psychiatry, 48,* 224–244.

Kaplan, P. S., Bachorowski, J., Smoski, M. J., & Hudenko, W. J. (2002). Infants of depressed mothers, although competent learners, fail to learn in response to their own mothers' infant-directed speech. *Psychological Science, 13*(3), 268–271.

Kaplan, P. S., Bachorowski, J., Smoski, M. J., & Zinser, M. (2001). Role of clinical diagnosis and medication use in effects of maternal depression on infant-directed speech. *Infancy, 2*(4) 537–548.

Kaplan, P. S., Bachorowski, J., & Zarlengo-Strouse, P. (1999). Child-directed speech produced by mothers with symptoms of depression fails to promote associative learning in 4-month-old infants. *Child Development, 70*(3), 560–570.

Kendler, K. S. (1996). Major depression and generalised anxiety disorder. Same genes, (partly) different environments – revisited. *British Journal of Psychiatry, 168*(Suppl. 30), 68–75.

Kochanska, G., Murray, K. T., & Harlan, E. T. (2000). Effortful control in early childhood: Continuity and change, antecedents, and implications for social development. *Developmental Psychology, 36*(2), 220–232.

Kochanska, G., Tjebkes, T. L., & Forman, D. R. (1998). Children's emerging regulation of conduct: Restraint, compliance, and internalization from infancy to the second year. *Child Development, 69*(5), 1378–1389.

Kurstjens, S., & Wolke, D. (2001). Effects of maternal depression on cognitive development of children over the first 7 years of life. *Journal of Child Psychology and Psychiatry and Allied Disciplines, 42,* 623–636.

Lee, L., Halpern, C. T., Hertz-Picciotto, I., Martin, S. L., & Suchindran, C. M. (2006). Child care and social support modify the association between maternal depressive symptoms and early childhood behaviour problems: A US national study. *Journal of Epidemiology and Community Health, 60,* 305–310.

Mannie, Z. N., Harmer, C. J., & Cowen, P. J. (2007). Increased waking salivary cortisol levels in young people at familial risk of depression. *American Journal of Psychiatry, 164,* 617–621.

Martins, C., & Gaffan, E. A., (2000). Effects of early maternal depression on patterns of infant–mother attachment: A meta-analytic investigation. *Journal of Child Psychology and Psychiatry, 41*(6), 737–746.

Maughan, A., Cicchetti, D., Toth, S. L., & Rogosch, F. A., (2007). Early-occurring maternal depression and maternal negativity in predicting young children's emotion regulation and socioemotional difficulties. *Journal of Abnormal Child Psychology, 35*(5), 685–703.

McMahon, C. A., Barnett, B., Kowalenko, N. M., & Tennant, C. C. (2006). Maternal attachment state of mind moderates the impact of postnatal depression on infant attachment. *Journal of Child Psychology and Psychiatry, 47,* 660–669.

Milgrom, J., Westley, D. T., & Gemmill, A. W. (2004). The mediating role of maternal responsiveness in some longer term effects of postnatal depression on infant development. *Infant Behavior and Development, 4,* 443–454.

Misri, S., Reebye, P., Corral, M., & Milis, L. (2004). The use of paroxetine and cognitive-behavioral therapy in postpartum depression and anxiety: A randomized controlled trial. *Journal of Clinical Psychiatry, 65,* 1236–1241.

Monk, C. S., Klein, R. G., Telzer, E. H., Schroth, E. A., Mannuzza, S., Moulton, J. L., et al. (2008). Amygdala and nucleus accumbens activation to emotional facial expressions in children and adolescents at risk for major depression. *American Journal of Psychiatry, 165,* 90–98.

Morrell, J., & Murray, L. (2003). Parenting and the development of conduct disorder and hyperactive symptoms in childhood: A prospective longitudinal study from 2 months to 8 years. *Journal of Child Psychology and Psychiatry and Allied Disciplines, 44*(4), 489–508.

Murray, L. (1992). The impact of postnatal depression on infant development. *Journal of Child Psychology and Psychiatry, 33*, 543–561.

Murray, L., Cooper, P. J., Wilson, A., & Romaniuk, H. (2003). Controlled trial of the short- and long-term effect of psychological treatment of post-partum depression, 2. Impact on the mother-child relationship and child outcome. *British Journal of Psychiatry, 182*, 420–427.

Murray, L., Fiori-Cowley, A., Hooper, R., & Cooper, P. (1996). The impact of postnatal depression and associated adversity on early mother–infant interactions and later infant outcome. *Child Development, 67*, 2512–2526.

Murray, L., Halligan, S., Adams, G., Patterson, P., & Goodyer, I. M. (2006). Socioemotional development in adolescents at risk for depression: The role of maternal depression and attachment style. *Development and Psychopathology, 18*, 489–516.

Murray, L., Halligan, S. L., Goodyer, I., & Herbert, J. (2010). Disturbances in early parenting of depressed mothers and cortisol secretion in offspring: A preliminary study. *Journal of Affective Disorders, 122*, 218–223.

Murray, L., Hipwell, A., Hooper, R., Stein, A., & Cooper, P. (1996). The cognitive development of 5-year-old children of postnatally depressed mothers. *Journal of Child Psychology and Psychiatry, 37*, 927–935.

Murray, L., Kempton, C., Woolgar, M., & Hooper, R. (1993). Depressed mothers' speech to their infants and its relation to infant gender and cognitive development. *Journal of Child Psychology and Psychiatry, 34*(7), 1083–1101.

Murray, L., & Ramchandani, P. (2007). Might prevention be better than cure? A perspective on improving infant sleep and maternal mental health: A cluster randomized trial. *Archives of Disease in Childhood, 92*, 943–944.

Murray, L., Sinclair, D., Cooper, P., Ducournau, P., Turner, P., & Stein, A. (1999). The socioemotional development of 5-year-old children of postnatally depressed mothers. *Journal of Child Psychology and Psychiatry and Allied Disciplines, 40*, 1259–1271.

Murray, L., Stanley, C., Hooper, R., King, F., & Fiori-Cowley, A. (1996). The role of infant factors in postnatal depression and mother–infant interactions. *Developmental Medicine and Child Neurology, 38*, 109–119.

Murray, L., Woolgar, M., Briers, S., & Hipwell, A. (1999). Children's social representations in dolls' house play and theory of mind tasks, and their relation to family adversity and child disturbance. *Social Development, 8*(2), 179–200.

Murray, L., Woolgar, M., Cooper, P., & Hipwell, A. (2001). Cognitive vulnerability to depression in 5-year-old children of depressed mothers. *Journal of Child Psychology and Psychiatry, 42*(7), 891–899.

NICHD, Early Child Care Research Network (1999). Chronicity of maternal depressive symptoms, maternal sensitivity and child functioning at 36 months. *Developmental Psychology, 35*(5), 1297–1310.

O'Connor, T. G., Ben-Shlomo, Y., Heron, J., Golding, J., Adams, D., & Glover, V. (2005). Prenatal anxiety predicts individual differences in cortisol in pre-adolescent children. *Biological Psychiatry, 58*, 211–217.

O'Hara, M., & Swain, A. (1996). Rates and risk of postpartum depression – A meta-analysis. *International Review of Psychiatry, 8*(1), 37–54.

Onozawa, K., Glover, V., Adams, D., Modi, N., & Kumar, R. C. (2001). Infant massage improves mother–infant interaction for mothers with postnatal depression. *Journal of Affective Disorders, 63*, 201–207.

Papousek, H., & Papousek, M. (1987). Intuitive parenting: A dialectic counterpart to the infant's integrative competence. In J. D. Osofsky (Ed.), *Handbook of infant development* (2nd ed., pp. 669–720). New York: John Wiley & Sons, Inc.

Patel, V., Rodrigues, M., & DeSouza, N. (2002). Gender, poverty, and postnatal depression: A study of mothers in Goa, India. *American Journal of Psychiatry, 159*, 43–47.

Pawlby, S., Hay, D., Sharp, D., Waters, C. S., & O'Keane, V. (2009). Antenatal depression predicts depression in adolescent offspring: Prospective longitudinal community based study. *Journal of Affective Disorders, 113*(3), 236–243.

Pawlby, S., Sharp, D., Hay, D., & O'Keane, V. (2008). Postnatal depression and child outcome at 11 years: The importance of accurate diagnosis. *Journal of Affective Disorders, 107*(1–3), 241–245.

Pelaez-Nogueras, M., Field, T., Cigales, M., Gonzalez, L., & Clasky, S. (1994). Infants of depressed mothers show less "depressed" behavior with their nursery teachers. *Infant Mental Health Journal, 15*(4), 358–367.

Petterson, S., & Burke-Albers, A. (2001). Effects of poverty and maternal depression on early child development. *Child Development, 72*(6), 1794–1813.

Philipps, L. H., & O'Hara, M.W. (1991). Prospective study of postpartum depression, 4½-year follow-up of women and children. *Journal of Abnormal Psychology, 100*(2), 151–155.

Posner, M. I., & Rothbart, M. K. (2000). Developing mechanisms of self-regulation. *Development and Psychopathology, 12*, 427–441.

Rahman, A., Bunn, J., Lovel, H., & Creed, F. (2007). Maternal depression increases infant risk of diarrhoeal illness: A cohort study. *Archives of Disease in Childhood, 92*, 24–28.

Rahman, A., Iqbal, Z., & Harrington, R. (2003). Life events, social support and depression in childbirth: Perspectives from a rural community in the developing world. *Psychological Medicine, 33*, 1161–1167.

Rahman, A., Iqbal, Z., Bunn, J., Lovel, H., & Harrington, R. (2004). Impact of maternal depression on infant nutritional status and illness. *Archives of General Psychiatry, 61*, 946–952.

Ramchandani, P., O'Connor, T. G., Evans, J., Heron, J., Murray, L., & Stein, A. (2008). The effects of pre- and postnatal depression in fathers: A natural experiment comparing the effects of exposure to depression on offspring. *Journal of Child Psychology and Psychiatry and Allied Disciplines, 49*(10), 1069–1078.

Ramchandani, P., Stein, A., Evans, J., O'Connor, T. G., & ALSPAC Study Team (2005). Paternal depression in the postnatal period and child development: A prospective population study. *Obstetrical and Gynecological Survey, 60*(12), 789–790.

Ramchandani, P. G., Stein, A., O'Connor, T., Heron, J., Murray, L., & Evans, J. (2008). Depression in men in the postnatal period and later child psychopathology: A population cohort study. *Journal of the American Academy of Child and Adolescent Psychiatry, 47*(4), 390–398.

Richman, N., & Graham, P. J. (1971). A Behavioural Screening Questionnaire for use with three-year-old children. Preliminary findings. *Journal of Child Psychology and Psychiatry and Allied Disciplines, 12*(1), 5–33.

Rosenblum, L. A., Coplan, J. D., Friedman, S., Bassoff, T., Gorman, J. M., & Andrews, M. W. (1994). Adverse early experiences affect noradrenergic and serotonergic functioning in adult primates. *Biological Psychiatry, 35*, 221–227.

Sameroff, A. J., & Emde, R. (Eds.) (1989). *Relationship disturbances in early childhood.* New York: Basic Books.

Schaffer, C. E., Davidson, R. J., & Saron, C. (1983). Frontal and parietal electroencephalogram asymmetry in depressed and nondepressed subjects. *Biological Psychiatry, 18*(7), 753–762.

Sharp, D., Hay, D. F., Pawlby, S., Schmucker, G., Allen, H., & Kumar, R. (1995). The impact of postnatal depression on boys' intellectual development. *Journal of Child Psychology and Psychiatry and Allied Disciplines, 36*, 1315–1336.

Sinclair, D., & Murray, L. (1998). The effects of postnatal depression on children's adjustment to school: Teacher reports. *British Journal of Psychiatry, 172*, 58–63.

Slater, A. (1995). Individual differences in infancy and later IQ. *Journal of Child Psychology and Psychiatry 36*(1), 69–112.

Southwick, S. M., Vythilingam, M., & Charney, D. S. (2005). The psychobiology of depression and resilience to stress: Implications for prevention and treatment. *Annual Review of Clinical Psychology and Allied Disciplines, 1*, 255–291.

St. James-Roberts, I., & Plewis, I. (1996). Individual differences, daily fluctuations, and developmental changes in amounts of infant waking, fussing, crying, feeding, and sleeping. *Child Development, 67*, 2527–2540.

Stanley, C., Murray, L., & Stein, A. (2004). The effect of postnatal depression on mother–infant interaction, infant response to the still-face perturbation, and performance on an instrumental learning task. *Development and Psychopathology, 16*, 1–18.

Stein, A., Gath, D. H., Butcher, J., Bond, A., Day, A., & Cooper, P. J. (1991). The relationship between post-natal depression and mother–child interaction. *British Journal of Psychiatry, 158*, 46–52.

Stern, D., Beebe, B., Jaffe, J., & Bennett, S. (1977). The infant's stimulus world during social interaction: A study of caregiver behaviors with particular reference to repetition and timing. In H. R. Schaffer (Ed.), *Studies in mother–infant interaction* (pp. 177–202). New York: Academic Press.

Stern, D. N., Spieker, S., & MacKain, K. (1982). Intonation contours as signals in maternal speech to prelinguistic infants. *Developmental Psychology, 18*, 727–735.

Thompson, L. A., & Trevathan, W. R. (2008). Cortisol reactivity, maternal sensitivity, and learning in 3-month-old infants. *Infant Behavior and Development, 31*, 92–106.

Tomarken, A. J., Davidson, R. J., & Henriques, J. B. (1990). Resting frontal brain asymmetry predicts affective responses to films. *Journal of Personality and Social Psychology, 59*, 791–801.

Tomlinson, M., Cooper, P. J., & Murray, L. (2005). The mother–infant relationship and infant attachment in a South African peri-urban settlement. *Child Development, 76*, 1044–1054.

Trevarthen, C. (1979). Communication and cooperation in early infancy: A description of primary intersubjectivity. In M. Bullowa (Ed.), *Before speech: The beginning of interpersonal communication* (pp. 321–347). New York: Cambridge University Press.

Tronick, E. Z. (1989). Emotions and emotional communication in infants. *American Psychologist, 44*(2), 112–119.

Tronick, E. Z., & Gianino, A. F. (1986). The transmission of maternal disturbance to the infant. *New Directions for Child and Adolescent Development, 34*, 5–11.

Tronick, E. Z., & Weinberg, M. K. (1997). Depressed mothers and infants: Failure to form dyadic states of consciousness. In L. Murray & P. Cooper (Eds.), *Postpartum depression and child development*. New York: Guilford.

Wachs, T. D., Black, M. M., & Engle, P. (2009). Maternal depression: A global threat to children's health, development, and behavior and to human rights. *Child Development Perspectives, 3*(1), 51–59.

Weinberg, M. K., Olson, K. L., Beeghly, M., & Tronick, M. Z. (2006). Making up is hard to do, especially for mothers with high levels of depressive symptoms and their infant sons. *Journal of Child Psychology and Psychiatry and Allied Disciplines, 47*(7), 670–683.

Weissman, M. M., Wickramaratne, P., & Prusoff, B. A. (1988). Early-onset major depression in parents and their children. *Journal of Affective Disorders, 15*, 269–277.

Weissman, M. M., Wickramaratne, P., Nomura, Y., Warner, V., Pilowsky, D., & Verdeli, H. (2006). Offspring of depressed parents, 20 years later. *American Journal of Psychiatry, 163*, 1001–1008.

Wisner, K. L., Perel, J. M., Peindl, K. S., Hanusa, B. H., Findling, R. L., & Rapport, D. (2001). Prevention of recurrent postpartum depression: A randomized clinical trial. *Journal of Clinical Psychiatry, 62*, 82–86.

Wisner, K. L., Perel, J. M., Peindl, K. S., Hanusa, B. H., Piontek, C. M., & Findling, R. L. (2004). Prevention of postpartum depression: A pilot randomized clinical trial. *American Journal of Psychiatry, 161*, 1290–1292.

Wrate, R. M., Rooney, A. C., Thomas, P. F., & Cox, J. L. (1985). Postnatal depression and child development: A 3-year follow-up study. *British Journal of Psychiatry, 146*, 622–627.

Wright, C. A., George, T. P., Burke, R., Gelfand, D. M., & Teti, D. M. (2000). Early maternal depression and children's adjustment to school. *Child Study Journal, 30*(3), 153–168.

Young, E. A., Vazquez, D. M., Jiang, H., & Pfeffer, C. R. (2006). Saliva cortisol and response to dexamethasone in children of depressed parents. *Biological Psychiatry, 60*, 831–836.

Zlochower, A., & Cohn, J. F. (1996). Vocal timing in face-to-face interaction of clinically depressed and non-depressed mothers and their 4 month old infants. *Infant Behavior and Development, 19*, 371–374.

PART III

Developmental Disorders

Introduction

Part III contains four chapters dealing with the nature of early developmental disorders. Chapter 9 by Berger, Hopkins, Bae, Hella, and Strickland deals with developmental assessment and the identification of infant cognitive and social-emotional problems. The chapter begins with a description of changes in the nature and goals of developmental assessment, noting the increasing emphasis on multilevel and multidimensional assessment. The first part of the chapter is focused on early cognitive assessment with an initial discussion of goals and criteria for developmental screening. Two types of developmental screening procedures are reviewed: parent report and examiner-administered. Examples of each type of screening procedure are described and the strengths and weaknesses of each are noted. A similar approach is taken in the following sections which review procedures for developmental assessment in infancy, neurobehavioral assessments used with very young infants and norm-referenced assessment procedures. Going beyond just instrument description, Berger and colleagues also discuss issues in early cognitive assessment that are particularly salient during the infancy period, such as rapidity of developmental change, infant sensitivity to the testing context and the predictive validity of infant cognitive assessment. The second portion of this chapter deals with the assessment of infant social-emotional development. In presenting this area Berger and colleagues note the close links between infant cognitive and social-emotional development, and emphasize the importance of including measures of caregiver–infant transactions when assessing social-emotional development. A variety of instruments for assessing infant social-emotional development are presented and discussed, with reference to their strengths and weaknesses, followed by a similar presentation of procedures designed to assess the nature of parent–infant relations. The chapter concludes with a brief discussion on potentially important future directions in infant assessment.

Chapter 10 by Young and Ozonoff deals with the development of autism spectrum disorders (ASDs) in infancy. The chapter begins with a presentation of the characteristics and developmental course of ASDs. This is followed by a detailed discussion of the various methodologies used to study ASDs in infancy and the strengths and weaknesses of these methods. Research methods reviewed include case studies, retrospective parental report, home movies or videos of infants later diagnosed with ASD, follow-up of infants at high risk for developing ASD (e.g., infants who have an older sib with the disorder) and ongoing use of screening instruments given to parents. In terms of meeting validity criteria, Young and Ozonoff emphasize that ASD markers need to occur in almost all cases of the disorder, but should not be seen with other developmental disorders. Based on these criteria, evidence on the validity of a variety of potential early markers of ASDs are reviewed. Behavioral markers that appear to meet these criteria include deficits in infants' social attention and responsivity, early deficits in nonverbal communication, language deficits starting around 24 months of age, deficits in shared affect appearing by 12 months of age and later appearing deficits in symbolic play. Although less evidence is available, early repetitive behavior and sensory processing deficits may also serve as markers of ASD. Based on their review, Young and Ozonoff discuss two current theoretical models that could be used to explain ASDs, namely brain-related deficits in social motivation and brain-related deficits in encoding social information. The chapter concludes with a brief discussion of clinical applications of these findings.

In contrast to the previous chapter's relatively restricted focus on ASDs, chapter 11 by Johnson and Appleyard reviews a broader area, namely psychosocial disorders in infancy other than ASDs. The chapter is based within the framework of developmental psychopathology theory, where infant adjustment or maladjustment is related to the developmental tasks faced by infants at different ages, and to multidimensional linkages between environmental and biological influences. The chapter begins with the presentation of a case study to define how a young infant can have significant emotional problems, followed by defining what is meant by the term "infant psychosocial disorder." Seven salient age-related infant developmental tasks are then listed. Johnson and Appleyard then discuss a variety of risk factors that can reduce the infant's ability to master these developmental tasks, including prenatal factors (e.g., maternal substance abuse or stress during pregnancy), parental mental illness (e.g., maternal depression), challenges to family functioning (e.g., lack of social support, poverty, domestic violence), severe deprivation (e.g., institutional rearing) and child abuse or neglect. This is followed by a presentation of approaches for classifying infant psychosocial disorders in three major areas: affective and relationship disorders (e.g., the various manifestations of attachment disorders), aggressive and oppositional disorders, and regulatory disorders (e.g., feeding and sleep problems). Finally, Johnson and Appleyard review the evidence for treatments that may be useful in treating infant psychosocial disorders, including traditional psychotherapy, behavioral interventions and a variety of interventions focused on facilitating parent–infant interactions.

Chapter 12 by Fidler, Daunhauer, Most, and Switzky deals with genetic disorders that result in early appearing intellectual disability. The chapter begins with discussion of changes occurring over the past century in terminology and criteria used to define intellectual disability. While noting that intellectual disabilities can result from a variety of biological and environmental causes, Fidler and colleagues focus on intellectual disabilities where there is a clear genetic etiology. They justify this choice based on evidence indicating that such genetic disorders can be detected prenatally or in the early neonatal period, which in some cases can result in early effective intervention (e.g., hypothyroidism, phenylketonuria), as well as the increasing evidence base on specific "behavioral phenotypes" associated with specific genetic disorders. Fidler and colleagues propose that identification of such behavioral phenotypes can also promote early treatment, by allowing clinicians to target specific functional behaviors for intervention. Evidence is then reviewed on behavioral phenotypes found for five genetic disorders associated with intellectual disability, two of which are relatively common (Down syndrome and Fragile X), while the remaining three syndromes are relatively rare (Williams, Prader–Willi and Smith–Magenis). Evidence is presented on diagnostic criteria and the behavioral phenotypes defined by patterns of cognitive development, language, social-emotional development and motor behavior for both Down syndrome and Fragile X. Because of their rarity less evidence is available on behavioral phenotypes for the remaining syndromes, but in addition to diagnostic criteria the authors present patterns of cognitive development, language and social-emotional development for Williams syndrome and Prader–Willi syndrome. Finally, evidence on diagnostic criteria and a potential behavioral phenotype is presented for infants with Smith–Magenis syndrome.

9

Infant Assessment

Susan P. Berger, Joyce Hopkins, Hyo Bae, Bryce Hella, and Jennifer Strickland

Introduction

Assessment of infant functioning has evolved over time. In the mid-twentieth century, the primary purpose was to document the progress of typically developing infants against normative standards in the hope of making predictions regarding long-term outcomes, particularly related to later intelligence and school performance. The Gesell Developmental Schedules (Gesell, 1925; Gesell & Amatruda, 1947; Gesell, Halverson, & Amatruda, 1940) and the Cattell Infant Intelligence Scale (Cattell, 1940) are two of the earliest infant assessment measures developed with this goal in mind. The Cattell was designed as a downward extension of the Stanford–Binet and yields a score analogous to an intelligence quotient (IQ). Over time, these measures (as well as others to follow) failed to demonstrate predictive validity. In addition, since they were standardized on small and relatively homogeneous samples, their applicability to more diverse populations was limited. As a result, use of these measures has declined significantly.

The focus of infant developmental evaluation has shifted from normative to diagnostic evaluation, and from an end in and of itself to a protocol used for designing intervention strategies during the last two decades. In the United States, two related occurrences have driven these changes.

First, improvements in medical technology have decreased mortality rates in gestationally younger and more fragile infants, while concomitantly increasing morbidities less commonly seen among full-term, healthy babies (Cooper, Berseth, Adams, & Weisman, 1998; Hack, Horbar, Malloy, Tyson, Wright, & Wright, 1991; McCormick, 1989, 1997). Available evidence suggests that between 5% and 8% of the current pediatric population experience significant developmental and/or behavioral challenges between 2 and 6 years of age (Aylward & Stancin, 2008; Pinto-Martin, Dunkle, Earls, Fliedner, & Landes, 2005). The earlier these children can be identified, the greater the possibility of intervening in the hopes of minimizing long-term disabilities.

Second, the enactment of PL 99-457 in 1986 and its 2004 follow-up, the Individuals with Disabilities Education Improvement Act (IDEA), mandated identification and early intervention for children from birth to 5 years of age with, or at risk for, developmental disabilities. Although eligibility criteria are determined on a state-by-state basis, all systems use standardized measures of development for decision-making involving services.

Currently, clinical application of infant assessment is both multilevel and multidimensional. The multilevel aspect of assessment refers to a spectrum from screening to full developmental evaluation. According to Wyly (1997), there are six possible reasons for undertaking infant assessment. These include screening, diagnosis, service eligibility determination, treatment planning, intervention evaluation, and parent education. Decisions about measures to use at each level are dependent on the clinical setting as well as the goals of any particular assessment.

The multidimensional component reflects the perspective that infant development unfolds in at least five interrelated domains (cognitive, social-emotional, communicative, adaptive, and physical), and that a full understanding of the infant's capacities and challenges requires taking a holistic approach across all areas of development. Many clinical assessment tools that are valid to use with children during the earliest years of life include most or all of these dimensions rather than focusing on an individual developmental component such as cognition. Individual domain scores are most frequently used contemporaneously to determine eligibility for early intervention services (e.g., a child whose scores demonstrate a 30% or greater delay in communication receives speech therapy). It is the cognitive component of infant assessments that is likely to be the predictor variable used in research in which outcomes of interest tend to be later cognitive capacities and/or academic achievement. In this chapter, we use the term "developmental assessment" because it best reflects the multidomain approach to testing infants. However, our emphasis will be on cognitive subscales as appropriate in both the discussion of individual scales and in discussing long-term outcomes.

Finally, it is widely acknowledged that context is a significant contributor to the development of young children. The primary context during infancy is the family, but may also include daycare providers or others who provide regular caregiving. Thus, the process of infant assessment involves collecting data from a variety of sources including parent interviews, informal observations, and standardized tests (Aylward & Stancin, 2008). Much of what a clinician may include in the interview or observational component of an assessment is idiosyncratic. Elements from promising research methodologies are often integrated into clinical encounters although they may not have been subjected to rigorous standardization for use in that setting. Many of these are detailed in other chapters in this Handbook (see chapters 6–8, 14, and 19 in volume 1) and will not be covered here. Rather, this chapter will focus on describing standardized measures of infant development that are commonly used in clinical infant programs while recognizing that these are only one component of a complete assessment.

Developmental Screening

The purposes of developmental screening are to identify infants within the general population who are at risk for developmental delay or disability and to make decisions about the need for further evaluation. To be practical for universal use, screening tools need to be brief, require minimal training to use or interpret, and be relatively easy to integrate into normative clinical contexts (e.g., pediatric primary care). Such tradeoffs affect the accuracy of most screening tools which demonstrate high rates of false positive scores (Gilliam & Mayes, 2000). This outcome is complicated by recommendations that psychometric standards for sensitivity, specificity, and predictive values be lower than accepted levels on full assessment measures (Aylward, 2004; Glascoe, 1997).

Two types of screening tools exist for use with an infant population: those that rely on parent report; and those that are directly administered by an examiner. Aylward (2004) suggests that parent-completed questionnaires are best considered "prescreening" instruments. Their use acknowledges the significance that should be placed on responding to parent concerns. Nevertheless, a parent's perspective is necessarily subjective and possibly biased. Rather than forming the crux of decision-making regarding further assessment, results from these tools should provide the impetus for a more direct, professional screening session. Further, a lack of concern by parents should not necessarily imply that there are no problems. Parents tend to miss subtle nuances in their child's behavior especially when they lack comparisons. The three most widely acknowledged parent-completed developmental screening tools appropriate for use with children during the first year of life are presented in Table 9.1.

The most widely used examiner-administered infant screening instruments are described in Table 9.2. (For more detailed explanations of these and other screening tools, see the American Academy of Pediatrics, 2006; Gilliam & Mayes, 2000.) It is important to note that while these instruments offer more detailed and reliable data about an infant's development than prescreening tools, they are not diagnostic measures nor do they provide standardized scores or cutoffs for disability criteria. The findings from screening tools should be predictive of scores on broader assessment measures. However, only the Battelle II Screener (Newborg, 2005) and the Bayley Infant Neurodevelopmental Screen (BINS; Aylward, 1995) have demonstrated significant correlations with in-depth assessment measures, and their reliability has been best against the specific broader measure from which they were derived (e.g., the Battelle Inventory and the Bayley Scales of Infant Development II, respectively).

A new addition to the screening toolbox that holds promise for future use is the Bayley-III Screening Test (Bayley, 2006). This measure is designed to screen the cognitive, language, and motor skills domains of children from 1 to 42 months of age. Included items were selected from the full Bayley-III, taking into consideration adequate coverage of content across domains and ages, psychometric standards and clinical value/sensitivity. The publishers suggest that a full screening should take between 15 and 25 minutes, though experience has shown that the higher time limit is more the norm, or even at the low end for expected time of administration. Cutpoints were developed for 3–6 month age bands yielding scores of "at-risk," "emerging" or "competent" for each of the five

Table 9.1 Selected parent report developmental screening instruments.

Name	Domains Assessed and Description	Scoring	Psychometrics	Standardization Sample Reported
Ages and Stages Questionnaires (ASQ) 2nd edition (Squires, Bricker, & Potter, 1999)	19 age-based questionnaires, 30 questions each. Domains: Fine & Gross Motor, Communication, Problem Solving, Personal/Social. Age range 4–60 months. Time required 10–15 minutes. Available in English, Spanish, French, and Korean versions	Answers: Yes, No, Not Yet Scored: Pass/Fail	Original sample: Sensitivity = .65–.90 Specificity = .81–.92 Test–retest reliability = .94 Inter-rater reliability = .94 Positive predictive value = .32–.64	$N = 2,008$ (risk and nonrisk); Varied SES; 2/3 Caucasian
Parents' Evaluation of Developmental Status (PEDS; Glascoe, 1997)	10 Questions. Age range Birth–8 years. Time required 2 minutes. Available in English, Spanish, and Vietnamese; can be licensed in Thai, Indonesian, Somali	Answers: Yes, No, A Little Concern Algorithm for low, medium, high risk for delay and for referral or further screening	Sensitivity = .74–.80 Specificity = .70–.80 Inter-rater and test-retest reliability range = .80–1.00, $M = .88$	$N = 771$; Varied SES and ethnicity
Child Development Review (Ireton, 1992)	6 general questions + 26 possible problems checklist. Age range 15 months–6 years. Time required approx. 5 minutes	Parents check areas of concern	Cut off points for concern included but no psychometrics reported	Not Reported

SES = socioeconomic status

Table 9.2 Selected examiner-administered developmental screening instruments.

Name	Domains Assessed and Description	Scoring	Psychometrics	Standardization Sample Reported
Battelle Developmental Inventory Screening Test, 2nd edition (Newborg, 2005)	Domains: Personal-Social, Adaptive, Gross & Fine Motor, Receptive & Expressive Language, Cognitive. Age range 0–96 months. Time required 15–35 minutes. Also available in Spanish	3-point scoring; cutoffs at 1.0, 1.5, and 2 SD below mean; percentile ranks, standard scores, age equivalents	Sensitivity and specificity (for broader age range 0–96 months) = .72–.88 Concurrent validity with full BDI range = .92–.99; Test–retest reliability range = .92–.99; Inter-rater reliability range = .94–.98	Nonclinical $N = 800$ Clinical $N = 160$ 86% Caucasian
Bayley Infant Neurodevelopmental Screen (BINS; Aylward, 1995)	Item sets: Basic Neurologic Functions, Expressive (motor, verbal), Receptive (visual, auditory), Cognitive Processes; 11–13 items in each set. Age range 3–24 months. Time required 10–15 minutes.	Items scored optimal/ nonoptimal; summary scores low, moderate, high risk	Sensitivity and specificity = .75–.86 across ages Concurrent validity with BSID-II, range .39–.82; Test–retest reliability range .71–.84; Inter-rater reliability range .79–.96	Nonclinical $N = 600$ Clinical $N = 303$

Measure	Description	Scoring	Psychometrics	Sample
Bayley-III Screener Bayley, 2006	Domains: Cognitive, Expressive & Receptive Language, Fine & Gross Motor. Age range 0–42 months. Time required 15–25 minutes	Cutpoints identified for at-risk, emerging and competent in each domain	Reliability: internal consistency: .82–.88 across subtests for all ages; test–retest: .80–.83 across subtests for all ages Concurrent validity with full Bayley-III: .42–.66 across subtests for 'at risk' category; .64–.78 across subtests for 'emerging' category; .89–.92 across subtests for 'proficient' category 0% 'at risk' identified as 'proficient' and 0% 'proficient" identified as "at risk'. Specificity = .77–1.00	
Brigance Infant and Toddler Screen-II Brigance & Glascoe, 2002	Domains: Fine & Gross Motor, Receptive & Expressive Language, Self-Help, Social-Emotional; 8–15 items for each age. Age range 0–23 months. Time required 10 minutes. Also available in Spanish	Overall score; Nonverbal and Communicative subscores	Sensitivity and specificity (for broader age range 0–90 months) .70–.82	$N = 1,156$; 73% Caucasian

subtests: cognitive, receptive language, expressive language, gross motor, and fine motor. Development of the Bayley-III Screening Test included rigorous assessment of the tool's internal consistency, test–retest reliability, convergent validity with the Bayley-III, and discriminant validity for use with special groups of children (e.g., those affected by prematurity, cerebral palsy or Down syndrome). At present the only data on its utility have been provided by the same researchers who were involved in the instrument's development. Thus it remains to be seen how useful it will prove to be for clinicians and early intervention service providers.

Developmental Assessment

Diagnosis and service eligibility determination

Norm-referenced measures of infant assessment are most frequently used to determine eligibility for early intervention services in the United States. These instruments have been standardized on a large number and, hopefully, representative sample of infants to determine how typically developing children of different ages perform on the relevant tasks. An individual infant's score is compared to a standard score for the reference group. That comparison forms the basis for decisions about whether an infant is developmentally delayed, which developmental areas might be affected, and what services are warranted within the limits of eligibility of any given state. Administration of these assessments is governed by a specific set of rules. Thus, they require significant training and qualifications of examiners. Table 9.3 compares the major norm-referenced infant assessment measures described below.

Bayley Scales.   The Bayley Scales of Infant Development (BSID-II; Bayley, 1993) have been the most widely used measures of infant development for more than a decade. Often considered the "gold standard" for infant developmental assessment, the BSID-II contains items that aggregate into Mental Developmental (MDI) and Psychomotor (PDI) Index scores ($M = 100$, $SD = 15$), as well as a Behavior Rating Scale that organizes the examiner's observations about an infant's behavior and interactions with others during the assessment. Criticism of a number of components of the BSID-II led to publication of the most recent (third) edition, the Bayley Scales of Infant and Toddler Development (Bayley-III; Bayley, 2006).

Perhaps the most obvious difference between the BSID-II and the Bayley-III is the inclusion of the word "Toddler" in the title of the third edition, despite both editions being applicable to use with 1–42-month-olds. The Bayley-III includes scales for five domains: Cognitive, Language, Motor, Adaptive and Social-Emotional. The Language and Motor domains are further differentiated into receptive/expressive and gross/fine, respectively. This restructuring is especially useful when assessing children beyond infancy (i.e., after a year of age) as developmental capacities become more differentiated and complex. Inclusion of all five of these domains was in response to criticism that the BSID-II did not reflect the range of areas covered by the IDEA legislation (Black & Matula, 2000). Items making up the first three scales are examiner-administered and intrinsic to the Bayley-III itself. The

Table 9.3 Infant developmental assessment instruments.

Name	Domains Assessed and Description	Examiner Qualifications	Psychometrics	Standardization Sample Reported
Bayley Scales of Infant Development II (BSID-II; Bayley, 1993)	Mental & Motor Development. Age range 1–42 months. Time required 60 minutes	Master's level or greater	Internal consistency = .78–.92 across scales Test–retest reliability = .83–.91 Inter-rater reliability = .96 Concurrent validity with McCarthy, WPPSI-R; Predictive validity: none	N = 1,700; Sample characteristic of the 1988 US Census
Bayley Scales of Infant and Toddler Development III (Bayley-III; Bayley, 2006)	Cognitive, Language (Expressive & Receptive), Motor (Gross & Fine), Social-emotional, Adaptive Behavior. Age range 1–42 months. Time required 50–90 minutes	Master's level or greater	Internal consistency = .76–.98 across scales Concurrent validity with WPPSI-R & PLS Predictive validity: none reported as of now	Nonclinical sample N = 1,700; Special needs sample N = 668; Sample representative of 2000 US census
Mullen Scales of Early Learning, AGS Edition (Mullen, 1995)	Gross & Fine Motor, Visual Reception, Receptive & Expressive Language. Age range 0–68 months. Time required 15–60 minutes	Minimal training requirements	Internal consistency = .53–.91 for scales Test–retest reliability = .82–.85 (1–24 months) Inter-rater reliability = .91–.99 Concurrent Validity with BSID & PLA Predictive Validity: none reported	N = 1,849; Sample representative of 1990 US census
Battelle Developmental Inventory 2nd edition (BDI; Newborg, 2005)	Personal-Social, Adaptive, Motor, Communication, Cognitive. Age range 0–95 months. Time required 60–90 minutes.	Minimal training requirements	Internal consistency = .98–.99 for total score Correlated with BSID-II, PLS, Vineland, WPPSI-R	N = 2,500; Sample representative of 2001 US census
Griffiths Mental Development Scales, Revised: Birth to 2 Years (Huntley, 1996)	Locomotor, Personal-Social, Hearing & Language, Eye & Hand Coordination. Age range 0–2 years. Time required 50–60 minutes	5-day training course required; typically administered by pediatricians and psychologists	Scores elevated relative to BSID-ll & BDI	N = 665; Standardized in the UK

Key: McCarthy = McCarthy Scales of Children's Abilities; PLA = Preschool Language Assessment; PLS = Preschool Language Scale; Vineland = Vineland Social-Emotional Early Childhood Scales; WPPSI = Wechsler Preschool & Primary Scale of Intelligence last two scales, completed using caregiver report, are adaptations of preexisting measures: the Adaptive Behavior Assessment System, 2nd edition (Harrison & Oakland, 2003) and the Greenspan Social-Emotional Growth Chart: A Screening Questionnaire for Infants and Young Children (Greenspan, 2004). The Greenspan instrument is described later in this chapter. The addition of these two scales is intended to enhance caregiver involvement in the assessment process and to allow for evaluation of functioning in areas that may not be evident during the testing session (Albers & Grieve, 2007; Bayley, 2006).

The BSID-II used "item sets" correlated with particular age ranges to determine start points for testing. Clinicians found this process confusing, especially when testing premature infants or those already identified as developmentally delayed. In the Bayley-III, the authors use more conventional basal and ceiling rules (i.e., a child has to pass three consecutive items as a start point and fail five consecutive items to discontinue testing).

The utility of the BSID-II MDI score has been questioned because it correlates poorly with later measures of mental development in childhood. As a result, scoring has been revised significantly in the Bayley-III. The Bayley-III now includes domain-specific composite scores ($M = 100$, $SD = 15$) for the Cognitive, Language and Motor domains and scaled scores ($M = 10$, $SD = 3$) in their subscales in lieu of a global MDI. The Social-Emotional and Adaptive tools use both scaled and composite scores as well. Confidence intervals, percentile ranks, and age equivalents for the subscales can also be calculated. Another new feature of the Bayley-III are growth charts that are designed to plot a child's growth along particular domains of development over time. The authors assert that the growth charts may be valuable in settings that repeatedly assess at-risk infants (e.g., neonatal follow-up clinics) and/or to monitor the effects of intervention services. Caution has been advocated in forming conclusions using the growth charts since their efficacy is currently untested in either research or clinical settings (Stancin & Aylward, 2008).

Substantial evidence of improved psychometric properties such as internal consistency and test–retest reliability has been presented (Bayley, 2006). A confirmatory factor analysis supports a three-factor structure with Cognitive, Language and Motor factors as separate entities. One of the goals for the revision was to improve intervention utility and predictive validity from the BSID-II. Whether this goal will be accomplished remains to be seen since the measure is still too new to draw any conclusions and more research is needed to evaluate the value of the Bayley-III (Albers & Grieve, 2007).

Mullen Scales of Early Learning, AGS Edition (MSEL).   The MSEL (Mullen, 1995) is a combined revision of two previously separate scales for infants and preschoolers and is applicable for use with children from birth to 68 months of age. The MSEL is based on a model in which information processing through visual and auditory modalities is a key element and intelligence is viewed as "a network of interrelated but functionally distinct cognitive skills" (Mullen, 1995, manual, p. 1). Thus the scales included for infants and toddlers are Gross Motor, Receptive and Expressive Language, Visual-Perceptual Skills and Visual-Motor Skills (including Fine Motor).

As strengths, the MSEL offers a reasonably short administration time and coverage of three areas required by federal IDEA legislation (motor, language, and cognition). T-scale scores ($M = 50$, $SD = 10$) are reported for each of the scales and a composite score may be calculated as well. Test items have been carefully included so that each is unique only to the scale in which it is included (e.g., Visual Receptive items such as stacking blocks do not require oral direction or response). Examiners may administer all or some of the scales without losing accuracy and the manual permits flexibility in the order of item administration in order to maintain rapport with the child (Mullen, 1995). A final strength of the MSEL is that administration is untimed.

There are several shortcomings recognized for the MSEL. The first is a lack of measurement of social-emotional development. To overcome this problem, use of the Vineland Social-Emotional Early Childhood Scales (Sparrow, Cicchetti, & Balla, 1998; see section on Social-Emotional Measures for details) is recommended to obtain a full developmental assessment. Second, it is suggested that the stages of development across the domains assessed by the MSEL be used to assist in intervention and educational planning. Bradley-Johnson (2001) notes there is a lack of empirical data supporting these stages. Caution should therefore be used in developing intervention plans from MSEL findings. Further, while the MSEL has adequate psychometric properties (see Table 9.3), this instrument was standardized about two decades ago and the sample consisted of children without known physical or mental disability. Updated standardization is warranted. Finally, the MSEL includes relatively few items for children under a year of age, possibly making it less valuable than would ideally be the case for this age group.

Battelle Developmental Inventory, 2nd edition (BDI-2).   The BDI-2 is included with other norm-referenced assessment measures because it assesses development in five domains (Adaptive, Personal-Social, Motor, Communication, and Cognition) and yields a developmental quotient score for each domain, a composite developmental quotient (M = 100, SD = 10), and scaled scores for subscales within the domains (M = 10, SD = 3). Percentile ranks and age equivalents can also be calculated (Newborg, 2005). However, one review (Bliss, 2007) describes the BDI-2 as criterion-referenced (see below) because it is most often used to determine children's functional abilities and to plan for early intervention, therapy, or school programming.

There are 450 items in a full BDI-2 assessment, taking 1–2 hours to administer. For most items, the examiner can collect data by direct administration, naturalistic observation, or through interviewing adults who are very familiar with the child (e.g., parent or daycare provider). Because children can obtain scores on all three of these administration methods, comparing a child's performance from observation versus interview versus using standardized norms derived from direct administration is problematic. In addition, the order of presentation of items can be varied, which can lead to difficulty in establishing basal and ceiling levels. Further, a full assessment is very long and might require testing over multiple sessions to determine a child's best performance.

On the other hand, there are some aspects of the BDI-2 that make it a relatively popular measure. First, a Spanish version is available. Second, examiner qualifications are not as rigorous as on some other norm-referenced measures. Third, guidelines are provided for adapting the tools to use with children who have physical, visual, or hearing impairments. Fourth, hand scoring is relatively easy, a scoring software package is also available, and a guide for interpreting scores is included in the examiner's manual. Finally, the large number of domains included in the BDI-2 permits early identification of the child's areas of strength and weakness as well as differentiation of overall and specific deficits. This can be especially useful in instructional planning and for monitoring intervention efficacy (Johnson & Marlow, 2006).

The Griffiths Mental Development Scales – Revised: Birth to 2 Years (GMDS 0–2). The GMDS 0–2 is an assessment measure more frequently used in the United Kingdom than in the United States (Huntley, 1996). The revised instrument is divided into two administration ages: from birth to 2 years and from 2 to 8 years. The infant version includes five scales (Locomotor, Personal and Social, Hearing and Language, Eye and Hand Co-ordination, and Performance) that are thought to have been developed in alignment with Gesell's developmental approach (Gilliam & Mayes, 2000). Raw scores are converted into age and percentile equivalents as well as a developmental quotient. One study comparing the original GMDS with earlier versions of the BSID and the BDI found that children's age equivalent scores were considerably higher on the Griffiths than on either of the other two measures (McLean, McCormick, & Baird, 1991). Scores for the 1996 validation sample were seriously elevated from the original sample (an average of 11 IQ points) as well. The discrepancy between GMDS 0–2 scores and scores on measures typically used in the United States probably accounts for their limited utility outside Europe.

Program planning and evaluation of infant progress

Knowing how a child compares globally with others in a reference group (e.g., by age or genetic disorder) says little about his/her particular strengths or challenges that need to be addressed in clinical service programs. As a result, norm-referenced measures have been criticized for their lack of utility in developing individualized intervention strategies for targeted children (Greenspan & Meisels, 1996). An alternative approach to assessment that is gaining favor within education and intervention programs involves the use of criterion-referenced systems of evaluation. At the core of this approach is testing for the achievement of particular skills against an established criterion (e.g., use of a complete pincer grasp, pointing to demonstrate a want or need, naming colors). Children's scores reflect the proportion of a skill area that has been mastered. How an infant performs on a criterion-based measure can thus be "translated directly into an individualized intervention plan by targeting those skills that the infant was expected to have mastered but as of yet had not" (Gilliam & Mayes, 2000, p. 245). Because their use is often embedded within programs, a criterion-referenced assessment often includes observations made by interdisciplinary team members in a variety of settings including those familiar to the infant (e.g., home). In school-age populations, questions have been raised about whether the use of criterion-referenced measures creates situations in which schools teach only to obtain higher test results without evidence that what is measured on the tests is critical to overall functioning. Though such issues have not yet been raised in clinical infant assessment, it is worth noting that there is the possibility that emphasis on achieving particular criteria may not be addressing crucial developmental landmarks, or those achievements that are meaningful mediators of developmental change.

There are many more criterion-based measures than norm-referenced ones and far too many to detail in this chapter. The Ounce Scale (Meisels, Dombro, Marsden, Weston,

& Jewkes, 2003), discussed in a later section of this chapter, is a promising recent addition in this grouping. Criterion-referenced procedures that are directly associated with particular intervention models are sometimes referred to as curriculum-based. The Carolina Curriculum (Johnson-Martin, Attermeier & Hacker, 2004) and the Hawaii Early Learning Profile (HELP; Parks, 1992) stand as two of the best-known examples of curricula with internally developed assessment systems. Despite their popularity for program planning, as well as for evaluating the progress of individual infants as a result of intervention, most of these measures have not been subjected to the same level of psychometric evaluation as norm-based tools.

Neurobehavioral developmental assessment: Parent education and clinical intervention with families

Over the past 100 years, a shift has taken place in our understanding of early infancy (Lester & Tronick, 2001). At the beginning of the twentieth century, infants' functioning was viewed as being highly reflexive and controlled by rudimentary brain stem activities. As researchers continued to study this developmental period, they began to recognize infants as active agents within their environment. Clinicians became increasingly interested in individual differences in arousal, self-control, habituation and other neurologically based infant characteristics. Due to this paradigm shift, clinicians and researchers developed tools to help assess these neurobehavioral functions of the newborn.

The three most commonly used neurobehavioral assessments of young infants are the Brazelton Neonatal Behavioral Assessment Scale – Third Edition (NBAS-3; Brazelton & Nugent, 1995), the Neonatal Intensive Care Unit Network Neurobehavioral Scale (NNNS; Lester & Tronick, 2004), and the Assessment of Preterm Infant Behavior (APIB; Als, Lester, Tronick, & Brazelton, 1982). These measures primarily aim to examine the infant's adaptation to the world, ability to interact with people and objects, and ability to self-regulate (Lester & Tronick, 2001). When determining which measure to use to assess very young infants, Lester and Tronick (2001) suggest using the NBAS-3 for full-term infants, the NNNS for high-risk or drug-exposed infants (either full-term or preterm) or the APIB for premature infants. When deciding between the NNNS and the APIB, it is suggested that the APIB be used for a detailed description of the infant's behavior, as APIB score interpretation is highly involved. The NBAS-3 and the APIB use a more unstructured assessment protocol than the NNNS, with the former focusing on eliciting optimal performance. The NNNS has a more standardized approach and assesses modal performance (Lester & Tronick, 2004).

The NBAS-3, NNNS, and APIB have been used by various types of clinicians in their work with parents (Boukydis, Bigsby, & Lester, 2004; Brazelton & Nugent, 1995; Browne & Talmi, 2005). These authors suggest taking a parent-centered interactive approach to the examinations, such that the newborn's behaviors and capacities can be demonstrated for parents to promote the development of a positive parent–child relationship. In addition, the neurobehavioral profile from the measures provides information regarding an infant's behavioral style and specific developmental needs. This can help a clinician develop a management plan for the infant's hospital stay, play a role in discharge decisions, guide parents in the infant's transition into the home, and determine early intervention eligibility (Lester & Tronick, 2001).

Research has been conducted on the clinical utility of these early neurobehavioral measures. In one study, neonatal nurses used an earlier version of the NBAS-3 to intervene with mothers and their 3-day-old infants (Worobey & Belsky, 1982). Clinicians provided verbal guidance as mothers administered the NBAS. One month later, researchers found that those mothers who had administered the NBAS with verbal guidance from a clinician displayed more positive interaction behaviors such as physical or verbal soothing, responsive vocalizations, and positive affect than other groups who did not receive the intervention. In addition, demonstrating infants' behavior to the mother using the APIB was related to mothers subsequent ratings as more knowledgeable, sensitive, and less stressed than mothers who did not receive any hospital-based intervention (Browne & Talmi, 2005). Such data suggest that an important clinical use of these measures is to enhance parents' ability to read their infants' cues, which may lead to a tailored home environment that is more sensitive to the newborn's needs.

Issues in Infant Assessment

Despite rapid advancement in the field of infant assessment and its methodology over the last decades, several issues remain. First, as illustrated in Table 9.3, available assessment instruments demonstrate varying degrees of psychometric rigor with respect to both validity and reliability. Second, efforts to assess very young children are complicated by the rapidity of their developmental change as well as by the integrated nature of functioning across developmental domains during infancy. For example, Aylward (2004) notes the difficulty of accurately testing infants with motor or sensory problems (also chapter 4 in this volume). Since all clinical measurement instruments used with infants involve substantial sensorimotor responses, limitations in these areas may preclude assessment in other domains such as cognition.

Third, the testing situation itself may influence responses in very young children more than it does in older children and adults. For example, the need to interact with and respond to directions from an unfamiliar adult may be hampered by developmentally appropriate stranger anxiety toward the end of the first year of life. Novelty also can affect how a child responds when presented with particular testing items. Familiar items may evoke previously developed response patterns while new ones may require more free exploration before the examiner is able to elicit a required response. Not all children will have had the same exposure to the testing items before an assessment, thus affecting the evaluation of a child's use and response on any given item. A related issue is test/item refusal that occurs commonly in this age group. With preschoolers, high rates of test refusal are associated with concurrent and later low IQ scores as well as other linguistic and neuropsychological problems (Langkamp & Brazy, 1999; Wocaldo & Rieger, 2000). In infants, item refusal may not reflect actual inability to complete a task as clearly as it does with older children, for the reasons stated above, but remains an area that merits consideration in determining the meaning of assessment scores.

We have previously discussed the lack of consensus regarding use of different types of assessment measures (norm- versus criterion-referenced). To a great extent, choice of instrument is, or should be, dependent on the purpose of the evaluation. However, even when choosing the best available tool for the purpose, expectations about assessment findings may be unrealistic. Initial evaluations are often completed in order to determine an infant's eligibility for early intervention services. In the United States, criteria for eligibility in any given state may be based on determinants such as percentage of delay in one or more domains, or on how many months' delay there is in development below a child's chronological age. Stancin and Aylward (2008, p. 149) argue that the need to "attribute this degree of preciseness … is neither realistic nor attainable." Even more importantly, such cutoffs have little clinical utility.

Among the most discussed issues in the literature on infant assessment has been whether there is predictive validity of test findings. Specifically, do scores on infant developmental assessments predict IQ, cognitive abilities, or school performance at some later date? Studies of infants of low to extremely low birth weight have provided a great deal of long-term outcome data on clinical populations. Evaluation of results from these studies was compromised by methodological problems such as small sample sizes, interchangeable use of birth weight and gestational age as predictor variables, test revisions that included questionable administration guidelines for premature infants, and shifting characteristics of the low birth weight population based on progress in medical treatment and technologies that resulted in declining mortality (Aylward, 2002). Excellent coverage of the breadth of current data and implications of the findings is available elsewhere (see, for example, Aylward, 2002, 2005; Hack et al., 2005; Vohr, 2007; Voss, Neubauer, Wachtendorf, Verhey, & Kattner, 2007).

In brief, studies appear to demonstrate differential continuity of outcome for infants with and without neurosensory dysfunction. When children have significant neurosensory dysfunction, early testing is moderately correlated with later measures of IQ (Hack et al., 2005). For those without neurosensory complications, early test scores only correlate with later IQ for those infants who score within the normal range for their corrected age (Hack et al., 2005). Predictive validity to IQ alone, however, does not reflect the full complexity of the issue of continuity. A significant portion of those children in the Hack et al. study without neurosensory issues who did poorly on assessments as infants had school-related problems and individualized educational plans (IEPs) in place at age 8 years. Because scores from infant assessments are composite measures of functioning across domains, there are some who question whether there should be any expectation of prediction from early testing to later defined IQ assessments (Vohr, 2007). Aylward (2005) suggests that, independent of IQ outcomes, poor performance on developmental assessment during infancy should be considered a marker for later disorders such as learning disability, attention problems, and issues with executive functioning that are more prevalent but of lower severity than mental retardation, cerebral palsy, and sensorineural vision and hearing impairments in today's former high-risk infants.

Although the field has not advanced far enough to accurately predict later outcome or IQ from infant assessment measures, this is not to say that the tests are not relevant clinically. Scores obtained from an infant assessment measure help clinicians examine how a child performs relative to normally developing peers and make decisions about the need for intervention services (Bayley, 2006). From there, the clinician is able to use the infant's developmental profile to aid in making individualized recommendations for service interventions.

Social-Emotional Assessment in Infancy

The assessment of social and emotional competence in infancy has a relatively brief history due to the earlier, almost exclusive, focus on cognitive development, discussed earlier in this chapter. This lack of attention to infant social-emotional development can be traced to several factors. First, as described at the beginning of this chapter, advances in neonatal medicine in the 1980s led to a dramatic increase in the survival rate of very premature infants (Cooper et al., 1998; Hack et al., 1991). However, as mortality decreased, concern shifted to the long-term outcome for these infants, since converging data indicated that they were at increased risk for later cognitive delays (Bendersky & Lewis, 1994; Cohen, Parmelee, Beckwith, & Sigman, 1986; Stanton, McGee, & Silva, 1991). Researchers and clinicians, therefore, focused on the assessment of infant cognitive development to determine which infants required early intervention to reduce their risk for later cognitive delays.

Second, the field of infant social-emotional evaluation has been hampered by a dearth of psychometrically sound assessment instruments. A prior recent review of measures of infant social-emotional development led Stack and Poulin-Dubois (1998, p. 37) to conclude that "such assessment measures remain scarce. Those measures that do exist are less refined and valid relative to those that exist for cognitive development." Previous versions of the BSID, considered to be the "gold standard" in the field of infant assessment, included the Infant Behavior Record, which can be considered a proxy measure of temperament. However, even the Bayley did not include a general measure of social-emotional development until its third revision in 2006 (Bayley, 2006).

Cognitive and social-emotional development, however, are inextricably intertwined. Accumulating evidence indicates that delays or problems in social-emotional functioning are as critical to long-term outcome as cognitive delays (Denham, Lydick, Mitchell-Copeland, & Sawyer, 1996; Shonkoff & Phillips, 2000). In addition, substantial data now demonstrate that infants and young children suffer from a range of psychiatric problems and disorders including Posttraumatic Stress Disorder, depression and anxiety (Briggs-Gowan, Carter, Moye Skuban, & McCue Horwitz, 2001; Luby & Morgan, 1997; Scheeringa, Peebles, Cook & Zeanah, 2001; for a review of infant mental health problems, see also chapter 11 in this volume). This growing awareness led to the need for psychometrically sound measures designed to assess social-emotional aspects of infant functioning.

The instruments developed include caregiver questionnaires and interviews, as well as strategies using direct observation during play or other situationally based paradigms, although the latter usually only provide descriptive, qualitative data. Some of these measures have been developed primarily for research use, whereas others have both clinical and research utility. A currently unpublished guide to screening and assessment measures for infants and toddlers, developed by the Illinois Association for Infant Mental

Health, includes 19 such measures (17 of which have been developed in the last seven years).

Before describing these measures, it is critical to understand the theoretical principles that have guided their design and development. First, it is widely recognized that infant social-emotional development occurs primarily within the context of the caregiver–infant relationship (Belsky, 2006; Sroufe, 2005). Parent–infant interaction and the caregiver–infant relationship provide the crucible for early infant social and emotional learning (Calkins, 1994; NICHD Early Child Care Research Network, 2006; Tronick, 1989; see also chapters 15 and 16 in volume 1). Extensive data indicate that during the first year of life, infants' rapidly developing perceptual and cognitive abilities are used to understand their social environment (Lewis, 1987), and that infants are able to discriminate social and non-social stimuli (Lewis, 1987; Stack & Poulin-Dubois, 1998). It is during interactions with their caregivers, however, that infants learn to initiate, respond, and modulate their social responses (Bornstein & Tamis-Lemonda, 2001). There is also ample evidence that affective and emotional regulation, important aspects of social-emotional functioning, develop within the context of this relationship (Volling, McElwain, Notaro, & Herrera, 2002).

A second guiding principle is that caregiver–infant interaction is a reciprocal, transactional process, whereby infant and caregiver mutually influence each other (Brazelton, Koslowski, & Main, 1974; Cohn & Tronick, 1988). Moreover, this process is a dynamic one, unfolding over time and changing in response to the infant's developing capacities. Individual differences in infant social-emotional functioning depend on the complex interplay between how each member of the caregiver–infant dyad adjusts their reactions to newly emerging developmental tasks.

Widespread recognition of the importance of the parent–infant relationship has led to the development of several measures designed to assess the quality of this relationship, most of which have been designed for research purposes, although there are several that can be used clinically as well.

The following review of assessment measures is divided into two sections: the first reviews instruments designed to assess social-emotional functioning of the infant, including instruments specifically designed to assess social-emotional development, as well as more general developmental assessments that include social-emotional function; and the second reviews measures of the caregiver–infant relationship that have clinical as well as research applications. Unlike measures of global or cognitive functioning discussed in earlier sections of this chapter, there is often a less clear distinction between screening and more comprehensive measures of social-emotional development. As a result, we have opted not to separate out these levels of measures but to indicate as clearly as possible where they fit along a clinical spectrum of utility.

Assessment of infant social-emotional functioning

Instruments to assess infant social-emotional development have been designed with two different purposes: to examine social and emotional development, as well as to determine if there are any delays in these areas of infant functioning; and to screen for possible psychiatric disorders and the need for further psychological/psychiatric assessment. The first four instruments (summarized in Table 9.4) were designed to assess normal social

Table 9.4 Measures of infant social and emotional development.

Name	Domains Assessed and Description	Scoring	Examiner Qualifications	Psychometrics	Standardization Sample Reported
ASQ:SE	Self-Regulation, Compliance, Autonomy, and Affect. Age range 3–66 months. Time required 10–15 minutes	Answers: Most of the time, Sometimes, Rarely. Total scores compared to cutoff scores	Parent completed; Interpreted by child development professionals (not further specified)	Test–retest reliability = .94; Inter-rater reliability = .95; Concurrent validity = .81–.95; Sensitivity = .75–.89; Specificity = .82–.96; Internal consistency = .67–.91 (overall alpha = .82)	N = 3,014; sample characteristic of the 2000 US Census
Vineland SEEC	Interpersonal Relationships, Play and Leisure Time, Coping Skills. Age range birth–71 months. Time required 15–20 minutes	Answers: usually performs, sometimes or partially performs, never performs, no opportunity for the child to perform, and don't know if the child performs	Interviewed/ interpreted by professional with child development and behavior expertise	Test–retest reliability = .71–.79; Internal consistency = .80–.87 (domain), .89–.97 (composite)	Normed on Vineland ABS national standardization sample (N = 1,200); sample characteristic of the 1980 US Census

Greenspan SEGC	Growing Self-Regulation & Interest in the World, Engaging in Relationships, Using Emotions in an Interactive Purposeful Manner, Using Interactive Emotional Signals to Communicate and Solve Problems, Using Symbols to Convey Intentions or Feelings & Express More Than Basic Needs, and Creating Logical Bridges Between Emotions & Ideas. Age range birth–42 months. Time required 5–15 minutes	Answers: full mastery, half of the time, some of the time, none of the time, can't tell	Administered by clinicians, educators, or paraprofessionals; Requires master's level or greater supervision	Internal consistency = .83–.94 (Social-Emotional), .76–.91 (Sensory Processing)	$N = 456$; sample characteristic of the 2000 US Census
Ounce Scale	Social-Emotional, Communication and Language, Cognitive, and Physical Development Age range birth–42 months. Time required: ongoing	Recorded observations of infant's behavior	Qualified professionals meeting appropriate early childhood training	N/A	N/A

Key: ASQ: SE = Ages and Stages Questionnaire: Social & Emotional; Vineland SEEC = Vineland Social-Emotional Early Childhood Scales; Greenspan SEGC = Greenspan Social-Emotional Growth Chart and emotional development. The rest of the measures (summarized in Table 9.5) either target emotional problems/disorders or combine a normative and clinical assessment for social-emotional problems.

Ages and Stages Questionnaires : Social-Emotional (ASQ:SE).   The ASQ:SE (Squires, Bricker & Twombly, 2003), a caregiver report instrument, screens for social and emotional competencies and delays in infants between 3 and 66 months of age. It was designed as a companion measure to the Ages and Stages Questionnaire (Squires, Bricker & Potter, 1999), a general developmental screen, in response to requests from early intervention programs (e.g., Head Start) for measures specifically addressing social and emotional behaviors (Squires, Bricker, Heo & Twombly, 2001). The conceptual frameworks used to develop this measure include social learning theory, developmental organizational theory (Cicchetti, 1993), and the marginal deviation model (Dishion, French, & Patterson, 1995).

One of the advantages of this instrument is that it provides cutoff scores that can be used to identify infants who may have delays in social-emotional functioning. These infants can then be referred for further assessment and, possibly, intervention. The ASQ:SE is easy to administer and has excellent psychometric properties (see Table 9.4). Despite these advantages, one problem with this measure is that African-American and Caucasian non-Hispanic children were underrepresented in the standardization sample. In addition, the standardization sample included very few children diagnosed with social-emotional problems.

The Vineland Social-Emotional Early Childhood Scales (SEEC).   The Vineland SEEC Scales (Sparrow et al., 1998), a structured parent interview measure, are a component of the Vineland Adaptive Behavior Scales: Expanded Form for infants and children from birth through 5 years 11 months of age. Three areas of social and emotional functioning are assessed: interpersonal relationships, which assesses how much the infant interacts with others; play and leisure time, which assesses the infant's play skills; and coping skills, which assesses the infant's sensitivity to others. In addition to standard scores in each of these domains, the interview yields a Composite Social-Emotional Score.

The SEEC is considered to have good psychometric properties (see Table 9.4), although test–retest reliability fell below acceptable limits when different administrators conducted the interview. Also, although exploratory factor analysis (EFA) was used to determine the domains, the authors provide little explanation for constructing a three-factor scale when the EFA indicated that a four-factor solution provided the best fit to the data. Another issue is that the factor analysis was conducted only on one age group, without explanation or discussion of its application across ages.

Despite these weaknesses, the Vineland SEEC provides the opportunity to identify an infant's strengths and weaknesses in specific areas of social-emotional behavior. Thus, this measure is useful in program planning and also in monitoring progress during intervention.

Greenspan Social-Emotional Growth Chart (SEGC).   The SEGC (Greenspan, 2004) is a screening measure of the infant's social-emotional strengths and weaknesses derived from

Table 9.5 Measures of infant social and emotional problems.

Name	Domains Assessed and Description	Scoring	Examiner Qualifications	Psychometrics	Standardization Sample Reported
TABS	Detached, Hypersensitive/-Active, Underreactive, Dysregulated. Age range 11–71 months. Time required 5 minutes (screen); 15 minutes (assessment)	Answers: parent checks yes (problem) or no (not a problem)	Completed by parent or paraprofessional; interpreted by child development professionals (not further specified)	Inter-rater reliability = .81–.94 Internal consistency = .88–.95 Factor loadings = .46–.69 Screen = 2.2% false negatives, 1.4% false positives	N = 833
ITSC	Self-Regulation, Attention, Sleep, Eating or Feeding, Dressing/Bathing or Touch, Movement, Listening and Language, Looking and Sight, Attachment/Emotional Functioning. Age range 7–30 months. Time required 10 minutes	Answers: most times, never/sometimes, past (i.e., the behavior occurred in the past)	Completed by parent or paraprofessional; interpreted by child development professionals (not further specified)	See text	Criterion referenced measure; N = 154 typically developing children, N = 67 children with identified regulatory problems
ITSEA/ BITSEA	Externalizing, Internalizing, Dysregulation, and Competence. Age range 12–36 months. Time required ITSEA: 20–30 minutes (questionnaire), 35–45 minutes (interview); BITSEA: 7–10 minutes	Answers: very true/often, somewhat true/ somewhat true/ sometimes, not true/rarely, no opportunity	ITSEA: master's level or greater BITSEA: administered by clinicians, educators or paraprofessionals with supervision	Test–retest reliability = .69–.91 Internal reliability = .59–.90 Parent inter-rater reliability = .72–.79 Content validity by confirmatory factor analysis	N = 1,517; assessed in 6-month age bands stratified by ethnicity, parent education, and region

Key: TABS = Temperament and Atypical Behavior Scale; ITSC = Infant Toddler Symptom Checklist; ITSEA/BITSEA = Infant-Toddler Social and Emotional Assessment/Brief Infant-Toddler Social and Emotional Assessment

Greenspan's developmental structuralist framework (Greenspan, Nover, & Scheuer, 1984). Greenspan describes his model as a "functional emotional developmental approach" that depicts emotions as precursors to mental abilities and social functioning. In this model, early relationship patterns, environmental factors, and individual differences in the infant coincide to form either adaptive or maladaptive infant behaviors. In addition to areas of strength and weakness, this measure also includes several items designed to assess sensory processing. It is intended for use with infants from birth to 42 months of age.

The SEGC has been adopted as the Social-Emotional subtest of the Bayley-III (Bayley, 2006) which was described in detail in the section on cognitive measures in this chapter. The 35-item social-emotional questionnaire is completed by parents or caregivers. Responses are stratified into six tasks of social-emotional development that are typically accomplished in the first 3½ years of life. The normative sample for the Social-Emotional domain is divided into nine developmental stages. The measure is supposed be administered at each developmental stage to assess whether the child is reaching specific emotional developmental milestones. Scores are plotted on a growth chart and compared with growth charts from previous screenings to highlight areas of improvement or concern.

According to the author, the standardization sample is representative of the 2000 US Census survey. However, psychometric data on this instrument are completely lacking. Other problems with this measure include the following: (1) it relies heavily on language ability to determine emotional status in the upper ages covered by this measure; (2) developmentally delayed children were not included in the standardization sample, which makes interpretation of low scores more difficult; and (3) the measure does not include standard scores. In spite of these issues the strong theoretical underpinnings of the SEGC argue for its face validity as a useful clinical assessment of whether an infant has achieved a particular emotional milestone in development, as well as in pinpointing any areas of concern. It seems critical to conduct further research to examine the reliability and validity of this measure before determining its long-term utility.

The Ounce Scale.   The Ounce Scale (Meisels et al., 2003), a recent addition to the assessment toolbox, shows promise for examining social-emotional development. Standardization and psychometric evaluation of this scale are currently underway, but it warrants some attention even at this preliminary phase of development because it is the only performance-based assessment of infant social-emotional development. The age range for the scale is from birth to 42 months. Several areas of social-emotional development are assessed including personal connections, feelings about self, and relationships with other children. In addition to providing a performance-based assessment of social-emotional development, the Ounce Scale also yields measures of other areas of functioning including communication and language, cognitive, and physical development, thus providing a comprehensive assessment of the infant's development. Another advantage of this measure is that it can be used with at-risk as well as typically developing children.

The instruments described next (see Table 9.5) can be used as one component of a comprehensive assessment. It is important to keep in mind, however, that determining if an infant meets diagnostic criteria for a specific disorder requires a comprehensive assessment of the infant and the parent–infant relationship (see chapter 11 in this volume).

The Temperament and Atypical Behavior Scale (TABS).   The TABS (Bagnato, Niesworth, Salvia, & Hunt, 1999), which the authors describe as a measure of "temperament and self-regulatory behavior" for children between 11 and 71 months of age, consists of a screener and a more comprehensive assessment tool. However, the name of this instrument is somewhat misleading because the items on both the screener and assessment tool assess problems in sensory regulation and behavior, rather than temperament. (A review of temperament measures is beyond the scope of this chapter; for a review of this topic, see chapter 20 in volume 1). The TABS yields four scores, all of which pertain to problems in sensory modulation, namely Detached, Hypersensitive/Active, Underreactive and Dysregulated.

The screening tool and assessment measure are designed to be used in tandem. That is, a caregiver first completes the 15-item screening checklist, and the more detailed 55-item assessment tool is completed only if the screener identifies an area of concern. The psychometric properties, including reliability and validity, seem to be adequate, and the moderately large normative sample included children with both typical and atypical development (see Table 9.5).

The TABS has both clinical and research applications, including determining eligibility for individualized program planning, interventions, monitoring progress, and outcome evaluations. Because this scale is norm-referenced, score interpretation aligns with most state eligibility criteria for early intervention services, as well as with the diagnostic classification system developed by the National Center for Clinical Infant Programs, DC:0–3R (Zero to Three, 2005). Other advantages of this instrument include its ease of administration (no special training required), as well as the fact that it takes only 5–15 minutes to complete. Therefore, despite its somewhat misleading name, this scale seems to be a useful, psychometrically sound instrument, particularly with reference to assessing problems in sensory regulation, a domain of emotional development that has recently received increasing attention (Ahn, Miller, Milberger, & McIntosh, 2004).

Infant Toddler Symptom Checklist (ITSC).   The ITSC (DeGangi, Poisson, Sickel, & Wiener, 1995) consists of a parent report screening questionnaire designed to identify potential sensory, attentional, emotional, or behavioral problems in infants between 7 and 30 months of age. This questionnaire includes nine domains (see Table 9.5), assessed across five different age ranges. However, not all domains are assessed in every age range. In addition, the domains in different age ranges vary in the number of descriptors used to identify problem behavior, and the wording of similar descriptor items varies between the age ranges. These inconsistencies do not allow clinicians or researchers to compare a child's scores across developmental stages and the inconsistencies are not explained in the item analysis. The test manual also does not include any description of the norming sample. More seriously, developers of the ITSC did not follow recommended test development guidelines for evidencing validity (American Educational Research Association, American Psychological Association, & National Council on Measurement in Education, 1985). Therefore, caution is indicated in utilizing this measure in the absence of additional validated components of a more comprehensive assessment.

The Infant-Toddler Social and Emotional Assessment (ITSEA) and Brief Infant-Toddler Social and Emotional Assessment (BITSEA).   The ITSEA (Carter & Briggs-Gowan, 2006) and its companion screening measure, the BITSEA (Briggs-Gowan & Carter, 2006), are to date the most comprehensive, psychometrically sound instruments for assessing social-emotional functioning in infants and toddlers. Both instruments consist of caregiver report questionnaires (see Table 9.5 for descriptive data on each of these instruments). In addition to social-emotional development, the ITSEA also assesses social and emotional problems and competencies. Symptoms assessed include those outlined in the DC:0–3R (Zero to Three, 2005) and relevant DSM diagnostic criteria.

The ITSEA consists of four broad domains (the first three are problem domains). The Externalizing domain includes subscales that assess aggression, defiance, and activity. Subscales of the Internalizing domain assess depression/withdrawal, anxiety, and separation distress. The Dysregulation domain has subscales for sleep disturbances, negative emotionality, eating and sensory problems. Finally, the Competence domain assesses compliance, attention, play, empathy, peer relations, and mastery motivation. There are also three Index Clusters: Maladaptive (Posttraumatic Stress Disorder, Tourette's disorder, toileting, sexualized behaviors, and Pica), Social Relatedness (approach, relatedness, and attention), and Atypical behaviors (e.g., atypical repetition).

The BITSEA (Briggs-Gowan & Carter, 2006) is a much briefer screening questionnaire, consisting of 42 items from the longer instrument. It includes two scales, a 31-item Problem scale and an 11-item Competence scale. Items were selected by expert opinion and from high factor-loading ITSEA items. Children with Problem scale scores greater than the 25th percentile and/or Competence scales below the 15th percentile are considered to be at risk and should be referred for a more comprehensive evaluation. The BITSEA does not require any specialized training to administer or score, which makes it very useful for a brief screening that includes an assessment of both social-emotional competence and problems.

As previously mentioned, both the ITSEA and the BITSEA have undergone extensive psychometric testing. The standardization sample for the ITSEA included a large, diverse sample of typically developing children, as well as those with developmental delays. Both scales have good internal consistency, test–retest reliability and have been shown to correlate with other parent report measures of child behavior problems, as well as independent behavioral observations (Carter, Briggs-Gowan, Jones, & Little, 2003; Carter, Little, Briggs-Gowan, & Kogan, 1999). The validity of the hypothesized scales was supported by confirmatory factor analyses (Carter et al., 2003).

The focus on both problems and competencies is a major strength of these questionnaires because competencies have been shown to play a mitigating role in the stability of problem behaviors (Elias, Gara, Schuyler, Branden-Muller, & Sayette, 1991). Also, recent data (Briggs-Gowan & Carter, 2008) indicate that the BITSEA correctly identified the majority of infants and toddlers who exhibited social-emotional problems in early elementary school, which suggests that it has excellent potential as an early screener for later psychiatric disorder.

Summary.   Growing awareness of the importance of infant social-emotional development had led to the recent development of a wide range of instruments designed to assess this aspect of infant functioning. Most of these measures depend on caregiver report, although there is one measure, the Ounce Scale, that uses direct observation. These instruments also vary widely in terms of their psychometric development. There are several questionnaires, including the ITSEA, the BITSEA, the AQS:SE and the Vineland SEEC, that have been developed through rigorous psychometric testing, including the use of large normative samples and "best practice" procedures for establishing reliability and validity. Other instruments, such as the ITSC and the Ounce Scale, await further validation, but are still useful for identifying infants in need of early intervention services, as well as those who should be referred for a more comprehensive diagnostic evaluation.

In addition to an assessment of the infant's functioning, there is widespread agreement that a comprehensive assessment of infant social-emotional development should also include an assessment of the caregiver–infant relationship. Many measures of this relationship, however, have been designed for research purposes, and are not readily applicable to the clinical setting, so they will not be reviewed here. Fortunately, there are several measures that have been designed for both clinical and research settings. These are described below. In addition to these measures, the 0–3 Diagnostic classification system (Zero to Three, 2005) includes a rating of the parent–child relationship, The Parent–Infant Relationship Global Assessment Scale (PIR-GAS; Zero to Three, 2005). This scale is described in chapter 11 in this volume, because it is used primarily as one axis (Axis II) of this classification system.

Assessment of the parent–infant relationship

The Parent-Child Early Relational Assessment (PCERA).   The PCERA (Clark, 1985, 1999) is a structured observational measure of infant–caregiver interaction for infants (and their caregivers) from birth through age 5. Caregiver–infant interaction is observed during four 5-minute situations (feeding, free play, structured task, and separation/reunion) with different activities depending on the infant's age (e.g., for infants less than 7 months of age the structured task consists of asking the caregiver to get the baby interested in shaking a rattle). Interactive quality is assessed in 29 caregiver domains (e.g., parental positive and negative affect, mirroring), 30 infant domains (e.g., positive and negative affect, social initiative and responsiveness), and 8 domains of dyadic functioning (e.g., joint attention, reciprocity), each of which are rated on seven-point Likert scales.

The PCERA is reported to have good inter-rater reliability and internal consistency (Clark, Tluczek, & Gallagher, 2004). Construct validity was established with a factor analysis supporting eight factors – three caregiver, three infant, and two dyadic (Clark, 1999). The three caregiver factors are: (a) Parental Affective Involvement and Verbalization; (b) Parental Negative Affect and Behavior; and (c) Parental Intrusiveness, Insensitivity and Inconsistency. Infant factors include: (a) Infant Positive Affect, Communicative and Social Skills; (b) Infant Quality of Play, Interest and Attentional Skills; and (c) Infant Dysregulation and Irritability. The two dyadic scales are: (a) Dyadic Mutuality and Reciprocity; and (b) Dyadic Disorganization and Tension. Predictive and discriminative validity also has been established (Clark, 1999; Clark, Hyde, Essex, & Klein, 1997).

The clinical utility of the PCERA has been documented in a recent study which showed that scores were sensitive to changes in caregiver–infant interaction following therapeutic intervention (Clark, Tluczek, & Wenzel, 2003). In addition to its utility in assessing the parent–infant relationship, this measure can also be used in combination with video replay with parents to assess their perception of their infants and their parenting skills (Clark et al., 2004). The author stipulates that training is required to use this scale, but does not specify the amount and type of training (Clark et al., 2004).

The Nursing Child Assessment Satellite Training Parent–Child Interaction Feeding and Teaching Task Scales (NCAST-PCI). The NCAST-PCI (Barnard, 1979; Kelly & Barnard, 2000; Sumner & Spietz, 1994) is an observational measure designed to assess the quality of parent–infant interaction from birth to 36 months of age during feeding and teaching activities. Caregiver and infant variables are assessed on a total of 149 behaviors: 76 in the Feeding Scale and 73 in the Teaching Scale. Each variable is rated on a dichotomous scale of "absent" or "present." There are four parent subscales, two child subscales and four total scales.

Generally, the psychometric properties of the scales are adequate (Barnard, 1979) and there are norms for White non-Hispanic, African-American and Hispanic parent–child pairs, although data suggest that they may be lower than reported in the manual. The Teaching Scales have been shown to have predictive validity in relation to children's language and cognitive outcomes at 3 and 5 years of age (Kelly, Morisset, Barnard, Hammond, & Booth, 1996). One of the disadvantages of the NCAST-PCI is that use of the scales requires fairly extensive training (5–7 days with a certified instructor). Also, the dichotomous ratings may make it less sensitive to change following intervention.

Future Directions in Infant Assessment

Infant assessment is still a relatively new and emerging field. Of the 15 developmental measures and the nine social-emotional measures discussed in this chapter, almost two thirds have been developed or revised in the last decade and only one dates to before 1992. Almost all would benefit from further psychometric testing. Most measures that rely exclusively on parent report especially could use further validation.

Much of the developmental assessment data to date comes from studies that looked at MDI scores on the BSID-II. The MDI has been criticized both as a composite score and as a scale on which passing items rely heavily on sensory and motor responses. The most recent edition of this measure, the Bayley-III, uses separate domain scales in lieu of a summed overall developmental score and attempts to minimize cross-domain responding in its item selection. Whether these changes will translate into predictive validity in targeted developmental streams remains to be seen. The addition of growth charts to the Bayley-III that are designed to demonstrate stability or change in level of functioning within domains over time is provocative as well, but these remain untested. The growth score may prove to be useful in predicting long-term outcome as it is possible that stability or inconsistency over time may be a better predictor of later functioning than an infant's score at any one point alone. Clearly, more research needs to be completed with the Bayley-III to determine if the new edition is a valuable addition to the infant assessment toolbox.

As infant researchers learn more about the remarkable capacities of the youngest of children, new methods of assessing individual children will no doubt become available to inform clinicians who work with infants and their families. Clinical practice, in general, is both art and science – perhaps more so when working with infants whose inner world must be inferred rather than overtly shared. Over and above what can be accomplished with standardized measures, it is useful to remember that a comprehensive developmental assessment requires a multidimensional approach to the evaluation of infant development and behavior in a family and cultural context. Becoming adept at interviewing and observing infant–parent interaction is equally important as testing to the assessment process. With many different instruments to choose from in infant assessment, the question of which measures to use will always be based in part on psychometric properties, in part on the purpose of the evaluation, and in part on clinical judgment of what formal information will adequately supplement other observations and interview material. In the end, components of any clinical infant assessment will probably be unique to individual clinicians.

References

Ahn, R. R., Miller, L. J., Milberger, S., & McIntosh, D. N. (2004). Prevalence of parents' perceptions of sensory processing disorders among kindergarten children. *American Journal of Occupational Therapy, 58,* 287–293.

Albers, C. A., & Grieve, A. J. (2007). Test review: Bayley Scales of Infant and Toddler Development (3rd edition). *Journal of Psychoeducational Assessment, 25,* 1880–1898.

Als, H., Lester, B. M., Tronick, E. Z., & Brazelton, T. B. (1982). Toward a systematic assessment of of pre-term infants' behavioral development. In H. E. Fitzgerald, B. M. Lester, & M. W. Yogman (Eds.), *Theory and research in behavioral pediatrics,* Vol. *1* (pp. 35–63). New York: Plenum.

American Academy of Pediatrics (2006). Identifying infants and young children with developmental disabilities in the medical home: An algorithm for developmental surveillance and screening. *Pediatrics, 18,* 405–420.

American Educational Research Association, American Psychological Association, & National Council on Measurement in Education (1985). *Standards for educational psychological testing.* Washington, DC: American Psychological Association.

Aylward, G. P. (1995). *Bayley Infant Neurodevelopmental Screener (BINS).* San Antonio, TX: The Psychological Corporation.

Aylward, G. P. (2002). Methodological issues in outcome studies of at-risk infants. *Journal of Pediatric Psychology, 27,* 37–45.

Aylward, G. P. (2004). Developmental assessment of infants and toddlers. In G. Goldstein, S. Beers (Vol. Eds.), & M. Hersen (Editor-in-Chief), *Comprehensive handbook of psychological assessment, Vol. 1. Intellectual and neuropsychological assessment* (pp. 87–97), Hoboken, NJ: Wiley.

Aylward, G. P. (2005). The conundrum of prediction. *Pediatrics, 116,* 491–492.

Aylward, G. P., & Stancin, T. (2008). 7a. Measurement and psychometric considerations. In M. Wolraich, D. Drotar, P. Dworkin, & E. Perrin (Eds.), *Developmental-Behavioral Pediatrics: Evidence and Practice* (pp. 123–130). Philadelphia: Mosby.

Bagnato, S. J., Niesworth, J. T., Salvia, J., & Hunt, F. M. (1999). *Temperament and Atypical Behavior Scale.* Baltimore, MD: Brookes Publishing.

Barnard, K. E. (1979). *Instructor's Learning Resource Manual*. Seattle: NCAST, University of Washington.

Bayley, N. (1993). *Bayley Scales of Infant Development – second edition*. San Antonio, TX: The Psychological Corporation.

Bayley, N. (2006). *Bayley Scales of Infant and Toddler Development – third edition*. San Antonio, TX: Harcourt Assessment.

Belsky, J. (2006). Determinants and consequences of infant–parent attachment. In L. Balter, & C. Tamis-LeMonda (Eds.), *Child psychology: A handbook of contemporary issues* (4th ed., pp. 3–78). New York: Psychology Press.

Bendersky, M., & Lewis, M. (1994). Environmental risk, biological risk, and developmental outcome. *Developmental Psychology, 30*, 484–494.

Black, M., & Matula, K. (2000). *Essentials of the Bayley Scales of Infant Development-II assessment*. New York: John Wiley & Sons.

Bliss, S. L. (2007). Test reviews: Newborg, J (2005). Battelle Developmental Inventory second edition. Itasca, IL: Riverside. *Journal of Psychoeducational Assessment, 25*, 409–415. On-line version at http://jpa.sagepub.com.

Bornstein, M. H., & Tamis-Lemonda, C. S. (2001). Mother–infant interaction. In G. Bremner, & A. Fogel (Eds.), *Blackwell handbook of infant development* (pp. 269–295). Malden, MA: Blackwell Publishing.

Boukydis, C. F. Z., Bigsby, R., & Lester, B. M. (2004). Clinical use of the neonatal intensive care unit network neurobehavioral scale. *Pediatrics, 113*, 679–689.

Bradley-Johnson, S. (2001). Cognitive assessment for the youngest children: A critical review of tests. *Journal of Psychoeducational Assessment, 19*, 19–44.

Brazelton, T. B., Koslowski, B., & Main, M. (1974). The origins of reciprocity: The early mother–infant interaction. In M. Lewis & L. A. Rosenblum (Eds.), *The effect of the infant on its caregiver*. New York: Wiley.

Brazelton, T. B., & Nugent, J. K. (1995). Neonatal Behavioral Assessment Scale (3rd ed.). London: MacKeith Press.

Brigance, A. H., & Glascoe, F. P. (2002). *Brigance Infant and Toddler Screens*. North Billerica, MA: Curriculum Associates.

Briggs-Gowan, M. J., & Carter, A. (2006). *Manual for the Brief Infant-Toddler Social and Emotional Assessment (BITSEA) Version 2*. San Antonio, TX: Psychological Corporation, Harcourt Press.

Briggs-Gowan, M. J., & Carter, A. S. (2008). Social-emotional screening status in early childhood predicts elementary school outcomes. *Pediatrics, 121*, 957–962.

Briggs-Gowan, M. J., Carter, A. S., Skuban, E. M., & Horwitz, S. McC. (2001). Prevalence of socio-emotional and behavioral problems in a community sample of 1- and 2-year-old children. *Journal of the American Academy of Child and Adolescent Psychiatry, 40*, 811–819.

Browne, J. V., & Talmi, A. (2005). Family based intervention to enhance infant–parent relationships in the neonatal intensive care unit. *Journal of Pediatric Psychology, 30*, 667–677.

Calkins, S. D. (1994). Origins and outcomes of individual differences in emotion regulation. In N. A. Fox (Ed.), *The development of emotion regulation*. Monographs of the Society for Research in Child Development, 59(2–3, Serial No. 240).

Carter, A. S., & Briggs-Gowan, M. J. (2006). *Manual for the Infant-Toddler Social and Emotional Assessment (ITSEA) Version 2*. San Antonio, TX: Psychological Corporation, Harcourt Press.

Carter, A. S., Briggs-Gowan, M. J., Jones, S. M., & Little, T. D. (2003). The infant-toddler social and emotional assessment (ITSEA): Factor structure, reliability, and validity. *Journal of Abnormal Child Psychology, 31*, 495–514.

Carter, A. S., Little, C., Briggs-Gowan, M. J., & Kogan, N. (1999). The infant-toddler social and emotional assessment (ITSEA): Comparing parent ratings to laboratory observations of task mastery, emotion regulation, coping behaviors and attachment status. *Infant Mental Health Journal, 20*, 375–392.

Cattell, P. (1940). *The measurement of intelligence in young children.* New York: Psychological Corporation.

Cicchetti, D. (1993). Developmental psychopathology: Reactions, reflections, projection. *Developmental Review, 13*, 471–502.

Clark, R. (1985). *The Parent-Child Early Relational Assessment. Instrument and manual.* Madison: Department of Psychiatry, University of Wisconsin Medical School.

Clark, R. (1999). The parent–child early relational assessment: A factorial validity study. *Educational and Psychological Measurement, 59*, 821–846.

Clark, R., Hyde, J. S., Essex, M. J., & Klein, M. S. (1997). Length of maternity leave and quality of mother–infant interactions. *Child Development, 68*, 364–383.

Clark, R., Tluczek, A., & Gallagher, K. C. (2004). Assessment of parent–child early relational disturbances. In R. DelCarmen-Wiggins & A. Carter (Eds.), *Handbook of infant, toddler, and preschool mental health assessment* (pp. 25–60). New York: Oxford University Press.

Clark, R., Tluczek, A., & Wenzel, A. (2003). Psychotherapy for postpartum depression: A preliminary report. *American Journal of Orthopsychiatry, 73*, 441–454.

Cohen, S., Parmelee, A., Jr., Beckwith, L., & Sigman, M. (1986). Cognitive development in preterm infants: Birth to 8 years. *Journal of Developmental and Behavioral Pediatrics, 7*, 102–110.

Cohn, J. F., & Tronick, E. Z. (1988). Mother–infant face-to-face interaction: Influence is bidirectional and unrelated to periodic cycles in either partner's behavior. *Developmental Psychology, 24*, 386–392.

Cooper, T. R., Berseth, C. L., Adams, J. M., & Weisman, L. E. (1998). Actuarial survival in the premature infant less than 30 weeks gestation. *Pediatrics, 101*, 975–978.

DeGangi, G., Poisson, S., Sickel, R., & Wiener, A. S. (1995). *The infant toddler symptom checklist.* San Antonio, TX: Psychological Corporation, Harcourt Press.

Denham, S. S., Lydick, S., Mitchell-Copeland, J., & Sawyer, L. (1996). Socioemotional assessment for atypical infants and preschoolers. In M. Lewis & M. W. Sullivan (Eds.), *Emotional development in atypical children.* Mahwah, NJ: Erlbaum.

Dishion, T. J., French, D. C., & Patterson, G. R. (1995). The development and ecology of antisocial behavior. In D. Cicchetti & D. J. Cohen (Eds.), *Developmental psychopathology*, Vol. 2: Risk, disorder, and adaptation (pp. 421–471). New York: John Wiley & Sons.

Elias, M. J., Gara, M. A., Schuyler, T. F., Branden-Muller, L. R., & Sayette, M. A. (1991). The promotion of social competence: Longitudinal study of a preventive school-based program. *American Journal of Orthopsychiatry, 61*, 409–417.

Gesell, A. (1925). *The mental growth of the preschool child.* New York: Harper.

Gesell, A., & Amatruda, C. S. (1947). *Developmental diagnosis* (2nd ed.). New York: Hoeber.

Gesell, A., Halverson, H. M., & Amatruda, C. S. (1940). *The first five years of life: A guide to the study of preschool children.* New York: Harper.

Gilliam, W. S., & Mayes, L. C. (2000). Developmental assessment of infants and toddlers. In C. H. Zeanah (Ed.), *Handbook of infant development* (2nd ed., pp. 236–248). New York: Guilford Press.

Glascoe, F. P. (1997). *Parent Evaluation of Developmental Status (PEDS).* www.pedstest.com.

Greenspan, S. I. (2004). *Greenspan Social-Emotional Growth Chart: A screening questionnaire for infants and young children.* San Antonio, TX: Harcourt Assessment.

Greenspan, S. I., & Meisels, S. J. (1996). Toward a new vision for the developmental assessement of infants and young children. In S. J. Meisels & E. Fenichel (Eds.), *New visions for the developmental assessment of infants and young children* (pp. 26–52). Washington, DC: Zero to Three.

Greenspan, S. I., Nover, R. A., & Scheuer, A. Q. (1984). A developmental diagnostic approach for infants, young children and their families. *Early Child Development and Care, 16,* 85–148.

Hack, M., Horbar, J. D., Malloy, M. H., Tyson, J. E., Wright E., & Wright L. (1991). Very low birth weight outcomes of the National Institute of Child Health and Human Development Neonatal Network. *Pediatrics, 87,* 587–597.

Hack, M., Taylor, H. G., Drotar, D., Schluchter, M., Carter, L., Wilson-Costello, D., et al. (2005). Poor predictive validity of the Bayley Scales of Infant Development for cognitive function of extremely low birth weight children at school age. *Pediatrics, 116,* 333–341.

Harrison, P. L., & Oakland, T. (2003). *Adaptive Behavior Assessment System* (2nd ed.). San Antonio, TX: the Psychological Corporation.

Huntley, M. (1996) *The Griffiths Mental Development Scales – Revised: Birth to 2 years.* Oxford: Hogrefe.

Ireton, H. (1992). *Child development review.* Minneapolis: Behavioral Science Systems.

Johnson, S., & Marlow, N. (2006). Developmental screen or developmental testing? *Early Human Development, 82,* 173–183.

Johnson-Martin, N. M., Attermeier, S. M., & Hacker, B. (2004). *The Carolina curriculum for infants and toddlers with special needs* (3rd ed.). Baltimore, MD: Brookes.

Kelly, J. F., & Barnard, K. E. (2000). Assessment of parent–child interaction: Implications for early intervention. In J. P. Shonkoff & S. J. Meisels (Eds.), *Handbook of Early Childhood Intervention* (pp. 258–289). New York: Cambridge University Press.

Kelly, J. F., Morisset, C. E., Barnard, K. E., Hammond, M. A., & Booth, C. L. (1996). The influence of early mother–child interaction on preschool cognitive/linguistic outcomes in a high-social-risk group. *Infant Mental Health Journal, 17,* 310–321.

Langkamp, D. L., & Brazy J. E. (1999). Risk for later school problems in preterm children who do not cooperate for preschool developmental testing. *Journal of Pediatrics, 135,* 756–760.

Lester, B. M., & Tronick, E. Z. (2001). Behavioral assessment scales: The NICU network neurobehavioral scale, the neonatal behavioral assessment scale, and the assessment of the preterm infant's behavior. In L. T. Singer & P. S. Zeskind (Eds.), *Biobehavioral assessment of the infant.* New York: Guilford Press.

Lester, B. M., & Tronick, E. Z. (2004). History and description of the neonatal intensive care unit network neurobehavioral scale. *Pediatrics, 113,* 634–640.

Lewis, M. (1987). Social development in infancy and early childhood. In J. Osofsky (Ed.), *Handbook of infant development* (pp. 419–493). New York: Wiley.

Luby, J. L., & Morgan, K. (1997). Characteristics of an infant/preschool psychiatric clinic sample: Implications for clinical assessment and nosology. *Infant Mental Health Journal, 18,* 209–220.

McCormick, M. C. (1989). Long-term follow-up of infants discharged from neonatal intensive care units. *Journal of the American Medical Association, 261,* 1767–1772.

McCormick, M. C. (1997). The outcome of very low birth weight infants: Are we asking the right questions? *Pediatrics, 99,* 869–876.

McLean, M., McCormick, K., & Baird, S. (1991). Concurrent validity of the Griffiths' Mental Development Scales with a population of children under 24 months. *Journal of Early Intervention, 15,* 338–344.

Meisels, S. J., Dombro, A. L., Marsden, D. B., Weston, D. R., & Jewkes, A. M. (2003). *The Ounce Scale.* Bloomington, MN: Pearson Assessments.

Mullen, E. M. (1995). *Mullen Scales of Early Learning: AGS edition*. Circle Pines, MN: American Guidance Service.

Newborg, J. (2005). *Battelle Developmental Inventory, 2nd edition*. Itasca, IL: Riverside.

NICHD Early Child Care Research Network (2006). Infant–mother attachment classification: Risk and protection in relation to changing maternal caregiving quality. *Developmental Psychology*, *42*(1), 38–58.

Parks, S. (1992). *Hawaii Early Learning Profile*. Palo Alto, CA: Vort Corporation.

Pinto-Martin, J., Dunkle, M., Earls, M., Fliedner, D., & Landes, C. (2005). Developmental stages of developmental screening. *American Journal of Public Health*, *95*, 826–833.

Scheeringa, M. S., Peebles, C. D., Cook, C. A., & Zeanah, C. H. (2001). Toward establishing procedural, criterion, and discriminant validity for PTSD in early childhood. *Journal of the American Academy of Child and Adolescent Psychiatry*, *40*, 52–60.

Shonkoff, J. P., & Phillips, D. A. (Eds.) (2000) *From neurons to neighborhoods: The science of early childhood development*. Washington, DC: National Academy Press.

Sparrow, S. S., Cicchetti, D. V., & Balla, D. A. (1998). *Vineland Social-Emotional Early Childhood Scales*. Bloomington, MN: Pearson Assessments.

Squires, J., Bricker, D., Heo, K., & Twombly, E. (2001). Identification of social-emotional problems in young children using a parent-completed screening measure. *Early Childhood Research Quarterly*, *16*, 405–419.

Squires, J., Bricker, D., & Potter, L. (1999). *Ages and stages questionnaires and users' guide, 2nd edition*, Baltimore, MD: Brookes Publishing.

Squires, J., Bricker, D., & Twombly, E. (2003). *Ages and stages questionnaires: Social emotional*. Baltimore, MD: Brookes Publishing.

Sroufe, L. A. (2005). Attachment and development: A prospective, longitudinal study from birth to adulthood. *Attachment & Human Development*, *7*, 349–367.

Stack, D. M., & Poulin-Dubois, D. (1998). Socioemotional and cognitive competency in infancy. In D. Pushkar, W. M. Bukowski, A. E. Schwartzman, & D. M. Stack (Eds.), *Improving competence across the lifespan* (pp. 37–57). New York: Plenum Press.

Stancin, T., & Aylward, G. P. (2008). 7c. Assessment of development and behavior. In M. Wolraich, D. Drotar, P. Dworkin, & E. Perrin (Eds.), *Developmental-behavioral pediatrics: Evidence and practice* (pp. 144–177). Philadelphia: Mosby.

Stanton, W., McGee, R., & Silva, P. (1991). Indices of perinatal complications, family background, child rearing, and health as predictors of early cognitive and motor development. *Pediatrics*, *88*, 954–959.

Sumner G., & Spietz, A. (1994). *NCAST Caregiver/parent–child interaction teaching manual*. Seattle: NCAST Publications. University of Washington, School of Nursing.

Tronick, E. Z. (1989). Emotions and emotional communication in infants. *American Psychologist*, *44*, 112–119.

Vohr, B. R. (2007). Progress in predicting outcomes for extremely low birth weight infants: Baby steps. *Acta Paediatrica*, *96*, 331–332.

Volling, B. L., McElwain, N. L., Notaro, P. C., & Herrera, C. (2002). Parents' emotional availability and infant emotional competence: Predictors of parent–infant attachment and emerging self-regulation. *Journal of Family Psychology*, *16*, 447–465.

Voss, W., Neubauer, A.-P., Wachtendorf, M., Verhey, J. F., & Kattner, E. (2007). Neurodevelopmental outcome in extremely low birth weight infants: What is the minimum age for reliable developmental prognosis? *Acta Paedriatrica*, *96*, 342–347.

Wocaldo, C., & Rieger, I. (2000). Very preterm children who do not cooperate with assessments at three years of age: Skill differences at five years. *Journal of Developmental and Behavioral Pediatrics*, *21*, 107–113.

Worobey, J., & Belsky, J. (1982). Employing the Brazelton Scale to influence mothering: An experimental comparison of three strategies. *Developmental Psychology, 18*, 736–743.

Wyly, M. V. (1997). *Infant assessment.* Boulder, CO: Westview Press.

Zero to Three (2005). *Diagnostic classification of mental health and developmental disorders of infancy and early childhood: Revised edition (DC:0–3R).* Washington, DC: Zero to Three Press.

10

The Early Development of Autism Spectrum Disorders

Gregory S. Young and Sally Ozonoff

Introduction

Autism spectrum disorders (ASDs) are a group of lifelong neurodevelopmental conditions that begin in the first three years of life. Behavioral features fall in the three areas of social relatedness, communication, and behaviors and interests. In the social domain, symptoms include impaired use of nonverbal behaviors to regulate social interaction (e.g., eye contact, facial expression, gestures), failure to develop age-appropriate peer relationships, little seeking of shared enjoyment or interests with other people, and limited social-emotional reciprocity. Communication deficits include delay in or absence of spoken language, difficulty in initiating or sustaining conversation, idiosyncratic or repetitive language, and imitation and pretend play deficits. In the behaviors and interests domain, there are often encompassing, unusual interests, inflexible adherence to non-functional routines, stereotyped body movements, and preoccupation with parts or sensory qualities of objects (American Psychiatric Association, 2000). To meet criteria for autistic disorder, an individual must demonstrate at least six of the 12 symptoms, with at least two coming from the social domain and one each from the communication and restricted behaviors/interests categories. At least one symptom must have been present before 36 months of age.

The early developmental course of autism appears to follow one of two broad onset patterns. The most common course involves the early onset of symptoms, often before 12 months of age (e.g., Osterling & Dawson, 1994). In approximately a third of cases, however, symptom onset does not occur until sometime in the second year of life, between 14 and 24 months of age (Fombonne & Chakrabarti, 2001; Lord, Shulman, & DiLavore, 2004), after a developmental regression or loss of previously acquired skills. The most frequently reported skill lost is language, although virtually all children who lose language lose social behaviors as well, such as eye contact, social interest, and engagement with others (Hoshino, Kaneko, Yashima, Kumashiro, Volkmar, & Cohen, 1987; Ozonoff, Williams, & Landa, 2005). It is often difficult to separate children who show a regression from children who show a developmental "stagnation," marked by a failure to continue making developmental gains in areas of social behaviors or language instead of a clear loss of skills (Siperstein & Volkmar, 2004). Moreover, many children with a reported regression already have a number of developmental delays prior to the regression itself (Ozonoff et al., 2005; Siperstein & Volkmar, 2004; Werner, Dawson, Munson, & Osterling, 2005). Although the heterogeneity in symptom onset and early developmental course might be due in part to a reliance on retrospective parent reports, a number of more recent studies using longitudinal observational methods have clearly confirmed that not all children with autism follow similar patterns and timing of early symptom onset and expression (e.g., Landa, Holman, & Garrett-Mayer, 2007; Werner & Dawson, 2005). It appears that children with autism may reach the threshold for diagnosis at different points in the first two years of life, involving different amounts and/or combinations of early signs, slowing development, lack of progression, and frank losses (Landa et al., 2007).

Although ASDs are considered lifelong, chronic conditions, there may be periods of waxing or waning of particular symptoms and in almost all cases there is improvement with age and development. Some studies suggest that improvement is most marked in preschool and early childhood, with functioning levels remaining stable and sometimes even worsening in adolescence and adulthood (Sigman & McGovern, 2005). Once diagnosed with an ASD, the vast majority of children will retain this diagnosis into adulthood (Piven, Harper, Palmer, & Arndt, 1996) and present with functional impairment throughout life (Howlin, 2003). In a very small proportion of cases, there are children who appear to "grow out of" an ASD diagnosis (Lovaas, 1987; Perry, Cohen & DeCarlo, 1995), although some do retain difficulties in other areas (Fein, Dixon, Paul, & Levin, 2005). Diagnosis at age 2 is remarkably reliable and stable, with 85–90% of children diagnosed at this age retaining the diagnosis over time (Kleinman et al., 2008; Moore & Goodson, 2003). Outcome is highly related to overall cognitive ability. Across all studies conducted to date, the most powerful predictors of outcome continue to be two factors identified decades ago: IQ scores and verbal ability at age 5 (Lotter, 1974; Rutter, 1983).

Early research suggested that autism (strictly defined, meeting full criteria) occurred at the rate of 4–6 affected individuals per 10,000 (Lotter, 1966). A study conducted in the mid-1980s broadened diagnostic criteria and found a rate of 10 per 10,000 in a total population screening of a circumscribed geographical region in Canada (Bryson, Clark, & Smith, 1988). Newer studies using standardized diagnostic measures and active ascertainment techniques have yielded prevalence estimates of 60–70 per 10,000 or approximately 1/150 across the spectrum of autism and 1/500 for children with the full syndrome of autistic disorder (Centers for Disease Control and Prevention, 2007). One obvious reason for the rise in rates is that more recent research has examined all ASDs, while early surveys looked at rates of only strictly defined autism. However, in studies that have broken down the rates by specific DSM-IV subtypes, it is clear that the prevalence of classic autism itself is higher. Chakrabarti and Fombonne (2001) reported a rate of 16.8 per 10,000 for autistic disorder, which is 3–4 times higher than suggested in the 1960s and 1970s and over 1.5 times higher than thought in the 1980s and 1990s. Therefore, ASDs are no longer considered rare conditions.

Although signs of autism are almost always present by the second birthday and a third of parents cite first concerns about their child's development prior to the first birthday (De Giacomo & Fombonne, 1998), clinical diagnoses are not typically made until the fourth year of life or later (Mandell, Novak, & Zubritsky, 2005). This lag between first signs and formal diagnosis raises a number of important questions: What does the very early development of autism look like? Are there early developmental markers in the first years of life that are unique and specific to the development of autism? Does development initially proceed normally only to regress later, or are subtle abnormalities present from birth that simply become magnified or evolve over time? Answering these questions is particularly important for the early identification and treatment of autism. Indeed, early diagnosis and intervention may help to prevent aspects of autism, such as self-imposed social isolation, from further interrupting and derailing typical socialization processes and compounding initial neurological insults (e.g., Mundy & Neal, 2001). Additionally, clarifying the early development of autism might help in understanding the etiology of the disorder; pinpointing the first detectable signs of autism may put us that much closer to pinpointing its ultimate causes.

This chapter will review research on the early development of children with autism between birth and 24 months of age. We will begin with an overview of the various research methodologies that have been used to examine the early developmental course of autism. We will then review specific research findings organized by symptom domain. Finally, we briefly consider the theoretical and clinical implications of this body of research.

Approaches to Researching the Early Development of Autism

One of the first methodologies employed to examine the early development of autism was the clinical case study. Kanner (1943) originally presented 11 case studies that included some degree of early developmental history, noting early abnormalities such as a lack of anticipatory responses to being picked up and feeding problems. A number of more recent case studies have also been presented that present prospective or at least contemporaneous clinical impressions and formal assessment data, providing a "real-time view" of autism as it develops in a single individual (e.g., Dawson, Osterling, Meltzoff, & Kuhl, 2000; Klin et al., 2004). Although case studies do not allow for group comparisons and statistical tests, they play an important role in gathering richly detailed data from which to generate new hypotheses to be tested at the group level. Case studies also provide a helpful foil to group-level research: group research often implies a homogeneity and universality of findings where case studies can offer remedial exceptions to help in refining conclusions derived from group design research.

A second methodology employed in researching the early development of autism has been the use of formalized retrospective parental reports. Although parent recall of early development is always an important component in the diagnostic process itself (i.e., a history of symptoms prior to age 3), a number of studies have employed detailed questionnaires and interviews to obtain a more specific picture of the early development of autism from birth. Although this methodology has the obvious advantage of getting data from someone who has lived with and observed the child on a daily basis from birth across many different settings, retrospective report methodology is particularly vulnerable to bias and error, especially if the parent is asked to recall specific behaviors from many years earlier, or has limited insight into child development.

A third methodology that has been used successfully is the systematic behavioral scoring of home video tapes of children with autism. Beginning in the 1970s, researchers have collected home movies from the infant and toddler years of children later diagnosed with autism, examining the early video records with an eye to identifying early behavioral signs of emerging autism. Given the ubiquity of home video cameras and the relative rarity of autism, this home movie methodology has proved a particularly efficient way to recruit relatively large groups of subjects with autism and collect longitudinal data on their early development, often from birth. An obvious shortcoming of this approach is the lack of standardization in the behavioral samples. Although many home movie studies have capitalized on the consistency in situations typically recorded by families (e.g., birthday parties, holiday celebrations), researchers must still contend with issues such as poor quality, spotty representation of development, lack of standardization, and biases about what is recorded (Palomo, Belinchón, & Ozonoff, 2006).

A fourth methodology for studying the early development of autism that has been employed more recently is the prospective follow-along study of infants who are at increased risk for developing autism. Specifically, these studies recruit infants early in their first year of life who have an older sibling already diagnosed with autism. Given the increased prevalence of autism in siblings (Bailey, Palferman, Heavey, & Le Couteur, 1998; Zwaigenbaum, Bryson, Rogers, Roberts, Brian, & Szatmari, 2005), this methodology of studying high-risk infants yields longitudinal developmental data collected in standardized laboratory settings. As such, this "infant sibling" methodology avoids many of the problems inherent in the above-mentioned approaches. It avoids the lack of standardization in home movie studies; it avoids the biases and errors inherent in recall of early development; and, unlike clinical case studies, it provides the power to statistically model and test hypotheses by comparing at-risk infants to typically developing infants or infants with other developmental delays. Nevertheless, infant-sibling studies are particularly expensive and inefficient to conduct in that they require the recruitment and close developmental monitoring of a large number of infants in order to generate a relatively small and perhaps less representative sample of infants who develop autism.

A final approach to examining the early development of autism has been the use of screening instruments administered to parents during routine visits to pediatric offices. This strategy has typically used a brief questionnaire that measures a limited number of key behaviors thought to be specific to autism. Infants who fail the screening tests can then be followed longitudinally and monitored for the development of autism. Similar to the infant-sibling methodology, the screening method has the advantage of obtaining detailed, standardized longitudinal data on a group of children showing early signs of autism. It also has the benefit of recruiting such at-risk children from the general population instead of only from families who currently have a child with autism, and further allows for the development of a useful measure for screening during routine office visits. The drawback of screening studies is that researchers must screen thousands of infants in order to recruit large enough groups of children who develop autism. Moreover, the difficulty inherent in verifying the sensitivity rates of screening measures (i.e., identifying the number of infants who are missed by the screening instrument but who do eventually develop autism) threatens the representativeness of the sample identified. Sample representativeness may also be adversely affected by failure to screen low-income families who may disproportionately miss routine pediatric visits.

Although each methodological approach has its strengths and weaknesses, it is important to note that research of any type on the early development of autism must demonstrate, at least to some degree, that a pathognomonic sign is both unique and universal to autism (cf. Fein, Pennington, Markowitz, Braverman, & Waterhouse, 1986). Ideally, assuming that autism is a homogenous disorder, any early developmental markers of autism should be universal in that such markers are manifest in all or most cases of autism. Markers should also be unique, such that they are found only or mostly in autism and not in other developmental disorders. These evidentiary criteria are very helpful for evaluating research findings. For the uniqueness criteria, the implication is that research on the early development of autism needs to include a useful comparison group (Shaked & Yirmiya, 2004). At the very least, the phenomenon under study should deviate from typical development, thereby necessitating a typically developing comparison group. A more stringent test of uniqueness, however, is that the phenomenon needs to be specific to autism and not simply an aspect of abnormal development in general. In the case of autism, this is particularly important given that it involves comorbid intellectual disability in approximately 75% of cases (American Psychiatric Association, 2000; for a more detailed discussion of intellectual disability, see chapter 12 in this volume). The criterion of universality implies that research findings should apply to all cases of autism in order to be considered of central importance to our understanding of the disorder.

However, given the realities of conducting such research, the criteria of uniqueness and universality should perhaps be taken as rough guides in evaluating the research literature. For instance, examining the specificity (uniqueness) of particular early markers for autism depends on defining homogenous comparison groups. Depending on the level of analysis, this could mean a separate control group for every associated feature in order to estimate specificity at a clinically useful resolution (e.g., a motor delay group, a specific language impairment group, a mental retardation group). Much of the research reviewed below involves at least one control group with typical development, and often a developmentally delayed group. The developmentally delayed groups, however, are most often heterogeneous, including children with Down syndrome, language delays, nonverbal delays, or general global delays all in the same group.

Even more problematic is that the criterion of universality implicitly assumes that autism is a homogeneous condition instead of an overarching category that may involve a number of specific phenotypes with distinct early developmental profiles. Importantly, some research has made distinctions between "classic autism" specifically and "autism spectrum disorders" more generally. ASD is viewed as a more inclusive category comprised of both classic autism and atypical autism, meeting criteria for pervasive developmental disorder not otherwise specified. More recent research, in particular, has combined these subtypes into the category of ASD, often in an effort to maximize statistical power when using methodologies that rely on screening or infant-sibling recruitment strategies (e.g., Wetherby, Woods, Allen, Cleary, Dickinson, & Lord, 2004; Zwaigenbaum et al., 2005). A small number of studies have also made distinctions between early onset autism and regression or late onset autism (e.g., Landa et al., 2007). Thus, the criterion of universality is often tempered by the breadth of the diagnostic category used in research. Therefore, it is important to treat the universality and specificity criteria as useful heuristics, rather than as absolute requirements for the centrality of an underlying deficit.

Despite the methodological difficulties involved in the research examining the early development of autism, the degree to which findings from each of these different methodologies converge on a similar picture should increase our confidence that we are able to provide some answers to the question of what autism looks like during the first two years of life. It is to this research that we turn in the next section, reviewing studies from all methodologies sequentially as we examine the literature in the domains of most relevance to early autism.

The Early Development of Autism

Social attention and responsivity

In typically developing infants, a strong preference for social responsivity and interaction appears to be present from birth. Research with typically developing infants from birth to 12 months has demonstrated early selective responsivity to a variety of social stimuli including faces (e.g., Turati, Simion, Milani, & Umiltà, 2002; Valenza, Simion, Cassia, & Umiltà, 1996), speech (e.g., Vouloumanos & Werker, 2007), biological motion (e.g., Simion, Regolin, & Bulf, 2008), and visual-gestural movements (Krentz & Corina, 2008). Research has also demonstrated that typically developing infants are exquisitely sensitive to social information as indexed by responses to still-face, social referencing, and joint attention research paradigms (e.g., Butterworth, 1991; Scaife & Bruner, 1975; Tronick, Als, Adamson, Wise, & Brazelton, 1978; Walden & Ogan, 1988; for a detailed discussion of the development of parent–child interaction in typical populations, see chapter 15 in volume 1). Early measures of social attention have also been shown to predict later social cognitive functioning such as theory of mind and understanding of intentions (e.g., Wellman, Lopez-Duran, LaBounty, & Hamilton, 2008; Wellman, Phillips, Dunphy-Lelii, & LaLonde, 2004). Given the importance and ubiquity of early social attention in typical development, in addition to the profound social deficits observed in autism, a careful consideration of the early development of basic orientation to and preference for social stimuli may provide important clues for understanding the early development of autism itself. Indeed, a number of authors have suggested that a deficit in basic social orienting processes is the earliest and most fundamental impairment in autism (Dawson, Meltzoff, Osterling, Rinaldi, & Brown, 1998; Mundy & Neal, 2001; Tantam, 1992).

Among the earliest case studies of autism provided by Kanner (1943), social withdrawal and unresponsiveness clearly appeared to be a defining feature of the disorder.

Kanner noted in particular that "almost all mothers of our patients recalled their astonishment at the children's failure to assume at any time an anticipatory posture preparatory to being picked up" (p. 242). Other case studies have detailed an early lack of responsiveness by 12 months of age to a variety of social stimuli such as voices, name calls, people, and faces (Clancy & McBride, 1969; Dawson et al., 2000; Eriksson & de Chateau, 1992; Green, Brennan, & Fein, 2002). A similar pattern of findings indicating early deficits in social attention and engagement, such as lack of eye contact, responding to joint attention, or orienting to name calls, has been found in studies using retrospective parent reports (e.g, Watson, Baranek, Crais, Reznick, Dykstra, & Perryman, 2007; Wimpory, Hobson, Williams, & Nash, 2000). In a parent report study by Werner et al. (2005), such social orientation deficits were found to discriminate children with autism from typically developing children as early as 6–9 months of age; when compared to children with developmental delays, however, such deficits did not discriminate the ASD group until 13–15 months of age.

A relatively large number of studies using home movies have similarly documented deficits in social attention and responsivity within the first two years of life (Adrien et al., 1991, 1993; Baranek, 1999; Bernabei, Camaioni, & Levi, 1998; Clifford, Young, & Williamson, 2006; Mars, Mauk, & Dowrick, 1998; Osterling & Dawson, 1994; Werner, Dawson, Osterling, & Dinno, 2000). These studies have consistently found deficits in looking to other people's faces and orienting to name calls as the most significantly discriminating behaviors between 8 and 12 months, not only when comparing ASD to typically developing infants, but also to those with developmental delay (Baranek, 1999).

Studies using direct behavioral observation have also found evidence for early deficits in behaviors such as eye contact and response to name. Swettenham et al. (1998) used a nine-item screening measure, the Checklist for Autism in Toddlers (CHAT; Baron-Cohen, Allen, & Gillberg, 1992) at 18 months of age to identify a group of children at risk for autism from a population sample of 16,000 children. The screening measure included items pertaining to gaze monitoring, gesture use, and pretend play. Of children who failed the screening measure at 18 months, 10 were identified who later received a diagnosis of autism at age 3. Detailed coding of video from these follow-up visits revealed that the group with autism demonstrated greater amounts of looking at objects and less time looking at people than the groups with developmental delay or typical development. The children with autism also exhibited fewer attentional shifts involving people than did the other groups. A second study using the same cohort (Charman, Swettenham, Baron-Cohen, Cox, Baird, & Drew, 1997) also found significantly less spontaneous looking to an adult who appeared to be in pain, and less triadic gaze between people and objects. A similar methodology, using children initially identified by a general screening measure – the Infant Toddler Checklist (ITC) – and later diagnosed with autism, was employed by Wetherby et al. (2004). Detailed coding of behavior samples collected at 20 months of age revealed that a lack of socially appropriate gaze and deficits in responding to name significantly discriminated children with ASD by age 3 from children with developmental delays.

More recently, a number of prospective studies using infant-sibling samples have examined early social attention and responsivity longitudinally in controlled laboratory settings. Zwaigenbaum et al. (2005) followed a group of 65 infant siblings and found that infants who exhibited decreased eye contact, decreased social interest, and a lack of responding to name calls during standardized behavior samples collected at 12 months of age were significantly more likely to receive a diagnosis of ASD at 24 months of age. Importantly, these infants could not be discriminated at 6 months of age on any variable, suggesting that deficits in social responsivity emerge slightly later in the first year of life. Similarly, Sullivan, Finelli, Marvin, Garrett-Mayer, Bauman, and Landa (2007) examined joint attention behaviors in 51 high-risk infant siblings and found that delays in following an adult's gaze at 14 months predicted a diagnosis of ASD at 24 months. Finally, Nadig, Ozonoff, Young, Rozga, Sigman, and Rogers (2007) investigated response to name in a group of high-risk infants seen prospectively from 6 months to 24 months and found that, out of 12 infants who clearly failed to respond to their name at 12 months, nine showed delays of some type by 24 months of age, and of these nine, five were specifically diagnosed with ASD by 24 months. Again, none of these infants could be discriminated on the basis of their response to name at 6 months from those who went on to develop typically.

In summary, results from numerous studies using a variety of methodologies and measures have revealed fairly consistent evidence that basic social attention and responsivity are disrupted very early in children with autism. Moreover, these early deficits appear to distinguish autism from typical development in the latter half of the first year and from developmental delay by early in the second year. Such specific early deficits in basic social attention and responsivity may, in turn, derail a variety of other developmental processes occurring within the second and third years, thereby compounding these early deficits with problems in other critical domains. Indeed, one such domain that may be particularly affected by early deficits in social attention and responsivity is language development. It is to this area that we now turn.

Communication and language

One of the most salient developmental milestones children reach during the first two years of life is the mastery and use of language as a tool for interacting with and negotiating their environment. During the latter half of the first year, for example, infants begin to develop an increasing repertoire of communicative deictic gestures such as protoimperative and protodeclarative pointing, ritualized requesting, and bids to be picked up (e.g., Bates, Camaioni, & Volterra, 1975; Camaioni, 2001). Coupled with the onset of babbling that usually begins between 6 and 9 months of age, these early communicative behaviors lead to an exponential growth in language acquisition, resulting in vocabularies of approximately 300 words and the regular use of multiple-word phrases or simple sentences by 24 months of age (Bloom, 1998; for a detailed discussion of communication development in typical populations, see chapters 13 on preverbal communication and 14 on language development in volume 1). Among individuals with autism, difficulties in language and communication can involve anything from subtle problems in the pragmatics of language use and difficulties maintaining conversations to profound delays or even absence of spoken language altogether. Given the ubiquity of language and communication impairments in autism, it is particularly informative to consider the early developmental roots of language such as the use of deictic gestures, the onset of babbling, and early vocabulary acquisition as early signs of autism.

Case studies of the early developmental history of individuals with autism have often noted early disruptions in language and communication development. For instance, Klin et al. (2004) reported a case study of a 15-month-old girl who was diagnosed with autism and noted that she stopped gesturing and vocalizing at 12–13 months of age and lost the few words she had acquired. Similar disruptions in early communication between 9 and 12 months have been noted in cases studies by Green et al. (2002), Eriksson and de Chateau (1992), and Dawson et al. (2000).

Retrospective parent report methodology has revealed that parents are particularly sensitive to disruptions in communication development in children with autism. Indeed, during standardized diagnostic interviews, De Giacomo and Fombonne (1998) found that a disruption in language development was reported by parents as a primary concern in the majority of children who were diagnosed with ASD (30% of parents at 12 months and 80% of parents by 24 months). Dahlgren and Gillberg (1989) used a parent questionnaire covering 130 autism-related symptoms over the first two years of life and found that parents of children with autism reported significantly less use of communicative bids to attract adults' attention than parents of children with mental retardation. Importantly, however, Dahlgren and Gillberg reported few other language-specific differences between the groups with autism and mental retardation, including the amount of babbling, use of inflection, or other gestures, a finding that raises questions about the specificity of early language delays to autism. The specificity of early language deficits was also addressed by Werner et al. (2005) who found that although parent reports showed children with ASD to have less social vocalizations and babbling than typically developing infants by 10–12 months, it was not until 19–21 months that language development, in the form of word usage and gestures (e.g., showing and pointing), was significantly lower in the ASD group than a developmentally delayed group. A second recent parent report study by Watson et al. (2007) comparing symptoms at 12 months of age in groups with ASD or developmental delay also suggested that delays in expressive language, including protoimperative and declarative gestures, were not significantly different, and thus not specific to autism.

In studies using screening questionnaires to identify at-risk samples, deficits in one aspect of communication at 18 months of age – protodeclarative pointing – were found to be one of the strongest predictors of later diagnoses of autism (e.g., Baron-Cohen et al., 1992; Robins, Fein, Barton, & Green, 2001). In the study by Wetherby et al. (2004) using the ITC, coding of behaviors during standardized behavioral assessments at 20 months of age revealed that the group with ASD had significantly less coordinated nonverbal communicative behavior (e.g., coordination of gestures, gaze, and vocalizations) and had more "unusual prosody" (e.g., odd intonation or rhythms in speech) than a group with developmental delays. A later study conducted by Wetherby, Watt, Morgan, & Shumway (2007) using similar methodology found ASD-specific differences at 20 months of age compared to a delay group in rates of communicative gestures and words, although the authors reported no differences on other language items such as phoneme or word production, or language comprehension.

In research using home video, a number of studies have documented significantly fewer communicative gestures in children with ASD by 12 months of age, but few differences in babbling or phoneme production (e.g., Colgan, Lanter, McComish, Watson, Crais, & Baranek, 2006; Osterling & Dawson, 1994; Werner et al., 2000). In a study specifically designed to address the specificity of delays such as language in the early development of autism, Osterling, Dawson, and Munson (2002) found that although infants with ASD and infants with mental retardation both exhibited significantly fewer gestures than typically developing infants at 12 months of age, the infants with ASD were no different from the infants with mental retardation in the amount of gestures observed at 12 months. Moreover, there were no differences between any of the groups in the frequency of vocalizations at 12 months.

An infant-sibling study reported by Mitchell et al. (2006; cf. Zwaigenbaum et al., 2005) compared scores on standardized measures of expressive and receptive language development for 146 infants from 12 to 18 months. A group of 15 infants later diagnosed at 24 months of age with ASD was compared to 82 high-risk infants who were not diagnosed with ASD and 49 typically developing controls. Analyses revealed significant delays in the infants with ASD in both language comprehension and use of gestures at 12 months of age compared to those without ASD. Similar delays in comprehension and use of gestures, as well as total expressive vocabulary, were also found at 18 months. Another infant-sibling study reported by Landa and Garrett-Mayer (2006) examined developmental trajectories of 87 infants from 6 to 24 months using a standardized observational measure of expressive and receptive language development. Twenty-four-month diagnoses yielded a group of 24 infants with ASD, 11 infants with a language delay, and 52 infants with typical development. Analyses revealed that the autism group exhibited slower rates of growth on language measures over time compared to both the language-delayed and typically developing groups, although it was not until 24 months of age that group differences in mean scores were detectable between the autism and language delay groups. Thus, the specificity of a language delay in the ASD group was only statistically evident by 24 months of age, despite overall trajectory differences between the ASD and language delay groups. A second report of this same infant-sibling sample by Landa et al. (2007) found that early use of gestures and vocalizations did discriminate a group of infants with early onset autism (identified by 14 months of age) from a group of infants with later onset autism (identified by 24 months of age).

In summary, research on the early development of language and communication behaviors in autism suggests that although there seem to be clear early differences between infants with autism and typically developing infants around 12 months of age, such differences primarily concern the use of communicative gestures rather than babbling or the amount of vocalizations. Throughout the second year of development, infants with autism clearly do not acquire receptive or expressive language to the same degree as typically developing children, and it is this particular deficit in language acquisition that appears to be the initial primary concern to parents. Nevertheless, the profile of early language deficits seen in infants with autism does not appear to differentiate them from infants with nonautistic developmental delays until 24 months of age. Indeed, results from a number of studies reviewed above, using a variety of methods, suggest there is little support for the specificity of language delays *per se* in autism prior to 24 months of age, despite the salience of such a deficit to parents.

Affect, imitation, and play

Although early deficits or disturbances in affect, imitation, and play have perhaps not always received the same amount of direct research attention as social orienting and language development, they are often the most important mediums within which primary social and communication symptoms of autism are most evident. Indeed, affect is important not only as a manifestation of internal state and state regulation, but also as a means of communicating within and negotiating social contexts (e.g., Witherington & Crichton, 2007; for a detailed discussion of emotional development in typical populations, see chapter 19 in volume 1). Thus affective disturbances in autism might involve not simply flat affect or emotion regulation difficulties, but also a disturbance in the use and interpretation of affect as a social signal, where expressions of joy or frustration might occur with little regard to the social context. Deficits in imitation and play may likewise become most evident as failures to engage in social reciprocity, or may be integral to deficits in language, where the imitation of words or the ability to use symbols is particularly important (for a detailed discussion of imitation in typical populations, see chapter 11 in volume 1). Some studies have thus examined the early development of these behaviors in very young children with autism.

Affect.   Among available case studies of autism atypical affective behavior has often been noted, including delayed onset of smiling, unusual quietness, a lack of physical affection such as "cuddliness," and a general lack of "affective contact" (e.g., Clancy & McBride, 1969; Kanner, 1943). In their prospective case study of an infant followed from birth, Dawson et al. (2000) note a restricted range of facial expressions and a lack of social smiling by 12–15 months. They also note poor state regulation and sleep problems during the first six months. Research using retrospective parent reports has found similar evidence for early affective disturbances (Dahlgren & Gillberg, 1989; Watson et al., 2007).

Direct behavioral observation research has also documented affective disturbances in children with autism. Wetherby et al. (2004) found that their sample of 20-month-old children identified by a screening instrument and later diagnosed with ASD had fewer shared smiles than a group who later exhibited developmental delays. Research with home movies has likewise consistently found a deficit in social smiling among children with autism (e.g., Adrien et al., 1993; Werner et al., 2000), even as early as 6 months of age (Maestro et al., 2002) and when compared to infants with developmental delay (Clifford et al., 2006). Finally, in a longitudinal infant-sibling study, Landa et al. (2007) found that 14-month-olds with early onset ASD had less shared positive affect than did infants with late onset ASD, subclinical autism, and nonaffected infant siblings. Through the age of 24 months, however, the late onset group exhibited a significantly negative developmental trajectory in shared positive affect and had an affective presentation at 24 months indistinguishable from the early onset group.

Imitation.   Studies that have assessed imitation in the first two years of life using case study methodology (Dawson et al., 2000; Green et al., 2002), retrospective parent report (Dahlgren & Gillberg, 1989; Ornitz, Guthrie, & Farley, 1977; Watson et al.,

2007), and behavioral observation (Charman et al., 1997; Mars et al., 1998; Zwaigenbaum et al., 2005) have consistently found disruptions among children with autism. For example, a behavioral observation study on 20-month-old infants who failed the CHAT screening measure at 18 months (Charman et al., 1997) examined object imitation skills in a group of 10 infants later identified with autism, 9 infants later identified with developmental delays, and 19 typically developing infants. Four actions on objects were modeled (e.g., pulling apart a dumbbell) and scored as pass/fail. Results revealed that children with autism imitated the modeled actions significantly less often than either of the control groups. Whereas the 20-month-old typically developing group imitated 82% of the time and the developmental delay group imitated 53% of the time, children with autism imitated the modeled actions on objects only 22% of the time. A study by Watson et al. (2007) using a retrospective parent report targeting development at 12 months found no differences between children with ASD and developmental delay on an imitation domain, although both groups imitated less than a typical group.

Play.   Despite the fact that deficits in symbolic play behaviors are part of the diagnostic criteria for autism under the communication and language symptom domain, there are very few studies that have looked at play in autism prior to 24 months. Dahlgren and Gillberg (1989) found that parents of children with autism endorsed play abnormalities during the first two years, such as "did not play like other children" and "would only play with hard objects," more frequently than parents of children with mental retardation or typical development. The initial development of the CHAT as a screening measure identified pretend play as a useful early marker at 18 months (Baron-Cohen et al., 1992). However, subsequent observational research has not been entirely supportive of play as a useful marker for autism (e.g., Landa et al., 2007; Wetherby et al., 2007). For example, research on samples screened with the CHAT did not find specific differences in spontaneous symbolic play between an ASD group and a group with developmental delay (Charman et al., 1997). Interestingly, the group with ASD demonstrated significantly less *prompted* play – when play acts were verbally prompted and physically modeled. Nevertheless, this performance difference is difficult to disentangle from confounding social attention and possible imitation deficits in the group with autism.

In summary, although fewer studies have directly assessed the developmental domains of affect, imitation, and play, it is clear that one of the most consistent findings is lack of shared positive emotion and social smiles around the first birthday or, in a few studies, in the second six months of life. Moreover, this early deficit in shared emotion may specifically discriminate autism from other developmental delays by 12 months and parallels deficits in social orientation at around the same developmental period. The domain of imitation has received less research attention in the very early development of autism, but does appear to be impaired at least when compared to typical development during the second year of life. In contrast, research findings on early play deficits in autism seem to suggest that symbolic play does not specifically differentiate children with autism from those with developmental delay prior to 24 months of age.

Repetitive and stereotyped behaviors

Repetitive and stereotyped behaviors in autism are commonly referred to as "positive symptoms" in that, unlike social and communication symptoms which are deficits, they are present where they would otherwise be absent in typically developing individuals. Although such symptoms are often clear markers for a diagnosis of autism in older children (Turner, 1999), their specificity to the autism phenotype in infancy is more difficult to establish since repetitive behaviors occur to some degree in typically developing infants and also in young children with mental retardation (Evans et al., 1997; Mahone, Bridges, Prahme, & Singer, 2004; Tan, Salgado, & Fahn, 1997; Thelen, 1979). Moreover, repetitive and stereotyped behavior symptoms of autism have frequently been described as appearing relatively later in childhood, between 3 and 4 years of age (e.g., Lord, 1995; Moore & Goodson, 2003; Stone et al., 1999) and, as such, may not be useful early markers of autism in the first two years of life.

Despite the presumed later onset of repetitive and stereotyped behaviors, however, numerous case studies have reported an early presence of such symptoms (Dawson et al., 2000; Eriksson & de Chateau, 1992; Green et al., 2002; Kanner, 1943). Studies using retrospective parent report have also documented group differences on a number of repetitive and stereotyped behaviors by 12 months of age (Watson et al., 2007; Werner et al., 2005).

A behavioral observation study conducted by Watt, Wetherby, Barber, and Morgan (2008) examined repetitive behaviors of 18–24-month-old children who initially failed a social communication screening measure and were later diagnosed with ASD. During a structured task using a variety of toys, Watt et al. coded several types of repetitive behaviors with objects and stereotyped body movements such as "bangs/taps object," "spins/wobbles object," and "rubs body." Findings revealed that, compared to both a group with developmental delay and a group of typically developing children, the group of children later diagnosed with ASD demonstrated higher frequencies and durations of repetitive and stereotyped behaviors both with objects and with body movements. Similar rates of repetitive movements and stereotypic behaviors have been found as early as 12 months of age in studies of high-risk infant siblings who later develop ASD (Loh et al., 2007), and repetitive use of objects differentiated them from a group with developmental delays in one study (Ozonoff, Macari, Young, Goldring, Thompson, & Rogers, 2008).

In contrast, research using home movies that has looked at younger ages has found relatively little evidence for repetitive and stereotyped behaviors. Baranek (1999) reported no differences in stereotypies between groups with classic autism, developmental delay, and typical development after review of home movies between 9 and 12 months of age. Nevertheless, she did report that increased mouthing was a significant component of a discriminant function analysis differentiating the autism group from both the developmental delay and the typical groups. Osterling et al. (2002) in a home movie study of first birthday parties found that both a group with ASD and a group with mental retardation exhibited more repetitive motor actions than a typically developing group, but found no significant difference between the ASD and mental retardation groups.

In summary, despite prior suggestions that repetitive and stereotyped behaviors are not part of the typical autism symptom profile prior to 3 or 4 years of age, a number of studies using both retrospective reports and behavioral observations have suggested that some types of repetitive and stereotypic behaviors are indeed present during the second year and as early as 12 months in some studies. Home movie studies have generally not captured early repetitive behaviors, but this may be because parents filming their child filter abnormal behavior or do not tend to videotape children involved in object play (Palomo et al., 2006). The evidence for diagnostic specificity of such symptoms is mixed and needs to be further studied.

Sensory processing

Although sensory processing abnormalities are not part of the DSM criteria for autism, they have long been considered an important feature of the disorder. Indeed, Kanner's (1943) initial description included numerous references to unusual sensory and perceptual reactions among the 11 cases described, and first-hand accounts of individuals with autism often stress sensory and perceptual aspects of the disorder (e.g., Grandin, 1992; Cesaroni & Garber, 1991). Most often, sensory abnormalities appear to be conceived of as hypersensitivity to sensory input such as sound (e.g., Hutt, Hutt, Lee, & Ounsted, 1964), but may also involve responses such as fascination with and obsessive focus on particular sensory inputs such as lights or spinning objects.

In addition to Kanner's (1943) numerous mentions of sensory abnormalities, more recent case studies (Dawson et al., 2000; Klin et al., 2004), studies using retrospective parent report data (Dahlgren & Gillberg, 1989; Watson et al., 2007), and studies using home movies (Baranek, 1999) have all documented early sensory abnormalities. In a study of repetitive and stereotyped behaviors in 20-month-old children with ASD, described above, Watt et al. (2008) also found more atypical tactile responses to objects and more atypical gaze fixations, such as holding objects close to the eyes or off to one side for visual inspection. Ozonoff et al. (2008), in a study that looked at atypical behaviors with objects in 12-month-old infant siblings, similarly found a significantly greater degree of unusual visual exploration of objects compared to a developmentally delayed and a typically developing group of 12-month-old infants.

Finally, in the prospective infant sibling study conducted by Zwaigenbaum et al. (2005), a task examining the ability to disengage visual attention from one stimulus presented centrally to another stimulus presented laterally was administered to infants at both 6 and 12 months of age. Findings revealed that decrements in the ability to disengage visual attention that occurred between 6 and 12 months of age were significantly associated with a diagnosis of ASD at 24 months of age. Although this particular finding does not suggest any particular hypersensitivity to visual stimuli, or any qualitatively "bizarre" visual behavior, it is consonant with a more general idea that basic sensory processing abnormalities are an early feature of the autism phenotype, perhaps even prior to 12 months of age.

Summary

Research on the early development of autism has examined a wide range of behaviors, from basic social orienting processes to language, repetitive behaviors, and sensory processing. Clearly, one of the most specific and universal early signs of autism consists of abnormalities in social orienting and responsivity. As noted, signs of significantly decreased social orientation are evident as early as 12 months of age, if not sooner, and involve significantly decreased social gaze, use of eye contact, and responding to name calls. Related to these early signs by around 12 months are clear reductions in coordinating smiles with social gaze and sharing positive affect during social interactions. These early deficits appear unique to infants with autism compared not only to typically developing infants, but also to infants with other developmental delays. Deficits in social orienting processes may also be related in some way to sensory processing abnormalities. Although relatively little research to date has addressed the nature of sensory processing abnormalities in the early development of autism, the few studies that have examined this domain have found unique early abnormalities, especially in visual processing specifically, a finding which may be functionally related to deficits in visual social orienting.

Research also suggests that a number of other deficits and abnormalities related to autism begin to emerge during the second year, including decreased use of gestures and spoken language, imitation, and emerging repetitive behaviors and stereotypies. Although few of these symptoms appear specific to autism when compared to children with other developmental delays at 12 months of age, these behaviors distinguish children with autism from children exhibiting other developmental delays by 24 months of age.

Although deficits in behaviors such as symbolic play have also been documented in autism, at least at later ages, evidence for specific impairments in play early in the development of autism prior to 24 months of age is equivocal. Deficits in symbolic play prior to 24 months have perhaps received too little attention to be ruled out as useful, unique markers of autism, although methodologically isolating a symbolic play deficit from other confounding deficits in social interaction, imitation, and language is challenging, especially given the often small sample sizes in such research.

A consistent finding in this literature is that there are no clearly documented deficits in the first six months of life and very few in the next six months of life. This challenges the traditional view (and Kanner's original suggestion) that behavioral signs of autism are evident from shortly after birth. This literature review suggests that signs of autism *emerge* over the first year and a half of life in a gradual process that involves both diminishment of certain key social behaviors and failure to progress in other more advanced social-communicative processes over time.

Theoretical and Clinical Implications

We began this chapter by asking what the very early development of autism looks like. The research reviewed above suggests that early behavioral signs and symptoms of autism most often emerge sometime between 9 and 12 months of age, with deficits in basic social attention and responsivity as one of the earliest apparent markers. We conclude this chapter with a brief consideration of what this early picture of autism might mean for theoretical models of autism and for clinical applications in the early diagnosis and treatment of autism.

Theoretical models

Given that a deficit in social attention and responsivity is one of the earliest and most specific behavioral signs of autism, a number of theoretical models have been proposed to account for how this might reflect the underlying causes of autism as well as the developmental consequences of such an early deficit. One such theoretical model proposes that the early lack of social attention and responsivity is reflective of a lack of social motivation (Bernier, Webb, & Dawson, 2006; Dawson et al., 1998, 2004; Mundy & Neal, 2001). Specifically, disruptions in a number of brain systems, including the amygdala, dopaminergic reward systems, and other limbic areas that mediate the assignation of reward value to stimuli, may lead to disruptions in motivation for selectively attending to social stimuli. This early disruption in preferential attention might then interrupt developmentally iterative socialization processes by failing to direct or capture an infant's attention in early social interactions – interactions which are critical for the learning of social cognitive skills and language and communication skills.

A second theoretical model proposes that the primary deficit in early social attention and responsivity may derive from abnormalities in brain systems that serve to encode social information in ways that are directly relevant to the self. As Meltzoff and Moore (1995) have suggested, autism may involve a primary inability to understand other people as "like me." At the neurophysiological level, a number of authors have further suggested that this primary inability may be due to disruptions in cortical systems involving mirror neurons that respond to both the perceptions of others' actions as well as to the observer's own actions (e.g., Oberman & Ramachandran, 2007; Williams, Whiten, Suddendorf, & Perrett, 2001). Abnormalities in these supramodal neurons may derail the otherwise naturally perceived relations between self and others, thereby undermining the development and maintenance of the neural architecture involved in social cognition. Given this resultant disconnect between self and others, early abnormalities in cortical systems involving mirror neurons may initially be manifest as a lack of preferential responding to social stimuli, in that stimuli that are "not like me" are of less relative interest. Such mirror neuron abnormalities may also be directly manifest as deficits in imitation, and later as deficits in more sophisticated areas such as empathy and theory of mind (Oberman & Ramachandran, 2007).

These two theoretical formulations – the mirror neuron and social reward models of autism – are not necessarily incompatible. Each may ultimately provide equally valid but only partial explanation for the underlying neurophysiological causes of autism. Indeed, these theoretical models have a particular difficulty accounting for positive symptoms such as repetitive and stereotyped behaviors, as well as sensory processing abnormalities. Likewise, other theoretical models of autism that propose basic attentional deficits (e.g., Courchesne et al., 1994), disruptions in temporal binding (e.g., Brock, Brown, Boucher, & Rippon, 2002; Rippon, Brock, Brown, & Boucher, 2007), or local processing bias (e.g., Happé & Frith, 2006) have equal difficulty accounting for the specific social and language deficits of autism. As such, each account may only help to explain part of the complicated and heterogeneous picture of autism. Moreover, it is clear that autism is a heterogeneous condition and "single etiology" models are unlikely to apply to all children on the spectrum. Finally, although each of the many theoretical models for autism has begun to outline the neurophysiological underpinnings of autism, they still do not speak to the ultimate etiological agents – the genetic and/or environmental factors that initially cause such far-reaching neurological consequences and their corresponding behavioral difficulties.

Clinical implications

Research on the early development of autism suggests that clinical surveillance and screening for autism beginning around 12 months of age may be particularly useful (for a detailed discussion of infant assessment over and above specific disorders, see chapter 9 in this volume). Indeed, the success of research detailing the earliest behavioral signs of autism has recently encouraged the American Academy of Pediatrics to issue a policy statement regarding the process of early surveillance and screening (Johnson et al., 2007). Among the early behavioral signs that clinicians or pediatricians are counseled to look for are "lack of appropriate gaze," "lack of recognition of mother's voice," and "lack of warm, joyful expressions with gaze," – precisely the behaviors shown in the research literature reviewed above to be the most discriminating of autism by around the first birthday. Nevertheless, early clinical identification faces numerous obstacles.

Although numerous brief screening measures have been developed, such as the CHAT and M-CHAT (Baron-Cohen et al., 1992; Robins et al., 2001) and the ITC (Wetherby et al., 2004), the sensitivity of such measures may be low or even unknown in the population at large, and may need to be supplemented by additional observations or interviews – extra work that, however minimal, may be prohibitively time-consuming for a busy pediatrician to complete. Results of screening measures, when completed by parent report, may also be colored by parents' own biased perceptions, recall, and knowledge of typical and atypical development. This may be especially true when asking parents about the more subtle and early signs such as decreased eye contact and response to name. Early screening also must continuously occur throughout the first several years of development, given the wide heterogeneity in symptom onset patterns, including developmental regressions as late as 24 months of age. For children with such late onset patterns, early developmental signs may be nonexistent, or may be so subtle as to escape detection, especially with brief parent screening questionnaires.

Despite these various caveats to the early detection of autism, it is clear that research over the last 10–20 years has given us a relatively clear and consistent picture of the early behavioral signs of autism. A variety of methodologies have converged on a picture of autism as it emerges during the latter half of the first year, providing a useful starting place for clinical surveillance and screening, as well as early intervention. This descriptive research has also provided a place in which to anchor new hypotheses about the neurophysiological mechanisms underlying the early symptom development in autism, and the underlying genetic and environmental interactions that may ultimately allow for a measure of prevention.

References

Adrien, J. L., Faure, M., Perrot, A., Hameury, L., Garreau, B., Barthelemy, C., et al. (1991). Autism and family home movies: Preliminary findings. *Journal of Autism and Developmental Disorders, 21*, 43–49.

Adrien, J. L., Lenoir, P., Martineau, J., Perrot, A., Hameury, L., Larmande, C., et al. (1993). Blind ratings of early symptoms of autism based upon family home movies. *Journal of the American Academy of Child and Adolescent Psychiatry, 32*, 617–626.

American Psychiatric Association (2000). *Diagnostic and statistical manual of mental disorders* (4th ed., text rev.). Washington, DC: Author.

Bailey, A., Palferman, S., Heavey, L., & Le Couteur, A. (1998). Autism: The phenotype in relatives. *Journal of Autism and Developmental Disorders, 28*, 369–392.

Baranek, G. T. (1999). Autism during infancy: A retrospective video analysis of sensory-motor and social behaviors at 9–12 months of age. *Journal of Autism and Developmental Disorders, 29*, 213–224.

Baron-Cohen, S., Allen, J., & Gillberg, C. (1992). Can autism be detected at 18 months? The needle, the haystack, and the CHAT. *British Journal of Psychiatry, 161*, 839–843.

Bates, E., Camaioni, L., & Volterra, V. (1975). The acquisition of performative prior to speech. *Merrill-Palmer Quarterly, 21*, 205–226.

Bernabei, P., Camaioni, L., & Levi, G. (1998). An evaluation of early development in children with autism and pervasive developmental disorders from home movies: Preliminary findings. *Autism, 2*, 243–258.

Bernier, R., Webb, S. J., & Dawson, G. (2006). Understanding impairments in social engagement in autism. In P. J. Marshall & N. A. Fox (Eds.), *The development of social engagement: Neurobiological perspectives* (pp. 304–330). New York: Oxford University Press.

Bloom, P. (1998). Language acquisition in its developmental context. In D. Kuhn & R. S. Siegler (Eds.), *Handbook of child psychology: Cognition, perception, and language* (Vol. 2, 5th ed., pp. 309–370). New York: John Wiley & Sons.

Brock, J., Brown, C. C., Boucher, J., & Rippon, G. (2002). The temporal binding deficit hypothesis of autism. *Development and Psychopathology, 14*, 209–224.

Bryson, S. E., Clark, B. S., & Smith, I. (1988). First report of a Canadian epidemiological study of autistic syndromes. *Journal of Child Psychology and Psychiatry, 29*, 433–445.

Butterworth, G. (1991). The ontogeny and phylogeny of joint visual attention. In A. Whiten (Ed.), *Natural theories of mind: Evolution, development and simulation of everyday mindreading* (pp. 223–232). Cambridge: Basil Blackwell.

Camaioni, L. (2001). Early language. In G. Bremner & A. Fogel (Eds.), *The Blackwell handbook of infant development* (pp. 404–426). Oxford: Blackwell.

Centers for Disease Control and Prevention (2007). Prevalence of autism spectrum disorders – autism and developmental disabilities monitoring network, 14 sites, United States, 2002. Surveillance summaries (February 9). *Morbidity and Mortality Weekly Report, 56*, 12–28.

Cesaroni, L., & Garber, M. (1991). Exploring the experience of autism through firsthand accounts. *Journal of Autism and Developmental Disorders, 21*, 303–313.

Chakrabarti, S., & Fombonne, E. (2001). Pervasive developmental disorders in preschool children. *Journal of the American Medical Association, 285*, 3093–3099.

Charman, T., Swettenham, J., Baron-Cohen, S., Cox, A., Baird, G., & Drew, A. (1997). Infants with autism: An investigation of empathy, pretend play, joint attention, and imitation. *Developmental Psychology, 33*, 781–789.

Clancy, H., & McBride, G. (1969). The autistic process and its treatment. *Journal of Child Psychology and Psychiatry, 10,* 233–244.

Clifford, S., Young, R., & Williamson, P. (2006). Assessing the early characteristics of autistic disorder using video analysis. *Journal of Autism and Developmental Disorders, 37,* 301–313.

Colgan, S. E., Lanter, E., McComish, C., Watson, L. R., Crais, E. R., & Baranek, G. T. (2006). Analysis of social interaction gestures in infants with autism. *Child Neuropsychology, 12,* 307–319.

Courchesne, E., Townsend, J. P., Akshoomoff, N. A., Yeung-Courchesne, R., Press, G. A., Murakami, J. W., et al. (1994). A new finding: Impairment in shifting attention in autistic and cerebellar patients. In S. H. Broman, & J. Grafman (Eds.), *Atypical cognitive deficits in developmental disorders: Implications for brain function* (pp. 101–137). Hillsdale, NJ: Lawrence Erlbaum Associates.

Dahlgren, S. O., & Gillberg, C. (1989). Symptoms in the first two years of life. *European Archives of Psychiatry and Neurological Sciences, 238,* 169–174.

Dawson, G., Meltzoff, A. N., Osterling, J., Rinaldi, J., & Brown, E. (1998). Children with autism fail to orient to naturally occurring social stimuli. *Journal of Autism and Developmental Disorders, 28,* 479–485.

Dawson, G., Osterling, J., Meltzoff, A. N., & Kuhl, P. (2000). Case study of the development of an infant with autism from birth to two years of age. *Journal of Applied Developmental Psychology, 21,* 299–313.

Dawson, G., Toth, K., Abbott, R., Osterling, J., Munson, J., Estes, A., et al. (2004). Early social attention impairments in autism: Social orienting, joint attention, and attention to distress. *Developmental Psychology, 40,* 271–283.

De Giacomo, A., & Fombonne, E. (1998). Parental recognition of developmental abnormalities in autism. *European Child and Adolescent Psychiatry, 7,* 131–136.

Eriksson, A., & de Chateau, P. (1992). Brief report: A girl aged two years and seven months with autistic disorder videotaped from birth. *Journal of Autism and Developmental Disorders, 22,* 127–129.

Evans, D. W., Leckman, J. F., Carter, A., Reznick, J. S., Henshaw, D., King, R. A., et al. (1997). Ritual, habit, and perfectionism: The prevalence and development of compulsive-like behavior in normal young children. *Child Development, 68,* 58–68.

Fein, D., Dixon, P., Paul, J., & Levin, H. (2005). Brief report: Pervasive developmental disorder can evolve into ADHD: Case illustrations. *Journal of Autism and Developmental Disorders, 35,* 525–534.

Fein, D., Pennington, B., Markowitz, P., Braverman, M., & Waterhouse, L. (1986). Toward a neuropsychological model of infantile autism: Are the social deficits primary? *Journal of the American Academy of Child Psychiatry, 25,* 198–212.

Fombonne, E., & Chakrabarti, S. (2001). No evidence for a new variant of measles-mumps-rubella-induced autism. *Pediatrics, 108,* E58.

Grandin, T. (1992) An inside view of autism. In E. Schopler & G. B. Mesibov (Eds.), *High functioning individuals with autism* (pp. 105–125). New York: Plenum Press.

Green, G., Brennan, L. C., & Fein, D. (2002). Intensive behavioral treatment for a toddler at high risk for autism. *Behavior Modification, 26,* 69–102.

Happé, F., & Frith, U. (2006). The weak coherence account: Detail-focused cognitive style in autism. *Journal of Autism and Developmental Disorders, 36,* 5–25.

Hoshino, Y., Kaneko, M., Yashima, Y., Kumashiro, H., Volkmar, F. R., & Cohen, D. J. (1987). Clinical features of autistic children with setback course in their infancy. *Japanese Journal of Psychiatry and Neurology, 41,* 237–245.

Howlin, P. (2003). Outcome in high-functioning adults with autism with and without early language delays: Implications for the differentiation between autism and Asperger syndrome. *Journal of Autism and Developmental Disorders, 33,* 3–13.

Hutt, C., Hutt, S. J., Lee, D., & Ounsted, C. (1964). Arousal and childhood autism. *Nature, 204,* 908–909.

Johnson, C. P., Myers, S. M., & American Academy of Pediatrics Council on Children with Disabilities (2007). Identification and evaluation of children with autism spectrum disorders. *Pediatrics, 120,* 1183–1215.

Kanner, L. (1943). Autistic disturbances of affective contact. *Nervous Child, 2,* 217–250.

Kleinman, J. M., Ventola, P. E., Pandey, J., Verbalis, A. D., Barton, M., Hodgson, S., et al. (2008). Diagnostic stability in very young children with autism spectrum disorders. *Journal of Autism and Developmental Disorders, 38,* 606–615.

Klin, A., Chawarska, K., Paul, R., Rubin, E., Morgan, T., Wiesner, L., et al. (2004). Autism in a 15-month-old child. *American Journal of Psychiatry, 161,* 1981–1988.

Krentz, U. C., & Corina, D. P. (2008). Preference for language in early infancy: The human language bias is not speech specific. *Developmental Science, 11,* 1–9.

Landa, R., & Garrett-Mayer, E. (2006). Development in infants with autism spectrum disorders: A prospective study. *Journal of Child Psychology and Psychiatry, 47,* 629–638.

Landa, R. J., Holman, K. C., & Garrett-Mayer, E. (2007). Social and communication development in toddlers with early and later diagnosis of autism spectrum disorders. *Archives of General Psychiatry, 64,* 853–864.

Loh, A., Soman, T., Brian, J., Bryson, S. E., Roberts, W., Szatmari, P., et al. (2007). Stereotyped motor behaviors associated with autism in high-risk infants: A pilot videotape analysis of a sibling sample. *Journal of Autism and Developmental Disorders, 37,* 25–36.

Lord, C. (1995). Follow-up of two-year-olds referred for possible autism. *Journal of Child Psychology and Psychiatry, 36,* 1365–1382.

Lord, C., Shulman, C., & DiLavore, P. (2004). Regression and word loss in autistic spectrum disorders. *Journal of Child Psychology and Psychiatry, 45,* 936–955.

Lotter, V. (1966). Epidemiology of autistic conditions in young children. I. Prevalence. *Social Psychiatry, 1,* 124–137.

Lotter, V. (1974). Factors related to outcome in autistic children. *Journal of Autism and Developmental Disorders, 4,* 263–277.

Lovaas, O. I. (1987). Behavioral treatment and normal educational and intellectual functioning in young autistic children. *Journal of Consulting and Clinical Psychology, 55,* 3–9.

Maestro, S., Muratori, F., Cavallaro, M. C., Pei, F., Stern, D., Golse, B., et al. (2002). Attentional skills during the first 6 months of age in autism spectrum disorder. *Journal of the American Academy of Child and Adolescent Psychiatry, 41,* 1–7.

Mahone, E., Bridges, D., Prahme, C., & Singer, H. (2004). Repetitive arm and hand movements (complex motor stereotypies) in children. *Journal of Pediatrics, 145,* 391–395.

Mandell, D. S., Novak, M. M., & Zubritsky, C. D. (2005). Factors associated with age of diagnosis among children with autism spectrum disorders. *Pediatrics, 116,* 1480–1486.

Mars, A., Mauk, J. E., & Dowrick, P. W. (1998). Symptoms of pervasive developmental disorders as observed in prediagnostic home videos of infants and toddlers. *Journal of Pediatrics, 132,* 500–504.

Meltzoff, A., & Moore, M. K. (1995). Infants' understanding of people and things: From body imitation to folk psychology. In J. L. Bermúdez, A. Marcel, & N. Eilan (Eds.), *The body and the self* (pp. 43–69). Cambridge, MA: MIT Press.

Mitchell, S., Brian, J., Zwaigenbaum, L., Roberts, W., Szatmari, P., Smith, I., et al. (2006). Early language and communication development of infants later diagnosed with autism spectrum disorder. *Developmental and Behavioral Pediatrics, 27,* S69–S78.

Moore, V., & Goodson, S. (2003). How well does early diagnosis of autism stand the test of time? Follow-up study of children assessed for autism at age 2 and development of an early diagnostic service. *Autism, 7*, 47–63.

Mundy, P., & Neal, A. R. (2001). Neural plasticity, joint attention, and a transactional social-orienting model of autism. In L. M. Glidden (Ed.), *International review of research in mental retardation, Vol. 23: Autism* (pp. 139–168). New York: Academic Press.

Nadig, A. S., Ozonoff, S., Young, G. S., Rozga, A., Sigman, M., & Rogers, S. J. (2007). A prospective study of response to name in infants at risk for autism. *Archives of Pediatric Adolescent Medicine, 161*, 378–383.

Oberman, L. M., & Ramachandran, V. (2007). The simulating social mind: The role of the mirror neuron system and simulation in the social and communicative deficits of autism spectrum disorder. *Psychological Bulletin, 133*, 310–327.

Ornitz, E. M., Guthrie, D., & Farley, A. H. (1977). The early development of autistic children. *Journal of Autism and Childhood Schizophrenia, 7*, 207–229.

Osterling, J., & Dawson, G. (1994). Early recognition of children with autism: A study of first birthday home videotapes. *Journal of Autism and Developmental Disorders, 24*, 247–257.

Osterling, J. A., Dawson, G., & Munson, J. A. (2002). Early recognition of 1-year-old infants with autism spectrum disorder versus mental retardation. *Development and Psychopathology, 14*, 239–251.

Ozonoff, S., Macari, S., Young, G. S., Goldring, S., Thompson, M., & Rogers, S. J. (2008). Atypical object exploration at 12 months of age is associated with autism in a prospective sample. *Autism, 12*(5), 457–472.

Ozonoff, S., Williams, B. J., & Landa, R. (2005). Parental report of the early development of children with regressive autism: The delays-plus-regression phenotype. *Autism, 9*, 495–520.

Palomo, R., Belinchón, M., & Ozonoff, S. (2006). Autism and family home movies: A comprehensive review. *Developmental and Behavioral Pediatrics, 27*, S59–S68.

Perry, R., Cohen, I., & DeCarlo, R. (1995). Applied behavioral analysis: Astonishing results? *Journal of the American Academy of Child & Adolescent Psychiatry, 34*, 1256.

Piven, J., Harper, J., Palmer, P., & Arndt, S. (1996). Course of behavioral change in autism: A retrospective study of high-IQ adolescents and adults. *Journal of the American Academy of Child and Adolescent Psychiatry, 35*, 523–529.

Rippon, G., Brock, J., Brown, C., & Boucher, J. (2007). Disordered connectivity in the autistic brain: Challenges for the 'new psychophysiology.' *International Journal of Psychophysiology, 63*, 164–172.

Robins, D. L., Fein, D., Barton, M. L., & Green, J. A. (2001). The modified checklist for autism in toddlers: An initial study investigating the early detection of autism and pervasive developmental disorders. *Journal of Autism and Developmental Disorders, 31*, 131–144.

Rutter, M. (1983). Cognitive deficits in the pathogenesis of autism. *Journal of Child Psychology and Psychiatry, 24*, 513–531.

Scaife, M., & Bruner, J. S. (1975). The capacity for joint visual attention in the infant. *Nature, 253*, 265–266.

Shaked, M., & Yirmiya, N. (2004). Matching procedures in autism research: Evidence from meta-analytic studies. *Journal of Autism and Developmental Disorders, 34*, 35–40.

Sigman, M., & McGovern, C. W. (2005). Improvement in cognitive and language skills from preschool to adolescence in autism. *Journal of Autism and Developmental Disorders, 35*, 15–23.

Simion, F., Regolin, L., & Bulf, H. (2008). A predisposition for biological motion in the newborn baby. *Proceedings of the National Academy of Sciences, 105*, 809–813.

Siperstein, R., & Volkmar, F. (2004). Brief report: Parental reporting of regression in children with pervasive developmental disorders. *Journal of Autism and Developmental Disorders, 34*, 731–734.

Stone, W. L., Lee, E. B., Ashford, L., Brissie, J., Hepburn, S. L., Coonrod, E. E., et al. (1999). Can autism be diagnosed accurately in children under 3 years? *Journal of Child Psychology and Psychiatry, 40*, 219–226.

Sullivan, M., Finelli, J., Marvin, A., Garrett-Mayer, E., Bauman, M., & Landa, R. (2007). Response to joint attention in toddlers at risk for autism spectrum disorder: A prospective study. *Journal of Autism and Developmental Disorders, 37*, 37–48.

Swettenham, J., Baron-Cohen, S., Charman, T., Cox, A., Baird, G., Drew, A., et al. (1998). The frequency and distribution of spontaneous attention shifts between social and nonsocial stimuli in autistic, typically developing, and nonautistic developmentally delayed infants. *Journal of Child Psychology and Psychiatry, 39*, 747–753.

Tan, A., Salgado, M., & Fahn, S. (1997). The characterization and outcome of stereotypic movements in nonautistic children. *Movement Disorders, 12*, 47–52.

Tantam, D. (1992). Characterizing the fundamental social handicap in autism. *Acta Paedopsychiatrica, 55*, 83–91.

Thelen, E. (1979). Rhythmical stereotypies in normal human infants. *Animal Behavior, 27*, 699–715.

Tronick, E., Als, H., Adamson, L., Wise, S., & Brazelton, B. (1978). The infant's response to entrapment between contradictory messages in face-to-face interaction. *Pediatrics, 62*, 403.

Turati, C., Simion, F., Milani, I., & Umiltà, C. (2002). Newborns' preference for faces: What is crucial? *Developmental Psychology, 38*, 875–882.

Turner, M. (1999). Annotation: Repetitive behavior in autism: A review of psychological research. *Journal of Child Psychology and Psychiatry, 40*, 839–849.

Valenza, E., Simion, F., Cassia, V. M., & Umiltà, C. (1996). Face preference at birth. *Journal of Experimental Psychology, Human Perception and Performance, 22*, 892–903.

Vouloumanos, A., & Werker, J. F. (2007). Listening to language at birth: Evidence for a bias for speech in neonates. *Developmental Science, 10*, 159–164.

Walden, T. A., & Ogan, T. A. (1988). The development of social referencing. *Child Development, 59*(5), 1230–1240.

Watson, L. R., Baranek, G. T., Crais, E. R., Reznick, J. S., Dykstra, J., & Perryman, T. (2007). The first year inventory: Retrospective parent responses to a questionnaire designed to identify one-year-olds at risk for autism. *Journal of Autism and Developmental Disorders, 37*, 49–61.

Watt, N., Wetherby, A. M., Barber, A., & Morgan, L. (2008). Repetitive and stereotyped behaviors in children with autism spectrum disorders in the second year of life. *Journal of Autism and Developmental Disorders, 38*(8), 1518–1533.

Wellman, H. M., Lopez-Duran, S., LaBounty, J., & Hamilton, B. (2008). Infant attention to intentional action predicts preschool theory of mind. *Developmental Psychology, 44*, 618–623.

Wellman, H. M., Phillips, A. T., Dunphy-Lelii, S., & LaLonde, N. (2004). Infant social attention predicts preschool social cognition. *Developmental Science, 7*, 283–288.

Werner, E., & Dawson, G. (2005). Validation of the phenomenon of autistic regression using home videotapes. *Archives of General Psychiatry, 62*, 889–895.

Werner, E., Dawson, G., Munson, J., & Osterling, J. (2005). Variation in early developmental course in autism and its relation with behavioral outcome at 3–4 years of age. *Journal of Autism and Developmental Disorders, 35*, 337–350.

Werner, E., Dawson, G., Osterling, J., & Dinno, N. (2000). Brief report: Recognition of autism spectrum disorder before one year of age: A retrospective study based on home videotapes. *Journal of Autism and Developmental Disorders, 30*, 157–162.

Wetherby, A. M., Watt, N., Morgan, L., & Shumway, S. (2007). Social communication profiles of children with autism spectrum disorders late in the second year of life. *Journal of Autism and Developmental Disorders, 37*, 960–975.

Wetherby, A. M., Woods, J., Allen, L., Cleary, J., Dickinson, H., & Lord, C. (2004). Early indicators of autism spectrum disorders in the second year of life. *Journal of Autism and Developmental Disorders, 34*, 473–493.

Williams, J. H. G., Whiten, A., Suddendorf, T., & Perrett, D. I. (2001). Imitation, mirror neurons and autism. *Neuroscience & Biobehavioral Reviews, 25*, 287–295.

Wimpory, D. C., Hobson, R. P., Williams, J. M. G., & Nash, S. (2000). Are infants with autism socially engaged? A study of recent retrospective parental reports. *Journal of Autism and Developmental Disorders, 30*, 525–536.

Witherington, D. C., & Crichton, J. A. (2007). Frameworks for understanding emotions and their development: Functionalist and dynamic systems approaches. *Emotion, 7*, 628–637.

Zwaigenbaum, L., Bryson, S., Rogers, T., Roberts, W., Brian, J., & Szatmari, P. (2005). Behavioral manifestations of autism in the first year of life. *International Journal of Developmental Neuroscience, 23*, 143–152.

11

Infant Psychosocial Disorders

Melissa R. Johnson and Karen Appleyard

Introduction

Many infant mental health practitioners have the experience of being asked by puzzled acquaintances, and sometimes even mental health colleagues, how a baby can have emotional problems. This question can best be answered through case example.

Joseph is a former 30-week premature infant whose parents sought help when he was 9 months old. Though his homecoming was much longed for, his parents found life with their infant to be increasingly stressful, with slow feeding, frequent wakening, long fussy periods, and extreme dislike of bathing and other routine care. His exhausted parents reported that he did not smile much, and they were not sure how to play with him. His mother acknowledged that she cried frequently and that it was hard to enjoy Joseph. They worried that he seemed unhappy and delayed. Evaluation and intervention included support and validation of the ordeal that this couple had experienced, education about development in preterm infants, supporting the mother to seek treatment for her postpartum mood disorder, helping the parents respect Joseph's sensory sensitivities, and supporting joyful dyadic interactions. The psychologist noted that Joseph and his mother both started appearing happier at the same time.

As this case example illustrates, infant psychosocial challenges are complex and multifaceted, affecting and affected by child, caregiver, and relationship functioning. The concept that infants and toddlers undergo rapid and critical development in their social and emotional functioning, equal in importance to their motor, intellectual, and language functioning, has roots in the turmoil of emerging early twentieth-century psychological thought. As far back as 1936, D. W. Winnicott said, "The child is also like the adult in being concerned with an outer and an inner world, with the appreciation of the outer by virtue of the richness of the inner, and the modification of the inner by experience of the outer" (1936, p. 74). Winnicott and his fellow pioneers in the fields of infant mental health, attachment, and early social learning (Ainsworth, Blehar, Waters, & Wall, 1978; Bowlby, 1982; Karen, 1994) started a process that continues to the present day, seeking to understand how these "outer and inner worlds" interact in healthy as well as in problematic ways.

A newborn human, at once competent and completely dependent, needs to learn to live in the interpersonal world of his or her family and broader community, while at the same time the family is getting to know this new individual. Considering how complex and delicate it is, it is not surprising that the process may go awry. Disruptions in this process, necessarily involving the child, the parent, and the interaction between the two, often result in the kinds of infant psychosocial disorders to be discussed in this chapter.

The infant psychosocial disorders of interest in this chapter are also defined by what they are not. They are considered separately from disruptions and delays that are primarily the result of neurophysiologic causes, such as genetically based cognitive disability and autism spectrum disorders (for discussion of these neurodevelopmental disorders, see chapters 12 and 10 in this volume, respectively). Visual, auditory, and motor impairments may affect social-emotional development as well, but these impairments are discussed in a separate chapter (chapter 4 in this volume). Psychosocial disorders also are somewhat arbitrarily distinguished from common, mild challenges of infancy such as difficult temperament, transient sleep disruptions and fussy periods, experienced by large numbers of otherwise well-developing children (see chapter 20 in volume 1). Discussion of assessment issues involving social-emotional disorders are discussed in chapter 9 in this volume.

We approach our discussion of infant psychosocial disorders using the developmental psychopathology framework, examining individual patterns of adaptation and maladaptation (disorder) as they relate to the salient developmental tasks of infancy, and the transactional nature of development – that is, the inherent linkage among previous adaptation, current environmental factors, biologic factors, and current function (Cicchetti & Toth, 1997; Sroufe, 1997). This framework also has the advantage of supporting intervention strategies that incorporate family, developmental, and social-emotional challenges in a transactional framework (Sameroff & Fiese, 2000). Approaching this discussion from the perspectives of the goals and tasks of the first two years of life helps focus on developmental progress, rather than pathology.

Psychosocial Tasks of Infancy and Toddlerhood

There have been many efforts to define the psychosocial tasks that infants and toddlers need to accomplish to develop into well-functioning children and adults. Although a comprehensive overview of all aspects and theories of infant social-emotional development is far beyond the scope of this chapter, seven core competencies that emerge repeatedly are highlighted and summarized in Table 11.1 (see also chapters 9, 16, 19, and 20 in volume 1). These tasks have been selected because of their key role in determining healthy psychosocial development in infants and toddlers and building the foundation for future emotional development.

Table 11.1 Psychosocial tasks of infancy and toddlerhood.

Task	Description	References
Relationship formation and development of attachment	Forming trusting, reliable, joyful relationship with primary caregivers. Starts in first 2 months, continues through toddler years	Cassidy & Shaver, 1999; Luby & Belden, 2006
Signaling needs	Increasingly differentiated responses to distress, indicating needs to caregivers	Carey & McDevitt, 1995
Developing range of affect	Capacity for widening range of emotions; ability to share, to detect signals from others, and to manage/regulate intensity	Emde, 1998; Greenspan, 1992; Wieder & Greenspan, 2006; Cole, Martin, & Dennis, 2004
Developing capacity to self-regulate biological needs	Feeding, sleeping, and elimination become organized and under increasing control, biological, cultural, and developmental factors influence process	Ferber, 2006; Kessler & Dawson, 1999; Marshall & Fox, 2006; Shonkoff & Phillips, 2000; Cozolino, 2006
Developing strategies for handling separation	Requires unique relationship with individual caregivers, understanding of presence/absence, ongoing maturation of attachment	Ainsworth et al., 1978; Greenspan & Brazelton, 2000; Sameroff & Emde, 1989; Sroufe, Egeland, Carlson, & Collins, 2005
Exploring the environment, tolerating frustration, and delaying gratification	Tasks highly dependent on development of a secure base, influenced by temperament. Problems with these tasks often relate to clinical concerns in toddlers	Smith, Calkins, & Keane, 2006; Lieberman, 1993; Brazelton, 1974; Denham, 1998; Fox & Calkins, 2003
Developing capacity for social interaction with peers	Capability to interact with other children (siblings/peers) and to engage in imaginative/social play	Brownell & Kopp, 2007; Linder, 1993

Environmental Challenges to Successful Mastery of Social-Emotional Tasks

The tasks summarized in Table 11.1, along with the increasing ability to follow rules and routines, are the hallmarks of a successful transition out of the toddler period into the preschool period. The question of why some children struggle to master these tasks is immensely complex. Since development and learning occur in the context of many environmental and relationship factors (Greenspan & Porges, 1984; Sroufe, 1997), it is apparent that any attempt to pull out separate "risk factors" from the infant's environment will involve oversimplification. Yet, some variables are so important as markers of risk, or as influencing factors, that they need to be discussed individually. In addition to the importance of understanding their impact on the infant, they also may help identify children and families in need of help, and may lead to strategies for prevention and intervention.

Prenatal factors

The impact of prenatal factors on many aspects of infant development, including health, growth, learning and social-emotional functioning, has been the subject of much study and debate for the last several decades (see chapter 1 in this volume). The continued evolution of this field highlights the difficulty of identifying single factors that reliably predict or affect outcomes in young children. Prenatal exposure of the fetus to alcohol is a known developmental risk factor (see chapter 3 in this volume), and fetal exposure to nicotine, other drugs and environmental chemicals also appears to have an impact on the developing brain and early behavior (Mayes & Ward, 2003; Wakschlag, Leventhal, Pine, Pickett, & Carter, 2006). However, recent research also indicates that the effects of prenatal exposure to drugs of abuse are more subtle and more intertwined with other risk variables than originally thought (Messinger et al., 2004). Further, psychosocially mediated stresses in the intrauterine environment may also impact infant behavior after birth. For example, recent findings indicate that after controlling for maternal and postnatal factors, stress and mood disturbance in pregnant women have negative effects on the sleep patterns of their infants as far out as 30 months (O'Connor et al., 2007; see also chapter 20 in volume 1).

Maternal depression and other parental mental illness

There is much evidence that maternal depression and other parental mental health disorders have major effects on infant psychosocial development (see chapter 8 in this volume), not only through genetic factors but also through perturbations of maternal–infant interaction, reduction in environmental responsivity to the child's needs, and maternal difficulty in assisting the infant in developing self-regulatory strategies (Hendrick & Daly, 2000; Morrell & Murray, 2003). Striking evidence exists that infants as young as 3 months detect and respond differentially to depressed or otherwise psychiatrically disordered mothers, in ways that influence not only the infants' emotional regulation and mood but also how the infants respond to other adults (Weinberg & Tronick, 1998). Furthermore, a longitudinal study found that parental depression appears to present a greater challenge to early childhood psychosocial development than schizophrenia (Sameroff & Seifer, 1990).

Parental social challenges

A number of intersecting and overlapping social factors demonstrate significant associations with infant psychosocial functioning. Prominent among these are: lack of social support, or social isolation; poverty; adolescent parenting; domestic violence; and exposure to disasters.

Social support from natural family and community sources, and adequacy of social networks, acts as a buffer against stress and as a promotive factor improving health and function in a variety of populations, including adolescent parents, single parents, parents in poverty, and other groups (Cochran & Niego, 1995; Logsdon, Birkimer, Ratterman, Cahill, & Cahill, 2002). Effects of social support have been found in relation to many outcomes, including parent–infant relationships, quality of the home environment and/ or parenting, and risk of maltreatment reports (Cochran & Niego, 1995; Corse, Schmid, & Trickett, 1990; Kotch, Browne, Dufort, & Winsor, 1999). These effects may be mediated by other processes, such as maternal attachment style (Green, Furrer, & McAllister, 2007), or moderated by individual characteristics such as neonatal irritability (Crockenberg, 1981). Subsequent research has also shown how social support directly provided to young children (from father figures, grandparents, etc.) relates to fewer internalizing and externalizing problems in later childhood (Appleyard, Egeland, & Sroufe, 2007).

Poverty is a related, though distinct, influence on early psychosocial development. Poverty impacts infants and young children through mediators that include increased stress around safety, health, nutrition, education, adequate housing, relationship stability, and childcare quality, that can affect parental adequacy and the child, both directly and indirectly (Aber, Jones, & Cohen, 2000). Clearly, many infants raised in poverty are successful in their psychosocial development. The study of social, interactional, temperamental, and genetic determinants of resilience in the face of these challenges, while beyond the scope of this chapter, is particularly important in the situation of poverty, because of the large numbers of children living in poverty (Bleiberg, 2002; Kim-Cohen, Moffitt, Caspi, & Taylor, 2004; see also chapters 5 and 6 in this volume).

Adolescent parenthood may impact infant psychosocial development in many ways: increased obstetric risks, the tendency of teens to focus on their own needs rather than those of another, the effect on economic and educational opportunities for the young mother, and the lower likelihood of a stable, long-term relationship with the father of the baby (Coley & Chase-Lansdale, 1998; Committee on Adolescence and Committee on Early Childhood and Adoption and Dependent Care, 2001). There is evidence that many of the maternal behaviors thought to facilitate success at the developmental tasks described above, such as talking, touching, and smiling at the baby, as well as realistic developmental expectations and supportive parenting practices, are less likely to be present in very young parents, though social support and better psychosocial function in the parent moderate these risks (East & Felice, 1996).

Domestic violence, typically abuse of the mother by a male partner, has recently received more attention in regard to its significant influence on the social-emotional development of children. Domestic violence has many negative effects on infants and toddlers (Osofsky, 1995), both directly and indirectly by damaging their mother's ability to parent. For example, domestic violence subjects infants to bewildering and frightening images, and can impair the infant's ability to develop a sense of security, safety, and positive, trusting relationships (Cunningham & Baker, 2007).

Another risk factor with potential adverse impacts on development of infants and toddlers is exposure to natural and man-made community disasters. The effects of disasters such as hurricane Katrina on young children and on their caregivers, may impact many dimensions of infant function both acutely and chronically (Osofsky & Osofsky, 2007; Zero to Three DC:0–3R Training Task Force, 2005).

Severe deprivation and maltreatment

The most significant risks for young children, maltreatment and global deprivation, disrupt psychobiological, cognitive, and especially socioemotional development (Cicchetti, 2003; Kaufman & Henrich, 2000). The most extreme and profound privation found primarily in institutional care settings in economically struggling countries has received recent attention as institutionalized children have been adopted by families in developed countries, primarily the United States and United Kingdom. Studies of children adopted before 42 months, after being in institutional care from birth (Rutter et al., 2001), and more recent comparisons of institutional and local foster care in 21–31-month-olds (Zeanah et al., 2005), yield complex results showing severe and long-lasting emotional effects in some young children and surprising resilience in others. A key finding of both studies is that the longer children remain in institutional settings, the lower is the likelihood of emotional and cognitive recovery. The variability in outcome for even very young infants and toddlers raises ethical, policy, and clinical questions that have yet to be resolved (Gunnar & Pollak, 2007).

Parental maltreatment, in the forms of physical or emotional abuse and failure to meet basic needs, has been a focus of infant mental health study for many years (Greenspan, Wieder, Nover, Lieberman, Lourie, & Robinson, 1987; see also chapter 7 in this volume). Clinicians and researchers have identified effects on the early attachment functioning of abused and neglected young children. In many cases abuse and neglect leads to devastating long-term consequences to emotional development (Toth & Cicchetti, 2004), especially in the absence of protective family and community factors (Dicker, Gordon, & Knitzer, 2001). For example, attachment disorders can be found in close to half of a sample of maltreated toddlers in foster care, and the mental health status of the biological mother is an important variable increasing the child's risk for this disorder (Zeanah, Scheeringa, Boris, Heller, Smyke, & Trapani, 2004).

In summary, the risk factors discussed above impair the accomplishment of salient developmental tasks, and thus may lead to the development of clinically significant psychosocial disorders.

Classifying Infant Psychosocial Disorders

Systems of classification for mental health dysfunction in early childhood are still emerging. Over the last decade and a half, an interdisciplinary and international collaboration of early childhood mental health professionals developed and revised a classification system, the Diagnostic Classification of Mental Health and Developmental Disorders in Infancy and Early Childhood (DC:0–3R; Lieberman, Wieder, & Fenichel, 1997; Zero to Three, 1994, 2005). The DC:0–3R draws upon the strengths of existing diagnostic classification systems, including multiaxial assessment and clinically and empirically based diagnostic criteria, and complements them with developmentally appropriate criteria for infants and toddlers as well as assessment of caregiving relationships and socioemotional functioning (Zero to Three, 1994, 2005). The system consists of five axes: three focusing on classification of key disorders and two addressing the assessment of individuals within contexts of development. The DC:0–3R is intended to complement, but not to replace, other classification systems, and a number of issues typically first diagnosed in infancy but not covered within the system still warrant assessment and treatment (e.g., pica, rumination disorder, obsessive-compulsive disorder, early disruptive behavior disorders) (Zero to Three, 2005). While the DC:0–3R and its predecessor have limitations, including the use of presumed causal factors as diagnostic labels as well as limited information on psychometric properties (Dunst, Storck, & Snyder, 2006), it nonetheless provides a very useful structure to consider these complex phenomena.

We will organize our discussion using the DC:0–3R system (complemented by other systems where applicable), divided into three key sections: affective and relationship disorders (anxiety disorders, depression, attachment disorders); aggressive and oppositional disorders; and regulatory disorders (focusing on feeding and sleep disorders and irritability; see also chapters 2 and 9 in this volume). Although, from a developmental psychopathology perspective, other disorders may be relevant and emerging in infancy and toddlerhood, such as attention deficit hyperactivity disorder, they are typically not diagnosed until after age 3, and thus will not be addressed in detail.

Relationship issues in diagnosis

Since infant–parent relationships are central to infant functioning, assessment of these relationships holds a primary role in the diagnostic process (Zeanah, Larrieu, Heller, & Valliere, 2000). Recommendations for infant–parent relationship assessment include aspects of parents' own experiences and internal representations of relationships as well as observed infant and parent behaviors during unstructured and structured interactions (Wieder & Greenspan, 2006; Zeanah et al., 2000). Several semi-structured interviews and observational techniques are available which demonstrate clinical utility and predictive validity; for detailed examples, see Zeanah et al. (2000) and chapter 9 in this volume. Within the DC:0–3R multiaxial system, following a review of infant and parent representations and behaviors, clinicians summarize the quality of relationship adaptation or disorder on Axis II, using the Parent–Infant Relationship Global Assessment Scale (PIR-

GAS; Zero to Three, 2005), a 100-point scale summarizing level of distress and impact on the child's functioning. The PIR-GAS relates to duration and intensity of problems in infants (von Hofacker & Papoušek, 1998) and significantly predicts later symptomatology (Aoki, Zeanah, Heller, & Bakshi, 2002).

Affective and relationship disorders

Anxiety disorders. We will primarily review the key diagnosis currently being researched, post-traumatic stress disorder (PTSD), and then discuss other anxiety disorders diagnosed in early childhood.

Post-traumatic stress disorder. PTSD reflects a set of symptoms experienced following exposure to a stressful or traumatic event or series of events (e.g., harm or injury to child or significant others, natural disaster, automobile accident, shooting, dog bite, ongoing maltreatment). Recent attention to PTSD in young children reflects an increased awareness of young children's exposure to and behavioral and emotional responses to traumatic events (Osofsky, 1995). Community and epidemiologic studies, however, of children under 24 months are lacking and many studies include mixed early childhood or only preschool samples – among them Lavigne et al. (1996) who demonstrated a relatively low prevalence of PTSD (0.1%). It is assumed that rates with infants and toddlers will be similarly low, due to developmental issues not taken into account in many classification systems.

According to the Diagnostic and Statistical Manual of Mental Disorders (DSM-IV-TR; American Psychiatric Association (APA), 2000), individuals with PTSD experience three types of symptoms: persistent re-experiencing of the traumatic event; avoidance of stimuli associated with the trauma; and increased arousal. Scheeringa and colleagues have recently conducted systematic studies of a set of developmentally appropriate alternative criteria for PTSD for infants, toddlers, and preschool children. These alternative criteria rely less on verbalization of subjective experiences, include behaviorally specific language relevant to young children (e.g., extreme tantrums, fussiness), add new criteria specific to young children (e.g., loss of developmental skills, new separation anxiety, new fears, new onset of aggression), and have a lower threshold of symptoms required for diagnosis. Studies with the revised criteria with mixed age samples (i.e., including infants, toddlers, and preschoolers) have demonstrated procedural, criterion, discriminant, and predictive validity (Scheeringa, Peebles, Cook, & Zeanah, 2001; Scheeringa, Zeanah, Myers, & Putnam, 2003, 2005). Further studies specifically with infant and toddler samples are needed.

For young children experiencing trauma, it is particularly important to emphasize the relational nature of trauma in early childhood. In early childhood, the parent–child attachment relationship plays a critical role in managing and regulating stress and stress hormones (cortisol), particularly for children who are behaviorally inhibited or prone to distress (Nachmias, Gunnar, Mangelsdorf, Parritz, & Buss, 1996). Parents' responses to trauma can negatively impact their own functioning, their ability to parent effectively, and their ability to be sensitive to their children's needs (Appleyard & Osofsky, 2003; Scheeringa & Zeanah, 2001).

The long-term influence of trauma on young children's socioemotional adjustment and relationship functioning is becoming clear. Despite conventional or common ideas that children may "forget" or "get over" such early experiences, both research and clinical literature document that PTSD symptoms from infancy and toddlerhood persist over time (Scheeringa et al., 2005) and may recur with subsequent reminders or later experiences of trauma (Kaplow, Saxe, Putnam, Pynoos, & Lieberman, 2006). Early efficacious treatment of PTSD in young children is imperative.

Other anxiety disorders diagnosed in infancy and early childhood. Anxiety in early childhood appears along a continuum from normal and developmentally appropriate anxiety (such as fear of strangers, developing between 7–12 months), to behaviorally inhibited temperament, to behaviors consistent with an anxiety disorder. Thus, identifying anxiety disorders in early childhood requires careful assessment and consideration of normal versus atypical development (Zero to Three, 2005).

The DC:0–3R system specifies four anxiety disorders that are reliable and appropriate for use with children ages 2 and older: separation anxiety disorder, specific phobia, social anxiety disorder (social phobia), and generalized anxiety disorder. The DC:0–3R recommends the use of "anxiety disorder not otherwise specified" (NOS) for anxiety that impairs functioning for children under 2. General criteria for diagnosis include persistent, pervasive, and uncontrollable anxiety that impairs functioning. Separation anxiety disorder involves developmentally inappropriate and excessive anxiety regarding separation from home or from significant caregivers or attachment figures. Specific phobia diagnosis involves a specific object or situation that elicits excessive fear or panic, and which the child (and parents) may avoid. Social anxiety disorder is characterized by strong and persistent fears of one or more social settings or situations with both children and adults (e.g., play dates, family gatherings, "circle time"), which the child and parent then avoid. Generalized anxiety disorder is marked by excessive anxiety and worry for an extended period (i.e., 6 months; Zero to Three, 2005).

Epidemiologic studies of anxiety disorders, specifically, in young children are limited. Keren, Feldman, and Tyano's (2001) study of a sample of infants referred to a community clinic reported that 7% were diagnosed with an affective disorder using the DC:0–3 system (which includes anxiety disorders along with depression, prolonged bereavement/grief reaction, and mixed disorder of emotional expressiveness). The epidemiologic study by Skovgaard et al. (2007) of 1½-year-olds estimated 2.8% of children as having DC0:3 affective disorders. Further research will be needed in this area for a comprehensive understanding of the diagnostic and treatment needs of anxiety disorders in young children.

Depression. The systematic study of depression in early childhood is a relatively recent development, though such disorders have long been discussed in the clinical literature. Psychoanalytic writings about "anaclitic depression" (Spitz, 1946) described infants in institutional settings and their striking emotional and developmental responses following temporary separation from or permanent loss of the primary caregiver (e.g., prolonged sadness and crying, lethargy, avoidance of eye contact, lack of response to alternative caregivers, loss of developmental skills). Spitz (1946) suggested that if the caregiver returned within 3 months, the infant could recuperate and regain functioning, but separations lasting longer than 3 months left permanent difficulties. Some case examples later, however, indicated that children with other supports in place (i.e., additional consistent, nurturing relationships) following the separation could be buffered from such permanent difficulty (Harmon, Wagonfeld, & Emde, 1982).

Despite these early clinical reports of significant depressed and withdrawn affect in young children, there was relatively little clinical research. Historically, the idea that prepubertal children could be diagnosed with depression was questioned on the assumption that they lack the cognitive and emotional maturity to experience the core symptoms associated with the disorder (for a review, see Luby, 2000; Luby, Heffelfinger, et al., 2003). Significant contributions from developmental research, however, have enriched our understanding of early affect expression and emotion regulation development (Denham, 1998; Lieberman, 1993). Moreover, research in the developmental psychopathology field illuminated the maladaptive course of emotional development in infants at high risk for affective disorders due to maternal depression (Field, 1992; see also chapter 8 in this volume).

Building upon the clinical literature and developmental research, recent efforts aim to clarify the nature and course of depressive disorders in early childhood. Zero to Three's (1994, 2005) classification system outlined criteria for the disorder, but has not yet tested their validity. Luby and colleagues, however, have modified and validated the current DSM-IV criteria for major depressive disorder (MDD) for preschool children by using developmental translations of depressive symptoms (e.g., behavioral changes in "activities and play" rather than "work or school"), modifying the assessment of preoccupation with death or suicidality through observation of persistent play themes, and eliminating the requirement of a 2-week duration of symptoms (Luby et al., 2002; Luby, Heffelfinger, et al., 2003; Luby, Mrakotsky, Heffelfinger, Brown, Hessler, & Spitznagel, 2003). These modifications would likely be relevant to infants and toddlers, but evidence for children under 24 months is not yet available.

Since this area of research is relatively new, prevalence studies are limited. As reported earlier, DC:0–3 affective disorders (which include depression as well as prolonged bereavement/grief reaction, anxiety disorders, and mixed disorder of emotional expressiveness) have been reported in infants at rates of 7% in clinic-referred infants (Keren et al., 2001) and 2.8% in an epidemiologic study of 1½-year-old children (Skovgaard et al., 2007). Clearly more research is needed on the specific symptom constellation and severity associated with depression in infants and toddlers.

Attachment disorders. The formation of attachment relationships is a key developmental process in early childhood (see chapter 16 in volume 1). Clinical interest in disordered or disturbed attachments stemmed from work with children experiencing extreme situations, such as privation and maltreatment (Aber & Allen, 1987; Spitz, 1946; see also chapter 7 in this volume). Formal classification of such disorders has been developed, describing disturbed social behavior in early childhood, evident across contexts, with etiological links to pathogenic care (APA, 2000; World Health Organization, 2004). The current criteria have been criticized for a number of reasons, including their limited utility (i.e., lack of operationalization of terms, failure to consider variability in functioning across relationships), lack of data supporting the criteria, and failure to consider relevant attachment and developmental research (see Stafford, Zeanah, & Scheeringa, 2003; Zeanah, 1996). Ultimately, the current diagnoses describe disorders resulting from a *failure to form an attachment*, rather than a *disturbed attachment relationship per se* (Zeanah & Boris, 2000).

The DC:0–3 classified a similar behavioral pattern under the category of *reactive attachment/maltreatment/deprivation disorder*, although DC:0–3R removed the term "*reactive* attachment" (Zero to Three, 1994, 2005). This system provides behavioral criteria for young children, and delineates descriptors of relationship problems under Axis II Relationship Disturbance (e.g., overinvolved, underinvolved, anxious/tense, angry/hostile), which may tap disturbed attachment relationships (versus lack of attachment). The criteria do not, however, define particular disorders of attachment.

To remedy these limitations and to validate these disorders in early childhood, Zeanah and colleagues developed a set of alternative criteria for classification of attachment disorders (Zeanah & Boris, 2000). This revised set of criteria includes a classification that follows current nosology (i.e., disorders of nonattachment), as well as classifications for extreme difficulties within specific attachment relationships (i.e., secure base distortions) and for behaviors following the loss of an attachment figure (i.e., disrupted attachment disorder). *Disorders of nonattachment* comprise two patterns in which no preferred attachment figure is identified: (1) nonattachment with emotional withdrawal (e.g., restricted comfort seeking or help seeking, poor emotional expression and self-regulation); and (2) nonattachment with indiscriminate sociability (e.g., seeking comfort or help from anyone, with little developmentally appropriate wariness of strangers).

Secure base disorders describe disturbed patterns of relating within selected attachment relationships. Such patterns appear to be relationship-specific, rather than generalized behaviors across social relationships (Zeanah & Boris, 2000). Four types of these distortions are being explored, including: *attachment disorder with self-endangerment* (i.e., exploring or engaging in dangerous activities without checking in with caregiver for protection and guidance), *attachment disorder with clinging/inhibited exploration* (i.e., extreme difficulties separating from caregiver), *attachment disorder with vigilance/hypercompliance* (i.e., vigilant and watchful of caregiver or hypercompliant with caregiver), and *attachment disorder with role reversal* (i.e., preoccupied with the parent's emotional and physical needs or controlling the caregiver's behaviors). Finally, Zeanah and colleagues describe *disrupted attachment disorder* as the behaviors of young children who experience the sudden loss of an attachment figure. The classic descriptions by Robertson and Robertson (1989) of children separated from their caregivers epitomize this disorder. Thus far, systematic studies to determine diagnostic validity and reliability as well as epidemiological data (e.g., prevalence, course of disorder) for attachment disorders are limited and require further study.

Aggressive and oppositional disorders

There is limited information regarding diagnosable aggressive and oppositional disorders in children under 2, but the evidence for their occurrence in children ages 2½ and older (Keenan & Wakschlag, 2000) indicates the importance of discussing early manifestations of these problems. Over a two-thirds of a century ago, Goodenough's (1931) detailed observational study of young children found that anger peaks in the second year of life. Given that one of the tasks of toddlerhood is the development of self-assertion, it is important to distinguish this normative task from clinical problems. A laboratory study of 23–26-month-old children found that defiance and self-assertion were distinct dimensions, and that negative maternal control related to more defiance (Crockenberg & Litman, 1990).

Longitudinal studies examining the course, stability, and predictors of aggression indicate that although most young children's aggression decreases over time (see review in Shaw, Gilliom, & Giovannelli, 2000), a number of factors in infancy may herald a pathway of continued disruptive behavior problems. In a longitudinal study of physical aggression in children followed from 5 through 42 months of age, 14% of the children were identified as early as 17 months as demonstrating high levels of physical aggression, best predicted by coercive maternal behavior and family dysfunction (Tremblay et al., 2004). Longitudinal evidence also demonstrates that infant temperament (specifically, unmanageability) is a precursor of later oppositional disorders (Rothbart & Bates, 2006). Other longitudinal studies have identified multiple early predictors of aggressive behavior over time, including infant temperament (e.g., negative emotionality, attention seeking, low frustration tolerance), parent characteristics and environmental supports (e.g., parent psychopathology and criminality, low social support, domestic violence), and parent–child relationship patterns (e.g., low maternal responsiveness, disorganized attachment) (see review in Shaw et al., 2000). Additionally, experiencing multiple risk factors appears to have a cumulative effect, such that the more risk factors present the higher the likelihood of behavioral problems across childhood and into adolescence (Appleyard, Egeland, van Dulmen, & Sroufe, 2005; Shaw, Winslow, Owens, & Hood, 1998). Thus, several lines of evidence support the contribution of both child and parenting factors to this important area of functioning in early childhood.

Regulatory disorders: Sleep behaviors, feeding disorders, and irritability

We will review difficulties with the regulation of states and biological needs in terms of sleep, feeding, and irritability, in particular due to their links with relationship dysfunction. Some researchers have suggested that sleep, feeding, and excessive crying disorders frequently co-occur and may, in fact, signify an underlying regulatory disorder (von Hofacker & Papoušek, 1998). Our focus here, however, will be on sleep, feeding, and irritability treated individually. It should be noted that some degree of difficulty in these areas is common in children with difficult temperament (see chapter 20 in volume 1).

Sleep behavior disorders. The development of a stable, consistent pattern of sleep is an important, though challenging, task over the first years of life. Parental reports of sleep problems in infants and toddlers are relatively common (Richman, 1981; Wolke, Meyer, Ohrt, & Riegel, 1995) at 15–25%. Possible contributing factors in the etiology of sleep dysfunctions include infant nutritional status, infant temperament or behavioral style, infant self-soothing/signaling behaviors, parent–infant bedtime interactions and sleep choices (e.g., co-sleeping), parental depression and anxiety, family stress, and parental conflict (Anders, Goodlin-Jones & Sadeh, 2000; Gaylor, Goodlin-Jones, & Anders, 2001; O'Connor et al., 2007; von Hofacker & Papoušek, 1998). The stability of early sleep problems is not yet clear, with estimates of consistent problems from infancy to early childhood ranging from 5% to 40% (Scher, Zuckerman, & Epstein, 2005). A recent study found significant longitudinal problems associated with stable early difficulties, such that early persistent night waking and difficulties with settling predicted higher child behavior problems at age 3 (Scher et al., 2005). Moreover, infant temperament (i.e., resistance to control) was found to increase the associations between sleep problems and externalizing behavior problem development across childhood (Goodnight, Bates, Staples, Pettit, & Dodge, 2007).

Differentiating between sleep problems and sleep disorders with reliable, developmentally appropriate criteria is crucial (Anders et al., 2000). However, little epidemiologic data are available on sleep disorders in young children. The DC 0–3:R (Zero to Three, 2005) and RDC-PA (Task Force on Research Diagnostic Criteria: Infancy and Preschool, 2003) diagnostic systems classify two forms of sleep behavior disorder for toddlers and young children: sleep-onset disorder (i.e., difficulty initiating sleep) and night-waking disorder (i.e., difficulty maintaining sleep). The diagnoses are not to be made prior to 12 months of age (when stable sleep patterns emerge) and behaviors must last at least 4 weeks, with five to seven episodes per week (Zero to Three, 2005).

A pilot study using this nosology revealed that the classification scheme diagnosed children at rates consistent with previous reports of sleep difficulties and that parents' reports of infants' signaling during night waking at 12 months predicted later diagnosis (Gaylor et al., 2001). Interestingly, there was discordance between objective diagnosis and parents' acknowledgment of the behaviors as problems (i.e., diagnosed children's parents did not always acknowledge problems), which the authors suggest may signify parents' adaptation to their young children's significant sleep problems (Gaylor et al., 2001). Since many assessments of children's sleep patterns rely on parental report, further study of sleep disorders in early childhood with combined objective assessments (e.g., videotaping, physiological measures) and parental reports linked to validated developmental norms is warranted to enhance our understanding and treatment of these problems.

Feeding behavior disorders.   Difficulties with feeding are a common concern for parents of young children. Feeding problems are reported to primary care physicians at a rate of 25–45% in typically developing young children and as high as 80% in developmentally delayed young children (Linscheid, Budd, & Rasnake, 2003). Feeding problems include such behaviors as food refusal, strict food preferences, food aversion or phobia, and non-optimal growth patterns (e.g., failure to thrive, obesity). Such problems may have long-term health and developmental implications due to their effect on infants' rapidly developing neurological and immune systems. The prevalence of feeding disorders *per se* is difficult to determine due to lack of consistent diagnostic criteria and methodological challenges (Benoit, 2000). More research is needed to better understand the epidemiology, course, and optimal treatment of these disorders. Failure to thrive is discussed in chapter 2 in this volume. We focus here on feeding difficulties separate from failure to thrive, such as relationship, behavioral, and medical factors which may or may not result in growth problems.

Feeding disorders may involve medical, nutritional, environmental, and relational issues. Medical disorders associated with feeding difficulties include *metabolic diseases, sensory defects* (e.g., blindness, hypersensitivity following tube feedings), *anatomic abnormalities* (e.g., cleft palate), *conditioned dysphagia* (e.g., gastroesophageal reflux), *disorders affecting appetite or ingestion* (e.g., depression), *disorders affecting suck/swallow behaviors* (e.g., bronchopulmonary dysplagia, tardive dyskinesia), and a variety of other *childhood disorders* (e.g., Prader–Willi syndrome, allergies) (Rudolph & Link, 2002). Other significant contributory factors include child characteristics that make the child less engaged in the feeding process (e.g., irritable temperament, lethargy) and family/environmental characteristics (e.g., chaotic home, parental psychosocial difficulties) or parent–child interaction difficulties (e.g., insensitivity, attachment difficulties) (APA, 2000; Davies et al., 2006).

Feeding behavior disorders are defined as occurring when an infant or young child "has difficulty establishing regular feeding patterns" (Zero to Three, 2005, p. 35), and are considered primary disorders when they do not co-occur with hunger and or interpersonal causes (e.g., separation, trauma). Specific subtypes of feeding disorders are identified which may be particularly useful for differential diagnosis and treatment (Chatoor, Ganiban, Harrison, & Hirsch, 2001; Chatoor, 2002). These subtypes include: *feeding disorder of state regulation* (i.e., infant cannot reach a calm state in which to feed), *feeding disorder of caregiver–infant relationship or reciprocity* (not solely caused by a physical disorder or pervasive developmental disorder), *infantile anorexia* (i.e., food refusal with significant growth delay not related to interactive difficulties, trauma, or medical conditions), *sensory food aversions* (leading to nutritional deficiencies or oral motor developmental delay), *feeding disorder associated with concurrent medical condition,* and *feeding disorder associated with insults to the gastrointestinal tract* (or *post-traumatic feeding disorder*) (Chatoor et al., 2001; Zero to Three, 2005).

Whereas most current diagnostic systems primarily focus on the behavior and characteristics of the child (with the exception of DC:0–3R's *feeding disorder of caregiver–infant relationship or reciprocity*), Davies et al. (2006) argue for a systemic and multidetermined diagnostic approach, underscoring the relational nature of many feeding disorders. The authors propose diagnostic criteria for *feeding disorder between parent and child,* which combines both child and relationship characteristics, and differentiates among particular relationship patterns related to a variety of feeding problems). This approach and Chatoor's classifications await further validation studies.

Irritability and excessive crying.   Babies who cry with exceptional frequency and/or duration, and toddlers who fuss, whine and throw tantrums more than is typical, may also be considered to have a regulatory disorder. These behaviors may have profound effects on infants' caregivers and environments. In younger babies, this behavior has traditionally been referred to as colic, though this term is becoming less common (see chapter 3 in this volume). The key diagnostic issues include inconsolable crying with problems in sleep–wake organization, parental overload and distress, and interactional failure (Ziegler, Wollwerth de Chuquisengo, & Papoušek, 2008). Assessment and intervention thus includes the infant's difficulty with calming, soothing, and other self-regulatory functions, along with its effect on the parents and on the new and fragile parent–infant interaction, taking into account physiological and psychosocial contributors in treatment strategies. A longitudinal study of infants with irritability and excessive crying found that these difficulties tended to persist into the second year of life and that affective dysregulation also later emerged (Papoušek & von Hofacker, 2008).

Because these issues are so widespread, the literature regarding their definition and treatment, and offering advice to parents, is extensive (Brazelton, 2003). The majority of professionals involved in the well-being of infants, toddlers and their families will likely encounter family challenges with irritability and excessive crying, and will find many opportunities for identification, intervention, and prevention of later disorders.

Interventions for Infant Psychosocial Disorders

Having outlined a variety of infant psychosocial disorders, we now turn to a review of available strategies and approaches to interventions with infants and young children. As with so many areas in psychology, the field is currently moving forward through increasingly rigorous assessment of treatment protocols with more or less standardized approaches. In this section, we will review some of the most promising and best-supported interventions strategies for infants and toddlers with psychosocial disruptions and disorders. It is very important to begin, however, by reflecting on the work that preceded these approaches and which provided the foundation for current empirically supported interventions.

Traditional approaches to infant psychosocial disorders

Clinicians and clinical researchers have been offering psychotherapeutic interventions to infants and toddlers for many years, typically in the context of treatment focused on the family (usually the mother). Earlier approaches, such as infant–parent psychotherapy, tended to focus on the application of psychodynamic principles to mother–infant dyads in a carefully observed and described manner (Fraiberg, Adelson, & Shapiro, 1975). The value of approaching infant behavioral concerns by developing a careful understanding of parental relationship history and current emotional functioning continues to be compellingly illustrated in current clinical literature (Acquarone, 2004; Bruschweiler-Stern, 2004) as well as in the emerging research literature on the impact of early attachment experiences on adult functioning (van IJzendoorn, 1995). Play therapy for the 0–2 age group has been used most in helping children cope with traumatic experiences, usually involves parental observation if not active participation, and typically strives to provide opportunities for expression of affect, desensitization, and mastery of the trauma through play (Gaensbauer & Siegel, 1995). There is emerging empirical evidence showing significant support for "traditional" interventions, such as parent–infant psychotherapy and play therapy (Cohen, Lojkasek, Muir, Muir, & Parker, 2002; Lieberman, Ippen, & Van Horn, 2006; Maldonado-Durán & Lartigue, 2002; Robert-Tissot et al., 1996), and thus the distinction between "traditional" and "evidence-based" may be less meaningful over time.

The field of early intervention is traditionally thought of as addressing cognitive and motor areas of development (see chapter 13 in this volume). However, early intervention programs have also played an important role in addressing children's psychosocial functioning through a focus on parental adaptation to child disability, the infant's contribution to family relationships, the practitioner–parent relationship, and sensitivity to the emotions experienced by the parents (Pawl & Milburn, 2006).

Evidence-based treatments

The above clinical approaches have served as foundations for and precursors to a range of new approaches that are being subjected to rigorous definition and testing, as part of the broad movement throughout psychology to provide evidence to support clinical practice. This section will review prominent work in this area.

Behavioral treatments.   There is a significant literature on the application of behavioral treatments to a variety of disorders in infants and toddlers, though not surprisingly there is more information on behavioral treatment for relatively discrete behaviors such as feeding and sleep problems than on relationship and affective disorders. For example, a review of literature published between 1970 and 1997 found 14 studies of empirically based pediatric feeding disorder treatments, many in the 0–2 population, all of which included some form of differential attention (Kerwin, 1999). Although behavioral approaches have proven to be successful, more needs to be done to understand the underlying learning principles, so that techniques can be modified as needed to meet the needs of individual children. For example, it is important to highlight the importance of appetite manipulation (Linscheid, 1999) and to move the application of well-documented treatments to the complex and variable "real world" problems presented by individual children (Linscheid, 2006).

Similar issues can be found in a review of empirically supported treatments to deal with sleep problems. A review of 41 studies found support for extinction as a strategy, with the caveat that many parents find that completely ignoring their child's crying is virtually impossible (Mindell, 1999). Fortunately, the same review found "probably efficacious" support for graduated extinction and scheduled awakenings (Mindell, 1999, p. 479). Parent training around the time of birth is also supported as an effective approach, as a prevention rather than an intervention strategy (Mindell, 1999).

Parent–infant treatments.   The developing relationship between infants and parents plays a crucial role in infant psychosocial functioning. As such, interventions which focus on enhancing this relationship to enhance infant adjustment constitute a burgeoning field of study. Although a comprehensive review of parent–infant interventions is beyond the scope of this chapter, we discuss here five intervention approaches which are developing a strong evidence base and which are widely used: Infant–Parent Psychotherapy, Attachment and Biobehavioral Catchup, Circle of Security, Interaction Guidance, and Parent–Child Interaction Therapy (for more thorough review, see Berlin, Ziv, Amaya-Jackson, & Greenberg, 2005; Oppenheim & Goldsmith, 2007; and Sameroff, McDonough, & Rosenblum, 2004). Table 11.2 provides a summary of the goals and strategies of each approach, and this section summarizes supporting research evidence.

Table 11.2 Evidence-based parent–child interventions for infant psychosocial disorders.

Intervention and References	Background and Goals	Strategies/Components/Approach
Infant–Parent Psychotherapy (Cicchetti et al., 2006; Lieberman et al., 2005)	• Designed to treat parent and infant simultaneously • Goals: to encourage healthy child development and trusting relationships	• Modalities include psychotherapy (play, emotional support, psychological interpretation), developmental guidance, and concrete assistance • Addresses parent's internal representations, expectations of child, and processing trauma
Attachment and Biobehavioral Catch-up (Dozier et al., 2005)	• Originally designed for foster infants • Goals: to enhance parental nurturing and to promote biobehavioral regulation in infants	• 10-week home-based program • Activities include emphasizing parental nurturance, following child's lead, creating predictable environments, and overriding own history or nonnurturing instincts
Circle of Security (Cooper, Hoffman, Powell, & Marvin, 2005; Marvin, Cooper, Hoffman, & Powell, 2002)	• Designed for high-risk dyads • Goal: to enhance attachment patterns to facilitate healthy child development by changing parental behaviors and representations of own caregiving history	• 20-week group-based parent education and psychotherapy program • Includes observational and interview assessment, teaching attachment concepts, and providing standardized, video-based treatment
Interaction Guidance (McDonough, 2004)	• Designed for families with multiple risk factors • Goal: to change problematic relationship patterns using strength-based, family systems approach	• 10–12 one-hour clinic-based sessions • Sessions include videotaping a family play session and reviewing videotape to provide immediate feedback, focusing on strengths and areas to change
Parent–Child Interaction Therapy (Herschell, Clazada, Eyberg, & McNeil, 2002)	• Designed for families of children ages 2–8 with significant behavioral and emotional problems, young children with separation anxiety disorder • Goals: to change family interactions and child behavior, integrating attachment and social learning theory	• Joint play sessions, therapist behind a one-way mirror using "bug-in-the-ear" technology • Two-stage model includes child-directed interaction (enhancing the parent–child interaction) and parent-directed interaction (enhancing parent's expectations of children, improving ability to set appropriate limits)

These interventions can be used for many of the disorders described above, particularly when the parent–infant relationship is compromised.

Infant–Parent Psychotherapy.   As described above, a number of clinical researchers are rigorously testing the effectiveness of some traditional early childhood interventions, including Infant–Parent Psychotherapy (or Child–Parent Psychotherapy). Infant–Parent Psychotherapy has been supported by findings from several randomized trials demonstrating increases in attachment security in maltreated infants and toddlers (Cicchetti, Rogosch, & Toth, 2006), enhanced cognitive and developmental outcomes for toddlers of depressed mothers (Cicchetti, Rogosch, & Toth, 2000; Toth, Rogosch, Manly, & Cicchetti, 2006), and improvement in children's behaviors and reductions in mothers' distress for preschoolers exposed to domestic violence (Lieberman, Van Horn, & Ippen, 2005).

Attachment and Biobehavioral Catch-up (ABC).   Dozier and colleagues' program was originally designed to educate and support relationships between foster infants and their foster parents. The intervention has been utilized with children with a variety of behavioral and emotional symptoms and distressed infant–parent dyads, and is being systematically evaluated in several randomized control trials. One recent study with foster children found that children in the ABC intervention group demonstrated enhanced regulatory capacities, demonstrated by more normal cortisol regulation and by fewer behavior problems (Dozier et al., 2006). Additionally, preliminary findings from a randomized trial with 100 infant–parent pairs indicate that those infants whose foster parents received the ABC treatment were more likely to be securely attached than those infants whose foster parents did not (Dozier, Peloso, Zirkel, & Lindheim, 2007). The intervention is currently undergoing a randomized trial with biological parents who have prior allegations of child neglect (Dozier, Lindheim, & Ackerman, 2005).

The Circle of Security Intervention.   Using this short-term, group-based technique, a recent pre–post evaluation of 65 low-income young children and their caregivers indicated promising changes such that 70% of children with disorganized attachments changed to organized (secure and insecure) attachment patterns, the majority of which were secure (Hoffman, Marvin, Cooper, & Powell, 2006). Taking into account evidence that insecure and disorganized attachment may be a risk factor for later psychopathology, particularly when combined with other risk factors (Lyons-Ruth & Jacobvitz, 1999; Sroufe, Egeland, Carlson, & Collins, 2005), these findings in the context of a relatively brief and structured intervention approach are encouraging.

Interaction Guidance.   This technique is a multigenerational approach to infant mental health problems rooted in family systems theory (McDonough, 2000, 2004), and has been applied to infants with regulatory disorders, behavior disorders and infant–parent interaction problems. Research evidence using this approach demonstrates significant reduction in child symptom reduction, improved dyadic interaction (i.e., less maternal intrusiveness and inappropriate/disrupted behavior, more cooperative infant behavior), enhanced maternal self-esteem, and reduced maternal negative affect (Benoit, Madigan,

Lecce, Shea, & Goldberg, 2001; Madigan, Hawkins, Goldberg, & Benoit, 2006; McDonough, 1995; Robert-Tissot et al., 1996).

Parent–Child Interaction Therapy.   This is a short-term, parent training program designed for families of children with significant behavioral and emotional problems, which has demonstrated clinically significant improvements in child behavior and parent management skills (Choate, Pincus, Eyberg, & Barlow, 2005; Querido & Eyberg, 2005). Although not designed specifically for infants and toddlers, it has been validated with children as young as 2–3 years, and may be an appropriate treatment approach when problems occur or begin in early childhood (Querido & Eyberg, 2005).

Conclusion

The study of psychosocial disruptions and disorders in our youngest children, and clinical efforts to diagnose and treat them, remains a work in progress. Yet, its deep roots in many areas of knowledge, from psychoanalysis to behavior therapy, from neurobiology to developmental psychopathology, from attachment theory to family systems, give it strength and promise. Great strides have been made in successfully intervening to help very young children and their families thrive emotionally and develop successfully, despite the biological, environmental, and interactive challenges that many face. Future research integrating new neurobiological discoveries with clinical research and more systematic study of factors that promote resilience in the face of challenge will likely enrich this effort. More integration among clinical and academic disciplines, as well as among theoretical perspectives, will further support progress toward making a lasting difference in the lives of children.

References

Aber, J. L., & Allen, J. (1987). Effects of maltreatment on young children's socioemotional development: An attachment theory perspective. *Developmental Psychology, 23*, 406–414.

Aber, J. L., Jones, S., & Cohen, J. (2000). The impact of poverty on the mental health and development of very young children. In C. H. Zeanah (Ed.), *Handbook of infant mental health* (2nd ed., pp. 113–128). New York: Guilford Press.

Acquarone, S. (2004). *Infant–parent psychotherapy.* New York: Karnac.

Ainsworth, M. D. S., Blehar, M. C., Waters, E., & Wall, S. (1978). *Patterns of attachment: A psychological study of the strange situation.* Hillsdale, NJ: Lawrence Erlbaum Associates.

American Psychiatric Association. (2000). *Diagnostic and statistical manual of mental disorders* (4th ed.). Washington, DC: Author.

Anders, T., Goodlin-Jones, B., & Sadeh, A., (2000). Sleep disorders. In C. H. Zeanah, Jr. (Ed.), *Handbook of infant mental health* (2nd ed., pp. 326–338). New York: Guilford Press.

Aoki, Y., Zeanah, C. H., Heller, S. S., & Bakshi, S. (2002). Parent–infant relationship global assessment scale: A study of its predictive validity. *Psychiatry and clinical neurosciences, 56*, 493–497.

Appleyard, K., Egeland, B., & Sroufe, L. A. (2007). Direct social support for young high risk children: Relations with behavioral and emotional problems over time. *Journal of Abnormal Child Psychology, 35,* 443–457.

Appleyard, K., Egeland, B., van Dulmen, M. H. M., & Sroufe, L. A. (2005). When more is not better: The role of cumulative risk in child behavior outcomes. *Journal of Child Psychology and Psychiatry, 46,* 235–245.

Appleyard, K., & Osofsky, J. D. (2003). Parenting after trauma: Supporting parents and caregivers in the treatment of children impacted by violence. *Infant Mental Health Journal, 24*(2), 111–125.

Benoit, D. (2000). Feeding disorders, failure to thrive, and obesity. In C. H. Zeanah, Jr. (Ed.), *Handbook of infant mental health* (2nd ed., pp. 339–352). New York: Guilford Press.

Benoit, D., Madigan, S., Lecce, S., Shea, B., & Goldberg, S. (2001). Atypical maternal behavior toward feeding-disordered infants before and after intervention. *Infant Mental Health Journal, 22,* 611–626.

Berlin, L. J., Ziv, Y., Amaya-Jackson, L., & Greenberg, M. T. (Eds.) (2005). *Enhancing early attachments: Theory, research, intervention, and policy.* New York: Guilford Press.

Bleiberg, E. (2002). Attachment, trauma, and self-reflection: Implications for later psychopathology. In J. M. Maldonado-Duran (Ed.), *Infant and toddler mental health: Models of clinical intervention with infants and their families* (pp. 33–56). Washington, DC: American Psychiatric Publishing.

Bowlby, J. (1982). *Attachment and loss, Vol. I: Attachment* (2nd ed.). New York: Basic Books. (Original work published 1969.)

Brazelton, T. B. (1974). *Toddlers and parents: A declaration of independence.* New York: Dell Publishing.

Brazelton, T. B. (2003). *Calming your fussy baby the Brazelton way.* Cambridge, MA: Perseus Publishing.

Brownell, C. A., & Kopp, C. B. (Eds.) (2007). *Socioemotional development in the toddler years.* New York: Guilford Press.

Bruschweiler-Stern, N. (2004). A multifocal neonatal intervention. In A. J. Sameroff, S. C. McDonough, & K. L. Rosenblum (Eds.), *Treating parent–infant relationship problems.* New York: Guilford Press.

Carey, W. B., & McDevitt, S. C. (1995). *Coping with children's temperament: A guide for professionals.* New York: Basic Books.

Cassidy, J., & Shaver, P. R. (Eds.) (1999). *Handbook of attachment: Theory, research, and clinical applications.* New York: Guilford Press.

Chatoor, I. (2002). Feeding disorders in infants and toddlers: Diagnosis and treatment. *Child and Adolescent Psychiatric Clinics of North America, 11,* 163–183.

Chatoor, I., Ganiban, J., Harrison, J., & Hirsch, R. (2001). Observation of feeding in the diagnosis of posttraumatic feeding disorder in infancy. *Journal of the American Academy of Child and Adolescent Psychiatry, 40,* 595–602.

Choate, M. L., Pincus, D. B., Eyberg, S. M., & Barlow, D. H. (2005). Parent–child interaction therapy for treatment of separation anxiety disorder in young children: A pilot study. *Cognitive and Behavioral Practice, 12,* 126–135.

Cicchetti, D. (2003). Neuroendocrine functioning in maltreated children. In D. Cicchetti & E. Walker (Eds.), *Neurodevelopmental mechanisms in psychopathology* (pp. 345–365). New York: Cambridge University Press.

Cicchetti, D., Rogosch, F. A., & Toth, S. L. (2000). The efficacy of toddler–parent psychotherapy for fostering cognitive development for offspring of depressed mothers. *Journal of Abnormal Child Psychology, 28,* 135–148.

Cicchetti, D., Rogosch, F. A., & Toth, S. L. (2006). Fostering secure attachment in infants in maltreating families through preventive interventions. *Development and Psychopathology, 18*, 623–649.

Cicchetti, D., & Toth, S. L. (1997). Transactional ecological systems in developmental psycho-pathology. In S. S. Luthar, J. A. Burack, D. Cicchetti, & J. R. Weisz (Eds.), *Developmental psychopathology: Perspectives on adjustment, risk, and disorder* (pp. 317–349). New York: Cambridge University Press.

Cochran, M., & Niego, S. (1995). Parenting and social networks. In M. H. Bornstein (Ed.), *Handbook of parenting: Volume 3, Status and social conditions of parenting* (pp. 393–418). Mahwah, NJ: Lawrence Erlbaum Associates.

Cohen, N. J., Lojkasek, M., Muir, E., Muir, R., & Parker, C. J. (2002). Six-month follow-up of two mother–infant psychotherapies: Convergence of therapeutic outcomes. *Infant Mental Health Journal, 23*, 362–380.

Cole, P. M., Martin, S. E., & Dennis, T. A. (2004). Emotional regulation as a scientific construct: Methodological challenges and directions for child development research. *Child Development, 7*, 317–333.

Coley, R. L., & Chase-Lansdale, L. (1998). Adolescent pregnancy and parenthood: Recent evidence and future directions. *American Psychologist, 53*, 152–166.

Committee on Adolescence and Committee on Early Childhood and Adoption, and Dependent Care (2001). Care of adolescent parents and their children. *Pediatrics, 107*, 429–434.

Cooper, G., Hoffman, K., Powell, B., & Marvin, R. (2005). The Circle of Security Intervention: Differential diagnosis and differential treatment. In L. J. Berlin, Y. Ziv, L. Amaya-Jackson, & M. T. Greenberg (Eds.), *Enhancing early attachments: Theory, research, intervention, and policy* (pp. 127–151). New York: Guilford Press.

Corse, S. J., Schmid, K., & Trickett, P. K. (1990). Social network characteristics of mothers in abusing and nonabusing families and their relationships to parenting beliefs. *Journal of Community Psychology, 18*, 44–59.

Cozolino, L. (2006). *The neuroscience of human relationships: Attachment and the developing social brain*. New York: Norton.

Crockenberg, S. (1981). Infant irritability, mother responsiveness, and social support influences on the security of infant–mother attachment. *Child Development, 52*, 857–865.

Crockenberg, S., & Litman, C. (1990). Autonomy as competence in 2-year-olds: Maternal correlates of child defiance, compliance, and self-assertion. *Developmental Psychology, 26*, 961–971.

Cunningham, A., & Baker, L. (2007). *Little eyes, little ears: How violence against a mother shapes children as they grow*. Ottowa: National Clearinghouse on Family Violence.

Davies, W. H., Satter, E., Berlin, K. S., Sato, A. F., Silverman, A. H., Fischer, E. A., et al. (2006). Reconceptualizing feeding and feeding disorders in interpersonal context: The case for a relational disorder. *Journal of Family Psychology, 20*, 409–417.

Denham, S. A. (1998). *Emotional development in young children*. New York: Guilford Press.

Dicker, S., Gordon, E., & Knitzer, J. (2001). *Promoting the emotional well-being of children and families, Policy Paper # 2: Improving the odds for the healthy development of young children in foster care*. New York: National Center for Children in Poverty, Mailman School of Public Health, Columbia University.

Dozier, M., Lindheim, O., & Ackerman, J. P. (2005). Attachment and biobehavioral catch-up. In L. J. Berlin, Y. Ziv, L. M. Amaya-Jackson, & M. T. Greenberg (Eds.), *Enhancing early attachments: Theory, research, intervention, and policy* (pp. 178–194). New York: Guilford Press.

Dozier, M., Peloso, E., Lindheim, O., Gordon, M. K., Manni, M., Sepulveda, S., et al. (2006). Developing evidence-based interventions for foster children: An example of a randomized clinical trial with infants and toddlers. *Journal of Social Issues, 62*, 767–785.

Dozier, M., Peloso, E., Zirkel, S., & Lindheim, O. J. (2007). Intervention effects on foster infants' attachments to new caregivers. In L. J. Berlin (Chair), *Interventions to support early attachments: New findings.* Symposium presented at the biennial meeting of the Society for Research in Child Development, Boston.

Dunst, C. J., Storck, A., & Snyder, D. (2006). Identification of infant and toddler social-emotional disorders using the DC:0–3 Diagnostic Classification System. *Cornerstones, 2,* 1–21.

East, P. L., & Felice, M. E. (1996). *Adolescent pregnancy and parenting: Findings from a racially diverse sample.* Mahwah, NJ: Lawrence Erlbaum Associates.

Emde, R. N. (1998). Early emotional development: New modes of thinking for research and intervention. *Pediatrics, 102* (Suppl., November), 1236–1243.

Ferber, R. (2006). *Solve your child's sleep problems: New, revised and expanded edition.* New York: Fireside.

Field, T. M. (1992). Infants of depressed mothers. *Development and Psychopathology, 4,* 49–66.

Fox, N. A., & Calkins, S. D. (2003). The development of self-control of emotion: Intrinsic and extrinsic influences. *Motivation and Emotion, 27,* 7–26.

Fraiberg, S., Adelson, E., & Shapiro, V. (1975). Ghosts in the nursery: A psychoanalytic approach to the problems of impaired infant–mother relationships. *Journal of the American Academy of Child Psychiatry, 14,* 387–421.

Gaensbauer, T. J., & Siegel, C. H. (1995). Therapeutic approaches to posttraumatic stress disorder in infants and toddlers. *Infant Mental Health Journal, 16,* 292–305.

Gaylor, E. E., Goodlin-Jones, B. L., & Anders, T. F. (2001). Classification of young children's sleep problems: A pilot study. *Journal of the American Academy of Child and Adolescent Psychiatry, 40,* 61–67.

Goodenough, F. L. (1931). *Anger in young children.* Minneapolis: University of Minnesota Press.

Goodnight, J. A., Bates, J. E., Staples, A. D., Pettit, G. S., & Dodge, K. A. (2007). Temperamental resistance to control increases the association between sleep problems and externalizing behavior development. *Journal of Family Psychology, 21,* 39–48.

Green, B. L., Furrer, C., & McAllister, C. (2007). How do relationships support parenting? Effects of attachment style and social support on parenting behavior in an at-risk population. *American Journal of Community Psychology, 40,* 96–108.

Greenspan, S. I. (1992). *Infancy and early childhood: The practice of clinical assessment and intervention with emotional and developmental challenges.* Madison, CT: International Universities Press.

Greenspan, S. I., & Brazelton, T. B. (2000). *The irreducible needs of children: What every child must have to grow, learn, and flourish.* New York: Perseus Books.

Greenspan, S. I., & Porges, S. W. (1984). Psychopathology in infancy and early childhood: Clinical perspectives on the organization of sensory and affective-thematic experience. *Child Development, 55,* 49–70.

Greenspan, S. I., Wieder, S., Nover, R. A., Lieberman, A. F., Lourie, R. S., & Robinson, S. E. (Eds.) (1987). *Infants in multirisk families: Case studies in preventive intervention.* Madison, CT: International Universities Press.

Gunnar, M., & Pollak, S. D. (2007). Supporting parents so that they can support their internationally adopted children: The larger challenge lurking behind the fatality statistics. *Child Maltreatment, 12,* 381–382.

Harmon, R. J., Wagonfeld, S., & Emde, R. N. (1982). Anaclitic depression: A follow-up from infancy to puberty. *Psychoanalytic Study of the Child, 37,* 67–94.

Hendrick, V., & Daly, K. (2000). Parental mental illness. In N. Halfon, E. Shulman, M. Hochstein, & M. Shannon (Eds.), *Building community systems for young children* (pp. i–26). Los Angeles: UCLA Center for Healthier Children, Families and Communities.

Herschell, A. D., Clazada, E. J., Eyberg, S. M., & McNeil, C. B. (2002). Parent–child interaction therapy: New directions in research. *Cognitive and Behavioral Practice*, *9*, 9–15.

Hoffman, K. T., Marvin, R. S., Cooper, G., & Powell, B. (2006). Changing toddlers' and preschoolers' attachment classifications: The Circle of Security Intervention. *Journal of Clinical and Consulting Psychology*, *74*, 1017–1026.

Kaplow, J. B., Saxe, G. N., Putnam, F. W., Pynoos, R. S., & Lieberman, A. F. (2006). The long-term consequences of early childhood trauma: A case study and discussion. *Psychiatry*, *69*, 362–375.

Karen, R. (1994). *Becoming attached*. New York: Oxford University Press.

Kaufman, J., & Henrich, C. (2000). Exposure to violence and early childhood trauma. In C. H. Zeanah (Ed.), *Handbook of infant mental health* (2nd ed., pp. 195–207). New York: Guilford Press.

Keenan, K., & Wakschlag, L. S. (2000). More than the terrible twos: The nature and severity of behavior problems in clinic-referred preschool children. *Journal of Abnormal Child Psychology*, *28*, 33–46.

Keren, M., Feldman, R., & Tyano, S. (2001). Diagnoses and interactive patterns of infants referred to a community-based infant mental health clinic. *Journal of the American Academy of Child and Adolescent Psychiatry*, *40*, 27–35.

Kessler, D. B., & Dawson, P. (1999). *Failure to thrive and pediatric undernutrition*. Baltimore, MD: Brookes Publishing.

Kim-Cohen, J., Moffitt, T. E., Caspi, A., & Taylor, A. (2004). Genetic and environmental processes in young children's resilience and vulnerability to socioeconomic deprivation. *Child Development*, *75*, 651–668.

Kerwin, M. E. (1999). Empirically supported treatments in pediatric psychology: Severe feeding problems. *Journal of Pediatric Psychology*, *24*, 193–214.

Kotch, J., Browne, D. C., Dufort, V., & Winsor, J. (1999). Predicting child maltreatment in the first 4 years of life from characteristics assessed in the neonatal period. *Child Abuse & Neglect*, *23*, 305–319.

Lavigne, J. V., Gibbons, R. D., Christoffel, K. K., Arend, R., Rosenbaum, D., Binns, H., et al. (1996). Prevalence rates and correlates of psychiatric disorders among preschool children. *Journal of the American Academy of Child and Adolescent Psychiatry*, *35*, 204–214.

Lieberman, A. F. (1993). *The emotional life of the toddler*. New York: Free Press.

Lieberman, A. F., Ippen, C. G., & Van Horn, P. (2006). Child–parent psychotherapy: 6-month follow-up of a randomized controlled trial. *Journal of the American Academy of Child and Adolescent Psychiatry*, *45*, 913–918.

Lieberman, A. F., Van Horn, P., & Ippen, C. G. (2005). Toward evidence-based treatment: Child–parent psychotherapy with preschoolers exposed to marital violence. *Journal of the American Academy of Child and Adolescent Psychiatry*, *44*, 1241–1248.

Lieberman, A., Wieder, S., & Fenichel, E. (Eds.) (1997). *DC:0–3 Casebook: A guide to the use of Zero to Three's "Diagnostic Classification of Mental Health and Developmental Disorders of Infancy and Early Childhood" in assessment and treatment planning*. Washington, DC: Zero to Three.

Linder, T. W. (1993). *Transdisciplinary play-based intervention*. Baltimore, MD: Brookes Publishing.

Linscheid, T. R. (1999). Commentary: Response to empirically supported treatments for feeding problems. *Journal of Pediatric Psychology*, *24*, 215–216.

Linscheid, T. R. (2006). Behavioral treatments for pediatric feeding disorders. *Behavior Modification*, *30*, 6–23.

Linscheid, T. R., Budd, K. S., & Rasnake, L. K. (2003). Pediatric feeding problems. In M. C. Roberts (Ed.), *Handbook of pediatric psychology* (3rd ed., pp. 481–498). New York: Guilford Press.

Logsdon, M. C., Birkimer, J. C., Ratterman, A., Cahill, K., & Cahill, N. (2002). Social support in pregnant and parenting adolescents: Research, critique, and recommendations. *Journal of Child and Adolescent Psychiatric Nursing, 15*, 75–83.

Luby, J. L. (2000). Depression. In C. H. Zeanah, Jr. (Ed.), *Handbook of infant mental health* (2nd ed., pp. 382–396). New York: Guilford Press.

Luby, J. L., & Belden, A. C. (2006). Mood disorders: Phenomenology and a developmental emotional reactivity model. In J. L. Luby (Ed.), *Handbook of preschool mental health: Development, disorders, and treatment* (pp. 209–230). New York: Guilford Press.

Luby, J. L., Heffelfinger, A. K., Mrakotsky, C., Brown, K. M., Hessler, M. J., Wallis, J. M., & Spitznagel, E. L. (2003). The clinical picture of depression in preschool children. *Journal of the American Academy of Child and Adolescent Psychiatry, 42*, 340–348.

Luby, J. L., Heffelfinger, A. K., Mrakotsky, C., Hessler, M. J., Brown, K. M., & Hildebrand, T. (2002). Preschool major depressive disorder: Preliminary validation for developmentally modified DSM-IV criteria. *Journal of the American Academy of Child and Adolescent Psychiatry, 41*, 928–937.

Luby, J. L., Mrakotsky, C., Heffelfinger, A., Brown, K., Hessler, M., & Spitznagel, E. (2003). Modification of DSM-IV criteria for depressed preschool children. *American Journal of Psychiatry, 160*, 1169–1172.

Lyons-Ruth, K., & Jacobvitz, D. (1999). Attachment disorganization: Unresolved loss, relational violence, and lapses in behavioral and attentional strategies. In J. Cassidy & P. R. Shaver (Eds.), *Handbook of attachment: Theory, research, and clinical applications* (pp. 520–554). New York: Guilford Press.

Madigan, S., Hawkins, E., Goldberg, S., & Benoit, D. (2006). Reduction of disrupted caregiver behavior using Modified Interaction Guidance. *Infant Mental Health Journal, 27*, 509–527.

Maldonado-Durán, J. M., & Lartigue, T. (2002). Multimodal parent–infant psychotherapy. In J. M. Maldonado-Durán (Ed.), *Infant and toddler mental health: Models of clinical intervention with infants and their families* (pp. 129–159). Washington, DC: American Psychiatric Publishing.

Marshall, P. J., & Fox, N. A. (Eds.) (2006). *The development of social engagement: Neurobiological perspectives*. New York: Oxford University Press.

Marvin, R., Cooper, G., Hoffman, K., & Powell, B. (2002). The Circle of Security project: Attachment-based intervention with caregiver-pre-school child dyads. *Attachment & Human Development, 4*, 107–124.

Mayes, L. C., & Ward, A. (2003). Principles of neurobehavioral teratology. In D. Cicchetti & E. F. Walker (Eds.), *Neurodevelopmental mechanisms in psychopathology* (pp. 3–33). New York: Cambridge University Press.

McDonough, S. C. (1995). Promoting positive early parent–infant relationships through interaction guidance. *Child and Adolescent Psychiatric Clinics of North America, 4*, 661–672.

McDonough, S. C. (2000). Interaction Guidance: An approach for difficult-to-engage families. In C. H. Zeanah (Ed.), *Handbook of infant mental health* (2nd ed., pp. 485–493). New York: Guilford Press.

McDonough, S. C. (2004). Interaction guidance: Promoting and nurturing the caregiving relationship. In A. J. Sameroff, S. C. McDonough, & K. L. Rosenblum (Eds.), *Treating parent–infant relationship problems: Strategies for intervention* (pp. 79–96). New York: Guilford Press.

Messinger, D. S., Bauer, C. R., Das, A., Seifer, R., Lester, B. M., Lagasse, L. L., et al. (2004). The maternal lifestyle study: Cognitive, motor, and behavioral outcomes of cocaine-exposed and opiate-exposed infants through three years of age. *Pediatrics, 113*, 1677–1685.

Mindell, J. A. (1999). Empirically supported treatments in pediatric psychology: Bedtime refusal and night wakings in young children. *Journal of Pediatric Psychology, 24*, 465–481.

Morrell, J., & Murray, L. (2003). Postnatal depression and the development of conduct disorder and hyperactive symptoms in childhood: A prospective longitudinal study from 2 months to 8 years. *Journal of Child Psychology and Psychiatry, 44,* 489–508.

Nachmias, M., Gunnar, M., Mangelsdorf, S., Parritz, R., & Buss, K. (1996). Behavioral inhibition and stress reactivity: The moderating role of attachment security. *Child Development, 67,* 508–522.

O'Connor, T. G., Caprariello, P., Blackmore, E. R., Gregory, A. M., Glover, V., Fleming, P., & the ALSPAC Study Team (2007). Prenatal mood disturbance predicts sleep problems in infancy and toddlerhood. *Early Human Development, 83,* 451–458.

Oppenheim, D., & Goldsmith, D. F. (Eds.) (2007). *Attachment theory in clinical work with children: Bridging the gap between research and practice.* New York: Guilford Press.

Osofsky, J. D. (1995). The effects of exposure to violence on young children. *American Psychologist, 50,* 782–788.

Osofsky, J. D., & Osofsky, H. J. (2007, March). *Katrina's children: Lessons learned about children in disasters.* Paper presented at the biennial meeting of the Society for Research on Child Development, Boston.

Papoušek, M., & von Hofacker, N. (2008). Clinging, romping, throwing tantrums: Disorders of behavioral and emotional regulation in older infants and toddlers. In M. Papoušek, N. Schieche, & H. Wurmser (Eds.), *Disorders of behavioral and emotional regulation in the first years of life: Early risks and intervention in the developing parent–infant relationship* (K. Kronenberg, Trans.) (pp. 169–199). Washington, DC: Zero to Three. (Original work published 2004.)

Pawl, J. H., & Milburn, L. A. (2006). Family- and relationship-centered principles and practices. In G. M. Foley & J. D. Hochman (Eds.), *Mental health in early intervention: Achieving unity in principles and practice* (pp. 191–226). Baltimore, MD: Brookes Publishing.

Querido, J. G., & Eyberg, S. M. (2005). Parent–child interaction therapy: Maintaining treatment gains of preschoolers with disruptive behavior disorders. In E. D. Hibbs & P. S. Jensen (Eds.), *Psychosocial treatments for child and adolescent disorders: Empirically based strategies for clinical practice* (2nd ed., pp. 575–597). Washington, DC: American Psychological Association.

Richman, N. (1981). A community survey of characteristics of one- to two-year-olds with sleep disruptions. *Journal of the American Academy of Child Psychiatry, 20,* 281–291.

Robert-Tissot, C., Cramer, B., Stern, D. N., Serpa, S. R., Bachmann, J.-P., Palacio-Espasa, F., et al. (1996). Outcome evaluation in brief mother–infant psychotherapies: Report on 75 cases. *Infant Mental Health Journal, 17,* 97–114.

Robertson, J., & Robertson, J. (1989) *Separations and the very young.* London: Free Association Books.

Rothbart, M. K., & Bates, J. E. (2006). Temperament. In N. Eisenberg, W. Damon, & R. M. Lerner (Eds.), *Handbook of child psychology: Vol. 3, Social, emotional, and personality development* (6th ed., pp. 99–166). Hoboken, NJ: John Wiley & Sons.

Rudolph, C. D., & Link, D. T. (2002). Feeding disorders in infants and children. *Pediatric Gastroenterology and Nutrition, 49,* 97–112.

Rutter, M. L., Kreppner, J. M., O'Connor, T. G., and the English and Romanian Adoptees Study Team (2001). Specificity and heterogeneity in children's responses to profound institutional privation. *British Journal of Psychiatry, 179,* 97–103.

Sameroff, A. J., & Emde, R. N. (Eds.) (1989). *Relationship disturbances in early childhood.* New York: Basic Books.

Sameroff, A. J., & Fiese, B. H. (2000). Transactional regulation: The developmental ecology of early intervention. In S. J. Meisels & J. Shonkoff (Eds.), *Handbook of early childhood intervention* (2nd ed., pp. 135–159). New York: Cambridge University Press.

Sameroff, A. J., McDonough, S. C., & Rosenblum, K. L. (Eds.) (2004). *Treating parent–infant problems: Strategies for intervention*. New York: Guilford Press.

Sameroff, A. J., & Seifer, R. (1990). Early contributors to developmental risk. In J. Rolf, A. S. Masten, D. Cicchetti, K. H. Nuechterlein, & S. Weintraub (Eds.), *Risk and protective factors in the development of psychopathology* (pp. 52–66). New York: Cambridge University Press.

Scheeringa, M. S., Peebles, C. D., Cook, C. A., & Zeanah, C. H. (2001). Toward establishing procedural, criterion, and discriminant validity for PTSD in early childhood. *Journal of the American Academy of Child and Adolescent Psychiatry, 40*, 52–60.

Scheeringa, M. S., & Zeanah, C. H. (2001). A relational perspective on PTSD in early childhood. *Journal of Traumatic Stress, 14*, 799–815.

Scheeringa, M. S., Zeanah, C. H., Myers, L., & Putnam, F. W. (2003). New findings on alternative criteria for PTSD in preschool children. *Journal of the American Academy of Child and Adolescent Psychiatry, 42*, 561–570.

Scheeringa, M. S., Zeanah, C. H., Myers, L., & Putnam, F. W. (2005). Predictive validity in a prospective follow-up of PTSD in preschool children. *Journal of the American Academy of Child and Adolescent Psychiatry, 44*, 899–906.

Scher, A., Zuckerman, S., & Epstein, R. (2005). Persistent night waking and settling difficulties across the first year: Early precursors of later behavioural problems? *Journal of Reproductive and Infant Psychology, 23*, 77–88.

Shaw, D. S., Gilliom, M., & Giovannelli, J. (2000). Aggressive behavior disorders. In C. H. Zeanah (Ed.), *Handbook of infant mental health* (2nd ed., pp. 397–411). New York: Guilford Press.

Shaw, D. S., Winslow, E. B., Owens, E. B., & Hood, N. (1998). Young children's adjustment to chronic family adversity: A longitudinal study of low-income families. *Journal of the American Academy of Child and Adolescent Psychiatry, 37*, 545–553.

Shonkoff, J. P., & Phillips, D. (Eds.) (2000). *From neurons to neighborhoods: The science of early childhood development*. Committee on Integrating the Science of Early Childhood Development. Washington, DC: National Academy Press.

Skovgaard, A. M., Houmann, T., Christiansen, E., Landorph, S., Jergensen, T., and CCC 2000 Study Team: Olsen, E. M., Heering, K., Kaas-Nielsen, S., Samberg, V., & Lichtenberg, A. (2007). The prevalence of mental health problems in children 1½ years of age – The Copenhagen Child Cohort 2000. *Journal of Child Psychology and Psychiatry, 48*, 62–70.

Smith, C. L., Calkins, S. D., & Keane, S. P. (2006). The relation of maternal behavior and attachment security to toddlers' emotions and emotional regulation. *Research in Human Development, 3*, 21–31.

Spitz, R. (1946). Anaclitic depression. *Psychoanalytic Study of the Child, 2*, 313–342.

Sroufe, L. A. (1997). Psychopathology as an outcome of development. *Development and Psychopathology, 9*, 251–268.

Sroufe, L. A., Egeland, B., Carlson, E. A., & Collins, W. A. (2005). *The development of the person: The Minnesota Study of Risk and Adaptation from Birth to Adulthood*. New York: Guilford Press.

Stafford, B., Zeanah, C. H., & Scheeringa, M. (2003). Exploring psychopathology in early childhood: PTSD and attachment disorders in DC: 0–3 and DSM-IV. *Infant Mental Health Journal, 24*, 398–409.

Task Force on Research Diagnostic Criteria: Infancy and Preschool (2003). Research diagnostic criteria for infants and preschool children: The process and empirical support. *Journal of the American Academy of Child and Adolescent Psychiatry, 42*(12), 1504–1512.

Toth, S. L., & Cicchetti, D. (2004). Child maltreatment and its impact on psychosocial child development. In R. E. Tremblay, R. G. Barr, & R. DeV. Peters (Eds.), *Encyclopedia on early childhood development* [Electronic Version] (pp. 1–8). Montreal: Centre of Excellence for Early Childhood Development.

Toth, S. L., Rogosch, F. A., Manly, J. T., & Cicchetti, D. (2006). The efficacy of toddler–parent psychotherapy to reorganize attachment in the young offspring of mothers with major depressive disorder: A randomized preventive trial. *Journal of Consulting and Clinical Psychology, 74,* 1006–1016.

Tremblay, R. E., Nagin, D. S., Séguin, J. R., Zoccolillo, M., Zelazo, P. D., Boivin, M., et al. (2004). Physical aggression during early childhood: Trajectories and predictors. *Pediatrics, 114,* e43–e49.

van IJzendoorn, M. H. (1995). Adult attachment representations, parental responsiveness, and infant attachment: A meta-analysis on the predictive validity of the adult attachment interview. *Psychological Bulletin, 117,* 387–403.

von Hofacker, N., & Papoušek, M. (1998). Disorders of excessive crying, feeding, and sleeping: The Munich Interdisciplinary Research and Intervention Program. *Infant Mental Health Journal, 19,* 180–201.

Wakschlag, L. S., Leventhal, B. L., Pine, D. S., Pickett, K. E., & Carter, A. S. (2006). Elucidating early mechanisms of developmental psychopathology: The case of prenatal smoking and disruptive behavior. *Child Development. 77,* 893–906.

Wieder, S., & Greenspan, S. I. (2006). Infant and early childhood mental health: The DIR model. In G. M. Foley & J. D. Hochman (Eds.), *Mental health in early intervention* (pp. 175–189). Baltimore, MD: Brooks Publishing.

Weinberg, M. K., & Tronick, E. Z. (1998). Emotional care of the at-risk infant: Emotional characteristics of infants associated with maternal depression and anxiety. *Pediatrics, 102* Supplement, 1298–1304.

Winnicott, D. W. (1936). Mental hygiene of the pre-school child. In R. Shepherd, J. Johns, & H. T. Robinson (Eds.) (1996), *D. W. Winnicott: Thinking about children* (pp. 59–76). Reading, MA: Addison-Wesley.

Wolke, D., Meyer, R., Ohrt, B., & Riegel, K. (1995). The incidence of sleeping problems in preterm and fullterm infants discharged from neonatal special care units: An epidemiological longitudinal study. *Journal of Child Psychology and Psychiatry, 36,* 203–233.

World Health Organization (2004). *The ICD-10 Classification of mental and behavioral disorders: Clinical observations and diagnostic guidelines.* Geneva: World Health Organization.

Zeanah, C. H. (1996). Beyond insecurity: A reconceptualization of attachment disorders in infancy. *Journal of Consulting and Clinical Psychology, 64,* 42–52.

Zeanah, C. H., & Boris, N. W. (2000). Disturbances and disorders of attachment in early childhood. In C. H. Zeanah (Ed.), *Handbook of infant mental health* (2nd ed., pp. 353–368). New York: Guilford Press.

Zeanah, C. H., Larrieu, J. A., Heller, S. S., & Valliere, J. (2000). Infant–parent relationship assessment. In C. H. Zeanah, Jr. (Ed.), *Handbook of infant mental health* (2nd ed., pp. 222–235). New York: Guilford Press.

Zeanah, C. H., Scheeringa, M., Boris, N. W., Heller, S. S., Smyke, A. T., & Trapani, J. (2004). Reactive attachment disorder in maltreated toddlers. *Child Abuse and Neglect, 28,* 877–888.

Zeanah, C. H., Smyke, A. T., Koga, S., Carlson, E., & the BEIP Core Group (2005). Attachment in institutionalized and community children in Romania. *Child Development, 76,* 1015–1028.

Zero to Three (1994). *Diagnostic classification of mental health and developmental disorders of infancy and early childhood.* Washington, DC: Zero to Three: National Center for Infants, Toddlers, and Families.

Zero to Three (2005). *Diagnostic classification of mental health and developmental disorders of infancy and early childhood: Revised edition (DC:0–3R).* Washington, DC: Zero to Three Press.

Zero to Three DC: 0–3R Training Task Force (2005). *Guidelines for the diagnosis of infants affected by disasters or major community violence.* Washington, DC: Zero to Three. www.zerotothree.org/

site/DocServer/DC03R_Disaster_Guidelines.pdf?docID=2105&AddInterest=1221   (accessed April 2008).

Ziegler, M., Wollwerth de Chuquisengo, R., & Papoušek, M. (2008). Excessive crying in infancy. In M. Papoušek, M. Schieche, & H. Wurmser (Eds.), *Disorders of behavioral and emotional regulation in the first years of life: Early risks and intervention in the developing parent–infant relationship* (K. Kronenberg, Trans.) (pp. 85–115). Washington, DC: Zero to Three. (Original work published 2004.)

12

Genetic Disorders Associated with Intellectual Disability: An Early Development Perspective

Deborah J. Fidler, Lisa Daunhauer, David E. Most, and Harvey Switzky

Since its inception, the field of intellectual disabilities has been defined by continued transformation. Throughout much of the twentieth century, changes in terminology, definitions, and philosophical approach to treatment marked the history of intellectual disability science and practice, with many of these changes reflecting the progress and shifts observable in the larger cultural and scientific context. Most notably, the field of intellectual disability research has been influenced by advances in biomedical sciences, in particular in the sophistication of genetics and embryology, as well as allied fields such as early intervention and early development science. In this chapter, the impact of evolving trends will be examined within the context of the early diagnosis of intellectual disability prenatally, in infancy, and in early childhood.

Changing Approaches to Intellectual Disability

Terminology

One critical change that has been made most recently involves the terminology used to define the population of interest, individuals who show a combination of impaired cognitive functioning and deficits in adaptive behavior. The term "intellectual disability", referring specifically to a limitation in one's intellect, has gained consensus most recently as the preferred term for educators, researchers, and clinicians. This term is often used together with the term "developmental disability," which refers specifically to an impairment or limitation involving an individual's developmental processes. These two terms have been adopted most widely internationally, though other terms, such as "learning disability" and "developmental handicap," are used in some parts of the world (Brown, 2007). In the United States, the adoption of the term "intellectual disability" is recent. For much of the twentieth century, terms used to define individuals with cognitive and adaptive behavior impairments were "mental deficiency" and, in later years, "mental retardation". While the term "mental deficiency" was phased out completely several decades ago, the term "mental retardation" has predominated in the United States until very recently. This shift in terminology is reflected most strongly in the changes made to the field's leading professional organization. In 2006, the American Association on Mental Retardation (AAMR) voted to change its name to the American Association on Intellectual and Developmental Disabilities (AAIDD).

Just as terminology has changed over time, similar shifts have been observed in the definitions of these terms as well, often with criteria for inclusion varying according to professional organization. Currently, the AAIDD defines intellectual disability as "a disability characterized by significant limitations both in intellectual functioning and in adaptive behavior as expressed in conceptual, social, and practical adaptive skills" (AAMR, 2002, p. 8). The AAIDD also specifies that the intelligence quotient (IQ) cutoff for intellectual disability is 70–75, and that the disability must also have originated earlier than age 18. The criteria for intellectual disability put forth by the American Psychiatric Association (APA, 2000) differ somewhat in the designation of a clear IQ cutoff of 70, though the designation of "concurrent limitations or alterations in adaptive functioning" (p. 41) and onset before age 18 are in line with the AAIDD definition. It is notable that the IQ cutoff designated by both the AAIDD and the APA has changed on several occasions from as low as 70 to as high as 85, with great implications for policy and service delivery. Similar shifts in the conceptualization of the adaptive behavior construct have also taken place in the latter half of the past century. See Switzky and Greenspan (2006) for a major review of these issues; see also chapter 10 in the present volume for detailed discussion of autism and autism spectrum disorders.

The role of etiology

Another critical change relates to the dimensions through which researchers categorize individuals with intellectual disability. The dominant paradigm for much of the twentieth century in the field of intellectual disability research was the "severity of impairment" approach, relying mainly on ranges of IQ scores to identify children as showing mild, moderate, severe, or profound impairment. However, in the latter part of the twentieth century, leaders in the field emphasized that the etiology, or the biological cause of an individual's impairments, were of potential importance in that different etiologies of impairment predispose children to different developmental outcomes (Burack, Hodapp, & Zigler, 1988; Dykens, 1995). Specifically, it was argued that there were at least two distinct groups of individuals with intellectual disability, those with "familial" etiologies, who inherited genes associated with low intelligence and/or experience impoverished environmental conditions such as low levels of early stimulation, and those with "organic" etiologies, who experienced a biological insult in the form of a genetic abnormality or a prenatal factor that led to the disability (Burack et al., 1988). Within this conceptualization, it is likely that the genetic factors that lead to outcomes associated with familial intellectual disability are more general in nature, referring to the inheritance of common gene variants that impact intellectual functioning, while the genetic factors associated with organic intellectual disability are likely to involve specific chromosomal or genetic abnormalities such as deletions, duplications, translocations, and aneuploidies. To date, 1,200 specific genetic disorders have been identified as being associated with intellectual disability (Moser, 2004).

This effort to improve our understanding of the various etiologies of intellectual disability has been aided by advances in biomedical research in the twentieth century. It is now understood that intellectual disability can result from environmental factors, genetic factors, and an interaction between the two. Environmental factors can include prenatal or postnatal malnutrition (e.g., absence of certain nutrients such as folic acid, vitamin A, or iodine) prenatal or postnatal exposure to certain environmental toxins, such as lead, mercury, and prenatal exposure to alcohol, tobacco, and illicit drugs (Percy, 2007). In addition, factors such as maternal health, prenatal exposure to maternal infections, and prematurity are also considered to be environmental etiologies of intellectual disability (for detailed discussion of nutritional deficiencies, prenatal risk factors, biomedical risks, and environmental toxins, see also chapters 2 and 3 in this volume). Environmental factors associated with intellectual disability can also involve the absence of important early experiences or chaotic family contexts that do not provide a young child with minimally nurturing contexts in which to develop (see chapter 15 in volume 1 on parenting and chapter 5 in this volume for detailed discussion of psychosocial risk factors). In this chapter, we focus our attention primarily on early developmental outcomes in genetic disorders associated with intellectual disability. It is important to note, however, that at this time, roughly 50% of individuals have no identifiable cause for their intellectual disability (McDermott, Durkin, Schupf, & Stein, 2007). For a wider discussion of familial intellectual disability and nongenetic organic causes of intellectual disability and early childhood, see Jacobson, Mulick, and Rojahn (2007) or Brown and Percy (2007).

Early diagnosis of genetic disorders

Until recently, diagnosis of disorders associated with intellectual disability often took place in early middle childhood, often coinciding with a child's initial exposure to formal school settings. However, with advances in the biomedical sciences, the diagnosis of disorders associated with intellectual disability is taking place as early as the first trimester of prenatal development. It is important to note that early diagnoses are mainly possible for organic forms of intellectual disability, particularly genetic disorders. Prenatal diagnosis of specific disorders is becoming more common as technologies such as prenatal ultrasound, nuchal translucency tests, maternal serum screening, and chorionic villi sampling become more widely used among pregnant women (Levine, 2002; Malone et al., 2005; Ormond, 1997; Pandya, Kuhn, Brizot, Cardy, & Nicolaides, 1994; Wapner et al., 2003). In some cases, such prenatal diagnoses can impact decisions relating to delivery options. Parents may also use this information for decision-making regarding therapeutic termination (Roberts, Stough, & Parrish, 2002). In other cases, prenatal diagnosis begins the process of adjustment to the role of parenting a child with intellectual or developmental disability.

In addition to prenatal diagnostic advances, early diagnosis of disorders associated with intellectual disability is becoming more common immediately after birth. Newborn screening procedures have become a common means of diagnosing disorders associated with intellectual disability in Western countries (American Academy of Pediatrics Newborn Screening Task Force, 2000). Disorders such as phenylketonuria, galactosemia, and congenital hypothyroidism are screened with blood samples taken from a newborn's heel (American Academy of Pediatrics et al., 2006; Koch, 1999). Standard screening in many Western countries also includes hearing testing, which in some cases can lead to more specific testing for specific disorders (Wrightson, 2007; see also chapter 4 in this volume on deafness). However, it is important to note that of the of the 1,200 known genetic disorders, very few are included in routine screening. For individuals born with one of the rarer disorders that are not included in any screening process, the road to obtaining accurate diagnosis can take substantially longer and can involve repeated genetic testing, numerous false leads, and in some cases substantial expense to the family. In addition, it should be noted that for children with idiopathic causes of intellectual disability, diagnosis is an ongoing process during early childhood and beyond, as delays become evident and pronounced (see chapter 9 in this volume for discussion of early intellectual assessment). In the near future, however, the search for a biological etiology for intellectual disability will likely be altered by the use of DNA microarray analysis (or "gene-chip" technology), which involves the most detailed analysis of variations in an individual's genotype available to date (see Ward, 2005).

Behavioral phenotypes

Percy (2007) describes several reasons why identifying and diagnosing the cause or contributing factors to a child's impairment may be important for families and practitioners. First, she notes that some genetic or hormonal disorders, such as inborn errors of metabolism, can be managed in a way that prevents or attenuates subsequent intellectual impairment. Screening for these disorders, such as phenylketonuria or hypothyroidism, can allow for medical and therapeutic interventions that minimize the degree to which these disorders progress. A second benefit noted by Percy (2007) is that identifying the specific etiology of a disability allows families to plan their future in an informed manner, including making decisions regarding subsequent pregnancies and the use of reproductive technology. The third reason is that some causes of intellectual disability are the result of environmental health hazards, such as exposure to mercury, lead, and other substances that are teratogenic and also hazardous in their exposure to young children. Identifying these causes can lead to preventive measures on an individual and a societal level. And finally, it is noted that identifying the etiology of intellectual disability can help individuals find appropriate interventions to improve their quality of life, and can also help researchers develop targeted interventions that specifically address the profile of needs associated with the disorder (Percy, 2007).

This last justification has propelled a great deal of research inquiry into identifying the behavioral outcomes, or the "behavioral phenotypes," associated with specific genetic disorders (Dykens, 1995; Hodapp & Dykens, 2005). There is now overwhelming empirical evidence that different genetic disorders predispose individuals to distinct outcomes involving a wide range of developmental performance areas, including cognitive, linguistic, social, emotional, motoric, and behavioral functioning (Dykens & Hodapp, 2001). These outcomes include patterns of strength and weakness in both cross-domain and within-domain performances in each of these areas. For example, in the area of information processing, it has been well documented that children with Down syndrome show a relative advantage for the short-term processing of visual over verbal information, while children with Williams syndrome tend to show the opposite pattern (Jarrold, Baddeley, & Hewes, 1999; Vicari, Carlesimo, & Caltegirone, 1995; Vicari, 2006). Behavioral propensities that have been associated with specific genetic disorders include hyperphagia (an extreme increase in appetite for and consumption of food) in Prader–Willi syndrome (PWS; see Dykens & Cassidy, 1996, for a review), self-injurious behavior in Smith–Magenis syndrome (Dykens & Smith, 1998), and an unusual crying behavior in 5p–syndrome (cri du chat syndrome; Cornish, Bramble & Standen, 2001). An enhancement of some aspects of social relatedness have been described in individuals with Williams syndrome (Fidler, Hepburn, Most, Philofsky, & Rogers, 2007; Pleska-Skwerer, Verbalis, & Schofield, 2006; Porter, Coltheart, & Langdon, 2007), while children with fragile X syndrome (FXS) are at higher risk of meeting criteria for autism or autism spectrum disorder, which impairs social relatedness (Demark, Feldman, & Holden, 2003; Farzin, Perry, & Hessl, 2006). Thus, genetic disorders associated with intellectual disability have the potential to impact a wide range of developmental outcomes beyond simply performance in areas of intellectual or cognitive functioning.

It has been argued that the characterization of these phenotypic profiles has great relevance for families, educators, and interventionists (Hodapp & Fidler, 1999), especially with regard to early development (Fidler, 2005; Fidler, Philofsky, & Hepburn, 2007; Hodapp & DesJardin, 2002; Hodapp & Fidler, 1999). For example, Fidler, Philofsky, and Hepburn (2007) argued for the potential effectiveness of an anticipatory guidance approach when working with families of young children with specific genetic disorders, wherein the literature on behavioral phenotypes might guide a clinician's treatment approach to be on the "lookout" for areas of potentially heightened vulnerability. With such an approach, it may be possible to identify early manifestations of outcomes in very young children in order to begin treatment before an area of difficulty becomes a pronounced area of weakness. However, rigorous treatment studies have not been conducted to support these potential benefits.

Emerging behavioral phenotypes in early childhood

Of particular relevance for this chapter is the notion that phenotypic profiles are the result of a dynamic developmental process that begins at the earliest moments of brain development and continues throughout the lifespan (Fidler, Philofsky, & Hepburn, 2007; Karmiloff-Smith, 1998). Researchers have begun to look beyond the cross-sectional phenotypic outcomes reported in research on children with different syndromes in middle and later childhood, and the developmental pathways leading to these end states have become the target of research as well (see Fidler, 2005).

This shift to a more developmental framework has resulted in evidence showing that behavioral phenotypes begin to emerge in detectable ways in the first few years of life (Fidler, 2005). For example, Karmiloff-Smith (1998) argues that intellectual and developmental disabilities are the result of a cumulative process of atypical brain and physiological development, and that, in the case of genetic disorders, this atypical process begins at the earliest moments of neurodevelopment. Studying changes in behavioral phenotypes over time places an emphasis on this dynamic developmental process, wherein the self-organization that generally occurs throughout development is strongly influenced by the constraints on gene expression that are caused by the genetic disorder. Such an approach provides a more complete understanding of the ways in which different disorders impact a child's ability to process information, communicate, relate to others socially, and function in adaptive ways. Beyond early childhood, there is also evidence that changes in behavioral profiles are observed at other critical points in development, such as adolescence and the transition to later adulthood (Dykens, Shah, Sagun, Beck, & King, 2002). From a treatment perspective, the subtle early manifestations of later, more pronounced outcomes found in middle childhood may serve as beneficial targets for early intervention in children with genetic disorders (Fidler, 2005). With this developmental view it may be possible to craft techniques that target the earliest manifestations of later more pronounced outcomes, in order to have a greater impact on development downstream.

Theoretical and practical issues in the study of emerging behavioral phenotypes

In order to study emerging behavioral phenotypes in early childhood, there are several theoretical and practical issues to consider. The first relates to the notion of developmental continuity and our ability to measure the manifestation of a specific construct throughout development. Of particular importance are issues related to heterotypic continuity (Fox & Henderson, 1999). This is because development is a cumulative and directional process, with each prior developmental achievement resting on the totality of all that came before it, and with each milestone representing a level of increasing developmental specificity and sophistication. Viewed in this way, the manifestation of a specific underlying construct, such as social relatedness or expressive language, evolves over time and takes many different forms throughout development, with the greatest changes observable in early childhood (Kagan, 1969). This type of heterotypic continuity is only identifiable within a developmental framework wherein an underlying hypothesis drives the link between two behaviors at different points in development (Caspi & Roberts, 1999). For example, to identify the early manifestation of a specific construct, such as middle childhood hypersociability in Williams syndrome, it is important to have a clear characterization of the nature of this unique behavioral profile in older children, a potential behavioral manifestation in early childhood, and a clear theoretical link between these two behaviors based on existing knowledge regarding these constructs. Longitudinal studies linking those two behaviors would provide empirical support for such proposed continuity. In this way, it may be possible to link candidate behavioral constructs in infancy or toddlerhood with their more complex form in later childhood in children with genetic disorders, even when homotypic continuities are unlikely.

In addition to these theoretical issues, there are also more practical issues to consider in the study of emerging behavioral phenotypes associated with specific genetic disorders. These issues relate to early diagnosis of genetic disorders, particularly those rarer disorders that are not included in prenatal and newborn screening. In order to be able to study the early behavioral manifestations of key constructs in specific disorders, it is important to have access to a large enough sample of infants, toddlers, and preschool age children with that particular disorder. However, as discussed earlier, while some genetic disorders are now included in routine screening procedures, the vast majority are not. Often, the diagnosis of less well-known disorders such as Williams syndrome does not take place until the second or third year of life or even later (Huang, Sadler, O'Riordan, & Robin, 2002; Morris, Demsey, Leonard, Dilts, & Blackburn, 1988). This poses a significant challenge to researchers interested in uncovering the early effects of genetic disorders that may not even be identified past the time frame of interest.

A further limitation relates to the literature that does exist regarding those disorders that have received research attention in early development. While some studies have been conducted on infants or young children with a small number of more common genetic disorders associated with intellectual disability, for the most part they have not been conducted in a way that tests systematic hypotheses regarding the early manifestation of phenotypic outcomes. In particular, Down syndrome and FXS have been researched in infancy (see below), yet few studies are posed with an eye toward questions regarding developmental continuity and potential targets for intervention to alter developmental trajectories.

Despite these limitations, it is possible to examine the existing literature on early development in those disorders that have received research attention in an attempt to offer a basic understanding of the early observed behaviors in each group. Although it is not yet possible to report findings from studies that have described behavioral trajectories and continuities from early childhood to adulthood, this first step can offer a clear picture that genetic disorders do impact development in its earliest stages, and that different disorders are impacted differentially even in the earliest years of life. In the following section, we consider the findings to date regarding early development in Down syndrome, Williams syndrome, FXS, PWS, and Smith–Magenis syndrome. These disorders have been selected because a great deal of innovative developmental and behavioral research is currently being conducted in these populations. We describe behavioral outcomes that have been characterized in infants, toddlers, and preschool-age children in order to identify the early behavioral manifestations of these disorders. (For a discussion of phenylketonuria, a genetic metabolic disorder, see chapter 3 in this volume.)

Early Development in Genetic Disorders Associated with Intellectual Disability

Down syndrome

Down syndrome is the most common genetic disorder associated with intellectual disability, occurring in approximately 1 in every 750 live births (Canfield et al., 2006). In 95% of cases, the cause of Down syndrome is the presence of an extra chromosome 21, which results from nondisjunction during meiosis. Several features of Down syndrome make it unique among other disorders. First, more prenatal tests are available to screen for Down syndrome than for any other genetic disorder associated with intellectual disability, with the latest, nuchal translucency technology, available as early as week 11 of gestation (Malone et al., 2005). Thus, when compared to all other disorders, Down syndrome is unique in that many more parents are informed of their child's diagnosis prior to the child's birth. In addition, Down syndrome was discovered over 150 years ago (Sherman, Allen, Bean, & Freeman, 2007) and remains the best-known and most commonly researched genetic disorder (see Fidler, 2005, for a review). Because of these issues, there is more information available regarding early development in Down syndrome than any other disorder. In this section, we review findings regarding early cognitive, social, emotional, motoric, and communication development in infants and young children with Down syndrome.

Cognition.   Most individuals with Down syndrome fall into the mild to moderate range of intellectual disability, with IQs ranging between 40 and 70 (Hodapp, Evans, & Gray, 1999). Early childhood is marked by a deceleration in the rate with which developmental milestones are achieved, and as a result, IQ scores tend to decline steadily in the first few years of life (Hodapp et al., 1999). Difficulty with instrumental ("means–end") thinking is observable in toddlers with Down syndrome on problem-solving tasks (Fidler, Philofsky, Hepburn, & Rogers, 2005), and may be detectable in earlier declines in contingency learning in 9-month-old infants with Down syndrome (Ohr & Fagen, 1994). Instrumental thinking deficits are also related to difficulties in toddler nonverbal communication behaviors (Fidler, Philofsky, et al., 2005). In terms of information processing, older individuals with Down syndrome show a distinct advantage for tasks that involve visual processing and a disadvantage for tasks that involve verbal and auditory processing (Jarrold et al., 1999; Klein & Mervis, 1999; Wang & Bellugi, 1994). The limited information that is available suggests a similar emerging profile of strengths in some areas of visual processing, such as visual imitation and memory (Heimann & Ullstadius, 1999; Karrer, Wojtascek, & Davis, 1995; Karrer, Karrer, Bloom, Chaney, & Davis, 1998), and deficits in vocal imitation and auditory brain stem responses (Mahoney, Glover, & Finger, 1981). Yet this occurs in the contexts of some deficits in visual processing in infancy as well (Berger & Cunningham, 1983; Miranda & Fantz, 1973), and thus it is important to recognize the complex nature of this profile.

Language.   Receptive language skills generally emerge with greater competence than expressive language skills in young children with Down syndrome (Chapman, 1999; Fabretti, Pizzuto, Vicari, & Voterra, 1997; Miller, 1999). In terms of expressive language delays, it has been hypothesized that there are two subgroups of young children with Down syndrome: one subgroup shows these delays from the onset of first words, and a second subgroup shows appropriate vocabulary acquisition, but shows expressive language lags in the onset of phrased speech (Miller, 1999). However, the origins of expressive language delays can be observed as early as the onset of prelinguistic vocalizations in infancy, where some features of vocal play and canonical babbling appear to develop atypically (Legerstee, Bowman, & Fels, 1992; Lynch, Oller, Steffens, Levine, Basinger, & Umbel, 1995), which can be a predictor of later expressive language skills (Lynch, Oller, Steffens, & Buder, 1995; Stoel-Gammon, 1992).

Despite these delays, young children with Down syndrome seem to show competence in some areas of early nonverbal communication. Young children with Down syndrome show mental age (MA) appropriate levels of nonverbal joint attention (Fidler, Philofsky, et al., 2005; Mundy, Kasari, Sigman, & Ruskin, 1995; Mundy, Sigman, Kasari, & Yirmiya, 1988; Wetherby, Yonclas, & Bryan, 1989) and show competence in the area of gestural communication (Caselli, Vicari, Longobardi, Lami, Pizzoli, & Stella, 1998; Iverson, Longobardi, & Caselli, 2003). Other areas of nonverbal communication that require the use of instrumental thinking skills, such as nonverbal requesting, appear to be impaired relative to other MA matched children (Fidler, Philofsky, et al., 2005; Mundy et al., 1988, 1995; Wetherby et al., 1989).

Social functioning.   The majority of young children with Down syndrome show MA appropriate functioning in the area of early social relatedness (see Fidler, 2006, for a review), though a small percentage of children with Down syndrome who meet criteria for comorbid autism or autism spectrum disorder show impairment in this area (Collacott, Cooper, & McGrother, 1992; Ghaziuddin, Tsai, & Ghaziuddin, 1992; Hepburn, Philofsky, Fidler, & Rogers, 2008; Kent, Evans, Paul, & Sharp, 1999; Pary & Hurley, 2002). For the majority of young children with Down syndrome who do not have comorbid autism, there is evidence of MA appropriate development of milestones associated with both dyadic and triadic social relatedness (see Fidler, 2006, for a review). However, evidence for atypicality can be observed in the increased looking behavior directed at parents in studies of infants with Down syndrome at 4 months, 6 months, and 9 months of age (Crown, Feldstein, Jasnow, & Beebe, 1992; Gunn, Berry, & Andrews, 1982). Interestingly, this increased looking behavior in infants with Down syndrome has been shown in ambiguous situations, but not in social referencing contexts (Kasari, Freeman, Mundy, & Sigman, 1995; Walden, Knieps, & Baxter, 1991). Enhanced social motivation can also be observed in toddlers and preschoolers with Down syndrome, who show more reciprocal turn-taking and other social initiations (object shows, invitations) when compared with typically developing children (Mundy et al., 1988; Sigman & Ruskin, 1999). Infants with Down syndrome may be more likely to show easy temperaments than typically developing infants, though evidence for this is somewhat mixed (see chapter 20 in volume 1). Other research on the emergence of a personality-motivation orientation in Down syndrome that involves poor task

persistence and an over-reliance on social strategies may shed further light on temperament and personality issues in this population (Fidler, 2006).

Motor skills.   As motor skills serve as a foundation for many other areas of functioning,
it is critical to note that many young children with Down syndrome show pronounced
delays in many areas of motor development. Infants with Down syndrome show atypical
reflexes, low muscle tone, and hyperflexibility, and many motor milestones such as sitting
without support, standing, and walking alone take place at least 6 months later than
observed in typically developing infants (Block, 1991; Harris & Shea, 1991). Evidence
of the atypical development of motor planning is also observed in toddlers with Down
syndrome (Fidler, Hepburn, Mankin, & Rogers, 2005), which may have important
implications for adaptive behavior skills and day-to-day functioning (Fidler, Philofsky,
et al., 2005).

Fragile X syndrome

Fragile X syndrome is one of the most commonly inherited forms of intellectual disability. In genetic studies during the 1970s, the distal X chromosome material appeared to
be tenuously connected to the remainder of the chromosome, thus it was described as
"fragile" (Sutherland, 1977). It is now known that FXS is caused by a mutation, or in
some cases a deletion, of the FMR-1 gene (Verkerk et al., 1991). The FMR-1 gene
contains a trinucleotide repeat (CGG) that in typical individuals occurs in sets of 6–40
(see Visootsak, Warren, Anido, & Graham, 2005, for a review). However, in individuals
who are FXS carriers (premutation), there is an expanded number of trinucleotide
repeats. In most individuals with FXS (full mutation) the repeats can number greater
than 200. The trinucleotide expansions or FMR-1 deletion disrupt the production of
a protein essential for brain functioning, FMRP. Decreased expression of the FMRP
protein affects the developmental pathways regulating physical appearance, intellect, and
behavior (Reiss & Dant, 2003). Generally higher levels of FMRP in an individual are
associated with better developmental outcomes (Bailey, Hatton, Tassone, Skinner, &
Taylor, 2001; Hagerman, 2002). Because FXS is carried on the X chromosome, both
males and females can be carriers (premutation) or have the syndrome (full mutation).
The likelihood of a trinucleotide expansion increases over generations. Therefore, it is
possible for unsuspecting parents to produce the first child with full mutation FXS
observed in a family. The incidence of FXS is 1 in 4,000 males and 1 in 8,000 females
(Turner, Webb, Wake, & Robinson, 1996). Given the discrepancy in incidence and
symptom severity between males and females, the preponderance of research on FXS
focuses on males.

Diagnosis.   Unlike Down syndrome, few dysmorphic physical features associated with
the FXS phenotype signal the presence of FXS in infants and young children because
these features are dependent on maturation. Many with FXS eventually will present with
prominent ears, long face, and in males, macroorchidism around the time of puberty
(Hagerman, 2002; Visootsak et al., 2005). Other physical features associated with FXS

include hypermobile joints, large head, hallucal crease, high-arched palate, hypotonia, and soft skin over the dorsum of the hands (Hagerman, 2002).

Due to the variability in delays and characteristics related to FXS, there is a substantial lag from when someone, usually a parent, notices a child is not achieving milestones to the referral for genetic testing. Most children eventually diagnosed with FXS are not identified with developmental delays until 18–24 months of age and genetic confirmation typically happens up to a year later (Bailey, Roberts, Mirrett, & Hatton, 2001). Consequently, many children do not receive a diagnosis until they are too old for early intervention.

Because physical appearance may not be useful in signaling a possible diagnosis of FXS, some clinicians recommend that every infant and toddler with developmental delays be genetically tested for FXS, particularly if those delays occur in the area of speech or in conjunction with a family history of intellectual disability (Visootsak et al., 2005). Early developmental delays are detectable in infants and young children with FXS through routine screenings (Mirrett, Bailey, Roberts & Hatton, 2004). Mirrett et al. found that 10 out of 11 boys with FXS were diagnosed with developmental delay with the Denver-II at 9 months of age and that the early Language Milestone Scale-2 found delays in 100% of these infants. Another research group used an ecologically relevant method to examine distinguishing behaviors in infants with FXS through observation of everyday activities. In a retrospective home video analysis of infants with FXS, Baranek et al. (2005) found that less sophisticated object play, repetitive use of objects, posturing, and more repetitive leg movements during activities differentiated the FXS group from infants with autism or other developmental delays.

Motor development.   Parents often notice early deficits in motor milestones and muscle tone in their children with FXS (Bailey, Skinner, & Sparkman, 2003; Rogers, Hepburn & Wehner, 2003). Infants and toddlers with FXS exhibit delayed motor skills from infancy (Bailey, Hatton, & Skinner, 1998; Kau, Reider, Payne, Meyer, & Freund, 2000; Partington, 1984; Prouty et al., 1988). In two small studies of infants with FXS, the infants sat independently at 10 months and walked independently around age 2 (20.6–23.4 months) (Partington, 1984; Prouty et al., 1988). In a longitudinal study of 2–6-year-olds with FXS, researchers found that not only were motor skills delayed, but that these skills developed at approximately half the rate of that found in typically developing children (Bailey et al., 1998). Importantly, this rate remained consistent from toddlerhood to 6 years of age. However, both motor skills and adaptive behaviors (e.g., feeding and dressing) were a relative strength for these children. Finally, there is some evidence that within-subject variability in motor development performance may be related to decreased FMRP protein expression (Bailey, Hatton, Tassone, Skinner, & Taylor, 2001).

Cognition and communication.   Similar to their longitudinal motor development findings, Bailey et al. (1998) report that 2–6-year-old children with FXS developed both cognition and communication at a rate that was approximately half the rate of their typically developing peers and that this rate remained consistent. Moreover, the performance level of these two domains was relatively lower than the level for motor skills. For example, the researchers highlighted that at the average assessment age (51 months), children's communication and cognitive performance was equivalent to the developmental ages of

22.4 and 24.9 months, respectively. In comparison, their motor performance was equivalent to a developmental age of 27.8 months (Bailey et al., 1998). As with motor skills, in this study lower FMRP levels were associated with lower cognitive performance (Bailey, Hatton, Tassone, Skinner, & Taylor, 2001).

Research indicates that older children with FXS experience relative strengths in receptive and expressive language (see Abbeduto, Brady, & Kover, 2007, for a review). Conversely, they experience challenges in using language socially (pragmatics) and following linguistic rules (morphosyntax; Abbeduto et al., 2007).

In a study of infants and toddlers, the FXS group demonstrated poorer visual inhibition in comparison to a Williams syndrome group (Cornish, Scerif, & Karmiloff-Smith, 2007). Similarly, toddlers with FXS made significant perseverative errors (kept pointing at previous correct responses) when searching for targets amongst distracters when compared to peers with either Williams syndrome or Down syndrome (Scerif, Cornish, Wilding, Driver, & Karmiloff-Smith, 2004). The authors made two interpretations: (1) that these early detected perseverative errors may be related to the inhibition difficulties reported in older children with FXS; and (2) this lack of inhibition may provide evidence for early executive control difficulties in FXS (Cornish et al., 2007; Scerif et al., 2004). Finally, Scerif, Cornish, Wilding, Driver, and Karmiloff-Smith (2006) noted that young children with FXS were capable of discriminating targets when paired with one, but not multiple, distracters.

Social-emotional functioning.   When compared to females, males with FXS tend to develop more behavioral issues including hyperactivity, gaze aversion, hand flapping, hand biting and other self-injurious or repetitive behaviors (Hagerman, 2002). In a study of preschoolers with FXS and a comparison group with mixed developmental disabilities, Kau et al. (2000) found that preschoolers with FXS demonstrated more social avoidance, more positive mood, higher activity level, and (surprisingly) less social withdrawal than IQ-matched peers with developmental delays. The authors noted that the less impaired social withdrawal finding was unexpected. The authors hypothesized that the reported positive mood in these preschoolers may differ from the irritability associated with older children with FXS because preschoolers face fewer demands (e.g., school, peer groups, and novel situations) than do school-age children. Rogers et al. (2003) found evidence that toddlers with FXS are reactive to sensory stimuli. Toddlers with FXS were rated by their parents to have more sensory reactivity to touch and more difficulty with auditory filtering than both a developmental delay group and a typically developing group.

Approximately 25% of older children and adults with FXS meet the diagnostic criteria for autism or present with autistic-like behaviors (Hatton et al., 2006; Rogers, Wehner, & Hagerman, 2001). In a study of toddlers and preschoolers with FXS, 33% of the FXS group met the criteria for autism (Rogers et al., 2001). The authors cautioned that this unexpectedly large finding may be related to assessing a younger (preschool) sample and to the recruitment strategy. The little evidence examining this in females indicates that autistic symptoms are not as common in female toddlers with FXS (6%; Hatton et al., 2006).

Infants and young children with FXS who meet the criteria for autism exhibit greater developmental delays and develop at a slower rate in all areas of development when compared to peers diagnosed solely with FXS (Bailey, Hatton, Mesibov, Ament, &

Skinner, 2000; Bailey, Hatton, Skinner, & Mesibov, 2001; Cohen, 1995; Philofsky, Hepburn, Hayes, Hagerman, & Rogers, 2004). Poor receptive language may be a marker for toddlers who have comorbid FXS and autism symptoms (Philofsky et al., 2004). It is still not known whether the children who both have a diagnosis of FXS and meet the criteria for autism are affected by a common pathway, influenced by other genes, or are demonstrating artifacts reflective of intellectual disabilities (Philofsky et al., 2004; Reiss & Dant, 2003; Rogers et al., 2001).

Prader–Willi syndrome

Prader–Willi syndrome is a genetic disorder that often (60–70% of cases) results from the partial deletion or translocation of the paternal contribution of chromosome 15 (15q11–q13 region; Chamberlain & Brannan, 2001; Ledbetter, Riccardi, Airhart, Strobel, Keenan, & Crawford, 1981). Less commonly (25–30%), PWS results from maternal uniparental disomy in which both copies of chromosome 15 are maternally contributed (Nicholls, Knoll, Butler, Karam, & Lalande, 1989). Infrequently (5%), PWS may also be the result of imprinting mutations, which involves a disruption of the process wherein specific genes are expressed uniquely based on parental origination (Chamberlain & Brannan, 2001). PWS is rare, occurring in 1 out of 10,000–15,000 individuals (Cassidy, 1997). The genetic involvement may disrupt hypothalamic functions in individuals with PWS (Cassidy, 1997).

While the syndrome varies individually, one of the quintessential characteristics of PWS is an insatiable appetite. The inability to feel sated is often accompanied by slow metabolism and compulsive food-seeking behaviors such as stealing and scavenging in PWS (see Dykens, 1999, for a review). This unfortunate combination of characteristics and behaviors can lead to obesity and life-threatening secondary complications (Dykens, 1999). Additionally, those with PWS often present with intellectual, communication, and behavioral challenges. They frequently have mild to moderate intellectual disability – although a range from typical to severe involvement is reported (Dykens, 1999). Moreover, compulsive behaviors including arranging, hoarding, skin picking and hair pulling are associated with the syndrome (Dimitropoulos, Blackford, Walden, & Thompson, 2006; Dykens & Cassidy, 1996). Finally, individuals with PWS resulting from maternal uniparental disomy have been reported to exhibit fewer maladaptive and compulsive behaviors (e.g., Dykens, Cassidy & King, 1999), but may have more autistic-like behaviors (Veltman, Craig, & Bolton, 2005).

Diagnosis.   Physical characteristics such as a narrow forehead, thin upper lip, fair skin and hair, short stature, small hands and feet, hypogonadism, thick saliva, and body temperature dysregulation are apparent in many individuals with PWS (Dykens, 1999; Holm et al., 1993). According to Holm et al., infants with PWS exhibit fewer signs and symptoms than older children or adults. Often described as "floppy," infants with PWS frequently have severe hypotonia (Thompson, Butler, MacLean, Joseph, & Delaney, 1999). Because this is a common feature within the syndrome, clinicians have suggested that PWS should be considered as a differential diagnosis for neonates with severe hypotonia (Trifirò et al., 2003). Problems with sucking, swallowing, and feeding are also common in infants with PWS (Wigren & Hansen, 2003). Paradoxically, while obesity may be a lifelong threat associated with the syndrome, infants with PWS can have failure-to-thrive syndrome. Infants with PWS may also have a weak cry and somnolence (Thompson et al., 1999). Additionally, infants with PWS may be prone to sleep disorders. Festen et al. (2007) found that 6% of a small sample of infants with PWS had obstructive sleep apnea syndrome and that this sleep disorder was associated with significantly delayed intellectual development. Similar to children with FXS, children with PWS are generally diagnosed at a mean age of 2.5 years (Wigren & Hansen, 2003), limiting the amount of time they can participate in early intervention.

Cognition and communication.   Infants and young children with PWS may have delayed motor milestones – sitting independently at approximately 12 months and walking independently at 24 months (Dykens & Cassidy, 1996). Myers, Whitman, Carrel, Moerchen, Bekx, and Allen (2007) found that infants with PWS who received growth hormone therapy demonstrated a modicum of improvement in both mobility and stability at 1 year of age in contrast to a control group. However, by age 2, the treatment group still scored in the 14th percentile for mobility. The sample was notable for large variability in both domains.

In terms of cognitive-linguistic development, researchers studying older children to adults with PWS have found relative weaknesses in auditory information processing and relative strengths in visual processing and spatial-perceptual organization (see Dykens, 1999, for a review). Myers et al. (2007) found significant improvements in language and cognitive performance for infants who had received growth hormone for one year in contrast to a control group. Despite these improvements, after two years of growth hormone therapy the PWS group remained delayed in both domains. Hiraiwa, Maegaki, Oka, and Ohno (2007) found that over half (52%) of a group of 2–5-year-olds with PWS were reported to have repetitive speech.

Social-emotional functioning.   There is a growing number of studies focusing on the early development of behavior problems in PWS. Hiraiwa et al. (2007) found that 50% of parents reported that their 2–5-year-old children with PWS exhibited "stubbornness." Additionally, 35% of these children were reported to tantrum, 35% were reported to engage in self-injurious behaviors such as skin picking, and 14% were reported to be labile. In the same study, 14% of this group was reported to have hyperphagia, or uncontrollable eating behavior. This concurs with other reports indicating that hyperphagia begins at 2–6 years of age in PWS (Dykens, 1999; Wigren & Hansen, 2003). Some parents of children with PWS reported observing their children engaging in compulsive behaviors (such as ordering, rearranging) as young as 2 years of age (Dimitropoulos, Feurer, Butler, & Thompson, 2001). Approximately half of these parents reported that their child with PWS exhibited compulsive behaviors by the time he or she entered kindergarten. A large proportion (40%) of the parents of 4–5-year-olds with PWS in this study reported that their child picked his or her own skin. However, Dimitropoulos et al. (2006) found that preschoolers with PWS did not demonstrate more severe ritualistic behaviors than children with idiopathic developmental delays. They also reported a positive, small relationship between the severity of nonfood-oriented ritualistic behavior and the severity of eating disorder in the PWS group. The researchers hypothesized that compulsive behaviors and hyperphagia may share an underlying neurological mechanism.

In a study of older children, those with PWS were reported to have poorer social competence than both children with Down syndrome and Williams syndrome (Rosner, Hodapp, Fidler, Sagun, & Dykens, 2004). While it is generally accepted that infants and young children with PWS are affectionate, compliant and cooperative, little is known about the specific early development of social behaviors in this population. Additionally, some individuals with PWS (toddler through adulthood) present with an autistic-like behavior (e.g., Descheemaeker, Govers, Vermeulen, & Fryns, 2006; Dykens, Sutcliffe, & Levitt, 2004; Veltman et al., 2005). More research is needed to understand how this may unfold in early development.

Williams syndrome

Williams syndrome (also called Williams–Beuren syndrome or infantile hypercalcemia) is a neurodevelopmental disorder first described in the 1960s (Beuren, Apitz, & Harmjanz, 1962; Williams, Barrett-Boyes, & Lowe, 1961). In the 1990s, researchers mapped the syndrome to a 1.5-megabase microdeletion of part of the long arm of chromosome 7, encompassing the gene that codes for elastin (Ewart et al., 1993). To date, 16 genes have been implicated in this region (e.g., 7q11.23), which is referred to as the "classic" or "common" deletion for Williams syndrome (Morris & Mervis, 1999). Prevalence of Williams syndrome is approximately 1 in every 25,000 live births (Bellugi, Lichtenberger, Jones, Lai, & St. George, 2000), though other estimates suggest a higher prevalence (Stromme, Bjornstad, & Ramstad, 2002). In addition to showing mild to severe intellectual disability, individuals with Williams syndrome generally demonstrate an uneven cognitive/linguistic profile including marked strengths in formal language processing and marked deficits in visuospatial processing (Klein & Mervis, 1999; Morris & Mervis, 1999). Also characteristic is an unusual social-emotional profile including social disinhibition but difficulty forming appropriate relationships (Jones et al., 2000). Williams syndrome children also show a distinct maladaptive behavior profile, which includes pervasive fears and anxieties that often impede individual and family functioning (Davies, Udwin, & Howlin, 1998; Einfeld, Tonge, & Rees, 2001; Sarimski, 1997; Udwin, Howlin, Davies, & Mannion, 1998).

Language and communication.   The majority of early development research in Williams syndrome focuses on the emergence of language, and how children with Williams syndrome follow delayed and deviant pathways in acquiring early language (Brock, 2007; Karmiloff-Smith & Thomas, 2003; Mervis & Robinson, 2000). Despite showing relative strengths in expressive language later in development, infants with Williams syndrome show delays in the onset of canonical babbling and first words, which are hypothesized to be related to delays in other motor milestones such as hand banging (Masataka, 2001). Many young children with Williams syndrome speak their first words before they point to refer to objects (Mervis & Bertrand, 1997), and children with Williams syndrome evidence a number of atypical patterns in the area of lexical development (as reviewed by Karmiloff-Smith, Grant, Berthoud, Davies, Howlin, & Udwin, 1997). In addition, young children with Williams syndrome show unusual prelinguistic communication patterns, with strengths observed in dyadic interaction skills, but pronounced difficulties observed in triadic interaction skills, such as initiating joint attention and initiating requesting (Laing et al., 2002).

Social-emotional functioning.   Early evidence of heightened sociability is found in reports that infants and toddlers with Williams syndrome focus on human faces and voices much more than typically developing infants, to the exclusion of focus on objects (Jones et al., 2000). Intense eye gaze directed to social partners has been observed in play settings and clinical settings, both with parents and strangers (Mervis et al., 2003). Fidler, Hepburn, Most, Philofsky, & Rogers (2007) also report heightened emotional responsivity in young children with Williams syndrome. They found that toddlers and preschoolers with Williams syndrome were more likely to mimic and imitate an experimenter's facial and vocal affect during laboratory experiments. However, they also note that this heightened imitation propensity did not afford young children with Williams syndrome any advantage in a related social decision-making task relative to developmental matched peers with other developmental disabilities.

Cognition.   The small literature on early cognitive abilities in Williams syndrome suggests that verbal abilities grow at a faster rate than nonverbal skills, with a significant discrepancy becoming evident by 8–9 years of age (Jarrold, Baddeley, Hewes & Phillips, 2001). Toddlers with Williams syndrome are also found to show poorer levels of sustained attention and exploration of the visual environment on spatial representation tasks, as well as difficulties with visual search tasks relative to developmentally matched children (Brown, Johnson, Paterson, Gilmore, Longhi & Karmiloff-Smith, 2003; Scerif et al., 2004).

Smith–Magenis syndrome

Smith–Magenis syndrome is a genetic disorder associated with intellectual disability that was first discovered in 1982. It is caused by a deletion on chromosome 17 (Del 17p11.2; Smith et al., 1986), though transmission from mother to daughter has been reported (Zori et al., 1993). The prevalence of Smith–Magenis syndrome is 1 in every 25,000 live births (Finucane, Dirrigl, & Simon, 2001; Greenberg, Guzzetta, & de Oca-Luna, 1991). Although individuals with Smith–Magenis syndrome show a distinct craniofacial appearance, the features of this appearance are subtle and difficult to detect without a familiarity with the disorder (Finucane et al., 2001). The most salient features in the Smith–Magenis syndrome behavioral phenotype include self-injurious behavior, sleep disturbances, and other maladaptive behaviors (Dykens & Smith, 1998; Smith, Dykens & Greenberg, 1998a, 1998b).

There is a limited amount of information available in the literature regarding early development in Smith–Magenis syndrome. Many infants with Smith–Magenis syndrome exhibit feeding difficulties, failure to thrive, and frequent ear infections (Udwin, Webber, & Horn, 2001). Additionally, a set of behavioral concerns have been reported in young children with Smith–Magenis syndrome, including hyperactivity, impulsivity, distractibility, sleeping difficulties, and self-injury (Dykens, Finucane, & Gayley, 1997; Greenberg et al., 1991; Smith et al., 1986; Udwin et al., 2001). A case report of three young children with Smith–Magenis syndrome suggested language delays, distractibility, and reduced frustration tolerance in all of them (Willekens, De Cock, & Fryns, 2000). In addition, by the age of 2–3 years, children in this study evidenced self-injury (head banging, hand, wrist or finger biting), sleep disturbance, and repetitive behaviors. A second case study of a 3-year-old girl with Smith–Magenis syndrome reports relative strengths in visual receptive performance and receptive language skills, with deficits in gross motor and expressive language (Fidler, Philofsky, & Hepburn, 2006). She also showed deficits in adaptive behavior relative to overall mental age, though notable strengths in imitation and nonverbal communication skills (joint attention, nonverbal requesting, integration of eye contact with gesture and vocalization) were observed as well.

Conclusions

Overall, the history of change that has characterized the field of intellectual disability research and practice in the twentieth century continues into the twenty-first century. Advances in biomedical sciences continue to alter the diagnosis process. Advances in developmental science and intervention research continue to deepen our understanding of the impact of different etiologies of disability on child outcomes, and the malleability of these outcomes based on timing, dosage, and intensity of intervention. Advances in behavioral phenotype research continue to change the way researchers and practitioners understand the similarities and differences among children with different syndromes associated with intellectual disability.

In particular, with rapid advances in our ability to characterize the genetic factors underlying atypical outcomes, it is likely that we will continue to identify new etiological factors leading to atypical outcomes. The technological advances associated with DNA microarray analyses, which provide the most comprehensive analysis of an individual's entire genome to date, will make it possible to identify subtle, as yet undiscovered genetic factors such as duplications and copy number variations, which may lead to more subtle variations in developmental outcome. One of the main challenges that this will pose to the field of intellectual disability research will be the extent to which these advances call into question some of the distinctions regarding familial and organic intellectual disability. It may be that some mild, familial cases of intellectual disability are caused by subtle genomic factors such as copy number variations, rather than, as currently conceptualized, by a set of genes associated with low intelligence. It will be critical for the field to keep pace with the rapid changes in diagnostic and biomedical technology, or behavioral science in intellectual disabilities will risk irrelevance.

In addition, it will be of critical importance to continue to identify interactions between environmental influences and genetic factors in the field of intellectual disability research. Though it is commonly known that environmental toxins such as lead and mercury can alter developmental trajectories from the earliest stages of prenatal development, there are likely additional environmental compounds that have more subtle effects on development throughout the life course. It has been hypothesized that some chemical agents found in commonly used materials such as plastic can have effects on physical development. It may also be that some children are more susceptible to such effects because of a genetic predisposition, while others are less so. These types of gene–environment interactions should continue to receive research attention as they offer additional promise for preventive intervention early in development.

Each of these issues, and the many others that have gone unmentioned, pose new challenges and questions to researchers and other professionals in the field of intellectual disability. What is the best way to educate children with different genetic disorders? How do we address the needs of families who receive a prenatal diagnosis of a genetic disorder? Are there newer and better ways to bridge basic scientific findings and intellectual disability practice? The twenty-first century is sure to bring about new questions that will continue to push the field of intellectual disability research and practice through its next period of change and growth.

References

Abbeduto, L., Brady, N., & Kover, S. T. (2007). Language development and fragile X syndrome: Profiles, syndrome-specificity, and within-syndrome differences. *Mental Retardation and Developmental Disabilities Research Reviews, 13*, 36–46.

American Academy of Pediatrics Newborn Screening Task Force (2000). Newborn screening: A blueprint for the future. *Pediatrics, 106*(Suppl.), 389–427.

American Academy of Pediatrics, Rose, S. R., Section on Endocrinology and Committee on Genetics, American Thyroid Association, Brown, R. S., Public Health Committee, Lawson Wilkings Pediatric Endocrine Society, et al. (2006). Update of newborn screening and therapy for congenital hypothyroidism. *Pediatrics, 117*, 2290–2303.

American Association on Mental Retardation (2002). *Mental retardation: Definition, classification, and systems of supports* (10th ed.). Washington, DC: Author.

American Psychiatric Association (2000). *Diagnostic and statistical manual of mental disorders* (4th ed.). Washington, DC: Author.

Bailey, D. B., Hatton, D. D., & Skinner, J. (1998). Early developmental trajectories of males with fragile X syndrome. *American Journal on Mental Retardation, 103*, 29–39.

Bailey, D. B., Hatton, D. D., Mesibov, G., Ament, N., & Skinner, M. (2000). Early development, temperament, and functional impairment in autism and fragile X syndrome. *Journal of Autism and Developmental Disorders, 30*, 49–59.

Bailey, D. B., Hatton, D. D., Skinner, M., & Mesibov, G. (2001). Autistic behavior, FMR1 protein, and developmental trajectories in young males with fragile X syndrome. *Journal of Autism and Developmental Disorders, 31*, 165–174.

Bailey, D. B., Hatton, D. D., Tassone, F., Skinner, M., & Taylor, A. K. (2001). Variability in FMRP and early development in males with fragile X syndrome. *American Journal on Mental Retardation, 106*, 16–27.

Bailey, D. B., Roberts, J. E., Mirrett, P., & Hatton, D. D. (2001). Identifying infants and toddlers with fragile X syndrome: Issues and recommendations. *Infants and Young Children, 14*, 24–33.

Bailey, D. B., Skinner, D., & Sparkman, K. L. (2003). Discovering fragile X syndrome: Family experiences and perceptions. *Pediatrics, 111*, 407–416.

Baranek, G. T., Danko, C. D., Skinner, M. L., Bailey, D. B., Hatton, D. D., Roberts, J. E., & Mirrett, P. L. (2005). Video analysis of sensory-motor features in infants with fragile X syndrome and 9–12 months of age. *Journal of Autism and Developmental Disorders, 35*, 645–656.

Bellugi, U., Lichtenberger, L., Jones, W., Lai, Z., & St. George, M. (2000). The neurocognitive profile of Williams syndrome: A complex pattern of strengths and weaknesses. *Journal of Cognitive Neuroscience, 12*(Suppl.), 7–29.

Berger, J., & Cunningham, C. C. (1983). Development of early vocal behaviors and interactions in Down's syndrome and nonhandicapped infant-mother pairs. *Developmental Psychology, 19*, 322–331.

Beuren, A. J., Apitz, J., & Harmjanz, D. (1962). Supravalvular aortic stenosis in association with mental retardation and certain facial appearances. *Circulation, 26*, 1235–1240.

Block, M. E. (1991). Motor development in children with Down syndrome: A review of the literature. *Adapted Physical Activity Quarterly, 8*, 179–209.

Brock, J. (2007). Language abilities in Williams syndrome: A critical review. *Development and Psychopathology, 19*, 97–127.

Brown, I. (2007). What is meant by intellectual and developmental disabilities. In I. Brown & M. Percy (Eds.), *A comprehensive guide to intellectual and developmental disabilities* (pp. 3–16). Baltimore, MD: Paul H. Brookes Press.

Brown, I., & Percy, M. (Eds.) (2007). *A comprehensive guide to intellectual and developmental disabilities.* Baltimore, MD: Paul H. Brookes Press.

Brown, J. H., Johnson, M. H., Paterson, S. J., Gilmore, R., Longhi, E., & Karmiloff-Smith, A. (2003). Spatial representation and attention in toddlers with Williams syndrome and Down syndrome. *Neuropsychologia, 41*, 1037–1046.

Burack, J. A., Hodapp, R. M., & Zigler, E. (1988). Issues in the classification of mental retardation: Differentiating among organic etiologies. *Journal of Child Psychology and Psychiatry, 29*, 765–779.

Canfield, M. A., Honein, M. A., Yuskiv, N., Xing, J., Mai, C. T., Collins, J. S., et al. (2006). National estimates and race/ethnic-specific variation of selected birth defects in the United States, 1999–2001. *Birth Defects Research A: Clinical Molecular Teratology, 76*, 747–756.

Caselli, M. C., Vicari, S., Longobardi, E., Lami, L., Pizzoli, C., & Stella, G. (1998). Gestures and words in early development of children with Down syndrome. *Journal of Speech, Language, and Hearing Research, 41*, 1125–1135.

Caspi, A., & Roberts, B. W. (1999). Personality continuity and change across the life course. In L. A. Pervin & O. P. John (Eds.), *Handbook of personality: Theory and research* (2nd ed., pp. 300–326). New York: Guilford Press.

Cassidy, S. B. (1997). Prader-Willi syndrome. *Journal of Medical Genetics, 34*, 395–400.

Chamberlain, S. J., & Brannan, C. I. (2001). The Prader-Willi syndrome imprinting center activates the paternally expressed murine Ube3a antisense transcript but represses paternal Ube3a. *Genomics, 73*, 316–322.

Chapman, R. S. (1999). Language development in children and adolescents with Down syndrome. In J. Miller, M. Leddy & L. A. Leavitt (Eds.), *Improving the communication of people with Down syndrome* (pp. 81–92). Baltimore, MD: Paul H. Brookes Press.

Cohen, I. L. (1995). Behavioral profiles of autistic and nonautistic fragile X males. *Developmental Brain Dysfunction, 8*, 252–269.

Collacott, R. A., Cooper, S. A., & McGrother, A. (1992). Differential rates of psychiatric disorders in adults with Down's syndrome compared to other mentally handicapped adults. *British Journal of Psychiatry, 161*, 671–674.

Cornish, K., Bramble, D., & Standen, P. (2001). Cri-du-chat syndrome: Toward a behavioral phenotype. *Mental Health Aspects of Developmental Disabilities, 4,* 156–160.

Cornish, K., Scerif, G., & Karmiloff-Smith, A. (2007). Tracing syndrome-specific trajectories of attention across the lifespan. *Cortex, 43,* 672–685.

Crown, C. L., Feldstein, S., Jasnow, M. D., & Beebe, B. (1992). Down's syndrome and infant gaze: Gaze behavior of Down's syndrome and nondelayed infants in interactions with their mothers. *European Journal of Child and Adolescent Psychiatry: Acta Paedopsychiatrica, 55,* 51–55.

Davies, M., Udwin, O., & Howlin, P. (1998). Adults with Williams syndrome: Preliminary study of social, emotional and behavioural difficulties. *British Journal of Psychiatry, 172,* 273–276.

Demark, J. L., Feldman, M. A., & Holden, J. J. A. (2003). Behavioral relationship between autism and fragile X syndrome. *American Journal on Mental Retardation, 108,* 314–326.

Descheemaeker, M.-J., Govers, V., Vermeulen, P., & Fryns, J. P. (2006). Pervasive developmental disorders in Prader-Willi syndrome: The Leuven experience in 59 subjects and controls. *American Journal of Medical Genetics Part A, 140A,* 1136–1142.

Dimitropoulos, A., Blackford, J., Walden, T., & Thompson, T. (2006). Compulsive behavior in Prader-Willi syndrome: Examining severity in early childhood. *Research in Developmental Disabilities, 27,* 190–202.

Dimitropoulos, A., Feurer, I. D., Butler, M. G., & Thompson, T. (2001). Emergence of compulsive behavior and tantrums in children with Prader-Willi syndrome. *American Journal on Mental Retardation, 106,* 39–51.

Dykens, E. M. (1995). Measuring behavioral phenotypes: Provocations from the "New Genetics". *American Journal on Mental Retardation, 99,* 522–532.

Dykens, E. M. (1999). Prader-Willi syndrome: Toward a behavioral phenotype. In H. Tager-Flusberg (Ed.), *Neurodevelopmental disorders* (pp. 137–154). Cambridge, MA: MIT Press.

Dykens, E. M., & Cassidy, S. B. (1996). Prader-Willi syndrome: Genetic, behavioral, and treatment issues. *Child and Adolescent Psychiatric Clinics of North America, 5,* 913–927.

Dykens, E. M., Cassidy, S. B., & King, B. H. (1999). Maladaptive behavior differences in Prader-Willi syndrome due to paternal deletion versus maternal uniparental disomy. *American Journal on Mental Retardation, 104,* 67–77.

Dykens, E. M., Finucane, B., & Gayley, C. (1997). Cognitive and behavioral profiles in persons with Smith-Magenis syndrome. *Journal of Autism and Developmental Disorders, 27,* 203–211.

Dykens, E. M., & Hodapp, R. M. (2001). Research in mental retardation: Toward an etiologic approach. *Journal of Child Psychology and Psychiatry, 42,* 49–71.

Dykens, E. M., Shah, B., Sagun, J., Beck, T., & King, B. H. (2002). Maladaptive behavior in children and adolescents with Down's syndrome. *Journal of Intellectual Disability Research, 46,* 484–492.

Dykens, E. M., & Smith, A. C. M. (1998). Distinctiveness and correlates of maladaptive behaviour in children and adolescents with Smith-Magenis syndrome. *Journal of Intellectual Disability Research, 42,* 481–489.

Dykens, E. M., Sutcliffe, J. S., & Levitt, P. (2004). Autism and 15q11-q13 disorders: Behavioral, genetic, and pathophysiological issues. *Mental Retardation and Developmental Disabilities Research Reviews, 10,* 284–291.

Einfeld, S. L., Tonge, B. J., & Rees, V. W. (2001). Longitudinal course of behavioral and emotional problems in Williams syndrome. *American Journal of Mental Retardation, 106*(1), 73–81.

Ewart, A. K., Morris, C. A., Atkinson, D., Jin, W., Sternes, K., Spallone, P., et al. (1993) Hemizygosity at the elastin locus in a developmental disorder. Williams syndrome. *Nature Genetics, 5,* 11–16.

Fabretti, D., Pizzuto, E., Vicari, S., & Voterra, V. (1997). A story description task in children with Down's syndrome: Lexical and morphosyntactic abilities. *Journal of Intellectual Disability Research, 41,* 165–179.

Farzin, F., Perry, H., & Hessl, D. (2006). Autism spectrum disorders and attention-deficit/hyperactivity disorder in boys with the fragile X permutation. *Journal of Developmental and Behavioral Pediatrics, 27,* S137–S144.

Festen, D. A. M., Wevers, M., DeWeerd, A. W., Van Den Bossche, R. A. S., Duivenvoorden, H. J., Otten, B. J., & Hokken-Koelega, A. C. S. (2007). Psychomotor development in infants with Prader-Willi syndrome and associations with sleep-related breathing disorders. *Pediatric Research, 62,* 221–224.

Fidler, D. J. (2005). The emerging Down syndrome behavioral phenotype in early childhood: Implications for practice. *Infants and Young Children, 18,* 86–103.

Fidler, D. J. (2006). The emergence of a syndrome-specific personality-motivation profile in young children with Down syndrome. In J.-A. Rondal & J. Perera (Eds.), *Down syndrome: Neurobehavioral specificity.* Chichester: John Wiley & Sons.

Fidler, D. J., Hepburn, S., Mankin, G., & Rogers, S. (2005). Praxis skills in young children with Down syndrome, other developmental disabilities, and typically developing children. *American Journal of Occupational Therapy, 59,* 129–138.

Fidler, D. J., Hepburn, S. L., Most, D. E., Philofsky, A., & Rogers, S. (2007). Emotional responsivity in young children with Williams syndrome. *American Journal on Mental Retardation, 112,* 194–206.

Fidler, D. J., Most, D. E., & Philofsky, A. (in press). The Down syndrome behavioral phenotype: Taking a developmental approach. *Down Syndrome: Research and Practice.*

Fidler, D. J., Philofsky, A., & Hepburn, S. (2006). A case study of early development in Smith-Magenis syndrome. *Focus on Autism and Other Developmental Disabilities, 21,* 130–137.

Fidler, D. J., Philofsky, A., & Hepburn, S. (2007). Language phenotypes and intervention planning: Bridging research and practice. *Mental Retardation and Developmental Disabilities Research Reviews, 13,* 47–57.

Fidler, D. J., Philofsky, A., Hepburn, S., & Rogers, S. (2005). Nonverbal requesting and problem solving in toddlers with Down syndrome. *American Journal on Mental Retardation, 110,* 312–322.

Finucane, B., Dirrigl, K. J., & Simon, E. W. (2001). Characterization of self-injurious behaviors in children and adults with Smith-Magenis syndrome. *American Journal on Mental Retardation, 2001,* 52–58.

Fox, N. A., & Henderson, H. A. (1999). Does infancy matter? Predicting social behavior from infant temperament. *Infant Behavior and Development, 22,* 445–455.

Ghaziuddin, M., Tsai, L., & Ghaziuddin, N. (1992). Autism in Down's syndrome: Presentation and diagnosis. *Journal of Intellectual Disability Research, 36,* 449–456.

Greenberg, F., Guzzetta, V., & de Oca-Luna, R. (1991). Molecular analysis of the Smith-Magenis syndrome: A possible contiguous-gene syndrome associated with del (17)(p11.2). *American Journal of Human Genetics, 49,* 1207–1218.

Gunn, P., Berry, P., & Andrews, R. J. (1982). Looking behavior of Down syndrome infants. *American Journal of Mental Deficiency, 87,* 344–347.

Hagerman, R. J. (2002). The physical and behavioral phenotype. In R. J. Hagerman and P. J. Hagerman, *Fragile X syndrome: Diagnosis, treatment and research* (pp. 3–109). Baltimore, MD: Johns Hopkins University Press.

Harris, S. R., & Shea, A. M. (1991). Down syndrome. In S. K. Campbell (Ed.), *Pediatric neurologic physical therapy* (2nd ed., pp. 131–168). Melbourne: Churchill Livingstone.

Hatton, D. D., Sideris, J., Skinner, M., Mankowsky, J., Bailey, D. B., Roberts, J., & Mirrett, P. L. (2006). Autistic behavior in children with fragile X syndrome: Prevalence, stability, and the impact of FMRP. *American Journal of Medical Genetics Part A, 140A*, 1804–1813.

Heimann, M., & Ullstadius, E. (1999). Neonatal imitation and imitation among children with autism and Down's syndrome. In J. Nadel & G. Butterworth (Eds.), *Imitation in infancy*, (pp. 235–253). Cambridge: Cambridge University Press.

Hepburn, S., Philofsky, A., Fidler, D. J., & Rogers, S. (2008). Autism symptoms in toddlers with Down syndrome: A descriptive study. *Journal of Applied Research in Intellectual Disabilities, 21*, 48–57.

Hiraiwa, R., Maegaki, Y., Oka, A., & Ohno, K. (2007). Behavioral and psychiatric disorders in Prader-Willi syndrome: A population study in Japan. *Brain & Development, 29*, 535–542.

Hodapp, R. M., & DesJardin, J. L. (2002). Genetic etiologies of mental retardation: Issues for interventions and interventionists. *Journal of Developmental and Physical Disabilities, 14*, 323–338.

Hodapp, R. M., & Dykens, E. M. (2005). Measuring behavior in genetic disorders of mental retardation. *Mental Retardation and Developmental Disabilities Research Reviews, 11*, 340–346.

Hodapp, R. M., Evans, D., & Gray, F. L. (1999). Intellectual development in children with Down syndrome. In J.-A. Rondal, J. Perera, & L. Nadel (Eds.), *Down syndrome: A review of current knowledge* (pp. 124–132). London: Whurr.

Hodapp, R. M., & Fidler, D. J. (1999). Special education and genetics: Connections for the 21st century. *Journal of Special Education, 33*, 130–137.

Holm, V. A., Cassidy, S. B., Butler, M. G., Hanchett, J. M., Greensway, L. R., Whitman, B. Y., & Greenberg, F. (1993). Prader-Willi syndrome: Consensus diagnostic criteria. *Pediatrics, 91*, 398–402.

Huang, L., Sadler, L., O'Riordan, M., & Robin, N. H. (2002). Delay in diagnosis of Williams syndrome. *Clinical Pediatrics, 41*, 257–261.

Iverson, J. M., Longobardi, E., & Caselli, M. C. (2003). Relationship between gestures and words in children with Down's syndrome and typically developing children in the early stages of communicative development. *International Journal of Language and Communication Disorders, 38*, 179–197.

Jacobson, J. W., Mulick, J. A., & Rojahn, J. (2007). *Handbook of intellectual and developmental disabilities*. New York: Springer.

Jarrold, C., Baddeley, A. D., & Hewes, A. K. (1999). Genetically dissociated components of working memory: Evidence from Down's and Williams syndrome. *Neuropsychologia, 37*, 637–651.

Jarrold, C., Baddleley, A., Hewes, A. K., & Phillips, C. (2001). A longitudinal assessment of diverging verbal and non-verbal abilities in the Williams syndrome phenotype. *Cortex, 37*, 423–431.

Jones, W., Bellugi, U., Lai, Z., Chiles, M., Reilly, J., Lincoln, A., & Adolphs, R. (2000). Hypersociability in Williams syndrome. *Journal of Cognitive Neuroscience, 12*(Suppl.), 30–46.

Kagan, J. (1969). The three faces of continuity in human development. In D. A. Goslin (Ed.), *Handbook of socialization theory and research* (pp. 983–1002). Chicago: Rand McNally.

Karmiloff-Smith, A. (1998). Development itself is the key to understanding developmental disorders. *Trends in Cognitive Sciences, 2*, 389–398.

Karmiloff-Smith, A., Grant, J., Berthoud, I., Davies, M., Howlin, P., & Udwin, O. (1997). Language and Williams syndrome: How intact is "intact"? *Child Development, 68*, 246–262.

Karmiloff-Smith, A., & Thomas, M. (2003). What can developmental disorders tell us about the neurocomputational constraints that shape development? The case of Williams syndrome. *Development and Psychopathology, 15*, 969–990.

Karrer, J. H., Karrer, R., Bloom, D., Chaney, L., & Davis, R. (1998). Event-related brain potentials during an extended visual recognition memory task depict delayed development of cerebral inhibitory processes among 6-month-old infants with Down syndrome. *International Journal of Psychophysiology, 29,* 167–200.

Karrer, R., Wojtascek, Z., & Davis, M. G. (1995). Event-related potentials and information processing in infants with Down syndrome. *American Journal on Mental Retardation, 100,* 146–159.

Kasari, C., Freeman, S., Mundy, P., & Sigman, M. D. (1995). Attention regulation by children with Down syndrome: Coordinated joint attention and social referencing looks. *American Journal on Mental Retardation, 100,* 128–136.

Kau, A. S. M., Reider, E. E., Payne, L., Meyer, W. A., & Freund, L. (2000). Early behavior signs of psychiatric phenotypes in fragile X syndrome. *American Journal on Mental Retardation, 105,* 266–299.

Kent, L., Evans, J., Paul, M., & Sharp, M. (1999). Comorbidity of autistic spectrum disorders in children with Down syndrome. *Developmental Medicine and Child Neurology, 41,* 153–158.

Klein, B. P., & Mervis, C. B. (1999). Contrasting patterns of cognitive abilities of 9- and 10-year-olds with Williams syndrome or Down syndrome. *Developmental Neuropsychology, 16*(2), 177–196.

Koch, R. K. (1999). Issues in newborn screening for phenylketonuria. *American Family Physician, 60,* 1462–1466.

Laing, E., Butterworth, G., Ansari, D., Gsodl, M., Longhi, E., Panagiotaki, G., et al. (2002). Atypical development of language and social communication in toddlers with Williams syndrome. *Developmental Science, 5,* 233–246.

Ledbetter, D. H., Riccardi, V. M., Airhart, S. D., Strobel, R. J., Keenan, B. S., & Crawford, J. D. (1981). Deletions of chromosome 15 as a cause of the Prader-Willi syndrome. *New England Journal of Medicine, 304,* 325–329.

Legerstee, M., Bowman, T. G., & Fels, S. (1992). People and objects affect the quality of vocalizations in infants with Down syndrome. *Early Development and Parenting, 1,* 149–156.

Levine, D. (2002). MR imaging of fetal central nervous system abnormalities. *Brain and Cognition, 50,* 432–448.

Lynch, M. P., Oller, D. K., Steffens, M. L., & Buder, E. H. (1995). Phrasing in prelinguistic vocalizations. *Developmental Psychobiology, 28,* 3–25.

Lynch, M. P., Oller, D. K., Steffens, M. L., Levine, S. L., Basinger, D. L., & Umbel, V. M. (1995). Development of speech-like vocalizations in infants with Down syndrome. *American Journal on Mental Retardation, 100,* 68–86.

Mahoney, G., Glover, A., & Finger, I. (1981). The relationship between language and sensorimotor development among Down syndrome and developmentally normal children. *American Journal of Mental Deficiency, 86,* 21–27.

Malone, F. D., Canick, J. A., Ball, R. H., Nyberg, D. A., Comstock, C. H., Bukowski, R., et al. (2005). First and second-trimester screening, or both, for Down's syndrome. *New England Journal of Medicine, 353,* 2001–2011.

Masataka, N. (2001). Why early linguistic milestones are delayed in children with Williams syndrome: Late onset of hand banging as a possible rate-limiting constraint on the emergence of canonical babbling. *Developmental Science, 4,* 158–164.

McDermott, S., Durkin, M. S., Schupf, N., & Stein, Z. A. (2007). Epidemiology and etiology of mental retardation. In J. Jacobson, J. A. Mulick & J. Rojahn (Eds.), *Handbook of Intellectual and Developmental Disabilities* (pp. 3–40). New York: Springer.

Mervis, C. B., & Bertrand, J. (1997). Developmental relations between cognition and language: Evidence from Williams syndrome. In L. B. Adamson & M. A. Romski (Eds.), *Communication and language acquisition: Discoveries from atypical development* (pp. 75–106). Baltimore, MD: Brookes.

Mervis, C. B., Morris, C. A., Klein-Tasman, B. P., Bertrand, J., Kwitny, S., Appelbaum, L. G., & Rice, C. E. (2003). Attentional characteristics of infants and toddlers with Williams syndrome during triadic interactions. *Developmental Neuropsychology, 23,* 243–268.

Mervis, C. B., & Robinson, B. F. (2000). Expressive vocabulary ability of toddlers with Williams syndrome or Down syndrome: A comparison. *Developmental Neuropsychology, 17,* 111–126.

Miller, J. F. (1999). Profiles of language development in children with Down syndrome. In J. Miller, M. Leddy, & L. A. Leavitt (Eds.), *Improving the communication of people with Down syndrome,* (pp. 11–40). Baltimore, MD: Brookes.

Miranda, S. B., & Fantz, R. L. (1973). Visual preferences of Down's syndrome and normal infants. *Child Development, 44,* 555–561.

Mirrett, P. L., Bailey, D. B., Roberts, J. E., & Hatton, D. D. (2004). Developmental screening and detection of developmental delays in infants and toddlers with fragile X syndrome. *Journal of Developmental and Behavioral Pediatrics, 25,* 21–27.

Morris, C. A., Demsey, S. A., Leonard, C. O., Dilts, C., & Blackburn, B. L. (1988). Natural history of Williams syndrome: Physical characteristics. *Journal of Pediatrics, 113,* 318–326.

Morris, C. A., & Mervis, C. B. (1999). Williams syndrome. In S. Goldstein & C. R. Reynolds (Ed.), *Handbook of neurodevelopmental and genetic disorders in children.* New York: Guilford Press.

Moser, H. W. (2004). Genetic causes of mental retardation. *Annals of the New York Academy of Sciences, 1038,* 44–48.

Mundy, P., Kasari, C., Sigman, M., & Ruskin, E. (1995). Nonverbal communication and early language acquisition in children with Down syndrome and normally developing children. *Journal of Speech and Hearing Research, 38,* 157–167.

Mundy, P., Sigman, M., Kasari, C., & Yirmiya, N. (1988). Nonverbal communication skills in Down syndrome children. *Child Development, 59,* 235–249.

Myers, S. E., Whitman, B. Y., Carrel, A. L., Moerchen, V., Bekx, M. T., & Allen, D. B. (2007). Two years of growth hormone therapy in young children with Prader-Willi syndrome: Physical and neurodevelopmental benefits. *American Journal of Medical Genetics Part A, 143A,* 443–448.

Nicholls, R. D., Knoll, J. H., Butler, M. G., Karam, S., & Lalande, M. (1989). Genetic imprinting suggested by maternal heterodisomy in nondeletion Prader-Willi syndrome. *Nature, 16,* 281–285.

Ohr, P. S., & Fagen, J. W. (1994). Contingency learning in 9-month-old infants with Down syndrome. *American Journal on Mental Retardation, 99,* 74–84.

Ormond, K. E. (1997). Update and review: Maternal serum screening. *Journal of Genetic Counseling, 6,* 395–417.

Pandya, P. P., Kuhn, P., Brizot, M., Cardy, D. L., & Nicolaides, K. H. (1994). Rapid detection of chromosome aneuploidies in fetal blood and chorionic villi by fluorescence in situ hybridization. *British Journal of Obstetrics and Gynaecology, 101,* 493–497.

Partington, M. W. (1984). The fragile X syndrome II: Preliminary data on growth and development in males. *American Journal of Medical Genetics, 17,* 175–194.

Pary, R. J., & Hurley, A. D. (2002). Down syndrome and autistic disorder. *Mental Health Aspects of Developmental Disabilities, 5,* 64–65.

Percy, M. (2007). Factors that cause or contribute to intellectual and developmental disabilities. In I. Brown & M. Percy (Eds.), *A Comprehensive Guide to Intellectual and Developmental Disabilities* (pp. 125–148). Baltimore, MD: Brookes.

Philofsky, A., Hepburn, S. L., Hayes, A., Hagerman, R., & Rogers, S. J. (2004). Linguistic and cognitive functioning and autism symptoms in young children with fragile X syndrome. *American Journal on Mental Retardation, 109*, 208–218.

Pleska-Skwerer, D., Verbalis, A., & Schofield, C. (2006). Social-perceptual abilities in adolescents and adults with Williams syndrome. *Cognitive Neuropsychology, 23*, 338–349.

Porter, M. A., Coltheart, M., & Langdon, R. (2007). The neuropsychological basis of hypersociability in Williams and Down syndrome. *Neuropsychologia, 45*, 2839–2849.

Prouty, L. A., Rogers, R. C., Sevenso, R. E., Dean, J. H., Palmer, K. K. Simensen, R. J., et al. (1988). Fragile X syndrome: Growth, development, and intellectual function. *American Journal of Medical Genetics, 30*, 123–142.

Reiss, A. L., & Dant, C. C. (2003). The behavioral neurogenetics of fragile X syndrome: Analyzing gene–brain-behavior relationships in children developmental psychopathologies. *Development and Psychopathology, 15*, 927–968.

Roberts, C. D., Stough, L. M., & Parrish, L. H. (2002). The role of genetic counseling in the elective termination of pregnancies involving fetuses with disabilities. *Journal of Special Education, 36*, 48–55.

Rogers, S. J., Hepburn, S. L., & Wehner, E. (2003). Parent reports of sensory symptoms in toddlers with autism and those with other developmental disorders. *Journal of Autism and Developmental Disorders, 33*, 631–642.

Rogers, S. J., Wehner, E. A., & Hagerman, R. (2001). The behavioral phenotype in fragile X: Symptoms of autism in very young children with fragile X syndrome, idiopathic autism, and other developmental disorders. *Journal of Developmental and Behavioral Pediatrics, 22*, 409–417.

Rosner, B. A., Hodapp, R. M., Fidler, D. J., Sagun, J. N., & Dykens, E. M. (2004). Social competence in persons with Prader-Willi, Williams and Down's syndrome. *Journal of Applied Research in Intellectual Disabilities, 17*, 209–217.

Sarimski, K. (1997). Behavioural phenotypes and family stress in three mental retardation syndromes. *European Child & Adolescent Psychiatry, 6*(1), 26–31.

Scerif, G., Cornish, K., Wilding, J., Driver, J., & Karmiloff-Smith, A. (2004). Visual search in typically developing toddlers and toddlers with fragile X or Williams syndrome. *Developmental Science, 7*, 116–130.

Scerif, G., Cornish, K., Wilding, J., Driver, J., & Karmiloff-Smith, A. (2006). Delineation of early attentional control difficulties in fragile X syndrome: Focus on neurocomputational changes. *Neuropsychologia, 45*, 1889–1898.

Sherman, S. L., Allen, E. G., Bean, L. H., & Freeman, S. B. (2007). Epidemiology of Down syndrome. *Mental Retardation and Developmental Disabilities Research Reviews, 13*, 221–227.

Sigman, M., & Ruskin, E. (1999). Continuity and change in the social competence of children with autism, Down syndrome, and developmental delays. *Monographs of the Society for Research in Child Development, 64*, v–114.

Smith, A. C. M., Dykens, E., & Greenberg, F. (1998a). Behavioral phenotype of Smith-Magenis syndrome (del 17p11.2). *American Journal of Medical Genetics, 81*, 179–185.

Smith, A. C. M., Dykens, E., & Greenberg, F. (1998b). Sleep disturbance in Smith-Magenis syndrome. *American Journal of Medical Genetics, 81*, 186–191.

Smith, A. C. M., McGavran, L., Robinson, J., Waldstein, G., Macfarlane, J., Zonona, J., et al. (1986). Interstitial deletion of (17)(p11.2p11.2) in nine patients. *American Journal of Medical Genetics, 24*, 393–414.

Stoel-Gammon, C. (1992). Prelinguistic vocal development: Measurement and predictions. In C. A. Ferguson, L. Menn, & C. Stoel-Gammon (Eds.), *Phonological development: Models, research, implications*, (pp. 439–456). Timonium, MD: York Press.

Stromme, P., Bjornstad, P. G., & Ramstad, K. (2002). Prevalence estimation of Williams syndrome. *Journal of Child Neurology, 17,* 269–271.

Sutherland, G. R. (1977). Fragile sites on human chromosomes: Demonstration of their dependence on the type of tissue culture medium. *Science, 197,* 265–266.

Switzky, H. N., & Greenspan, S. (Eds.) (2006). *What is Mental Retardation? Ideas for an Evolving Disability in the 21st Century.* Washington, DC: American Association on Mental Retardation.

Thompson, T., Butler, M. G., MacLean, W. E., Joseph, B., & Delaney, D. (1999). Cognition, behavior, neurochemistry, and genetics in Prader-Willi syndrome. In H. Tager-Flusberg (Ed.), *Neurodevelopmental disorders* (pp. 155–177). Cambridge, MA: MIT Press.

Trifirò, G., Livieri, C., Bosio, L., Gargantini, L., Corrias, A., Pozzan, G., et al. (2003). Neonatal hypotonia: Don't forget the Prader-Willi syndrome. *Acta Paediatrica, 92,* 1085–1089.

Turner, G., Webb, T., Wake, S., & Robinson, H. (1996). Prevalence of fragile X syndrome. *American Journal of Medical Genetics, 64,* 98–103.

Udwin, O., Howlin, P., Davies, M., & Mannion, E. (1998). Community care for adults with Williams syndrome: How families cope and the availability of support networks. *Journal of Intellectual Disability Research, 42*(3), 238–245.

Udwin, O., Webber, C., & Horn, I. (2001). Abilities and attainment in Smith-Magenis syndrome. *Developmental Medicine and Child Neurology, 43,* 823–828.

Veltman, M. W. M., Craig, E. E., & Bolton, P. F. (2005). Autism spectrum disorders in Prader–Willi and Angelman syndromes: A systematic review. *Pediatrics Genetics, 15,* 243–254.

Verkerk, A. J. M., Pieretti, J. S., Sutcliffe, Y.-H., Fu, D. P., Kuhl, A., Pizzuti, O., et al. (1991). Identification of a gene (FMR-1) containing a CGG repeat coincident with a breakpoint cluster region exhibiting length variation in fragile X syndrome. *Cell, 65,* 905–914.

Vicari, S. (2006). Motor development and neuropsychological patterns in persons with Down syndrome. *Behavior Genetics, 36*(3), 355–364.

Vicari, S., Carlesimo, A., & Caltegirone, C. (1995). Short-term memory in persons with intellectual disabilities and Down syndrome. *Journal of Intellectual Disabilities Research, 39,* 532–537.

Visootsak, J., Warren, S. T., Anido, A., & Graham, J. M. (2005). Fragile X syndrome: An update and review for the primary pediatrician. *Clinical Pediatrics, 44,* 371–381.

Walden, T., Knieps, L., & Baxter, A. (1991). Contingent provision of social referential information by parents of children with and without developmental delays. *American Journal on Mental Retardation, 96,* 177–187.

Wang, P. P., & Bellugi, U. (1994). Evidence from two genetic syndromes for a dissociation between verbal and visuo-spatial short-term memory. *Journal of Clinical and Experimental Neuropsychology, 16,* 317–322.

Wapner, R., Thom, E., Simpson, J. L., Pergament, E., Silver, R., Filkins, K., et al. (2003). First-trimester screening for trisomies 21 and 18. *New England Journal of Medicine, 349,* 1405–1413.

Ward, K. (2005). Microarray technology in obstetrics and gynecology: A guide for clinicians. *American Journal of Obstetrics and Gynecology, 195,* 364–372.

Wetherby, A. M., Yonclas, D. G., & Bryan, A. A. (1989). Communicative profiles of preschool children with handicaps: Implications for early identification. *Journal of Speech and Hearing Disorders, 54,* 148–158.

Wigren, M., & Hansen, S. (2003). Prader-Willi syndrome: Clinical picture, psychosocial support and current management. *Child Care, Health & Development, 29,* 449–456.

Williams, J. C. P., Barrett-Boyes, B. G., & Lowe, J. B. (1961). Supravalvular aortic stenosis. *Circulation, 14,* 1311–1318.

Willekens, D., De Cock, P., & Fryns, J. P. (2000). Three young children with Smith-Magenis syndrome: Their distinct, recognizable behavioral phenotype as the most important clinical symptoms. *Genetic Counseling, 11*, 103–110.

Wrightson, A. S. (2007). Universal newborn hearing screening. *American Family Physician, 75*, 1349–1352.

Zori, R. T., Lupski, J. R., Heju, Z., Greenberg, F., Killian, J. M., Gray, B. A., et al. (1993). Clinical, cytogenic, and molecular evidence for an infant with Smith-Magenis syndrome born from a mother having a mosaic 17p11.2p12 deletion. *American Journal of Medical Genetics, 47*, 504–511.

PART IV

Intervention and Policy Issues

Introduction

This final part of the book contains three chapters dealing with issues involved in early intervention programs. Chapter 13 by Powell reviews early intervention programs for at-risk infants and young children. The chapter begins with a brief discussion of the various societal and conceptual factors that have led to the current emphasis on early intervention. Powell then distinguishes between three types of intervention programs: programs where the primary focus is child-centered, programs where the primary focus is on parents or families, and programs that focus on both child and family. A number of intervention programs that are primarily child-focused are described and the developmental outcomes found with such programs are reviewed. A similar review is carried out for intervention programs that are primarily parent-focused. In the section on parenting-focused programs Powell distinguishes between parenting interventions that focus primarily on a specific outcome dimension (e.g., facilitating the mother–infant relationship) versus programs that focus on multiple aspects of parenting (e.g., providing parents with links to social support, community resources and information on parenting and child development). Programs that focus on both parent and child are then reviewed and described. Cutting across program types, Powell then goes on to discuss three critical dimensions of early intervention programs that have been associated with infant and child developmental outcomes. These dimensions involve program content, program intensity and program staffing. The chapter concludes with a discussion of critical future directions in the early intervention field, including the need to identify individual characteristics that moderate the impact of early interventions, and to understand societal changes that may change the goals of early interventions.

Chapter 14 by Friedman, Melhuish, and Hill deals with the many issues involved in childcare for infants and young children. The chapter is framed within an ecological perspective, wherein provision of childcare and childcare setting characteristics derive from contextual and societal features. Childcare provision and setting characteristics in turn influence the experiences of children in childcare. While the authors offer a standard definition of childcare, they are careful to point out that childcare settings and infants' and young children's experiences within childcare can be highly variable. Initial presentation of these conceptual issues is followed by a discussion of assessment of the childcare environment, with specific reference to issues involving quality of childcare. Friedman and colleagues then review evidence on the developmental consequences of infants' being in childcare. Outcome domains that have been associated with early childcare include attachment security, social competence, behavioral problems and cognitive and language development. Based on their review, Friedman and colleagues conclude that childcare in infancy has a moderate influence on developmental outcomes, that conclusions about the negative consequences of early childcare may have been overstated given the evidence, and that quality of the childcare environment is critical, particularly for outcomes involving cognitive or language development. The chapter concludes with a discussion of directions for future research in early childcare, including targeting childcare experiences to specific developmental outcomes such as the early development of social skills, and a greater use of randomized control studies.

Chapter 15 is by Barratt and Fener on linking together infancy research with public policy and practice. The framework of this chapter is based on Bronfenbrenner's ecological model in which infants are influenced by patterns of parenting practices, and parenting practices are influenced by local, state and national public policy decisions (e.g., policies on parental leave after the birth of an infant, policies on work requirements for low-income mothers receiving state or federal income supplementation). Barratt and Fener provide a detailed description of policy-driven programs that impact on infants and young children and/or their parents from low-income families such as healthcare for pregnant women, healthcare coverage for children, preventing teenage pregnancy, providing adequate nutrition to women, infants, and children, income support and subsidized childcare. Because there is decentralization (i.e., policies are made at the national level but are actually implemented at the state or local level), Barratt and Fener are able to identify gaps between policy and actual practice. For example, not all potentially eligible infants or parents are covered by available programs, or there is not complete coverage, or there are time limits on the amount of support that can be given. In addition to coverage issues, there are other gaps between policy and practice, such as families not being aware of programs, parents not wanting to participate, or parents not being able to get to locations where services are being offered. The chapter concludes with a detailed discussion of the role university-based infancy researchers can play in this process. University-based infancy researchers can be an unbiased source of information to policy makers and practitioners with regard to knowledge about known influences on infant development and the consequences of developmental risks. In addition, Barratt and Fener emphasize that universities must become actively involved in promoting interdisciplinary coordination and in committing resources to link research knowledge with ongoing practice in the field of infant development.

13

Early Intervention

Douglas R. Powell

Early intervention refers to "a broad array of activities designed to enhance a young child's development" (Ramey & Ramey, 1998, p. 110). A myriad of early intervention programs throughout the world today emanate from a simple yet powerful idea: providing appropriate developmental supports during infancy can lead to long-term positive outcomes for children at risk. The simplicity of this concept is a striking contrast to the complexity of identifying effective ways to promote the well-being of children whose development is compromised by environmental or individual factors. Intervention research has not kept pace with the press for new and expanded programs. Nonetheless, there is a growing scientific base to guide decisions about the form and substance of early interventions.

A logical starting point in the search for effective intervention approaches is a critical consideration of program designs and features that hold the promise of contributing to significant improvements in children's outcomes. Advances in the field of early intervention require an unpacking of programs. To this end, this chapter examines basic program designs that vary in the structure and content of work with families; summarizes available evidence on three features of programs that may be critical in influencing program outcome; and briefly discusses several needed directions in early intervention research. The chapter draws mostly from research on early intervention programs targeted at children at risk due to environmental factors, particularly poverty, low birth weight, and prematurity. The studies were conducted chiefly but not exclusively with programs in the United States.

Expansion of early intervention programs has been driven by four widespread issues: the deleterious and long-term effects of poverty on young children (for further discussion on poverty and development, see chapters 5 and 6 in this volume); stunning statistics about the incidence of child abuse and neglect (for detailed discussion of child abuse and neglect, see chapter 7 in this volume); images of families as increasingly less capable of providing optimal child-rearing environments for young children (for discussion of issues involved in parenting and child rearing, see chapter 15 in volume 1); an "earlier is better" assumption that prevention efforts at the beginning points of life are a prudent investment in the development of social capital.

Growth of the Internet has improved the accessibility of information for indirectly gauging the progress of policies and programs aimed at reversing troubling trends such as infant mortality rates, proportion of lower-birth-weight babies, proportion of babies immunized against childhood diseases, rates of babies born to adolescent mothers, and proportion of infants and toddlers who are victims of physical abuse. Information on the status of young children is gathered and disseminated by well-regarded agencies such as the Kids Count project of the Annie E. Casey Foundation (www.kidscount. org), the Child Well-Being Index of the Foundation for Child Development (www.fcd-us.org), and the Key National Indicators of Well-Being report issued by the Federal Interagency Forum on Child and Family Statistics (www.childstats.gov). Internationally, progress in meeting the United Nations Millennium Development Goals – which include eradicating extreme poverty and hunger, reducing child mortality, and improving maternal health – is tracked and available at the United Nations website (www. mdgmonitor.org).

Basic Program Designs

A major decision in the design of early intervention programs is how much and what type of programmatic room to make for families (Powell, 2006). Structural and substantive questions are pertinent here. The structural question involves the extent to which intervention with the family and/or the child is considered central to altering children's developmental trajectories. Programmatic responses to this question differ in whether the focus of intervention services is primarily on the child; the parent or family; or both the child and parent/family. The substantive question pertains to the domain(s) of services aimed at parents or other family members. Across intervention designs there is a wide range of content from a particular parenting behavior to a broad set of family functions, including economic self-sufficiency.

Theoretical and empirical bases of contrasting approaches to the design of early intervention reflect the state of scholarly literature on child development. Intervention programs may be situated in different theoretical perspectives regarding whether the primary locus of forces regulating developmental change is internal or external to the child, or a product of interaction between internal and external forces (Cowan, Powell, & Cowan, 1998). Similarly, intervention designs may be mapped onto contrasting positions in the debate about the magnitude of family effects on children (e.g., Collins, Maccoby, Steinberg, Hetherington, & Bornstein, 2000; Harris, 1995, 1998; Okagaki & Luster, 2005; Rowe, 1994). Notable here is Harris's (2002) argument that changes in child behavior via intervention in the home environment will not transfer to changes in a child's behavior at school or in other settings that do not involve the parent. In addition, interventions that embrace broad content boundaries in services to parents are congruent with developmental theory and research regarding the contexts of family functioning, particularly family connections with systems of formal and informal resources at neighborhood and community levels (see chapter 5 in this volume).

The merits of child- and family-oriented programs have long been debated in the early intervention literature (e.g., Zigler & Berman, 1983), with some scholars concluding that direct work with the child is superior to indirect (via parent/family) intervention (e.g., Ramey & Ramey, 1998). Although there is a growing corpus of research on effects of particular early intervention programs, there is a dearth of studies that employ an experimental design to compare the effectiveness of child- versus parent-oriented approaches. In one of the few studies on this issue Wasik, Ramey, Bryant, and Sparling (1990) randomly assigned infants from low-income families to participate in a daily center-based program plus a weekly home visit aimed at the parent or to a weekly home visit condition. Services were provided for five years. The daily center-based program combined with a home visit had significant effects on children's cognitive development, but the home visit condition alone had no effects on child or parent. The study did not include a center-based condition without a home visit.

Similarly, the merits of family-versus parent-focused programs have also been debated. Some of the early calls for intervention programs to attend to the supportiveness of family contexts were theoretically based, driven by an ecological framework as well as a view of traditional parent education practices as disempowering (e.g., Bronfenbrenner, 1978; Cochran & Woolever, 1983). Currently in the early intervention field, this perspective seems to have widespread support (e.g., Shonkoff & Phillips, 2000). However, there is limited research to guide decisions on how narrow or wide to define the substantive boundaries of work with parents of infants. A meta-analysis of 88 preventive interventions focused on enhancing parental sensitivity and infant attachment found that interventions with a clear-cut behavioral focus on parental sensitivity were more effective than interventions with a broader content focus that included attention to social support (Bakermans-Kranenburg, van IJzendoorn, & Juffer, 2003). Also, several large-scale studies of multisite interventions that provided a range of services to parents found minimal or no positive intervention effects on parents or children. These studies are described in a subsequent section of this chapter.

Feasibility considerations also shape intervention design decisions. Lags in the time it may take for some services for parents (e.g., reading instruction; mental health counseling) to translate into meaningful improvements in interactions with their child lend support to early interventions that include direct work with the child. Limited availability of facilities for center-based programs in some communities may lead to the use of home-based delivery systems. Also, some parents may be unwilling to regularly place their infant in a center-based program whereas other parents may view a center-based program as a valuable childcare resource and be unavailable for home visits due to work or school schedules.

Characteristics of basic early intervention designs are described below. The designs are organized by whether the intervention gives primary focus to the child, to the parent/family, or to both child and parent/family. The term "primary" is salient because it is rare to find an intervention that has no contact with parents, especially during the infancy period. Programs differ, then, in the amount and type of attention given to parents. Each section describes one or several interventions as illustrations of a particular program design.

Primary focus on child

Developed countries.   Interventions that seek to work directly with the child typically do so through a center-based program of early education and care. This type of intervention may provide occasional opportunities for parents to be involved in the program (e.g., monthly group meeting providing parenting education). Generally parent participation is encouraged but not required, and thus is viewed as an adjunct to direct work with the child. Interventions that work directly with the child may do so in the home or a clinic rather than a center-based program. This is common in programs where professionals provide individualized services to a child with a disability. To improve the intensity of a one-on-one intervention approach, there usually is serious effort to teach and encourage the parent to implement a protocol of activities in between the child's periodic sessions with a professional. Accordingly, individualized interventions often are focused on both child and parent.

Illustrative of a center-based program design is the Abecedarian Project, launched in 1972 at the Frank Porter Graham Child Development Institute at the University of North Carolina, Chapel Hill. The project's goal was to determine whether an education-ally focused full-day childcare program beginning in infancy could prevent nonorganically caused mild mental retardation in children from high-risk families (Ramey, Dorval, & Baker-Ward, 1983). The target sample was children at risk for developmental retardation and school failure, based on sociodemographic factors which were weighted and com-bined into a risk index. The families were low-income and mostly African American. Infants entered the childcare program at a mean age of 4.4 months and the center oper-ated 8 hours a day, 5 days a week for 50 weeks per year.

The infant Abecedarian program, based on the Learningames curriculum for infants and toddlers (Sparling & Lewis, 1979), focused on cognitive, language, perceptual-motor, and social development. Teachers maintained a developmental chart for each child in order to tailor curriculum experiences to individual child functioning. Program provisions for parent participation included regular parent–teacher conferences focused on the child's growth and development, scheduled group discussions on child and family development topics, and access to project social workers who were available to provide direct and indirect assistance with housing, social services, and counseling on individual and family matters (Ramey & Ramey, 1992). Published reports of the Abecedarian project do not include implementation data on actual levels and forms of parent participation.

A total of 111 infants from 109 eligible families were randomly assigned to the early childhood program or to a control group. Four cohorts of approximately 28 children were selected for the study over a 5-year period (Ramey et al., 1983). Outcome data indicate that the Abecedarian intervention prevented intellectual decline during the pre-school period (Ramey & Campbell, 1984), and contributed to improved reading and math performance when children were 8 and 15 years of age (Campbell & Ramey, 1994, 1995) and to lower rates of placement in special education during the 10 years children attended school prior to age 15 years (Ramey, Campbell, Burchinal, Skimmer, Gardner, & Ramey, 2000). A follow-up at 21 years of age found that participants in the early intervention group earned significantly higher scores on intellectual and academic measures, had acquired significantly more years of total education, and showed a reduction in teenage pregnancy compared to participants in the control group (Campbell, Ramey, Pungello, Sparling, & Miller-Johnson, 2002).

Evaluation of the Abecedarian Project also examined effects on parents. It appears that adolescent parents benefited the most. At the time of their child's kindergarten entry, more teenage parents in the intervention (46%) than in the control group (13%) had graduated from high school (Campbell, Breitmayer, & Ramey, 1986) and when children were 15 years of age more teenage parents of participants in the intervention group (80%) than teenage parents whose children were in the control group (28%) had attained post-secondary education. Employment rates were also higher for the intervention group than for the control group (Ramey et al., 2000).

Developing countries.   Center-based programs for infants are less prevalent in developing countries due to limited space and staffing resources. A serious challenge is to provide quality education experiences for young children when funding is scarce. For example, a report of an initiative to establish preschool centers in 350 tribal villages in the Indian state of Orissa indicated that it was common to find toddlers in classrooms with older children even though frequently "the play degenerated into fighting and the teachers could only try to keep the peace" (Bernard van Leer Foundation, 2008, p. 44). In addition to funding problems, deeply rooted values in some cultures may view home and family rather than center-based programs as the appropriate setting for infant care.

None of the interventions included in a recent review of outcome evaluations of center-based early education programs in developing countries targeted children younger than 2 years of age; most programs began when children were 3 or 4 years of age (Engle et al., 2007). Further, in many developing countries the nutritional and health deficiencies of infants may be viewed as a more pressing issue than the cognitive and social domains addressed by center-based early childhood programs (Walker et al., 2007). Interventions focused on health outcomes generally work through parents and are described in the next section.

Primary focus on parent

Many early intervention programs aimed at infants work with parents (almost exclusively mothers) in an attempt to have an influence on the child's family experiences, including parent–child interactions. Home visiting is especially common. Among the benefits of home visiting are the program worker's opportunity to secure first-hand information about the home and family circumstances in which the child is being reared, including the opportunity to tailor program content to family preferences and conditions. However, studies indicate that, as an early intervention delivery strategy, home visiting programs in general yield modest to no effects (Sweet & Appelbaum, 2004), although results of some individual program evaluations point to more robust positive effects. Parent-focused interventions that differ by giving attention to single- versus multiple-content domains are described below.

Single-content domain.   Attachment theory provides a productive theoretical framework for early interventions that seek to improve the quality of mother–infant relationships. Such interventions view a secure attachment relationship as the basis for well-being, including social development. A mental representation of others as trustworthy and responsive and of the self as worthy of love and respect are core dimensions of a secure attachment relationship (see chapter 16 in volume 1). Major contributors to a secure attachment relationship are parents' mental representations of attachment (representational level) and their sensitivity to the infant (behavioral level; Juffer, Bakermans-Kranenburg, & van IJzendoorn, 2008).

The Video-feedback Intervention to Promote Positive Parenting (VIPP) developed at Leiden University in the Netherlands is illustrative of this approach (Juffer et al., 2008). Parents are offered short-term behaviorally focused intervention or a combination of behaviorally and representationally focused interventions, both aimed at enhancing parental sensitivity and positive parent–child interactions. The VIPP programs make use of videotaped interactions of parent–child interaction. Mother and infant are videotaped during daily situations (e.g., bathing, mealtime) for 10–30 minutes. The videotapes are discussed with the parent to focus on actual behaviors (as observed rather than remembered) of the child and the parent. Attention is given to segments involving positive interactions as well as potentially negative interactions, and to the infants' signals and expressions. The intent is to strengthen the mother's accurate perception of infant signals and adequate response to signals. Home visitors also have the option of providing written information to the parent. VIPP interventions that include attention to parents' representations of the attachment relationship include additional discussion with the parent about past and present attachment relationships. The program is implemented in the home for four to eight sessions. The intervention has been tested in a variety of settings, including Italy and the United Kingdom, with different populations and found to be effective with nonclinical families as well as families in which parents or child suffer from psychological or health problems (Bakermans-Kranenburg, Juffer, & Van IJzendoorn, 1998; Juffer et al., 2008; for further discussion of other interventions for depressed mothers or for infants with psychological or behavioral disorders, see chapters 8 and 11 in this volume).

In addition to attachment-focused early interventions, parenting education programs focused on school-related outcomes have been an active part of the early intervention field since the 1960s. A prominent model is the Parents as Teachers (PAT) Program, which provides home visits (called *personal visits* because some may be conducted in a setting other than the home) that offer age-appropriate activities and child development information aimed at strengthening the quality of mother–child interaction and the home learning environment. There also are periodic group meetings of parents, developmental screenings, and referrals to community services. School readiness is a major program goal. A number of randomized trials of PAT have been conducted with low-income populations. A three-site study conducted in geographically dispersed urban areas found few statistically significant effects at the end of two years in the program (child's second birthday). Specifically, of 28 measures of parent outcomes, only three were statistically significant (e.g., higher frequency of telling stories, saying nursery rhymes, and singing with the child), and there were no significant child outcomes (Wagner, Spiker, & Linn,

2002). In a separate randomized trial of PAT with primarily Latino parents and with adolescent parents, both in different locations in California, there were small and inconsistent positive effects on parent knowledge, attitudes, and behavior, and no gains in child development or health when experimental and control groups were compared overall (Wagner & Clayton, 1999). A qualitative study focused on why the PAT program was not more effective in the two California trials found that home visitors emphasized their social support role and generally did not discuss parenting behaviors that appeared to be in need of change or improvement, even though program goals emphasized the latter outcomes (Hebbeler & Gerlach-Downie, 2002).

Multiple-content domains. Reviewers of the early intervention literature have long argued that parenting education programs aimed at low-income populations are unlikely to yield positive effects because they do not address major sources of stress faced by parents living in poverty (e.g., Chilman, 1973). Partly in response to this argument, the PAT program was examined in an intervention condition that combined the program's content in parenting knowledge and skills with attention to personal and family life issues through case management. The intervention was tested in an experiment in which adolescent mothers were randomly assigned to the intervention (PAT content plus case management) or to a control group. Results indicated that intervention group mothers were more accepting of their children's behavior and there were significantly fewer opened cases of child abuse or neglect compared to control group participants. Intervention children experienced gains of 1 or 2 months in cognitive development compared to control group children, a small effect size that may not be educationally beneficial. There were no significant intervention effects on a range of other outcome variables, however (Wagner & Clayton, 1999).

The case management approach to supporting families of very young children was subjected to investigation in the Comprehensive Child Development Center Program (CCDP). The CCDP is a multisite initiative aimed at improving the physical, social, emotional, and intellectual development of children in low-income families from birth to age 5 years. The primary means of intervention was case management work with parents and other family members. The project's name is misleading because the initiative did not provide services directly to children other than developmental screening. Case management was central to the intervention in that case managers were to assess goals and service needs of individual family members and the family as a whole, develop a service plan, refer the family to services in the community, and provide counseling and support to family members. The program also provided parenting education for the mother or primary caregiver and arranged for developmentally appropriate early childhood experiences for all children (Goodson, Layzer, St. Pierre, Bernstein, & Lopez, 2000).

An experimental study of CCDP's effects was conducted in 21 sites, with data collected annually for a five-year period. Results are easily summarized: CCDP did not produce any important positive effects on participating parents or children when compared with control group families. Specifically, CCDP had no statistically significant effects on participating mothers' economic self-sufficiency or parenting skills. There were no program effects on children's cognitive or social-emotional development or health. Also, there were no differential effects on subgroups of participants (e.g., adolescent parents). Further, the length of time a family was enrolled in CCDP was not associated with statistically significant differences in outcomes achieved. Positive change that occurred in the lives of CCDP families (e.g., mothers in the labor force) also occurred in control group families (Goodson et al., 2000).

It is informative to contrast characteristics and results of the CCDP intervention with the Nurse–Family Partnership (NFP; previously known as the Nurse Home Visiting Program), also targeted at low-income families. The NFP does not employ the "case management" label or approach. However, one of its strategies for improving child and parent outcomes is to help first-time young mothers make productive connections with informal social support networks and community services, including health and human services that can reduce situational stressors encountered by low-income families. Home visitors also provide information on child development, particularly on how to promote sensitive and responsive caregiving (e.g., understanding and responding to infant cues). The goals of the NFP are to improve the outcomes of pregnancy, the quality of caregiving (and related child health and developmental outcomes), and maternal life course development (Olds, Kitzman, Cole, & Robinson, 1997). Home visits follow a detailed protocol and last between 75 and 90 minutes each. Visits begin during pregnancy and continue during the first two years of the child's life. Visits are made every week to two weeks, with frequency varying by stage of pregnancy, child age, and the mother's needs.

The NFP has been tested in three successive randomized trials. The original trial with predominantly European Americans conducted in semirural Elmira, New York, found positive intervention effects on rates of child abuse and neglect, maternal welfare dependence, spacing of successive pregnancies, and maternal criminal behavior related to use of alcohol and other drugs (Olds, Eckenrode, et al., 1997; Olds, Henderson, Chamberlin, & Tatelbaum, 1986). Positive intervention effects were concentrated on poor, unmarried teenage mothers. A 15-year follow-up of adolescents born to low-income women who participated in NFP both during pregnancy and postnatally, and who were unmarried, found fewer instances of running away, fewer arrests, fewer convictions and violations of probation, fewer lifetime sex partners, and fewer days having consumed alcohol in the prior 6 months than youth in the comparison group (Olds, Henderson, Kitzman, Eckenrode, Cole, & Tatelbaum, 1998).

In a subsequent randomized trial conducted with primarily African American women in Memphis, Tennessee, nurse-visited mothers had higher quality home environments and held fewer child-rearing beliefs associated with child abuse and neglect, including belief in physical punishment and unrealistic expectations for infants, compared to comparison group mothers when their children were 24 months of age. Also, compared to control group participants, fewer women visited by nurses during pregnancy had pregnancy-induced hypertension or hypertension in the years after delivery. In addition, women visited by nurses during pregnancy and the first two years of the child's life had fewer healthcare encounters for children in which injuries or ingestions were detected, fewer days that children were hospitalized for injuries or ingestions, and fewer second pregnancies. However, there was no intervention effect on maternal teaching behavior, use of well-child care, immunization status, the child's mental development, or parent report of child behavior problems (Kitzman, Cole, Yoos, & Olds, 1997). In a three-year follow-up of the Memphis trial, intervention mothers had fewer subsequent pregnancies and fewer months of welfare and food stamp use (Kitzman et al., 2000).

In the most recent trial of the NFP, conducted in Denver, Colorado, with a low-income population of first-time mothers (45% Hispanic), nurse-visited infants at 6 months of age were less likely to exhibit emotional vulnerability in response to fear stimuli, and infants born to women with low psychological resources (mental health, sense of mastery, intelligence) were less likely to exhibit low emotional vitality in response to joy and anger stimuli. At 21 months, nurse-visited children born to women with low psychological resources were less likely to exhibit language delays and at 24 months they exhibited superior mental developmental compared to their control group counterparts. In comparison to control group participants, nurse-visited smokers also had greater reductions in nicotine levels from intake to the end of pregnancy. Further, by the study child's second birthday women visited by nurses had fewer subsequent pregnancies and births and during the second year after the birth of their first child they worked more than women in the control group. There were no intervention effects on women's educational achievement or use of welfare or children's behavior problems (Olds et al., 2002).

In sharp contrast to CCDP and many other home visiting initiatives, NFP home visitors are nurses. An experimental study designed to determine whether paraprofessionals could produce positive results when trained in delivering the NFP found that paraprofessionals produced small effects that rarely achieved statistical or clinical significance whereas, as noted earlier, nurses produced significant effects on a wide range of maternal and child outcomes (Olds et al., 2002).

Focus on child and parent

The third and final basic program design considered in this chapter entails intervention services to both child and parent with approximately equal levels of intensity. This may occur concurrently or sequentially. Interest in this design has been high since the early 1970s when Bronfenbrenner (1974) concluded from a review of early intervention programs that significant family involvement was key to sustaining positive effects in the long term.

The Early Head Start program provides services to both child and parent, beginning in infancy or prenatally, through home visits, a center-based childcare program, and parent group meetings. An experimental study of the program in 17 different sites found that, at age 3 years, children in the Early Head Start Program performed better than control group children in cognitive and language development, displayed higher emotional engagement with the parent and sustained attention with play objects, and were lower in aggressive behavior. Early Head Start parents were more emotionally supportive, provided more language and learning stimulation, read to their children more, and spanked less than control parents (Love et al., 2005). The study found that results were strongest in a *mixed-approach* program in which children and families received home-based and/or center-based services, concurrently or at different times, and when performance standards were fully implemented early. Programs offering the mixed-approach strategy were compared to programs offering child development services through weekly *home visits* and parent–child group socialization activities twice a month, and to *center-based* programs that provided childcare plus parenting education and a minimum of two home visits a year to each family (Love et al., 2005). Because children and families were not randomly assigned to the three program models examined in this study, results do not address the question of whether working with both parent and child (mixed model) is superior to working with primarily with the child or the parent.

The Infant Health and Development Program (IHDP) was an eight-site experimental study of a three-year intervention with low-birth-weight, premature infants that included home visits through age 3 years; a full-day child development center 50 weeks a year, beginning when children were 1 year of age; and parent group meetings during the second and third years. The home visits provided information and skill development in child health and development, using the Partners for Learning curriculum (Sparling & Lewis, 1995) that also was used in the child development center (Ramey, Sparling, Bryant, & Wasik, 1997). Home visits also provided parents with training in problem-solving skills, using a curriculum that views problem-solving as a cognitive-behavioral process that includes both thinking and action components (Wasik, Bryant, Lyons, Sparling, & Ramey, 1997). At 3 years of age, at the end of the intervention, IHDP children had significantly higher intelligence test scores and receptive vocabulary test scores and lower scores on a parental measure of reported behavior problems than children in the comparison group. Benefits were more pronounced among heavier low-birth-weight than in light low-birth-weight infants (IHDP, 1990). There were no intervention effects on the home environment at 12 months, but at 36 months the home environments of intervention families were rated higher than comparison families. Intervention mothers scored higher than comparison group mothers on a self-report measure of problem-solving skills, but there were no differences between intervention and comparison group mothers on a measure of coping with health and daily living at 36 months (Wasik, Bryant, Sparling, & Ramey, 1997) and on measures of knowledge or concepts of child development at 12, 24, or 36 months (Benasich, Brooks-Gunn, Spiker, & Black, 1997).

Identifying Critical Features of Interventions

Patterns of findings in studies involving different levels and types of intervention with parents highlighted in the previous section suggest that a program's delivery system (center- or home-based) and scope of work with families may not be the only factors contributing to child outcomes. For instance, in the parent-focused interventions addressing broad content boundaries, one program (CCDP) was fully ineffective whereas another program (NFP) has demonstrated significant intervention effects on mothers and children in three randomized trials. There are numerous differences between the interventions, including the content of work with parents, approach to staffing (professional vs. paraprofessional), and target population (first-time young mothers vs. any low-income family with one or more young children).

An intervention is not one variable but a composite of program variables that are organized in complex ways (Campbell, 1986). Advances in the field of early intervention require an identification of program features and configurations of program features that contribute to positive outcomes. An empirically based understanding of critical elements of an intervention is key to efforts to take a program to scale; omitting or significantly altering a program component may diminish or eliminate an intervention's effectiveness. Beginning in the mid-1980s, the focus of many early intervention studies was broadened to include questions about "what works" and "what works for whom" (Guralnick, 1997; Korfmacher, 2001; Powell, 2005). This is a methodologically challenging area of investigation that has mostly employed correlational methods to identify variables that warrant more systematic examination in an experimental study. Dimensions of three potentially critical features of intervention design are described below.

Content

Guidance on developmentally appropriate practices in group- and home-based early education and care programs is readily available from professional associations such the National Association for the Education of Young Children and the American Academy of Pediatrics. Nutrition standards are available from the World Health Organization (www.who.int/en/) and other organizations with a focus on developing countries.

Expert information to inform decisions about the content of work with parents is less plentiful. For example, the CCDP and IHDP interventions offer contrasting approaches to facilitating parent connections family support systems. Case managers in the CCDP helped families make connections with community services after conducting an assessment of family needs. The IHDP's problem-solving curriculum sought to strengthen parents' skills in identifying their own problems, generating and weighing alternative responses, and evaluating the effects of implementation (Wasik, Bryant, Sparling, & Ramey, 1997). The interventions, then, pursued different substantive routes or theories of change toward the same goal of improving the supportiveness of family contexts. As reported above, the problem-solving curriculum appeared to have small effects whereas the case management strategy, as implemented by the CCDP, was ineffective.

An important decision regarding the content of interventions with parents is the extent to which the substantive emphasis is on parenting behaviors or family interactions, versus information about some aspect of child development or parenting. Programs that provide information primarily or exclusively to parents presumably operate under the tenuous assumption that parents will act on the information they receive. The link between cognition and behavior is complex (Sigel, 1992) and there are limited empirical data to support a view of causal role of parent cognitions (particularly parental beliefs about child development) in determining parenting behavior (Okagaki & Bingham, 2005).

The content of early intervention also may be conceptualized as relationships between the intervener and family members, including children. For example, the Program for Infant/Toddler Care, which contributed in a major way to national training of Early Head Start staff, is a relationship-based curriculum which emphasizes relationship planning, not lesson planning (Lally & Mangione, 2009). Caregiver responsiveness is a major theme of recommended practices in infant care (Lally, Griffin, Fenichel, Segal, Szanton, & Weissbourd, 2003; see chapter 14 in this volume). Quality of relationships with parents may be viewed as a complement or pathway to providing information about parenting practices. For example, one early intervention program developed therapeutic relationships with mothers that include demonstrations of ways to handle family relationships and problems (e.g., Booth, Mitchell, Barnard, & Spieker, 1989). In a review of early family intervention studies, Heinicke and Ponce (1999) suggested that the relationship between the family and the intervener was central to achieving positive intervention effects on maternal functioning and quality of family and community support. However, broadening the intervention lens beyond the mother–child relationship raises important questions about the involvement of fathers in programs. Families involved in early intervention programs may differ from the modal family type that developmental scientists have examined in father–child relationship studies (Marsiglio, Amato, Day, & Lamb, 2000). More than one male may play a fathering role in an infant's life (e.g., nonresident biological father, resident stepfather, grandfather, or other male relative; Roggman, Fitzgerald, Bradley, & Raikes, 2002). In addition, the gatekeeping role of women in nonresident fathers' and stepfathers' relationships with their children may need careful attention in program designs and actions (Raikes, Summers, & Roggman, 2005).

Whether parents and other family members view predetermined content of an early intervention program as pertinent to their needs and circumstances may contribute to their level of engagement with the program. Several interventions aimed at parents of older children have gathered data from prospective program participants as part of the program development process, in an attempt to ensure a good match between the presentation of program content and interests of targeted participants (e.g., Powell & Peet, 2008). Parent engagement of early intervention programs is discussed in greater detail below.

Intensity

There are four dimensions of intervention intensity: the point at which an intervention begins with a child; length or duration or an intervention; frequency of contact with a child or family; and the extent to which participants are actively engaged in a program.

An "earlier is better" perspective undergirds the field of early intervention but there is limited empirical information about the precise timing of work with infants and their families. In the Bakermans-Kranenburg et al. (2003) meta-analysis of interventions focused on parental sensitivity and infant attachment security, programs starting six months after birth or later were somewhat more effective than interventions starting prenatally or within the first six months of life.

A "more is better" view also is prevalent in the early intervention field. However, research on the relation of intervention duration to outcomes is compromised by high rates of participant attrition. For example, in the aforementioned three-site study of the PAT program 22% of participants never began any visits and 35% received some visits but dropped out by the assessment at the second year of the study. High rates of attrition in the three study sites led to cancellation of data collection at the third year (Wagner et al., 2002). Results of the Bakermans-Kranenburg et al. (2003) meta-analysis do not support a "more is better" perspective. Interventions with fewer than five sessions were as effective as interventions with 5–16 sessions, but interventions with more than 16 sessions were less effective than interventions with a small number of sessions. A related issue is the quality of developmental supports available to children after the termination of an intervention. Some of the children enrolled in the five-year Abecedarian project were randomly assigned to an educational support program in kindergarten through second grade. Examination of this follow-up assistance compared to no special assistance found that the school-age intervention helped to maintain preschool benefits for reading (Campbell et al., 2002).

Experimental studies of the frequency of intervention contact with infants and/or their families are rare. A common research strategy here is to look at dose–response relations. The main problem of this correlational approach is the lack of control for population characteristics that may function as confounds. The only published investigation of systematically varied levels of program frequency is a study by Powell and Grantham-McGregor (1989) conducted in Jamaica. Random assignment to different frequencies of home visiting (twice a month, once a month, control condition) was by neighborhood, not family, in one sample, whereas families in a second sample were randomly assigned to weekly home visits or a control condition. Results of separate analyses of the two samples indicate that bimonthly visits had a small influence on children's developmental outcomes and that there were significant developmental improvements in children whose families received weekly home visits compared to children in the control group.

Studies suggest that participants' active engagement of program content is predictive of outcomes. An analysis of the IHDP data found that parent and child active experiences in the intervention (as assessed by parent's interest in the intervention activities during the home visit and child's mastery of tasks taught at the child development center) were stronger predictors of child IQ and quality of home environment scores at age 3 years than program exposure (i.e., number of contacts in home and child development center) and rate of participation (i.e., number of activities presented per visit to parent in the home or per day to the child at the center). A higher level of active experience of both child and parent was more strongly associated with child IQ and home environment quality than a high level of active experience on the part of the child only or the parent only (Liaw, Meisels, & Brooks-Gunn, 1995).

An intervention's pedagogical strategies for engaging parents may be linked to issues regarding the relation of program intensity to magnitude of outcomes. For example, a didactic presentation of information to parents without any discussion is presumably less intense than a guided discussion with a program participant about new information. Similarly, information that is tailored to a parent's interests or circumstances, including an infant's developmental status, may be more intense than general information that may or may not be directly pertinent to the status of a particular parent or infant. Perhaps more intensive than any of these strategies is constructive feedback to individuals based on observations of their parenting behaviors. As described earlier, some interventions use videotapes of parent–child interactions and of infant behaviors to guide discussions with a parent about child development and parenting. The Bakermans-Kranenburg et al. (2003) meta-analysis found that interventions with video feedback were more effective than interventions without this method. Another pedagogical consideration is the pace with which new information is presented. One intervention study found that the rate at which a curriculum emphasizing adult–child interactions was implemented in home visits and in a child development center added significantly to the prediction of children's IQ scores at 3 years of age (Sparling, Lewis, Ramey, Wasik, Bryant, & LaVange, 1991).

Staffing

A common staffing pattern in early intervention programs is to employ paraprofessionals as the primary worker with infants and their families. Many factors potentially contribute to the use of paraprofessionals. In some communities such as geographically remote regions or developing countries, professionals such as nurses may not be available to provide intervention services. Some programs employ paraprofessionals because they are expected to provide a high level of personal credibility that facilitates recruiting and retaining hard-to-reach families, including parental acceptance of a program and its core messages or recommendations. Many paraprofessional staff persons are former partici-pants in an early intervention program and have had life experiences similar to those of targeted program participants (Powell, 1993). Yet another factor is the expected financial benefits of employing less expensive staff and an opportunity to serve more infants (e.g., two paraprofessional staff members for the cost of one professional). However, the extant literature suggests that these anticipated benefits may not be fully realized. Paraprofessionals may find it easier to provide material support, such as transportation for a mother or infant to a clinic appointment (Musick & Stott, 2000), but may have difficulty talking with parents about problematic parenting behaviors and may avoid discussing sensitive issues (e.g., adolescent pregnancy) that the paraprofessional also has experienced. With regard to expected financial benefits, a cost–benefit analysis indicates that the amount of training and supervision of paraprofessionals may erase economic benefits (Harkavy & Bond, 1992).

An experimental study, discussed earlier, of the NFP intervention with first-time, low-income mothers in Denver, Colorado, addressed the question of whether paraprofession-als can produce significant gains for mothers or children. Results indicated that, when staff (paraprofessionals or nurses) were trained in the NFP model, families working with paraprofessionals demonstrated small improvements that rarely achieved statistical or clinical significance. Nurses produced significant effects on a wide range of maternal and child outcomes. For most outcomes on which either paraprofessionals or nurses produced significant effects, the paraprofessionals typically had effects that were half of the size of those produced by nurses (Olds et al., 2002). Mothers' ratings of the helping relationship did not differ between nurses and paraprofessionals (Korfmacher, O'Brien, Hiatt, & Olds, 1999). The investigators speculate that nurses may have higher levels of legitimacy than paraprofessionals in the eyes of parents to address their health-related concerns and therefore may have more power to engage parents and support adaptive behavior change. However, generalization of the Olds et al. (2002) findings is limited to programs serving first-time, low-income mothers with a program model focused on improving health outcomes.

A needed research direction is to determine effects of professionals versus paraprofes-sionals in content other than health issues. A meta-analysis of 60 home visiting programs found that staff type was inconsistently related to intervention effect sizes. Use of professional home visitors was associated with higher effect sizes than was use of paraprofessionals regarding child cognitive outcomes, but use of paraprofessional home visitors was associated with higher effect sizes than were professional and nonprofessional home visitors regarding child abuse outcomes (Sweet & Appelbaum, 2004).

Future Directions

Missing in the preceding sections of this chapter is delineation of population and contextual conditions that are associated and not associated with the effectiveness of a particular program design or feature. This is risky in a field that is prone to promulgating sweeping and inappropriate generalizations about intervention effects (Shonkoff, 2000). Few intervention models have been examined in successive trials with different populations, and when a series of trials has been conducted (notably NFP) a key population characteristic (first-time mother) has been held constant. The next wave of research needs to systematically investigate "for whom" questions without resorting to population subgroup analyses that negate the benefits of random assignment. A major challenge in the intervention field is to find a meaningful balance between general research-based principles of early intervention and accommodation of population-specific characteristics.

Attention to several levels of context is needed. The societal context of early intervention programs deserves our attention as results of long-term follow-up studies of programs spark renewed interest in an intervention model implemented decades ago. Demographic and community variables change over time and conditions that were supportive of a program in one era may be less prevalent at a different time. Illustrative here is the dramatic change in the labor force participation of women in the United States. One of the best-designed studies of an early intervention program, the Parent–Child Development Center initiative, was carried out at a time when many women did not work outside of the home and were available for extensive periods of program participation (Andrews et al., 1982). These norms changed dramatically in the late 1970s and by the 1990s the employability skills of low-income adults were a prominent domestic issue, prompting welfare reform policies that emphasize job skills and work. Accordingly, early intervention programs aimed at low-income populations significantly reduced parent involvement components because parents were not available for participation and/or embraced welfare-to-work goals by providing job and self-sufficiency skills training (Smith & Zaslow, 1995) and abandoned or significantly reduced the attention to parents' child-rearing knowledge and skills. Parenting education became a less pressing need in the eyes of policy-makers and parents (Powell, 2006).

There is some evidence to suggest that agency characteristics are associated with implementation of a well-defined early intervention (e.g., Duggan et al., 2000). Consider results of the 21-site CCDP initiative. Positive effects on children and parents were secured in one of the sites, leading investigators to speculate on site and agency characteristics that might have contributed to effects (Goodson et al., 2000). Critics of the

CCDP study argue that the intervention was taken to scale prematurely (Gilliam, Ripple, Zigler, & Leiter, 2000). Organizational capacity to carry out an intervention with fidelity appears to have been a factor in the unevenness of the Early Head Start study. Some agencies participating in this study never fully implemented federally mandated components of the Early Head Start program. Rigorous research on this topic is needed if resources are to be used prudently in expanding an intervention model in multiple locations.

Lastly, the community context of an intervention is valuable to investigate in early intervention research because the formal and informal supports available to a child and family during and after participation in an intervention program may well contribute to intervention effects in the short and long term. Early intervention is unlikely to serve as an inoculation for life (Klebanov & Brooks-Gunn, 2006). Existing intervention programs generally work from the inside out, from the infant and family to the community. Yet inadequate health, educational, and social services, unsafe neighborhoods, and dysfunctional patterns of social life are debilitating conditions for an intervention to counteract. An equally important starting point for interventions is to move inward, from a community's formal and informal resources to families and infants.

References

Andrews, S. R., Blumenthal, J. B., Johnson, D. L., Kahn, A. J., Ferguson, C. J., Lasater, R. M., et al. (1982). The skills of mothering: A study of parent child development centers. *Monographs of the Society for Research in Child Development, 47* (6, Serial No. 198).

Bakermans-Kranenburg, M. J., Juffer, E., & van IJzendoorn, M. H. (1998). Intervention with video feedback and attachment discussions: Does type of maternal insecurity make a difference? *Infant Mental Health Journal, 19*, 202–219.

Bakermans-Kranenburg, M. J., van IJzendoorn, M. H., & Juffer, F. (2003). Less is more: Meta-analysis of sensitivity and attachment interventions in early childhood. *Psychological Bulletin, 129*, 195–215.

Benasich, A. A., Brooks-Gunn, J., Spiker, D., & Black, G. W. (1997). Maternal attitudes and knowledge about child development. In R. T. Gross, D. Spiker, & C. W. Haynes (Eds.), *Helping low birth weight, premature babies: Infant Health and Development Program* (pp. 290–303). Stanford, CA: Stanford University Press.

Bernard van Leer Foundation (2008). Low-cost ways of improving quality in early childhood education. *Early Childhood Matters, 110*, 44–46.

Booth, C. L., Mitchell, S. K., Barnard, K. E., & Spieker, S. J. (1989). Development of maternal social skills in multiproblem families: Effects on the mother–child relationship. *Developmental Psychology, 25*, 403–412.

Bronfenbrenner, U. (1974). *Is early intervention effective? Vol. 2. A report on longitudinal evaluations of preschool programs.* Washington, DC: Department of Health, Education and Welfare, Office of Child Development.

Bronfenbrenner, U. (1978). Who needs parent education? *Teachers College Record, 79*, 767–787.

Campbell, D. T. (1986). Relabeling internal and external validity for applied social scientists. In W. M. K. Trochim (Ed.), *Advances in quasi-experimental design and analysis* (pp. 67–77). San Francisco: Jossey-Bass.

Campbell, F. A., Breitmayer, B. J., & Ramey, C. T. (1986). Disadvantaged teenage mothers and their children: Consequences of educational day care. *Family Relations, 35*, 63–68.

Campbell, F. A., & Ramey, C. T. (1994). Effects of early intervention on intellectual and academic achievement: A follow-up study of children from low-income families. *Child Development, 65,* 684–698.

Campbell, F. A., & Ramey, C. T. (1995). Cognitive and school outcomes for high risk African American students at middle adolescence: Positive effects of early intervention. *American Educational Research Journal, 32,* 743–772.

Campbell, F. A., Ramey, C. T., Pungello, E., Sparling, J., & Miller-Johnson, S. (2002). Early childhood education: Young adult outcomes from the Abecedarian project. *Applied Developmental Science, 6,* 42–57.

Chilman, C. S. (1973). Programs for disadvantaged parents. In B. M. Caldwell & H. N. Ricciuti (Eds.), *Review of child development research* (Vol. 3, pp. 403–465). Chicago: University of Chicago Press.

Cochran, M., & Woolever, F. (1983). Beyond the deficit model: The empowerment of parents with information and informal supports. In I. Sigel & L. Laosa (Eds.), *Changing families* (pp. 225–245). New York: Plenum.

Collins, W. A., Maccoby, E. E., Steinberg, L., Hetherington, E. M., & Bornstein, M. H. (2000). Contemporary research on parenting: The case for nature *and* nurture. *American Psychologist, 55,* 218–232.

Cowan, P. A., Powell, D. R., & Cowan, C. P. (1998). Parenting interventions: A family systems perspective. In W. Damon (Editor-in-Chief), I. E. Sigel, & K. A. Renninger (Vol. Eds.), *Handbook of child psychology: Vol. 4. Child psychology in practice* (5th ed., pp. 1113–1132). New York: Wiley.

Duggan, A., Windham, A., McFarlane, E., Fuddy, L., Rohde, C., Buchbinder, S., et al. (2000). Hawaii's Health Start program of home visiting for at-risk families: Evaluation of family identification, family engagement, and service delivery. *Pediatrics, 105,* 250–259.

Engle, P. L., Black, M. M., Behrman, J. R., de Mello, M. C., Gertler, P. J., Kapiriri, L., et al. (2007). Strategies to avoid the loss of developmental potential in more than 200 million children in the developing world. *Lancet, 369,* 229–242.

Gilliam, W. S., Ripple, C. H., Zigler, E. F., & Leiter, C. (2000). Evaluating child and family demonstration initiatives: Lessons from the Comprehensive Child Development Program. *Early Childhood Research Quarterly, 15,* 41–59.

Goodson, B. D., Layzer, J. I., St. Pierre, R. G., Bernstein, L. S., & Lopez, M. (2000). Effectiveness of a comprehensive, 5-year family support program for low-income children and their families: Findings from the Comprehensive Child Development Program. *Early Childhood Research Quarterly, 15,* 3–39.

Guralnick, M. J. (1997). Second-generation research in the field of early intervention. In M. J. Guralnick (Ed.), *The effectiveness of early intervention* (pp. 3–20). Baltimore, MD: Brookes.

Harkavy, O., & Bond, J. T. (1992). Program operations: Time allocation and cost analysis. In M. Larner, R. Halpern, & O. Harkavy (Eds.), *Fair start for children: Lessons learned from seven demonstration projects* (pp. 198–217). New Haven, CT: Yale University Press.

Harris, J. R. (1995). Where is the child's environment? A group socialization theory of development. *Psychological Review, 102,* 458–489.

Harris, J. R. (1998). *The nurture assumption.* New York: Free Press.

Harris, J. R. (2002). Beyond the nurture assumption: Testing hypotheses about the child's environment. In J. G. Borkowski, S. L. Ramey, & M. Bristol-Power (Eds.), *Parenting and the child's world: Influences on academic, intellectual, and social-emotional development* (pp. 3–20). Mahwah, NJ: Erlbaum.

Hebbeler, K. M., & Gerlach-Downie, S. G. (2002). Inside the black box of home visiting: A qualitative analysis of why intended outcomes were not achieved. *Early Childhood Research Quarterly, 17,* 28–51.

Heinicke, C. M., & Ponce, V. A. (1999). Relationship-based early family intervention. In D. Cicchetti & S. L. Toth (Eds.), *Developmental approaches to prevention and intervention* (pp. 153–193). Rochester, NY: University of Rochester Press.

Infant Health and Development Program (1990). Enhancing the outcomes of low birth-weight, premature infants: A multisite, randomized trial. *Journal of the American Medical Association, 263,* 3035–3042.

Juffer, F., Bakermans-Kranenburg, M. J., & van IJzendoorn, M. H. (Eds.) (2008). *Promoting positive parenting: An attachment-based intervention.* New York: Erlbaum.

Kitzman, H. J., Cole, R., Yoos, H. L., & Olds, D. (1997). Challenges experienced by home visitors: A qualitative study of program implementation. *Journal of Community Psychology, 25,* 95–109.

Kitzman, H., Olds, D. L., Sidora, K., Henderson, C. R., Hanks, C., Cole, R., et al. (2000). Enduring effects of nurse home visitation on maternal life course: A 3-year follow-up of a randomized trial. *Journal of the American Medical Association, 283,* 1983–1989.

Klebanov, P., & Brooks-Gunn, J. (2006). Cumulative, human capital, and psychological risk in the context of early intervention: Links with IQ at ages 3, 5, and 8. *Annals of the New York Academy of Sciences, 1094,* 63–82.

Korfmacher, J. (2001). Early childhood interventions: Now what? In H. E. Fitzgerald, K. H. Karraker, & T. Luster (Eds.), *Infant development: Ecological perspectives* (pp. 275–294). New York: Routledge Palmer.

Korfmacher, J., O'Brien, R., Hiatt, S., & Olds, D. (1999). Differences in program implementation between nurses and paraprofessionals providing home visits during pregnancy and infancy: A randomized trial. *American Journal of Public Health, 89,* 1847–1851.

Lally, R., Griffin, A., Fenichel, E., Segal, M., Szanton, E., & Weissbourd, B. (2003). *Caring for infants and toddlers in groups: Developmentally appropriate practice.* Washington, DC: Zero to Three.

Lally, J. R., & Mangione, P. L. (2009). The Program for Infant Toddler Care. In J. P. Roopnarine & J. E. Johnson (Eds.), *Approaches to early childhood education* (5th ed., pp. 25–47). Englewood Cliffs, NJ: Prentice Hall.

Liaw, F., Meisels, S. J., & Brooks-Gunn, J. (1995). Effects of experience of early intervention on low birth weight, premature children: Infant Health and Development Program. *Early Childhood Research Quarterly, 10,* 405–431.

Love, M. J., Kisker, E. E., Ross, C., Raikes, H., Constantine, J., Boller, K., et al. (2005). The effectiveness of Early Head Start for 3-year-old children and their parents: Lessons for policy and programs. *Developmental Psychology, 41,* 885–901.

Marsiglio, W., Amato, P., Day, R. D., & Lamb, M. E. (2000). Scholarship on fatherhood in the 1990s and beyond. *Journal of Marriage and the Family, 62,* 1173–1191.

Musick, J., & Stott, F. (2000). Paraprofessionals revisited and reconsidered. In J. P. Shonkoff & S. J. Meisels (Eds.), *Handbook of early childhood intervention* (2nd ed., pp. 439–453). New York: Cambridge University Press.

Okagaki, L., & Bingham, G. (2005). Parents' social cognitions and their parenting behaviors. In T. Luster & L. Okagaki (Eds.), *Parenting: An ecological perspective* (2nd ed., pp. 3–33). Mahwah, NJ: Erlbaum.

Okagaki, L., & Luster, T. (2005). Research on parental socialization of child outcomes: Current controversies and future directions. In T. Luster & L. Okagaki (Eds.), *Parenting: An ecological perspective* (2nd ed., pp. 377–401). Mahwah, NJ: Erlbaum.

Olds, D., Eckenrode, J., Henderson, C. R., Jr., Kitzman, H., Powers, J., Cole, R., et al. (1997). Long-term effects of home visitation on maternal life course and child abuse and neglect: 15-year follow-up of a randomized trial. *Journal of the American Medical Association, 278,* 637–643.

Olds, D., Henderson, C. R., Chamberlin, R., & Tatelbaum, R. (1986). Preventing child abuse and neglect: A randomized trial of nurse home visitation. *Pediatrics, 78,* 65–78.

Olds, D. L., Henderson, C. C., Jr., Kitzman, H., Eckenrode, J., Cole, R., & Tatelbaum, R. (1998). The promise of home visitation: Results of two randomized trials. *Journal of Community Psychology, 26,* 5–21.

Olds, D., Kitzman, H., Cole, R., & Robinson, J. (1997). Theoretical foundations of a program of home visitation for pregnant women and parents of young children. *Journal of Community Psychology, 26,* 85–100.

Olds, D. L., Robinson, J., O'Brien, R., Luckey, D. W., Pettitt, L. M., Henderson, C. T., et al. (2002). Home visiting by paraprofessionals and by nurses: A randomized, controlled trial. *Pediatrics, 110,* 486–496.

Powell, C., & Grantham-McGregor, S. (1989). Home visiting of varying frequency and child development. *Pediatrics, 84,* 157–164.

Powell, D. R. (1993). Inside home visiting programs. *Future of Children, 3,* 23–38.

Powell, D. R. (2005). Searches for what works in parenting interventions. In T. Luster & L. Okagaki (Eds.), *Parenting: An ecological perspective* (2nd ed., pp. 342–373). Mahwah, NJ: Erlbaum.

Powell, D. R. (2006). Families and early childhood interventions. In W. Damon, R. M. Lerner (Series Ed.), K. A. Renninger, & I. E. Sigel (Vol. Eds.), *Handbook of child psychology, Vol. 4: Child psychology in practice* (6th ed., pp. 548–591). Hoboken, NJ: John Wiley & Sons.

Powell, D. R., & Peet, S. H. (2008). Development and outcomes of a community-based intervention to improve parents' use of inquiry in informal learning contexts. *Journal of Applied Developmental Psychology, 29,* 259–273.

Raikes, H. H., Summers, J. A., & Roggman, L. A. (2005). Father involvement in Early Head Start programs. *Fathering, 3,* 29–58.

Ramey, C. T., & Campbell, F. A. (1984). Preventive education for high-risk children: Cognitive consequences of the Carolina Abecedarian Project. *American Journal of Mental Deficiency, 88,* 454–465.

Ramey, C. T., Campbell, F. A., Burchinal, M., Skimmer, M. L., Gardner, D. M., & Ramey, S. L. (2000). Persistent effects of early childhood education on high-risk children and their mothers. *Applied Developmental Science, 4,* 2–14.

Ramey, C. T., Dorval, B., & Baker-Ward, L. (1983). Group day care and socially disadvantaged families: Effects on the child and the family. In S. Kilmer (Ed.), *Advances in early education and day care* (Vol. 3, pp. 69–106). Greenwich, CT: JAI Press.

Ramey, C. T., & Ramey, S. L. (1992). Effective early intervention. *Mental Retardation, 30,* 337–345.

Ramey, C. T., & Ramey, S. L. (1998). Early intervention and early experience. *American Psychologist, 53,* 109–120.

Ramey, C. T., Sparling, J. J., Bryant, D. M., & Wasik, B. H. (1997). The intervention model. In R. T. Gross, D. Spiker, & C. W. Haynes (Eds.), *Helping low birth weight, premature babies: Infant Health and Development Program* (pp. 17–26). Stanford, CA: Stanford University Press.

Roggman, L. A., Fitzgerald, H. E., Bradley, R. H., & Raikes, H. (2002). Methodological, measurement, and design issues in studying fathers: An interdisciplinary perspective. In C. S. Tamis-LeMonda & N. Cabrera (Eds.), *Handbook of father involvement: Multidisciplinary perspectives* (pp. 1–30). Mahwah, NJ: Erlbaum.

Rowe, D. C. (1994). *Limits of family influence.* New York: Guilford.

Shonkoff, J. P. (2000). Science, policy, and practice: Three cultures in search of a shared mission. *Child Development, 71,* 181–187.

Shonkoff, J. P., & Phillips, D. A. (Eds.) (2000). *From neurons to neighborhoods: Science of early childhood development.* Washington, DC: National Academy Press.

Sigel, I. E. (1992). The belief behavior connections: A resolvable dilemma? In I. E. Sigel, A. V. McGillicuddy-DeLisi, & J. J. Goodnow (Eds.), *Parental belief systems: The psychological consequences for children* (2nd ed., pp. 433–456). Hillsdale, NJ: Erlbaum.

Smith, S., & Zaslow, M. (1995). Rationale and policy context fort two-generation interventions. In S. Smith (Ed.), *Two generation programs for families in poverty: A new intervention strategy* (pp. 1–35). Norwood, NJ: Ablex.

Sparling, J., & Lewis, I. (1979). *Learningames for the first 3 years: A guide to parent–child play.* New York: Walker.

Sparling, J., & Lewis, I. (1995). *Partners for learning: Birth to 36 months.* Lewisville, NC: Kaplan.

Sparling, J., Lewis, I., Ramey, C. T., Wasik, B. H., Bryant, D. M., & LaVange, L. M. (1991). Partners: A curriculum to help premature, low birthweight infants get off to a good start. *Topics in Early Childhood Special Education, 11,* 36–55.

Sweet, M. A., & Appelbaum, M. I. (2004). Is home visiting an effective strategy? A meta-analytic review of home visiting programs for families with young children. *Child Development, 75,* 1435–1456.

Wagner, M. M., & Clayton, S. L. (1999). Parents as Teachers program: Results from two demonstrations. *Future of Children, 9,* 91–115.

Wagner, M., Spiker, D., & Linn, M. I. (2002). Effectiveness of the Parents as Teachers program with low-income parents and children. *Topics in Early Childhood Special Education, 22,* 67–81.

Walker, S. P., Wachs, T. D., Gardner, J. M., Lozoff, B., Wasserman, G. A., Pollitt, E., et al. (2007). Child development: Risk factors for adverse outcomes in developing countries. *Lancet, 369,* 145–157.

Wasik, B. H., Bryant, D. M., Lyons, C., Sparling, J. J., & Ramey, C. T. (1997). Home visiting. In R. T. Gross, D. Spiker, & C. W. Haynes (Eds.), *Helping low birth weight, premature babies: Infant Health and Development Program* (pp. 27–41). Stanford, CA: Stanford University Press.

Wasik, B. H., Bryant, D. M., Sparling, J. J., & Ramey, C. T. (1997). Maternal problem solving. In R. T. Gross, D. Spiker, & C. W. Haynes (Eds.), *Helping low birth weight, premature babies: Infant Health and Development Program* (pp. 276–289). Stanford, CA: Stanford University Press.

Wasik, B. H., Ramey, C. T., Bryant, D. M., & Sparling, J. J. (1990). A longitudinal study of two early intervention strategies: Project CARE. *Child Development, 61,* 1682–1696.

Zigler, E., & Berman, W. (1983). Discerning the future of early childhood intervention. *American Psychologist, 40,* 894–906.

14

Childcare Research at the Dawn of a New Millennium: An Update

Sarah L. Friedman, Edward Melhuish, and Candace Hill

Introduction

This chapter updates the publication by Friedman, Randolph, and Kochanoff (2001) about infant childcare. The continued interest in childcare and its relation to children's development reflects the fact that the employment of mothers of infants has been steadily increasing in recent decades and become the norm in many countries (Melhuish & Petrogiannis, 2006). Theory and research findings suggest that the link between childcare and children's development is dependent upon context, or social ecology (Bronfenbrenner, 1999). The social ecology in which childcare is embedded includes cultural and social contexts such as ideology and labor markets. These influence the availability of childcare, the types of childcare, and the experiences children have in childcare (Melhuish, 2005). Most industrialized societies have seen marked increases in maternal employment in the last 30 years. For example, in the USA in 1975, 39% of mothers with a preschool child were in employment. By 2000 this had increased to 67%. However, much of this was part-time employment and over 60% of preschool children had at least one parent who did not work full-time. Such changes resulted in the number of US preschool children being in childcare increasing from 4.3 million in 1977 to 12.4 million (over 50% of children) by 1997 (Smith, 2002). Countries have responded differently to the increased demand for childcare. In some countries, childcare provision is seen as a state responsibility. For example, Sweden had 85% of mothers of preschool children in employment in the early 1990s, and provided high levels of publicly funded childcare. In English-speaking countries in the twentieth century, childcare was a private concern with little public funding. In these circumstances, the quality and type of childcare is more diverse. For example, in the USA, in the 1990s, where mothers were employed, 10% of infant childcare was center-based, 24% was family daycare, nanny or babysitter, 28% was provided by a relative, and 20% was by the father (Ehrle, Adams, & Trout, 2001). Most childcare in the USA is funded by parents and the quality varies considerably, partly because states have markedly different regulations concerning childcare. Where childcare costs fall to parents, parents are likely to choose on the basis of cost, particularly as information on quality is not readily available.

Where childcare is publicly funded, cost constraints are reduced, and quality of childcare is usually regulated to acceptable minimum standards, and there is investment in training for childcare providers. Parental leave affects the provision and nature of infant childcare profoundly and parental leave varies markedly between countries. Sweden and Norway have had parental leave in excess of 12 months post birth for some time, and childcare in the first year of life has almost disappeared, yet extensive public funding and high staff training led to high overall quality of childcare (e.g., Hwang, 2006). In the UK recognition of the costs and difficulties associated with providing high-quality childcare in the first year consistently on a large scale has led to the recent extension of parental leave to 12 months post birth (Melhuish, 2007). Similar phenomena are apparent in other European countries (Moss & Wall, 2007). Consequently, the range of quality, quantity and age of use for childcare varies markedly between societies. These aspects are likely to mediate the links between childcare and child development, and such variation between societies would be expected to produce different patterns of association between childcare and child development. Hence it is rash to generalize results from one society to others with very different systems of childcare provision. Figure 14.1 (adapted from Melhuish, 2005) presents the social ecology of childcare and the hierarchical links through several mediating levels to children's outcomes.

The widespread increase in childcare use leads to increased interest in whether the features of childcare are linked to developmental outcomes. As indicated by Friedman et al. (2001), psychological theory and cultural beliefs about the central role of maternal care in the early years have led to concerns that placing infants in childcare may interfere with their attachment to their mothers, and their social and cognitive development. Studies published since 2001 indicate that some of the concerns are unwarranted, with other concerns finding modest support. In addition, childcare has been associated with

LEVEL	UNIT OF STUDY
SOCIETY	Culture and social context (e.g., labor markets and ideology) ↓
INSTITUTIONS	Childcare provision ↓
SETTINGS	Daycare center, individual daycare, etc. ↓
SOCIAL EXPERIENCE	Patterns of interaction ↓
INDIVIDUAL	Children's development

Figure 14.1   Ecological perspective on childcare and influences upon children (adapted from Melhuish, 2005).

modest positive child development outcomes. Finally, the links between childcare and developmental outcomes were found to vary depending on family and child characteristics. In this chapter we describe the conceptualization of childcare, its assessment and the state of knowledge about childcare and child development. We also suggest some future research directions.

Conceptualizing Childcare

Typically the term "childcare" refers to the routine care of children during the hours when their mothers are occupied elsewhere. This care is frequently provided by hired help, for pay. Most mothers use childcare to allow them to hold a job, run a business, or go to school. Some use childcare to allow them to undertake volunteer work, social obligations, or other activities that cannot be carried out while taking care of a young child.

Some define childcare as nonparental care (Lamb, 1997), which assumes parents are interchangeable, and if the father is the primary care provider when the mother works there is no need to be concerned about potential negative impact of this arrangement on child–mother attachment or on the child's social or cognitive development. Others define childcare as nonmaternal care (NICHD Early Childcare Research Network (ECCRN), 1996, 2000a), thereby including care by the child's father when the mother works as a type of childcare.

Childcare is not a unitary concept. Childcare settings are different along many dimensions. Friedman and Amadeo (1999) have described childcare settings in terms of who provides care, where care is provided, how care is provided, and the children's experience in childcare. For example, childcare can be described in terms of the identity of the provider, his or her characteristics (e.g., education level; experience as childcare provider) or relation to the child (e.g., grandparent; nonrelative). Childcare can be provided in the child's home or elsewhere. Children may receive care at a relative's home, a childcare home, or a childcare center. The recipients of care may be an individual child or several children of the same or different ages, of the same gender or ethnicity, or of different gender or ethnicity. Childcare can be highly professional, with well-planned daily routines for providing experiences that promote child development, or it can be custodial. Children may experience the childcare setting as a place with loving adults, with friends to spend time with and to play with. They may experience it as a place with interesting things to do. At the other extreme are children who experience childcare as a place where adults are harsh, the noise level is high and where there is little to do or enjoy. Children vary in terms of the amounts of childcare they experience from a few hours per week to full-time childcare, for more than 30 hours per week. Some children experience stability in childcare. Others go to different settings in any given week or their parents move them from one childcare setting to another to accommodate family finances and transient residential patterns.

Childcare can be conceptualized in terms of aspects of the environment experienced directly or indirectly by the child based on Bronfenbrenner's (1988, 1999) ecological model. For example, children in childcare directly experience others talking or responding to them, the presence of peers and the availability of toys, books, decorations, and television. They also experience caregiver turnover, stability, and multiplicity of care arrangements. Caregiver turnover and stability in daily childcare are associated with poorer developmental outcomes (de Schipper, van IJzendoorn, & Tavecchio, 2004; Whitebook, Howes, & Phillips, 1990), whereas multiplicity of arrangements is associated with both positive and negative outcomes, depending on the quality and stability of care (Morrisey, 2008; Tran & Weinraub, 2006). The education level of the caregiver is experienced indirectly through the quality of care received. Caregivers with higher educational attainment typically provide a higher-quality environment (Burchinal, Roberts, Nabors, & Bryant, 1996; Clarke-Stewart, 1987; Dunn, 1993; NICHD ECCRN, 1999a). Similarly, children indirectly experience the salary their caregivers receive and conditions of employment, in that caregivers with low income or poor employment conditions tend to leave their jobs for better ones, thereby leading to instability in childcare. These characteristics of childcare have guided the assessment of childcare environments.

The Assessment of Childcare

Assessments of the childcare environment need to be tailored to the goals of the assessment. Existing measures are associated with three practical assessment goals and the conceptualizations associated with these. Friedman and Amadeo (1999) classified the methods for assessing childcare in three ways: assessments for state licensing; assessments for accreditation; and research assessments to scientifically evaluate the effects of childcare on children's psychological development. In general, the assessment of the quality of care is guided by what researchers consider as quality of care and this is based on their value judgments and theoretical orientation. Quality care is care that leads to outcomes that are valued. In North America, Europe and many other countries, society values children who are curious and imaginative, who use language effectively for communication, and who are considerate of peers and adults. We value assertiveness but not aggression. We value skill in problem-solving, creativity, and academic achievement. So we look in childcare environments for predictors of such outcomes. These predictors include sensitivity and responsiveness to children's positive and negative affect, treating of children with respect, talking to children and answering their questions. The childcare predictors also include the extent to which childcare environments facilitate learning and positive interaction among peers. The more distal measures of quality include adult–child ratio, group size, and the provider's educational level and training in child development. These distal aspects of the childcare environment are childcare characteristics that set the conditions for higher-quality proximal care (Phillips & Howes, 1987). It is noteworthy that the distal measures of childcare are related to the proximal measures and through them are linked to the developmental outcomes of children (NICHD ECCRN, 2002a). Typically childcare regulations will refer to distal measures of quality as these are more readily observable, and open to regulatory control. For a summary of the links between different measures of the childcare environment, see Friedman and Amadeo (1999).

Recently, Child Trends (Halle & Vick, 2007) has issued a compendium of measures of quality in early childhood care and education settings for a variety of purposes including program improvement, monitoring/accreditation and/or research/evaluation. The measures assess quality of care in settings as diverse as home-based and center-based programs, and only those measures with known psychometric information were included. The compendium provides extensive information, is very timely, and aids systematic evaluations of the quality of childcare. One measure mentioned in that compendium allowed the estimation of the quality of US childcare (NICHD ECCRN, 2000a). Based on two different studies, one with nationally representative data and another with in-depth observational data about the quality of childcare, the authors concluded that positive caregiving is rare for 8.1% of children in the United States aged 1–3 years, infrequent for 53.2% of the children, occasional for 29.6%, and typical for only 9% of children. Another study revealed that 9% of children in center-based arrangements experienced low-quality care, 66% were in medium quality (i.e., adequate) care, and 24% were in high-quality care, while 36% of children in home-based arrangements were in low-quality care, 57% were in medium-quality (i.e., adequate) care, and 7% were in high-quality care (Flanagan & West, 2004; Mulligan & Flanagan, 2006). Reports of childcare quality in Canada indicate similarly wide variation (Doherty, Lero, Goelman, LaGrange, & Tougas, 2000; Doherty, Lero, Goelman, Tougas, & LaGrange, 2000).

The State of Knowledge about Childcare and Child Development

The research methodology pertaining to childcare and its links to child development has evolved over the years, within the context of studies of childcare as used by the general population as well as within studies of childcare used as an intervention for high-risk families.[1] Early research started with small studies of samples of convenience with no consideration given to variations in family background and experiences. Childcare was conceptualized as nonparental care or nonmaternal care and treated as a uniform experience. Variations in the childcare experience in terms of age of entry, hours of care, or quality of care were not considered. Over the years researchers have become interested in the developmental consequences of variations in the childcare experience and, therefore, focused on more and more aspects of childcare and children's experiences in childcare. Likewise, the idea that what is considered optimal childcare may vary with the child's age influenced the construction of assessments of the childcare environment. The need to statistically control for family characteristics in analyses of the effects of childcare on child development became more obvious as it became clear that family variables predict both the selection of childcare and the same child outcomes that childcare variables are expected to predict (Baumrind, 1989; Bornstein & Tamis-LeMonda, 1989; Dowsett, Huston, Imes, & Gennetian, 2008; Feinstein, 2003; Friedman & Cocking, 1986; Hungerford & Cox, 2006; Melhuish, Sylva, Sammons, Siraj-Blatchford, Taggart, & Phan, 2008a; Morrisey, 2008; NICHD ECCRN, 1997a). Assessments of family control variables became more differentiated, and quantitative analyses became more sophisticated in enabling statistical control of all variables other than the specific childcare target variables. Questions about the specificity of quality and of the links between aspects of childcare quality and children's developmental outcomes came to dominate the research (and in some countries, the policy) agenda. In parallel, researchers came to realize that childcare and its links to developmental outcomes may vary for children from different family backgrounds or with different developmental limitations or needs. The increasing domination of the ecological theoretical model as a framework for studying human development on the one hand, and the increased interest in studying nationally representative samples on the other hand, have led to the most recent wave of large-scale longitudinal studies that collect data about childcare as a tool that families use in rearing their children (Friedman et al., 2001).

Most research regarding childcare and developmental outcomes does not allow us to draw firm conclusions about causal effects. The same literature can, however, tell us about associations between childcare and children's performance in social, emotional, and cognitive development. This is the case because most studies did not randomly assign children to the childcare group or to the exclusive maternal care group. Instead, children were studied in the settings that their parents selected. Therefore, even after controlling for obvious family variables, findings may be due not only to childcare but also to unmeasured and uncontrolled family characteristics that determine both the selection of childcare and the developmental outcomes of children.

Despite the recognition that one cannot infer causality from studies that do not randomly assign children to childcare conditions, the investigators of the NICHD Study of Early Childcare and Youth Development (NICHD ECCRN, 2003a) examined the possibility that longitudinal research designs might allow researchers to infer causality with some level of confidence. They used their longitudinal data about childcare and children's developmental outcomes to explore five propositions that, if all were to be met, would support a causal argument. Three out of the five propositions were supported: associations between care and outcomes remained even with the child and family factors controlled; associations between care and outcomes were domain-specific; and outcomes were predicted by quality of earlier care with current care controlled. The fourth proposition, that association between quality of care and child outcomes would be significant with earlier child abilities controlled, received limited support. There was no support for the fifth proposition, that quality and outcomes would exhibit dose–response relations. Possibly these last two propositions were not met because measures of quality were not sufficiently discriminating, or the study did not have sufficient diversity of quality. Nonetheless since not all propositions were met, it appears that the data from the NICHD study cannot be used to infer causality, although neither can causality be ruled out. In summary, the study designs and the analytical methods of natural history studies (as opposed to studies that randomly assign some children to childcare and others to none) limit conclusions, such that any interpretations of cause and effect cannot be confirmed. However, the findings of natural history studies and other studies reporting on statistical links between variables of interest provide directions for future research that will use other research methodologies. Below, we highlight some findings from childcare research conducted to date.

Childcare and the Development of Children who Experienced Childcare in Infancy

Childcare and security of attachment

One focus of intense investigation by researchers of childcare was the relation between childcare and the child's sense of trust in the mother (security of attachment). Detailed information about attachment in infancy can be found in chapter 16 in volume 1. Bowlby's (1973) theory of attachment suggests the possibility that routine daily separations from the mother would be associated with less opportunity for the infant and mother to form close and warm relationships that are characterized by maternal sensitivity to the needs of the infant and the infant's trust in the mother as a source of security (Barglow, Vaughn, & Molitor, 1987; Jaeger & Weinraub, 1990; Owen & Cox, 1988). Some studies indirectly gave support to this proposition as shown by analyses based on clusters of small studies (Belsky & Rovine, 1988; Clarke-Stewart, 1989; Lamb, Sternberg & Prodromidis, 1992). For example, in the analysis by Belsky and Rovine (1988), 43% of the infants in early and extensive care were classified as insecurely attached to their mother, while only 26% of the infants with more limited childcare exposure were insecurely attached. The hypothesis that routine daily separations from the mother interfered with the cultivation of maternal sensitivity and the building of the child's trust in the mother was not directly validated, however. The studies did not evaluate maternal sensitivity and the findings could be due to attributes of the childcare experience. In studies of mother–child interaction where the mother's sensitivity and responsiveness are evaluated, usually there is no statistically significant link between the amount of childcare and mothers' behaviors toward their young children (e.g., Burchinal, Bryant, Lee, & Ramey, 1992; Egeland & Heister, 1995). However, the NICHD ECCRN (1999b) found that the more hours the child spent in childcare, the less responsive the mother and the less engaged the child. Similar results are reported by Belsky (1999) and by investigators who focused on the first six months of life (Campbell, Cohn, & Meyers, 1995; Stifter, Coulehan, & Fish, 1993).

Recently, three studies (NICHD ECCRN, 1997b, 2001a; Roggman, Langlois, Hubbs-Tait, & Reiser-Danner, 1994) failed to replicate the attachment findings from earlier studies. Also a study by Sagi, Van IJzendoorn, Aviezer, Donnell, and Mayseless (1994) of 48 kibbutz children in Israel suggests that for many children (though not for all) minimal daily contact with parents may be sufficient for the formation of secure attachment. Friedman and Boyle (2008) used such evidence to argue that in the US sample of the NICHD study, the amount of consistent and sensitive care typically provided by employed mothers on weekdays and on the weekend may well be sufficient for the formation of secure attachment. They also argued that the absence of main effects of childcare on attachment could also be due to the fact that in the US today, employed mothers are involved in parenting to a similar extent to mothers who are not in the workforce. The data from the NICHD Study of Early Childcare and Youth Development indicate that mothers of infants spending more than 30 hours per week in childcare, compared with those whose infants spent 0 hours in childcare, interacted only 12 hours less per week with their infants. Further, children in childcare and those in exclusive maternal care did not differ in the quality of child–mother interactions or child outcomes, including attachment security at 15 months (Booth, Clarke-Stewart, Vandell, McCartney, & Owen, 2002). Similar results are also reported by Huston and Aronson (2005) who found that maternal employment reduced time with infants, but that employed mothers compensated by decreasing the time spent on activities that interfere with time devoted to the child. These findings on 7-month-olds may be representative of child–mother interactions more generally. Such considerations may explain, at least in part, the absence of main effects of childcare on attachment security in the sample of the NICHD study. The results would not necessarily generalize to samples in which employed mothers were substantially less involved in parenting than mothers who were not in the workforce or to mothers who did not invest the amount and quality of parenting necessary for the formation of secure attachment.

While studies based on the NICHD sample failed to replicate earlier findings linking childcare to insecure attachment, the findings from the NICHD study are also rather complex. The first NICHD attachment paper (NICHD ECCRN, 1997b) revealed that infants were less likely to be securely attached when poor quality of care was combined with either low maternal sensitivity/responsiveness, more than minimal amounts of childcare, or more than one care arrangement. Also, in a second attachment paper (NICHD ECCRN, 2001a), it was found once again that when maternal sensitivity was low, more hours per week in childcare somewhat increased the probability that children would be insecurely attached to their mothers. Thus greater amounts of childcare can be a *risk factor* when combined with another risk factor (e.g., poor responsiveness at home). Conversely, responsive home environments, responsive childcare, and stable childcare can be regarded as *protective factors*. These more nuanced findings suggest that the relation between childcare and attachment security needs to be considered in the context of other factors that are linked to the development of secure attachment. Friedman & Boyle (2008) advised the specification of the conditions under which the relations between childcare and child–mother attachment may be associated with insecure attachment, so that theoretically derived conditions could be empirically tested and theory refined using empirical results.

Childcare, social competence, and behavior problems

Since families have an important role in socializing their children, one could argue that the role of the family might be diminished, or at least altered, when children are in childcare, thereby possibly leading to less favorable social development. Children of employed mothers or in childcare have been found to be at higher risk for poor social adjustment than children not in childcare, even after controlling for family variables (Baydar & Brooks-Gunn, 1991; Belsky, 1988, 1990; Crockenberg & Litman, 1991; Egeland & Heister, 1995). Results from the NICHD Study of Early Childcare and Youth Development partially support these findings but effects are of modest magnitude (e.g., NICHD ECCRN, 1999b, 2001b, 2002b, 2003b, 2003c, 2003d, 2006; Belsky, Burchinal, McCartney, Vandell, Clarke-Stewart & Owen, 2007). The outcomes studied in the

NICHD study include mother–child relations, social competence, peer interaction, and behavioral problems. For example, NICHD ECCRN (2006) reports on the relations between childcare variables and outcomes at 15, 24, 36, and 54 months of age and estimates the magnitude of the effects using different approaches. Children in higher quality of care, as compared to those in lower quality of care, were rated by their caregivers as displaying modestly to moderately more social skills at 24 months and at 54 months of age and less conflict with their teachers at 54 months. Hours in childcare from birth onward were also linked to social outcomes: children with more hours in childcare per week were rated by their caregivers as showing modestly more problem behaviors at 36 months of age and at 54 months and more caregiver–child conflict at 54 months; children who spent more hours in childcare were observed to exhibit somewhat more negative behavior with a peer at 54 months of age; and, it was found that more care in childcare centers (as distinguished from other types of care) was modestly related to more positive interactions during peer play at 54 months of age. However, more attendance at center care was also linked to lower ratings of social skills by the caregiver at 24 and 36 months of age and to higher ratings of problem behaviors at 36 months of age. In another paper, the same authors note that "the overwhelming majority of children did not score in the at risk range, even when considering those experiencing the most childcare" (NICHD ECCRN, 2003b, p. 996), as the ratings of behavior problems were within the normal range and the proportion of children with behavioral problems in the clinical range was not higher than expected in the population (NICHD ECCRN, 2003e). Follow-up of the children through third grade (NICHD ECCRN, 2005b) revealed that more time in early childcare no longer predicted previously reported behavior problems (NICHD ECCRN, 2002b) but, in contrast to findings at 54 months, more time spent in childcare was associated with lower social competence. In a follow-up report on outcomes through sixth grade (mean age 12 years), teacher-reported externalizing behaviors and teacher–child conflict were not predicted by hours in childcare overall, with only more exposure to center childcare predicting more teacher-reported externalizing problems (Belsky et al., 2007).

The findings from the NICHD Study of Early Childcare and Youth Development led to speculation concerning the generalizability of the findings, particularly as the study may not have included as wide a range of childcare quality as exists in the US generally, or indeed elsewhere. Love et al. (2003) review findings from the Sydney (Australia) Family Development Project (SFDP), the Haifa (Israel)–NICHD (US) merged data, and the Early Head Start program evaluation in the US. By doing so, the authors expanded the diversity of families and the diversity of childcare and lowered the correlation between quality of care and family socioeconomic status that exists in the NICHD study. Taken together, the three studies point to the limited generalizability of the findings from the NICHD study. Although some of the findings reported by Love et al. (2003) corroborate the NICHD study findings, other outcomes raise questions as to whether the association between early childcare quality and social-emotional development reported by the NICHD study would hold in a more diverse sample of children and families and in a wider range of childcare settings. Votruba-Drzal, Coley, and Chase-Lansdale (2004) in a study of 2–4 years old children from low-income families found that higher levels of childcare quality were modestly associated with improvements in children's socioemotional development over time, and extensive hours in childcare were linked to increases in children's quantitative skills and decreases in behavioral problems. These results about the negative correlation between hours in care and behavioral problems that were found with low-income families are different from the findings of the NICHD study that are based on a sample from the general population. Others have suggested, based on the education research literature (both ethnographic and experimental) with older children, that the NICHD findings regarding the link between more hours in care and children's poorer social outcomes may not be inherent to childcare but rather to the extent to which childcare settings cultivate positive social development (Maccoby & Lewis, 2003). Based on the literature, these authors suggest that childcare practices should focus on attachment to the school and the peer group, constructivist learning, intrinsic and internalized motivation, and social development, if they are to nurture the positive social development of young children, and to teach and reinforce positive social skills.

Recent research has also examined the conditions under which childcare characteristics are associated (or not) with children's social and emotional outcomes. The investigators of the NICHD study (NICHD ECCRN, 2002c) found that children from minority and single-parent families were rated as less prosocial by their mothers when in low-quality childcare. However, family risk interacted with childcare quality in only one out of five analyses, and did not interact with childcare quantity at all. Cote, Borge, Geoffroy, Rutter, and Tremblay (2008) analyzed data from 1,358 Canadian families with young children. Family risk was calculated using information about socioeconomic status, family functioning, maternal depression, maternal age at the child's birth, and the extent to which the family was intact. Family risk was found to moderate the link between (whether or not the child was in) childcare and the child's physical aggression. Exclusive maternal care in infancy was associated with lower levels of physical aggression in children from low-risk families but not in children from high-risk families. Family risk and the child's gender moderated the link between childcare and emotional problems. Exclusive maternal care in infancy was associated with lower levels of emotional difficulties among girls from low-risk families but not among boys or among boys and girls from high-risk families. Future research is likely to further elucidate the characteristics of families and children that moderate the relations between childcare characteristics and childcare.

Childcare and cognitive and language development

Socioemotional and cognitive/linguistic development are interdependent (e.g., Kopp, 1997; Lazarus, 1991; Lewis & Michalson, 1983). Therefore, the assumed disruption of the parent–child relationship due to extensive childcare could affect cognitive development (e.g., van IJzendoorn, Dijkstra, & Bus, 1995). The evidence about the effects of the *amount of childcare* on cognitive and language development has been mixed (e.g., Hayes, Palmer, & Zaslow, 1990; Lamb, 1997). Some studies reported a positive relation between the amounts of infant care and school performance in middle childhood (Andersson, 1992; Broberg, Wessels, Lamb, & Hwang, 1997; Field, 1991), while some reported that early positive effects dissipated over time (Chin-Quee & Scarr, 1994). Yet others reported poorer later performance for children who were placed in childcare when they were infants, especially if placed in care in the first year of life (Baydar & Brooks-

Gunn, 1991; Baum, 2003; Brooks-Gunn, Han, & Waldfogel, 2002; Cote et al., 2008; Joshi & Verropoulou, 1999; Vandell & Corasaniti, 1990). In attempting to explain such disparities, Melhuish (1991, 2005) has argued that negative, neutral, and positive effects may occur for different populations depending on the relative balance of quality of care at home and in childcare. With quality of care in both settings equivalent, there is likely to be little effect from attending childcare. Where quality of care in childcare is superior to the home, then children receiving childcare are likely to show beneficial effects, as seen in several studies of children from disadvantaged families receiving good-quality childcare (e.g., Ramey, Dorval, & Baker-Ward, 1983; Votruba-Drzal et al., 2004). However, where the quality of childcare is inferior to that at home, then negative or detrimental effects may occur, as reported in studies where children attend poor-quality childcare (e.g., Melhuish, Lloyd, Martin, & Mooney, 1990). This model would predict that the strongest effects of quality would occur for disadvantaged families, which has some empirical support (e.g., McCartney, Dearing, Taylor, & Bub, 2007; Peisner-Feinberg et al., 2001).

In the NICHD Study of Early Childcare and Youth Development, the relation between amount of childcare in the first three years of life and the cognitive/linguistic performance of the children was not statistically significant (Burchinal & Clarke-Stewart, 2007; NICHD ECCRN, 2000b, 2006). The picture emerging from studies of the relations between the *quality of childcare* experienced during infancy and children's cognitive and language development is more consistent. Higher quality of care was found to be associated with better performance (Belsky et al., 2007; Burchinal et al., 1996; Galinsky, Howes, Kontos, & Shinn, 1994; Howes & Smith, 1995; Howes, Smith, & Galinsky, 1995; Melhuish et al., 1990; NICHD ECCRN, 2000b, 2003b, 2005a, 2005b, 2006; Phillips, McCartney, & Scarr, 1987). A recent study based on the NICHD sample points to the fact that children in poverty and their families benefit from quality of childcare more than children and families with higher incomes (McCartney et al., 2007). This finding, based on a natural history study, is in line with studies showing that interventions targeted at children of the poor and at minority children can be beneficial (e.g., Love et al., 2002; Ramey & Campbell, 1991). A detailed review on infant intervention programs is given in chapter 13 in this volume.

Summary

Both the positive and negative statistical associations between features of childcare and different developmental outcomes are modest and typically have effect sizes upon child outcomes that are smaller than those found for family and home factors[2] (NICHD ECCRN, 2003e, 2006). In some instances, family variables but not childcare variables predict children's outcomes (NICHD ECCRN, 2003e). Therefore, the scientific literature suggests that the serious concerns about possible negative links between childcare and children's development were largely unwarranted. In addition, the associations between hours in care and teacher-reported behavior problems, which received a lot of publicity, pertain to behaviors within the normal range, and do not suggest clinical problems requiring professional intervention. In much research the quality of childcare has regularly been linked to effects on children's development, particularly cognitive and language development, with the effects being mediated by family characteristics. Nuanced analyses suggest that the relations between childcare features and children's outcomes sometimes vary for children who are different in terms of their age, gender, race, or socio-economic background. Therefore, questions about childcare and child development always need to be examined in a way that takes into account specific groups of children and their life circumstances.

Directions for Future Research

We would like to see the next wave of childcare research focus on developing interventions to maximize the beneficial effects of childcare and to minimize its modest risks. We predict that such a direction would be useful and productive for several reasons. Childcare is now a prevalent tool for helping families rear their infants and toddlers, and is already used as a form of intervention with high-risk families. This historical trend presents society and scientists with a tremendous opportunity to contribute to the well-being and development of children. Now that we know that childcare does not present the antici-pated developmental risks (Friedman et al., 2001), the door is open to use knowledge that has accumulated over the last thirty to forty years to maximize the educational and developmental role of childcare. There is ample scientific knowledge that can serve as a basis for developing interventions aimed at supporting the psychological development of very young children and there are also methods for evaluating the impact of educational interventions.

The goal of developing interventions for the childcare context is in harmony with the current zeitgeist. There is a growing awareness that early experiences of children shape their brain development, their cognitive and social development (e.g., Fantuzzo, Rouse, McDermott, Sekino, Childs, & Weiss, 2005; Shonkoff & Phillips, 2000; Snow, Bums, & Griffin, 1998). In addition, there is growing recognition that the achievement gap between children from different sectors of society needs to be closed because of the implications for the life chances of the individuals involved and for the social fabric and the economic success of the countries that the children live in. The closing of the gap can be achieved through interventions aimed at raising the academic performance of children of the poor, ethnic minorities, and immigrants (e.g., Ramey & Campbell, 1991; Rouse, Brooks-Gunn, & McLanahan, 2005). It is likely that the earlier such interventions start, the greater their effects. Further, it has been argued that the education of young children from all walks of life is a smart investment in the economic future of their socie-ties (Heckman, 2006; Melhuish & Petrogiannis, 2006; Rolnick & Grunewald, 2003). But in spite of the fact that the first three years of life are very important for acquiring cognitive and social skills that lay the basis for school readiness and future achievements, there is still a very narrow public agenda to develop interventions that would benefit infants and toddlers. To change this state of affairs and to meet important societal edu-cational goals, we recommend that resources be devoted to the development of interven-tions that target specific cognitive, linguistic, and social skills of infants and young children. As already mentioned, this effort can be guided by the scientific literature that is already rich in ideas relevant to the development of such interventions. For example, research on quality of childcare and effectiveness of interventions can be further developed using research techniques that enable the estimation of childcare/institution effectiveness in terms of demonstrated influences upon child outcomes (e.g., Melhuish et al., 2008b). Such approaches can answer the question of whether a particular experience/institution makes a difference to the expected developmental trajectory of a child. We further suggest that these ideas need to be examined for their relevance to different groups of childcare providers and to the children under their care.

One example of an area in which specific interventions would be helpful is that of teaching infants and toddlers how to deal with frustrations and to get along with peers and care providers. The fact that young children in extensive childcare are perceived by their care providers as having more behavior problems than children who are exposed to fewer childcare hours indicates that children in extensive care need further support for developing social skills. Other areas in which intervention programs could be developed are moral development and cultural knowledge and pride. The transmission of moral values and of the traditions of the culture is at the heart of child-rearing, and different cultures have different values. In the United States, an important socialization goal of ethnic minority parents is fostering a sense of ethnic pride in children (Harrison, Wilson, Pine, Chan, & Buriel, 1990). Latino families value social skills as much as or more than they value cognitive skills. They discourage competitive behavior that sets the child apart from the group (Parke, 1997). Their emphasis on cooperation and social sensitivity may differ, at least to some extent, from the emphasis that mainstream American culture places on the same values. Yet there are no studies about the links between childcare and moral development or about the extent to which children in childcare have knowledge about and pride in their family cultural traditions. This is the case because the transmission of these values is not considered an index of the quality of childcare. Interventions could also be developed to sensitize childcare providers to cultural differences regarding discipline. In the US, childcare settings are expected to be authoritative, such that limits are negotiated in cooperation by the adult and the child (Baumrind, 1989). Also, childcare settings are expected to discipline children verbally. But African American parents often favor physical punishment that is not coupled with the withdrawal of affection (Parke, 1997). Chinese American parents often believe in strict discipline in the context of deep caring and teaching right from wrong (Parke, 1997). Consequently, their teaching and discipline style may well appear more controlling than that of European American parents. Given their child-rearing values, African American and Chinese American parents may be less than fully satisfied with the quality of authoritative childcare settings designed with European American values in mind.

A related direction of future research is the evaluation of the impact of interventions aimed at improving the cognitive and social development of children. Such evaluations are essential since not all programs that are designed to improve children's cognitive, linguistic, or social outcomes are successful in doing so. Consider findings from the What Works Clearinghouse of the Institute of Education Sciences that reviews curricula and practices designed to improve the school readiness of 3–5-year-old children. Of 24 literacy specific interventions reviewed as of July 18, 2008 and covering one or more of four areas of literacy – oral language, print knowledge, phonological processing, early reading/ writing – only nine had rigorous evidence of positive effectiveness and another nine were potentially effective (http://ies.ed.gov/ncee/wwc/reports/topic.aspx?tid=13). The impact of interventions is best evaluated using methods that allow the investigators to conclude that the intervention brought about the desired outcomes. One method that allows researchers to come to such conclusions is that of randomized controlled studies in which children are assigned at random either to the intervention group or to a control group. Those in the control group receive either a different intervention or whatever practices are current at the time ("business as usual"). The performance of the intervention group children following the intervention period is compared to the performance of the children in the control group. The intervention is found to be effective if the intervention group performs significantly better than the control group. The scientific literature includes some randomized control evaluations of psychological interventions in the early years and these can serve as the foundation for the next wave of childcare research (for a review see Melhuish, 2004). These studies provide evidence that high-quality childcare for disadvantaged children can produce benefits for cognitive, language, and social development and that low-quality childcare has either no effects or negative effects. Another method that can provide information about the extent to which the intervention led to the desired performance at the end of the intervention is the regression discontinuity (RD) design, in which participants are assigned to program or comparison groups solely on the basis of a cutoff score on a preprogram measure. For example, the Early Reading First evaluation (Jackson et al., 2007) took advantage of the fact that the US Department of Education established criteria for scoring applications for getting funds to implement the intervention. It awarded grants to the applicants with the highest scores, progressing down the score distribution until all the funding available for the fiscal year was allocated. Applicants below the cutoff line were not awarded grants. Impact estimates were obtained by comparing child outcomes and teacher practices in funded sites to those in unfunded sites, controlling for the applications' scores.

Friedman et al. (2001) suggested directions for future research that are still valid. They subsumed their suggestions under four headings: expanding the research focus to include a more diverse group of children; expanding research on the families of children who are in childcare, on care providers, and employers of parents of young children; expanding research on quality of childcare; and expanding research about parents' knowledge and decision-making regarding childcare. While endorsing these research directions, we now believe that future research about childcare should also focus, perhaps primarily, on the two topics that we mentioned earlier and in doing so draw on ideas that were explored in the "Future Directions" section of Friedman et al. (2001). The two topics that we mentioned above are the development of interventions to maximize children's developmental outcomes and the evaluation of such interventions in terms of their impact on the cognitive, linguistic, and social development of infants and toddlers.

Conclusion

The current provision and use of childcare is largely a product of economic realities and social changes that have led to a steady increase over the last 30–40 years in the participation of women in the workforce. It has come into being to help families with their child-rearing responsibilities. Childcare reflects the societal and personal values and the resources of the people who create it and participate in it. It is a human creation, which, in turn, shapes the life of its creators. Because childcare is a societal product and a child-rearing tool, its characteristics and its links to family and children's developmental outcomes will need to be continuously reinvented and evaluated. This chapter updates what we learned from childcare research and suggests what we need to learn in the future in order to maximize the utility of childcare to the society it serves, and indeed partially shapes.

Notes

1. This chapter focuses on research on childcare used by the general population, referring to studies of childcare as intervention only occasionally, when appropriate. See chapter 13 in this volume for discussion of intervention studies.
2. The effect size for childcare quality ranges from between half to a third as large for cognitive, language and academic outcomes, but is twice the parenting effect sizes for some social outcomes.

References

Andersson, B. E. (1992). Effects of day-care on cognitive and socioemotional competence of thirteen-year-old Swedish school children. *Child Development, 63*, 20–36.

Barglow, P., Vaughn, B. E., & Molitor, N. (1987). Effects of maternal absence due to employment on the quality of infant–mother attachment in a low-risk sample. *Child Development, 58*, 945–954.

Baum, C. L. (2003). Does early maternal employment harm child development? An analysis of the potential benefits of leave taking. *Journal of Labor Economics, 21*(2), 409–448.

Baumrind, D. (1989). Rearing competent children. In W. Damon (Ed.), *Child development today and tomorrow* (pp. 349–378). San Francisco: Jossey-Bass.

Baydar, N., & Brooks-Gunn, J. (1991). Effects of maternal employment and child-care arrangements on preschoolers' cognitive and behavioral outcomes: Evidence from the children of the National Longitudinal Survey of Youth. *Developmental Psychology, 27*, 932–945.

Belsky, J. (1988). Infant day care and socioemotional development: The United States. *Journal of Child Psychology and Psychiatry and Allied Disciplines, 29*, 397–406.

Belsky, J. (1990). Parental and nonparental childcare and children's socioemotional development: A decade in review. *Journal of Marriage and the Family, 52*, 885–904.

Belsky, J. (1999). Quantity of nonmaternal care and boys' problem behavior/adjustment at ages 3 and 5: Exploring the mediating role of parenting. *Psychiatry, 62*, 1–20.

Belsky, J., Burchinal, M., McCartney, K., Vandell, D. L., Clarke-Stewart, A., & Owen, M. T. (2007). Are there long-term effects of early childcare? *Child Development. 78*, 681–701.

Belsky, J., & Rovine, M. J. (1988). Nonmaternal care in the first year of life and the security of infant–parent attachment. *Child Development, 59*, 157–167.

Booth, C. L., Clarke-Stewart, K. A., Vandell, D. L., McCartney, K., & Owen, M. T. (2002). Child-care usage and mother–infant "quality time." *Journal of Marriage and Family, 64*(1), 16–26.

Bornstein, M. H., & Tamis-LeMonda, C. S. (1989). Maternal responsiveness and cognitive development in children. *New Directions for Child Development, 43*, 49–61.

Bowlby, J. (1973). *Attachment and loss: Vol. 2. Separation.* New York: Basic Books.

Broberg, A. G., Wessels, H., Lamb, M. E., & Hwang, C. P. (1997). Effects of day care on the development of cognitive abilities in 8-year-olds: A longitudinal study. *Developmental Psychology, 33*, 62–69.

Bronfenbrenner, U. (1988). Interacting systems in human development. In *Persons in context: Developmental processes* (pp. 25–49). New York: Cambridge University Press.

Bronfenbrenner, U. (1999). Environments in developmental perspective: Theoretical and operational models. In S. L. Friedman & T. D. Wachs (Eds.), *Measuring environment across the life span: Emerging methods and concepts* (pp. 3–28). Washington, DC: American Psychological Association.

Brooks-Gunn, J., Han, W. J., & Waldfogel, J. (2002). Maternal employment and child cognitive outcomes in the first three years of life: The NICHD Study of Early Childcare. *Child Development, 73*, 1052–1072.

Burchinal, M. R., Bryant, D. M., Lee, M. W., & Ramey, C. T. (1992). Early day care, infant–mother attachment, and maternal responsiveness in the infant's first year. *Early Childhood Research Quarterly, 7*, 383–396.

Burchinal, M. R., & Clarke-Stewart, K. A. (2007). Maternal employment and child cognitive outcomes: The importance of analytic approach. *Developmental Psychology, 43*, 1140–1155.

Burchinal, M. R., Roberts, J. E., Nabors, L. A., & Bryant, D. M. (1996). Quality of center childcare and infant cognitive and language development. *Child Development, 67*, 606–620.

Campbell, S. B., Cohn, J. F., & Meyers, T. (1995). Depression in first-time mothers: Mother–infant interaction and depression chronicity. *Developmental Psychology, 31*, 349–357.

Chin-Quee, D. S., & Scarr, S. (1994). Lack of early childcare effects on school-age children's social competence and academic achievement. *Early Development and Parenting, 3*(2), 103–112.

Clarke-Stewart, K. A. (1987). Predicting child development from childcare forms and features: The Chicago study. In D. A. Phillips (Ed.), *Quality in childcare: What does research tell us?* (pp. 21–42). Washington, DC: National Association for the Education of Young Children.

Clarke-Stewart, K. A. (1989). Infant day care: Maligned or malignant? *American Psychologist, 44*, 266–273.

Cote, S. M., Borge, A., Geoffroy, M. C., Rutter, M., & Tremblay, R. E. (2008). Nonmaternal care in infancy and emotional/behavioral difficulties at 4 years old: Moderation by family risk characteristics. *Developmental Psychology. 44*, 155–168.

Crockenberg, S., & Litman, C. (1991). Effects of maternal employment on maternal and 2-year-old child behavior. *Child Development, 62*, 930–953.

de Schipper, J. C., van IJzendoorn, M. H., & Tavecchio, L. W. C. (2004). Stability in center day care: Relations with children's well being and problem behavior in day care. *Social Development, 13*, 531–550.

Doherty, G., Lero, D. S., Goelman, H., LaGrange, A., & Tougas, J. (2000). *You bet I care! A Canada-wide study on wages, working conditions, and practices in childcare centers.* Ontario: University of Guelph, Centre for Families, Work and Well Being.

Doherty, G., Lero, D. S., Goelman, H., Tougas, J., & LaGrange, A. (2000). *Caring and learning environments: Quality in regulated family child care across Canada. You bet I care!* Ontario: University of Guelph, Centre for Families, Work and Well Being.

Dowsett, C. J., Huston, A. C., Imes, A. E., & Gennetian, L. (2008). Structural and process features in three types of childcare for children from high and low income families. *Early Childhood Research Quarterly. 23*, 69–93.

Dunn, L. (1993). Proximal and distal features of day care quality and children's development. *Early Childhood Research Quarterly, 8,* 167–192.

Egeland, B., & Heister, M. (1995). The long-term consequences of infant day-care and mother–infant attachment. *Child Development, 66,* 474–485.

Ehrle, J., Adams, G., & Trout, K. (2001). *Who's caring for our youngest children? Childcare patterns for infants and toddlers.* Washington, DC: Urban Institute Press.

Fantuzzo, J. W., Rouse, H., McDermott, P. A., Sekino, Y., Childs, S., & Weiss, A. (2005). Early childhood experiences and kindergarten success: A population-based study of a large urban setting. *School Psychology Review, 34,* 571–588.

Feinstein, L. (2003). Inequality in the early cognitive development of British children in the 1970 cohort. *Economica, 70,* 73–98

Field, T. (1991). Quality infant day care and grade school behavior and performance. *Child Development, 62,* 863–870.

Flanagan, K., and West, J. (2004). *Children born in 2001: First results from the base year of the Early Childhood Longitudinal Study, Birth Cohort (ECLS-B)* (NCES 2005–036). Washington, DC: National Center for Education Statistics, US Department of Education.

Friedman, S. L., & Amadeo, J. (1999). The childcare environment: Conceptualizations, assessments, and issues. In S. L. Friedman & T. D. Wachs (Eds.), *Measuring environment across the life span: Emerging methods and concepts* (pp. 127–165). Washington, DC: American Psychological Association.

Friedman, S. L., & Boyle, D. E. (2008). Attachment in US children experiencing nonmaternal care in the early 1990s. *Attachment and Human Development, 10*(3), 225–261.

Friedman, S. L., & Cocking, R. R. (1986). Instructional influences on cognition and on the brain. In S. L. Friedman, K. A. Klivington, & R. W. Peterson (Eds.), *The brain, cognition, and education* (pp. 319–346). Orlando, FL: Academic Press.

Friedman, S. L., Randolph, S., & Kochanoff, A. (2001). Childcare research at the dawn of a new millennium: Taking stock of what we know. In G. Bremner & A. Fogel (Eds.), *Blackwell handbook of infancy research.* Oxford: Blackwell.

Galinsky, E., Howes, C., Kontos, S., & Shinn, M. (1994). *The study of children in family childcare and relative care: Highlights of findings.* New York: Families and Work Institute.

Halle, T., & Vick, J. E. (2007). *Quality in early childhood care and education settings: A compendium of measures.* Washington, DC: Child Trends, for the Office of Planning, Research and Evaluation, Administration for Children and Families, US Department of Health and Human Services.

Harrison, A. O., Wilson, M. N., Pine, C. J., Chan, S. Q., & Buriel, R. (1990). Family ecologies of ethnic minority children. *Child Development, 61,* 347–362.

Hayes, C. D., Palmer, J. L., & Zaslow, M. J. (1990). *Who cares for America's children?* Washington, DC: National Academy Press.

Heckman, J. (2006). Skill formation and the economics of investing in disadvantaged children. *Science, 312,* 1900–1902.

Howes, C., & Smith, E. W. (1995). Relations among childcare quality, teacher behavior, children's play activities, emotional security, and cognitive activity in childcare. *Early Childhood Research Quarterly, 10,* 381–404.

Howes, C., Smith, E., & Galinsky, E. (1995). *The Florida Childcare Quality Improvement Study.* New York: Families and Work Institute.

Hungerford, A., & Cox, M. (2006). Family factors in childcare research published. *Evaluation Review, 30,* 631–655.

Huston, A. C., & Aronson, S. R. (2005). Mothers' time with infant and time in employment as predictors of mother–child relationships and children's early development. *Child Development, 76,* 467–482.

Hwang, C. P. (2006). Policy and research on childcare in Sweden. In E. Melhuish & K. Petrogiannis (Eds.), *Early childhood care and education: International perspectives* (pp. 77–94). London: Routledge.

Jackson, R., McCoy, A., Pistorino, C., Wilkinson, A., Burghardt, J., Clark, M., et al. (2007). National evaluation of Early Reading First. US Department of Education NCEE 2007–4007.

Jaeger, E., & Weinraub, M. (1990). Early nonmaternal care and infant attachment: In search of process. *New Directions for Child Development, 49,* 71–90.

Joshi, H., & Verropoulou, G. (1999, October). Maternal employment and child outcomes: Analyses of the NCDS (1958 Birth Cohort) second generation. Presented at the Equality Action Seminar, 11 Downing Street, London.

Kopp, C. B. (1997). Young children: Emotion management, instrumental control, and plans. In S. L. Friedman & E. K. Scholnick (Eds.), *Why, how and when do we plan? The developmental psychology of planning* (pp. 103–124). Hillsdale, NJ: Lawrence Erlbaum Associates.

Lamb, M. E. (1997). Nonparental childcare: Context, quality, correlates, and consequences. In W. Damon (Series Ed.), I. E. Sigel & K. A. Renninger (Vol. Eds.), *Handbook of child psychology: Child psychology in practice* (4th ed., pp. 783–915). New York: Wiley.

Lamb, M. E., Sternberg, K. J., & Prodromidis, M. (1992). Nonmaternal care and the security of infant–mother attachment: A reanalysis of the data. *Infant Behavior and Development, 15,* 71–83.

Lazarus, R. S. (1991). *Emotion and adaptation.* New York: Oxford University Press.

Lewis, M., & Michalson, L. (1983). *Children's emotions and moods.* New York: Plenum Press.

Love, J., Kisker, E. E., Ross, C. M. Schochet, P. Z., Brooks-Gunn, J., Paulsell, D., et al. (2002). *Making a difference in the lives of infants and toddlers and their families: The impacts of Early Head Start. Volume 1: Final Technical Report.* Princeton, NJ: Mathematica Policy Research Inc. Available at http://www.mathematica-mpr.com/PDFs/ehsfinalvol1.pdf

Love, J. M., Harrison, L., Sagi-Schwartz, A., van IJzendoorn, M., Ross, C., Ungerer, J. A., et al. (2003). Childcare quality matters: How conclusions vary by context. *Child Development. 74,* 1021–1033.

Maccoby, E. E., & Lewis, C. (2003). Less day care or different day care? *Child Development, 74,* 1069–1075.

McCartney, K., Dearing, E., Taylor, B. A., & Bub, K. L. (2007). Quality childcare supports the achievement of low-income children: Direct and indirect pathways through caregiving and the home environment. *Journal of Applied Developmental Psychology, 28,* 411–426.

Melhuish, E. C. (1991). Research issues in day care. In P. Moss & E. C. Melhuish (Eds.), *Current issues in day care for young children: Research and policy implications.* London: HMSO.

Melhuish, E. C. (2004). *A literature review of the impact of early years provision upon young children, with emphasis given to children from disadvantaged backgrounds: Report to the Comptroller and Auditor General.* London: National Audit Office. Available at www.nao.org.uk/publications/nao_reports/03–04/268_literaturereview.pdf.

Melhuish, E. C. (2005). Daycare. In B. Hopkins et al. (Eds.) *Cambridge encyclopaedia of child development.* Cambridge: Cambridge University Press.

Melhuish E. C. (2007). Developments in early childhood care and education in the UK. *SRCD Developments, 50*(2), 1–9.

Melhuish, E. C., Lloyd, E., Martin, S., & Mooney, A. (1990). Type of childcare at 18 months: II Relations with cognitive and language development. *Journal of Child Psychology and Psychiatry, 31,* 861–870.

Melhuish, E. C., & Petrogiannis, K. (Eds.) (2006). *Early childhood care and education: International perspectives on policy and research.* London & New York: Routledge.

Melhuish, E. C., Sylva, K., Sammons, P., Siraj-Blatchford, I., Taggart, B., & Phan, M. (2008a). Effects of the home learning environment and preschool center experience upon literacy and numeracy development in early primary school. *Journal of Social Issues, 64*, 157–188.

Melhuish, E. C., Sylva, K., Sammons, P., Siraj-Blatchford, I., Taggart, B., Phan, M. B., & Malin, A. (2008b). Pre-school influences on mathematics achievement. *Science, 321*(5893), 1161–1162.

Morrisey, T. W. (2008). Familial factors associated with the use of multiple childcare arrangements. *Journal of Marriage and the Family, 70*, 549–563.

Moss, P., & Wall, K. (2007). International review of leave policies and related research 2007. London: BERR. Available at www.berr.gov.uk/files/file40677.pdf.

Mulligan, G. M., & Flanagan, K. D. (2006). Findings from the 2-year old follow-up of the early childhood longitudinal study, birth cohort (ECLS-B). US Department of Education. National Center for Education Statistics, Institute of Education Sciences 2006–043.

NICHD Early Childcare Research Network (1996). Characteristics of infant childcare: Factors contributing to positive caregiving. *Early Childhood Research Quarterly, 11*, 269–306.

NICHD Early Childcare Research Network (1997a). Familial factors associated with the characteristics of nonmaternal care for infants. *Journal of Marriage and the Family, 59*, 389–408.

NICHD Early Childcare Research Network (1997b). The effects of infant childcare on infant–mother attachment security: Results of the NICHD Study of Early Childcare. *Child Development, 68*, 860–879.

NICHD Early Childcare Research Network (1999a). Child outcomes when childcare center classes meet recommended standards for quality. *American Journal of Public Health, 89*, 1072–1077.

NICHD Early Childcare Research Network (1999b). Childcare and mother–child interaction in the first three years of life. *Developmental Psychology, 35*(6), 1399–1413.

NICHD Early Childcare Research Network (2000a). Characteristics and quality of childcare for toddlers and preschoolers. *Journal of Applied Developmental Science, 4*(3), 116–135.

NICHD Early Childcare Research Network (2000b). The relation of childcare to cognitive and language development. *Child Development, 71*(4), 960–980.

NICHD Early Childcare Research Network (2001a). Childcare and family predictors of preschool attachment and stability from infancy. *Developmental Psychology, 37*, 847–862.

NICHD Early Childcare Research Network (2001b). Childcare and children's peer interaction at 24 and 36 months: The NICHD Study of Early Childcare. *Child Development, 72*, 1478–1500.

NICHD Early Child Care Research Network (2002a). Child-care structure > process > outcome: Direct and indirect effects of child-care quality on young children's development. *Psychological Science, 13*, 199–206.

NICHD Early Childcare Research Network (2002b). Early childcare and children's development prior to school entry: Results from the NICHD Study of Early Childcare. *American Educational Research Journal, 39*, 133–164.

NICHD Early Childcare Research Network (2002c). The interaction of childcare and family risk in relation to child development at 24 and 36 months. *Applied Developmental Science, 6*, 144–156.

NICHD Early Childcare Research Network (2003a). Does quality of childcare affect child outcomes at age 4½? *Developmental Psychology, 39*, 451–469.

NICHD Early Childcare Research Network (2003b). Does amount of time spent in childcare predict socioemotional adjustment during the transition to kindergarten? *Child Development, 74*, 976–1005.

NICHD Early Childcare Research Network (2003c). Early childcare and mother–child interaction from 36 months through first grade. *Infant Behavior and Development, 26*, 345–370.

NICHD Early Childcare Research Network (2003d). Social functioning in first grade: Associations with earlier home and childcare predictors and with current classroom experiences. *Child Development, 74*(6), 1639–1662.

NICHD Early Child Care Research Network (2003e). Families matter – even for kids in child care. *Journal of Developmental and Behavioral Pediatrics, 24*, 58–62.

NICHD Early Childcare Research Network (Eds.) (2005a) *Childcare and Child Development.* New York: Guilford Press.

NICHD Early Childcare Research Network (2005b). Early childcare and children's development in the primary grades: Follow-up results from the NICHD Study of Early Childcare. *American Educational Research Journal, 42*(3), 537–571.

NICHD Early Childcare Research Network (2006). Childcare effect sizes for the NICHD Study of Early Childcare and Youth Development. *American Psychologist, 61*(2), 99–116.

Owen, M. T., & Cox, M. (1988). Maternal employment and the transition to parenthood. In A. E. Gottfried & A. W. Gottfried (Eds.), *Maternal employment and children's development: Longitudinal research* (pp. 85–119). New York: Plenum Press.

Parke, R. (1997). Socialization in the family: Ethnic and ecological perspectives. In W. Damon (Series Ed.) & N. Eisenberg (Vol. Ed.), *Handbook of child psychology: Vol. 3. Social, emotional, and personality development* (5th ed., pp. 463–552). New York: Wiley.

Peisner-Feinberg, E., Burchinal, M., Clifford, R., Culkin, M., Howes, C., Kagan, S., & Yazejian, N. (2001). The relation of preschool child care quality to children's cognitive and social developmental trajectories through second grade. *Child Development, 72*, 1534–1553.

Phillips, D. A., & Howes, C. (1987). Indicators of quality in childcare: Review of research. In D. A. Phillips (Ed.), *Quality in childcare: What does the research show us?* (pp. 1–19). Washington, DC: National Association for the Education of Young Children.

Phillips, D. A, McCartney, K., & Scarr, S. (1987). Child-care quality and children's social development. *Development Psychology, 23*, 537–543.

Ramey, C. T., & Campbell, F. A. (1991). Poverty, early childhood education, and academic competence: The Abecedarian experiment. In A. C. Huston (Ed.), *Children in poverty: Child development and public policy* (pp. 190–221). Cambridge, MA: Cambridge University Press.

Ramey, C. T., Dorval, R., & Baker-Ward, A. (1983). Group day care and socially disadvantaged families: Effects on the child and the family. In S. Kilmer (Ed.), *Advances in early education and day care* (Vol. III, pp. 69–106). Greenwich, CT: JAI Press.

Roggman, L. A., Langlois, J. H., Hubbs-Tait, L., & Rieser-Danner, L. A. (1994). Infant daycare attachment, and the "file drawer problem." *Child Development, 65*, 1429–1443.

Rolnick, A., & Grunewald, R. (2003). Early childhood development: Economic development with high public return. *Fedgazette,* March.

Rouse, C., Brooks-Gunn, J., & McLanahan, S. (2005). Introducing the issue. In *School readiness: Closing racial and ethnic gaps. The Future of Children, 15*, 5–14.

Sagi, A., van IJzendoorn, M. H., Aviezer, O., Donnell, F., & Mayseless, O. (1994). Sleeping out of home in a kibbutz communal arrangement: It makes a difference for infant–mother attachment. *Child Development, 65*, 992–1004.

Shonkoff, J. P., & Phillips, D. A. (Eds.) (2000). *From neurons to neighborhoods: The science of early childhood development.* Committee on Integrating the Science of Early Childhood Development. Washington, DC: National Academy Press.

Smith, K. (2002). Who's minding the kids? Childcare arrangements: Spring 1997. Current Population reports: Household Economic Studies. Washington, DC: US Dept. of Commerce (pp. 70–86).

Snow, C. E., Bums, S., & Griffin, P. (Eds.) (1998). *Preventing reading difficulties in young children.* Washington, DC: National Academy Press.

Stifter, C. A., Coulehan, C. M., & Fish, M. (1993). Linking employment to attachment: The mediating effects of maternal separation anxiety and interactive behavior. *Child Development, 64,* 1451–1460.

Tran, H., & Weinraub, M. (2006). Childcare effects in context: Quality, stability and multiplicity in nonmaternal childcare arrangements during the first 15 months of life. *Developmental Psychology, 42,* 566–582.

Van IJzendoorn, M. H., Dijkstra, J., & Bus, A. G. (1995). Attachment, intelligence and language: A meta-analysis. *Social Development, 4,* 115–128.

Vandell, D., & Corasaniti, M. (1990). Childcare and the family: Complex contributors to child development. *New Directions for Child Development, 49,* 23–37.

Votruba-Drzal, E., Coley, R. L., & Chase-Lansdale, P. L. (2004). Child care and low-income children's development: Direct and moderated effects. *Child Development, 75,* 296–312.

Whitebook, M., Howes, C., & Phillips, D. (1990). *Who cares? Childcare teachers and the quality of care in America (Final report).* National Childcare Staffing Study. Oakland, CA: Childcare Employee Project.

15

Infancy Research, Policy, and Practice

Marguerite Barratt and Erica Fener

Introduction

If we are to create an "engaged university" (Kellogg Commission on the Future of State and Land-Grant Universities, 1999), it is imperative that we take the vast knowledge about infants that resides on campuses, and is summarized so well in these two volumes, and see its application to the everyday lives of infants. The "scholarship of engagement" (Boyer, 1996) has the potential to forge a direct path between what we know broadly about infants and its application for each infant in the context of his or her own family, community, state, and nation. At the moment, that path is very meandering.

Infancy researchers, such as the ones writing in these volumes, clearly care very deeply about the well-being of infants and each one can delineate the implications of his or her work for infants and their families. But the link between knowledge and action based on that knowledge could be much stronger. Policies are in place to implement some of what we know is important for infants, a number of which will be reviewed in this chapter. Further, some communities have created their own programs to address the needs of infants. But it will become clear that we know so much more than is being implemented in the everyday lives of infants. To address this, a number of mechanisms for pulling together research, policy, and practice will be presented.

Theoretical Framework

Bronfenbrenner's (1979) conceptualization of the multiple influences on children provides a useful framework for this examination of the application of infancy research to the lives of infants. At the level of the microsystem, infants are influenced by mothers, fathers, childcare providers, and others who come into direct contact with them. At the level of the exosystem, infants and their caregivers are influenced by the organizations and systems in which they participate. Examples include (1) childcare programs that organize the care infants receive; (2) employers who set constraints on parents of infants; (3) community programs that support families; and (4) local, state, and national policies that affect infants. As public policies and community programs are reviewed, these influences will be addressed.

Researchers are often unfamiliar with the lived experiences of infants in families who are different from their own. From the ivory tower of the university it is easy to forget that the poorest families in the United States are young families with infants, and that over 12 million of those infants are living in single-parent families with limited support and resources (Oser & Cohen, 2003; for a detailed review of poverty in the United States see chapter 5 in the present volume). The decade-long trend of declining poverty in the 1990s ended in 2000. By 2005, 43% of infants were born into low-income families and 21% lived in poor families. Furthermore, of the 2.7 million infants and toddlers who lived in low-income families, more than half were in single-parent homes (National Center for Children in Poverty, 2009). Of the female-headed single-parent households with children under 5, over 45% of the household income levels fell below the federal poverty line.

From the ivory tower of the university it is also easy to lose contact with the policy context of early development and how all aspects of a child's life (familial demographic, financial circumstances) can be supported by federal programs in order to improve developmental outcome. The ecological perspective being adopted in this chapter makes it essential to consider infant development in the context of families, communities, states, and nations.

The academy has begun to extend efforts to collaborate with the policy arena towards developing well-informed policy. The University of Wisconsin-Madison's Policy Institute for Family Impact Seminars is an example of academia developing an infrastructure to inform policy-makers about research and researchers about policy (Policy Institute for Family Impact Seminars, 2009). The Institute pulls together nonpartisan, solution-oriented research investigating the impact of current programs and policies on US families, with the goal of informing and improving family-oriented programs and policies. Twenty-nine states have family impact seminars focused on providing information for state policy-makers, including officials responsible for policy implementation.

Policy and Practice

The United States will be used as a case example in considering the policy context of infancy. The US is geographically large and encompasses cultural, ethnic, and racial diversity. In the US there is an income spread that is larger than that in many other countries, such that we have significant numbers of infants in extremely poor families and significant numbers of infants in very rich families. In the US, over 4 million infants are born each year, and almost half of African American and Hispanic infants are born into poverty (Oser & Cohen, 2003).

As policies affecting the lives of infants in the US are described, it is worth keeping in mind that the United States is precisely that, a collection of states. Increasingly, federal legislation provides block grant funding to states and provides some broad guidelines within which that money can be spent. States then are free to make individual choices about exactly how to implement federal policies, and states can even request waivers of federal statutory limitations.

As a further development, states are undergoing a devolutionary process of delegating decision-making to local levels. For example, in Michigan, all counties or collaboratives of counties have established a multi-purpose collaborative body to bring together the public and private human service funding organizations for regular meetings and decision-making (Michigan Department of Community Health, 2008). These collaboratives usually include social services, health, education, and public health, and they are asked to work together to make community-level decisions about implementation of policy. Collaborative programs have forged successful efforts in their communities. Examples include the Great Parents, Great Start program, where parental education for families with young children includes information, support, and access to community services (Michigan Department of Education, 2009).

This means that, in the US, policies affecting infants are often made at the federal level, adjusted at the state level, and implemented at the community level. Accordingly, it is complex to describe infancy policy. For example, it will be apparent in the descriptions below that federal legislation allows states to cover costs of some services to poor families whose incomes exceed the minimums. The following review includes policies in the US affecting medical care, nutrition, income support, developmental assessment and support, childcare, safety, and supports and education for parents. Some of the research base for the policies and descriptions of the policies themselves are also included.

Medical care

Prenatal care. It is clear that prenatal care contributes significantly to the well-being of infants. Research shows that infants are less likely to be born preterm when mothers receive prenatal care, and comprehensive prenatal care for low-income women has been shown to reduce infant complications (Lowry & Beikirch, 1998). Prenatal care beginning in the first trimester is one of the Healthy People 2010 goals in the United States (US Department of Health and Human Services (USDHHS), 2000). The 1987 baseline data indicated that 76% of mothers giving birth had prenatal care during the first trimester; for 2002 it was 84%; the goal for 2010 is 90%, and progress is being made towards this target (Office of Disease Prevention and Health Promotion, US Department of Health and Human Services, 2006). As part of the federal Medicaid program for low-income families, states provide programs that cover the costs of prenatal care for low-income pregnant women whose incomes are at or below 133% of the federal poverty level (Centers for Medicare and Medicaid Services, 2005). Individual states may choose to cover women at a higher percentage of the poverty level; expanded Medicaid eligibility in some states can go to 185% of the federal poverty level. In the United States, 41% of births are covered by Medicaid (Kaiser Family Foundation, 2007). In many states, there is a presumptive eligibility for this coverage such that pregnant women are provided with temporary coverage immediately on the basis of an application completed at many clinics (including public health departments and family planning clinics). This process facilitates early and immediate access to prenatal care. To assure continuity of care, once eligibility is established, Medicaid coverage continues until 60 days after the end of the pregnancy.

Healthcare for infants and children.   Although it is clear that healthcare for infants contributes to well-being, historically infants in the US were not all receiving routine well-child care, or timely treatment of acute and chronic medical problems. However, the US has made great strides in improving immunization for children. For example, the percentage of children aged 19–35 months who are fully immunized has stabilized at about 82% from 2003 to 2006; while this is a great improvement over 69% in 1994, there is still a distance to go (Child Trends Databank, 2007b).

Healthy People 2010 targets 100% healthcare coverage for children (USDHHS, 2000). After 2000, a decline in the nation's economy led to increased participation in federal programs by struggling families (Center on Budget and Policy Priorities, 2007). In the US, Medicaid is administered by each state to provide coverage of medical expenses for children in poor families where the family income is at or below 133% of the federal poverty level. In addition, under the Children's Health Insurance Program (CHIP), many states have created low-cost insurance programs for families who are not quite poor enough to qualify for Medicaid. In 2006, about 13% of children were covered by Medicaid or other public health insurance (i.e., CHIP), totaling over 38 million families that relied on federal support to meet their healthcare needs (Center on Budget and Policy Priorities, 2007). To address the high cost of care for infants and children with disabilities, the Family Opportunity Act authorized in 2004 gives states the option of allowing families of disabled children, who do not qualify for Medicaid but are below 250% of the federal poverty level, to purchase health coverage through Medicaid. In 2006, 88% of children were covered by health insurance (Child Trends Databank, 2007a). In February 2009, President Obama signed the Children's Health Insurance Reauthorization Act that will expand coverage to an additional 4 million children (National Conference of State Legislatures, 2009).

The medical expenses of middle-income and well-off families are usually covered by private insurance provided or subsidized by employers. In between the group of poor children whose insurance is covered by public funds, and the better-off children whose insurance is covered by employers, 11.7% of young children are not covered by medical insurance. However, not all coverage problems are financial. Beyond the financial barriers, other significant barriers to medical care include scheduling difficulties, transportation difficulties, cultural and language barriers, dissatisfaction with services, and lack of information about financial supports (Child Trends Databank, 2007a; Omar, Schiffman, & Bauer, 1998; Riportella-Muller, Selby-Harrington, Richardson, Donat, Luchok, & Quade, 1996).

Healthcare for parents.   Medicaid insures poor children, but usually not their parents. A significant body of research (e.g., Weinberg & Tronick, 1998) indicates that maternal depression and anxiety, as well as other forms of mental illness, interfere with the development of a healthy mother and infant relationship (for detailed discussion of maternal depression see chapter 8 in this volume). Healthy People 2010 (USDHHS, 2000) includes a goal of having at least half of mothers suffering from depression receiving treatment; currently less than one quarter receive treatment. The American Psychological Association reported in 2008 that 9–16% of new mothers experience postpartum depression; reducing that percentage is a current national goal.

Developmental deficits in children of substance-abusing mothers are partly attributable to the chaotic environments these mothers provide for their infants (e.g., Mayes, 1995), and healthcare can include substance abuse treatment. Research indicates that rates of premature birth, low birth weight, and infant mortality rates were significantly improved for women who participated in a residential substance abuse treatment program while pregnant (Rosack, 2001). This line of evidence suggests the importance of healthy parents for infants' well-being, yet the US has not invested broadly in the health of parents. UNICEF (2009) ranked the US lower on maternal mortality than many other countries (for detailed discussion of the impact of poverty in developing countries see chapter 6 in the present volume).

Teen parents

While the overall birth rate among teenagers in the US continued to decline in 2005, continuing the trend from the 1990s, the rate of teenage pregnancy remains alarming with more than 750,000 teenagers becoming pregnant each year, and about 420,000 giving birth. Furthermore, about a quarter of teen mothers under age 18 have a second baby within two years after the birth of their first baby. The approximately 4% of teenagers who have a baby often face overwhelming challenges during new motherhood, including health and psychosocial risks. These risk factors include: a higher average of smoking during pregnancy than women over age 25, higher rates of premature delivery and pregnancy complications (e.g., anemia and high blood pressure), and lower rates of prenatal care than any other age group.

Additionally, teenagers who have children before age 18 are less likely to graduate from high school (i.e., only 40% become high school graduates) and are more likely to live in poverty than women who delay childbearing. For example, more than 75% of all unmarried teen mothers go on welfare within five years of the birth of their first child. These factors also negatively impact the children of teen parents. About 78% of children born to teenage mothers who are unmarried and high-school dropouts live in poverty, and about half of children born to a teenage mother experience academic difficulties and drop out of school before graduating (March of Dimes, 2007).

To deal with these issues on the national level, the March of Dimes established the National Day to Prevent Teen Pregnancy (May 7, 2008). The initiative was designed to reach hundreds of thousands of teens nationwide to increase awareness and improve decision-making skills via activities surrounding teen pregnancy, including participation in an online quiz that asks teens to reflect on the best course of action in a number of tough and realistic sexual situations. Additionally, states utilize federal funds to develop programs to assist teen parents and maximize the potential for mother and child health, as well as educational and developmental success. For example, the Illinois Department of Human Services developed the Teen Parent Services program that targets pregnant or low-income parents who are aged 20 or younger and do not have a high school diploma (or its equivalent) (Illinois Department of Human Services, 2009).

Nutrition

Prenatal nutrition.   In the US, the federal Special Supplemental Nutrition Program for Women, Infants and Children (WIC) provides nutritious food via vouchers to pregnant women and mothers of children under the age of 5 who are poor and at nutritional risk. WIC eligibility includes family incomes at or below 185% of the federal poverty level. Nutritional risk includes such risk factors as anemia, underweight, and poor eating patterns. Through WIC, women also receive individual counseling, education about healthy eating during pregnancy, screening for anemia, and healthcare referrals. The WIC program serves approximately 8.7 million individuals; 45% of pregnant women participate. Over 80% of WIC infants meet eligibility due to their mother's "at-risk" status during pregnancy (USDA Food and Nutrition Service, 2007). Women enrolled in the WIC program have been shown to be less likely to deliver infants who are small for gestational age (Ahluwalia, Hogan, Grummer-Strawn, Colville, & Peterson, 1998) and less likely to die in the first year (Moss & Carver, 1998).

Breastfeeding.   Healthy People 2010 has a goal of 25% breastfeeding at 1 year. Even though that is also the recommendation of the American Academy of Pediatrics (1997), the current level is only 16%. WIC also has prenatal and postpartum programs that target increasing breastfeeding. In 2005, in line with the aim of Healthy People 2010, the USDA Food and Nutrition Service (FNS) outlined their strategic plan to increase the percentage of breastfed infants to 60% by the year 2010. In 2006 that goal was nearly reached, with 58% of infants being breastfed. FNS indicates an increase in enrollment of mothers in the breastfeeding initiation program for WIC infants. Research suggests that breastfed infants have fewer ear infections, allergies, and respiratory infections, and are less likely to die of sudden infant death syndrome (Stuart-Macadam & Dettwyler, 1995). Mothers who breastfeed their infants return more quickly to their prepregnancy weight and are less likely to develop breast cancer premenopausally. Differing from the FNS initiatives, the goals of Health People 2010 are differentiated by age milestones. In 1998, 64% of mother breastfed their newborns and 39% breastfed through 6 months. Healthy People 2010 aims for 75% breastfeeding in the newborn period and 50% breastfeeding at 6 month (USDHHS, 1991, 2000). Income-eligible women (at or below 185% poverty) who are breastfeeding their infants receive vouchers for healthy foods from WIC to provide the extra nourishment that their bodies need during lactation. Increased breastfeeding in low-income women served by WIC can result in significant cost savings (Heinig, 1998). Some communities, clinics, and hospitals employ lactation consultants to provide access to information and individual consultation to breastfeeding women.

Other communities have developed peer support programs through which women volunteers support new mothers who are breastfeeding, although the research evidence on the effectiveness of these peer support programs is equivocal (e.g., Arlotti, Cottrell, Lee, & Curtin, 1998; Caulfield et al., 1998; Morrow et al., 1999).

Nutrition for infants.   Accumulated evidence suggests the importance of nutrition during the first years (see chapter 2 in this volume for further details), yet for low-income families in the US there may not be enough food for children. WIC provides vouchers for healthy food for income-eligible children up to 5 years old, as well as nutrition education for their parents. It is estimated that every $1 spent on WIC results in $1.77 to $3.13 in Medicaid savings for newborns and their mothers. The program has been proven to increase prenatal care, reduce incidence of low birth weight and fetal mortality, reduce anemia and overall enhance nutrition. With the decline in the nation's economy, the need continues to increase, but potentially eligible infants, children, and mothers remain unserved.

The Child and Adult Care Food Program is a federal program that is a downward extension of the school lunch program, which subsidizes the cost of snacks and meals served to children in childcare programs. Children whose families have incomes at or below 130% of the federal poverty level receive these foods free; between 130% and 185% of the poverty level, the price is reduced. The Child and Adult Care Food Program also provides oversight for menus and education for childcare providers. Another federal program that helps with nutrition for families with infants is the Food Stamp Program, which provides income-eligible parents with vouchers that stretch their food dollars. About 80% of food stamp participants live in households with children, and participation has increased from 17.2 million in 2000 to almost 27 million in 2006 (Center on Budget and Policy Priorities, 2007). While declines in the economy partly account for this trend, changes in legislation and programs also created a more easily navigated process for states and families to increase participation of eligible families (Children's Defense Fund, 2004). Parent education about nutrition, food safety, purchase of food, and food preparation is the focus of the Expanded Food and Nutrition Education Program (EFNEP) offered nationwide in nearly 800 counties by the Extension branch of each state's land-grant university. As a longstanding outreach effort of the land-grant university in each state, extension services provide this education to small groups and in homes. Educators follow a research-based learning model and impact data has indicated effective results (US Department of Agriculture, 2009).

State and community initiatives to address infant nutrition issues also include the development of local food pantries that provide food for families in need. Food distributed by food pantries is made available through volunteer donations (local food drives) as well as food banks that accept large donations of food and organize their distribution through local food pantries. Food pantries are also a source of formula and diapers for infants, and so particularly serve families with young children. However, local food pantries each create their own guidelines, and many have barriers that limit the food that infants and their families actually make use of (Tableman, 1999). For example, families may be limited to receiving food once a month or to accepting only bags with specific items.

Income support

Welfare.   In the US, the federal income support program, Aid to Families with Dependent Children, was replaced in 1996 by Temporary Assistance to Needy Families (TANF) in an effort to move families off the welfare rolls and into the world of work (Zaslow, Tout, Smith, & Moore, 1998). This program provides some financial support for the 21% of children under 6 years old who live in poverty (National Center for Children in Poverty, 2009). However, with TANF, families now have lifetime limits on receiving support such that only 60 months of support may be received, and work requirements are part of the program. Families who exceed the number of months and families who do not meet work requirements are "sanctioned" and often may not receive federal support, although states are given some flexibility in this.

Preliminary research indicates a potential false sense of success for significant changes made during the 1990s in federal and state income support on infant outcomes. The decline in participation in income support programs in the 1990s, including Food Stamps, Medicaid and state health insurance programs, was partly accounted for by the strong US economy (35%), changes in social welfare reform and political variables (12%); only 28% was accounted for by an increase in family income (Wilde, Cook, Gundersen, Nord, & Tiehen, 2000). States are offered federal incentives to reduce participation in TANF programs through work requirements. As a condition of the receipt of TANF, states are required to achieve two minimum work participation rates. The first, the overall work participation rate, requires that 50% of all families receiving assistance must participate in at least some work activities in the fiscal year. The second, the work participation rate for adults in two-parent families, requires that 90% of two-parent families participate in at least some work program activities in the fiscal year.

States that successfully meet their work participation rates receive a reduction in their maintenance of effort requirement (i.e., required work participation rates are set lower for the following fiscal year). Failure to meet the required work participation rates may result in a financial penalty to a state under federal regulations. While these efforts may successfully get parents back into the work force and make them less reliant on federal program support, they underline the need for improved access to quality childcare for poor working families.

Child support.   In the US today, 39% of infants are born to single mothers and 84% of births to teen mothers were outside marriage (Anderson, Ikramullah, & Keith, 2008). Noncustodial parents, usually fathers, are often obligated to provide financial support for their minor children; the collection of child support has been facilitated by procedures that make it easier to establish paternity. Hospitals are now required to make available official forms that fathers can complete to establish their paternity, and mothers are given the opportunity to provide information to help track down putative fathers and determine paternity. When paternity is established, courts often order noncustodial parents to provide child support, and procedures have been established to make it relatively straightforward to collect child support. For example, wages are garnished at the point when child support is ordered, and income tax refunds and lottery winnings are intercepted when child support is owed.

These procedures, some of which derive from the Personal Responsibility and Work Opportunity Reconciliation Act of 1996, go part of the distance toward providing financial resources for the support of infants (Zaslow et al., 1998). However, according to the Office of Child Support Enforcement, two thirds of the current $92.3 billion in unpaid child support is owed by extremely poor noncustodial parents. Some states are developing programs that assist noncustodial parents, predominately fathers, in becoming more financially secure and better able to provide for their children. For example, the Georgia Fatherhood Services Network program (http://dhr.georgia.gov), created by the state's Department of Human Resources, provided employability assessment, skills training, job-readiness training, and job placement to unemployed and underemployed noncustodial fathers. The program lasts approximately 4–6 months and requires participants to meet at least 50% of their child support obligation. Evaluation studies indicated that by 2001, 47% of participants were employed and able to pay their full child support. New York City's Office of Child Support Enforcement developed the Step Through Employment Program (STEP), which facilitates a collaborative effort between the Manhattan Family Court and several community-based organizations to provide employment programs for noncustodial parents, including job training and job placement.

Earned income tax credit.   This federal program provides refundable credits for low-income families in the United States. The money can be provided monthly or in an annual lump sum. As an income support program for working parents, this has been particularly effective in lifting families out of poverty (Scholz, 2000). Some states also have a state earned income tax credit. Other federal programs include the Economic Growth & Tax Relief Reconciliation Act of 2001, which increased the per-child tax credit and the eligible dependent childcare amount, and the Child and Dependent Care Credit, which provides a tax credit based on a percentage of expenses for childcare, daycare, or adult daycare services. To qualify, parents must have a dependent child aged 12 or younger, or a dependent who cannot care for himself or herself.

Developmental assessment and support

The US does not have a public health system through which each infant passes for medical regular check-ups. This is in contrast to other countries such as Japan where all infants receive developmental and physical checkups at 3 or 4 months of age. For poor children who are served by Medicaid, each child in the US should receive Early and Periodic Screening, Diagnosis, and Treatment (EPSDT) services that include a review of medical history, physical measurements, sensory screening, mental and developmental assessment, and other checking. With the assignment of Medicaid patients to health maintenance organizations for medical care, this has become the responsibility of medical care providers (Health Resources and Services Administration, 2009).

For children not served by Medicaid, each state has developed Child Find programs, including media campaigns, to help identify children with developmental delays or sensory impairments who would be eligible for services under the Individuals with

Disabilities Act (Part C). Programs include early intervention, preschool special educa-tion, Head Start, and Title V programs for children with special healthcare needs. Where delays or impairments are detected, each state has a lead agency responsible for providing supportive services to children between birth and 3 years old who have handicapping conditions. The specific services that are needed are developed jointly by families and professionals and documented in an individualized family service plan. States have also utilized federal funds to develop local level infrastructures to more accurately identify children in need of services, improve service delivery and quality, and ensure healthy developmental outcomes. For example, the Infant and Toddler Connection of Virginia is a system of services and supports to promote positive developmental outcomes for infants and toddlers with developmental delays or disabilities by providing occupational therapy, speech and language therapy, and psychological services (www.infantva.org).

Childcare

In the US, over half of mothers with infants work outside the home. This is a remarkable increase from the 31% of mothers in 1976 who worked outside the home. Furthermore, only 19% of infants and toddlers in low-income families (1 million) have both parents unemployed (Douglas-Hall, Chau, & Koball, 2006). This rebuffs the myth that low-income mothers are predominately stay-at-home mothers, and further asserts the need for affordable quality childcare.

Parents utilize many different options for childcare. A few infants accompany their mothers to work, some are cared for by their father while the mother works (particularly mothers who work evening and night shifts), and others are cared for by relatives. The US Census Bureau in 2008 reported that grandparents serve as the primary caregivers for about 20% of the 11.3 million preschoolers whose mothers are employed, and about 25% of children under 5 are cared for by paid providers in the infants' home, in family childcare settings, or in childcare centers. In addition, differences across ethnicity were found, with African American grandparents being the most likely to provide childcare if the mother is unemployed, but Asian grandparents being the most likely to provide childcare if the mother is working.

What does a good childcare program look like? Experts agree on fundamentals that are required of "good" childcare programs, which include: health and safety standards, developmentally and culturally appropriate activities, limited group size, adequate staff training in child development and early childhood education, warm staff–child interac-tions, adequate provider salaries, and adequate indoor and outdoor space (for details on childcare quality issues, see chapter 14 in this volume). The three most critical compo-nents are structural, including appropriate child-to-caregiver ratios, group sizes, and provider qualifications. Research has found a relation between quality of childcare and cognitive development, school readiness, social competence, peer interactions, and overall adjustment (NICHD Early Child Care Research Network, 1998, 1999). For example, children in poor quality childcare more often exhibit aggression and delays in reading skills. According to the National Institutes of Health, the most critical predictors of child outcome were quality of childcare and overall parenting, further emphasizing the need for improved access to quality childcare (for further information, see chapter 14 in this volume).

There is an emerging consensus in the literature that supports the assertion that by paying attention to structural aspects of childcare, the overall care provided to infants and toddlers in childcare programs can be enhanced. Childcare programs that have one adult taking care of no more than three infants, that keep infants in groups of six or fewer, and that have trained childcare providers are providing the most supportive care (e.g., American Public Health Association and American Academy of Pediatrics, 1992). For example, in those programs providers are most likely to be nurturing (i.e., warm staff–child interactions; NICHD Early Child Care Research Network, 1996). However, NICHD Early Child Care Research Network (1999) indicates that 20% of infants from ten communities across the US were in childcare programs that meet *none* of these standards. This is important to note because of the link between quality of childcare in infancy and adaptive socioemotional development (NICHD Early Child Care Research Network, 1998).

Quality childcare is often very expensive, which creates a barrier to accessing adequate care for poor families. The US Census Bureau reported in 2005 that poor families (who paid for childcare) spent 29% of their monthly income on childcare, compared with only 6% for families at the poverty level or above. In an effort to combat this burden on poor families, federal programs attempt to offer financial support for families in funding quality childcare. For example, the Best Beginnings childcare scholarship program provides funding for qualified low-income families who send their infants and children to licensed childcare centers, registered group or family childcare homes, or unregistered childcare providers. Scholarships with similar requirements are also available via TANF. In the context of welfare reform and the Personal Responsibility and Work Opportunity Reconciliation Act of 1996, considerable public money from the TANF program has been put into paying for childcare for infants whose mothers are returning to work (Zaslow et al., 1998). Each state has developed its own procedures for determining reimbursement rates and procedures. In many states, that care is largely provided by friends and relatives who are exempt from state regulations (Capizzano, Adams, & Sonenstein, 2000). The Federal Child and Dependent Care Credit reduces taxes for certain working families with childcare expenses (Internal Revenue Service, 2008).

Infant safety

In 2001, over 27,000 deaths of children under 1 occurred in the US, which is more than all the deaths combined among those aged 1–19 years. One quarter of American children receive injuries needing medical attention each year (US Bureau of the Census, 1996), and unintentional injuries are the leading cause of death in children aged 1–4 years (National Center for Health Statistics, 2007). In the US, policies related to the safety of infants have largely been the responsibility of state departments of public health or community health programs. Their efforts include media campaigns, booklets, and policy changes. The federal agency, the Centers for Disease Control (CDC), provides support for these efforts and tracks their impacts. Messages about car-seat safety, placing children on their backs to prevent sudden infant death syndrome, crib safety, and safe walkers are part of these efforts. For example, Healthy People 2010 aims to increase the number of infants who are placed on their backs to sleep from 35% to 70% (USDHHS, 2000). Some safety topics are more specialized, such as the importance of testing rural well water for nitrates from fertilizer runoff. Other topics are very general, such as the safe food-handling procedures that are even described on some grocery bags. Because of the aging housing stock in the United States, screening for lead poisoning is an important part of the safety of young children (for discussion of the nature and consequences of lead exposure, see chapter 3 in this volume). The CDC's Childhood Lead Poisoning Prevention Program is committed to the Healthy People goal of eliminating elevated blood lead levels in children by 2010. Federal funds and support services assist state and local childhood lead poisoning prevention programs.

Infant mortality

The National Center for Health Statistics (2007) indicates no significant improvement in the rate of infant mortality in the United States since 2000. The US rate was approximately 7.0 per 1000 births in 2003 (Mathews & MacDorman, 2006). This ranks the US 33rd in the world, below many other industrialized countries, with some American cities having an infant mortality rate higher than rates in Third World countries. In recent years, some areas of the US have seen a rise in infant mortality, (e.g., Mississippi's rate rose from 6.9 in 2003 to 11.4 in 2005). Researchers have questioned the negative impact of cuts in welfare programs and Medicaid on access to quality healthcare and subsequent increase in infant mortality. Studies indicate that the main causes of infant death in poor Southern regions included premature birth and low birth weight, sudden infant death syndrome, congenital defects, and, among poor teenage mothers in particular, deaths from accidents and disease.

Infant mortality in the US is particularly linked with lack of early prenatal care, preterm birth, and extreme disadvantage. Healthy People 2010 aims to cut infant mortality to 4.5% (USDHHS, 2000). The key to decreasing infant mortality is prevention, and there are several policy initiatives that target improving prevention efforts for main causes of infant mortality and that target infants who are at risk for increased rates of infant mortality. For example, birth defects account for more than 20% of all infant deaths, and over 37 states have birth defect prevention programs. Programs also extend to international efforts (e.g., the World Health Organization's cleft palate project). In addition, there are discrepant rates of infant mortality across ethnicity. The infant mortality rate among African Americans is twice the national average (14.1 deaths per 1,000 live births versus 6.9 deaths per 1,000 live births for Caucasian infants), while the sudden infant death syndrome rate among American Indian and Alaska Natives is 2.3 times the rate for Caucasians. The Office of Minority and Health's goal is to eliminate disparities among racial and ethnic groups with infant mortality rates above the national average, including American Indian, Alaska Native, and Puerto Rican populations, by 2010. Currently, the CDC is funding programs to further investigate infant mortality to better inform prevention program and policy development (e.g., improving the investigation of infant deaths).

Abuse and neglect

According to the DHHS, an estimated 3 million children each year are reported as suspected victims of abuse and neglect, and approximately 900,000 of these reports are substantiated (for details on the nature and consequences of abuse and neglect in infancy, see chapter 7 in this volume). Infants and toddlers have the highest victimization rate, with infants representing the largest number of children victimized of any age group (Children's Defense Fund, 2004). Each state has created a system of child welfare services for addressing issues of abuse and neglect. Where a report of neglect or abuse is substantiated, states use some combination of case work, criminal prosecution, mandatory parenting education, and foster care to protect children from future maltreatment. Approximately 4% of all children under the age of 1 are in foster care. In addition to formal foster-care systems run by public, secular, and nonprofit agencies, additional children are in informal care with relatives (kin care) as a result of abuse and neglect or suspicions of abuse and neglect.

Policy at the federal level has also targeted preventing child abuse and ensuring the proper care and treatment of children who have been abused and/or neglected. A major step in those efforts was the Child Abuse Prevention and Treatment Act (CAPTA), amended most recently in 1946 (Administration for Children and Families, 2009). CAPTA provides federal funding in support of states' prevention, assessment, investigation, prosecution, and treatment programs. Additionally, CAPTA provides grant support to public agencies and nonprofit organizations for demonstration programs and projects, as well as supporting research, evaluation, technical assistance and data collection activities. This legislation has also established the Office on Child Abuse and Neglect (CAPTA, section 101) and mandated the creation of the National Clearinghouse on Child Abuse and Neglect Information (section 103; www.childwelfare.gov/).

Supporting parents

Family Resource Centers.   Beginning in the 1980s and continuing today, Family Resource Centers were developed as a strategy to support parents. The idea was that communities could better support the development of infants and children if they would centralize parents' access to information and support (Little, 1998). Family Resource Centers have offered parent education classes, parent support groups, respite care for children in stressed families, and other programs. For example, in Wisconsin support from state governments as well as from the Children's Trust Fund (2007) has been instrumental in establishing and continuing 21 centers.

Home-visiting programs.   Since the 1990s, many communities and professionals in the US have created home-visiting programs to welcome new infants and to educate and support parents. Programs use nurse home visitors, social workers, paraprofessionals, and volunteers to optimize the development of infants, particularly high-risk infants, through supportive and educational services. It is estimated that more than half a million pregnant women, infants, and their families in the US are being served by home-visiting programs (Gomby, Culross, & Behrman, 1999). Evaluations of current home-visiting models suggest documented ongoing effectiveness (Olds, 2002; Sweet and Appelbaum, 2004). For example, the Nursing Home Visitation Program has been documented as having a long-run impact and, in this program, benefits seem to particularly accrue to high-risk families (Karoly et al., 1998; Olds, 2002).

Early Head Start.   As a downward extension of the widespread federally funded Head Start program for 3- and 4-year-olds, Early Head Start (www.ehsnrc.org) began in 1994 to serve income-eligible pregnant women and families with children under 3 years of age. Currently hundreds of sites nationally offer flexible services designed around each child, each family, and each community. With a focus on promoting children's development, pregnant women, infants, and young children are served with a combination of home visits and group activities. A national evaluation of effectiveness indicated significantly better cognitive, language, and socioemotional development by Early Head Start participants than their peers (Mathematica Policy Research, Inc., 2009).

Parental leave.   In the US, the Family Medical Leave Act of 1993 (FMLA) requires employers to grant employees up to 12 weeks of unpaid leave for the birth and care of the newborn child of the employee, for adoptive or foster placement with the employee of a son or daughter, to care for an immediate family member (spouse, child, or parent) with a serious health condition, or to take medical leave when the employee is unable to work because of a serious health condition (Employment Standards Administration: Wage and Hour Division, 2009). However, this only applies to parents who work for employers with over 50 employees, which leaves many parents vulnerable to financial difficulties in the midst of trying to cope with major life events. While this leave is not required to be paid leave, some employers allow parents to use accumulated sick leave and vacation time toward the 12 weeks. Some employers also make paternity leave available for fathers in addition to the maternity leave offered to mothers.

A few states have implemented innovative programs and parental leave policies that are slightly different from the federal law. For example, in 2002, California became the first state to enact a comprehensive paid family leave program for workers, where most workers will be paid about 55% of their salary for 6 weeks of leave to care for a new child (by birth, adoption, or foster care) or sick child (Employment Standards Administration: Wage and Hour Division, 2002).

Policies in the US are in stark contrast to other countries, which offer periods of paid leave that may include part-time pay over a period of more than a year (e.g., Sweden, Finland). Recent federal proposals may lead to allowing states to use unemployment funds to cover some paid parental leave. Research suggests that maternity leave of less than 6 weeks is a risk factor for depression (Hyde, Essex, Clark, & Klein, 1996) and that shorter leave periods are associated with less optimal mother–infant interaction (Clark, Hyde, Essex, & Klein, 1997).

Policy Summary

This review of policies in the United States has described *how* programs should work and *who* should be able to participate. And indeed, some of the information that researchers know is reflected in those policies. However, many families do not make use of the programs for which they are eligible. Some families are unaware of their eligibility, while others do not want to participate in stigmatized programs. Some families run up against barriers of transportation, red tape, or waiting lists, and other families only receive partial services. For example, a record review in North Carolina indicated that only portions of the EPSDT protocols were being administered (Richardson, Selby-Harrington, Krowchuk, Cross, & Williams, 1994). Clearly policies do not reflect much of what we know about infants, and what has been enacted into policy is not necessarily being implemented and having impact.

To differentiate between the ideal and reality, imagine a poor single American mother's negotiation through the policy maze. Welfare support from TANF will pay a monthly stipend for a time, although there may be work requirements. The amount of support for a single mother and her infant is small, for example about $145 per month in Mississippi (Division of Economic Assistance, n.d.). The case worker who enrolls the mother and infant may or may not also be empowered to enroll the family for Food Stamps (now called the Supplemental Nutrition Assistance Program), Medicaid, or state-funded child health insurance, and even if empowered to enroll for these programs, may not be knowledgeable about the intricacies of eligibility (USDA Food and Nutrition Service, 2008). Food stamps might provide about an additional $150 toward food costs for this mother and infant, and WIC provides coupons that can be redeemed for specific nutritious food at most stores. Enrollment for WIC supplemental food is probably a separate stop, with questions about financial and nutritional need; eligibility for home-visiting and socialization experiences for Early Head Start or a locally organized home-visiting program is also probably a separate stop in communities that offer these services. In many states there is now public support or help in finding a job and finding childcare, but considerable leg work is involved, perhaps with the infant in tow. In other words, although policies provide numerous supports for needy families with infants, most communities have not made access to supports a convenient process.

Public information

While academic researchers have accumulated huge amounts of knowledge about infants, the public is clamoring for help in solving many social problems that begin in infancy. Legislatures across the US are considering and enacting initiatives that address the early years. For example, North Carolina has its Smart Start initiative for supporting infants, young children, and their families (Smart Start, 2009). A national initiative, Fight Crime: Invest in Kids (www.fightcrime.org/), is focusing increasing attention on early childhood.

The public appetite for information about infants also has been fed by organizations that are not part of universities such as Families and Work Institute, Zero to Three (www.

zerotothree.org/site/PageServer) and Children's Defense Fund (www.childrensdefense. org), which provide print and Web materials as well as leadership.

Engaged university

Where is the academy in this dialogue? Infancy researchers need to share what they know so that families, communities, states, and nations can put that knowledge into action. Policy-makers, practitioners, and citizens need to be welcome when they make inquiries of the academy and need to find a willingness to enter into two-way dialogue. Infancy researchers can also play an important role in helping the public interpret what it is hearing. Researchers can help differentiate among what we know solidly, what is suggested by research, what we are pretty sure is not true, and what we know is not true.

Movement toward becoming engaged universities is guided by the Kellogg Commission's (1999) report to the National Association of State Universities and Land-Grant Colleges, *Returning to Our Roots: The Engaged Institution*. This report can facilitate our efforts to effect the application of infancy research to the lives of infants. An engaged university is responsive and respectful. The academy has to do more than provide expert answers to the questions that it thinks communities and practitioners should be asking about infants. Instead, the academy needs to participate in a two-way dialogue where we learn about the knowledge that is emerging in practice and about the questions that are important to families, practitioners, and policy-makers. It is this dialogue that will lead to changes on and off campus.

An engaged university holds to academic neutrality. In other words, when we become involved in contentious issues, can we "maintain the university in the role of neutral facilitator and source of information" (Kellogg Commission, 1999, p. x)? Communities, policy-makers, and citizens ask a variety of questions such as: "Does brain science indicate that windows of opportunity close at the end of the first three years?"; "Can we prevent child abuse in our community with home visiting?"; "Does breastfeeding make children smarter?"; "At what age should parents begin reading to their children?"; "Can appropriate care of infants raise IQ 40 points?"; "What about Mozart for babies?"; "When should my infant start using a keyboard?" The academy treads a fine line in sticking to what we know and providing useful information in answer to questions like these.

The engaged university will need to work hard at coordination if it is to be useful (Kellogg Commission, 1999). Can we work together across traditional disciplinary boundaries, across unit boundaries on campuses, and across campuses? If the academy can coordinate across these boundaries, it will also enhance accessibility to communities, policy-makers, and citizens. When the academy coordinates its efforts to address relevant questions, we will know who else is doing the infancy research on our campus and on neighboring campuses. Then it will not matter who is the point of access because we can make useful referrals within our networked academy.

If universities commit to becoming engaged universities, they will integrate this engagement across the research, teaching, and service missions of the university (Kellogg Commission, 1999). For example, the Interdepartmental Graduate Specialization in Infant Studies at Michigan State University is a multidisciplinary effort involving a dozen departments, and it provides students with coursework, seminars, and an internship experience that prepares them to work with infants in a number of fields (Department of Family and Child Ecology, 2007).

Universities that make a commitment to engagement also commit resources to these efforts. "The most successful engagement efforts appear to be those associated with strong and healthy relationships with partners in government, business, and the nonprofit world" (Kellogg Commission, 1999, p. x). Our professional organizations recognize these needs. The American Psychological Association offers an annual award for Distinguished Contribution to Psychology in the Public Interest (e.g., American Psychological Association, 1999), and the work of the 1995 awardee, Dr. David Riley, included infancy work (American Psychological Association, 1996). The Society for Research in Child Development now publishes applied and policy studies in its journal, *Child Development* (Zigler, 1998), includes topical syntheses in *Child Development Perspectives*, and for some time has regularly published the *Social Policy Report*. Of particular interest is the Social Policy Report, "Beyond 'Giving Science Away': How University-Community Partnerships Inform Youth Programs, Research and Policy" (Denner, Cooper, Lopez, & Dunbar, 1999).

The new research agendas for infancy will include multidisciplinary action research agendas shaped jointly by families, service providers, government, business, and scholars. With this collaboration between the academy and the off-campus world, what the academy knows – about perception and cognition; about social, emotional, and communicative development; about risk factors; and about the context of early development – will be put to use by families, the practitioners who serve them, policy-makers, and communities to optimize the development of infants.

References

Administration for Children and Families (2009). Child Abuse Prevention and Treatment Act. www.acf.hhs.gov/programs/cb/laws_policies/cblaws/capta/index.htm (accessed March 2009).

Ahluwalia, I. B., Hogan, V. K., Grummer-Strawn, L., Colville, W. R., & Peterson, A. (1998). The effect of WIC participation on small-for-gestational-age births: Michigan, 1992. *American Journal of Public Health, 88*, 1374–1376.

American Academy of Pediatrics Work Group on Breastfeeding (1997). Breastfeeding and the use of human milk. *Pediatrics, 100*, 1035–1039.

American Psychological Association (1996). Award for Distinguished Contribution to Psychology in the Public Interest: David A. Riley. *American Psychologist, 51*, 336–341.

American Psychological Association (1999). Award for Distinguished Contribution to Psychology in the Public Interest: Bonnie Strickland. *American Psychologist, 54*, 246.

American Public Health Association and American Academy of Pediatrics Collaborative Project (1992). *Caring for our children – national health and safety performance standards: Guidelines for out-of-home child care programs.* Washington, DC: American Public Health Association.

Anderson, K., Ikramullah, E., & Keith, J. (2008). *Facts at a glance: A fact sheet reporting national, state-level and city-level trends in teen childbearing [Brochure].* Menlo Park, CA: The William and Flora Hewlett Foundation.

Arlotti, J. P., Cottrell, B. H., Lee, S. H., & Curtin, J. J. (1998). Breastfeeding among low-income women with and without peer support. *Journal of Community Health Nursing, 15*, 163–178.

Boyer, E. L. (1996). The scholarship of engagement. *Journal of Public Service and Outreach, 1,* 11–20.

Bronfenbrenner, U. (1979). *The ecology of human development. Experiments by nature and design.* Cambridge, MA: Harvard University Press.

Capizzano, J., Adams, G., & Sonenstein, F. (2000). *Child care arrangements for children under five: Variation across states* (Series B, No. B-7). Washington, DC: Urban Institute.

Caulfield, L. E., Gross, S. M., Bentley, M. E., Bronner, Y., Kessler, L., Jenson, J., et al. (1998). WIC-based interventions to promote breastfeeding among African-American women in Baltimore: Effects of breastfeeding initiation and continuation. *Journal of Human Lactation, 14,* 15–22.

Center on Budget and Policy Priorities (2007). *More Americans, including more children, now lack health insurance. Center on Budget and Policy Priorities.* www.cbpp.org/8-28-07health.htm (accessed March 2008).

Centers for Medicare and Medicaid Services (2005). *Technical summary of Medicaid program.* www.cms.hhs.gov/MedicaidGenInfo/03_TechnicalSummary.asp#TopOfPage (accessed March 2009).

Child Trends Databank (2007a). *Health care coverage.* www.childtrendsdatabank.org/indicators/26HealthCareCoverage.cfm (accessed March 2009).

Child Trends Databank (2007b). *Immunization.* www.childtrendsdatabank.org/indicators/17Immunization.cfm (accessed March 2009).

Children's Defense Fund (2004). *The state of America's children.* Washington, DC: Author.

Children's Trust Fund (2007). Family resource centers meet the needs of their communities. http://wctf.state.wi.us/home/FRC.htm (accessed March 2009).

Clark, R., Hyde, J. S., Essex, M. J., & Klein, M. H. (1997). Length of maternity leave and quality of mother–infant interactions. *Child Development, 68,* 364–383.

Denner, J., Cooper, C. R., Lopez, E. M., & Dunbar, N. (1999). Beyond "giving science away": How university-community partnerships inform youth programs, research, and policy. In *Social Policy Report* (Vol. *13,* No.1). Ann Arbor, MI: Society for Research in Child Development.

Department of Family and Child Ecology (2007). Interdepartmental graduate specialization in infancy & early childhood. www.fce.msu.edu/InfantStudyEndorsement/IGSISInformation.htm (accessed March 2009).

Division of Economic Assistance (n.d.). TANF – Temporary Assistance for Needy Families. www.mdhs.state.ms.us/ea_tanf.html (accessed March 2009).

Douglas-Hall, A., Chau, M., & Koball, H. (2006). Basic facts about low-income children: Birth to age 3. www.nccp.org/publications/pub_679.html (accessed March 2008).

Employment Standards Administration: Wage and Hour Division (2002). *Federal vs. California family and medical leave laws.* www.dol.gov/esa/whd/fmla/ (accessed March 2009).

Employment Standards Administration: Wage and Hour Division (2009). *Family and Medical Leave Act.* www.dol.gov/esa/whd/fmla/ (accessed March 2009).

Gomby, D. S., Culross, P. L., & Behrman, R. E. (1999). Home visiting: Recent program evaluations – analysis and recommendations. *Future of Children, 9,* 4–26.

Health Resources and Services Administration (2009). *EPSDT program background.* www.hrsa.gov/epsdt/overview.htm (accessed March 2009).

Heinig, M. J. (1998). Breastfeeding and the bottom line: Why are the cost savings of breastfeeding such a hard sell? *Journal of Human Lactation, 14,* 87–88.

Hyde, J. S., Essex, M. J., Clark, R., & Klein, M. H. (1996). Parental leave: Policy and research. *Journal of Social Issues, 52,* 91–109.

Illinois Department of Human Services, *Teen parent family services.* www.dhs.state.il.us (accessed March 2009).

Internal Revenue Service (2008). *Claiming the child and dependent care credit.* www.irs.gov/newsroom/article/0,,id=106189,00.html (accessed March 2009).

Kaiser Family Foundation (2007). *Issue Brief: An update on women's health policy. Medicaid's role for women.* www.kff.org/womenshealth/upload/7213_03.pdf (accessed March 2008).

Karoly, L. A., Greenwood, P. W., Everingham, S. M. S., Hoube, J., Kilburn, M. R., Rydell, C. P., et al. (1998). *Investing in our children: What we know and don't know about the costs and benefits of early childhood interventions* (Doc. No. MR-898-TCWF). Santa Monica, CA: RAND Corporation.

Kellogg Commission on the Future of State and Land-Grant Universities (1999). *Returning to our roots: The engaged institution.* Washington, DC: National Association of State Universities and Land-Grant Colleges.

Little, P. M. D. (1998, October). Family Resource Centers: Where school readiness happens. *Early Childhood Digest.* www.ed.gov/offices/OERI/ECI/digests/98october.htm.

Lowry, L. W., & Beikirch, P. (1998). Effect of comprehensive care on pregnancy outcomes. *Applied Nursing Research, 11*(2), 55–61.

March of Dimes (2007). Fact sheets: Teen pregnancy. *March of Dimes.* www.marchofdimes.com/professionals/14332_1159.asp (accessed March 2008).

Mathematica Policy Research, Inc. (2009). *Early Head Start research and evaluation.* www.mathematica-mpr.com/earlycare/ehstoc.asp (accessed March 2009).

Mathews, T. J., & MacDorman, M. F. (2006). Infant mortality statistics from 2003 period linked birth/infant death data set [Electronic version]. *National Vital Statistics Reports, 54*(5).

Mayes, L. C. (1995). Substance abuse and parenting. In M. H. Bornstein (Ed.), *Handbook of parenting: Vol.4. Applied and practical parenting* (pp. 101–125). Mahwah, NJ: Erlbaum.

Michigan Department of Community Health (2008). *Community collaboratives.* www.michigan.gov/mdch/0,1607,7–132–2941_4868_7145–14660–,00.html (accessed March 2009).

Michigan Department of Education (2009). *Great parents, great start.* www.michigan.gov/mde/0,1607,7–140–73477–,00.html (accessed March 2009).

Morrow, A. L., Guerrero, M. L., Shults, J., Calva, J. J., Lutter, C., Bravo, J., et al. (1999). Efficacy of home-based peer counseling to promote exclusive breastfeeding: A randomised controlled trial. *Lancet, 353,* 1226–1231.

Moss, N. E., & Carver, K. (1998). The effect of WIC and Medicaid on infant mortality in the United States. *American Journal of Public Health, 1998,* 1354–1361.

National Center for Children in Poverty (2009). *Demographics of young, low-income children.* www.nccp.org/profiles/state_profile.php?state=US&id=8 (accessed March 2009).

National Center for Health Statistics (2007). Centers for Disease Control and Prevention [Electronic version]. *National Vital Statistics System 2004 Mortality Statistics.*

National Conference of State Legislatures (2009). *State children's health insurance program.* www.ncsl.org/programs/health/chiphome.htm (accessed March 2009).

NICHD Early Child Care Research Network (1996). Characteristics of infant child care: Factors contributing to positive caregiving. *Early Childhood Research Quarterly, 11,* 269–306.

NICHD Early Child Care Research Network (1998). Early child care and self-control, compliance, and problem behavior at twenty-four and thirty-six months. *Child Developments, 69,* 1145–1170.

NICHD Early Child Care Research Network (1999). Child outcomes when child care center classes meet recommended standards for quality. *American Journal of Public Health, 89,* 1072–1077.

Office of Disease Prevention and Health Promotion, US Department of Health and Human Services (2006). Figure 16–1. Progress quotient chart for focus area 16: Maternal, infant, and child health. www.healthypeople.gov/Data/midcourse/html/tables/pq/PQ-16.htm (accessed March 2009).

Olds, D. L. (2002). Prenatal and infancy home visiting by nurses: From randomized trials to community replication. *Prevention Science, 3,* 153–172.

Omar, M. A., Schiffman, R. F., & Bauer, P. (1998). Recipient and provider perspectives of barriers to rural prenatal care. *Journal of Community Health Nursing, 15,* 237–249.

Oser, C., & Cohen, J. (2003). *America's babies, The Zero to Three Policy Center's data book.* Washington, DC: Zero to Three Policy Center.

Policy Institute for Family Impact Seminars (2009). *Connecting policymakers and professionals to build research-based family policy.* http://familyimpactseminars.org/ (accessed March 2009).

Richardson, L. A., Selby-Harrington, M. L., Krowchuk, H. V., Cross, A. W., & Williams, D. (1994). Comprehensiveness of well child checkups for children receiving Medicaid: A pilot study. *Journal of Pediatric Health Care, 8,* 212–220.

Riportella-Muller, R., Selby-Harrington, M. L., Richardson, L. A., Donat, P. L. N., Luchok, K. J., & Quade, D. (1996). Barriers to the use of preventive health care services for children. *Public Health Reports, 111,* 72–77.

Rosack, J. (2001). Moms in drug abuse treatment have healthier children [Electronic version]. *Psychiatric News, 36*(19), 5.

Scholz, J. K. (2000). Not perfect, but still pretty good: The Earned Income Tax Credit and other policies to support low-income working families. In *Helping poor kids succeed: Welfare, tax, and early intervention policies* (Wisconsin Family Impact Seminars Briefing Report). Madison: University of Wisconsin, School of Human Ecology.

Smart Start (2009). Smart Start and the North Carolina Partnership for Children, Inc. www.smartstart-nc.org/ (accessed March 2009).

Stuart-Macadam, P., & Dettwyler, K. A. (Eds.) (1995). *Breastfeeding: Biocultural perspectives.* New York: Aldine de Gruyter.

Sweet, M., & Appelbaum, M. (2004). Is home visiting an effecting strategy? A meta-analytic review of home visiting programs for families with young children. *Child Development, 75,* 1435–1456.

Tableman, B. (Ed.) (1999). *Overcoming hunger in the United States* (Best Practice Briefs No. 8, 1998–99). East Lansing: Michigan State University, Outreach Partnerships.

UNICEF (2009). *The state of the world's children: Maternal and newborn health.* New York: UNICEF.

US Bureau of the Census (1996). *Statistical abstract of the United States, 1996* (116th ed.). Washington, DC: US Department of Commerce.

US Department of Agriculture (2009). *Nutrition.* www.csrees.usda.gov/nea/food/efnep/about. html (accessed March 2009).

US Department of Agriculture Food and Nutrition Service (2007). WIC participant and program characteristics 2006: Summary. www.fns.usda.gov/oane/menu/Published/WIC/FILES/PC2006Summary.pdf (accessed March 2008).

US Department of Agriculture Food and Nutrition Service (2008). *Supplemental Nutrition Assistance Program.* www.fns.usda.gov/FSP/ (accessed March 2009).

US Department of Health and Human Services (2000). *Healthy People 2010* (Conference Edition, 2 vols.). www.health.gov/healthypeople/.

US Department of Health and Human Services, National Clearinghouse on Child Abuse and Neglect Information (1995). *Child maltreatment: Reports from the states to the National Center on Child Abuse and Neglect* (No. HE 23.1018). Washington, DC: Author.

US Department of Health and Human Services, Public Health Service (1991). *Healthy People 2000: National health promotion and disease prevention objectives* (DHHS Publication No. PHS 91–50212). Washington, DC: US Government Printing Office.

Weinberg, M. K., & Tronick, E. Z. (1998). The impact of maternal psychiatric illness on infant development. *Journal of Clinical Psychiatry, 59*(2), 53–61.

Wilde, P., Cook, P., Gundersen, C., Nord, M., & Tiehen, L. (2000). *The decline in food stamp program participation in the 1990s.* Food assistance and nutrition research report No. FANRR7 [Electronic version]. USDA Economic Research Service.

Zaslow, M., Tout, K., Smith, S., & Moore, K. (1998). Implications of the 1996 welfare legislation for children: A research perspective. In H. G. Thomas (Ed.), *Social Policy Report* (Vol. *12*, No. 3). Ann Arbor, MI: Society for Research in Child Development.

Zigler, E. (1998). A place of value for applied and policy studies. *Child Development, 69*, 532–542.

Author Index

Aamo, T. O. 207
Aaron-Jones, N. 195
Aase, J. M. 73
Abbeduto, L. 319
Abel, E. 71, 75
Abels, M. 153
Aber, J. L. 119, 167, 172, 284, 289
Abrahám, H. 26
Abrams, M. 36
Abrams, R. M. 23
Acemoglu, D. 124
Achenbach, T. M. 200
Ackerman, J. P. 297
Acquarone, S. 294
Adair, L. S. 34
Adams, D. 196, 208
Adams, G. 206, 360, 390
Adams, J. M. 226
Adams, W. G. 69
Adamson, L. 262
Adelson, E. 294
Adrien, J. L. 263, 267
Ahlström, M. 94
Ahluwalia, I. B. 385
Ahn, R. R. 247
Ainsworth, M. D. S. 88, 281, 282
Airhart, S. D. 320
Aitkens, S. 101
Albers, A. B. 125

Albers, C. A. 234
Albright, M. 42, 49
Alexander, R. 179
Alexandra, H. 196–7, 200
Ali, M. 68, 69, 70, 71
Aligne, C. A. 39
Allen, D. B. 321
Allen, E. G. 315
Allen, H. 197
Allen, J. 263, 289
Allen, J. P. 172
Allen, L. 262
Allen, L. H. 40
Allen, M. 93
Alpern, L. 201
Alperstein, G. 63
Als, H. 95, 237, 262
Altham, P. M. 206
Amadeo, J. 361, 362, 363, 366
Amato, P. R. 127, 350
Amatruda, C. S. 226
Amaya-Jackson, L. 295
Ament, N. 320
Amin, S. B. 24
Amlie, R. N. 24
Ammerman, R. 168
Amsden, L. B. 121
Anders, T. 292
Andersen, E. 98

Andersen, M. J. 198
Anderson, C. B. 48
Anderson, J. W. 64
Anderson, K. 387
Andersson, B. E. 368
Andre, M. 22
Andresen, G. 48
Andrew, A. K. 100
Andrews, M. 43
Andrews, M. W. 196
Andrews, R. J. 316
Andrews, S. R. 353
Angelo, W. A. 74
Angelsen, N. K. 45
Angold, A. 120, 201
Ani, C. 121
Anido, A. 317
Annest, J. L. 76
Aoki, Y. 287
Apitz, J. 322
Appelbaum, M. I. 343, 353, 393
Appleby, L. 207
Appleton, K. M. 42
Appleyard, K. 284, 287, 291
Arbib, M. A. 88
Arenz, S. 44
Ariagno, R. L. 22
Arias, A. 179
Arimond, M. 46
Arlotti, J. P. 386
Armstrong, K. 167
Arndt, S. 258
Aronson, S. R. 366
Arrazola, O. 158
Artal, R. 66
Aseltine, R. H. 206
Ashworth, A. 40, 147
Assel, M. A. 47
Assunção, A. M. 147
Astley, S. 74
Asten, P. 197
Atkinson, L. 194
Atkinson, M. K. 182
Atlemeier, W. 167
Attermeier, S. M. 237
Auinger, P. 39
Austin, M. P. 209
Avery, L. S. 182
Aviezer, O. 365
Aylward, G. P. 227–8, 230, 234, 238–9

Bachorowski, J. 194, 199
Baddeley, A. 312, 323
Baer, J. 172
Baghurst, P. 45
Bagnato, S. J. 247
Bailey, A. 260
Bailey, D. B. 317, 318–20
Baird, G. 263
Baird, L. 91
Baird, S. 236
Baker, L. 285
Baker-Henningham, H. 158
Baker-Ward, L. 342, 369
Bakermans-Kraneburg, M. 182, 341, 344, 350, 351
Bakker, M. K. 17
Bakketeig, L. S. 45
Bakshi, S. 287
Baldwin, V. 100
Balla, D. A. 235
Bamford, J. 90
Banks, J. 116
Bankston, C. 128
Bar-Hamburger, R. 16
Baranek, G. T. 263, 266, 269–70, 318
Barber, A. 269
Barber, N. 126
Barglow, P. 365
Barker, D. J. 18
Barker, L. 43
Barlow, D. H. 298
Barnard, K. E. 250, 350
Barnes, R. H. 36
Barnett, B. 194, 197
Barnett, D. 167, 172, 178
Barnett, W. S. 129
Baron-Cohen, S. 263, 265, 268, 273
Barraza, V. 196
Barrett, L. R. 67
Barrett-Boyes, B. G. 322
Barron, R. M. 124
Barros, F. C. 45
Bartels, M. 196
Barth, R. 166, 169
Barton, M. L. 265
Basinger, D. L. 316
Bassoff, T. 196
Bassuk, E. L. 123
Bateman, D. 16
Bates, E. 93, 264

Bates, J. 173, 178–9, 291, 292
Baudin, J. 78
Bauer, P. J. 14, 16, 383
Baughcum, A. E. 48
Baum, C. L. 369
Bauman, M. 264
Baumrind, D. 46, 47, 49, 363, 371
Baxter, A. 316
Baydar, N. 366, 368–9
Bayley, N. 228, 231–4, 240, 246
Bean, L. H. 315
Beard, J. L. 36, 39
Beardshaw, T. 157
Beasley, M. 151
Beauchamp, G. K. 27
Beck, T. 313
Beckwith, L. 172, 240
Bedford, H. 68
Beebe, B. 48, 193, 316
Beeghly, M. 193
Behnke, M. 16
Behrman, J. R. 49, 158
Behrman, R. E. 393
Beikirch, P. 382
Bekman, S. 158
Bekx, M. T. 321
Belden, A. C. 282
Belfield, C. R. 129
Belinchón, M. 260
Belizán, J. 147
Bell, M. 167
Bell, T. 50
Bellinger, D. 72, 79
Bellugi, U. 315, 322
Belsky, J. 36, 166–9, 172, 178, 204, 238,
    241, 365, 366–7, 369
Ben-Shlomo, Y. 196
Benasich, A. A. 348
Bendersky, M. 240
Bennett, S. 193
Benoit, D. 292, 297–8
Bentley, M. E. 40
Berg, A. T. 169
Berger, J. 315
Bergmann, R. 44
Berkman, D. S. 34
Berle, J. O. 207
Berlin, I. 62
Berlin, L. 120, 125, 126, 178, 295
Berliner, L. 181

Berman, W. 341
Bernabei, P. 263
Bernier, R. 272
Bernstein, L. S. 345
Berry, C. 36
Berry, P. 316
Berseth, C. L. 226
Berthoud, I. 323
Bertrand, J. 322
Bettes, B. A. 194
Beuren, A. J. 322
Bhutta, Z. A. 50
Bianco, L. E. 36
Bierer, L. 173
Bigelow, A. 96, 99
Bigelow, K. 182
Bigsby, R. 237
Bilheimer, L. 50
Bingham, G. 349
Birch, E. E. 41–2
Birch, H. G. 63, 76
Birch, L. L. 46, 47, 48, 49
Birkimer, J. C. 284
Biterman, D. 115, 125
Bithoney, W. G. 42
Bjornstad, P. G. 322
Black, B. 63
Black, G. W. 348
Black, J. E. 25, 177
Black, M. 176, 232
Black, M. M. 34, 36, 39–41, 43, 45–7,
    49–50, 143, 148, 155, 158–9, 192
Black, R. E. 39, 147, 148
Blackburn, B. L. 314
Blackford, J. 320
Blair, P. S. 76
Blamey, P. J. 93
Blanden, J. 123
Blehar, M. C. 88, 281
Bleiberg, E. 284
Bleichrodt, N. 38
Blessing, J. S. 194
Bliss, S. L. 235
Block, M. E. 317
Bloom, D. 315
Bloom, P. 264
Blössner, M. 147
Blundell, R. 116
Boath, L. 209
Bogin, B. 13

Boivin, M. 66, 150
Bond, A. 194
Bond, J. T. 352
Boney-McGoy, S. 178
Bonvillian, J. D. 93
Booth, C. L. 250, 350, 366
Bor, W. 198
Borders, A. E. B. 121
Borge, A. 368
Boris, N. 172, 285, 290
Börjeson, M. 115, 125
Borkowski, J. G. 125
Bornstein, M. 141, 143, 153, 241, 340, 363
Bosma, J. F. 45
Bosquet, M. 42, 49
Boucher, J. 272
Boukydis, C. F. Z. 237
Bounds, W. 46
Bowlby, J. 167, 365
Bowman, T. G. 316
Boyce, P. M. 192
Boyer, E. L. 380
Boyle, D. E. 365
Boyle, M. 126
Bradbury, B. 115, 116, 118
Bradford, W. H. 67, 68
Bradley, E. 209
Bradley, R. H. 123, 128, 143, 154, 350
Bradley-Johnson, S. 235
Brady, N. 319
Brady-Smith, C. 125
Bramble, D. 312
Brambring, M. 95–6, 99
Branden-Muller, L. R. 248
Brandolini, A. 118
Brannan, C. I. 320
Brannmark, J. G. 207
Braunwald, K. 167, 173
Braverman, M. 261
Brayden, R. 167, 171, 182
Brazelton, B. 95, 262
Brazelton, T. 172, 193, 237, 241, 282, 294
Brazy, J. E. 238
Breilid, H. 207
Breinbauer, C. 204
Breitmayer, J. 343
Brennan, L. C. 263
Brennan, P. 42, 198, 200, 203
Brenner, R. A. 79

Brent, R. L. 72
Breznitz, Z. 194
Brian, J. 260
Brice, A. 40
Bricker, D. 229, 244
Bridges, D. 269
Briers, S. 206
Brigance, A. H. 231
Briggs-Gowan, M. J. 240, 247–8
Britton, H. L. 45
Britton, J. R. 45
Brizot, M. 310
Broadhurst, D. 176
Broberg, A. G. 368
Brock, J. 272, 322
Brodei, F. H. 99
Brody, G. H. 125
Bronfenbrenner, U. 36, 124, 143, 166, 341, 347, 359, 361–2, 380
Brooks, L. 93
Brooks, M. G. 123
Brooks-Gunn, J. 115, 117–21, 123–30, 348, 351, 354, 366, 368–9, 370
Brown, C. 272
Brown, C. H. 148
Brown, E. 262
Brown, G. 205
Brown, I. 309, 310
Brown, J. 176
Brown, J. H. 323
Brown, K. 289
Brown, S. F. 88
Browne, D. C. 284
Browne, J. V. 237, 238
Brownell, C. A. 194, 282
Browning, C. 117
Bruce, D. 178
Bruneforth, M. 153
Bruner, J. S. 262
Brunet, A. 19
Bruschweiler-Stern, N. 294
Brust, J. C. 16
Bryan, A. A. 316
Bryant, D. M. 341, 348–9, 352, 362, 365
Bryson, S. E. 258, 260
Bub, K. L. 369
Buchel, F. 124
Buckner, J. C. 123
Budd, K. S. 46, 292

Buder, E. H. 316
Budetti, P. 36
Buescher, P. A. 50
Bugental, D. B. 196
Bulf, H. 262
Bulkow, L. R. 67
Bums, S. 370
Bunn, J. 210
Burack, J. A. 309–10
Burchinal, M. 126, 128–9, 342, 362, 365, 366, 369
Buriel, R. 371
Burke, R. 202
Burke-Albers, A. 197
Bus, A. G. 368
Buss, K. 287
Butcher, J. 194
Butler, M. 179
Butler, M. G. 320, 321
Butler, P. 36
Butte, N. F. 44
Butterworth, G. 262
Butz, A. M. 71
Byck, G. R. 118

Cabral de Mello, M. 198
Cadzow, S. 167, 171, 178
Caffey, J. 76
Cagney, K. A. 117
Cahill, K. 284
Cahill, N. 284
Caldas, S. J. 128
Calderón, J. 149
Calkins, S. D. 241, 282
Caltegirone, C. 312
Camaioni, L. 263, 264
Campbell, D. T. 348
Campbell, F. A. 129–30, 342–3, 351, 369–70
Campbell, J. 97, 98
Campbell, S. B. 193, 194, 208, 365
Canfield, M. A. 315
Cannari, L. 118
Canterford, L. 121
Capizzano, J. 390
Caplan, H. L. 196–7, 200
Cardy, D. L. 310
Carey, W. B. 282
Carlesimo, A. 312
Carlin, J. B. 121

Carlson, E. A. 282, 297
Carlson, S. E. 41
Carlson, S. J. 43
Carlson, V. 167, 173
Carlson, W. 172–3
Carothers, S. S. 125
Carrel, A. L. 321
Carruth, B. 46
Carter, A. S. 240, 247–8, 283
Carter, J. A. 150
Carver, K. 385
Caselli, M. C. 316
Casey, B. J. 25
Casey, P. 43
Caspi, A. 284, 313
Cassia, V. M. 262
Cassidy, J. 125, 282
Cassidy, S. B. 312, 320, 321
Castillo-Duran, C. 40
Castoldi, A. F. 17
Caulfield, L. E. 36, 47, 49, 386
Ceci, S. J. 36
Cesaroni, L. 270
Chaffin, M. 169, 176
Chakrabarti, S. 257, 258
Chamberlain, S. J. 320
Chamberlin, R. 346
Chan, S. Q. 371
Chandler, N. 76
Chaney, L. 315
Chang, S. M. 34, 148, 158
Chang-Lopez, S. M. 148
Chapman, R. S. 316
Charier, L. 74
Charman, T. 263, 268
Charney, D. S. 206
Chase-Lansdale, P. L. 127, 284, 367
Chasin, J. 93
Chatoor, I. 293
Chau, M. 389
Checkley, W. 34
Chen, A. 73
Chen, C. J. 149
Chen, C. M. 149
Chen, D. 101, 102
Chen, W. 41
Chernoff, R. 183
Childs, S. 370
Chilman, C. S. 345

Chin-Quee, D. S. 368
Chiriboga, C. A. 16
Cho, E. 196, 202
Choate, M. L. 298
Chou, H. Y. 149
Choudhury, N. 147
Christoffel, K. 168
Christopher, K. 125
Chu, S. Y. 80
Chun, B. 168
Chute, P. M. 91
Ciampi, A. 19
Cicchetti, D. 166–7, 169, 172, 178, 200,
    202, 208, 235, 244, 281, 285, 296–7
Cigales, M. 208
Clancy, H. 263, 267
Clandinin, M. T. 41
Clark, B. S. 258
Clark, J. 72
Clark, K. E. 15
Clark, M. 71, 73
Clark, R. 207, 249–50, 393
Clarke-Stewart, K. A. 362, 365, 366, 369
Clarren, S. 74
Clasky, S. 208
Claussen, A. H. 39, 119
Clayton, S. L. 345
Clazada, A. J. 296
Cleary, J. 262
Clibbens, J. 93
Clifford, S. 263, 267
Cochran, M. 284, 341
Cocking, R. R. 363
Coder, J. 116
Cogill, S. R. 196–7, 200
Cogswell, M. E. 121
Cohen, D. J. 258
Cohen, I. 258, 319
Cohen, J. 284, 381
Cohen, N. 94
Cohen, N. J. 294
Cohen, P. 176
Cohen, P. J. 196
Cohen, S. 240
Cohn, J. F. 193–4, 208, 241, 365
Cole, N. 121
Cole, P. M. 282
Coley, R. L. 127, 284, 367
Colgan, S. E. 266

Coll, C. G. 123, 128
Collacott, R. A. 316
Collins, K. S. 36
Collins, W. A. 282, 297, 340
Colten, M. E. 206
Coltheart, M. 312
Colville, W. R. 385
Combs-Orme, T. 183
Compton, S. N. 120
Concato, J. 45
Conger, K. J. 127
Conger, R. D. 124, 125, 127
Connell, D. 193
Connell-Carrick, K. 165–9, 171–2, 175–6,
    177, 178–9, 181, 182–3
Conti-Ramsden, G. 98, 99
Coohey, C. 167, 169, 171, 176, 182
Cook, C. A. 240, 287
Cook, D. G. 44
Cook, J. T. 43, 121
Cook, P. 193, 197, 202, 387
Coolbear, J. 194
Cooper, C. R. 396
Cooper, G. 296, 297
Cooper, P. J. 150, 158, 194, 203, 207, 209,
    210
Cooper, S. A. 316
Cooper, T. R. 226, 240
Coplan, J. D. 196
Copper, P. J. 90
Corasaniti, M. 369
Corbett, S. S. 43
Corina, D. P. 262
Cornish, A. M. 197
Cornish, K. 312, 319
Corral, M. 207
Corse, S. 168, 284
Corvalan, C. 34
Corwyn, R. F. 123, 128, 154
Costanzo, P. 46, 49
Costello, E. J. 120, 122, 125
Cote, S. M. 368, 369
Cottrell, B. H. 386
Coulehan, C. M. 365
Courchesne, E. 272
Cowan, P. A. 340
Cowen, C. P. 340
Cox, A. 263
Cox, A. D. 195

Cox, E. O. 89
Cox, J. L. 201
Cox, M. 363, 365
Cox, M. J. 126, 128
Coy, K. C. 208
Cozolino, L. 282
Crais, E. R. 263, 266
Cravioto, J. 70
Crawford, D. 129
Crawford, J. D. 320
Crawford, S. 183
Crawley, H. 207
Creasy, R. K. 65
Creed, F. 155
Creedy, D. 209
Crepin, G. 23
Crichton, J. A. 267
Crittenden, P. 167–8, 172, 176, 178
Crockenberg, S. 284, 291, 366
Cross, A. W. 394
Crown, C. L. 193, 316
Crozier, J. 178
Cueto, S. 158
Cuijpers, P. 207
Culhane, J. F. 147
Culross, P. L. 393
Cummings, P. 167
Cunningham, A. 285
Cunningham, C. C. 315
Cunningham, F. G. 27
Cunningham, M. 89
Currie, J. M. 117, 118, 120, 130
Curtin, J. J. 386
Cusack, T. 71

Dabholkar, A. S. 12, 23
Daelman, M. 101
Daelmans, B. 198
Dahlgren, S. O. 265, 267, 268, 270
Dakroub, H. 179
Dalaker, J. 119
Dale, G. 174
D'Alessio, G. 118
D'Allest, A. M. 22
Daly, K. 283
Dalzell, L. E. 24
Dang, T. T. 129
Daniels, J. L. 17
Dant, C. C. 317, 320

Darling, N. 43, 47
Davalos, M. 195
Davenport, B. R. 173
David, O. 72
Davidson, K. K. 48
Davidson, M. C. 25
Davidson, R. J. 205
Davies, M. 322, 323
Davies, W. H. 293
Davis, A. 90
Davis, J. M. 74
Davis, M. G. 315
Davis, R. 315
Davis, S. F. 68
Dawson, G. 195, 201, 205, 257–9, 262–3, 265–7, 269–70, 272
Dawson, P. 282
Day, A. 194
Day, R. D. 350
Dearing, E. 122, 128, 369
DeBoer, T. 14
DeCarlo, R. 258
DeCasper, A. J. 26–7
Decavalas, G. O. 16
de Chateau, P. 263, 265, 269
De Cock, K. M. 150
De Cock, P. 324
DeGangi, G. A. 204, 247
De Giacomo, A. 259, 265
de Haan, M. 177
de Jong van den Berg, L. T. 17
Delaney, D. 320
Delange, F. 38
De Licardie, E. R. 70
de Lonlay, P. 77
Del Valle, C. 208
Demark, J. L. 312
Demsey, S. A. 314
Denham, S. A. 282, 289
Denham, S. S. 240
Denner, J. 396
Dennis, C. L. 207, 209
Dennis, T. A. 282
de Oca-Luna, R. 323
De Onis, M. 35, 44, 147
deRegnier, R-A. 24, 26–7
Descheemaeker, M-J. 322
de Schipper, J. C. 362
Desjardins, J. L. 312

Desmond, M. M. 16
DeSouza, N. 210
Dettwyler, K. A. 385
Devaney, B. 50
Devisé, I. 97
de Walle, H. E. 17
Dewey, K. G. 44
Diaz, J. 158
DiBlasio, F. 176
Dick, J. 71
Dicker, S. 183, 285
Dickinson, H. 262
Diego, M. A. 19, 195, 205
Dierssen, M. 12
Dietrich, K. N. 72, 73
Dietrich, M. 167
Dijkstra, J. 368
DiLavore, P. 257
Dilts, C. 314
Dimitropoulos, A. 320, 321
D'Imperio, R. 172
Dinno, N. 263
Dionne, G. 66
Dirrigl, K. J. 323
DiScala, C. 167, 169
Dishion, T. J. 244
Dixon, J. 181
Dixon, P. 258
Dobbing, J. 36
Doctor, R. 182
Dodge, K. A. 122, 173, 178, 292
Doherty, G. 363
Dombro, A. L. 236–7
Donat, P. L. N. 383
Donn, S. M. 16
Donnell, F. 365
Dooley, M. 126
Dorval, R. 342, 369
Douglas-Hall, A. 389
Doussard-Roosevelt, J. 204
Dow, A. 150
Dowrick, P. W. 263
Dowsett, C. J. 363
Dozier, M. 296, 297
Dramaix, M. 38
Drapeau, P. 12
Drew, A. 263
Drewett, F. R. 43, 76
Driskell, J. A. 40

Driver, J. 319
Droegemueller, W. 76, 165
Drotar, D. 42
Dubner, A. 181
Dubowitz, H. 43, 172, 174, 176
Ducournau, P. 194, 202
Dufort, V. 284
Duggan, A. 353
Duhamel, L. 24
Dunbar, N. 396
Duncan, G. J. 115, 117–21, 122, 123, 127
Dunifon, R. 127
Dunkelberg, E. 150, 152
Dunkle, M. 227
Dunlea, A. 100
Dunn, L. 362
Dunphy-Lelii, S. 262
Dunst, C. J. 286
Durkin, M. S. 310
Dykens, E. M. 309, 312–13, 320–4
Dykstra, J. 263

Earley, C. J. 36
Earls, M. 227
East, P. L. 285
Eaton, M. A. 66
Eckenrode, J. 167, 169, 346
Edwald, G. 173
Edwards, S. 158
Egeland, B. 42, 48–9, 126, 167, 172, 174,
   176–8, 282, 284, 291, 297, 365, 366
Eggermont, J. J. 23
Ehrle, J. 360
Eilander, A. 41
Einfeld, S. L. 322
Ek, U. 94–5
Ekman, P. 205
El-Bastawissi, A. Y. 50
El Amin, A. 67
Elder, G. H. 124, 125, 127
Elias, M. J. 248
Elliman, D. 68
Elliott, D. 181
Ellis, K. J. 44
Ellwood, D. 119
Emde, R. 204, 282, 289
Emmett, P. M. 76
Emond, A. M. 76
England, P. 125

Engle, P. L. 142–3, 145, 151–2, 154–5, 157, 158–9, 192, 343
English, D. J. 172
English, K. 125
Ensminger, M. E. 119
Epstein, R. 292
Erickson, M. 174, 176, 177, 178, 182
Erikkson, A. 263, 265, 269
Erkam, U. 91
Erting, C. 92
Eshel, N. 198
Eshel, R. 13
Essex, M. J. 196, 201–2, 249, 393
Estes, N. 75
Evans, D. 315
Evans, D. W. 269
Evans, G. W. 125, 128
Evans, J. 210, 316
Evans, R. 92
Ewart, A. K. 322
Eyberg, S. M. 296, 298

Fabretti, D. 316
Fagen, J. W. 199, 315
Fahn, S. 269
Faiella, I. 118
Faith, M. 47, 48
Famularo, R. 169, 178
Fantuzzo, J. W. 370
Fantz, R. L. 315
Faragher, B. 207
Farley, A. H. 267
Farzin, F. 312
Fattal-Valevski, A. 13
Faver, C. 183
Fawzi, W. W. 67, 148
Fein, D. 258, 261, 263, 265
Feinstein, L. 363
Feldman, M. A. 312
Feldman, R. 46, 288
Feldstein, S. 193, 316
Felice, M. E. 285
Fels, S. 316
Fenichel, E. 286, 349
Fenton, T. 169, 178
Ferber, R. 282
Fergusson, D. M. 45, 123–4, 182
Fernald, A. 194
Fernald, L. 147

Fernando, S. D. 150
Fernell, E. 95
Festen, D. A. M. 321
Feurer, I. D. 321
Fidler, D. 312–13, 315–17, 322, 323–4
Field, T. 20, 193, 195–6, 199, 204, 208, 368
Fiese, B. H. 281
Fifer, W. P. 26, 27
Findling, R. L. 209
Finelli, J. 264
Finger, I. 315
Finkelhor, D. 178, 181
Finnegan, L. P. 16
Finucane, B. 323, 324
Fiori-Cowley, A. 192–4, 197, 198, 204
Fischer, T. K. 71
Fish, M. 365
Fisher, J. O. 46, 48
Fitzgerald, H. E. 350
Flanagan, K. D. 363
Fleckenstein, L. K. 199
Fliedner, D. 227
Flores, R. 49
Fogel, A. 88
Folven, R. J. 93
Fombonne, E. 257, 258–9, 265
Forman, D. R. 204, 208
Forrest, D. 178
Forshaw, M. 90
Forster, M. F. 129
Fosarelli, P. 71
Fosdahl, M. A. 67
Foster, G. 143, 150, 151
Fothergill, K. E. 119
Fountoulakis, M. 12
Fox, M. K. 121
Fox, N. A. 195, 282, 313
Fraiberg, S. 95, 97, 294
Francis, L. A. 47, 49
Frank, D. A. 79–80
Frazier, J. 167
Fredericks, H. 100
Fredriksen, P. M. 67
Freeman, S. 315, 316
Freeman, V. 121
Freinkel, N. 64
Freisthler, B. 168
French, D. C. 244

Freund, L. 318
Frey, K. 195
Frick, J. R. 124
Fricke, D. 47
Friedman, B. 126
Friedman, S. 64, 196
Friedman, S. L. 359–66, 370, 372
Friedrich, R. 181
Friel, J. K. 40
Friesen, W. V. 205
Frith, U. 272
Frodi, A. 167
Frongillo, E. A. 154
Fryns, J. P. 322, 324
Fuligni, A. S. 120
Furrer, C. 284
Furstenberg, F. J. 125

Gabbe, S. G. 65
Gaensbauer, T. J. 294
Gaffan, E. A. 194
Galinsky, E. 369
Gallagher, A. C. 249
Galler, J. R. 67
Ganiban, J. 178, 293
Gannon-Rowley, T. 129
Gao, Q. 126
Gara, M. A. 248
Garber, M. 270
Garcia, R. 193
Garcia Coll, C. T. 128
Gardella, C. 72
Gardner, D. M. 342
Garrett, M. E. 13
Garrett-Mayer, E. 258, 264, 266
Gath, D. H. 194
Gaudin, J. M. 172, 176, 182
Gauthier, Y. 126
Gayley, C. 324
Gaylor, E. 292
Geers, A. 93
Gelfand, D. M. 202, 204
Gelles, R. 167, 168
Gellin, B. G. 67
Gemmill, A. W. 197
Gennettian, L. A. 129, 363
Gentile, L. 125
Gentile, S. 17
Geoffroy, M. C. 368

George, T. P. 202
Georgieff, M. K. 13, 14, 24, 26, 64–6
Gerhardt, K. J. 23
Gerlach-Downie, S. G. 345
Gernay, J. 158
Gershater-Molko, R. 182
Gesell, A. 226
Gessner, B. 169, 178
Geva, R. 13
Ghaziuddin, M. 316
Ghodsian, M. 200
Ghuman, S. 158
Gianino, A. F. 204
Gibson, R. A. 41
Gil, D. 167
Gilbreth, J. G. 127
Gillberg, C. 95, 263, 265, 267–8, 270
Gilliam, M. 291
Gilliam, W. S. 228, 236, 354
Gillman, M. W. 44
Gilman, R. H. 34
Gilmore, R. 323
Gilson, R. A. 45
Giovannelli, J. 291
Gjerde, P. F. 206
Glascoe, F. P. 228, 229, 231
Glassman, M. 126
Gleitman, L. 97
Glover, A. 315
Glover, V. 196, 208
Gnat, D. 38
Goddard, H. H. 74
Goddijn, M. 10
Godfrey, K. M. 66
Goelman, H. 363
Goerge, R. 176
Goetghebuer, T. 67
Goldberg, S. 298
Goldenberg, R. L. 147
Goldin-Meadow, S. 96
Golding, J. 196
Goldring, S. 269
Goldsmith, D. F. 295
Goldstein, S. 193, 204
Gomby, D. S. 393
Gomolin, R. H. 94
Gonnella, C. 125
Gonnella, J. S. 62–3
Gonzalez, L. 208

Goodenough, F. L. 291
Goodlin-Jones, B. 292
Goodman, J. H. 209
Goodnight, J. A. 292
Goodson, B. D. 345, 346, 353
Goodson, S. 258, 269
Goodyer, I. 196, 206
Gorden, M. 42
Gordon, E. 183, 285
Gore, S. 206
Gorman, J. M. 196
Gorman, K. S. 147, 148
Gorman, L. L. 208
Gotlib, I. H. 204
Govers, V. 322
Gowen, J. 177
Graham, J. M. 317
Graham, P. J. 200
Grandin, T. 270
Grandjean, P. 17
Grant, H. 182
Grant, J. 323
Grantham-McGregor, S. M. 34, 38, 40, 67,
    79–80, 121, 144–5, 147–8, 154, 157,
    158, 351
Gray, F. L. 315
Graziani, L. 24
Green, A. 167
Green, B. L. 284
Green, G. 263, 265, 267, 269
Green, J. A. 265
Green, M. F. 17
Greenberg, F. 323, 324
Greenberg, M. T. 295
Greenough, W. T. 25, 177
Greenspan, S. 204, 234, 236, 244, 246,
    282–3, 285, 286, 309
Gregg, P. 123
Gregson, S. 151
Grieve, A. J. 234
Griffin, A. 349
Griffin, P. 370
Grisham, K. 75
Grobman, W. A. 121
Gronwaldt, V. 45
Grotevant, H. 179
Grummer-Strawn, L. 43, 44, 385
Grunewald, R. 130, 370
Grunfeld, E. 62

Guérini, C. 88
Guerra, A. 121
Guger, S. 194
Guillet, R. 24
Gultiano, S. 158
Gundersen, C. 387
Gunn, P. 316
Gunnar, M. 285, 287
Gunter, E. W. 121
Guo, G. 126
Guralnick, M. J. 349
Gurwitz, A. 77
Gussow, J. D. 63, 76
Guthertz, M. 204
Guthrie, C. A. 48
Guy, L. 193
Guzzetta, V. 323

Hack, M. 226, 239, 240
Hacker, B. 237
Hagerman, R. J. 317–18, 319, 320
Halbreich, U. 210
Halle, T. 363
Halligan, S. L. 196, 203, 206
Halpern, C. T. 208
Halpern, J. 38
Halterman, J. S. 39
Halverson, H. M. 226
Hamadani, J. D. 40, 154, 158
Hamilton, B. 169, 262
Hammen, C. 42, 198, 203
Hammond, M. A. 250
Han, W. J. 127, 369
Haney, M. 101, 102
Hannigan, B. 71, 75
Hansen, S. 321
Hanusa, B. H. 209
Happé, F. 272
Har, S. 208
Harder, T. 44
Hardy, P. 121
Hardy, R. 45
Harel, S. 13, 16
Harkavy, O. 352
Harlan, E. T. 204
Harmer, C. J. 196
Harmjanz, D. 322
Harmon, R. J. 289
Harold, G. T. 201

Harper, J. 258
Harrington, D. 176
Harrington, R. 210
Harris, J. R. 340
Harris, K. M. 126
Harris, M. 92–3
Harris, P. 73
Harris, S. R. 317
Harris, T. 205, 206
Harrison, A. O. 371
Harrison, J. 293
Harrison, P. 173
Harrison, P. L. 234
Hart, S. 40
Harter, K. S. M. 126
Haschke, F. 121
Hashimi, S. 75
Hatton, D. D. 317, 318–20
Hauser, W. A. 16
Hawkins, E. 298
Hay, D. F. 197, 201, 203
Hay, T. 169
Haydon, P. G. 12
Hayes, A. 320
Hayes, C. D. 368
Healy, B. 204
Heavey, L. 260
Hebbeler, K. M. 345
Heckman, J. 115, 124, 126, 129–30, 370
Heclo, H. 118
Heffelfinger, A. K. 289
Heimann, M. 315
Heinecke, C. M. 350
Heinig, M. J. 44, 385
Heisler, A. 183
Heister, M. 365, 366
Heller, S. 172, 285, 286–7
Henderson, H. A. 313
Henderson, C. R. 346
Hendrick, V. 283
Henrich, C. 285
Henriques, J. B. 205
Henshaw, C. 209
Hepburn, S. 312–13, 315–18, 320, 323–4
Hepper, P. G. 23
Herbert, J. 196, 206
Hernandez, D. 119, 127
Hernandez-Reif, M. 195
Heron, J. 196, 210

Herrera, C. 241
Herrera, M. G. 67
Herrera, V. 179
Herschell, A. D. 296
Hertz-Picciotto, I. 208
Hertzman, C. 129, 152, 158
Hessl, D. 195, 196, 312
Hessler, M. 289
Hetherington, E. M. 340
Hetherington, J. 73
Hevner, R. F. 26
Hewes, A. K. 312, 323
Hiatt, S. 352
Hill, J. 205
Hilpert, P. L. 24
Hipwell, A. 197, 198, 202, 206
Hiraiwa, R. 321
Hirsch, R. 293
Hittelman, J. 74
Hobcroft, J. 115
Hobson, R. P. 263
Hod, M. 64
Hodapp, R. M. 309, 312, 315, 322
Hoddicott, J. 49
Hodges, V. 172
Hodgkinson, A. 208
Hodnett, E. 207
Hofer, S. M. 49
Hoffbrand, S. 207, 209
Hoffman, D. R. 41–2
Hoffman, K. 296, 297
Hoffman, R. A. 94
Hoffmann, N. 173
Hogan, V. K. 385
Hohman, M. 176
Holden, J. J. A. 312
Holditch-Davis, D. 63
Holl, J. L. 121
Hollenberg, J. 169
Hollins, K. 18
Holm, I. 67
Holm, V. A. 320
Holman, K. C. 258
Holt, L. E. 67
Hong, K. Z. 117, 120
Honig, A. S. 39
Hood, N. 291
Hooper, R. 90, 192–4, 197, 209
Hopkins, J. 208

Hopkins, R. 71
Hopkinson, J. M. 44
Horbar, J. D. 226
Horn, I. 324
Horowitz, J. A. 208
Horta, B. L. 45
Horwood, J. 182
Horwood, L. J. 45
Hoshino, Y. 258
Hossain, Z. 208
Howard, L. 207, 209
Howes, C. 362, 369
Howlin, P. 258, 322, 323
Hu, H. 71, 72
Huang, C. C. 126
Huang, L. 314
Hubbs-Tait, L. 365
Huda, S. N. 38, 154, 158
Hudenko, W. J. 194
Hughes, S. 46–7, 48
Humber, K. 174
Hundscheid, D. C. 41
Hung, S. S. 117
Hungerford, A. 194, 363
Hunt, F. M. 247
Hunter, B. 129
Huntley, M. 233, 236
Hurley, A. D. 316
Hurley, K. M. 36, 43, 45, 46, 47, 49
Hurtado, E. K. 39, 119, 121
Huston, A. C. 363, 366
Hutt, C. 270
Hutt, S. J. 170
Huttenlocher, P. R. 12, 23
Huttunen, M. 20
Hwang, C. P. 360, 368
Hyde, J. S. 249, 393
Hykin, J. 25
Hymbaugh, K. J. 73

Iannotti, L. L. 39
Iceland, J. 116, 117
Ikramullah, E. 387
Imes, A. E. 363
Incesulu, A. 91
Ippen, C. G. 294, 297
Iqbal, Z. 210
Ireton, H. 229
Irwin, L. B. 152

Isabella, R. A. 204
Iverson, J. 96, 97, 316

Jackson, A. P. 126
Jackson, R. 372
Jacobsen, G. 45
Jacobson, J. W. 310
Jacobson, L. 95
Jacobvitz, D. 297
Jafari, H. S. 69
Jaffe, J. 193, 204
Jager, E. 365
Jagnow, C. P. 27
Jain, A. 45
Jameson, P. B. 204
Jamieson, J. R. 92
Janoff, E. 71
Janssen, M. 101
Jäntti, M. 118
Jarrold, C. 312, 315, 323
Jasnow, M. D. 193, 316
Jenkins, S. P. 115
Jewkes, A. M. 237
Jiang, H. 196
Johnson, C. P. 273
Johnson, D. E. 66
Johnson, J. 176
Johnson, L. 169
Johnson, M. H. 323
Johnson, S. 236
Johnson, S. L. 48, 49
Johnson-Martin, N. M. 237
Johnston, F. 67, 70, 76
Jones, A. 66
Jones, B. C. 36
Jones, K. L. 74
Jones, L. 169, 176
Jones, N. A. 195
Jones, S. 284
Jones, S. M. 248
Jones, W. 322
Joorman, J. 204
Joseph, B. 320
Joshi, H. E. 123, 129, 369
Juffer, F. 182, 341, 344

Kaczorowski, J. M. 39
Kaffman, A. 196
Kagan, J. 313

Kagitcibasi, C. 158
Kahn, A. J. 115
Kain, J. 34
Kaiser, L. 40
Kalin, N. H. 196
Kallischnigg, G. 44
Kaltenbach, K. 16
Kamerman, S. B. 115, 116, 117, 126, 129
Kaminer, R. 167, 169
Kaneko, M. 258
Kanner, L. 259, 262–3, 267, 269–71
Kanoy, K. W. 126
Kaplan, P. S. 194, 199
Kaplow, J. 178, 288
Karam, S. 320
Kariger, P. 154
Karkun, S. 210
Karlsson, J-O. 103
Karmiloff-Smith, A. 313, 319, 322–3
Karoly, L. A. 393
Karp, H. 79
Karp, M. 64
Karp, R. J. 73–6, 79–80
Karrer, J. H. 315
Karrer, R. 315
Kasari, C. 316
Kashinath, K. 158
Kattner, E. 239
Katz, R. 200
Kau, A. D. M. 318, 319
Kaufman, J. 167, 285
Kaushal, N. 126
Keane, S. P. 282
Keeler, G. 120
Keenan, B. S. 320
Keenan, K. 290
Keith, J. 387
Kekelis, L. 98
Kelleher, K. 169
Keller, H. 100, 153, 158
Kelly, J. F. 250
Kempe, C. H. 76, 165
Kempton, C. 90, 194
Kendall, J. 174
Kendall-Tackett, K. 181
Kendler, K. S. 205
Kenny, D. A. 124
Kent, L. 316
Keren, M. 46, 288, 289

Kerr, M. 176
Kerwin, M. E. 295
Kessler, D. B. 42, 282
Kessler, M. 182
Keules, D. 74
Khatun, F. 158
Khosla, S. 148
Kiernan, K. 115
Kihara, M. 150
Kilpatrick, A. 176
Kim-Cohen, J. 284
King, B. H. 313, 320
King, E. 158
King, F. 102
King, S. 19
Kinney, H. C. 26
Kinscherff, R. 169, 178
Kirk, K. 93
Kisilevsky, B. S. 26
Kitson, W. 178
Kitzman, H. 346–7
Klaus, M. 45
Klebanov, P. K. 117, 123, 128, 354
Klein, B. P. 315, 322
Klein, M. 196, 201–2, 249
Klein, M. H. 393
Klein, N. K. 39
Klein, R. E. 148
Kleinman, J. M. 258
Kleinman, R. E. 36, 37, 42
Klesges, R. C. 49
Klin, A. 259, 265, 270
Knieps, L. 316
Knitzer, J. 285
Knoll, J. H. 320
Koball, H. 389
Koch, R. K. 311
Kochanoff, A. 359
Kochanska, G. 204
Koester, L. S. 93
Kogan, N. 248
Kohen, D. 125, 126, 128–9
Koletzko, B. 44
Kolko, D. J. 178
Kolling, P. 17
Kontos, S. 369
Kopp, C. B. 282, 368
Korenman, S. 119, 121, 128
Korfmacher, J. 349, 352

Koslowski, B. 241
Kosofsky, B. E. 14
Kossmann, J. 67
Kosztolányi, G. 26
Kotch, J. 284
Kover, S. T. 319
Kowalenko, N. M. 194, 197
Kozlowski, B. 193
Kraemer, H. 202
Kramer, M. S. 44, 45, 147
Krause, P. 124
Krauss, M. 167
Krebs, N. F. 34
Krentz, U. C. 262
Krentzel, C. P. 79
Kreuzer, J. A. 24
Krishna, A. 153
Krishnakumar, A. 43
Krowchuk, H. V. 394
Krueger, A. B. 126
Kuczmarski, R. J. 35
Kugiumutzakis, G. 88
Kuhl, P. 259
Kuhn, P. 310
Kulcsar, E. 204
Kumar, J. 148
Kumar, R. 197, 200, 208
Kumashiro, H. 258
Kurstjens, S. 197
Kurtzberg, D. 24
Kurz-Reimer, K. 182

LaBounty, J. 361, 365, 368
Lachmann, F. 48
LaGrange, A. 363
Lai, Z. 322
Laing, E. 323
Lakhani, A. 153
Lalande, M. 320
Lally, J. R. 349
Lally, R. 349
LaLonde, N. 262
Lamb, M. E. 361, 365, 368
Lami, L. 316
Lamm, B. 153
Landa, R. 258, 262, 264, 266, 267–8
Landau, B. 97
Landes, C. 227
Landman, M. 150, 210

Landon, M. B. 65
Landry, S. H. 47
Landsford, J. 178–9
Lang, S. 45
Langdon, R. 312
Langkamp, D. L. 238
Langlois, J. H. 365
Lanphear, B. P. 71, 72
Lanter, E. 266
Lany, J. 96
LaPlante, D. P. 19
Larrien, J. 172, 286
Larsen, K. E. 208
Larsen, P. S. 44
Larson, L. C. 50
Lartigue, T. 294
La Scala, E. 168
Laub, J. H. 119
Laugier, J. 24
LaVange, L. M. 352
Lavigne, J. V. 287
Layzer, J. I. 345
Lazarus, R. S. 368
Le Brocque, R. 42
Lecanuet, J. P. 23
Lecce, S. 298
Le Couteur, A. 260
Ledbetter, D. H. 320
Lee, B. 176
Lee, D. 270
Lee, L. 208
Lee, M. W. 365
Lee, P. J. 78
Legerstee, M. 316
Leiter, C. 354
Leitner, Y. 13
Lemieux, K. 173
Lenihan, A. J. 50
Lenneberg, E. H. 99
Leonard, C. O. 314
Leonard, W. R. 13
Lepine, J. 154
Lerner, C. 50
Lero, D. S. 363
Lescano, A. G. 34
Leschot, N. J. 10
Lester, B. M. 237–8
Letson, G. W. 67, 68
Leventhal, B. L. 283

Leventhal, J. 45, 169
Levi, G. 263
Levi, T. 115, 120, 129, 130
Levin, H. 258
Levine, D. 310
Levine, S. L. 316
Levitsky, D. A. 36
Levitt, C. 179
Levitt, P. 322
Lewis, C. 367
Lewis, I. 342, 348, 358
Lewis, M. 240, 241, 368
Leyendecker, B. 47
Li, G. 167
Li, R. 43
Li, Y. 91
Liaw, F. 351
Lichtenberger, L. 322
Lidow, M. S. 15
Lieber, C. S. 71, 75
Lieberman, A. F. 282, 285–6, 288–9, 294,
    296, 297
Lilburn, M. 78
Lima, R. C. 45
Lind, T. 40
Linden, G. 115
Linder, T. W. 282
Lindheim, O. 297
Lindsay, J. 167
Link, D. T. 293
Linn, M. I. 344
Linscheid, T. R. 46, 292, 295
Linver, M. R. 118, 126, 128
Lipman, E. L. 126
Lira, P. I. 40, 147
Litman, C. 291, 366
Little, P. M. D. 392
Little, T. D. 248
Liu, X. 72, 73
Llanos, A. 41–2
Lloyd, E. 369
Loftin, C. 157
Logan, S. 43
Logsdon, M. C. 284
Loh, A. 269
Lohman, B. J. 127
Lojkasek, M. 294
Longhi, E. 323
Longobardi, E. 316

Lonnerdal, B. 44
Looker, A. C. 121
Loots, G. 97
Lopez, E. M. 396
Lopez, M. 345
Lopez, S. L. 34
Lopez-Duran, S. 262
Lopman, B. 151
Lord, C. 257, 262, 269
Lotter, V. 258
Lourie, R. S. 285
Lovaas, O. I. 258
Love, J. M. 130, 367, 369
Love, M. J. 347–8
Lovel, H. 210
Low, J. A. 13
Lowe, J. B. 322
Lowry, L. W. 382
Lozoff, B. 39, 66, 67
Lubec, G. 12
Luby, J. L. 240, 282, 289
Luchok, K. J. 383
Ludwig, J. 116, 120
Ludy-Dobson, C. 178
Lukashov, I. 16
Lumley, J. 209
Lundy, B. 195
Lusk, D. 151, 152
Luster, T. 340
Lustig, S. 154
Luthar, S. 116, 172
Lutzker, J. 182
Lydick, S. 240
Lynch, M. 166, 169, 172, 316
Lyons, C. 348
Lyons-Ruth, K. 42, 49, 104, 193, 201, 297
Lyubchik, A. 42

Maas, Y. G. 22
Mabughi, N. 118
McAdoo, H. P. 128
McAllister, C. 284
Macari, S. 269
McBride, G. 263, 267
McCartney, K. 122, 366, 369
McCarton, C. 123, 125, 130
McCarty, C. A. 42
McCloskey, L. 179
McClure, B. 42, 49

Maccoby, E. E. 46, 47, 49, 340, 367
McComish, C. 266
McConnachie, H. R. 99
McCormick, M. C. 123, 130, 148, 226, 236
McCue Horwitz, S. 240
McCulloch, A. 123, 128, 129
McCullough, A. L. 40
McDermott, P. A. 370
McDermott, S. 310
McDevitt, S. C. 282
MacDonald, D. 150
McDonough, S. C. 295, 296, 297–8
MacDorman, M. F. 391
McElwain, N. L. 241
McFayden, R. 178
McGee, R. 240
McGovern, C. W. 258
McGrother, A. 316
McIntosh, D. N. 247
MacKain, K. 199
McKean, C. M. 24
McLanahan, S. 119, 122, 124–5, 370
McLaren, D. S. 67
McLean, M. 236
MacLean, W. E. 320
McLeer, S. 181
McLeod, J. D. 125
McLoyd, V. C. C. 125
McMahon, C. A. 194, 197
McMahon, R. J. 42
McNamara, R. K. 41
McNeil, C. B. 296
Madge, N. 76
Madigan, S. 297–8
Maegaki, Y. 321
Maestas y Moores, J. 92
Maestro, S. 267
Magnusson, K. A. 116, 120
Magwaza, A. 158
Mahone, E. 269
Mahoney, G. 315
Maillot, F. 78
Main, M. 167, 172, 193, 241
Makrides, M. 41, 45
Maldonado-Durán, J. M. 294
Male, C. 121
Malloy, M. H. 226
Malone, F. D. 310, 315
Malphurs, J. 208

Maluccio, A. 166
Maluccio, J. A. 49
Mandell, D. S. 259
Mangelsdorf, S. 287
Mangione, P. L. 349
Mankin, G. 317
Manly, J. T. 297
Mann, D. 178
Mannie, Z. N. 196, 206
Mannion, E. 322
Manolopoulos, R. 50
Marcynyszyn, L. A. 125
Margrand, N. A. 126
Marino, R. V. 73
Maritato, N. 115
Markowitz, D. 67, 76
Markowitz, P. 261
Marlow, N. 13, 236
Marmot, M. G. 63
Mars, A. 263, 268
Marschark, M. 91, 93
Marsden, D. B. 236–7
Marshall, D. B. 172
Marshall, P. J. 282
Marsiglio, W. 350
Martin, J. 46, 47, 49
Martin, R. M. 44
Martin, S. 369
Martin, S. L. 208
Martin, W. H. 24
Martines, J. 198
Martinez, C. 172
Martinez, F. 158
Martinez-Piedra, R. 71
Martins, C. 194, 203
Martorell, G. A. 196
Martorell, R. 49, 148
Marvin, R. 296, 297
Masataka, N. 322
Maso, M. 93
Masterov, D. V. 126
Mastrogiannis, D. S. 16
Mathews, T. J. 391
Matias, R. 193, 208
Mattia, F. 24
Mattson, S. N. 14
Matula, K. 232
Maughan, A. 202, 205
Mauk, J. E. 263

Maurice, E. 43
Maurin, E. 124
Maxfield, M. 179
May, P. A. 73
May, T. 68, 69–70
Mayer, S. E. 117, 120, 122, 124, 128
Mayes, L. C. 15, 228, 236, 283, 384
Mayseless, O. 365
Meadow-Orlans, K. 90, 91, 92
Meadows, A. T. 62
Meaney, M. J. 196
Mednick, S. A. 20
Meeks Gardner, J. 40, 148
Mei, Z. 44
Meisels, S. J. 236–7, 246, 351
Mejer, L. 115
Melgar-Quinonez, H. 121
Melhuish, E. C. 359, 360, 363, 369–72
Meltzoff, A. N. 88, 259, 262, 272
Mena, P. 41–2
Mendelsohn, A. L. 71, 72
Mendez, M. A. 34
Mennella, J. A. 27
Mennerick, S. 20
Menon, P. 154
Menon, V. 148
Meriq, V. 34
Merle, K. S. 24
Merlob, P. 64
Merrit, D. 168
Mervis, C. B. 315, 322, 323
Mesibov, G. 319–20
Messinger, D. S. 283
Meyer, R. 291
Meyer, T. 93
Meyer, W. A. 318
Meyers, T. 193, 365
Mezger, J. 169
Michael, M. G. 100, 101
Michaelsen, K. F. 44
Michailevskaya, V. 16
Michalson, L. 368
Micklewright, J. 115, 124
Miech, R. 201
Milani, I. 262
Milberger, S. 247
Milburn, L. A. 295
Milgrom, J. 197, 199
Milis, L. 207

Millar, W. S. 158
Miller, J. E. 119, 121, 128
Miller, J. F. 316
Miller, L. J. 247
Miller-Johnson, S. 129, 178, 343
Mills, A. 197
Mills, J. L. 79
Mills, M. 195
Mills, M. M. 66
Mindell, J. A. 295
Miranda, S. B. 315
Mirmiran, M. 22
Mirrett, P. 318
Misri, S. 207
Mitchell, D. C. 48
Mitchell, S. 266
Mitchell, S. K. 350
Mitchell-Copeland, J. 240
Miyamoto, R. 93
Modi, N. 208
Moerchen, V. 321
Moffitt, T. E. 284
Mohan, R. 194
Molamu, L. 150
Mølbak, K. 71
Molitor, N. 365
Moller, K. A. 74
Molteno, C. 150, 210
Monasch, R. 151
Monk, C. S. 204
Montie, J. 129
Moog, J. 93
Moon, C. M. 27
Mooney, A. 369
Moore, K. 387
Moore, M. 169
Moore, M. K. 272
Moore, V. 99, 258, 269
Morenoff, J. D. 117, 129
Morenza, L. 158
Morgan, K. 240
Morgan, L. 265, 269
Morgan, S. P. 125
Morishima, T. 71
Morisset, C. E. 250
Morley, D. W. 78
Morrell, J. 205, 283
Morris, C. A. 314, 322
Morris, P. A. 129, 143

Morris, S. E. 45
Morris, S. S. 40, 147
Morrisey, T. W. 362, 363
Morrow, A. L. 386
Morrow, C. E. 16
Moser, H. W. 310
Moses-Kolko, E. L. 17
Moss, N. E. 385
Moss, P. 360
Most, D. E. 312, 323
Most, T. 91
Mott, F. L. 127
Motta, R. 181
Mrakotsky, C. 289
Mueller, S. 46
Muir, E. 294
Muir, R. 294
Mulford, R. 99, 100
Mulick, J. A. 310
Mullany, L. 147
Mullen, E. M. 233, 234–5
Muller, R. 173
Mulligan, G. M. 363
Mundy, P. 259, 262, 272, 316
Munson, J. 258, 266
Mupuala, A. 150
Murray, K. T. 204
Murray, L. 90, 150, 192–4, 196–206, 207, 209–10, 283
Murray-Kolb, L. E. 39
Musheno, K. 165
Musick, J. 352
Muth, P. 169
Myers, L. 287
Myers, S. E. 321

Nabors, L. A. 362
Nachmias, M. 287
Nadel, J. 88
Nadig, A. S. 264
Nafstad, A. 101
Naiman, J. L. 67
Najman, J. M. 198
Narayan, D. 152–3
Nash, S. 263
Nassogne, M. C. 77
Nawrocki, T. 195
Neal, A. R. 259, 262, 272
Nearing, G. 208

Neault, N. B. 121
Needleman, H. L. 72
Nelson, C. A. 11, 14, 24, 26, 122, 177
Nelson, C. S. 80
Nelson, K. 93, 99
Nelson, M. D. 50
Nestel, P. 67
Neubauer, A-P. 239
Neuman, M. 115
Nevins, M. E. 91
Newborg, J. 228, 230, 233, 235
Newton, C. R. 150
Niccols, A. 15, 194
Nicholls, R. D. 320
Nicklas, T. A. 46, 48
Nicolaides, K. H. 310
Niego, S. 284
Niesworth, J. T. 247
Nikolopoulos, T. 93
Nold, J. L. 64, 65, 66
Nommsen, L. A. 44
Nomura, Y. 203
Nonnemaker, J. M. 125
Nord, M. 43, 387
Nores, M. 129
Norris, M. 99
Norström, H. 103
Notaro, P. C. 241
Novak, G. P. 24
Novak, M. M. 259
Nover, R. A. 246, 285
Novotny, T. 71
Nugent, J. K. 237
Nye, C. 40

Oakland, T. 234
Oates, R. 178
Oberlander, S. 46
Oberman, L. M. 272
O'Brien, K. L. 69
O'Brien, R. 352
Ochoa, D. Q. 80
O'Connel, B. 93
O'Connor, T. G. 196, 210, 283, 292
O'Donnell, K. S. 38
O'Donoghue, G. 93
Offord, D. 126
Ogan, T. A. 262
O'Grady Hynes, M. 92

O'Hara, M. 192, 200, 208
O'Hara, P. S. 199, 315
Ohno, K. 321
Ohr, P. S. 199, 315
Ohrt, B. 291
Oka, A. 321
Okagaki, L. 340, 349
O'Keane, V. 203
Olds, D. 346–7, 352, 393
Oller, D. K. 316
Olson, K. L. 193
Olstad, M. 67
O'Malley, K. 75
Omar, M. A. 383
Onozawa, K. 208
Onyang, A. W. 44
Ooylan, L. M. 40
Oppenheim, D. 295
Oppenheimer, R. 167
O'Riordan, M. 314
Orlando, M. S. 24
Ormond, K. E. 310
Ornitz, E. M. 267
Ornoy, A. 16
Ortiz, N. 158
Orzol, S. M. 43
Osberger, M. J. 93
Osendarp, S. J. 41
Oser, C. 381
Oski, F. A. 39, 67
Osmond, C. 18
Osofsky, H. J. 285
Osofsky, J. D. 285, 287
Osredkar, D. 22
Osterling, J. A. 195, 257–9, 262, 263, 266, 269
Ousted, C. 167, 270
Ovadia, J. 64
Owen, A. L. 50
Owen, C. G. 44
Owen, G. M. 50
Owen, M. T. 365, 366
Owens, E. B. 291
Oxley, H. 129
Ozonoff, S. 258, 260, 264, 269, 270

Paglia, A. 194
Paley, B. 126
Palferman, S. 260

Palmer, J. L. 368
Palmer, P. 258
Palomo, R. 260, 270
Panagiotides, H. 195
Panambulam, A. 77, 78, 79
Pandya, P. P. 310
Papas, M. A. 36, 43, 46, 47, 49
Papousek, H. 193
Papousek, M. 193, 287, 291, 292–4
Paris-Delrue, L. 23
Parke, R. 371
Parker, C. J. 294
Parker, K. C. H. 194
Parker-Corell, A. 178
Parkes, S. 237
Parks, D. J. 67
Parlakian, R. 50
Parmelee, A. 240
Parrish, L. H. 311
Parritz, R. 287
Partington, M. W. 318
Pary, R. J. 316
Patel, V. 210
Paterson, S. J. 323
Patole, S. 41
Patterson, G. 178, 244
Patterson, P. 206
Paul, J. 258
Paul, M. 316
Paul, P. V. 100, 101
Paus, T. 12
Pawl, J. H. 295
Pawlby, S. 197, 201, 203
Payne, L. 318
Payne, M. 168
Peacock, A. 178
Pecora, P. 166
Pedersen, E. D. 92
Pedersen, J. 64
Peebles, C. D. 240, 287
Peerson, J. M. 44
Peet, S. H. 350
Peindl, K. S. 209
Peisner-Feinberg, E. 369
Pelaez-Nogueras, M. 208
Pellizzari, M. 129
Peloso, E. 297
Pennington, B. 261
Percy, M. 310, 311–12

Perel, J. M. 209
Perez, E. M. 39
Perez-Pereira, M. 98, 99
Perrett, D. I. 272
Perry, B. D. 172, 177, 178, 179–81
Perry, H. 312
Perry, R. 258
Perryman, T. 263
Persson, L. A. 121
Pérusse, D. 66
Peters, J. C. 48
Peters, R. 50
Peterson, A. 385
Peterson, M. 174
Petesch, P. 152–3
Petrogiannis, K. 359, 370
Petry, C. D. 13, 66
Petterson, S. M. 125, 197
Pettit, G. 173, 178–9, 292
Pezé, A. 88
Pfeffer, C. R. 196
Phan, M. B. 363
Philipps, L. H. 200
Phillips, A. T. 262
Phillips, C. 323
Phillips, D. A. 63, 66–7, 76, 127, 140, 143,
     240, 282, 341, 362, 369–70
Phillips, I. W. 66
Phillips, N. M. 66
Phillips, S. M. 43
Philofsky, A. 312–13, 315–17, 320, 323–4
Piccinini, C. A. 158
Pickens, J. 195
Pickens, N. 195
Pickett, K. E. 117, 283
Pilchen, M. 38
Pilowsky, D. 203
Pincus, D. B. 298
Pine, D. S. 283
Pine, C. J. 371
Pinto-Martin, J. 227
Piontek, C. M. 209
Pischke, J. S. 124
Pisoni, D. B. 93
Pittman, L. D. 127
Piven, J. 258
Pizzoli, C. 316
Pizzuto, E. 316
Plagemann, A. 44

Pleska-Skwerer, D. 312
Plessinger, M. A. 15
Plewis, I. 204
Plikaytis, B. D. 69
Plomin, R. 48
Plotnik, R. D. 125, 166
Poisson, S. 247
Polansky, N. 176
Pole, M. 179
Pollak, S. 177, 285
Pollard, R. 177, 179, 181
Pollitt, E. 148
Ponce, V. A. 350
Porges, S. 204, 283
Porter, K. B. 40
Porter, M. A. 312
Posner, M. I. 204
Potter, L. 229, 244
Potterton, J. L. 152
Poulin-Dubois, D. 240, 241
Pound, A. 195
Powell, B. 296, 297
Powell, C. A. 34, 148, 158, 351
Powell, D. R. 340, 349–50, 352, 353
Power, T. G. 46
Prabucki, K. M. 39
Prahme, C. 269
Preisler, G. 91–4, 96–7, 98, 101, 103
Prezioso, C. 92
Proctor, B. D. 119
Prodromidis, M. 365
Prouty, L. A. 318
Prusoff, B. A. 192
Puckering, A. 195
Pungello, E. P. 129, 343
Putnam, F. W. 287, 288
Pynoos, R. S. 288

Qazi, Q. 74
Quade, D. 383
Querido, J. G. 298
Querleu, D. 23, 26
Quigg, A. 43, 46
Quinn, P. 45

Radcliffe, J. 72, 73
Ragan, N. B. 72
Rahman, A. 155, 210
Rahman, K. M. 38

Raiha, N. 174
Raikes, H. 350
Rainwater, L. 116, 119
Rakic, S. 11
Ramachandran, V. 272
Ramchandani, P. 204, 210
Ramey, C. T. 129, 339, 341–3, 348–9, 352, 365, 369, 370
Ramkalawan, T. 90
Ramstad, K. 322
Randolph, S. 359
Rao, M. R. 79
Rao, N. 158
Rapoport, D. 209
Rapoport, L. 48
Rasnake, L. K. 46, 292
Ratsatsi, D. 153
Ratterman, A. 284
Raudenbush, S. W. 117
Ravallion, M. 152
Rayburn, W. F. 13
Rebello, P. B. 154
Reebye, P. 207
Reece, R. 167
Rees, V. W. 322
Regolin, L. 262
Reider, E. E. 318
Reidy, K. 46
Reiss, A. L. 317, 329
Renard, X. 23
Renfrew, M. J. 45
Resing, W. 38
Resnick, J. S. 263
Resnik, R. 65
Rezvani, I. 77, 78
Rhoads, G. G. 72
Ribner, D. R. 199
Riccardi, V. M. 320
Ricci, L. 178
Richards, M. 45
Richards, P. G. 77
Richardson, L. A. 383, 394
Richman, N. 200, 291
Richter, L. 143, 150, 151
Ridder, E. 182
Riegel, K. 291
Rieger, I. 238
Riksen-Walraven, J. M. 101
Riley, D. 396

Riley, E. P. 14
Rinaldi, J. 262
Riportella-Muller, R. 383
Ripple, C. H. 354
Rippon, G. 272
Risley-Curtiss, C. 183
Rivera, F. 167
Rivet, C. 88
Rizley, R. 166, 169
Rizzolatti, G. 88
Robbins, A. K. 93
Robert Tissot, C. 294, 298
Roberts, B. W. 313
Roberts, C. D. 311
Roberts, J. E. 318, 362
Roberts, W. 260
Robertson, J. 290
Robertson, M. L. 13
Robin, N. H. 314
Robinshaw, H. M. 92
Robinson, B. F. 322
Robinson, H. 317
Robinson, J. 346
Robinson, K. A. 69
Robinson, S. E. 285
Rodbroe, I. 101
Rodewald, L. E. 70, 80
Rodrigues, M. 210
Roebuck, T. M. 14
Rogan, W. J. 71, 72, 73
Rogers, S. 312, 315–16, 317, 323
Rogers, S. J. 264, 269, 318–20
Rogers, T. 260
Roggman, L. A. 350, 365
Rogosch, F. A. 200, 202, 208, 297
Rojahn, J. 310
Rojas, J. 34
Rolnick, A. 130, 370
Romaniuk, H. 207
Rooney, A. C. 201
Rosack, J. 384
Rose, D. 117
Rose-Jacobs, R. 43
Roseboom, T. J. 13
Rosen, J. F. 72
Rosenberg, T. 94
Rosenblum, K. L. 295
Rosenblum, L. A. 196
Rosner, B. A. 322

Ross, K. 125, 153
Rothbart, M. K. 204, 291
Rouse, C. E. 124, 370
Rouse, H. 370
Rovine, M. 172, 365
Rowe, D. C. 340
Rowland, C. 97
Royal, J. 71
Rozga, A. 264
Ruback, R. 179
Ruckerl, R. 44
Rudolf, M. C. 43
Rudolph, C. D. 293
Ruel, M. T. 46
Ruggerio, K. 181
Rumm, P. 167
Rusecki, Y. 64
Ruskin, E. 316
Rutter, M. 76, 168, 258, 285, 368
Ryan, G. W. 76

Sachs, J. 153
Sadeh, A. 292
Sadler, L. 314
Sagi, A. 365
Sagun, J. 313, 322
St George, M. 322
St James-Roberts, I. 203–4
St Pierre, R. G. 345
Saito, S. 151
Salamy, A. 24
Salgado, M. 269
Saliba, E. 24
Salmon, J. 129
Salpekar, N. 125
Salvia, J. 247
Salzinger, S. 176
Sam, L. K. 93
Sameroff, A. 76, 204, 281–2, 284, 295
Samet, J. M. 73
Sammons, P. 363
Sampson, R. J. 117, 119, 129
Samuelson, G. 44
Sandberg, D. 193
Sanders, S. 24
Sanderson, S. 48
Sanson, A. 120
Santoli, J. M. 80
Sarimski, K. 322

Sarkar, S. 16
Saron, C. D. 205
Sasone, R. 179
Sass-Lehrer, M. 91
Sasseen, K. 50
Saudubray, J. M. 77
Sawyer, L. 240
Sawyer, M. 121
Saxe, G. N. 288
Sayette, M. A. 248
Sazalwal, S. 40, 148
Scaife, M. 262
Scanlon, K. S. 47
Scannapieco, M. 165–9, 171–2, 175–9,
    181–3
Scarr, S. 368, 369
Scerif, G. 319, 323
Schaal, B. 23
Schaffer, C. E. 205
Scheeringa, M. S. 240, 285, 287–8, 290
Schein, J. 91
Schempf, A. H. 15
Scher, A. 292
Scher, J. 63
Scherr, L. 143
Schettler, T. 148
Scheuer, A. Q. 246
Schich, S. 178
Schiffman, R. F. 383
Schisterman, R. F. 79
Schlotz, W. 66
Schmid, K. 168, 284
Schmitz, N. 19
Schmucker, G. 197
Schnaas, L. 72
Schneider-Rosen, K. 173
Schoenfeld, A. 64
Schofield, C. 312
Scholl, T. O. 70, 73
Scholmerich, A. 47
Scholz, J. K. 388
Schore, J. 50
Schubiner, H. 14
Schulte, M. C. 48
Schulter, C. 118
Schulzke, S. M. 41
Schupf, N. 310
Schuyler, T. F. 248
Schwartz, J. 71

Schwartz, T. 63
Schweinhart, L. J. 129
Schweke, W. 130
Sciolo, L. 173
Scola, P. 68
Scott, K. G. 39, 119
Sedlak, A. 176
Seeler, R. 71
Segal, M. 349
Sege, R. 167
Séguin, J. R. 66
Seifer, R. 284
Sekino, Y. 370
Selby-Harrington, M. L. 383, 394
Seleme, I. 158
Self, J. 195
Selim, T. 118
Selten, J. P. 20
Sen, A. 152
Senulis, J. A. 205
Seress, L. 26
Sermijn, J. 97
Sethuranaman, K. 147
Shaffer, J. 179
Shah, B. 313
Shahidullah, B. S. 23
Shaked, M. 261
Shankar, A. H. 148
Shapiro, V. 294
Shapiro, W. H. 94
Sharp, D. 197, 201, 203
Sharp, M. 316
Shaver, P. R. 282
Shaw, D. S. 291
Shea, A. M. 317
Shea, B. 298
Shelly, R. O. 94
Sherman, S. L. 315
Sherman, T. 194
Sherry, B. 47
Shillam, P. 71
Shillington, A. 176
Shilton, P. 176
Shinn, M. 369
Shonkoff, J. P. 63, 66–7, 76, 127, 140, 143,
    240, 282, 341, 353, 370
Shore, C. 93
Shore, R. 179
Shrimpton, R. 42

Shulman, C. 257
Shumway, S. 265
Sia, C. C. 62, 79–80
Sickel, R. 247
Sidappa, A. 14
Siddiqi, A. 152, 157–8
Siegel, C. H. 294
Siermann, C. 115
Sigel, I. E. 349
Sigma, M. 240
Sigman, M. 258, 264, 316
Silva, P. 240
Silver, H. K. 76, 165
Silverman, F. N. 76, 165
Silverman, R. D. 68, 69–70
Simion, F. 262
Simmer, K. 41
Simon, E. W. 323
Simonoff, E. 34
Simons, R. L. 125
Sinclair, D. 194, 201, 202
Singer, H. 269
Singer, L. T. 16
Singer, V. 174
Singleton, R. J. 69
Sinha, P. 177
Siperstein, R. 258
Siraj-Blatchford, I. 363
Skimmer, M. L. 342
Skinner, D. 318
Skinner, J. 46
Skinner, M. 317, 318–20
Skovgaard, A. M. 288, 289
Skuban, E. M. 240
Slater, A. 199
Sloman, J. 79
Smeeding, T. 115, 116, 120, 125, 129
Smeriglio, V. 148
Smicikas-Wright, H. 48
Smider, N. A. 201
Smith, A. C. M. 312, 323, 324
Smith, C. L. 282
Smith, D. W. 74
Smith, E. O. 44
Smith, E. W. 369
Smith, G. D. 44
Smith, I. 258
Smith, J. P. 116
Smith, J. R. 117, 122, 123, 125

Smith, K. 359
Smith, K. E. 47
Smith, P. J. 80
Smith, R. S. 116, 125
Smith, S. 353, 387
Smith, W. 179
Smoski, M. J. 194
Smyke, A. T. 285
Snodgrass, J. J. 13
Snow, C. E. 370
Snyder, D. 286
Solera, C. 129
Solomon, J. 167, 172
Soma, D. 174
Sonenstein, F. 390
Song, H. K. 117, 120
Song, Y. 115, 118
Souriau, J. 101
Southwick, S. M. 206
Soutullo, D. 195
Sparkman, K. L. 318
Sparling, J. J. 341–3, 348–9, 352
Sparrow, S. S. 235, 244
Spaulding, P. J. 99
Speiker, S. J. 194
Spence, M. J. 27
Spencer, P. E. 90, 91, 93
Spieker, S. 199, 350
Spietz, A. 250
Spigset, O. 207
Spiker, D. 344, 348
Spitz, R. 288, 289
Spitznagel, E. 289
Squires, J. 229, 244
Sroufe, L. A. 48, 167, 172, 241, 281–2, 283, 284, 291, 297
Stack, D. M. 240, 241
Stafford, B. 290
Stancin, T. 227, 234, 239
Standen, P. 312
Stanley, C. 192, 194, 198
Stanley, J. R. 13
Stanton, W. 240
Staples, A. D. 292
Starr, A. 24
Starr, R. 176
Starr, R. H. 43
Steele, B. F. 76, 165
Steen, V. M. 207

Steffens, M. L. 316
Stein, A. 90, 194, 197–8, 202, 210
Stein, J. 148, 149
Stein, Z. A. 310
Steinberg, A. G. 91
Steinberg, L. 47, 340
Stella, G. 316
Stephens, D. S. 68
Stern, D. 88, 193, 199
Sternberg, K. J. 365
Stewart, A. J. 172
Stewart, K. 124
Stewart, S. 151
Stewart Brown, S. 63
Stier, D. M. 169
Stifter, C. A. 365
Stoel-Gammon, C. 316
Stokoe, W. 92
Stoltzfus, R. J. 147
Stone, W. L. 269
Storck, A. 286
Stott, F. 352
Stough, L. M. 311
Straus, M. 168, 169
Strauss, R. S. 13
Streissguth, A. P. 73, 74, 75
Strobel, R. J. 320
Stromme, P. 322
Strykowski, B. F. 117
Stuart, S. 208
Stuart-Macadam, P. 385
Studdert-Kennedy, M. 88
Suchindran, C. M. 208
Suddendorf, T. 272
Sullivan, M. 264
Summers, J. A. 350
Sumner, G. 250
Sun, A. 176
Sun, Y. 125
Sunar, D. 158
Susman, E. 168
Sutcliffe, J. S. 322
Sutherland, G. R. 317
Svirsky, M. 93
Swain, A. 192
Swank, P. R. 47
Swartz, L. 150, 210
Sweet, M. A. 343, 353, 393
Swettenham, J. 263

Switzky, H. N. 309
Sylva, K. 363
Sywulka, S. M. 154
Szanton, E. 340
Szatmari, P. 260
Szilagyi, P. G. 39

Tableman, B. 386
Tachibanaki, T. 116, 120
Taggart, B. 363
Talbot, L. 204
Talge, N. M. 19
Talmi, A. 237, 238
Tamis-LeMonda, C. 42, 49, 241, 363
Tamplin, A. 206
Tan, A. 269
Tang, D. 149
Tantam, D. 262
Tassone, F. 317, 318–19
Tatelbaum, R. 346
Tattersall, H. 90
Tavecchio, L. C. 362
Taveras, E. M. 44
Taylor, A. 284
Taylor, A. K. 317, 318–19
Taylor, B. A. 122, 369
Taylor, C. 121
Taylor, D. G. 172
Taylor, M. G. 24
Tejani, N. 16
Tencer, H. 96
Tennant, C. C. 194, 197
Teti, D. M. 202, 204
The, H. W. 149
Thelen, E. 269
Thoman, E. B. 22
Thomas, K. M. 25, 26, 177
Thomas, M. 322
Thomas, P. F. 201
Thompson, L. A. 199
Thompson, M. 269
Thompson, T. 320, 321
Thomsen, B. L. 44
Thorén, A. 98
Tibbitts, R. 93
Tiehen, L. 387
Tielsch, J. M. 39
Tilly, C. 152
Timperio, A. 129

Tjebkes, T. L. 204
Tluczek, A. 207, 249
Tofail, F. 154
Tomarken, A. J. 205
Tomkins, A. 38
Tomlinson, M. 150, 210
Tonge, B. J. 322
Tornóczky, T. 26
Toth, S. 200, 203, 208, 281, 285, 297
Touati, G. 77
Tougas, J. 363
Tout, K. 387
Traci, M. A. 93
Tran, H. 362
Transler, C. 41
Trapani, J. 285
Trask, C. L. 14
Tremblay, R. E. 66, 122, 291, 368
Trevarthen, C. 88–9, 102, 193
Trevathan, W. R. 199
Trickett, P. 167, 168, 169, 284
Trifirò, G. 321
Tronick, E. Z. 88–9, 95, 193, 204, 237–8,
       241, 262, 284, 383–4
Tronick, M. Z. 193
Tröster, H. 95–6
Trout, K. 360
Tsai, L. 316
Tsai, S. Y. 149
Tsaih, S. W. 71
Tucker, D. 167
Turati, C. 262
Turner, G. 317
Turner, M. 269
Turner, P. 194
Tvingstedt, A-L. 94
Twombly, E. 244
Tyano, S. 46, 288
Tyson, J. E. 226

Uauy, R. 34, 41–2
Udwin, O. 322, 323, 324
Ulleland, C. 74
Ullstadius, E. 315
Umbel, V. M. 316
Umiltà, C. 262
Ungerer, J. A. 197
Urquiza, A. 174
Urwin, C. 96, 97

Valenti, M. 148
Valenza, E. 262
Valliere, J. 286
Vandell, D. L. 366, 369
van den Berg, P. B. 17
van Dijk, J. P. M. 101
Van Dulmen, M. H. M. 291
Van Horn, P. 294, 297
Van IJzendoorn, M. 182, 294, 341, 344, 362, 365, 368
Van Os, J. 20
Van Rie, A. 150, 151
van Straten, A. 207
van't Hof, M. A. 121
Vaughan, H. G. 24
Vaughn, B. E. 365
Vazir, S. 158
Vazquez, D. M. 196
Vega-Lahr, N. 193
Vellet, S. 47
Veltman, M. W. M. 320, 322
Verbalis, A. 312
Verdeli, H. 203
Verhey, J. F. 239
Verkerk, A. J. M. 317
Verma, U. 16
Vermeulen, P. 322
Vernon-Feagans, L. 128
Verropoulou, G. 369
Versyp, F. 23
Vertongen, F. 38
Vicari, S. 312, 316
Vick, J. E. 363
Victora, C. G. 34, 35, 45
Vietze, P. 167
Vig, S. 167, 169
Vik, T. 45, 79
Villar, J. 147, 148
Visootsak, J. 317, 318
Visser, A. 101
Vleminckx, K. 115
Voeller, K. 72
Vohr, B. R. 239
Volker, S. 153
Volkmar, F. R. 258
Vøllestad, N. 67
Volling, B. L. 241
Vollmer, J. 49
Volpe, J. J. 10, 14, 15

Volterra, V. 264, 316
Vondra, J. 178
Von Hofacker, N. 287, 291, 292, 294
vonKries, R. 44
Voss, W. 239
Votruba-Drzal, E. 127, 128
Vouloumanos, A. 262
Vuori-Christiansen, L. 158
Vural, M. 91
Vyrostek, S. B. 76, 77
Vythilingham, M. 206

Waber, D. P. 158
Wachs, T. D. 36, 63, 67, 76, 80, 143, 148, 152, 155, 192, 210
Wachtendorf, M. 239
Wadworth, M. E. 45
Wagner, G. G. 124
Wagner, M. 344–5, 350
Wagonfeld, S. 289
Waisbren, S. E. 78
Wake, M. 121
Wake, S. 317
Wakschlag, L. S. 283, 290
Walberg, H. J. 117
Walden, T. 262, 316, 320
Waldfogel, J. 115, 126, 127, 369
Walker, D. M. 13
Walker, S. P. 34, 62, 70, 143, 144, 146–8, 150, 152, 158, 343
Wall, K. 360
Wall, S. 88, 281
Wallace, C. S. 25, 177
Wallace, K. E. 125
Wallinga, D. 148
Walzman, S. 93–4
Wang, P. P. 315
Wang, X. 20
Wapner, R. 310
Ward, A. 283
Ward, J. I. 67
Ward, K. 311
Wardle, J. 48
Ware, J. H. 71, 73
Warner, R. 207
Warner, V. 203
Warren, D. 99
Warren, S. T. 317
Wasik, B. H. 341, 348, 349, 352

Wasserman, G. A. 149
Waterhouse, L. 261
Waters, C. S. 203
Waters, E. 88, 281
Waters, O. 48
Waterston, T. 63
Watson, J. B. 20
Watson, L. R. 263, 265–8, 269, 270
Watt, N. 265, 269, 270
Watts, H. 151
Webb, S. J. 272
Webb, T. 317
Webber, C. 324
Wehner, E. 318, 319
Weinberg, K. 89
Weinberg, M. K. 193–4, 204, 284, 383–4
Weinfield, N. S. 126
Weinraub, M. 362, 365
Weinreb, L. F. 123
Weintrob, N. 64–5
Weisman, L. E. 226
Weiss, A. 370
Weissbourd, B. 349
Weissman, M. M. 192, 203
Weitzdoerfer, R. 12
Weitzman, L. 24
Weitzman, M. 72
Wellman, H. M. 262
Wendland-Carro, J. 158
Wenger, J. D. 69
Wenzel, A. 207, 249
Werker, J. F. 262
Werner, E. E. 116, 125, 258, 263, 265–6, 267, 269
Werner-Wilson, R. J. 173
Wershil, B. 77
Wesch, D. 182
Wessels, H. 368
West, A. 209
West, J. 363
West, K. P. 40
Westley, D. T. 197
Weston, D. R. 236–7
Wetherby, A. 262, 265, 267–9, 273, 316
Wewerka, S. 14, 24, 26
Whaley, G. J. L. 126
Whincup, P. H. 44
Whipple, E. 178
Whitaker, R. C. 43

White, H. R. 179
Whitebook, M. 362
Whiten, A. 272
Whitman, B. Y. 321
Whitman, T. L. 125
Whittaker, J. 166
Whitton, A. 207
Wickramaratne, P. 192, 203
Widom, C. 173, 179
Wieder, S. 282, 285, 286
Wiener, S. 247
Wiesinger, J. 36
Wigren, M. 321
Wilbur, M. A. 79
Wilde, P. 387
Wilding, J. 319
Wilkinson, R. G. 117
Williams, B. J. 258
Williams, D. 394
Williams, G. M. 198
Williams, J. C. P. 322
Williams, J. H. G. 272
Williams, J. M. G. 263
Williams, L. 181
Williamson, P. 263
Willikens, D. 324
Wilson, A. 207
Wilson, G. S. 16
Wilson, I. 90
Wilson, M. N. 371
Wimpory, D. C. 263
Winnicott, D. 88, 280
Winslow, E. B. 291
Winsor, J. 284
Wirtz, S. 174
Wise, S. 262
Wisner, K. L. 209
Wisniewski, K. E. 12
Witherington, D. C. 267
Wobken, J. D. 66
Wocaldo, C. 238
Wodarski, J. S. 182
Wojtascek, Z. 315
Wolfe, R. 42
Wolff, P. 38
Wolfner, G. 167, 168
Wolke, D. 197, 291
Wolkind, S. 168, 200
Wollworth de Chuquisengo, R. 293

Wong, W. W. 44
Woods, J. 262
Woods, J. R. J. 15
Woodward, L. J. 123–4
Woody, E. 46, 49
Woolever, F. 341
Woolfrey, J. 49
Woolgar, M. 90, 194, 202, 206, 210
Woolridge, M. W. 45
Worobey, J. 238
Wrate, R. M. 201
Wright, C. A. 202
Wright, C. M. 43
Wright, E. 226
Wright, L. 226
Wright, R. J. 71
Wright, R. O. 71
Wright, S. 90
Wrightson, A. S. 311
Wyly, M. V. 227

Xiang, Z. 129

Yamada, E. 195
Yanoff, J. M. 73
Yashima, Y. 258
Yesmin, S. 154
Yeung, W. J. 117–18, 122, 124, 126, 128
Yip, R. 39
Yirmiya, N. 261, 316
Yolken, R. 71
Yonclas, D. G. 316
Yoos, H. L. 346

Yoshinaga-Itano, C. 90
Young, A. 90
Young, E. A. 196
Young, G. S. 264, 269
Young, R. 263
Yovski, R. D. 153
Yu, S. 115, 118

Zahlsen, K. 207
Zaidman-Zait, A. 91
Zajicek, E. 200
Zarlengo-Strouse, P. 199
Zaslow, M. 353, 368, 387–8, 390
Zeanah, C. H. 240, 285, 286–7, 290
Zecevic, N. 11
Zhou, S. J. 45
Ziegler, M. 293
Ziegler, P. 46
Zigler, E. 167, 172, 309, 341, 354, 396
Zinser, M. 194
Zirkel, S. 297
Ziv, Y. 295
Zlochower, A. 194
Zock, P. L. 41
Zori, R. T. 323
Zorumski, C. F. 20
Zubieta, A. C. 121
Zubritsky, C. D. 259
Zuckerman, S. 292
Zuravin, S. 176
Zuze, L. 153
Zwaigenbaum, L. 260, 262, 263–4, 266, 268, 270

Subject Index

Abecedarian Project 129–30, 342–3, 351
absolute poverty 113, 117–18, 152
adaptation patterns 281
Adaptive Behavior Assessment System 234
Adaptive Behavior Scales 244
Administration for Children and Families 392
adolescent parenthood 284–5
adolescent psychiatric disturbance 203
adrenocorticotropic hormone (ACTH) 19
affect, autism and 267, 282
affect attunement 88, 96
affective disorders 224, 286, 287–90
African Network for the Care of Children
    Affected by HIV/AIDS 150
agency, lack of 153
Ages and Stages Questionnaire: Social-
    Emotional 229, 242, 244, 249
aggressive disorders 224, 286, 290–1
Aid to Families with Dependent
    Children 387
alcohol
    child neglect and 149–50
    effects of 14–15, 18, 21, 145
    FAS 14–15, 73–6, 149–50, 283, 310
ALSPAC Study Team 210
American Academy of Pediatrics 36, 42–3,
    67–8, 71, 228, 273, 349, 385, 390
    Injury Prevention Program 76
    Newborn Screening Task Force 311

American Association on Intellectual and
    Developmental Disabilities 309
American Association on Mental
    Retardation 309
American College of Obstetricians and
    Gynecologists 49
American Dietetic Association 40, 43
American Educational Research
    Association 247
American Psychiatric Association 173, 257,
    261, 287, 289, 293, 309
American Psychological Association 247, 384,
    396
American Public Health Association 390
American Sign Language 93
amino acids 78
amniotic fluid 27
"anaclitic depression" 288–9
anatomic development 9–12
anemia 37, 39, 70, 119, 145, 147
animal models/studies 18–19, 42
Annie E. Casey Foundation 340
anophthalmia 94, 95
antibiotics 67
antidepressants 16–17, 207, 209
anxiety 18, 203, 287–8
apoptosis 11
arachidonic acid 41
arsenic 146, 148, 149

assessment
  of childcare 362–3
  developmental 223, 227, 232–8, 250–1,
    388–9
  independent (depression) 201–2
  infant functioning 223, 226–51
  social-emotional 240–50
Assessment of Preterm Infant Behavior
    (APIB) 237, 238
attachment 104, 126, 282
  and biobehavioral catch-up 295–7
  disorders 167, 285, 289–90
  impaired 172–4
  maltreatment and 167, 172–4, 177–8,
    182–3
  postnatal depression and 90, 194–9
  security 45, 344, 365–6
attention 199
  social 257, 262–4, 271, 272
attention deficit disorder 89
attention deficit hyperactivity disorder 14,
    205, 286
auditory brainstem response 24
auditory cortex 12, 23
auditory development 12, 22–5, 26–7
auditory processing disorders 89
authoritarian parenting style 47, 49
authoritative parenting style 47, 49
autism spectrum disorders 2–3, 40, 89, 94,
    223–4, 257–73, 309, 312, 316, 319
autosomes 10
axilla 65
axon 11

bacterial infection 67, 70–1
battered child syndrome 165
Battelle Developmental Inventory 228, 230,
    233, 235–6
Bayley Infant Neurodevelopment Screen
    (BINS) 228, 230
Bayley Mental Development Index 197
Bayley Scales of Infant Development 122,
    128, 154, 174, 198, 228, 230–4, 240
Bayley Scales of Infant and Toddler
    Development 228, 231–4, 246, 250
Behavior Rating Scale 232
Behavior Screening Questionnaire 200
behavioral observation 267–8, 269
behavioral phenotypes 225, 311–14, 324

behavioral problems 200–6, 366–8
behavioral treatments 295
Bernard van Leer Foundation 156
Best Beginnings program 390
Bielefeld Observations Scales 99
bioecological risks
  fetal development 7, 9–28
  health 7, 62–80
  infant nutrition 7, 33–52
  sensory disabilities 8, 87–104
biological needs 282
biological outcomes (depression) 195–6
biological processes, depression and 205
biological risk 62, 144–50, 151–2
birth weight 33, 35, 42
  low 50, 128, 144–9, 152, 239, 348,
    386
Blacksmith Institute 148
blind children 87, 94–100, 104
body mass index (BMI) 34, 35
borderline personality disorder 173
brachial plexus 65
brain development
  anatomic development 9–12
  fetal 7, 9–28
  influences on 12–20
brain systems, autism and 272
brainstem 12, 21, 23, 24
breastfeeding 121, 207
  developing countries 145, 147, 150
  nutrition 35–7, 41, 43–5, 50, 385–6
Brief Infant-Toddler Social and Emotional
    Assessment 245, 247–8, 249
Brigance Infant and Toddler Screen 231

calcium 37
Cambridge longitudinal study 194, 197, 198,
    202–3, 204–5, 206
Canadian National Children's Agenda 120
carbohydrates 37, 40
caregivers 208
  communication 88–9, 96–8, 101–4
  see also childcare; parent(s)
Carolina Curriculum 237
case management approach 345, 346
case studies 280
  autism 224, 259–60, 267, 270
Cattell Infant Intelligence Scale 226
center-based interventions 341–3, 347–8

Center on Budget and Policy Priorities 383, 386
Centers for Disease Control and Prevention 35, 71, 73, 258, 390–1
Centers for Medicare and Medicaid Services 382
central nervous system 10–11, 17, 63–4, 70, 76, 78, 89
cephalopelvic disproportion 65
cerebral cortex 11, 12, 22, 24
cerebral palsy 103
Checklist for Autism in Toddlers (CHAT) 263, 268, 273
child-focused intervention 337, 341, 342–3, 347–8
child abuse 2, 76–7, 114, 146, 165–83, 285, 339
    interventions/treatment 180, 182–3
    policies 392
    theoretical perspective 166–74
    see also child neglect; physical abuse; sexual abuse
Child and Adult Care Food Program, 386
Child Behavior Checklist (CBCL) 200
Child and Dependent Care Credit 388
child development
    childcare experience and 365–70
    outcomes (poverty) 119–24
    postnatal depression and 192–211
    state of knowledge 363–4
Child Development Review 229
Child Feeding Questionnaire 49
Child Find programs 388–9
child maltreatment 114, 165–83, 285, 392
    attachment and 172–4
    infants and toddlers 174–82
    interventions and treatment 182–3
    protective factors 169, 171–2
    risk factors 169–72
    theoretical perspective 166–74
    see also child abuse; child neglect
child neglect 2, 114, 146, 149–50, 165–83, 285, 339
    effects of 174–7
    interventions and treatment 182–3
    policies 392
    theoretical perspective 166–74
child stimulation (lack) 145, 153–4
child support 127, 387–8

Child Trends 363, 383
Child Well-Being Index of the Foundation for Child Development 340
childcare 342, 347–8
    assessment of 362–3
    child development and 365–70
    definition/conceptualization 361–2
    policy and practice 389–90
    quality 338, 368–9, 371–2, 389–90
    research 337–8, 359–73
    state of knowledge 363–4
Children's Defense Fund 386, 392, 395
Children's Health Insurance Program 383
Children's Trust Fund 392
cholera 70–1
choline 21
chorionic villi sampling 310
chromosomal abnormalities 10, 12–13, 21
chromosomes 10
chronic illness 63
circle of security 295, 296, 297
cleft palate project 391
clinical intervention with families 237–8, 341
cocaine 15–16, 21
cochlear implant 91, 92, 93–4
Cochrane Reviews 40, 41
cognition
    Down syndrome 315
    Fragile X syndrome 318–19
    Prader–Willi syndrome 321
    Williams syndrome 323
cognitive assessment 223, 240
cognitive behavior therapy 207
cognitive development 20, 38–9, 240
    childcare and 338, 360–1, 364, 368–9, 370, 371–2
    depression and 196–9
cognitive outcomes (of poverty) 122–3
colic 79, 293
colony effects 77
Committee on Ways and Means (US Department of Agriculture) 117, 121, 130
communication
    autism and 257, 264–6
    Fragile X syndrome 318–19
    Prader–Willi syndrome 321
    sensory disabilities 8, 87–104
    Williams syndrome 322–3

community-level effects 128–9
competence model 89
competent infant 87–8
Comprehensive Child Development Center
    Program 345–6, 347, 348, 349, 353–4
conflict/emergencies 145, 154
congenital cataract 95
congenital glaucoma 95
congenital infections 68, 69
consanguinity 77
contagion effect (of distress) 204
content (interventions) 337, 349–50
contingency learning 315
controlling feeding style 46–8, 49
Convention for the Rights of the Child
    (CRC) 156
copy number variations 324
corpus callosum 22
cortisol 19, 20, 196, 199, 206, 287
corticotrophin-releasing hormone (CRH) 19
cost of living 117, 119
counseling (postnatal depression) 207
cretinism 38
cri du chat syndrome 312
criterion-referenced procedures 236–7, 239
crying, excessive 293–4, 295
cultural context/values 143–4, 153–4, 158,
    371
cytokines 42
cytomegalic inclusion disease 68, 69

DC:0–3R system 286, 288–90, 292, 293
deaf-blind children 87, 100–2, 104
deaf children 87, 89–94, 104, 311
deficit model 89, 128
demandingness/control, parental 46–9
dendrites 11
dentate gyrus 26
Department of Family and Child
    Ecology 396
depression
    antidepressants 16–17, 207, 209
    in early childhood 288–9
    see also maternal depression
deprivation (severe/global) 285
developed countries 342–3
    impact of poverty 113, 115–30
developing countries 210, 343
    infant development 113–14, 140–59

developmental-ecological theory (DET) 35–6,
    39, 40, 43, 50
developmental assessment 223, 227, 232–8,
    250–1, 388–9
developmental disability 308
developmental disorders 1–2
    autism 223–4, 257–73
    genetic disorders 224–5, 308–25
    infant assessment 223, 226–51
    psychosocial disorders 224, 280–98
developmental handicap 309
developmental organizational theory 244
developmental psychopathology theory 224,
    281
developmental screening 223, 228–32
diabetes 62, 64–7
diagnosis
    developmental assessment 232–6
    Fragile X syndrome 317–18
    genetic disorders (early) 310–11
    Prader–Willi syndrome 320–1
    relationship issues 286–7
diarrheal disorders 34, 70, 71, 146
direct models 36
disabilities 383
    intellectual 224–5, 261, 308–25
    sensory functional 8, 87–104
disorganized-disoriented attachment
    patterns 167, 172–3, 178
distress contagion 204
"divalent cation" 72
DNA microarray analysis 311, 324
docosahexanoic acid (DHA) 41
dopamine 20, 39, 78
dose–response relations 351, 364
Down syndrome 12–13, 225, 261, 312, 314,
    315–17
drugs 283, 310
    antidepressants 16–17, 207, 209
    brain development and 14–18, 21
dyslexia 89
dysregulation of emotion 199

early child development (ECD) program 154,
    157–9
Early Childcare Research Network (ECCRN)
    361, 362–3, 364, 365–9, 389–90
Early Head Start program 347, 349, 354,
    367, 393

early intervention 337, 339–54
Early and Periodic Screening, Diagnosis and
    Treatment (EPSDT) 388, 394
Early Reading First 372
earned income tax credits 388
ecological/transactional model 166, 169–72
ecological model 2, 143, 166–9
    childcare 337–8, 359, 360, 364
    infancy research/policy 338, 380–96
ecological systems theory 124
Economic Growth and Tax Relief
    Reconciliation Act (2001) 388
education 123–4, 156
    see also school(s)
electroencephalogram (EEG) 20, 21–2, 195,
    196, 205–6
emergencies/conflicts 145, 154
emotion 143, 199, 206, 267
emotional abuse 165, 173, 285
emotional development 338, 364, 368
emotional problems 224, 280–98, 364
employment 127, 359, 360, 387–8, 393
    see also unemployment
endangerment standard 178
engaged university 380, 395–6
environmental challenges 283–5
environmental risk factors 144, 171
environmental toxins 1, 17, 21, 310, 325
Erb palsy 65
ethnic minority parents 371
etiology, role of 3, 309–10, 311
eugenics movement 73–4
event-related potentials 21, 24, 26
evidence-based treatments 294, 295–8
evoked potentials (EPs) 21
examiner-administered developmental
    screening 223, 228, 230–1
exosystem 167–8, 381
Expanded Food and Nutrition Education
    Program (EFNEP) 386
experience-dependent development 25, 177
exploratory factor analysis (EFA) 244

facial expressions 27, 88, 95, 96–7, 101
failure to thrive 34, 42–3, 292, 321
families
    environment 46–9, 152
    interventions with 237–8, 341
    risk, childcare and 368, 370

fathers 127, 200, 209–10, 350, 387–8
fats 37, 40
Federal Child and Dependent Care
    Credit 390
Federal Interagency Forum on Child and
    Family Statistics 340
feeding
    behavior/styles 45–9, 50, 51–2
    behavior disorders 292–3, 295
    skills 33, 45–9
fertility rate 118, 150, 157
fetal alcohol syndrome (FAS) 14–15, 73–6,
    149–50, 283, 310
fetal development 7, 9–28
fetal programming 18–20
Fight Crime: Invest in Kids 394
"fight or flight" responses 179
fluoxetine 207
FMRP protein 317, 318, 319
folic acid 13, 21, 40
follow-along studies (autism) 224, 260
food 27, 117
    insecurity 43, 50
    pantries 386
    see also feeding; nutrition
Food Stamps Program 121, 386, 387, 394
foster care 392
Fragile X syndrome 225, 312, 314, 317–20
Frank Porter Graham Child Development
    Institute 342
frontal cortex 19
frustration (tolerance of) 282
fuel-mediated teratogenesis 64
functional magnetic resonance imaging
    (fMRI) 21, 25

galactosemia 311
gastrointestinal disorders 70
"gene chip" technology 311
general responsiveness (depression) 198–9
generalized anxiety disorder 288
genetic disorders, intellectual disability
    and 224–5, 308–25
Georgia Fatherhood Services Network 388
Gesell Developmental Schedules 226, 236
gestation 9, 10, 11
gestational age 10, 42
gestational diabetes mellitus 62, 64–7
glial cells 12

Global Monitoring Report Team 142, 153, 156
grandparents (childcare role) 389
gratification delay 282
Great Parents, Great Start program 382
Greenspan Social-Emotional Growth Chart (GSEGC) 234, 243, 244, 246
Griffiths Mental Development Scales 233, 236
gross national income (GNI) per capita 141
Group B *streptococcus* 69
growth 44
  hormone therapy 321
  nutrition and 33–5

harm standard 178
Hawaii Early Learning Profile 237
head circumference 34, 66
Head Start program 389
health 7, 62–80
Health Resources and Services Administration 388
healthcare policies 383–4
Healthy People 2010 382, 383–5, 391
hearing *see* auditory development; deaf-blind children; deaf children
height-for-age 42
  stunting 34, 144–5, 146–7, 151
hematopoiesis 66
hemoglobin synthesis 39
hepatic detoxification 75
herd immunity, loss of 68, 69
heroin 16
herpes simplex 68, 69
heterotypic continuity 313–14
HIB vaccine 68, 69
hippocampus 19, 26
HIV/AIDS 39, 142–4, 146, 150–2, 155
home-visiting programs 158, 341, 343–4, 346–8, 353, 392–3, 394
home environment, investment in 127–9
Home Observation for Measurement of the Environment (HOME) 127, 128, 154
home videos 224, 260, 263, 265–6, 269
homicide rates 168
homotypic continuities 314
hormonal influences, prenatal 19
HPA-axis functioning 195–6, 206
Human Resources Development Canada 120

human rights 140, 155–7
hydroxylation, failure of 78
hyperbilirubinemia 65
hpyerglycemia 64
hyperphagia 321, 322
hyperviscosity syndrome 66
hypocalcemia 65
hypoglycemia 64, 65–6
hypothalamus 19
hypothyroidism 38, 311
hypotonia 320–1

illicit drugs 15–16, 21
Illinois Association for Infant Mental Health 240–1
Illinois Department of Human Services 385
illness, development and 7, 62–80
imitation 88
  autism and 257, 267–8, 271, 272
immunization 67–70, 71, 383
impaired attachment 172–4
inborn errors of metabolism 77–9, 311
income support 129, 387–8
income transfer 129, 130
independent assessments 201–2
indirect models 36
individualized educational plans 239
Individuals with Disabilities Education Improvement Act (IDEA) 227, 234
indulgent parenting style 47, 48
industrialized countries (comparisons) 141–2
infancy
  psychosocial tasks 281–2
  research (policy) 338, 380–96
infant–parent psychotherapy 294–7
infant-sibling studies (autism) 224, 260, 263–4, 266, 270
Infant-Toddler Social and Emotional Assessment (ITSEA) 245, 247–8, 249
infant assessment 223, 226–51
Infant Behavior Record 240
infant development 1–2
  developing countries 113–14, 140–59
Infant Health and Development Program (IHDP) 123, 148, 348, 349, 351
infant mortality 141–2, 391–2
infant nutrition *see* nutrition
infant progress (evaluation) 236–7
infant psychosocial disorders 224, 280–98

infant safety 390–1
Infant Toddler Checklist 263, 265, 273
Infant and Toddler Connection of
    Virginia 389
Infant Toddler Symptom Checklist 245, 247,
    249
infantile hypercalcemia 322–3
infants, maltreatment in 174–82
infection 145, 146, 150
infectious illnesses 62, 67–71
influenza 67, 68
information processing 312, 313, 315
injury 76–7, 178
    see also physical abuse; sexual abuse;
        violence
Institute of Education Sciences 371
Institute of Medicine 49, 68
instrumental thinking 315
insulin production 64, 65
intellectual delay 89
intellectual disability
    changing approaches 308–14
    comorbid, autism and 261
    genetic disorders 224–5, 308–25
intellectual functioning 44–5
intensity (interventions) 337, 350–2
interaction
    guidance 295, 296, 297–8
    mother–infant 114, 192–211
    therapy 295, 296, 298
Interdepartmental Graduate Specialization in
    Infant Studies 395–6
internal working model 167, 173, 177
intersubjectivity 88
interventions
    childcare research 337–8, 359–73
    clinical (families) 237–8
    early 337, 339–54
    evidence-based 294, 295–8
    identifying critical features 348–53
    infancy research 338, 380–96
    infant psychosocial disorders 294–8
    postnatal depression 206–9
    program designs 339, 340–8
intrauterine growth retardation (IUGR) 66,
    75, 145, 147
investment model, parental 124, 127–9
iodine deficiency 38–9, 145, 146, 147
IQ scores 38, 43, 72, 73, 351–2

developing countries 145, 146–7
genetic disorders 309, 315
infant assessment 226, 238–9
postnatal depression and 197, 199
poverty and 121–3, 126, 128
iron deficiency 13–14, 21
developing countries 144–5, 147–8
health and 66–7, 70
nutrition and 37, 39–40, 50
poverty and 119, 121
irritability 293–4, 295
islet cell hyperplasia 65

Joint Learning Initiative 152, 155
"Jukes" family 73–4

Kaiser Family Foundation 382
"Kallikak" family 73–4
Kellogg Commission 380, 395–6
kernicterus 67
Key National Indicators of Well-Being 340
Kids Count project 340
Klumpke palsy 65

language/language development 88
    autism and 257–8, 264–6
    blind children 98, 99–100
    childcare and 368–9, 370, 372
    deaf children 92–4
    Down syndrome 316
    Williams syndrome 322–3
lead poisoning 71–3, 75–6, 145, 148–9, 310,
    325, 391
learning 26–7, 102, 308–9, 348
    opportunities 145, 152–4, 155
    social (theory) 244
Learningames curriculum 342
long-chain polyunsaturated fatty acids 21,
    41–2
Longitudinal Study of Australian
    Children 120

M-CHAT 273
macronutrients 36, 37–8
macrosomia 64, 65
macrosystem 168–9
magnetic resonance imaging (MRI) 24–5
magnetoencephalography 21
major depressive disorders (MDD) 289

malaria 70, 145, 150

malnutrition 13, 42, 43, 70, 75
  developing countries 144–7, 151

man-made disasters 285

manganese 146, 148

Manhattan Family Court 388

March of Dimes 384

marginal deviation model 244

marijuana 15

marital conflict 125, 167, 200, 201–2

maternal depression 16–18, 20, 42, 125, 383–4
  developing countries 145, 154–5
  postnatal 114, 192–211
  psychosocial disorders and 283–4, 289

maternal hostility/coercion 204–5

maternal responsiveness 146, 153, 365

maternal sensitivity 125, 127–8, 194, 205,
    365, 366

maternal serum screening 310

maternal stress, prenatal 19–20

maternity leave 360, 393

Mathematica Policy Research, Inc. 393

measles 67, 68, 69

median income 116, 118

mediational model 124

Medicaid 382–3, 386–8, 391, 394

medical care (policies) 382–4

"medical home" 62, 79–80

Medicare 382

medication, brain development and 14–18

melanin 78

memory 13–14, 26–7

meningioencephalitis 68

mental deficiency 309

Mental Development Index 232, 234, 250

mental health 18, 20, 49, 283–6

mental retardation 309, 342
  autism and 261, 265–6, 269

mercury 17, 148, 310, 325

metabolic rate 13

metabolism, inborn errors 77–9, 311

methadone 16

methylmercury 17, 18, 21

Michigan Department of Community
    Health 382

micronutrients 36, 38–42, 148

microsystem 167, 380–1

migration 154

Millennium Development Goals 156–7, 340

mirror neuron model 272–3

miscarriage 10

mixed-approach program 347–8

MMR vaccine 68, 69

monoamines 14, 15

monosomy 10

moral development/values 371

mortality rates
  infant 141–2, 391–2
  maternal 384
  neonatal 11, 18

mothers
  –infant interactions 114, 192–211
  see also maternal *entries*

motor development/skills 317, 318

Mullen Scales of Early Learning: AGS
    Edition 233, 234–5

Multicenter Growth Reference Study 35

multiple-content domains 345–7

mumps 68, 69

myelination 12, 14, 21, 23, 41

narcotics 16
  see also drugs

National Association for the Education of
    Young Children 349

National Center for Children in Poverty 381,
    387

National Center for Clinical Infant
    Programs 247, 248, 249

National Center for Health Statistics 35, 390,
    391

National Center on Shaken Baby Syndrome
    (NCSBS) 179–80

National Clearinghouse on Child Abuse and
    Neglect (NCCAN) 179, 181, 392

National Conference on State Legislatures 383

National Council on Measurement in
    Education 247

National Day to Prevent Teen Pregnancy 384

National Diabetes Quality Improvement
    Alliance 64

National Institute of Child Health/Human
    Development 194, 198–9, 208, 241
  ECCRN 361–9, 389–90

National Institute of Health and Child
    Development 122, 125, 127–8, 204

National Institute of Neurological Disorders
    and Strokes (NINDS) 180

National Institutes of Health 389–90
National Longitudinal Survey of Youth 122, 123
National Maternal and Child Health surveys 197
National Scientific Council for the Developing Child 122, 152, 157
natural disasters 285
NCAST-PCI 250
needs 143–4, 282
neighborhood characteristics 128–9
Neonatal Behavioral Assessment Scale 208, 237–8
neonatal death 11, 18
Neonatal Intensive Care Unit Network Neurobehavioral Scale 237
neural development, depression and 195
neural networks 11, 25
neural tube 11, 21, 40
neurobehavioral development 13–18, 20–2
neuronal migration 11, 15, 21
neurons 11, 15, 20, 21
neurotransmitters 11, 13–15, 17, 18, 39
New York City's Office of Child Support Enforcement 388
NHANES III 39
nicotine 149, 283
norepinephrine 20
norm-referenced assessment measures 223, 232–6, 239
nuchal translucency tests 310, 315
Nurse–Family Partnership 346–8, 352–3
Nursing Home Visitation Program 393
nurturance, parental 46–9
nutrition 7
  brain development and 13–14, 21
  developmental theory 35–6
  failure to thrive 34, 42–3, 292, 321
  human growth 33–5, 36–42
  nutrient requirements 36–42
  nutritional deficiencies 144–7
  policy and practice 385–8
  see also feeding; food

obesity 35, 44, 48–9, 50, 121
Office of Child Support Enforcement 388
Office of Disease Prevention and Health Promotion 382
Office of Minority and Health 391

ontogenic development 166–7
opportunity structure 153
oppositional disorders 224, 286, 290–1
orphans and vulnerable children 151
Organisation for Economic Co-operation and Development (OECD) 116, 120, 121
Ounce Scale 236–7, 243, 246, 248–9

"palebral fissure" 74
Panel Study of Income Dynamics 123
paraprofessionals 352–3
parasitic diseases/infections 68, 70
parent(s)
  -completed screening 223, 228–9
  education 237–8
  feeding styles/behavior and 46–9
  -focused intervention 337, 343–8
  healthcare for 383–4
  –infant relationship 249–50, 286–7
  –infant treatments 295–7, 298
  loss of/illness of 146
  single 125–6, 381, 384, 387
  supporting (policies) 392–3
  teenage 179, 384–5, 387, 391
  see also fathers; mothers
Parent–Child Development Center 353
parental investment model 124, 127–9
parental leave 360, 393
parental reports 224, 259–60, 263, 265, 267–8, 270, 273
parental sensitivity 341, 350
parental social challenges 284–5
parenting style 126–7
Parents as Teachers (PAT) program 346–7, 350
Parents' Evaluation of Developmental Status 229
paroxetine 207
Partners for Learning curriculum 348
PCERA 249–50
Peabody Individual Assessment Test 123
Peabody Picture Vocabulary Test 123
peripheral nervous system 12, 21
Perry Preschool Project 129, 130
Personal Responsibility and Work Opportunity Reconciliation Act (1996) 388, 390
personal visits 344
pervasive developmental disorder 68, 69

pesticides 146, 148
pharmacological interventions 207, 209
phenylalanine (PHA) 78
phenylketonuria (PKU) 78–9, 311, 314
phobias 288
physical abuse 165–6, 173, 174, 175,
    177–80, 285
physical outcomes (of poverty) 120–1
PIR-GAS 249, 286–7
pituitary gland 19
placental abruption 15
play 97–8, 101–2, 202, 294
    autism and 267, 268, 271
pneumonia 67, 68, 69
polio 67, 68
policy
    infancy research and 338, 380–96
    resource-poor countries 155–9
Policy Institute for Family Impact
    Seminars 381
pollution 17, 148–9
polychlorinated biphenyls (PCBs) 17
polycyclic aromatic hydrocarbons 149
polycythemia 65, 66
positive symptoms (autism) 269
post-traumatic stress disorder (PTSD) 175,
    178, 181, 287–8
postnatal depression 114, 192–211
postnatal health/illness 7, 62–80
poverty 1, 43, 71, 94, 168, 284, 369
    absolute 113, 117–18, 152
    in developed countries 113, 115–30
    in developing countries 151–3, 154
    early intervention 339, 345
    policy and 381–3, 384, 388
    relative 113, 116–18
Prader–Willi syndrome 225, 293, 312, 314,
    320–2
prefrontal cortex 12
prenatal
    care (policy) 382–3
    learning and memory 26–7
    maternal stress 19–20
    nutrition 385
    risk factors 68–9, 72, 74–5, 283
prevention of mother to child transmission
    (PMTCT) services 150
preventive interventions 209, 341
pro-inflammatory cytokines 42

problem-solving skills 348, 349
program content (interventions) 337, 349
program design (interventions) 339–48
Program for Infant/Toddler Care 349
program intensity (intervention) 337,
    350–2
program planning/evaluation 236–7
program staffing 337, 352–3
programmed cell death 11
promoting learning through active interaction
    (PLAI) 102
protective factors 169, 171–2, 366
proteins 37–8, 40
protodeclarative pointing 265
psychiatric problems 200–6
psychoanalytic therapy 207
psychological risk factors 145, 146, 152
psychometrics 233, 238, 240, 242–50
Psychomotor Index (PDI) 232
psychosocial disorders 224, 280–98
    case example 280–1
    classifying 286–94
    interventions for 294–8
    social-emotional tasks 283–5
    tasks 281–2
psychosocial risks 113–14, 151–2
    child abuse/neglect 114, 165–83
    infant development 113–14, 140–59
    postnatal depression 114, 192–211
    poverty 113, 115–30
psychotherapeutic interventions 207–8, 294,
    295, 296, 297
public information (policies) 394–5
public policy 338, 380–96
punishment 154, 168, 178, 371

rapid eye movement (REM) sleep 22, 23
reactive attachment disorder 173
recognition memory 26, 27
red cell production 41
regression discontinuity (RD) 372
regulatory disorders 224, 286, 291–4
relationship
    disorders 224, 287–90
    formation 282
    issues (psychosocial disorders) 286–7
    parent–infant 249–50, 286–7
relative poverty 113, 116–18
repetitive behaviors 269–70, 271, 272

research 1, 2
    childcare provision 337–8, 359–73
    infancy (policy/practice) 338, 380–96
responsiveness, parental 46–9
responsivity, social 257, 262–4, 271–2
retinoblastoma 94
retinopathy of prematurity 94–5, 99
risk(s) 1
    bioecological *see* bioecological risks
    biological 62, 144–50, 151–2
    in developing countries 144–55
    factors 169–72, 224, 283–5, 366
rubella 67, 68, 69
rural families 153
Rutter Scale 201

safety, infant (policies) 390–1
scholarship of engagement 380
school 386
    attendance 124, 142, 153
    readiness 123, 126, 127, 344
screening
    developmental 223, 228–32
    genetic disorders 310–11, 314
    instruments (autism) 224, 260–1, 265,
        273
seasonal affective disorder 203
security of attachment 45, 338, 344, 365–6
selective serotonin reuptake inhibitors
    (SSRIs) 17, 207
self-regulation 204, 237, 242–3, 245, 247,
    282, 283, 293
sensitive feeding style 46–7, 49
sensory functional disabilities 8, 87–104
sensory processing 270, 271, 272
separation 282, 288
serotonin 17, 42, 207
serotonin reuptake inhibitors 207
service eligibility determination 232–6
severity of impairment approach 309
sex chromosomes 10
sexual abuse 165–6, 173, 175, 180–2
shaken baby syndrome 76–7, 178, 179–80
sign language 91–3, 94, 102, 104
single-content domain 344–5
"single etiology" models 273
single parents 125–6, 381, 384, 387
sleep behavior disorders 283, 291–2, 295,
    321

sleep states 21–2, 23
smallpox 67, 68
Smart Start 394
smell experience 27
smiling 88, 267, 284
Smith–Magenis syndrome 225, 312, 314,
    323–4
smoking 310, 384
social-emotional assessment 240–50
social-emotional functioning
    Fragile X syndrome 319–20
    Prader–Willi syndrome 321–2
    Williams syndrome 323
social-emotional tasks 283–5
social anxiety disorder 288
social attention/responsivity 257, 262–4, 271,
    272
social capital 119, 340
social change 153
social cognition 88, 206, 262
social competence 338, 366–8
social development, childcare and 338, 360,
    364, 368–71, 372
social dialogues 88
social ecology (of childcare) 337–8, 359, 360,
    364
social exclusion 152
social functioning 46, 316–17
social gradient theory 63
social interaction (with peers) 282
social isolation 182, 259, 284
social learning theory 244
social orientation deficit 262, 263, 267, 271
social reward model 272–3
social support 182–3, 207, 284–5, 346
Society for Research in Child
    Development 396
socioeconomic status (SES) 119, 124, 128,
    153, 158, 168, 202, 229
socioemotional
    outcomes (of poverty) 121–2
    problems, depression and 200–6
Speak for the Child project 151–2
Special Supplemental Nutrition Program 39,
    50, 385, 394
specific phobia 288
speech 26–7, 89, 92, 94, 97, 98
spina bifida 11, 13
spinal cord 12

staffing (interventions) 337, 352–3
Stanford–Binet test 226
Step Through Employment Program 388
stereotyped behaviors (in autism) 269–70, 271, 272
stillbirth 11
stress
    maternal (prenatal) 19–20
    PTSD 175, 178, 181, 287–8
stress hormones 152, 287
Study of Early Childcare 208
Study of Early Childcare and Youth Development 365, 366–7, 369
stunting 34, 144–5, 146–7, 151
substance abuse 14, 15, 384
sudden infant death syndrome 385, 391
SUNY Downstate Medical Center 64
Supplemental Nutrition Assistance Program 39, 50, 385, 394
Swedish Sign Language 93
Sydney Family Development Project 367
synapse formation 23, 25
synaptic elaboration 11–12
synaptogenesis 12
syphilis 68, 69

Task Force on Research Diagnostic Criteria (RDC-PA) 292
taste experience 27
teenage parents 179, 384–5, 387, 391
Temperament and Atypical Behavior Scale (TABS) 245, 247
Temporary Assistance to Needy Families (TANF) 387, 390, 394
teratogenic effects (drug use) 75
thyroid failure 38
time, investment in 127
Title V program 389
tobacco 310, 384
toddlers
    maltreatment of 174–7
    psychosocial tasks 281–2
toxic stressors 152
toxins
    brain development and 14–18, 21
    exposure to 1, 145, 146, 148–50, 152
    see also alcohol; drugs; lead poisoning; mercury; methylmercury; smoking
toxoplasmosis 68, 69

trinucleotide expansions 317
trisomy 10
tuberculosis 67, 69
Type D attachment 167, 172–3, 178
tyrosine 78

ultrasound monitoring 9, 10, 20, 310
UNAIDS 150
unemployment 115, 124, 126, 167, 389, 393
UNICEF 39, 140, 141–2, 147, 151, 153, 154, 156, 168, 384
uninvolved parenting style 47, 48
United Nations
    Committee on the Rights of the Child (UNCRC) 156
    General Assembly 156
    Millennium Development Goals 156–7, 340
    see also UNAIDS; UNICEF
urbanization 153
US Department of Agriculture 385, 386
US Department of Health and Human Services 165, 172, 174, 178, 183, 382–3, 385, 391–2

vaccination 67–70, 71, 383
varicella 67, 69
video films 224, 260, 263, 265–6, 269–70, 344, 351
Vineland Social-Emotional Early Childhood Scales 235, 242, 244, 249
violence 145
    domestic 125, 167–9, 200–2, 285
    physical abuse 165–6, 173–5, 177–80, 285
    punishment 154, 168, 178, 371
viral agents 71
visual impairment 87, 94–100, 104
Vitamin A deficiency 38, 40, 67, 94, 146
Vitamin B6 deficiency 38, 40
Vitamin B9 deficiency 38, 40
Vitamin B12 deficiency 38, 41
Vitamin D deficiency 37

wealth 116, 117, 118, 119
weight-for-age 34, 42
weight-for-height 34, 42, 119
weight-for-length 34
welfare programs 129, 387–8, 391

What Works Clearinghouse 371–2
Williams–Beuren syndrome 322
Williams syndrome 225, 312, 314, 322–3
Woodcock–Johnson math/reading
   assessment 122–3
work participation rate 387
working poor 118
World Bank 49, 141, 142

World Health Organization 38–9, 43, 70–1,
   147, 149–50, 289, 349, 391
   Multicenter Growth Reference Study 35
   Social Commission on Health 157

Zero to Three 50, 249, 285–7, 289–90, 292,
   293, 394–5
zinc deficiency 37, 40, 146, 148

Contents of Volume 1

List of Contributors   viii

Introduction to Volume 1: Basic Research   1
J. Gavin Bremner and Theodore D. Wachs

1   Historical Reflections on Infancy   3
    Alan Fogel

Part I   Perceptual and Cognitive Development   **33**

    Introduction   35

2   Visual Perception   40
    Alan Slater, Patricia Riddell, Paul C. Quinn, Olivier Pascalis, Kang Lee,
    and David J. Kelly

3   Auditory Development   81
    Denis Burnham and Karen Mattock

4   Intermodal Perception and Selective Attention to Intersensory Redundancy:
    Implications for Typical Social Development and Autism   120
    Lorraine E. Bahrick

5   Action in Infancy – Perspectives, Concepts, and Challenges   167
    Ad W. Smitsman and Daniela Corbetta

6   Cognitive Development: Knowledge of the Physical World   204
     J. Gavin Bremner

7   Perceptual Categorization and Concepts   243
     David H. Rakison

8   Infant Learning and Memory   271
     Carolyn Rovee-Collier and Rachel Barr

9   Functional Brain Development during Infancy   295
     Mark H. Johnson

Part II   Social Cognition, Communication, and Language   315

     Introduction   317

10   Emerging Self-Concept   320
     Philippe Rochat

11   The Importance of Imitation for Theories of Social-Cognitive Development   345
     Andrew N. Meltzoff and Rebecca A. Williamson

12   Engaging Minds in the First Year: The Developing Awareness of
     Attention and Intention   365
     Vasudevi Reddy

13   Preverbal Communication   394
     Andrew Lock and Patricia Zukow-Goldring

14   Early Language   426
     George Hollich

Part III   Social-Emotional Development   451

     Introduction   453

15   Parent–Infant Interaction   458
     Marc H. Bornstein and Catherine S. Tamis-LeMonda

16   Attachment in Infancy   483
     Germán Posada and Garene Kaloustian

17   Early Social Cognitive Skills at Play in Toddlers' Peer Interactions 510
     Hildy Ross, Marcia Vickar, and Michal Perlman

18 Touch and Physical Contact during Infancy: Discovering the Richness
   of the Forgotten Sense   532
   Dale M. Stack

19 Emotion and its Development in Infancy   568
   David C. Witherington, Joseph J. Campos, Jennifer A. Harriger,
   Cheryl Bryan, and Tessa E. Margett

20 Temperament   592
   Theodore D. Wachs and John E. Bates

21 Culture and Infancy   623
   Charles M. Super and Sara Harkness

Author Index   650
Subject Index   684

Contents of Volume 2: Applied and Policy Issues   705